# STITCHES

Azreay'l

## Gotham Books

30 N Gould St.
Ste. 20820, Sheridan, WY 82801
https://gothambooksinc.com/

Phone: 1 (307) 464-7800

© 2023 Azreay'l. All rights reserved.

No part of this book may be reproduced, stored in a retrieval system, or transmitted by any means without the written permission of the author.

Published by Gotham Books (September 8, 2023)

ISBN: 979-8-88775-528-1 (H)
ISBN: 979-8-88775-526-7 (P)
ISBN: 979-8-88775-527-4 (E)

Because of the dynamic nature of the Internet, any web addresses or links contained in this book may have changed since publication and may no longer be valid.

The views expressed in this work are solely those of the author and do not necessarily reflect the views of the publisher, and the publisher hereby disclaims any responsibility for them.

# TABLE OF CONTENTS

DEDICATION ................................................................... 7
SPECIAL ACKNOWLEDGMENT AND COMMITMENT ...... 8
MEET THE AUTHOR ............................................................ 10
PLAN OF ACTION AND MILESTONES (POA&M) .............. 12
DISCLAIMER ...................................................................... 13
PROLOGUE ......................................................................... 14
CHAPTER ONE ................................................................... 29
CHAPTER TWO .................................................................. 69
CHAPTER THREE ............................................................... 108
CHAPTER FOUR ................................................................. 153
CHAPTER FIVE ................................................................... 194
CHAPTER SIX ..................................................................... 242
CHAPTER SEVEN ............................................................... 288
CHAPTER EIGHT ................................................................ 328
CHAPTER NINE .................................................................. 378
CHAPTER TEN .................................................................... 424

# DEDICATION

This novel is in loving commemoration of my grandmother, Cora Fikes-Battle, who was 86 years young when she went with the Lord! She was a cornerstone of our family, very spiritual, fun, loving and strong. While writing this novel, I knew that she would have approved of this comedy and the toning down of the content since the first version, which I toned down tremendously.

As a kid, she sewed strong values into my life and brought meaningfully mannerisms and encouraged manly values from a female's perspective into my world as I know it.

To this day, her words, rearing, and training are interwoven deeply into the core of my being. The relentless love she brought to our family makes me very proud to know that my life has evolved and God granted me the opportunity to be the grandson of this loving woman.

# SPECIAL ACKNOWLEDGMENT AND COMMITMENT

Above all things, I give thanks and praise wholeheartedly to Almighty God and my Lord, Jesus Christ, who laid down HIS life for all.

I realize I am nothing without the Almighty ONE! HE gives me every breath I breathe, so I am continually grateful.

God has blessed me with the ability to explore my talents in; inventing, songwriting, literary writing, business planning, and business development. HE has enabled me to dream dreams and live them.

HE is my Lord, my Healer, Savior, and Deliverer, at my best or worst. In my trials and tribulations, there is one thing consistent: HE has been, is, and will always be, according to HIS Word, on which I stand. God First! HE is God alone!

Here is a special toast to my developmental stage fans; a toast to those who previously previewed *STITCHES* in its rarest form through various online excerpts. Thanks to the generous strangers who pulled no punches in their critiques. It is your welcome comments, appraisals, and constructive criticism that helped STITCHES reach its destiny.

Cover illustration: James Steidl

My hat goes off to my great cover illustrator, James Steidl, and his terrific staff at jgroupstudios. For excellent illustrations for many occasions, view James and his team's marvelous works at www.jgroupstudios.com.

*STITCHES*, now listed on Gotham Book' website, my new business website – www.dynamicdimenzion.com, sites of leading booksellers, and other official sites!

Bravo, Zulu, to my adept editor! Thanks for your quality time and endless efforts to make *STITCHES* a delightful read. With your help, *STITCHES* has received professional reviews, constructive criticism, and the required polishing before production.

For new authors: You can never do it all with just spell and grammar check alone. ~smile~

My learning experience is that you write one way, proof another, and go to production another. Of course, there are a gazillion other little gadgets with which to contend..., LOL. Just enjoy what you do and have fun doing it!

For future fans: Thanks in advance for your eager eyes, which first caught STITCHES' beautiful cover, drawing you near and sparking your curiosity. Your excellent taste has not gone unnoticed, my dear friends.

# MEET THE AUTHOR

Who is Azreay'l? He is a; freelance, amateur author, inventor, poet, business developer, songwriter, business planner, and visionary. He lives in Newport News, Virginia, with his lovely wife, Mary.

The most amazing gifts he possesses are those revealed from the North (Heaven), manifested through very vivid imagination, dreams, daydreams, and nightmares. The spiritual intervention he receives is the blessing he receives for his talents and work.

He joined the U.S. Armed Forces in 1980, served in the Army & Navy, retiring from the Navy in June 2001. He served 20 years of faithful and honorable military service and retired as a highly decorated Chief Petty Officer - Enlisted Surface Warfare Specialist (ESWS).

Azreay'l concentrates his writing on the success of being a mixed genre author. His first four novels are under the copyrights of the Library of Congress (LOC).

He is ecstatic about the release of his three new patented inventions – GRID-LOCX (a new strategic board game), the Viral Shield (VS-2000), clear face, Personal Protective Equipment (PPE) mask and CLICK! (a new strategic board game). He works diligently on his mega-billion-dollar valuation business plans for his future global-enterprise venture(s): Dynamic Dimenzions, LLC, a mega job creator, that ties multiple LLCs together, i.e., STITCHUZ, and JVINCO, to name a few of over 50 business concepts and portfolios under the Dynamic Dimenzions, LLC's umbrella.

**Advice to new authors:** Regardless of the world which is full of critics; those jealous of your accomplishments and envious because they can never reach the goals you are achieving, so they try to discourage you. Forget about em', as my old, Italian buddy would say! Just go for it, enjoy what you do, and have fun doing it! Nothing hurts a failure but a try..., some knowledgeable person once quoted.

As for Azreay'l, if he's not working the 9-5 IT Security or sky-lighting in intelligence operations; he's drafting the next new invention, detailing a prototype, detailing an intense plot for a future novel, or working on that subsequent inclusion or expansion for his enterprise business model.

## Azreay'l's hobbies:

- Mixed-genre writing
- Inventing
- Drafting leading company business plans
- Developing strong business models

# PLAN OF ACTION AND MILESTONES (POA&M)

## NOVELS

### Other novels by Azreay'l. Now Showing!!!
*"MadUSoul's Crossing"* – Spine tingling and nail biting, Horror
*"Tainted Obsessions"* – Suspense, Erotica
*"Liberty Call... Port of Spain"* – Hilariously funny, Comedy

### Other novels by Azreay'l in the makings!!!
*"The Mirror in the Mirror"* – Bone-chilling, Horror
*"To… Nowhere"* – Suspense, Inspiration
*"Forgotten Sorrows"* – Heart and mind-melting, Inspiration
*"Drugged"* - Heart and mind-melting, Inspiration

## GOALS

<u>Short-term:</u> To be an established, well-known mixed-genre author, inventor, invention-publisher financier, and chairman of the board of directors for my future businesses.

<u>Long-term goals:</u> Become a business planner, developer for several new Dynamic Dimenzions, LLC's companies and portfolios. To develop into a thriving, generous venture capitalist and philanthropist, focused on impacting the lives of those in need while improving the lives of others.

# Disclaimer

What is STITCHES? It is merely a compilation of words pulled together from one's vision; the author. They are simply thoughts that have crossed the minds of many generations before us, those with us, and those to come. They are words written yet playfully scripted to soothe the mind.

This novel is for relaxation, pleasurable reading, entertainment, and laughter, which is a remedy to heal the body and soul.

I love everyone with a brotherly love instilled in me from birth. No matter who you are or what you claim to be, it is not my place to judge, for we should not judge first unless we be judged; but we all shall one day be judged before the All-Mighty.

The locations, titles, positions, and comical setting is an outreach into my civil past and the things I did or saw while growing up as a born and raised citizen.

The characters are only a reflection of the characters in our society, so you cannot separate the mixed groups depicted but we must always discern between good and evil. This novel does not reflect upon or target any group. Still, it is a compilation of various groups that make up our society, so the make-up crosses an equally mixed gender based on our society.

God gives us free will in his love for us, but the things HE despises, we will grow to despise in our soul purely from our love for HIM as we grow, mature, and wax old.

**NOTE:** By procedures, the publisher runs all novels against quality plagiarism software, and removes any perceived indications of plagiarism from this document. Still, in a case of oversight, I will gladly add a citation in my next novel if such plagiarism is ever noted.

Sit back, relax, sip on your favorite glass of wine; a drink of class, or some bubbly while I present to you…, "STITCHES."

~smile~
**Freedom of speech…, there is nothing like it, so enjoy!**

# Prologue

A long time ago, no..., four scores, no..., hmm..., once upon a time..., hmm..., hecky (heck) naw (no)! Hmm..., 2018, in the deepest part of Alabama, along the Alabamy River, near the tremendous disoriented swamps and Couchieman Trail, sits a small town - Petersonville.

Crickets chirp in orchestration on a calm Saturday night, with lightning bugs lighting the jet black, low skyline, while slowly fading in thick weeds.

Miles away, in LeeLeeville, a sudden, heavy downpour pounds upon dark, cold asphalt with trails of lightning glowing along the horizon, moving closer and rapidly.

Forty-knot winds come out of nowhere, settling then gusting with thunder roaring until tapering off to a dull roar.

In another city, Fikesville, moderate traffic picks up in a community of seven hundred or more.

Torrential downpours blow sideways, with distant street lights piercing through darkness, revealing Lil' Bobby's dilapidated general store.

A rusty soda pop sign sways, pushed by gusts of continual winds that anxiously rise and diminish, suddenly.

The door to Lil' Bobby's store slams open, sticking against dry, red clay, until rocking to and fro, from resisting the winds.

Out front, a five-year-old lad eases to the edge of the shelter. He pulls gum from his pocket, playfully throwing the wrapper to the wet ground.

Suddenly, a gust of wind comes, lifting the wrapper and gliding it gracefully until persistently clinging to blades of grass.

The wrapper stays longer yet slowly begins rocking until a stronger gust forcefully blows it as if a joyful game, until abruptly altering its directions until landing a ways off, on John "Boogey" and Nattie Johnson's front porch minutes later.

Distant sirens proliferate, and Boogey's old hound, Luke, howls.

A full moon appears from behind dark, thick clouds when suddenly a rusty water pail flings high; the chain tightening when Luke charges with brute force toward now, moderate sirens.

Blue flashing lights swiftly appear along a thick tree line on the main stretch of road; a deputy's cruiser leading yet leaving other emergent vehicle lights in the dust when coming up to eighty miles per hour.

On a crowded street, a county over, and in Mundson, Boogey of Fikesville, and Winton, first cousins, pull up in Winton's rust-bucket, blocks from the renowned STITCHES Comedy House.

Winton sits anxiously awaiting a group of women to pass when embarrassingly pushing the broken driver's side window up with both hands. When the window jams, his face becomes fierce when looking back, and sliding rubber into the track.

"Man, you the tightest sucker I know!" Boogey declares, excited. "This window has been broken for what…, three years? And you're too darn tight to buy a freakin' ten-cent screw."

Winton's nervous hands ease back in anticipation of the window dropping. He cuts his beady eyes at Boogey, bursting into a crazy, long, uncontrollable laugh until he in tears when his liquor high he had polished off on the drive over adds fuel to his crazy laughter. Winton takes his time gaining control until sitting in a firm stare. "You're one to talk! Your car is down for four freakin' years, and who the heck knows why?" Winton says when the headrest falls backward, dangling when they jump, simultaneously.

Boogey's eyes shoot back in disbelief, and a sly grin emerges when grabbing the door handle, barely pulling on it when it breaks off. "Ahh, man!" he shouts, eye-to-eye with Winton, whose shoulders are constantly jerking from laughing so hard.

Winton eases out and heads to the front near the passenger side.

Boogey struggles, getting the handle in the striped socket, until finally opening the door. He comes up slow, losing his balance when the dead weight of the door drops to the pavement.

Instantly, a loud clamor of laughter comes, causing Boogey and Winton to slightly turn and find four women; two heavyset and two skinnies, bent over, and laughing out loud.

Boogey grips the handle tighter, jerking and clenching the door against the frame. "What the hell, Winton!" Boogey nervously whispers, discovering a broken hinge on the ground, barely submerged in water.

Winton finally notices that the women are paying them no mind, when rushing and seizing the door, helping to lift it high.

They rock the door, losing their grip when it heavily slams into the pavement again.

Winton sprints to the trunk, pulling out bungee cords then runs back over, swiftly strapping the door to the frame. He sneakily motions Boogey to let go and Boogey does with hands fearfully extended forward while looking back at the women.

Seconds later, the club's door flies open, and a short, round female sprints out, slowing down to pull down her too-short skirt and adjust her wide, Santa belt over her big, pot belly.

"Girl, slow down before you hurt yourself," a thinner girl yells, laughing and causing others to join in.

"Girl, please, I got this!" the short woman responds, pointing to the tall blonde's face. "Trust me..., blam! Pilates got this!" She motions both hands over her round figure as if in a business product presentation.

Boogey, Winton, and the four women make eye contact.

Two of the women's faces are cheery, and the other two frowns but Boogey and Winton smile with unwelcome eyes swarming over the two hottest women's bodies.

"What the hell are you looking at with your dingy self?" the short, round female yells, looking Winton over with an unwelcoming stare when thrusting her head forward and shoulder backward fast, making Winton hesitantly jump.

"Who the hell are you calling dingy?" Winton lividly responds. "Out here looking like a beached whale; you need to take Santa's extended belt back so he can corral his reindeers," Winton utters in crazy, great laughter.

"Come on, man, leave them alone!" Boogey exclaims, slightly guiding Winton away yet beaming.

"Ugh, ugh, ugh..., Santa? Look here, yah (you) raggedy tooth fool!" she exclaims, bending forward and swerving to look sexy. She throws her weave to one side when a squeal, then loud pop shatters the buckle.

The tall, skinny girl instantly begins high-stepping then yelps, unsure of what just hit her leg.

Everyone laughs, and some bend over, catching their breaths, with others joining in the laughter spotting the metal pieces sprawled over the pavement.

Winton backs up, seeing the short woman's tight fists and finally her tears. "No, you don't just lie about freakin' Pilates! Riiiggghhht..., the only thing you do with Pilates is probably eat'em'." Winton bursts into a crazy hee-haw, until sounding like a seasoned turkey. He stares longer, then lights into her with more humorous jokes.

Her two taller friends immediately stop laughing and grow so fierce that Winton will not let up, so they exchange offensive words, with the other two laughing harder as Winton tares deeper into the short woman.

The short woman turns red. "Come on! Don't pay Jeff and Mutt; I mean Dick and Butt, no mind! They need to go somewhere and wash that saw funk off," she says, gazing over their faded company name tags.

"What!" Boogey says with a mean stare. "Come on, Wint! We came for the show, not to listen to busted chicken heads clucking!" Boogey says, almost cross-eyed from the high when exchanging more offensive words.

The women linger around longer then wander alongside Winton's car after Boogey and Winton enter the club.

One woman pulls out a sharp, shiny knife, scrolling alongside the car making a deep, long scrape, leaving no damage to the rusted metal.

The tall brunette lights a cigarette, backing closer and throws a match through the barely cracked-open back window.

The short female starts talking more trash until walking away, heading for the club again, ready to go inside and fight Winton.

Seconds pass when the other tall, thin female notices smoke billowing from Winton's car. She pulls her friends away with fast-clicking, stampede-sounding heels that grow loud until fading around the corner.

A bouncer motions a frisked guy away motioning over Boogey and Winton.

Boogey senses the man's feminine tone; watching him size Winton up until blowing Winton a kiss. "You first!" Boogey says, shoving Winton in is back, and deep into the bouncer.

Winton resists the bouncer's advances until he's swung around expeditiously, and pressed against the wall. He feels something hard pressed against his butt and his eyes instantly shoot over to Boogey like sad puppy eyes with a diminishing smile.

"Any weapons, honey bun?" the bouncer utters, lightly blowing in his ear with dimming eyes.

Winton smiles and frowns, finding Boogey's surprised and then fast frowning face.

Boogey sees another bouncer and frantically waves. "Here..., over here!" Boogey yells, over loud laughter pouring out of the entertainment room when trying to squeeze past Winton.

The bouncer grabs Boogey at the collar. "You're next, big daddy," he utters, bringing a well-manicured finger to Boogey's face when speedily turning to Winton.

Boogey waves until the other bouncer approaches and begins wanding Boogey.

The bouncer looks off, discovering the other bouncer running a finger through Winton's greasy, permed-out hair. "Pokie, frisk him, or you two get a darn room!" he yells, walking over and slightly shoving Pokie.

Boogey counts off a few bills, looking back and finding Winton hurrying over. "Wint, if I was a betting man, I'd bet on you busting slob with him if I wasn't here," he exclaims, staring in Winton's shameful face.

"Man, you done lost your rabid ass mind? I love women too much for that!" Winton declares, frowning.

"Yeah..., right! You seemed to be loving that grinding just a little too much for me, buddy," Boogey exclaims, frowning more.

"Man, you crazy as heck! I just know how to follow security protocol," Winton responds in a more serious tone.

"Proto my butt...! Didn't you hear him say, Pokie? Hmm..., Poke this and Poke that..., Pokie gone, keep on until he gone (is going to) poke something!" Boogey declares, finding Winton lagging behind and looking again when bursting into a crazy laugh when finding Winton playfully walking wide-legged. "No wonder he wanted you! Hell..., you walk like you are packing, I reckon."

"You better ask somebody, chump!" Winton says when walking even more wide-legged.

"Man, go on with that silly crap! I know better, but for real, for real..., you ain't (aren't) packing nothing, but a heat rash if anything." Boogey laughs harder.

The commentator soon appears on stage. "For the main attraction!" he yells, hearing loud cheers. People clap then clap louder when the DJ cranks up a new tune. "Up next, out of Kinston, North Carolina, by way of Newport News, Virginia," he yells, pointing to slow, opening curtains. "My man, Keyonton Worthingtoooonnn!" he shrieks even louder.

The crowd grows wilder until slowly tapering off to a moderate roar.

"Forget that! Yawl better get on your feet and show my man some love!" he yells, hugging the famous comedian and passing him the mic.

"Good evening, Mundson! I said..., good evening Mundson!" Keyonton yells, pointing to the DJ when another new beat blazes from the Fiktek quality speakers.

Most patrons hold their drinks high or put them down, dancing when Keyonton goes into a crazy-looking dance, cracking folks up or leaving them in tears.

Boogey and Winton shuffle into the small room, squeezing past tightly packed patrons looking for a seat, and finding standing room only.

Keyonton signals the DJ, and the beat stops when he bursts into a crazy laugh. "I know yawl ain't (haven't) seen that one because I got that from a crack house. Now, I didn't tell you that to say I'm a crackhead, but I have relatives who are crackheads. Come on, now! There's at least one in every family these days..., right! I mean, it's a sad epidemic, but now you know, crackhead family members..., heck, you can't help but love em' because they keep you laughing. Hell..., mine helps keep food on my table. Yeah, I have a cousin, and I love this brother, ya (you) feel me? You know, I even take him on tours just to get fresh material.

So, check it; this is what I learned here, in Mundson, and in a crack house: Are you ready?" he screams, smiling as the crowd gets quieter. "What happens in crack houses stays in the crack houses!"

A patron exits the entertainment when the crowd bursts into laughter.

Mild sirens grow louder and fade when the door closes.

'Ok, so check it…, we're here a hot minute and ole cuz scopes out a hot little down-home spot that turns out to be, nothing but what? A freakin' crack house…, now you go figure! So, we're in this smoked-out joint; and I mean there are all kinds of freak-a-zoids in there, and some are new at the crack game, and I know this because they still have breasts and booty. Man! So tell me this…, why is it that when it comes to crack, the first thing to go is the booty and breasts?" He laughs. "So anyway, hours later, we're still there, not because I'm a crackhead; hell, my cousin is the damn crackhead!" he yells, winking. "But anyway, lo and behold, I found the hottest honey, ever; I mean, baby girl is so fine, so I'm thinking candlelight, babies, and then I wake up,' he says, laughing.

"Tell me, Mundson, why do you gotta pay tricks first, not even knowing their performance level? I mean, if I'm paying, I at least want a profession-AL (professional). I'm just saying! Naw, naw, I'm just saying! It's not like I've been serviced or anything because I'm not a crackhead. Hel…, my cousin is the damn crackhead! Shucks, I want mine when you are at your bizzest (best). Huh, mess around all cracked up and amputate something, shucks…,

Come on, Mundson! Whose to say she ain't gonna awake and forget you already paid. Huh? In that case, I guarantee we gone be remodeling up in that mother!" he exclaims, regaining his thought. "Man, can you see a skinny brother like me in jail for choking a crackhead out?" He laughs even harder. "Shoot, ain't no rusty tail man gone be humping on this." He laughs, slightly bent over and rubbing his flat butt.

"There is a permanent stamp that reads: 'one way, do not enter, road closed, stop, and all on one sign!' Hell, it hurts to drop a load, so ain't gonna be no damn back-to-back pain."

Keyonton sees a hottie walking to her seat "Man!" he hesitantly says. "Look at this fat hammer over here! Babe, Babe, Babe! Umm…, those luscious, thick thighs in black, glitter spandex. I thought spandex was out of style, but girl, you bringing them back!" he exclaims, when the crowd bursts into great laughter.

'Ok, back to the story…, well, anyways, I holler for a minute,' he utters, laughing and winking. 'Before I knew it, we were outside, and I mean, ole girl has a tight hairdo, classy outfit, nails done, and a soft accent…, well the accent…, ok, well let's just say the Azreay'l Cognac was in full effect.

Anyway, we go over to her place, which she claims is five blocks, but seriously; it felt like every bit of sixteen with me three sheets to the wind, but anyways, forty blocks later, we finally arrive and still have to climb what looks like the freakin' Eiffel Tower. I'm buzzing like crazy and thinking, 'It's not even 4 AM, and this chick is still a dime.' He reminisces.

'Ok, so we finally get in, and man, I will be..., not a damn drop of lights in this joint! The first thing she says is no worries because she's going to blow my mind,' he says, giggling senselessly. 'At that point, I tried not to laugh in her face, so I politely smiled, pulled out a wad and said..., just blow a fourth, and I'll keep the rest. Before I knew it, my hands were empty. So anyway, she lights a candle, rummages around, and pulls out her crack tools and her reserve stash. Let me tell you, I've never seen them this close, so I'm in suspense because she is a true professional, and I am gone (going to) get me some damn good jokes. Like magic, her voice turns deep, like with spasms. I mean, my mind goes crazy thinking of jokes from this venture.' he laughs.

'Before I know it, she flops down in a chair, chants, and freezes. With my scary, giggly tail; I get serious instantly, thinking, overdose when checking for a pulse, and nothing! You would think I would do CPR, call 911..., uh, uh, no..., not I! I reach for her bra, for my moolah! Now how 'bout her tight fist gone grab my hand in a kung-fu grip with a Chinese twist, leaving me vulnerable. She was so strong that my thoughts of knocking this trick out diminished fast, and without a plan B. She held me, and then eased off to a touch as soft as cotton, staggering, and standing, then releases me, yet pulls me until I stumble over this mess all over the floor.

So anyway, we walk in the back, and she pushes into me, pulling my clothes off, and trusts that I'm trying just as fast until butt-balled, but she's still fully dressed!

All of a sudden she gets quiet, shushing me and killing my high. I start thinking: robbery, mugging, jacking, or whatever. I turn, and she drops back, sprawled over the bed, so I undress this beautiful thang, kissing soft, silky thighs until hearing a light knock then a whisper. I perceive someone is calling Kechia when swiftly turning to handle mine when something slimy and hard brushes across my chin.

I mean comeooonnn! Man, I am hoping for a belt buckle, purse, bean bag, or anything. I mean I go straight delusional, willing to accept anything but what I think it is, but it diminishes when something flexes like a stiff plank. Violated! Violated! I don't think I ever spit or threw up that much in my whole entire life! Ok..., so now my high is bye-bye, and I spring up, staggering then jostling into something.

Something slumps over me from behind before I make out what it is, and I'm just fighting until I find out it's a mountain of dirty clothes. I mean..., I'm literally covered in this dirty, filthy, stinking laundry.

I tell you, I don't know what is in these clothes, but they are heeaaavvy, and even though you might not think I work out. Ok, so I think one push-up and wham, the clothes are off, but it's like darn kryptonite. Hell..., even Superman would be in a world of hurt.

Comeooonnn people! I literally smell perfume, piss, turds, and sometimes a mixture. So, I fight more, and I'm about to gain footing when hearing Kechia clearer, when the deep voice calls who…, Keith and even clearer. Ughhhhh! Man, my mind instantly goes from robbery, mugging, and gangbanging, to death. Yeah, I said it…, death, and I mean death by Bunga-Bunga! Now that's when they just bust through your back door, tearing through all the no entry signs I said earlier, and you just take it until you die. Hell…, I was so scared that for a second, I hear African butt music and continual butt banging bongos in rhythm, which clear my mind instantly when thinking about survival.' he says, giggling.

'I quickly bury myself, allowing time to see, when hearing more voices calling Keith. Instantly, Kechia's earlier, sweet voice turns into the deepest voice ever, kinda like my daddy's when I was a lad.

Out of nowhere, the posse converges, and I find Keith leaning, cutting on a lamp. I was like, man…, what? This mother got lights! Out of nowhere, something flops over one of my eyes. Would you believe it? A stankin', freakin' balloon skin and smelling like straight doo-to-the-do-to-the-do-do-do and perfumed when I start quietly oozing out mouths full of chunks, realizing I have to hold my scream or lose my virginity. Now, again, need I remind you of all the signs posted?' Keyonton declares, with a serious look.

'Ok, so one uncovered eye, a wide-open, very sensitive nose, and a heart-racing five hundred miles an hour. My eye wanders swiftly, as if in a professional five-hundred raceway. So, anyway…, five hungry, cracked-up feminine acting dudes and little ole me about to pass out; scared as heck that they may hear my heartbeat, because, shoot, I hear it. How about Keith gone (is going to) walk to the pile, picking off a few clothes, working his way down with his dangling pirate…, I mean dangling private inches from my face, looking like a doll baby's arm. Well, hell, come to think of it, even though I hate to say it, it looked like a damn pirate! Shoot, instantly, my manhood shriveled up inside my body, and my butt packed up and left town.

So…, now comes a fresh scent: butt, cigarettes, liquor, and some other funk, probably from an earlier booty-pumping party. The top of my head lightens as Keith drills down further until a guy points, and Keith turns and bends over, with nothing but butt sprawled so wide that a heavy-duty flashlight could fit inside, missing all sides. Ok…, more chunks, plus I'm breathing slowly and wondering if I even have a pulse. I close my eyes fast, refusing to look down his brown, endless tunnel, swiftly pinning my eyes to the floor, when his long fingernails grab my fresh, clean threads. Oh, I am straight sober now…, and watching him dig his beforehand, unrecognized big paws deep in my pant pockets, pulling out my liquor flask and then wad of the fifties.

His friends instantly spot the roll, and you would have thought it was a damn Super Bowl party up in this mother, with laughter and continual high fives flying, and at my expense. Yeah, the conversation went a little like this: 'Girl, it's your treat, let's go to the smokehouse,' the smallest one says. 'Hey, whose threads?' another asks, sizing them up then slipping into them faster than a cat can lick its butt.

'Like I know,' Keith utters, picking up his dingy panties and turning to me to put them on. 'So anyway, I keep my eyes closed, and when I think he has them on, I peek, finding five to seven dark-brown doughnut rings in his drawers. Let me tell you..., for real, for real, now I am dry heaving.

I discover the biggest guy with my silk handkerchief, continually sniffing until flipping it, seeing my white engraved initials, which he sniffs even harder, like a predator.

They rush Keith to get dressed, and I start plotting my exit..., oh no, there was no waiting on the brain to catch up. I watch them anxiously, keeping their eyes on the wad that is so thick; Keith couldn't close his big hand. I finally look off and find this big burly dude off in the corner, still sniffing my handkerchief, then sniffing in the air like a dog.

The light goes out and light shines in from the street.

Their footsteps soon fade, with mumbling then fading voices, and I spot the first one in a turn with a candle leading the way while their voices transform back to that of women until the door slams.

Ok, this is it! I've been waiting for this big break, so I sit with a clear nose and another eye uncovered, vigilantly listening..., so vigilant that I could have heard a rat pissing on cotton three blocks away. I judge the walk back in my mind, springing forward, and leaving the lights off, speedily ravaging through clothes, when something sharp pierces my ribs and something heavy slumps over me. I tell you..., I am sweating like a Thanksgiving buttered turkey wrapped in aluminum, on broil, on Thanksgiving Day,' Keyonton giggles.

'Don't move, or I'll gut you like a hog,' the deep, manly voice growls with a thick hand around my neck, cutting off my circulation while sniffing against my flesh like the monster in the movie, Predator.

'Let me tell you..., my mind goes five hundred miles per hour, and my butt clenches so tight that it feels like it's filled with concrete. My mind goes think..., think..., and I'm thinking creatively, trying to figure out where this is going, then an idea comes. Anything, just name it, I say, trying to see where his mind is.

On your knees and get at this, Johnson; then I'm going to crack you open like a pretty, green, sweet pea!' the deep, booming voice resonates throughout the grim room in a serious yet very convincing tone.'

'Wait, be reasonable; we can both benefit,' I say, leveraging my options of escaping death. 'There's no need for the knife because Candy makes it happen, babe,' I say, creating a quick, fantasy, and erotic name to make him think I'm about it, 'bout it.

Well..., he quiets for seconds, sizing me up, then slips the knife in his back pocket with his hand tighter around my throat, lifting me to my tiptoes until completely cutting off my circulation.'

'Well? Candy was it?' he declares, tightening his brute grip.

'See..., ugh, ugh..., naw, you ain't gone treat Candy any kind of way! You take it out, cause Candy loves some aggressioness,' Keyonton chuckles. 'Agressioness..., is that even a word? Anyway that is what I said, cringing from the thought of touching a man's pirate..., I mean private. Before I know it, shoot..., I hear that big ole belt buckle rattle, sounding like a wind chime; and then that zipper, huh..., sounding like one of those old, long, Army duffle bags..., you know, the ones they made back in world war one. Huh..., then comes the thick, long trousers hitting the floor like fast coliseum dropping curtains. Huh..., right now! I already know, it's gone be either medium-well, charred porterhouse in a restaurant later or burnt tube steak in this crappy room. So I slowly kneel, tensing with all the power I can muster, and send an instant, powerhouse driver straight to his musty sacks. You know..., the ole one-two when the left jab stops stealthily, going numb instantly, with the right still digging deeper until driving him to his tiptoes and hearing his boots' in a delayed slam to the floor.

This hulk side dude falls to his knees in a deep moan, springing upward when something hits the floor, a metal ball of some sort. I shake off my left, clutching his thick herringbone to recoup some of my stolen loot, hearing fast running footsteps and soft, giggly voices outside.

Exhausted, I tiptoed to the window, feeling relief finding a fire escape, when swiftly making my way down, and looking at the shiny engraved chain when I ran under a light that read, 'To my lover, Iron Ball Vegas.' Well, needless to say, the emblem went to the gutter, but this here is a nice damn herringbone, huh?' Keyonton yells, extending it forward from around his neck. 'And most of all..., my booty thanks me every day,' Keyonton says, holding the thick, shiny necklace higher until it glistens from the bright stage lights. "And guess what? I don't do crack houses, and damn sho (sure) ain't doing Vegas!" Keyonton boldly exclaims, laughing until snickering, non-stop, and causing people to laugh even harder with the greater uproar.

Boogey and Winton are into laughter when a waitress walks up, taking orders.

Keyonton looks down at the red stage timer numbers, displaying his last thirty minutes when pulling the microphone closer. "Man, you gotta love this place, the land of milk and honey, but that is one place I was not about to milk nor give up the honey!" he exclaims, bending and patting his butt while in a crazy twisting move, almost as if dancing backward. He looks around, finding a Sailor then two Soldiers walking past in uniforms. "But on a serious note..., my hat goes off to our young Soldiers and Troops fighting in foreign lands. Come on! Give them a round of applause!" he declares, holding the mic under one arm while clapping and pointing at the three making their way back to their seats, with drinks.

The crowd cheers, whistling until almost everyone is cheering in a great uproar.

"God help us all, because we're for sure a stiff-necked people; you know, like in biblical times," he says, looking like he had an out-of-body experience when trying to gather his thoughts. "Yeah, the world has changed, drastically. Unemployment's on the rise. I just read that milk is three-sixty a gallon, gas five ninety-five a gallon, and ink five thousand a gallon; now ain't that some crap?"

Suddenly, there is a loud outburst from a deep drunken voice. "Dude..., you stole that..., it's already been used! I heard it last week, in San Dawg (San Diego)!" a drunken young man yells, standing and slightly swaying.

"Used, huh? Hmm..., well that's the same thing your mother said about my glow-in-the dark prophylactic."

The room grows furious with laughter, and the man's grin turns sour.

"Aight (All right)! You got me on that one," he says, throwing up both thumbs and pretending to be cool.

"Naw, what I got was your mama, in a love promise but one-night stance, but I got you by the busted elongated shaped water balloon which your sister was playing with the next morning until I snatched it."

Again, the young man throws up two thumbs, knowing he's been had.

"So where was I before my son, the great magician..., Swazeelee interrupted," Keyonton utters, in deep thoughts until shaking his head as if still in disbelief. "Man, I still don't know how you got out of that prophylactic, especially after dousing it in moonshine, gasoline, and burning it. Hmm, could be why you drink so much, I reckon!" Keyonton declares, laughing until the room tapers off.

Keyonton looks over his shoulder bringing a finger to his lips in a low tone. "Man, there was a guy backstage eating fried chicken and it got me hungry than a champ, just thinking about how country folks throw down: rocky mountain oysters, hog maws, hog balls, how 'bout them shitterling, I mean chitterlings, umm!" he shouts, hearing hog maws screamed out in a delayed response.

"Only thing is I haven't seen any Chinese restaurants yet!" he exclaims, running his fingers under his chin with his eyes cut upwards with a finger to his temple as if thinking when fixing his mouth, strangely. "Now that is some good eating," he says, throwing his voice to that of a foreign accent: da beef, wit (with) da (the) broccoli, shimpa wit da egg foo young, house expa (extra) spesha (special) fried-rice," he says in an even more excellent impersonation. "Man, we are off up in those Chinese joints not knowing a thing they are saying. But look..., there's nothing funnier than a five-hundred-pound person at a Chinese buffet. Whew, the sight of that poor, little Chinese man when they walk up in there. The little Chinese man be looking at the man's swollen stomach as if it is a foreign object. I saw a Chinese man one day, just ah screaming, crying, 'Yo (your) stomach ah (is) too big for little buffet; you need to go to the farm and eat wit (with) cow, pig or horse but you, no buffet! Buffet no good for you, and no good for me; bankrupt little buffet, put little Chinese man out of business!' Keyonton says, laughing.

Keyonton goes on with more jokes and then smiles, pulling the microphone closer when the crowd is finally, almost calm.

Keyonton goes into several other jokes when wrapping up his set when his mind slips back to another food joke when he hears and finally sees a patron run past the stage, calling Keyonton, Iron Ball. "Iron Ball huh? While we are at it, is there an Iron Ball Vegas in the house?" Keyonton shouts, senselessly giggling but playfully pretending he is about to swallow the microphone.

Two tall figures emerge from the back of the dark, smoke-filled room, and Keyonton puts his hand up, shielding the stage lights and motioning the DJ to play his exit theme song.

Out of nowhere, a glass loudly smashes against the wall and the DJ scratches and then halts the track.

"I'm Iron Ball! I'm Iron Ball, dam nit!" the deep, too-familiar voice resonates. His name is barely heard until repeating it, but louder as the room draws so quiet that you could hear a pin drop.

All eyes stare between Keyonton and the dark figures when a full-figured, hourglass shaped body prances to the stage, followed by a tall, thick-built man as they clear the thick, smoke curtain and materialize into view, halfway down the aisle.

Keyonton's smile turns into pure horror and he unknowingly shrieks like a little girl through the microphone running in circles and dropping the mic while wading through the flimsy curtains until stepping on the hem and bringing the curtains to the floor. "I'm Key, and that's my time, folks!" he nervously yells, running backward.

Keith and Vegas give chase until intercepted by bouncers when turning, shoving each other, and sprinting for the main entrance.

Mild winds ease through the streets, raising a strong, burnt smell.

Commotion from bystanders in the hall roars in a moderate tone until laughter.

Distant clouds draw near as distant lightning and thunder slowly fades.

Boogey and Winton exit through an opened side door behind a large crowd.

Winton slows down looking for Boogey then shuffles to catch up when a hand reaches forward, swiping a few good swipes until grabbing a handful of Winton's booty. Winton's head then eyes go back quick, finding the bouncer, Pokie, winking and picking up his pace until turning, when dropping something and Winton looks back finding him fading into the crowd.

Boogey and Winton rush out onto the main street and pass a fire marshal standing near the front door, asking folks questions.

"What the hell!" Winton exclaims, running and leaving Boogey with tears instantly forming as his eyes roam over wet, busted windows, charred seats, and other half-busted windows with thick, black smoke billowing out.

The fire marshal finally looks back, finding Boogey and Winton talking to a firefighter. "Sir, is this your car?" the marshal asks, walking up and leading Winton, the most hysterical, off to the side for minutes until the marshal is called away.

Boogey and Winton keep chatting and looking for the women until most people disperse. They open the doors, and gallons of water pour out until leveled with the deep-cut floorboards.

"What you gone do now?" Boogey asks with concerned and sad eyes.

"Nothing..., nothing to do..., I bet it was those trifling tail wenches!" Winton utters, kicking the passenger door and jumping back when it falls off.

They stay for over an hour, getting most of the water out with old rags from the trunk, and then cover the front seat with thick quilts from the five and dime a few days earlier, climbing inside and sitting in deep thought.

Suddenly, headlights unknowingly come on at the corner when a car rolls toward them with bright lights beaming.

Winton wipes the last tear, finally leaning and digging in his pockets for keys, when loud laughter bursts out as the car pulls alongside.

Boogey looks meanly into the women's laughing faces.

"What's up, Cap'n (captain), fireball?" the female driver yells in deep laughter when Winton finally notices them.

Winton's face turns cherry red, and he grows furious when springing up with both hands stretched forward, hogtied by the seat belt around his neck when slammed into the side of his car, hanging and gagging.

The girl in the back leans out, holding something hidden until spraying pink, silly string all over Winton's face.

Boogey jumps in disbelief, letting go of the door, which slams to the concrete when he jumps out.

Winton finally gets somewhat loose and comes up expressly; still half bent over, trying to unbuckle.

The female driver guns the engine, with tires squealing; leaving deep burn marks.

Boogey squints, reading some of the license plate when a car crosses his line of sight, and he spots something off to the side, moving pronto toward the corner, in a streak, finally realizing it is Winton.

The driver turns, flooring the engine, and then swerves, gaining control.

Winton runs back to his car, patting his pockets fast until finding the keys in the trunk and snatching them. His tight fist slams into the roof, and he kicks the door but misses the freeboard, driving metal deep into his shin, and nipping the bone. His mouth drops open expressly, without a sound, and tears heavily flow as he begins dancing around in agonizing pain.

Boogey finally looks over the cab, discovering Winton jumping slowly with an agonizing stare and raised eyebrows. He soon registers what happened when seeing Winton fade and sees his hands at his shin, rubbing fast. "They're club hoppers Wint, so you'll see them again; I can almost guarantee it!" Boogey declares, finding Winton jumping again, with his mouth torn wide open when Winton's yelp pours out, causing Boogey to jump.

Boogey ducks down on the side of the car, on his knees, slipping his index finger in his mouth to keep from bursting into laughter. His belly heavily giggles, but he remains silent until he is almost in control when crawling an inch or two and looking up, finding Winton's saw dust-covered boots inches away.

Boogey's eyes go down and back fast, nippily rubbing through the puddle of muddy water, pretending to be searching for something.

"What is it? What are you doing?" Winton asks with fierce, bloodshot eyes.

"Hinges…, I'm looking for the screw that might have come out."

Winton stares at Boogey's red neck longer then his face when Boogey comes up, with Winton shaking his head. "Laugh, laugh, laugh, you're just a laughing fool, aren't you; you'll laugh at anything. Get this door up, and let's get the heck out of here, you laughing hyena!" Winton yells, with a more severe frown when heavily limping away.

# CHAPTER ONE

## Hilarious From The Comedy Club

In the woods, and miles from Boogey's house, two men in a shabby house carry out a deceptive plot to deter a friend's son from joining a gang.

The taller man peels off adhesive, electronic gun leads, giggling while attaching them to a friend's body; staging a fake drug scene when hearing an engine turn off.

Four young guys sit high, still puffing marijuana in a 1957 Classic in pure darkness until lowered by the automatic suspension when easing out, slowly and quietly shutting doors.

One guy loads a gun, unknowingly carrying the activator for the electronic gun leads attached to the man's body in the house.

The four quietly ease onto the porch; the one with a gun nervously bringing up the rear with nervous and fast wandering eyes.

The front door squeaks on rusty hinges, and everyone is visible when loud shrieks ring out with rumbling and loud shots echoing through the dense forest.

Silence falls, and the tall man fakes being unconscious, and the short man fakes his death with fake blood spewing when feeling dizzy from pills taken to lower his blood pressure until there is no pulse, intentionally.

The four young men spring back against the wall and then jump forward, nervously collecting all costly valuables.

The leader takes a black, cloth bag that looks as if it contains drugs and money.

The three pats down the two imposters, and the leader instantly quiets them when hearing a distant engine.

The four rush to the window, eight eyes gazing through dusty screens and over the lawn while hearts race until overpowered by a small Baby-Ben clock on the worn-down mantle.

The old, worn screen door flings open, and the four springs forward with boots slamming into the dust; shuffling fast yet taking baby steps while fighting to pull up, below the butt-cut, sagging, low-rider trousers.

Gunshots ring out, and bullets fly hot on their trails but intentionally higher over heads as the tall man stands emptying a clip while hooting, cursing, reloading, and then firing again. He aims, slightly offsetting, ensuring a miss when hearing another engine and finding another car's park lights approaching, slowly.

Headlights lunge forward, and the leader plows down tall stalks of tobacco when a tightly held electronic gun extends from the car window, clicking and misfiring.

The tall man tucks the gun in his trousers, dancing fast to get the hot barrel off his thigh when Texas four-stepping until making some silly move when the gun falls, prematurely firing. He jumps back, staring at park lights again, grabbing the gun, and shuffling inside to find his friend giggling, stumbling, and pulling off the fake blood-covered shirt and electronic leads. "I think it worked; let's go to Plan B!"

Hours later, over at Boogey's, a loud ring comes from inside the pitch-dark house, and Boogey's run-down boots shuffle over the grit-covered, run-down floor. He fights to stand on long legs from the deep, sunken-in, busted spring couch.

The phone stops ringing after the second ring.

Boogey's wife, Nattie, sets a cool glass of fruit punch next to his seat, sitting with a plate of food.

Boogey leans, accidentally letting out a loud, obnoxious fart.

"Really!" Nattie frowns. "Yah, nasty sucker! You coulda (could have) took yo' (your) stankin' tail outside! I'm eating!" she yells, fanning over and around her plate.

"Oh, woman, quit yo (your) lip popping! Hell..., it slipped, I reckon. Shucks! Can't even fart in peace without you opening yo (your) ole pie trap!" He grabs the seat of his pants, pulling out a hand full of his sticky drawers.

"Trap? You need a trap in those skid-marked covered drawers," she hollers, rolling her eyes and staring at a commercial when frowning again.

Now, Boogey and Nattie love each other and have been together so long that they have become bittersweet; speaking their minds with it never coming out just right. They do little things to degrade each other, either in fun or out of pure anger.

Nattie would sometimes hang his pissy sheets or soiled underwear on the porch or write crazy things on the dusty car windows, to name a few.

On the other hand, Boogey does unbecoming things as well, like tying her unused tampons to her Sunday hat, slipping laxatives in her drinks, etc.

The mischief over the years has grown to a very long list, but at this point, the pranks have become a competitive sport of some sort.

Boogey finally stands, pissed, with his serious face impetuously growing into a sly grin when the phone rings again, and he slowly walk over, pulling it to his ear.

Nattie snatches a dingy pillow, covering her face when hearing him light off another almost silent but deadly fart and the stench instantly grows. "What the heck have you been eating, reindeers?" she grumbles, swiftly running to the bedroom with her plate, and slamming the door.

"Uh yello (hello)!" Boogey finally answers, sluggishly seizing another handful of sticky drawers and swishing until in a mild, short-lived dance when shifting on both feet.

The voice on the other end mumbles a few words, and Boogey flips on a dim lamp, scrambling over the junky table.

"Ok, call it to me again," Boogey says, verifying. "And Tiny says it will hit?" he inquires, looking at the clock and realizing he has fifteen minutes before the lottery closes out. The phone's handle drops freely, jerking, banging, and dangling inches from the floor. Boogey busts through the screen door which bangs loudly against the house, and then retracts halfway on worn-out springs. Boogey's boots lunge forward, missing five steps as he stumbles and almost trips, when a hand touches the ground, rebalancing.

"What the...!" Nattie shrieks, peeking out and finding dust rising and Boogey homing in on the country store like a heat-seeking missile. She shakes her head, pulls the screen shut, and heads for the kitchen.

Boogey walks onto a sidewalk, hearing dogs howling, then a silenced, non-flashing ambulance speed past on the dark, main road with just dim parking lights on.

Two deputies' cruisers flash by when the next cruiser swerves, barely missing a row of tall, slow-moving, proud ducks.

Boogey nosily looks back, discovering people on porches with some shuffling out of the store, finding red and blue lights fading over the hill.

A few folks mumble when the phone inside the store rings.

Folks converge outside with eyes still piercing into pure darkness toward the emergency lights that reflect against the long tree line, in the bend of the road.

A sudden, missile sound furiously grows when the sheriff's car fades out of darkness; no lights or siren. He swerves, laying into the horn when pedestrians scatter and the siren and headlights finally come with flames bursting out of dual exhaust pipes.

A scream blares out of nowhere, startling everyone when several items loudly smash, and the store's screen door bursts wide open, slamming into the wall and retracting, expeditiously.

"What the...!" Boogey utters, scratching his greasy head.

Everyone stares at the tall female who runs hysterically into the middle of the street then in the wrong direction, turning and bursting through the crowd with a liquor bottle under one arm as if going in for a Super Bowl touchdown. Her heels skid until clicking when coming to a screeching halt, turning and running back through the crowd toward her car.

"I told y'all (you all) she ain't wrapped tight. I reckon she needs some serious meds or something," Boogey shouts, shaking his head in disbelief.

"She's 'bout a pint low! I think her cracker fell off hu (her) cheese," the short, bifocal old man beside Boogey shouts, staring at her in disbelief as well.

"What? It's cheese off the cracker! Huh..., you need the darn meds; some talk-straight pills so you ain't back-asswards (ass-backward), I reckon!" Boogey burst into laughter.

"What?" the man asks, somewhat dumbfounded.

"Oh, nothing," Boogey says, smiling when hearing the woman's transmission grinding when going into gear.

There comes a loud squeal and a slight hint of burnt rubber when folks fan, stepping back, watching the car jerk slowly when taking off fast then creeping at an even slower pace.

"Hell..., she's better off running home, I reckon!" Boogey exclaims, laughing harder when the gears grind louder until thrown into high gear as folks stare at the taillights until they slowly vanish over the hill.

In Boogey and Nattie's house, Nattie's head finally turns, slowly following the phone cord to the floor and she soon hears a screaming voice and numbers being punched when picking it up. "Who da (the) heck dis (this) be?"

"Me, Nat! Nattie, it's me..., Wint!"

"Winton! What the heck does yo (your) trifling tail want?"

"Where's Boogey? I think we lost our connection."

"Connection? Oh, you lost a connection alright..., got that fool after those there numbers, again. Now, you listen here!" she declares with one eyebrow slightly raised. "Don't call here wit (with) that crap, you hea (hear) me? You got it, slick..., you got that?" she yells.

"I know, Nat, but Tiny guarantees its gone (going to) be a sure winner!"

"What? Man, the heck wit (with) that cracked-out, palm-reading heffa! If she told ya'll that there was free, alien poontang on the moon, you two fools would probably be stowaways in a cargo hold, I reckon. I can't believe you got Boogey mixed up with that fake, palm-reading fool..., doggone!"

"Yeah, Nattie, but what if he hits..., you know..., the big gon (one)?"

"Hit what? Shucks, you'd do better to hit the side of a tobacco barn with a slingshot. Now, gone with that bull, Wint! Don't make me slap the piss oucha (out of you)! Keep on, and I reckon I'll bust a cap in that narrow tail of yours!"

Winton burst out in a heavy yet quiet giggle, continually staring deep into the mirror until sucking his gut in and out, flexing. "I hear you, but look hea (here), I ain't gone take kind to idle tail threats, so you just run along and tell Boogey to call me, ASAP!"

"Oh yeah, and when I do..., it will be a cold day in Hades, sucker! And another thing; if my threats are so idle, don't bother sleeping light tonight!" she screams, slamming the phone down.

Winton jerks the phone away with a finger in his ear to stop the ringing.

Meanwhile, a short, manly silhouette stands alongside Boogey's house with white eyes gazing while quietly rummaging through mason jars, illegally tapping into Boogey's underground moonshine spout.

Outside the store, six feet, one-hundred-forty-pound, fifty-two-year-old Boogey, medium-built with a dark, heavy tan, lifts his hole-riddled hat, running his fingers through his grey-streaked permed hair. His size-fourteen brogans slam against the concrete, knocking away dust.

The general store's door opens, and a kid stands unintentionally blocking the doorway, gawking with his jaws flapping until blowing a giant bubble and bursting into a silly laugh.

Boogey scratches his temple, losing his patience when jumping in a firm stance, frightening the kid. "Boy! Get your snotty nose tail out my way!" Boogey yells, cutting his eyes back when the kid scrambles past, almost knocking Boogey down.

Other patrons rush up, following Boogey inside; huddling yet quiet and nosy.

"What is wrong with that crazy old hag, busting out of here like a bat out of Hell?" Boogey asks the attendant while picking up a few overturned wine bottles.

"I'm not sure, but it seemed urgent," the male stocker says, interrupting.

"All I know is a deputy said she needs to get home pronto," the cashier says, coming from around the counter, sweeping.

Boogey swishes around the thick wad of tobacco, nervously swallowing when frowning and hacking up a thick wad mixed with phlegm, causing folks to cringe when he takes a deep swallow.

A different old man walks up behind Boogey, puffing hard on his cigar.

Boogey frowns, looking back a few times, putting up with the pungent stench when a giant ring of smoke glides over his head like a halo, and mild to loud giggles rings out. Boogey looks back again, frowning when another ring floats by, slower with loud, silly laughter following. Boogey turns in an instant. "Look!" Boogey declares, eye-to-eye. "I'm a grown tail man, not one of your silly, shy-tail kids."

The man nervously stares, frowning until bursting into a weird, long laugh.

Boogey turns away, pacing, yet swiftly clenching his cheeks and fighting hard to hold it when silently expelling gas which sounds like air from a straw and tapers off to that of a spear gun.

The old man backs away fast, grabbing his neck, pretending he's shot when double-timing backward, and staggering to the couch near the cast-iron heater.

"You..., you..., you..., nasty buzzard!" Boogey screams, moving up in the line, and intentionally spreading the powerhouse scent.

"Whoo wee! That there sure is a hummana, humdinger," an old, granny-glass-wearing lady stutters, backing away expressly in a backward dance, and causing others to disperse, speedily.

Boogey puts on a convincing face. "Yeah, what she said! You common dog!" Boogey points to the man who is staring back with wide eyes as if mesmerized.

The old man frowns harder, jumping up with bulged eyes, puffing more circles faster to cut off the overpowering scent while continually fanning.

The female cashier slams the register shut, backing away, and grabs a can of air freshener, vigorously spraying a thick mist until folks almost vanish.

The old man burst into a loud laugh. "Dang son! That brought tears to my cataracts; yes, it did. Doc says my eyes would never make tears again, but I'll be doggone!" He wipes his overly watery eyes, giggling harder.

Boogey extends a wadded dollar out with two minutes to spare.

The clerk puts down the can, retrieves his money and a pink slip, which she pulls from his tight grip in a normal, yet playful spirit.

"How are you doing, Tamyi?" Boogey asks, staring at her faded name tag.

"For the umpteenth time, it's Tommi!" She frowns, rolling her eyes.

"Hmm..., spells T_a_y_m_i, Taayyymmii!" he utters in a slurred, silly speech.

"Yeah, and I explained to your non-reading tail before, so get it right or don't say it at all, ya (you) pissy tail drunk!" she declares, shutting him down in embarrassment.

Boogey's shoulders slightly droop, hearing murmurs and several giggles, but he swiftly recalls being told that the numbers would hit when a big smile comes, instantly. "Taymi, Tommi, Hommie, Mommie, Slanky, Stanky, but sure as hell is cranky," he senselessly declares, staring into her frown. "Now, give me my numbers!"

The clerk punches in the numbers, banging the machine when the display light blinks, and the machine re-energizes when she runs his numbers, throwing the tickets on the counter.

Boogey grabs his tickets, backing away when the short man walks up teary-eyed, still laughing. "Man..., that funk was terrible..., whew..., it was so bad that you almost shut down the dang lottry (lottery) network!"

"What? I done tolt (told) you, it won't me! I ain't never smelt nothing that darn bad! It was you since you think it's so darn funny," Boogey says, trying to convince everyone who stares with frowns, still pinching their noses while dispersing from the line as Boogey passes again.

The old man straightens his face, instantly bursting into a loud irritating laugh until almost choking.

Another old lady walks up, patting his back until thrusting her tight, fist into his back.

"Enough already!" the old man shouts, slowly swiveling around on one heel. "You need a man with all that strength," he says, turning to the ninety-year-old and holding up a trembling balled tight fist. He slowly turns from her, seriously staring at Boogey, when bursting into an irritating laugh. "Hey Boog, I bet those scruffy drawers look like Jeff's two-ton truck has been popping wheelies in them," the old man says, laughing while Boogey stares eye-to-eye, still pretending to be innocent.

Boogey stares at his buck teeth. "Yeah..., and those teeth are as yellow as Jeff's darn truck. Walking around here with butter-me-not teeth..., teeth so yellow you can make a darn pound cake; and please, please sanitize that stank breath! Huh, the mayor should give you the key to the city, to the sewage plant, that is!" Boogey declares, chuckling hard until laughing out loud when tilting his head forward. "Ladies, my deepest apology for this jive time turkey!" Boogey shouts, finally tilting his hat toward a few ladies standing side-by-side.

"You the jivester, ya (you) slick-head fool!" the old man says with a straight face.

"Oh, kiss where the sun doesn't shine!" Boogey yells, playfully patting his butt with dust shooting out of the dry-rotted material.

"Yeah, then toss my salad!" the man shrieks, bending, leaning, and lifting a leg.

"Salad? What? A salad is all you got? Shucks, I don't even like salad unless tossed with ranch," Boogey utters, scratching his head, and confused about the comment.

"Ok, deal..., ranch it is, so start tossing, Bubba!" The man excitedly begins unbuckling.

A whirlwind of laughter comes, with everyone in tears and some almost crying.

"Whoo wee! Boogey, I think you messed on yourself!" a short lady exclaims, smelling an even more pungent stench as Boogey passes, when everyone grabs their noses, backing away fast.

In Boogey's dimly-lit living room, the birdcage rattles as their parakeet (Bud), a sixteen-inch white cockatiel, shakes its head, regaining his vision. "Dang, Nattie! Is Boogey at those numbers again?" Bud asks, shaking off sleep.

"Oh shut up, Bud!" she yells, walking around the filthy, cluttered living room.

"Well screw…!"

"Ott! Ott! You betta not, Bud! I double dare you! Say it, and I'll put soap in your mouth until you gag your puny bird brain out!" Nattie shrieks, frowning.

Bud spits, getting the heavily perfumed soap off his mind until his head goes up and down, looking through the dirty screen. "Where is that dang Boogey now, Natt?"

"Ah Bud, shut up!" she shrieks, looking over her shoulder.

"Ah, screw…!"

"What!" she screams, heading for the kitchen in a mad dash until stopping to let him know she is dead serious.

Bud rolls his eyes upward, whistling a known tune; letting her know he is ignoring her until she looks back and finally sees Boogey.

Boogey comes up on the first step. He looks back, spotting two cruisers rolling past in the opposite direction and stares longer until a coroner's car slowly rolls past.

"Boogey! Get yo (your) nosy as…!" Bud yells, cutting the curse word short when hearing Nattie's fast shuffling feet across the gritty floor.

Boogey comes to the top step, rushing inside and passing the cage, which slightly bounces as Bud fights to get away from the fresh, funky scent.

"Uh…! Boogey! Boogey! Boogey! Whooa! Come on now, main (man)! You're too old for this crap main (man)!" Bud yells.

Nattie steps into the living room, frowning and backing down fast. "Whooaaa, Daddy! Whooa! Man get yo' (your) stankin' tail out of dis (this) house! On the back porch, now! Woo!" she screams, marching him out with the broom, and shutting the screen door.

Boogey's brogans stomp, sadly dragging across the crooked wooden porch.

"Boogey, get yo' tail out of dis (this) house, now!" Bud repeats, sounding just like Nattie and causing Boogey to look back over his shoulder with excited eyes.

Nattie searches a change of clothing for him.

Boogey flips Bud a finger through the mirror with his head pressed into the screen.

"Punk! You want some of this?" I'll...," Bud yells, flexing his chest forward.

"What did I tell you about that mouth, Bud?" Nattie shrieks from the bedroom.

"Yah..., dookie man! Boogey is the dookie man! A dookie man!"

Boogey creeps inside, clutching a glass for a hit of moonshine.

"Man, what did I tell you? Now, give me dem (them) boots so I can sit them on the back porch," Nattie screams, holding her nose while watching him unlace them with his back to the screen.

"Forget that! Haven't you heard about the overpopulation of brown recluse spiders around these woods? Huh..., mess around and make somebody lose a toe or foot," he declares, in a menacing stare, laughing.

Nattie points him to the door again, turning and walking into the bedroom when Bud swears. "Don't make me come in there, Bud!" Nattie yells, pulling clean underwear from the busted chest when the drawer's face and a handful of clothes fall to the floor.

Boogey flips on the porch light, sliding the wooden chair across the deck and about to sit.

"Ott, Ott..., don't even think about sitting your stankin' tail there!" Nattie shouts, handing him clean clothes. She rushes to the sink, running water in a pail with lye soap, then rushes back to the door, passing it to him.

Boogey washes and dresses and minutes later walk in embarrassed.

Five-feet, six-inch, fifty-year-old Nattie, slender built, shuts the front door, covering the bird's cage with a torn sheet when Bud makes it his business to be nosy when peeking through several frayed holes.

"Oh..., Winton said to call," she says in a nasty tone easing in a chair, frowning.

"Maybe tomorrow," he says, turning on the television and sitting.

Nattie thinks about their debt until she finally bursts into tears. "What we gone (going to) do, Boog?"

"What do you mean?" he asks, playing clueless.

"The bills, car, rent..., everything. Bill collectors call daily, and we can barely afford to keep a roof over our heads!" she utters, putting her shaking head down.

"We're going to hit the number, Nat..., I can feel it, I tell yah (you)," he responds, feeling foolish but still believing.

Nattie's head comes up in a rush. "Lottery! That is all you think about! There is so much wasted bill money on a dang lottery! I think you'll play the lottery before you pay bills if you had it your way!" she exclaims, livid.

"Don't talk like you lost your last red cent, woman! Huh..., Lottery? Shucks! I only play but a dollar, here and there; you would think I spent a whole check on it, I reckon. Just get off my back, I tell you…, get off my back, now!" Boogey yells in anger.

"You need to face your responsibilities!" she declares, leaning back.

Boogey swiftly jumps, pissed when unbuckling his trousers, dropping them and grabbing them, balled tight in his fist. "Who wears the freakin' pants around here?" he shrieks when leaning back, throwing them at her.

Nattie comes unglued when springing up, ducking, and slowly rocking in a fighting stance. "You done lost your ever-loving, cotton-picking mind now, throwing those darn turdy trousers at me!" she screams, now bouncing like a professional boxer.

"Turdy? Those are washed!"

"Yeah, but you didn't wash that butt well!" she says with an evil stare.

Boogey walks around heaps of clothes until his trembling, long index finger comes to her face. "Leave me alone before I double bank ya (you)!"

Nattie come toe-to-toe, not blinking but biting her bottom lip in a frown. "One freakin' dollar!" she shrieks. "One dollar? Dollars make hundreds. Yeah, a dollar maybe, but every freakin time you pass a stoe (store)!"

Boogey turns, and Nattie's eyes immediately drift to the dark, long, faded stain in his drawers.

Nattie's cheeks puff and she laughs uncontrollably, trying hard to stop.

Boogey frowns with raised eyebrows. "He..., he..., he..., ha..., ha..., ha...; always giggling! Laugh, laugh, laugh..., laugh your tail off!" he declares, stepping away. "I'm feeling lucky; I know we gone hit, and when we do..., whoo wee!" he utters, with his fist balled tight and high. "You can buy anything you want!" he shouts, almost smiling.

Nattie sadly shakes her head. "You know…, you use to be a young fool with wild, non-accomplishable dreams, but that is what I fell in love with, and now…, well, now you're just an older fool with even bigger, un-accomplishable dreams, like that there, lottery," she says in a sad tone.

"Young fool, old fool, huh..., well, it means the same. You would have ended up with that clown, Freddy, had I not come along. Now that there, Freddy; now he be the dang fool! Just think, he spent all that time in school, warming seats to do what…, end up a business mascot? Obviously, he went for the free hot meals, tatto (potato) spuds, and sugar prunes!" Boogey bursts into an unstoppable, silly laugh until in endless tears. "Everyone has some kind of talent, but I seriously think Freddy pissed his away."

Nattie holds back until her face is cherry red. "Screw you!" she finally screams at the top of her voice and out of anger. "Every time, look..., every time you throw Freddy in my face. Yeah, he may shake his tail for a living, but you look hea (here), he has nice things and ain't broke as hell all the time, like yo (your) broke butt!" she angrily shrieks, feeling somewhat relieved.

Harsh words bring Boogey into a deep depression when his head goes low. "So, that's how you see me, Natt!" he asks, walking toward the bedroom without looking back. "Really..., so that's how you see me, now?"

Boogey enters the bedroom, slamming the door and scratching his head. He stands in deep thoughts when pulling out a flask, taking a few swallows with a torn-up face, then the worst face when taking another straight hit. He bends, swaying into the television. His hair spikes from static electricity until cutting the television off. He looks in the mirror at his new hair duo and jumps back in a fighting stance, silently giggling until feeling around in the dark. He makes it to the bed, easing under the worn-out silk sheets, shuffling and constantly untangling his scaly feet for minutes.

At Winton's house, his family settles in when Winton walks out with a beer. He looks at his neighbor's house, finding his neighbor's shadow moving expressly by each window, heading for the front door. His eyes wander over his charred seats, shaking his head before going inside and coming out with half a gallon of Azreay'l Scotch. Winton cracks the seal, slipping it behind the seat when hearing dry, fast crunchy leaves and turning, finding his neighbor slowing and creeping up.

"Sup, Winton?" His neighbor heavily sways with a small mason jar in hand.

"Sup, John?" Winton exclaims, sliding the scotch further alongside the couch and even farther out of view.

"Oh, nothing; I saw you up and decided to see what you are up to."

"Chillin'..., about to call it a night," Winton responds, sneakily glaring at him.

They look away, neither saying a word until Winton mentions it being late again.

"I heard that," John says, maneuvering until the bottle is slightly visible.

"Aight John, I'm gonna have to say good night," Winton says, staring at his watch then at John's red, glassy eyes.

"Ok, later dude," John utters, still stiff as a board and swaying more.

Winton steps toward the door, and John plops down on the busted, dry-rotten, porch couch.

"Man, what a pretty view. I think I'm gonna enjoy it for a minute; that's if you don't mind," John says, looking back at Winton, somewhat serious.

"Do I mind? Heck yeah, I mind! Man, I'm not gonna have you out here with my family inside. When I hear noise in my yard at night, I need to know I can bust a cap in some hind parts and not worry about who it is."

"I'll be extra quiet, I promise." John winks in an intoxicating frown.

"No way, dude…, ah bye-bye!" Winton declares, still pretending that he has concerns for his family, when pointing him away. Winton shuts the door, peeking, and finds John behind a tree, glancing back until playing a game of cat and mouse for minutes when the curtains shut, expeditiously.

John breaks out in a serious stagger, sprinting for Winton's front door, slowing down feet away when Winton whistles loudly and deeply barks like a big pit bull, following up with deep, vicious growls.

John picks up his steps, jetting alongside the house into the backyard, toward an old, broken-down truck, which he expressly leaps onto, denting the rusty metal while dancing, fearfully. He peeks into the darkness, nervously shaking his head, finally remembering Winton doesn't even have a dog when shaking his head and smiling.

Winton cracks the door open, dragging the bottle inside. "Silly sucker!" he whispers, smiling, and quietly giggling, then laughing harder.

John gets his laugh out, then creeps to the front, fumbling around, alongside the couch until a cool barrel touches the back of his head.

"One wrong move, sucker!" Winton's wife, Nelle, a five-six, stout woman exclaims, frowning while tightening her thin gown.

John's hands rise slowly. "It's me…, Nelle…, John! I ain't gone hurt you, gul (girl)," he whispers in a soft, whiney voice. "It's me, your neighbor…, John!"

"Boi! Get your tail away from my house! I could have put a plug in you!" she declares, watching Winton burst through the door, laughing himself almost to death.

Winton uncontrollably giggles until almost gagging. "I told you about messing around out here in the dark!" Winton utters, giggling harder when seeing John's torn-up, teary, sweaty face.

Nelle slides the pistol into her robe, laughing until finally choking from the heavy smell.

Winton's eyes grow big when she covers her mouth and nose, nippily sliding his arms around her, and quickly guiding her to the door. "You need to get inside…, the smog," he says, swiftly guiding her more.

Nelle fans harder with wandering eyes until staring at the black seats. "Uh, uh, uh! What happened to the darn car, Wint?" she asks, walking back to the car and backing away fast when the scent gets too strong for her asthma.

"Well..., at work..., yeah, at work… this dude's car next to ours caught on fire, but the fire department put it out before it burned too badly."

"Oh yeah?" she says, beaming then playfully dancing until kicking up a heap of dust until they can hardly see one another.

Winton and John fan hard, backing away until on the porch. "What are you all that excited about?" Winton finally asks, fanning more.

"Cause we can get a new car when his insurance pays off, right?" She walks out of the dust cloud, a few shades darker when cheerily easing onto the porch.

"Whoa, whoa, whoa!" Winton declares in deep thought. "Well, that ain't happening because he didn't have insurance. The fire marshal says it is an act of nature or something; lightning hits the car, kaboom, fire, and smoke. Tell her, John," Winton exclaims, winking at John.

John looks at Winton as Nelle turns, hearing a passing car's horn. He eases out his jar, wiggling it, and then shoots it down to his side when she looks back at him.

Winton motions 'no' with his head and a mean look, then smiles, looking at Nelle and John again.

John sticks his finger up as if in an elementary class, about to ask a question when deep in thought, before Nelle sees him.

Winton rapidly shakes his head, 'yes,' then looks down, pissed.

"You're right; a friend who works in insurance told me about the nature clause," John expressly utters, swallowing hard with a knot in his throat and sounding like a bullfrog.

"Oh heck no, we are not going off that bull!" Nelle declares, unconvinced. "I'll call our insurance company first thing in the morning," she says, walking inside and easing the door shut.

Winton walks inside and brings the bottle out along with a shot glass.

Winton and John drop to the couch, shaking their heads, giggling.

Winton tops off his own shot glass then fills one-fifth of the jar and stops.

"Yeah, come to think of it, Nelle, you can get paid big time!" John says in a mild tone and gets louder when Winton pours it to the rim to shut him up.

Before long, the two reminisce about past crazy prank phone calls until Winton goes inside, bringing out a radio, and minutes later, they are singing at the top of their drunken voices.

Out of nowhere, John mentions the phone pranks again when Winton goes inside and comes out with another bottle, phone book, and the phone.

Winton flops down, dialing and putting the phone on speaker.

"Main Moon, may I help you su (sir) or ma'am?" the soft-spoken, feminine Oriental voice answers.

"Yes, pickup, please," Winton says, giggling, and covering the phone.

"Go head wit (with) your order, sau (sir)," she says in a mild, pleasant tone.

"Yes, uh, uh..., how about an order of some Dumb Chick and uh, uh, a side of Two Dumb Nuts, and Two Dumb Fools!" Winton declares, covering the mouthpiece, and giggling senselessly. "Oh and ah, ah..., two dumb sluts!"

The Chinese girl continues scribbling then slows the pen strokes with eyes gazing up and down the list when her mouth drops open. "Wha..., (what)! Why you call wit dumb shit? Screw you..., you can suc (suck) an egg and cho kon (choke on) it!" she shrieks, slamming down the phone.

Winton bursts into deep laughter, slouching until rolling to the wood deck in even deeper laughter when the phone rings back, prompting him to answer in speaker mode.

"Hey! Dummy! You call wit (with) stupid, dumb shit! I got yo (your) number! I know where you live cock suckkeerr! I come to yo (your) house; bang bang mamsaun (your wife) when you at work and love hu (her) for a very, very longtime! She say..., she say...; you hung like King Kong, Ching Chong, not little Chinese man myth!" the deep-voiced, pissed Chinaman utters.

The phone goes dead, and Winton instantly feels somewhat sober.

John tears up, rolling in laughter, seeing Winton's scary face when going into an even crazier laugh, and reaching for the phone. "Hey, hey..., my turn," he says, pulling at the phone until almost wrestling with Winton.

Winton jerks the phone tightly in his chest. "Enough! Enough!" Winton declares, shocked until smiling and drooling with an alcohol-numbed face. "Look at the time..., look at the time!" Winton declares, placing the cap tight on the bottle when John's jar comes forward, shaking.

"Come on, man, I got you, I got you, Babe!" John declares, unconvincingly.

"Got me? Why is it that I just missed you every time I ask you about liquor, or you just poured your last out for your lil' dead homies?" Winton declares, staring.

"Why are you bringing up old Romper Room stuff?" John asks in an overly drunken stare.

Winton pours half a jar, bringing a smile to John's drunken, numb face.

"Yeah, boi! That's what I'm talking about!" John says, staggering and stumbling in a forward lean, and about to fall face-first until balancing and protecting the jar at all costs.

Winton walks off and inside, shaking his head when finding Nelle sprawled over the floor, laughing hard and barely able to catch her breath. "What in the world…?" he asks, setting the liquor and glass down.

"Did you see that fool 'bout to break his darn neck?" she lightly shrieks. "He wasn't even about letting that liquor spill!" she laughs until John stops in his tracks, curiously looking back.

At Boogey's house, Boogey snores in the bedroom, waking himself then lye there listening for Nattie. He soon hears water running in the kitchen, followed by her flexing the old school ice tray before the dropping cubes. He continually listens until hearing her making her way to the room when turning over and pretending to be asleep. He begins faking a mild snore while monitoring his rhythm.

The squeaky door opens with light shining over heaps of clothes, barely lighting the room until she backs against the door, allowing just a thin beam to shine inside.

Boogey barely cracks an eyelid, finding her overshadowing him, discovering her moving things around on the nightstand until placing a bowl down. He sees mild streams of steam vanish when she stirs in the bowl with her index finger, causing fast-melting ice to bump lightly against the bowl. Boogey takes a deep breath, pulling his hand from underneath the pillow should something crazy pop off, and finds her instantly reaching for his hand. He hears soft giggles as she glances at him but lies very curious until remembering a ridiculous magazine article she had mentioned days ago, concerning homemade truth serums; when getting his snoring back in rhythm, thinking of anything serious to keep from bursting into laughter.

Nattie grabs his hand again, softly giggling and holding it with a light grip, kneeling and senselessly giggling, knowing this whole ordeal is silly.

Boogey breathes heavier, scenting the room with booze, so she thinks he is pissy drunk. He watches, hoping she will hurry before he bursts into laughter.

Nattie gets control of her laugh; almost knocking the bowl over then holds his hand but can't stop giggling until feeling sweaty fingers when whispering his name.

Boogey softly moans when she eases his fingers deeper into the water.

She stirs his fingers more until still, calling to him a second time.

He moans, pretending to be in a trance. "Grandma?" he moans in a slur.

Nattie's face lights up, amazed that it works while heavily meditating and dipping his fingers more until calling out to him again.

"Grandma Shelley? Wow..., grandma! You are an ugly heffa now; what the hell happened to you?" he shrieks, slightly jerking back as if frightened.

Nattie bursts into a silly laugh, gently easing onto the side of the mattress.

Boogey continual laughs inside. "Grandma, where are you going? Can I come? Grandma..., did you hear me?" Boogey asks, trying to get Nattie more involved.

"Yes, you can, Babe!" Nattie utters, in his grandmother's impersonated voice, gently stroking his face. Come on Boogey Woogy," she says, using the pet name his grandmother had given him. "How's that beautiful wife of yours, Nattie?" she murmurs.

"Grandma, oh Grandma..., beautiful? Oh, Grandma, that ugly heffa ain't changed a bit, always talking about that lame tail Freddy; you know, Wilbur, and Sheila Anne's silly-tail, nappy head boy. Huh..., well either him or whining about me spending a dollar here or there on that lotree (lottery)," he says, slightly peeking.

"Boy, watch yo (your) mouf (mouth)..., well, anyway, I can't say I do know him, but Nattie is a great woman, so stop with this Freddy mess!" Nattie frowns.

"I'll be da...!" Boogey exclaims, curving the curse word when Nattie hauls off with a firm slap to his face. "Uh, Grandma, why do you do that?" he asks, jerking, and peeking with an ugly, painful frown when rubbing the sting.

"Don't mimic me, boy! I've been watching Nattie, and she means well, so just keep Freddy's name outcha (out of your) mouth!" Nattie mildly shrieks, grinning.

"Screw that!" he whispers when Nattie leans back, double slapping him this time. "Forget that...!" Boogey begins to say when Nattie hauls off with another hard slap that leaves him almost cross-eyed.

"Grandma! I tell you..., I love you to death, but if you hit me one more time, we're going to be doing some refurbishing up in this mother...!" Boogey says, cutting off the curse word while holding a tightly sprung fist as a tear runs down his frowned face.

Nattie looks at his bluish skin until he yawns, turning over and working his jaw to see if it's broken. She sits longer until grabbing the bowl and heading for the kitchen, smiling and shaking her head.

Boogey shifts his jaw more, rubbing his face until hearing the water faucet.

Nattie finally eases in the kitchen chair with her mind running through his offensive comments until yawning and putting her head on the edge of the table for a while, unknowingly nodding off. Her head rocks for minutes until drooling and repositioning several times to keep from falling over. She finally loses her balance seconds later, flipping headfirst in a slight spin when her head bounces off another chair's back panels. "What the...," she lightly moans, embarrassed while moving her numb neck. She sees double and shakes her head, walking to the mirror. "What in the Sam Hill?" She bangs her head with the palm of her hand to realign her crossed eyes.

There comes a loud thump, and she freezes until it comes again, finally recognizing it is a strong wind against the door. She grows quiet, clutching a knife from the rack when slowly opening the door. Her heart races until she slams the screen shut and secures it with a thick, bent nail. Her eyes adjust slowly, finding shadows of clothes from the line on the ground and near the outhouse when the dark, dreary look runs chills down her spine. She slams the door swiftly, then locks it, heading for the bedroom, smelling liquor mingled with some other strange odor.

She speedily changes clothes, sits on the bed, rolls her hair, and slips her black-bottomed feet under the dingy covers, sliding them out at the foot and rocking her until she is fast asleep.

An hour or so later, the dog's heavy barks wake Nattie, then fade off fast when a large rock sails past the dog's fathead, causing the dog to run away yet cautiously creep to the house again until yelping loudly when hit broadside, in a wide turn.

Nattie maneuvers, seizing the shotgun. She eases to the window, aiming at a swaying straw hat while listening to a whispering voice. She swiftly flows to a shelf of rock salt, loading it, and eases a few extra shells into her robe pocket, nervously jumping when seeing the birdcage swinging. She eases the curtain back, quickening her aim with her face pressed hard against the cool glass, looking for the hat again or a body. Her eyes wander over the dimly-lit yard when pushing back, and anxiously making her way through the dark living room, then the kitchen, nervously unlatching the lock to the back door.

The door eases open with the barrel slowly extends through the busted screen when a brisk wind flings the door outward.

Nattie slips one foot onto a flimsy deck board, adjusting her sight to darkness when the yard begins to materialize, slowly.

Several dogs bark, causing her to train the gun to the strongest fading bark, finding a staggering, manly silhouette expressly heading down a dirt path.

"Hey!" Nattie calls out, cocking her head speedily to one side with her arms tensed in anticipation of the powerhouse recoil when seeing the body barely in view and easing to the edge of the porch.

The spring-loaded door slams shut, startling her when her reflex causes her to fire one, un-aimed round, high in the trees, knocking down rotten branches.

She retrains quickly, with wandering eyes stealthy looking when the man's straw hat fades. She let off another round with buckshot whistling past his head within inches, and he ducks down in the high weeds, with shots flying past the dog.

The man low crawls then slides down an embankment, yelling when she reloads, firing off another un-aimed round.

"Awrrrp! Awrrrp! Awrrrp!" the dog yelps at a high pitch, running off in the weeds. "Awrrrp! Awrrrp! Awrrrp!" he yelps in a fast-fading sound while limping and increasing distance.

"Shoot! I missed that so-and-so!" Nattie shrieks, loudly snapping her fingers to her side rapidly and nervously backing up with her hands anxiously swiping for the door handle. She slings the screen door back, slightly turning and bursting through the door, falling forward with loud gunfire echoing inside when the gun slides, slamming into the wall and blasting a hole in the baseboard.

"Ahh! Shiii...! What in the world is going on in there, Natt?" the bird shrieks, frightened with the cage swinging from side to side from Bud anxiously and nosily looking then jumping to see through various ripped holes.

Nattie impetuously shuffles to her knees, diving and coming up, stealthily.

"What the...!" Bud shrieks again, seeing her rush up with dirty slippers beating down the dusty floor; and the barrel aimed at the cage.

Nattie grabs the bedroom door frame, spinning and launching into the room. She leaps onto the crooked bed, unbalanced and falls backward, propelled into the dresser when the shotgun round shatters the mirror.

Boogey jerks and falls back asleep.

Nattie bounces up, twisting her foot on clothes and junk strewn over the floor, slightly spinning and falling, yet struggling to unravel the covers while yelping. She low-crawls to the bed, pronto, pounding on Boogey's chest, but gets no response when freezing in place, listening. Nattie's face transforms into its ugliest stare ever until furiously pounding on Boogey and momentarily listening when barely hearing his heartbeat. She breathes a sigh of relief until, nervously thinking, she hears a door shut. "A prowler, a Peeking Tom!" she vigorously shrieks, shaking Boogey until his hand drops to the floor on top of faulty, frayed, live electrical wiring.

Boogey's upper body and legs lunge upward, slamming hard into the mattress when the lamp dims, brightens, and then goes out, leaving them in pure darkness until bright street lights from the firehouse grow brighter.

Nattie springs up pulling the curtains back and securing them open by a bent nail. She fearfully looks around with the smell of fried pork skins growing stronger. She sees smoke near Boogey's hand, but does not give it any thought. "Boog! What did I tell you about eating poke (pork) skins in bed, or is that your sweaty feet?" she says with her back to him when looking at the gun and then for the bag of pork rinds.

Nattie grabs the shotgun, putting all her weight into it until falling back with it and rolling, then bouncing up and quieting when hearing something drug through the kitchen floor. She reaches for Boogey's pants, pulling out a buck knife, flipping it open, and instantly, the blade extends past the door as she tiptoes out, listening until hearing her heart beating.

She lays the knife down, nervously reloading, and then freezes with scary eyes when hearing glass shatter, causing her to jerk the gun with her adrenaline; driving the barrel deep into her forehead, gashing it. "Uh…!" she whispers, feeling the throbbing pain and the slight trail of blood drip just above her eyebrow.

Nattie grabs a candle and matches from the table, backing up, and trying to figure out how to light it while easing the barrel onto the lopsided recliner. She tucks the butt under her arms, striking the match then peeks into the kitchen, smelling something burning, and freaks out when finding the tip of her long hair burning upward. "Ahhh!" she shrieks, releasing the gun and blasting a hole in the bedroom wall, braising Boogey's thigh; sending him upward, and dancing until hopping on the floor.

Boogey screams, grabbing his leg silently, running around fast, in circles, in pain until jumping back on the low riding bed with his mouth still torn open, when suddenly, a delayed, louder scream comes, then a deeper squawk.

Nattie drops the candle, unknowingly setting the dusty carpet on fire and viciously fans to put her hair out until it's smoldering. She looks at what looks like a light, panicking when finding the carpet on fire and dancing in circles, stomping.

Boogey finally bursts through the door, finding Nattie with the gun. "Have you lost your cotton-picking mind, woman?" he screams in tears, with snot hanging and confused when staring at her bloody face.

"Shush!" she whispers with an index finger to her lips, passing him the candle and looking for the matchbox, which she finds near the couch leg.

Boogey slightly bites his finger, leveraging the pain while flipping on the light switch, but nothing when a pan loudly slams to the floor and runs around on its edge for seconds before lying flat.

Nattie fearfully looks back into Boogey's watery eyes and heavily frowning face when he stuffs a salty handkerchief in his mouth, lighting a candle and holding it while biting down harder. Tears continually fall as Boogey's blurry eyes wander to his hand when feeling a slight tingle. He tries wiggling his fingers but can't when his eyes widen, and he vigorously shakes his numb hand, mumbling when looking at Nattie's frightened face. He stares at his hand again when Nattie flinches, instantly feeling the heat at the base of her neck when jumping back and expressly clutching Boogey's wrist, pushing the candle away.

Boogey hysterically looks at his limp, burnt wrist, flapping it until uncontrollably slapping his face. He nibbles a finger with no feeling, until biting down hard and accidentally breaking the skin when feeling teeth on the bone with no pain. He licks his lips, finally feeling something wet when tasting salt, realizing its blood.

"Shush!" Nattie declares, staring at his bloody chin and then gawking at his watery eyes and frown, which worsens from the excruciating pain when his nerves return. His mouth opens wide to scream but instead, he bites down on the salty rag.

Instantly, they hear a louder noise and freeze in total silence with eyes wandering to the bottom of the screen door, discovering the rescreened patch ripped back about twelve inches wide.

Boogey slowly trains the candle flame, increasingly lighting the room.

"Ahhhh!" Nattie shrieks with her hair, standing tall when eye-to-eye with a fat, oversized possum hanging from the cabinet, loudly hissing with its sharp claws inches from her face, and in a few fast swipes.

Boogey screams in a muffled, feminine voice, fighting for the gun when the candle flickers, then goes out as they quiet long enough to hear the candle roll off.

The possum instantly quiets, listening to them, then hisses again when clawing with continual, eerie sounds.

Boogey grabs Nattie and the gun, dragging her across the living room and into a pile of junk then coat rack, which spins fast with sleeves high over their heads until one lands on Boogey's shoulder as he comes up. He screams, releasing Nattie, then jumps, turning, and wrestling the rack to the floor, punching, kicking, and yelping.

"Wait a minute! Wait a minute! You darn idiot! It's a darn coat rack, a freakin' coat rack!" Nattie shrieks until it finally registers when he stops and low-crawls, coming to his feet, slowly.

Boogey looks around cautiously, limping over for another candle and nippily lighting it while Nattie trains the shotgun, and they advance toward the kitchen.

They inch inside, peeking with fast, wandering eyes, finding the possum's wobbly tail vanishing through the hole in the screen and into darkness.

Boogey steps back, opening the fuse panel, energizing the lights.

They look the kitchen over quickly, and Nattie creeps over and shuts the door.

Boogey looks longer then eases into a kitchen chair. "What is the name of Sam Dilbert Jenkins, are you doing with a gun and the door open this late?" he asks in a mean tone and even a meaner stare when looking at the bruise at this thigh.

"Outside..., someone was outside..., at the window..., yeah, the window?" she says in an uneasy voice.

"Yeah, like who? Did you actually see them or thought you saw them or just heard something?" Boogey asks, briskly rubbings his wrist and salt-burning thigh.

Nattie's eyes fearfully wandered up to where the possum was, finding her secret stash in a pretty, pink bottle which is tilted over and barely visible.

Boogey's eyes finally follow hers when easing up, barely spotting the unfamiliar bottle when jumping up, reaching for it. He pops the top, deeply inhaling the too-familiar smell of his special shine deep in his nostrils.

"Someone was out there, alright..., yo (your) drunk tail. Something probably blew against the window and spooked you! Hell, I didn't even know you were a drinker. Huh..., so you have to steal from your own people, now?" Boogey goes silent, easing back and just staring at her until her head goes down in shame. Out here sneaking around, like an undercover alcoholic," he says, finding her rocking, shamefully. "Shucks, can't even get a break in your own home. Crackheads to the right, tack heads to the left, and here I am stuck with an Alc head," he senselessly articulates, drilling more to piss her off.

"What's that? What's that senseless mess you just made up?" she asks, raising her head and looking in his eyes with a frown. "Alc what?"

"You heard me: Alc head..., alcoholic head, yeah..., that would be you! Look it up in the dictionary, and find your recent picture in the latest edition; probably peeking around a corner with a bottle turned up..., I reckon!" he says, pointing to her with a sturdy index finger. He lays down the bottle cap, turns up her little flask, and takes the whole bottle down, then slams it down, shattering it over the table and causing Nattie to jump.

Nattie shakes her head, staring while he eases up. Ahh...!" she shrieks, with one hand on top of the table and the other on the bottom, flipping the table and bouncing back and forth in a fighting stance with tightly balled fists. "Come on! Come on..., ain't nothing but air and opportunity!" she shrieks, swinging with a few stealth uppercuts and loudly sucking in air. "Come on; all the air is gone now, darn it; ain't nothing but a darn opportunity!"

"Huh..., now, go head wit (with) that bull, Natt! I ain't never hit you, and I ain't gone be forced to now, but if you tempt me, you gone be the first, and doggonit, gone wish you were the last! Leave me be now because you don't want that bad luck on ya (you)!" He cuts his eyes over at her.

"Naw, you gone take this beat-down, chump! I'm fed up, Boog!" she shrieks. "I ought to knock your head off your darn shoulders!" she yells with tears dropping.

"You better go now, Nattie!" Boogey screams, ducking a couple more instantaneous jabs. "You better stop before I knock you out, now!" Boogey shrieks, taking a stance and bouncing as if about to deliver a few devastating jabs of his own. "You gone keep on, and this hea (here) gone be one whipping you gone wish you neva (never) had guul (girl)," Boogie shrieks, staring deep in her eyes until her bouncing finally settles. Boogey leans down slowly, flips the table over, then walks out when Nattie flies through the doorway, lunging onto his back with her legs tightly wrapped around his waist. Boogey stumbles forward, losing his balance when almost invisible hands wrap around his neck.

He tries pulling her hands loose until losing consciousness when dropping back into the wall, crushing her thin body, and feeling her hands loosen and quickly tighten. Boogey comes straight up, running from one wall to another as if a wrestler in a ring, spinning inches away and smashing her until she falls away, slowly sliding down the dingy sheetrock, almost passed out.

"I told you to gone wit (with) that mess, Natt! Now, look at you!" He looks back, discovers her shaking off the dizziness and crawling to her knees. Boogey steps a few feet away while she is on all fours, staring with hair covering her eyes, roaming the floor, closely following his footsteps as he walks up.

With one last step, Nattie surprisingly lunges upward, speedily slamming her head into his groin, dropping him to his knees with a massive vein at his temple. He instantly cups his inseam as she falls back and drops flat on her behind.

The following morning, Sunday, before sunrise, the rooster crows, waking Boogey, but he lies tossing and turning until the twelfth, tired crow grows, even louder than the others.

Nattie's ashy, white flower bag-kicking-looking feet slide into dingy bunny slippers, sluggishly pulling from the bed and heading for the kitchen. She shields her bloodshot eyes from the bright light, tripping over a chair and expressly falling forward with fast, shuffling feet and somewhat balancing with her head crashing into a deep, collard green pot hanging low on the wall. Nattie's head throbs badly; feeling like something is wrapped tightly around it when she nervously knocks the pot to the floor. She drops in a chair, watching the pot still spinning then rock until it is still when senselessly giggling yet shamefully making sure Boogey didn't see her when gawking at the deep dent and shaking her head. She eases up, pulls out an iron skillet, opens the refrigerator, and pulls out a muskrat.

Boogey scratches his thigh, hacking up phlegm. He stumbles to the bathroom with deep, brown stains in his drawers, looking almost like a large, spray-painted exclamation mark. He removes his T-shirt, leaning into the mirror, smiling. 'Hot dog! If I have to say so myself, sir, that is one nice tan you've got there, Mr. Johnson.' He turns sideways to better view his five shades of pale skin. Boogey turns on the sink faucet, adjusting the temperature hotter and fogs the bathroom, giving off a fresh steamy appearance. Boogey grabs a hole-filled, green rag, washing his face, then a dingy yellow one, for his feet, then the red, for his private and backside.

Boogey soon smells muskrat until overpowered by fresh, wild onions. He dresses, propping his foot on the bed, lacing his rugged boots, unknowingly leaving mud stains smeared lightly across the spread. He eases out, maneuvering around the junky living room, removing the torn sheet from Bud's cage, when Bud drops down, nibbling seeds, and then stops, looking up at Boogey with his head half-tilted.

"What do you say there, little buddy!" Boogey utters, turning the television to the news and watching the headlines of a disappearance, when creeping into the kitchen, quietly fiddling through junk mail lying on the table.

"Coffee?" Nattie asks, looking over her shoulder and finally noticing him.

"Sure," Boogey answers, grabbing a cup from the wall. "I was just watching a shooting, and they can't seem to find that body." He pours the coffee, then walk out the back door and slams the screen door. Boogey stretches, smiling until glaring at the sun with bright rays slightly warming his face. He looks off, staring at the neighbor's barn, until finding his neighbor, Sam, on a high tractor when his boots shuffle. He leaps from the next-to-last step, and coffee shoots over his coveralls and down his pant leg.

Dust rises to his knees as Boogey takes off in a drunken trot, making it to the wood and metal swing gate, finding Sam pulling up and waving.

Boogey's callused hand grips the cup tighter, placing it on a beam while opening the gate and heading over to five-foot-four, slender-built

Sam, who is parking. Boogey leads in on the headliners to see what Sam knows, then talks a spell until hearing Nattie's voice.

"I think Nattie's calling." Sam scratches his head through his duorag.

Boogey strikes up another conversation, walking toward Sam's place.

They talked about inventions, seeing how Boogey always loved hearing Sam's theories on the inventions he was going to someday market.

Before long, Sam walks inside and comes out with an old scrapbook with over ten inventions he claims are his own.

Boogey stares attentively, finding initials other than Sam's on documents when giving him the evil eye but keeping the infractions to himself.

Sam continues to speak until he shifts to investments, realizing that Boogey has no idea about either, then moves on to something else until he looks up and hears a triangular chime, which Nattie bangs around, loudly.

"Sounds like breakfast is calling." Sam helps Boogey out of the lowrider couch.

"That it does, Mr. Sam…, that it does," Boogey says, shaking Sam's hand when leveling out on his feet. Boogey bids him a good day and strikes out, whistling something like Dixie while looking up, finding Nattie going inside.

Nattie meditates on her plot for revenge from his harsh comments about Freddy when rummaging through dirty laundry. She pulls out drunken, pissy sheets that he had hidden days ago when peeping out the window, spotting the tip of Boogey's fathead, when swiftly hooking the sheet on nails attached to a dilapidated roof post. She sprints inside, easing into her favorite chair, when the phone rings.

Boogey finally comes up the steep hill, ducking when discovering over a hundred blackbirds feasting on Bud's birdseed that Nattie accidentally spilled from the shed to the porch. He quietly creeps until several feet away, striking out, yelling and screaming like a lunatic. His boots stomp fast; his hands going forward while his body slumps, hoping to catch at least one of the fat birds for dinner but gets none.

Nattie continues in conversation with their daughter, Melissa, about Melissa's oldest daughter's recital until finding Boogey expressly zigzagging when dropping the phone and bursting into an obnoxious laugh. She clutches her side, doing everything to stop laughing.

Melissa holds, shrieking fearfully, trying to get Nattie's attention.

Nattie looks away, then back again, finding Boogey out of breath when grabbing a post and catching his breath.

Nattie hears a mild, muffled scream when picking up the phone, laughing.

Boogey leans forward; hands on his knees, totally exhausted, and minutes later, he heads for the back door.

Nattie continues talking and hiding her smile.

Boogey walks inside, finding her shoulders jerking when waving her off and hurrying for the bathroom. He shaves, pulling out a thirty-year-old bottle of aftershave, blowing dust, and coughing until choking. He turns on the dust-covered radio hanging on a metal clothes hanger wire, picking up static until fine-tuning and accidentally intercepting rap when bobbing and easing the volume up a few notches. He shifts his head left-to-right, up-and-down until finding Nattie's hairbrush and pulling it to his mouth, rapping while moving his hand as if he's some young rapper.

Bud listens, swinging until making some strange move when the cage rocks, and Bud begins rapping, adding words to make the song gangster.

Boogey removes his shirt, performing silly moves from back in high school.

Nattie finally gets wind of the commotion and hangs up. She sits curiously listening until walking into the living room, finding Bud stiff as a board, so she walks off.

Bud peeks, looking for her then raps lower when the volume fluctuates, and Bud quiets, shrugging his shoulders and swinging before moving; flopping his wings, and looking like he's jumpstarting a motorcycle.

Before long, Nattie is swaying her hips until breaking out in the stinky leg dance and a few others she has no rhythm for, but she is getting down in her mind.

The song finally ends with another song mixing, but a more upbeat one when Boogey does a few more undiscovered dances until moonwalking his way toward the door and the strong scent of muskrat.

"Boogey, your food is getting cold!" Nattie hollers, dancing until dropping low in a crazier dance.

Boogey unknowingly eases up on her, spanking her backside when she backs deeper into him, dancing harder.

Bud sings his heart out until finally looking over, freezing and whistling loud. "Oooh! Naw! Heck naw! That's just nasty!"

Nattie and Boogey keep getting down until the whistle grows louder.

Bud flaps harder, rising to the top of the cage and banging his head. He bangs hard one last time, knocking the cage to the floor, causing Boogey and Nattie to stop in their tracks and rush over.

Bud quiets, peeking out of one eye, and pretending to be dead.

Boogey fights to get the door open, and Nattie flops down on the edge of the couch with tears welling while closely watching. "Bud, Bud, talk to me, lil' buddy!" Boogey cries in excitement. Boogey's hand strokes Bud's head and then chest.

Bud takes light breaths, remaining motionless as possible as a tear of laughter unnoticeably falls when he closes his eyes even tighter.

Nattie eases her head down when Boogey's hand falls below Bud's stomach, then lower, and instantly, Bud cracks an eye slightly open, staring at Boogey.

Boogey strokes further downward when both Bud's eyes fly open. "Hey, ain't none of that freaky mess going on in this mother..., hey Boogey!"

"Oh, my little, Bud!" Boogey says when Nattie's smile grows on her damp face.

"Bud!" Nattie shouts, wiping tears before rushing to check on the food left cooking on the stove.

Boogey sits Bud on his shoulder. "No more getting excited! You could have killed yourself." Boogey extends his hands out so Bud can walk along both arms.

"Hmm..., that nasty dance could kill me, so don't ever do that again..., promise!"

"Ok, buddy." Boogey stands Bud on the couch while setting the cage back up.

Nattie feeds Bud then rushes, preparing breakfast and waiting for Boogey.

She grows restive using too much pepper and then sits uncontrollably sneezing until she subconsciously digs in her nose. The second joint of her finger vanishes when digging for a crusty booger; not realizing Boogey is standing there.

"Darn, woman! A few more centimeters and you're sure to be scratching your brain..., I reckon," Boogey utters when she rapidly retracts her hand to her lap.

Seconds later, Boogey's eyes wander over to her fingers which slowly inch toward him as he draws back, bursting into laughter. "Woman, if you don't wash those buggerfied fingers, you better!"

"Oh yeah..., oh, yeah," she mumbles, laughing while rushing, washing, and drying her hands before easing into the chair and joining hands in prayer.

Within minutes, the dog eases up, clawing and pulling at the corner of the reattached, busted screen until it almost falls off. "Stop! Stop! I said..., stop it!" Boogey yells, listening to vicious growls.

The dog ignores Boogey until hearing shuffling feet and chair legs screech, when Boogey slides back.

The dog takes off running for the tall weeds.

Boogey stares over his shoulder at the dusty clock. "Man, look at the time! Look at the time!" he declares, taking one last sip of black coffee.

A loud horn blows and Nattie makes her way up front, passing Boogey's coat.

Boogey flings the door open, kissing Nattie. "See you later, little buddy," he says, looking over at Bud before rushing off. He comes up on the passenger side and stops, leaning down, looking over at Winton, then the charred front seats when climbing in the back seat.

Winton impatiently waits then looks over his shoulder. "Oh, so I'm your chauffeur, now?" Winton asks, frowning.

"Man, I ain't got time to play around with that raggedy-tail door this morning!"

Winton leans forward for seconds as if in a daze when throwing his head back, letting off a loud cry of laughter. He looks back at Boogey then at the porch. "Tell me something..., you still sleep on the left side, right?"

Boogey sits in silence, thinking hard. "What? What kind of question is that? Heeellll yeah..., chump, always the left, the manly side, you perm-head sucker! Now, you wouldn't know anything about manly, now would you?" Boogey declares, getting smart.

"Huh..., yeah..., then that's your side! Man, get your pissy tail upfront!" Winton shrieks, pointing at the deep yellow, pissy sheet slightly swaying in the wind.

Winton blows, finding Nattie peeking with possum, white-looking teeth through the dusty screen.

Boogey grabs the handle, pissed when springing up and out, closing the door and climbing in the front seat, strapping down the door.

Winton brings the car to the road, stopping with dust rushing past the hood when heavily fanning. He hits the gas then slams on the brakes when two chicken trucks race by; the rear truck passing and swerving in front, then speeding off.

Winton cautiously inches out, pulling over at the general store and then further off the road. He swiftly slides out, looking around and then back inside. "Hey..., can I get you anything, Boog?"

"Yeah, a handful of wrapped gum and a winning ticket," Boogey replies.

"How many and what kind?" Winton asks, looking at Boogey's hands slowly and nervously running from his thigh to his kneecaps.

"Five pieces, I reckon, and one easy pick." Boogey watches a car pull in slowly and park when slightly cutting his eyes away, then back at Winton's hand, which shoots out, for money, like two empty cups.

"Gone wit' (with) that mess, Boog!" Winton exclaims, speedily opening and closing his hand even faster until his dry, dusty hands sound like number two grit sandpaper.

"What? Man, go ahead with that crap! Gone get the gum and number, yah (you) tight rascal! Man, yo (your) tail is so tight it smokes when you walk."

"Tight my foot!" Winton continually opens and closes his hand more until a light, powdery dust rises.

"Keep on, and those hands gone start, a damn campfire," Boogey says, shrugging his shoulders, leaning and giggling when still finding Winton's hand out. "Are you serious?" Boogey asks, staring.

"As serious as a cat walking on a hot tin roof in summer in a double-knit suit, tie and turtleneck," Winton says, not blinking.

Boogey leans to one side, reaching deep in his pocket, pulling out a tightly-balled dollar bill when Winton's eyebrows rise, thinking Boogey is pushing something off as money when coins roll out.

"Let me hold something for some smokes," Winton says, smiling when the money unravels, and he sees the five-dollar bill rolled with the one.

"Huh..., most likely, but not hardly, pal. This is my lucky lotto dollar," Boogey says, passing the hot five and three dimes from his tight grip.

"Tight? Man, your grip is so tight, old George or whoever is on the dime, and the five is cheery," Winton says, reading their names when a dime falls. Winton flings the door open, pulling out several mysterious things that have his face frowning when trying to make out what it is. He slams the door, fighting to get his high-water pants to his ankles, and then pulls a five from his cap's liner while crossing the street.

Winton looks up the street, hearing a car door, and a big, sly grin comes when he discovers Big Hank standing next to a shiny, new Cadillac. He stops and leans back, gazing at Hank's two sexy working girls, when waving to Hank. "Hey, hey, hey..., Big Bank Hank!"

"What's up, Wint, Spent!" Hank senselessly declares in a senseless rhyme.

"What's up, Baabeee! What you got for me, main (man)?"

"What you need, Big Bank can handle, Baaabeee!" Hank utters in a deep, irritating voice when pulling another drag from his burned-down cigar, inches from burning his lip. He leans forward, slightly pulling up his trousers by the suspenders.

Winton finds Boogey being nosy, so he guides Hank to the store with his head cut back over his shoulder, spotting Boogey trying to see his hands.

"What you need, Baabee!" Hank brushes off his double knitted threads when several patrons look over with disgusted stares.

Winton motions Hank with a nod, directing him down a long, narrow aisle. "A couple of dimes and five hundred if you can spare it,"

Winton mumbles with fast wandering and attentive eyes, putting his head down when spotting a nosy man.

Hank sneakily smiles, pulling out money and drugs, invisibly loading Winton quickly, and backing away even faster. "So, when can I expect payment with full interest; you already know the rates? Cause time is money, Baabee!" Hank cheerfully smiles.

"Next Friday; is that cool because you know I'm good for it, main (man)," Winton says, swallowing hard.

"Aight now..., and don't be acting a fool because folks been saying you ain't been paying on time! Man..., I can tell you straight up, that you ain't gone be playing with mine like that because I'll come up in your house, Jack! Boom..., boom..., boom..., wife, kids, and all..., even the dog!" Hank says snappily to show he is serious.

"Come on, Hank, you know I ain't gone dip on you like that, main (man)."

"Come correct, cause I'd hate to send folks you don't know up in your crib (house), every day, all day; no breaks and no holidays." Hank says, plucking dirt from under his long nails, until accidentally popping some on Winton's lip when Winton starts spitting and swiping.

Winton thinks more about the situation and threats when taking another deep swallow. He finally remembers hearing about Hank slapping a man and then reregisters Hank's shiesty lifestyle and his friends while watching Hank's mouth moving, not hearing a word until a thick finger snaps and then a fat hand waves.

"Are you alright?" Hank asks with a concerned stare.

"Yeah..., yeah..., but on second thought, maybe I don't really need this," Winton nervously says, pulling the loot and drugs out while cautiously looking around.

"Ok..., you sure? Well, if not, let's see...," Hank says, pulling out a rundown calculator with heavy faded numbers. Hmmm..., five minutes times five hundred dollars plus the dimes..., hmmm," he utters with one cigar-burning eye tightly closed.

"What? You're charging interest for holding it?" Winton declares with his eyes wide from excitement, instantly noticing Hank is no longer the cheerful big guy.

"Time is money, dawg!" Hank exclaims, turning the calculator to Winton when Winton's eyes bulge out of his head.

The front door slams, causing everyone but Winton, who is still in shock, to look.

Hank's eyes bulge, shoving Winton down fast by the top of his head while still glimpsing over a shelf until squinting when finding Sheriff Big John with his arms stretched wide while yawning before he leans in for a hot cup of coffee.

Hank's big fist grabs Winton in the chest, snatching him halfway up. "It's yours..., you own it once it leaves these hands, so pay interest now or in full on payday." Hank slides his other drugs into another secret pocket, in his jacket while keeping a steady eye peeled on the sheriff until looking back and down at Winton, mean and growling like a mean pit-bull with his mouth stuck out on one side.

"Screw me! Screw me!" Winton utters in slow motion, nervously easing up and expressly patting his clothes down when slipping the loot and drugs back into his pocket. He finally comes up over the ledge of the shelf, instantly spotting the tip of the sheriff's hat then the shiny badge.

The sheriff scratches his head, looking through the front window at the two women in the unidentified car.

Winton and Hank stay low, nippily dispersing down different aisles.

Hank slips over to the wall, easing out the side door and vanishes.

Winton rushes for a door near the back of the store where he hides the drugs in the bathroom and then exits. He wanders down a few aisles, coming up from time to time, looking at the sheriff's back.

Boogey's eyes wander over the store until spotting a shadow extending from the side of the store, outward and across the road, when bobbing and weaving, looking for Winton before looking for the sheriff again.

The sheriff anxiously watches the girl in the backseat continually run her fingers through the girl in the front seat hair.

Within seconds, Hank's shadow fades backward, then expands, retracting again until some of his brims extend past the corner when his big hand waves, pointing to the front of the store until one girl spots the sheriff.

The female driver stares until the sheriff's hat goes upward when he begins sniffing heavily in the air then turns away.

Winton trails the sheriff, ducking down aisles to remain undetected, and sees the sheriff when his head tilts back again as the sheriff makes it over by the register.

Mild chatter from several patrons ceases when the sheriff walks near the soda machine near the back, putting in a few coins.

Winton tiptoes, nervously grabbing a handful of gum, throwing it over the counter, then asks for the ticket.

The cashier drops his change, and tickets, backing away while staring high over Winton's shoulder as a light shadow slowly towers over Winton.

Winton trembles, picking up the ticket with heavy shaking hands then the gum, dropping a few pieces and picking it up fast when turning fast with his nose pressed deep into the top of the sheriff's stomach. "Excuse me, Mr. Sheriff, top of the morning to you, mister, sir," Winton nervously says, backing down in a frown and frightened stare.

"Well, well, well..., well I'll be; if it ain't ole Winton' Trouble Making' Mo (Moore)...!"

"Yes, su (sir)," Winton nervously yet anxiously tilts his cap, taking a few quick steps past the sheriff, instantly feeling his shirt tighten at the chest and front collar.

The sheriff grips Winton tighter, pulling him close until Winton's heels drag until swung around swiftly and pressed against a wall. The sheriff's nose runs over Winton's body, sniffing with one eyebrow raised. "Is that weed I smell, Mr. Mo (Moore), or is it your nasty, dirty hair wax?"

"Probably mu..., mu..., stankin' hair, su (sir)," Winton nervously responds.

The sheriff releases Winton, shoving him against another drink machine, when a white and black patron back away in a rush and the clerk freezes.

Winton comes off the machine slightly, and the sheriff grabs both shoulders, slinging him into the machine even harder, and Winton goes spread eagle. His hands and legs go wide as accustomed from previous encounters.

The sheriff thoroughly frisks Winton until his wide hand crosses Winton's secret stash, and Winton slumps down, but the sheriff pulls him up, shoving him into the drink machine like a rag doll.

The sheriff's hands run down Winton's trousers, patting the wad again when sliding his hands deep into Winton's pocket, pulling out the money, and leaving Winton's pockets looking like rabbit ears. "Three strikes, Mr. Mo (Moore)! My, my, my! What do we have here, Junior!" the sheriff yells, excitedly gazing at the thick wad and flipping through the worn-out singles and a few twenties.

"Bill money," Winton nervously responds, with sweat heavily dripping.

"Come again?" the sheriff says, raising an eyebrow when looking around at other patrons who turn their heads away, quickly. The sheriff unbuttons and flips open his shirt pocket, slipping the thick wad inside before looking at other patrons who look away even faster. "Hell..., payday ain't for another week down at the old mill, huh? So the way I see it, this here is dirty money..., darn drug money, you slew-footed snake!" the sheriff shrieks, expeditiously gripping Winton's neck.

"Yes su (sir), another week, but bill money, Sheriff, su (sir)," Winton nervously says with teary eyes when thoughts of Hank punishing him flashes in his mind.

"Hell..., I seriously doubt it!" the sheriff shrieks, twisting Winton until pressing Winton's face tight against the soda machine with foaming saliva dripping and snot oozing onto his chin. The sheriff slaps his leather holster loudly, drawing his long-barreled gun and cocking it while easing it to Winton's temple. "Now, boi…, you gonna tell me about this hea (here) money right now, and the only thing I don't want to hear is anything along the lines of bills or paying bills; you hear me?" Big John utters with flaring nostrils and cocked eyes.

"Sheriff…, I," Winton says when almost transparently slapped twice and sailing through the air; feet off the floor. He lands near the red hot, wood-burning heater, backing off fast when the sheriff's big boot stops him from backing down.

The sheriff strains, pushing Winton forward and forcing him headfirst into the hot COTTIER logo, seeing grease dripping and slightly hearing something sizzling when lightly burning and smoking his forehead.

"Ahh!" Winton shrieks, swiftly sitting with hot, permed hair slapping across his forehead when screaming louder and shaking his head when his mouth opens wide, trying more to convince the sheriff.

The sheriff straddles himself until standing over Winton with his gun-toting hand trembling when cutting his eyes to his little audience before leaning into Winton. "Dagon it, Wint! I've got all damn day; you jive-tail turkey!" he murmurs. "You don't want me to drag you to my jail and put it on you like the last time 'cause it will be somethin' to tell the captain, Jack!" he says with his dull, scuffed boots patting expeditiously until slowing and then stopping when hearing an engine rev.

The sheriff's head pops up, finding the Cadillac in front of the store and making a U-turn closer to the store. He jerks downward, looking at Winton, who jumps with his arms over his head from the sudden movement. "You better start talking quick, you stankin' hair fool!" the sheriff shouts when the front door springs open and the owner, Lil' Bobby, walks in sleepy-eyed until seeing the sheriff's gun drawn.

Lil' Bobby drops his bag lunch, rushing for the counter, impetuously motioning for his shotgun; pumping it and aiming at Winton's head. "Sherriff!" he exclaims, coming alongside with one eyebrow raised, finding Winton with his new branding and his eyes closed tighter, whining then crying. "You caught this thievin' punk red-handed, I know it?" Lil' Bobby anxiously says.

The female driver anxiously slams on squeaky brakes when the sheriff grabs Lil' Bobby's gun by the barrel, guiding it down to his side. "I got this, Lil' Bobby, so go tend to your business," Big John says, looking at Lil' Bob even meaner.

Lil' Bobby backs away slowly, looking at the clerk until motioning her over with questions on the incident.

Boogey stares at Hank's brake lights and the hookers in excitement.

Hank's shadow widely projects against the side of the car when Hank breaks out in a stride, leaping when feet away and diving through the open door with his body halfway out, kicking while screaming in a muffled tone.

The tires squeal, burning rubber, leaving a black trail and scent of burnt rubber.

The sheriff shoves Winton away, double-timing in a wide-legged sprint when finally remembering whose car it was. He cautiously approaches each aisle, pointing the gun at the window, finding a thick cloud of black dust fading, slowly.

Hank's hood slightly rises with the rear of the car fishtailing then straightening as the female driver floors it, while exchanging seats with Hank while barreling toward the expressway. "Oooh wee…! You should have seen how the sheriff had Winton up against the drink machine!" the female in the front seat yells excitedly while still turning and twisting until releasing the steering wheel.

Hank floors the engine, dropping the needle off the odometer reading. "Oh well, that's on him; he had just better have my stuff, or the sheriff will be the least of his worries," Hank utters, bringing the car up to top speed when entering the expressway and carelessly swerving when reaching under the seat for his gun.

"Hot dangit!" the sheriff shrieks, discovering the side door wide open. He backs off the door quickly, throwing his hat down when sliding a few feet and turning back to pick it up. He runs down another aisle wide-legged, finding Lil' Bobby's head peeking out when he tries to slow down but knees him in the head, knocking him into the couch.

"Ohh!" Lil' Bobby screams, holding his bloody face.

"Dangit, Lil' Bobby!" the sheriff screams, cutting a corner and trying to balance when crashing into a high stack of dog food, leaving it strewn over the floor.

Lil' Bob rocks, feeling light-headed when leaning and rolling to the floor.

Big John busts through the front door, shoving the gun in the holster when it almost falls. His finger accidentally slides in the trigger well, reaching to lock the leather flap when firing into the tip of his boot. "Ahh…!" the sheriff screams, limping in circles until flinging the door open and dropping in the seat.

Boogey bites the side of his index fingers in tears, to keep from blurting out and then chuckles until his belly is heavily bouncing. He slowly comes over the dash seconds later, teary-eyed and secretly staring at the sheriff.

The sheriff bends forward, noticing it's only cut at the sole, and pats his pocket faster until keys jingle, pulling them out when he drops down, cranking up, and slamming the door.

Boogey's watery eyes drop to the sheriff's bright tail lights until they go out, then hears burning rubber when the sheriff cuts the wheel sharp, still backing down fast and looking near Winton's busted car. Boogey's head slips below the dash again, and he bursts into even greater laughter until sliding down further.

The sheriff slams on the breaks, looking around, trying to find out where the loud laughter is coming from when patrons wander outside looking around. The sheriff's eyebrows sharply rise when stepping into the gas, burning rubber as the car fishtails until gaining control and speeding to the top of the hill. His fast, wandering eyes scan the high and low roads until he spots Hank on the expressway when slamming the brakes and throwing the cruiser in reverse; radioing his deputies. The sheriff flips a switch, then more switches, lighting up five dash gauges. He guns the engine with his head thrown back and his hat flying in the back window, heavily vibrating from the wind.

Winton stays in the fetal position, listening until it is tranquil, then peeks, finding Lil' Bobby with the front door held open. Winton comes up fast and quiet, swaying and catching his balance when wiping snot on his sleeves; cutting down an aisle fast and creeping out the side door. He approaches the front side of the store, hearing Boogey's too-familiar loud laughter until finding the top of Boogey's head jerking for minutes until the laughter finally tapers off.

Everyone's eyes stay peeled on the fast fading, flashing cruiser lights until jumping when seeing Winton's shadow alongside the store as he inches out, until eye-to-eye with Lil' Bobby.

"You..., you...!" Lil' Bobby shrieks with wide, quickened eyes. "Quick..., my smoke pole! My smoke pole! Quick!" he shrieks, watching Winton take off across the street, fast and wide-legged.

Winton sprints faster until his metal taps spark when sliding a few feet and letting off a long streak of sparks that look like sparkles.

Boogey's eyes widen from the commotion until feeling the car swaying when Winton grabs the handle, shaking the car and almost breaking off the handle.

Winton looks back, finding the clerk handing Lil' Bobby the gun when he jumps in, turning the ignition and patting the pedal fast.

"What's going on?" Boogey nervously shrieks, noticing the slight, red, faint wood stove logo on his forehead when nervously eye to eye.

Winton slams his foot down, missing the pedal, when seeing Lil' Bobby shove a lady to one side. He cuts the wheel sharp with the tires squealing and smoking with dust rising high.

Lil' Bobby trips over the threshold, falling to his knees, prematurely blowing a hole in the shelter's roof.

Boogey and Winton duck, then duck again, hearing a second blast.

Winton sweats profusely. "Crooked damn sheriff!"

"What? The sheriff? Why..., What..., what happened?"

"Chump took five hundred off me!" Winton declares, wiping teary eyes.

"What?" Boogey asks with suspicious eyes and smiling until bursting into a crazy, uncontrollable laugh. "Like your broke tail had five hundred. Man, are you smoking that mess again? What are you getting me caught up in, Wint? What..., you mixed up in some mess with Hank?"

"What? Five hundred, I meant fifty," Winton says, looking ahead with his lying, nervous eyes constantly cutting over at Boogey.

Boogey stares with a meaner face. "You heard me..., you caught up with Hank? Man, look..., Hank is a pure T-fool, so don't even think about getting caught up with his money or drugs! Shucks, he just shot a fool over five cents last night."

Minutes later, Hank exits a ramp, making a sharp turn into a cornfield, cutting off the park lights when parking and listening.

Within minutes, they hear a stealth approaching siren then see the sheriff speed past at what looks like two hundred miles per hour with his tailpipe red, hot, rattling, and smoking black.

Winton slows, remaining under the limit yet nervously looking back. "Man, I wanted to swing back by the house for a ham sammage (sandwich)," he says, looking at his watch back-to-back.

"Yeah, right, you spent the whole morning screwing around in the store, so you might as well wipe that sammage (sandwich) right off your busted mind, not to mention your usual smoking and joking before work!" Boogey declares, deep in thought.

Boogey sees a lottery sign as they shoot past. "Wint, Wint, turn back..., I just had a strange feeling, dude!" Boogey yells, continuously patting Winton's shoulder.

"Man, you always got a feeling and ain't hit nothing over fifty." Winton looks over his shoulder at the rapidly fading store and lottery sign.

Boogey taps faster until Winton fights the wheel, slowing when making the turn. Seconds later, he swerves into the lot, finding an old lady getting out of her car.

Boogey meets the old lady, holding the door open until she grabs it with an angry look. He sprints inside first, letting the inner door slam in the woman's face.

The old woman curses when rushing in and down aisles until discovering him walking up to the counter.

"You getting lotto?" he asks a middle-aged woman staring over various colorful beads.

"Oh no, honey, I'm here for the beads," she says, fanning out her dress, smiling.

Boogey closes the counter, staring at the male clerk. "Yeah, one easy pick; the big game, please," he utters, anxiously tapping the counter's edge when the horn blows. Boogey retrieves the tickets, counting the change and slipping it into his pocket while looking at a few products on the shelf behind the clerk.

The old lady comes up from behind Boogey with her cane high, leaning forward and slowly rocking back, aligning with the back of his head when Boogey extends the dollar forward.

The hook shoots down his collar, speedily snatching him back to one side, then continually around in a few circles with both their boots continually slamming against the hardwood floor.

Boogey continuously stumbles, squealing like a female with one foot expressly going over the other, still swung around more until dizzy when flying forward. He falls into a display, knocking over boxes, and kicking, trying to free his head from a crushed box, and he does when jumping up fiercely and in a fighting stance with wandering eyes.

"He ran out, that way…, that way!" the old lady shrieks, pointing a shaky finger with one hand, with the cane in the other, toward the door.

Boogey grabs the ticket from the floor, rushing to the window when Winton blows again, then lays into the horn for seconds while looking at his watch.

Thirty minutes later, Winton and Boogey finally pull up to the saw mill, hearing the work whistle sound as soon as the transmission goes into park. They grab their lunches, rush past the main office, and find two owners going over something while scribbling over a whiteboard. They look forward simultaneously, finding a friend, Tunk, nodding and placing their time cards in the storage rack before walking off.

"Thanks, Tunk!" Boogey says, waving when Winton waves as they rush inside the dressing room to put on safety gear.

Tunk proceeds into the yard, hurrying up to three patiently waiting guys nodding and smiling. They dig deep in their pockets, passing Tunk a dollar each before dispersing in laughter.

Boogey and Winton rush out into the breezeway, with Boogey leading, and Winton follows closely until a slap on the back when his uniform rise high at the collar, causing Winton to lose his balance, when falling backward.

"Hey, hey, hey!" Winton shouts, swinging while coming to his tiptoes.

The owner's tall, heavyset son lowers Winton, flashing his blank timecard in his face.

"What! What? I clocked in already!" Winton says, quieting while staring into empty squares.

"The hell you did; you're late!" the owner's son shouts, frowning.

"What? The heck I am, shoot! I don't see you pulling Boogey's card! Huh! If I am late…, he's late!" Winton yells, finally shaking himself free. Winton steps forward briskly, pulling Boogey's card and finding it stamped when cutting his eyes around, to find Boogey's frowned face and fat, balled fist, for dimming him out.

"Wint, you're walking a thin line! You're out of here if you're late one more time, so help me!" the son shrieks with a fat, tight, clenched fist to his face.

"Yeah, yeah, yeah!" Winton responds, snatching his card and slipping Boogey's back into the rack. He clocks in, slowly looking in his peripheral vision for Boogey when turning and nervously looking for Boogey. Winton slowly advances in the yard and comes around a stack of trees, finding Boogey, Tunk, and five different guys in deep laughter when stopping, backing and coming up on the other side, hidden and eavesdropping.

"I told ya'll I was going to get that chump!" Tunk yells, laughing, dancing crazy, and pointing to Boogey.

Winton's steamy face and red eyes wander over Tunk's red, laughing face, then over at the others, then slowly at Boogey, finding him reaching deep in both pockets and coming up short.

"I know I betted four times more, so I got you tomorrow. I spent some on the way in, but here's three," Boogey says, passing three tightly balled bills when his foreman yells from a distance, and they all scatter.

Everyone goes about their day but minutes before lunch, Winton convinces Tunk's boss that the trash needs to go out.

Winton hides when spotting Tunk on a forklift with a load of dross, heading for the incinerator. He eagerly watches him pass, then ducks past the front office, sneaking into the parking lot, retrieving a clothes hanger from his car. He pops Tunk's back door lock, seizing his bagged lunch.

Winton sprints for his car, reaching in his cooler, pulling out funky Limburger Cheese, his favorite, smearing half the container over the middle of the sandwich before smashing it, then giggling while sneaking the bag back into Tunk's car and locking it.

The lunch whistle finally blows and everyone lines up, clocking out. Some exit through the narrow hallway while others wander to the picnic area inside the gate.

Tunk keeps an eye on Winton when walking past, knowing how playful and vindictive he is, especially after the timecard incident.

"Aight, Tunk, we even!" Winton yells from a distance, veering off with Boogey and walking to his car.

Winton and Boogey come from behind a long delivery truck, and there is a loud shriek of laughter with find five guys converging around Winton's burnt car.

The men take turns glancing inside and bursting into a peal of even greater laughter, while two just stand back shaking their heads.

Winton wipes away his smile, looking down and then up, discovering Boogey's shaking head. "What?" Winton asks, shamefully.

"What my tail! You'd dime your dead momma out, wouldn't you?" Boogey asks, shaking his head in disbelief.

Winton and Boogey retrieve their lunch, and Winton convinces Boogey to sit at the table vice in the car and not far from Tunk and Tunk's cousin. They walk up on the picnic tables, finding a younger man joking when breaking out their lunches, and joining in the laughing.

Tunk is distracted when Winton asks him to pass the salt but then dives into his bag, pulling out his spicy, homemade chicken sandwich, when a stench rushes past his nostrils then waves off. His eyebrows rise, and he stares around the table, finding Winton's watery eyes and jerking shoulders when freezing in deep thought.

"Dang, Wint!" Boogey yells, backing away from the table with his food covered.

"Huh..., what? It won't me," Wint responds, laughing even harder with heavy tears dropping.

"Who cut that one?" Tunk asks, backing up and taking a big bite with the funk getting stronger. He walks back over to the guys, barely smelling the funk but still fanning. He tare through the center after the next bite, and the thick load of Limburger clings to the roof of his mouth and smears over his mustache.

Winton sees the thick glob at his top lip, bursting into a burst of deep, uncontrollable laughter and pointing.

The scent triples as mustard-hating Tunk jerks the sandwich away, seeing mayo mixed with an unfamiliar mustard color. His eyes instantly roll over to Winton, and the sandwich falls to the ground when leaning in a slow stance like a ram, charging Winton at full speed.

Winton double-times, dodging around a few transport carts, then spins out, making faces with his hands.

Tunk takes several swipes, missing until his fiery, red eyes are filled with tears. "You have done it now, Wint!" Tunk falls back, running toward the office.

Winton goes into a more resounding laugh and can't stop laughing when rushing over, telling the guys what he had done when they all burst into laughter; all except Tunk's cousin, whose face draws serious.

The cousin stands, finding Tunk running in stealth mode until stomping and kicking up dust near the back of the mill. He anxiously watches Tunk climb onto a forklift, soon spotting black smoke pouring out of the stack when Tunk guns the engine harder, making more smoke barrel out from the exhaust with light winds blowing sand around when he barrels forward.

Boogey is in tears until his eyes clear, finding Tunk's cousin with a serious, stale face until beaming with eyes somewhat still peeled on the plowing cloud of high dust shooting up over the back of the long building. Boogey stands amazed at the high smoke and sand cloud until guiding along the cousin's line of sight, finding the monster-like sand-fire ball, when rapidly nudging Winton's shin and causes him to jump back from the brogans driven in his shin.

Winton's eyes finally follow Boogey's gesture when biting his sandwich even slower until freezing with his mouth still full when dropping the sandwich, easing up slowly, and patting his pockets for his keys. He shifts his weight, falling over, and springing up, still feeling for his keys while scurrying toward his car.

The huge, wind-driven dust ball maneuvers somewhat, shifting its direction while Tunk is aggressively making his way past the back of the main office, heading for the parking lot.

Winton rushes up to the door with trembling hands. He slides the key around the lock several times, scraping rust until sliding the key inside.

The owner and his son walk out jumping back, finally registering the high dust cloud and yellow machinery bearing down on them. They scream, eye to eye, almost bracing one another when diving to one side, in a flower bed, barely missed.

Tunk's bloodshot eyes fill with more tears, and his dusty sleeve continually swipes at his dirt-smeared face, clearing his blurred vision as he heads for his target with determination.

Winton finally gets the engine going, throwing it into gear, and skidding wheels when spotting the forklift bursting through the locked shipping gate at a high rate of speed.

Tunk spots Winton's tail end, cutting the wheel hard until uncontrollably rocking when tilting the lift over and sliding fifty yards into the big boss's new car.

Instantly, everyone stands in awe, and Tunk's cousin rushes up, out of nowhere, slinging the cage open, and trying to pull Tunk out.

Within minutes, bright police cruiser lights swarm the parking lot.

Winton pulls off at the end of the second lot, watching two guys along with the owners pointing and waving for him to come back. Still, he continually sits, uncontrollably laughing until pulling away and heading down the street. Winton keeps his eyes pierced in the rearview mirror until leaning, spotting a cop manhandling Tunk against the cruiser and cuffing him.

Winton looks out of the side mirror, spotting another officer running to his cruiser to give chase when he slows and cuts the wheel hard, ducking into another vacant parking lot. He punches the gas, comes up on the far side of the building, and then slows, listening to the loud siren until it passes the cubbyhole and fades.

Winton pulls up minutes later and parks, greeted by an officer outside his cruiser, still writing up the incident. He eases out and finds Tunk with a mean frown and jumps when turning, finding the owners pointing to him with frowns. Winton freezes, seeing Tunk's face against the window, steaming the glass while slightly transforming until looking like a pit bull when the car rocks and Tunk's growling voice grows louder, with more curse words than a seasoned Sailor.

The owner's son rushes up to Winton. "Arrest him too, for causing this ruckus!" the son shouts over Tunk's screams, which silences, still enraged when the big boss points at the cruiser's window.

"Look, I have no reason to arrest him, based on the witnesses' statements. No one saw Winton, here, do a thing," he says, looking over the report again for Tunk's real name. "Now, Jeffery here is charged with destruction of property and resisting arrest," he says, tearing off a duplicate copy of the police report.

# CHAPTER TWO

### Pranksters Awakened

In Fikesville, a tall, neatly dressed, six feet tall man stands in a café, handing a cashier a crisp twenty-dollar bill. The un-ordained, thirty-four-year-old Ronald, nicknamed Rev, watches the waiter count change. "Thank you, young lady," he says, holding out his hand.

She drops the last coin in his hand with a stale look and sadly looks away.

"Have a blessed day, and remember that God loves you and can handle whatever it is that keeps your beautiful face from shining the way HE created it to," he utters, staring at her with a smile.

She rolls her teary eyes with an attitude, ignoring him when rudely motioning a lady behind him forward.

"Have a blessed day!" He lays a hefty tip on the counter, backing away with eyes dead-set on her.

"Good evening, Rev!" a frail-looking woman from behind him says, cheerily.

"Evening, Sistah, it was great seeing you at bible study," he says, shaking her hand gently when distracted by another patron's gesture, and unintentionally holding her hand a little longer than expected.

Several folks jump, hearing the register slam, finding the cashier's jowls banging out a wad of gum.

The cashier stares at what she perceives is a too-friendly handshake while frowning in disgust and shaking her head with a smirk. "Get a hotel room, you two!" she shouts, laughing like a lunatic while looking at patrons, then a coworker, who frowns back at her before walking away.

The woman snatches her hand back in embarrassment with eyes rapidly wander over the quiet café, finding nosy patrons leaning or rising to see the culprits.

Ronald too looks around, embarrassed, when the room draws quiet, and those making eye contact put their heads down, pretending not to be looking. "Well, have a blessed day, Sistah," he says out loud, to his member to get the pressure off, then turns to the cashier. "And you..., don't give Satan his due..., don't let him ride and definitely don't let him drive," he says, nodding to a few folks while slipping on his hat. Ronald looks at the cashier with a fading smile, seeing her mischievous stare that grows more concentrated. "I see you, Satan," Rev barely whispers, watching her diminishing smile when her eyes transform to pure black marbles before her head drops, without him noticing.

Minutes later, several stores down, the tiny bell on the door rings at the barbershop, and the door jerks open.

"What's up, my Brotha?" the short, stout barber and owner says, pulling clippers back from a customer's head and greeting Rev with a firm handshake.

Other barbers smile, greeting Rev with nods, gestures, or low-toned greetings.

"Good evening, everyone," Rev says, with a hand on the owner's shoulder while looking over at a young, nappy-head boy, fifteen or so, in the third barber's chair.

Rev walks off, hanging his hat on the rack then sits, and instantly, the hard wrap volume goes down to a dull roar. Rev's eyes wander to the television when the radio goes off, and the television's volume goes up.

A female newscaster appears, walking around the house of the missing young man, the woman in the store's son, when the picture shifts to the morgue as the mystery is clearly revealed to viewers.

A kid sits against the wall, watching his best friend in the third barber's chair until a burst of laughter comes when the barber tries getting the comb through his knotty head and almost pulls him out of the chair.

"Boy, you gone (are going to) pay extra with this knotty as..., head," the barber utters, cutting his eyes over at Rev when cutting the profanity short.

Rev looks up, then off, pretending not to have heard him when the owner frowns, staring over low cut glasses at the barber, and nodding a dissatisfied gesture.

The teen in the barber's chair holds his laugh then bursts into a silly giggle, closing his eyes and peeking to find the barber shaking a can of sheen until discharged with a dense fog heavily surrounding the chair.

"Uh-huh..., and an extra buck thirty-five for using up my sheen on this bug-infested fro!" he exclaims, frowning. "Oh..., snap!" the barber shouts, jumping back and almost into the sink when a cockroach peeks out of the fro and ducks inside again.

The teen's friend fearfully jumps onto the seat, easing one foot down while leaning in to see what the barber saw.

"What? What is it?" the owner asks, rushing over to the station with eyes cut over at the newly refurbished row of chairs. "Boi, get your feet out of my new leather; I just had them reupholstered. Now, get down!" he shouts, looking under-eyed over bifocals. "What the...," the owner shouts, finding the teen with the bug issue smiling with his eyes still closed.

A fracas ensues as everyone shuffles to the barber's chair.

"What the...!" the teen's friend shouts, rushing up beside the owner, who plucks the friend's Mohawk cut hairdo from his language.

"Watch your mouth or see your way out!" the owner says.

The third barber peeks again, then scrambles to the corner, ravaging through things until grabbing a straw broom.

The teen's eyes finally peeks open, finding feet shuffling, when springing up, swatting and knocking the cockroach onto the back of the fourth barber's jacket.

The owner backs down frantically, calling to the fourth barber until he looks in the mirror, swatting when the roach is halfway up his back when high-stepping, and ripping coat buttons. He frantically slides out of the jacket, throwing it, and the bug lands on a drunk, former boxing champ who has managed to sleep through all the commotion.

The owner snatches the broom and, without a second thought, slams the broom straws into the boxer's chest, crushing the roach.

The boxer's eyes instantly shoot open in a loud and fearful scream. He instantly springs up in a boxing stance, drunkenly wobbling and swinging at anybody close but misses from his slow, drunken reaction.

The exciting shop turns into laughter.

Rev manages to calm the boxer more after he finally cools down and stands swaying when the owner apologizes, telling him what transpired until the boxer's red, drunken eyes fill with tears of laughter.

Minutes later, the laughter tapers off and then picks back up when someone points at the teen running the comb through his head so fast that the sheen smokes.

The teen's barber heads back to his station when the teen jumps, clutching the clippers and cutting a trench down the middle of his head.

"Hey, hey!" the barber screams, finally noticing he has the scissors in the other hand. "Hey, hey, hey..., slow down there, young blood! Have a seat, and I'll cut it all off in case there's a nest," he shouts when everyone bursts into laughter.

Rev massages his pained abs longer; still, half bent over and frowning in laughter while walking, half slumped toward the bathroom.

Twenty minutes later, the teen stands waiting for change when Rev walks up.

"Hey, look ah here..., you need to pull those britches up on your behind, young man" the owner says, looking over bifocals.

"What? What did you say, old man?" the kid responds, backing up to the door. "Naw, see..., what you need to do is stay up, out my business," the teen says, easing the door open against his back while rubbing across his fresh, new, bald cut.

"You heard me; walking around with your dirty draws showing! You act like it's a new style; real, classy ladies don't want no bum! Where are your parents?" he declares, prepping his clipper with one eyebrow raised.

"My parents? My parents? Oh..., umm..., up your butt and 'round (around) the cona (corner)!" the teen yells, shoving his friend through the door when the clippers slam onto the counter.

The owner screams, lunging forward with both hands wide spread apart.

"Kids these days," Rev exclaims, shaking his head while sitting, and smiling. "This new generation is something else," he utters, seeing the barber shake out his cover. "You didn't see this backlash until our so-called leaders removed religion out of schools," Rev says, shaking his head.

"Yeah..., and when they removed it from the schools, they removed it out of the homes as well," the owner says, shaking his head.

"Well they didn't totally remove it but no one bothered to ask the extent of removal, so it just vanished. The thing was, they could not force the kids to pray, but a hand few should not have stopped prayer in schools all together. We should be ashamed that we as Christians did not stand up for that cause," Rev says.

"Yeah..., do you remember back in the days when schools issued punishment? Now those were the days...; licks sounded like firecrackers," the boxer anxiously says in a hard laugh.

"Oh yeah, they need to bring that back today. Kids are so hooked on threatening their parents; talking about calling 911, but what parents need to do is strip them down to nothing like old times and get some of that naked meat! No abuse but discipline only," the owner says, when stopping and prepping his clippers. "Just think about it; we continually do things that are an abomination, and we can break out of these additions if we truly love God, who gives us free will. Even Sodom and Gomorrah were destroyed for things that are an abomination to God, but we are a lot worse than them," the owner declares.

"Well, for one thing, there are not too many who even know what things are an abomination to God, or what an abomination really means, but it is as simple as reading the Bible; searching the Web, or asking someone like a pastor; and let me correct that statement, a real pastor," another barber says.

"Yeah, but most pastors avoid preaching certain things, especially things that are an abomination. The Word is great to us and for us, but it goes against the grain, so many will choose their fleshly desires over true Godly love. Many pastors know they will lose money if they preach Word-for-Word, so they hide the truth, not caring if someone loses their soul. I believe that even today, Sodom and Gomorrah cry out from the bottomless pit, pointing to us," Rev utters, finally peeking at his watch.

The following morning brings an anticipated brisk wind over Boogey and Nattie's house.

Nattie gets up early, plotting against Boogey, who awakens to hammering and later, country ham frying until rushing in his nostrils.

Boogey lies shaking a leg then breaks out of the sheets with a woody from a full bladder. Seconds later, he rushes out of the bathroom, dresses, and sits at the kitchen table.

Nattie walks in, kissing his forehead, and he looks at her confused as she set his coffee down and bends, looking deep in the refrigerator.

Boogey tries not to stare but finds her fighting to hold back her smirk which he pays no mind. He eats and afterward plays with Bud, trying to figure out what the hammering was when going into deep thought. "Natt, what the heck was all that dang racket earlier?" he asks, removing the busted sheet completely from the birdcage.

Nattie laughs hard and can't answer from bending over the junky kitchen counter when accidentally knocking over a heap of pots and pans.

Out of nowhere, dim headlights shine upon the house, and a weak horn blows when high beams flash a few times.

"I'm outta here..., see ya!" Boogey mumbles, bursting through the door. He rushes into the yard, speedily looking back when hearing Wint in a loud, crazy laugh.

Boogey sees Nattie's white eyes and dentures transform into that of a sneaky possum when she fades from the window, covering her mouth in tears of laughter and falling back on the couch.

Boogey finally looks off to his right, finding a dingy material waving in the mild wind when squinting, instantly recognizing his heavily-stained, skid-marked underwear. He grows embarrassed, bursting into a silly laugh. "Man, let's get the heck out of here; that Natt is silly as hell, always playing practical jokes. How is she gonna mess up a good pair of drawers with black and brown crayons?"

"Practical..., huh?" Winton asks, reaching for the door handle when Boogey motions him back inside.

"Man, Young Anderson is waiting for you to screw up so he can fire you, so come on before you make us late!" Boogey yells, pissed at Nattie's trifling plot when taking a deep swallow with shocked eyes.

Winton burst into an uncontrollable laugh while backing up, turning, and pulling up to the main road with the signal light flashing. He cuts his squinty eyes at Boogey, tapping the gas, with Boogey's hand flexing each time in anticipation of Boogey tapping his shoulder, and he does as soon as the front tires hit the pavement.

Boogey stares eye-to-eye. "Winton, come on, I've got a strong feeling, main (man)," Boogey says, nervously patting his own knees.

"Man, you always get a feeling that fizzles out to nothing. The only feelings you have are those dollars burning your hands," Winton says, fighting the wheel and abruptly stopping.

Nattie eases up to the dingy screen door staring at Wint's bright tail lights, shaking her head in disbelief.

Boogey shuffles inside, and his eyes light up, finding no one in line.

A stocky man intercepts Boogey, trying to get to the register first when Boogey's wadded bill flies high, landing and bouncing on the counter when the clerks catch it before it falls to the floor.

"One on the big one!" Boogey shouts, staring at the man's fiery, red face as he stares back with a mean face. "Excuse me…, were you in line?" Boogey asks, trying to ease the tension.

"Huh! I bet if I had my gun, you'd get educated real quick, now wouldn't you?" the man stays in a stale stare.

"If? Hmm…, if? Well, if bullfrogs had wings, they wouldn't be hopping around, bumping their butts, now would they?" Boogey sarcastically says, grabbing the ticket and rushing out the door.

The horn blows. "Come on before you get me fired!" Winton shouts, frowning.

Boogey climbs in, in laughter, putting the ticket in his pocket.

"What? What?" Winton asks, easing onto the main road and checking traffic.

"Some old dude in there tried to clown me; talking about…, if he had his gun. Hell…, I should've had mine and made him suck that cool barrel like a baby's bottle," Boogey says, senselessly giggling.

Winton and Boogey approach the city, miles from the saw mill when traffic begins to move slower.

Instantly, Winton gets cut off by an old, beaten up, heavily primed van with mud splattered over heavily-plastered bumper stickers. He slowly inches up to the bumper, and they sit with the bright morning rays burning their face until flipping down their visors. Winton stares longer then at the van's side mirror, discovering a blonde's pretty face, until noticing her hand flipping around slowly until giving him the middle finger, from being so nosy.

Traffic moves a little then stops for a while until moderately moving until coming to a standstill but longer this time.

Winton stares over a few stickers, reading until drawing Boogey's attention to the hot mess. "What a dummy…, like people have time to read all that crap!" Winton utters, squinting. "If…, you…, like…, taters…, honk your horn." Winton reads the less difficult sticker that he had seen and heard someone say when abruptly laying into the horn and continuously honking until Boogey is in tears of laughter.

Boogey reads more with a slightly tilted head when the van's heavy-weighted, right side leans less when lightened with the traffic beginning to flow.

Suddenly, the sunrays vanish and Boogey and Winton immediately recognize the five-hundred-pound beast leaning into the van's open back door.

The big man pulls out a sledgehammer and steps to Winton's side with a mean look. "You got a freakin' problem with that horn, then I'll fix it for ya (you)!" he yells, swiftly drawing the hammer back while Winton's trembling hand points to the bumper stickers in a speechless stutter.

The sledgehammer almost invisibly drops something fierce into the window, forcing Winton sideways and into Boogey's lap.

The next few whacks drive through the steering column; the last whack stuck and leaving the horn blaring, non-stop.

The huge man vigorously pulls on the handle, frantically shaking the car until falling back when the stock slides from his sweaty grip; the head still lodged in the busted steering column. He shuffles, yelping until looking up, finding Boogey and Winton slowly yet barely glancing over the door frame when he begins kicking in the door with steel toe boots, continually.

The female van driver steps out, walking to the rear.

"Hot diggity, dog!" Winton declares, easing from Boogey fast, with Boogey sitting upright: both seeing the sexy young woman in the tight, white spandex bottom, filled with thick hips, and her thin, blue top, filled with gigantic twins.

Winton eases back and Boogey pushes Winton away hard, trying to get a good look.

Winton snatches the hammerhead, rocking it hard until free then throws it to the ground, barely missing the man's fathead. He snatches the ground wire for the horn, silencing it then stares in the man's mean face, nippily cutting the wheel in a near head-on collision when slamming on brakes with several cars skidding.

The big man springs up, watching his woman climb back in and slam the door. He sprints to the driver's side, throwing the hammer in the back and shoving her over while expressly positioning in the chair.

The tires squeal abruptly, burning thick, black rubber when coming up to top speed and slowing at each crossing.

Within minutes, Boogey and Winton fly into the saw mill's parking lot, rushing past a visiting owner who looks at his watch, shaking his head before going into the office.

They clock in, and the work whistle sounds off when rushing, dressing in their safety gear, and hurrying to the middle of the mill yard.

Winton slows, bending and loosening his stomach muscles until stopping.

"What? What is it?" Boogey anxiously asks, looking at his strange face and sweat beads swarming over his forehead.

"Bathroom..., go! Go!" Winton yells, clenching his cheeks tight until able to take baby steps yet farting with each step. His hand slips to his sunken butt, and laughter fades in over by the band saw when he looks back, finding folks pointing and laughing.

Winton makes it a few feet from the door, stopping and standing longer. He slides forward, inch-by-inch still passing gas with each step, until on the gritted concrete in a slow, forward moonwalk when slipping inside and tiptoeing.

Another worker walks out, slamming the door and looking at Winton strangely.

Winton loosens his belt, hearing a strain and several deep breaths between strains.

Old Man Anderson sits in a stall with his legs spread apart, both arms pressed against each stall wall, straining his guts out, until his face is bright red.

Winton peeks, seeing the wall of an empty stall bowing with each strain when holding his laugh, about to lose it but frowns, not wanting to mess his pants. He eases over, bracing the sink when peeking through the door's crack again, finding Old Man Anderson with his eyes closed in a strain with veins popping out of his forehead.

Winton eases off slowly, going from stall to stall until finally finding one somewhat clean. He unzips, dropping down about the same time Old Man Anderson strains, hard with a loud and obnoxious fart following.

"Fire in the hole!" Winton screams in a loud, animated, and comical voice.

Old Man Anderson freezes, frowning and mumbling low-level curse words when a big saw starts up.

Winton glances through the door's crack discovering Boogey's supervisor at the sink.

"Can't even use the bathroom in private..., yah (you) sorry soin' so! Hell..., what sorry sucker said that?" Old Man Anderson mumbles louder.

The supervisor opens a few stalls, finding a cleaner one beside Winton.

Winton rushes and within minutes, he leaves the unflushed toilet, creeping out and into the yard.

The van turns at the corner near the mill, and the driver slows with eyes wandering over each lot when out of nowhere, the woman grows excited. "There, there it is! There..., there!" she screams as if hitting the freakin' lottery jackpot.

The man jerks the wheel hard and swerves into the mill's lot, jumping out, pulling the hammer out, then a dirty, dusty visor cap covered in tobacco finger print stains. He raises the hammer with eyes roaming over the capital letters "HAMMER OF THEOSIS" heavily engraved in the stock. The big man draws back, taking a few good whacks until dancing to the music mildly blaring from the van, while working his way from the front to the back. Afterward, he eases out a big knife, flattening tires.

Winton and Boogey run into each other, hearing a loud cheer when finding everyone's backs at the fence and cheering louder while looking forward, after each whack.

One man walks off, heading to his station, when spotting Winton. "Hey, Wint, is that your car out there being remodeled?" a lead foreman asks, laughing hard and in tears before taking off and directing a crane with a heavy load.

Winton fights through the crowd, finally seeing what remains of his car when the big man throws up a middle finger at Winton, smiling. "Hey, you! How about them dea (there) tatas, chump!" he yells, jumping in when the girlfriend speeds off.

"Wow..., man!" Winton anxiously shouts, kicking up dust and dropping tears.

A siren blares after the van passes a deputy with flashers finally on when speeding into the lot.

Boogey comes up from behind Winton, patting his back, comforting him yet holding his laugh while looking at the car, on all fours, and looking like it just came off a smasher.

"You sure are screwing up, not being on your station, Wint! One more point, and you're out!" his supervisor yells when Winton rushes off with teary eyes.

Winton is called to the office minutes later to make a statement with the police and then wait for a tow truck. He signs forms and then goes inside and contacts his insurer to find out that his policy is substandard when feeling sick. He exits and heads into the yard then spins out, finding Twon, swishing like a woman near the bathroom.

Winton waits a while before going inside, then waits longer when his stomach cramps. He sprints, taking the furthest stall, sitting, and listening to Twon's muffled voice drowned out by a generator when Winton pulls out a flask, taking several hits.

"So, what's up? Twon asks, talking to one of his flings on his cell phone.

Winton's eyes go wide as he freezes and looks shocked with his mouth dropped open.

"Can you hear me? I said what's up?" Twon says as the engine shuts down.

"Sup?" Winton says low, peeking through a crack to ensure no one else is there.

"What you doing? You want some, huh? I know you do," Twon responds to his fling with a girlish laugh.

"You mean, right now?" Winton declares with his eyes wide open, in shock.

"If you're what I like, we need a room so I can hollllaaa!" Twon says, digging dirt from under his nails with the phone to one ear and slightly deaf in the other.

"Hotel? Oh…, ok, but who's paying?" Winton asks, excitedly peeking through the crack.

"Look! Would you shut the hell up! Ugh…,! Naw, boo, not you; this idiot in the other stall that keeps answering me. Now, what were you saying, Babe?" Twon asks.

Winton sinks deep in embarrassment, thinking and timing himself to come out, simultaneously when flushing after hearing Twon hang up, and they meet at the sink.

"Sorry," Winton utters, holding out his cell. "Guess we were on the phone at the same time, huh," he says, sticking his chest out, and acting manly.

"Yeah, whateva! Ugh…, I mean, ugh!" Twon declares, slowly twisting his curvaceous hips and walking out.

Winton stares, mesmerized by Twon's perfect, girlish figure, until he fades through the door.

A foreman sits on the toilet, looking through the seam of the stall at Winton's head which lustfully shakes until looking back in the mirror.

"Uh, now that is fine; I'd knock the dust off that!" he whispers when the foreman bursts into loud laughter, causing Winton to put his head down and rush out.

Winton meets his claims adjuster later, who gives him a few hundred dollar bills and rental keys to a car that looks worse than his own. He walks into the lot at lunch time pulling out his flask and climbing in the rental; watching guys come out then heads inside for Boogey, finding Young Anderson on his cellular with his back to him.

The bathroom door swings open, and Young Anderson nods to Boogey when Winton's index finger and trigger thumb come up, inches behind Anderson's head; Winton blazes as if in a shootout, until his other hand comes up, replicating the first.

Boogey finds Winton leaning back, blazing more until seeing someone in the window. "Three o'clock! Three o'clock!" Boogey whispers, finding Old Man Anderson's eyes and mouth tore open, to the gesture of violence, in disbelief.

Winton finally notices movement and begins clowning with Boogey turns with more ridiculous moves that end with him doing the robot and calling Boogey before running off. He turns the corner fast, looking for Boogey, and passes a bush discovering Boogey in tears, with his back against the wall and hands on his knees.

"Aiii..., hii..., hii! Your trifling tail is cold-busted! Old Man Anderson caught you red-handed, sucker!" Boogey screams, laughing to catch up, until on Winton's heels.

Boogey happily passes a few cars that he thinks is Winton's rental then goes slower after they pass the last car, finding the old heap parked off by itself.

Winton climbs in and keeps from looking over at Boogey and the strange sounds he is making with heavy jumping shoulders when a heavy burst of laughter shoots out in a long scream, followed by more screams of laughter when Winton pulls out, heading for the heart of downtown.

Within minutes, Winton stops at the red light and waits for a few cars to pass, then makes a turn when Boogey taps him.

Boogey's eyes stay glued on Winton and the tightly gripped steering wheel. "Winton, come on, dude!" he exclaims, looking at the lottery sign fade by slowly.

"Yeah, yeah, yeah! Another feeling, huh?"

"No, but we got time, and I got a dollar," Boogey says, staring at the distant sign in the side view mirror until the car turns, doubles back and pulls into the lot. He jumps out, rushing to the counter, where the clerk stands, stacking boxes. Boogey grows impatient and slaps the dollar down in his big hands. "The big one!" he declares, slapping the counter louder while anxiously looking around.

Winton sits staring at a female getting out of her SUV with her kids.

Boogey rushes, climbing in, holding up the ticket, and kissing it.

Winton's lustful eyes stay on the woman, who smiles when he slams on the brakes and Boogey flies forward. He speedily rolls down the window and then steps on the gas, finally noticing the SUV rocking from side to side, with a big man inside venting with his firm index finger pointed at Winton.

Winton makes it to the next block, finding Boogey in a daze when seeing movement out of the corner of his eye.

Boogey stares and then leans forward, squinting when finding Freddy in a monkey suit with the costume head under his arm. "I'll be..., what the..., I'll be damn if it ain't ah, ah, ah, Freddy...," he stutters, bursting into a peal of deep laughter. "He ought to stop that mess, out here shaking his butt at his age; that's for the young'uns," Boogey says, looking until no longer able to see him in the bend in the road.

"Freddy? Freddy who..., Holmes?"

"Hell naw..., Freddy from high school; Nattie's old crush," Boogey utters, looking back and getting one last glimpse in another turn.

"Are you serious? What? Where?"

"At the joint back there with an ape suit on," Boogey says, laughing harder until tears are dripping on his cheeks.

"For real?" Winton declares in a slurred speech, looking over his shoulder and finding the distant costume figure striking a pose at the red light. "Well, I thought he was shaking his booty down at the Chicken Shack," Winton says, driving further before turning into the strip mall with the Chinese restaurant.

"Then he's working two jobs because that was definitely him. Uh, uh, uh..., why did Freddy's spend all the time in school, taking up a desk, just to shake his butt later in life?"

"A job is a job; somebody gotta do it, right?" Winton exclaims.

"I guess so..., I'm just glad it is not me or your drunk tail!" he declares, finally getting a good whiff of Winton's strong, liquored breath. Man, you need to give up liquor because it hits you too fast, and you wear drunk, too darn well!" Boogey says, finally noticing his heavier, slurred speech.

"If push comes to shove, you would be out there shaking that booty too," Winton utters, bursting into an irritating, drunken laugh.

"Huh, I think I'll hustle off stuff beside the street first," Boogey says, laughing.

Winton parks, quickly turning up his flask when finding Boogey's back to him.

"Look at ya (you)..., ya (you) lush...! I'm surprised your supervisor, or the boss didn't smell that strong stench. You gone (are going to) mess around and screw yourself right out of a good darn job!" Boogey declares, staring into Winton's bloodshot eyes.

Winton's door swings open, and his legs feel wobbly when swiftly bracing the door, and looking over the roof at Boogey.

"You pissy-tail drunk, and yes..., I saw you stumbling," Boogey says, shaking his head in disbelief.

They approach the door, and a deep bass with rap grows until glancing through the glass door bursting into laughter, seeing the young non-Chinese looking man with his back turned, dancing like he has two left feet. They watch the man getting down longer before easing to the door.

The bell rings, instantly causing the non-Chinese looking man to pretend to be stirring something in the wok while drawn to normalcy when turning the music low. He stays low, embarrassed until coming up with napkins and a serious face.

Boogey and Winton hear metal utensils continuously banging against other metal works until a strong aroma of fried rice rises deep in their nostrils.

Boogey lifts a menu, glancing over a few pictures before drifting over the prices. He opens his mouth to order, finding the non-Chinese looking man whispering to the older non-Chinese looking cook who stares at Boogey, shaking his head with a mean look.

Boogey looks back, finding Winton slithering into a chair, the alcohol nippily taking full effect with his eyes slightly dim then crossed, and his mouth banging out twelve or more pieces of minty gum and popping it loudly.

Boogey's eyes wander over all the gum wrappers strewn over the table, shaking his head in disbelief. "You need to get that monkey off yo (your) back!" Boogey says, ordering his dish and passing his dingy, cracked credit card.

The young non-Chinese looking man stares at the card, calling the old non-Chinese looking man, over who laughs, sucking his teeth. He shakes his head, reaching on the top shelf, passing the young non-Chinese looking man a handful of checks before heading back to the steamy wok.

The young non-Chinese looking man stares at Boogey, glimpsing the checks before sliding them into the drawer. He swipes the card swiftly, but nothing registers, then swipes again, and the LED flashes 'declined' in bright, bold letters. "Huh! – Ping chong ting ping tong ye, yong!" he shrieks.

Without warning, Winton stumbles and slams into the counter, and the young non-Chinese looking man jumps, looking at Boogey with a mean stare, then into Winton's crossed eyes.

"Never mind him; he's had too many human, Guinee pig, lab tests today. I think they must have maxed him out," Boogey exclaims, seriously staring at Winton's foolish looking face.

The young non-Chinese looking man's face turns bright red. "No good! Credit card no good, sua (sir)..., yo (your) broke..., always come wit (with) credit card, no good, you..., you! You never have money! Always cumma (coming) hea (here) wit (with) credit no good, check no good and money probably, no good. No more, sua (sir), no more!" he yells in a slow, whiny voice.

Winton leans back and throws a tight, rolled twenty on the counter out of nowhere.

The young non-Chinese looking man thinks it is trash, unraveling it to find half a twenty. "Dis joke, huh? He, he..., ha, ha!" he senselessly shrieks. "You think dis a joke, huh..., drunk butt?" he screams, forcefully mushing Winton back by his forehead.

Winton loses his balance, dropping back with a loud slap when his feet go high.

"What the...," Boogey yells with a tight fist toward the young man, who backs up with a mean stare, shouting several curse words.

"You want some, huh, punk?" the young non-Chinese looking man yells, looking over his shoulder. "Mi ping ting a ling ding ding ting, pag, chow ling ting yen bang!" he yells even louder when the rotten-toothed old man immediately appears from behind saloon-style double doors with a two-feet machete high over his head, rocking back-and-forth like a crazed lunatic.

"Hey, hey, hey..., calm down, little angry man! Nobody means you any harm!" Boogey utters, feeling Winton tugging at his leg to stand. Boogey balances when Winton kneels with all his strength, putting his weight up on Boogey before falling into him when they disappear beneath the counter's ledge, struggling to get up.

The non-Chinese looking men ease to the edge until on tiptoes when Boogey's hand finally comes up; then, his fat head reappears but dips down quickly when Winton pulls up against him again.

"Get out of my stoe (store)! You..., you get out, I say! Get out!" the old non-Chinese looking man hollers in a thundering voice that does not match his appearance.

"The twenty?" Boogey says, looking at the half-twenty still on the counter.

"Ahhh...," the old non-Chinese looking man shrieks, swiftly raising the machete high, slipping on the wet floor, and causing the machete to come down on the counter in brute force, splitting the half twenty in half.

"Ok..., ok, we were just leaving," Boogey nervously yells, trying to calm down.

"We didn't want this crap anyway!" Winton blurts out in a high, drunken slur.

The old non-Chinese looking man's face turns fiery red, instantly. "Crap! Crap!" he shrieks. "All the time you come hea (here), you come hea (here) all da (the) time and what.., you order? You order crap..., you eat crap!"

Winton stares in disbelief then breaks out in a devious laugh, shaking his head and slightly staggering backward.

Winton and Boogey back up more with eyes glued on the non-Chinese looking men as they scroll from behind the counter; their mouths filled with more curse words than a seasoned Sailor can say in a lifetime.

Winton stumbles past Boogey. "Now what..., punks? What! What!" Winton sluggishly screams, swiftly brandishing a rusty-looking .22.

Both non-Chinese looking men's arms go high, and the one with the machete goes even higher.

"Ping ting ding ding the ding ding ding dong this, you mother...!" Winton shouts in a drunken voice with glassy, snake eyes.

"Wint! Wint! You done lost your freakin' mind?" Boogey stutters with wide eyes and his heart rapidly pounding until almost hyperventilating.

"Sorry sua (sir!) Sorry sua!" the non-Chinese looking men beg, almost simultaneously.

"I'll take that!" Winton snatches the machetes, motioning them to the kitchen.

Boogey nervously looks around, realizing he has to stick around to clear up the mess, so he follows them, watching Winton closely as he motions them to the floor.

The front door swiftly opens and slams shut fast, and Boogey nervously jumps, turning and looking into the eyes of his high school sweetheart, Clarice, who he has not seen in a while, walking up to the counter, smiling.

"Boogey? Umm..., if it ain't Boogey..., Boogey 'Lover Boy' Johnson!" she yells with a big smile of lust.

"Clarice...," he responds excitedly, motioning Wint by pointing undercover.

"Wow..., you're working in a Chinese restaurant, now?" She laughs. "Well, I would have never known," she says, giggling.

"Oh naw..., naw..., hellz naw! You see, me and ole Winton..., you remember Wint, right? Well, we own this hea (here) little joint (place) but still work the mill til we get on our feet," he says, surprisingly finding a deputy's car pulling up across the street.

"Yeah, I remember that crazy-tail Winton; who can forget that silly tail clown? Last I heard, he was the towns drunk." She laughs, and Boogey grows tense with eyes cut quickly back at Winton then even faster at her.

"Yo, mama!" Winton barely mumbles, catching himself when frowning under-eyed and looking toward the counter, still out of view.

Clarice's mouth drops open in shock. "Boog..., look..., why didn't you tell me Winton was here?" she whispers, jerking her shoulder in a peal of frightening laughter.

"Winton? Girl, naw..., he ain't here, right now. My little Chinese cook was talking about a new, authentic dish called..., yohamma! You see..., the H in the word is silent, but they have a hard time saying it right. Well, look..., anyway, I'm about to head out, but what can I get you?" Boogey asks, still attentive to the deputy who is now sitting on the hood, talking to a beautiful, blonde female pharmacist.

"Large broccoli and shrimp, crab rangoon and fried rice," she exclaims, grabbing her purse and fiddling inside for seconds.

"Did you hear that, Pang?" Boogey yells, coming up on his tiptoes, looking into Winton's drunken eyes and then down into the old non-Chinese looking man's eyes when motioning Winton to get the old man over and hot on the wok.

Within seconds, Boogey and Clarice look toward the back, hearing loud, metal utensils banging as the old man begins whipping up the meal.

Boogey looks back again, finding Winton nodding with crossed eyes.

The old non-Chinese looking man turns two woks on high, banging the food out and sometimes staring teary-eyed when maneuvering and bringing Clarice into view. He finds Winton nodding and Boogey's back to him when he slowly grabs Clarice a few soy sauce packets and utensils, whispering for help when she starts moving her lips in unison to make out his words.

Boogey stares at Clarice with stale eyes, immediately blocking the non-Chinese looking man with advertising signs on the counter and motioning Winton to back the man away when reaching for her food.

"It's great seeing you, Boog!" she says, hoping for aggression in a reconnection. "Well, I better get going because I like my food hot, like my man." She winks. "Maybe we can get together for old time's sake while I'm here," she says, holding out the crisp fifty-dollar bill.

"Maybe...," he responds, nervously cutting his eyes over at the deputy. "But hey, your money's no good here, beautiful." He closes her hand and swallows hard when the deputy walks toward the restaurant but suddenly fades off, to the driver's side of his cruiser.

"Make it your business to come by Momma's, please! There's nothing wrong with seeing an old friend, right?" she says, winking, picking up the bag and walking away.

The old non-Chinese looking man backs up to the hot wok and a light trail of smoke billows when he sticks the long tongs inside, slowly churning with his back still to the wok.

Winton playfully points the gun directly at the young non-Chinese looking man's face, and the man's face grows fearful, slightly transitioning into a smile when realizing the gun is fake. He continually stares at Winton until finding Winton leaning against the prep table, slightly snoring with his droopy eyes almost closed.

Boogey's eyes stay fixated on Clarice's hourglass shape that stretches her too-tight knit, tan skirt until she fades out of sight.

The young non-Chinese looking man looks at his father. "Dey hon liu said sue dam binang," he whispers very low when the father swiftly swings a fiery spatula, slapping Winton in the face, and it sticks, leaving a light burn mark when Winton peels away, screaming and instantly sober.

Boogey freezes in fear, leaning over the counter, finding Winton lifted high by the young non-Chinese looking man with legs collapsed together, going higher.

Winton drops the BB gun accidentally, scrambling for it yet falling forward until both hands are searing while pressed hard in the bottom of each red, hot, burning wok until springing back under heavy pressure. He wavers and wobbles until falling flat on his butt, jerking, kicking, and springing up fast, trying to balance.

Both non-Chinese looking men take off out the back door, with the old man yelping even louder than his son, who ducks down, taking off swiftly and even faster when veering off down the long, steep hill.

Winton drops to his knees, continually screaming, when Boogey bursts through the double doors, snatching him up by the collar, rushing him to the ice machines, and burying his hands deep.

Boogey repeats the process until Winton's hands cool, then swings Winton around, dipping both hands in globs of cool butter before easing back, giggling. His shoulders go up and down heavily, watching Winton moving his hands expressly in and out of the butter like an old Kung Fu teacher, constantly digging his hands in hot gravel in movies.

Boogey can't hold the laughter any longer when in tears and a silent cry until his shoulders are heavily jumping again until finally settling minutes later. Deep in thought, Boogey flips open the drawer, pulling his checks out and cramming them in his pocket, when out of nowhere, he jumps, seeing the two non-Chinese looking men peeking through the front window before backing away in a flash, and bumping into each other.

The non-Chinese looking men run frantically and stop at the busy road, continually waving to the deputy who has his back to them; flirting with two new females outside the cleaners.

A call keys up on the walkie-talkie, and the deputy jumps, hearing a robbery and shooting in progress when expressly jumping in his cruiser. He throws the car in reverse, expressly stopping, discovering the old non-Chinese looking man hanging from the side mirror with feet drawn in, tight.

"What the...?" the deputy yells, flipping on the blue, flashing lights.

"We've been robbed! Robbed, I tell you! The men are still there!" the younger non-Chinese looking screams, pointing toward the restaurant when seeing movement in the kitchen.

"Look, I have to answer this call first, but I'll dispatch another car," the officer says, prying the man's little Kung Fu grip hands from the door and watching him fall when hitting the siren and speeding off.

"Cops…, cops…, let's hit it!" Boogey shrieks, shoving Winton and bursting through the wooden back screen door. Boogey scans their surroundings fast, spotting houses down the hill when pointing. "Quick! Quick!" Boogey nervously screams, forcing Winton in the back again until stumbling then grabbing Winton by the collar to help Winton gain his drunken balance.

They go faster until finally reaching the bottom, veering off and taking cover in the dense woods where they duck, and Boogey begins murmuring a plan.

Minutes later, Boogey trots beside a house, coming to the front fast, and knocking.

Winton peeps from a thick bush, finding a woman walking away from her baby still in the high chair when running to the clothesline. His head pops up seconds later; a swift hand removing two sun hats and sundresses when hearing the baby screaming and finding him pointing when ducking behind several rows of sheets.

The woman cracks the door open after the second ring, looking into Boogey's sad eyes.

"Excuse me, but can I use your phone? My car broke down a block away. I promise I'll only be a sec; then I'll be out of your hair, scout's honor."

Her hand finally comes to her chest in fear realizing she made a bad mistake opening the door to a stranger. "One sec," she nervously says, closing and locking the door. She reappears seconds later, cracking the door but this time with her foot at the door and a baseball bat in hand, easing the cordless phone out when finally registering the baby screaming again when easing the door shut and locking it.

Winton looks again, seeing the woman with her back to him and the whiny kid pointing and screaming when ducking low and coming up high, running toward the woods with his arms full of flopping clothing.

Boogey knocks lightly, and the woman eases the door open, reaching for the phone when Boogey thanks her, smiling and easing the door shut. He walks past her car, looking back swiftly when grabbing sunshades hanging from the visor and several scarves. He takes off in a mad dash and shoots through the thick bushes, rushing into the dense woods, spotting Winton when slowing and almost out of breath.

Ten minutes or so later, the two appear at the far end and backside of the strip mall, peeking out for seconds.

Winton steps out, strutting with a hat, dress, shades, and dusty brogans slamming against the concrete. He turns at the corner strutting along the front of the strip mall, passing people who stop and look at him strangely until he touches his face and expressly pulls the scarf over his mustache.

Winton closes the rental with shaking hands, hurrying to get the key in when the lock clicks. He backs up with his boots raised high, jumping, and finding Big John staring him down when the dress sways forward, slightly covering his brogans.

"Excuse me, ma'am," the sheriff utters, dipping his wide brim and intentionally grabbing a handful of narrow butt in a disgusting stare when stepping to one side.

"Ooh, Ooh!" Winton moans in a giggly, high, girly pitch.

The sheriff stops, sniffing a few good times when the slight stench of Winton's familiar hair grease rushes in his nostrils and fades off quickly.

Winton jumps in the car with his head peeled down to the console. He sits longer pretending to be looking for something until inching his head up, staring at the sheriff's back when throwing the car in reverse. Winton backs out slowly, keeping his eyes on the sheriff until recapturing him in the rear and side-view mirrors with him getting smaller.

The sheriff continues looking through the restaurant window, until slamming his back against the wall and drawing his gun. He leans forward and off to the side, peeking through the window, hearing low Chinese sounding voices getting louder as the owners rush up from the other side of the street.

Winton swerves expressly around to the side of the strip mall, stopping when Boogey rushes up, jumping inside. He steps into the gas then slows when exiting the parking lot and entering Main Street.

Boogey immediately wrestles out of the woman's clothing and when miles from the mill, Boogey sits in a daze and then bursts into laughter, looking over at Winton.

"What now? You're always giggling about something," Winton says, looking at Boogey's red, teary face while Boogey is tearing off the last piece of ridiculous clothing.

"For one, get rid of that ridiculous outfit, and two, the guys know about the bouncer." Boogey looks down with guilty eyes, instantly gripping the dashboard when Winton slams on the brakes with cars, blowing horns, skidding and swerving.

"What the..., Boog! You actually told them that crap?" Winton steps into the gas hearing and seeing a long distant, longhorn blaring truck on a collision course.

Other cars pull up behind or abruptly alongside, blowing with fists or middle fingers high until Winton swerves off and into a vacant lot.

"Now, now..., it won't me..., the guys went to the club, and the bouncer asked for you. He probably remembered your uniform and name tag. The guys even said your name's plastered in the stalls: 'Something to the effect of..., for a good time, call Wint,' but not sure if it was one stall or all of them," Boogey says, slightly beaming. "And I sure as heck don't know how he would have your phone number."

Later that night, Rev has bible study in his brother's garage.

Folks arrive early and sit talking amongst themselves and get loud until Rev walks in, leading off in a short song and then lengthy prayer.

Rev opens his eyes and looks over the small group, finding an older lady pointing to another lady, smiling. "Rev…, Sistah Mettlin has a song to share."

Rev smiles, motioning the middle-aged woman to the front. "So tell me, Sistah, what will you be sharing with us tonight?"

The woman smiles, looking down bashfully and then up. Well, my baby sister Liz wrote this song, and it's not complete, but I told her I would share it at service," she responds, glowing. "It's called Tears After Tears," she nods, slightly clearing her voice when lighting into the song.

*Tears after tears Years after years*
*Big smile on my face but hiding lots of fears*
*Don't know how hard it is to feel*
*Stressed out depression is for real*
*Every day contemplate on suicide*
*Though I'll be better dead than to be alive*

*The Bible is telling me otherwise*
*Now I sit here with tears in my eyes*
*He said I love you; you'll always be mine*
*The Lord brought the truth to a corrupted mind*

*No More Fear, No More Pain, No More Sorrow, Lord in Your Name*
*Nothing Will Separate Me from You Again*
*You're My Hope, My Father, and My Friend*

*Tears after tears, Years after years*
*Hold a smile on my face but hiding lots of fears*
*Behind my smile, I'm crying. Lord, inside I'm dying*
*My pain outweighs my fear. I keep dying year after year*

*The Bible telling me otherwise*
*Now I sit here with tears in my eyes*
*He said I love you; you'll always be mine*
*The Lord brought the truth to a corrupted mind*

*No More Fear, No More Pain, No More Sorrow Lord In Your name*
*Nothing Will Separate Me From You again*
*You're My Hope, My Father, and My Friend'*

Sistah Mettlin ends it, rocking in tears and slightly humming the tune when another woman repeats a verse or two with the room in an uproar of praise.

After praising the woman for the great song, Rev waits for everyone to settle down. "We will read from the Book of Matthew tonight," he says, running his finger over a few verses, which he reads and then explains in great detail.

An hour later, his assistant signals that it is time to bring the session to an end. "And another thing..., stop being lazy. Pick up this Bible and read it yourself. How do you think these slick, so-called pastors are getting their congregation in bed? Because they are too lazy to read. When you read, you have the power to save your own Soul. If any pastor says one word that contradicts the Bible, you need to first ask for clarification in case you misunderstood and when he confirms, and you know it is still wrong, you need to start looking for another church. What does God say? Don't take away from His word and don't add to it..., that means the ingredients are unchangeable and already perfect. Guard your Soul and stop turning your Soul over to men and women that twist even one of God's words because Satan was a perfectionist at it and Satan's children are even more craftier today. Be careful who you trust with your Soul and your life. Take ole Pastor Zelle across town; sitting up in his church, and you know it's his only because his name is plastered all over it. You know it..., and what does it say..., Zelle's house of worship..., huh..., must be a house of Satan worship! Zelle is twisting and turning God's words daily for his benefit and pleasure. Jesus says..., there is only one way to the FATHER, but not ole Zelle..., Zelle says there are a lot of ways! So who are you going to trust? A man that came into this world clueless and void of everything; grew up to lean to his own understanding and is now bold enough to override the Word of our Lord Jesus Christ? Want to try God! All I have to say is buyer beware..., be very, very aware!"

Rev looks at his watch. "We'll..., we'll wrap things up here because the Sandman is riding some of you tonight," he says, smiling and getting smiles in return. "Have you noticed how sleepy you get when opening your Bible? Well, that's how easy it is for Satan to manipulate you. When you come off that bed, even before getting out of bed, praise God and give Him your time," he utters with a smile and then a serious stare.

Oh..., there is something sad and pitiful that I want to share with you before we get out of here. I was watching a pastor of television the other night and he was telling me about this man he spoke to that told him that he put his wallet under the bed to remind him that he needs to pray." Rev burst into an uncontrollable laughter. "Now what was disturbing is that the pastor thought it was something glorious to hear, but in reality its pitiful to say the least if you have to use your wallet to remind you to pray; poor ole Soul; both the man and the pastor.

I mean what happens if you lose your legs and can't get down there anymore; will you stop praying all together? God gives you the breath to breathe and the legs and knees to get down on your knees and the best you can do is come up with some lame reminder. I bet you don't have to put that wallet or anything under that bed when remember to worship Satan. Poor pastor, but we need to pray for that man and the pastor. This is what some have come to when thinking of Almighty God." He closes his Bible, raising his hand for everyone to stand in prayer.

The following morning, Tuesday, Rev heads to the café, parking and sitting a spell, enjoying the scenery, when hearing sirens closing. He looks in his rearview, spotting two officers rushing past when easing out, and before he can open the door to the restaurant, it flies open with the impertinent waitress brought out in cuffs and in tears. Rev stands off to the side, overhearing a co-worker telling a lady that the waiter had been fighting her boss after being accused of stealing.

The waitress stands continually looking down, slightly resisting, until her eyes wander across Rev's shiny shoes, slowly following the creased pant leg to the suit coat until staring deep into Rev's eyes. She resists without strength when the officers shove her but can't guide her when she unknowingly transforms into evil and then back, finally breaking her stare and allowing the cops to rush her to the cruiser.

Rev backs up in fear, holding his chest. He watches the officer bow her head inside when she flops down and looks over at Rev, staring. He continues looking at the beautiful girl, having pity until tears form when seeing her face transform demonically when he fearfully grabs his chest again and rushes inside.

At the mill, on the first break, ten men sit, shooting the breeze (chatting), when a young man walks up with his headset on, bobbing.

Boogey looks at him, laughing.

"Hey, young blood, how about pulling those britches up? Nobody wants to see your drawings," an old man says, shaking his head.

"What? Look..., just step off, old head!" the young guy exclaims, turning and lifting himself on top of a wooden crate.

"Young folks are having freakin' problems and bad luck because they are hard headed. Their dress code is screwed all up, and you wonder why folks ain't hiring. Oh yeah, they are hiring alright, just not your trifling behind!" the old man says in a deep voice, pulling out his cigarettes and spanking the packet. "If you tried to court my daughter, walking around deformed with a long upper body and midget lower body, I would kick you square in your tail!" the old man laughs with others joining in the laughter.

"Well, that's just it, old head!" the young boy says, leaning forward, spitting. "I wouldn't come to your old, broken-down house to see your busted daughter anyway!"

Old man Lewis cuts his smile short, standing stealthily and slowly making his way over to the young boy, who keeps pretending to be tough. Lewis' hand slides in his pocket, gripping his Hawk-Bill knife while sliding one leg out and digging deeper to make sure he has a firm grip while looking around at quiet faces.

"If anything, if I come over, I'll be laying pipe with the Mrs.," the boy stupidly utters, laughing until freezing with a cool hand and something cooler and sharp at his neck.

Several men laugh, but Boogey breaks out in a wide-legged, ridiculous run, grabbing Lewis's hand, and fighting his firm resistance. "Easy..., easy!" Boogey whispers, trembling while easing the blade back from the boy's neck. He looks into Lewis' bloodshot eyes when tears fall from cigarette smoke burning Lewis' eyes. "Come on..., Lew, this punk ain't even worth it, man; you're going back to jail for sure, so spare him; let it go! What about your family, main (man)!"

Lewis stares into the young guys' eyes, lowering his head with his eyes full of tears, but keeps an eye on him until his head cocks, seeing the boy's slow smile.

"Uh, oh...," someone declares when the sound of a single firecracker echoes, and everyone ducks watching the boy's limp body sail into a pile of boxes.

Louder laughter comes, and everyone falls all over the place, trying to gain their composure.

The laughter grows even louder, watching the young boy fight his way out, instantly staggering back into the boxes.

Boogey and Winton go to a famous hamburger joint at lunch, and Boogey recommends passing the tax place to get a few good laughs at Freddy's expense.

They grab carryout, and Winton makes his way to the tax place, and sure enough, Freddy is out there shaking it and making several crazy dance moves; some they had never seen. They sit chuckling with tears continually dropping while watching Freddy go at it nonstop. They laugh so hard that food drops and their tears make some of their submarine sandwich bread soggy.

Minutes later, Winton heads back with minutes to spare and, minutes later, backs in next to a black, shiny car.

Boogey and Winton glance over at the two pretty faces in the front, the other three in the back, and the driver's pretty, soft-looking, tanned skin.

Boogey stares at the woman's pretty, soft-looking fingers, immediately recalling the bouncer having the same ring and tattoo.

The driver's hand flips over with the index finger motioning Winton over.

"You..., she..., I mean, he wants you, Wint! Boogey rushes around to the driver's side. "I'll cover you on the timecard, but make it quick..., I mean pronto, lover boy," Boogey says, rushing to clock in and tell the crew.

Winton slowly eases out with a smile, seeing all the other cheerful, hot chicks.

The driver eases out in an overly tight jumper, closing the door and leaning against it; adjusting shades; the wig, curls, and breasts.

"Sup, ladies?" Winton says, leaning in and pointing to the girl behind the driver's seat, who has the prettiest face. His eyes glaze over the voluptuous bouncer, whom he still does not recognize.

"See! Uh, uh! How are you gonna stand here and disrespect me?" the bouncer yells, taking off the shades with a balled fist snatching Winton in the collar when he finally recognizes the bouncer, and his body tenses.

Out of nowhere, loud and chanting voices rise in Winton's ear when he cuts his eyes over near the fence, finding a vast audience.

The bouncer pins Winton against the car with Winton's feet slightly dangling. "Hmm..., naw, see, you gonna make this up to me," he says, lowering Winton and interlocking all fingers with Winton's when squeezing tight, causing Winton to dip down and break out in a death cry until on his knees, begging.

"Hey, Adam! Adam's Apple!" a mill worker hollers until it's chanted in unison.

Winton strains, hearing the chants until it fades under the loud saw and whistle.

A lead foreman runs to the gate, running the guys back to work.

The bouncer reaches inside his bra, pulling out a card. "Here's my number, and don't play me because you have not seen stalking until you've had me stalk you!" he says, giving Winton a long wet kiss when backing away with his skirt bulging a foot outward when adjusting it, climbing in and speeding off.

Winton continually watches the car, then turns slowly, finding a few guys and Boogey still looking with bucked eyes and their mouths dropped open. Without warning, he jumps, kicking up gravel, swearing, and throwing up a fist, pretending to be livid when heading for the yard with his face torn up.

Twon passes Winton, winking. "Were you serious about getting with this? How much?" Twon asks, seeing Winton smiling then straightening his face when seeing guys off to the side, staring when looking down fast.

On their next break, the guys rush up and continually disparage Winton, but he just sits, taking it like a champ and playing it down.

Winton finds Boogey looking up, whistling with his hand in his pocket. "What about dem (them) Skins..., dem (them) Boys?" Boogey hollers to get the heat off.

Before long, the men are talking about sports and laughing.

Winton soon feels the conversation heading to the incident again when his eyes wander, finding the guy who was slapped, lying on the crate in a fetal position, taking a catnap. He motions for Lewis to pass him the brown spray paint and then stands by the young guy until the loud saw cranks up. Winton giggles looking back a few times when spraying a long streak down the young guy's exposed underwear, and when the whistle blows, everyone allows the boy to pass and then bursts into laughter.

After work, Boogey and Winton sit in Winton's car about to crank up when a lowrider sports car pulls up.

The young man with the painted drawers runs out of the breezeway, jumping in the backseat.

Winton and Boogey watch as the male passenger passes a joint and liquor to the young guy in the back, shaking their heads.

Crickets chime in just before Winton cranks up, and within thirty minutes, the general store comes into view with Boogey motioning Winton to stop.

"Nattie's right, Boog..., you have a serious problem with this lottery, man," Winton utters when Boogey lunges forward and out.

"Can I get you something?" Boogey asks, looking back.

"Yeah, an ice-cold one." Winton beams. "At least, if I spend money, I'm getting something out of it." Winton reaches into his pocket, pulling out two dollars.

"Right..., a DUI, bigger potbelly, or long or strong urination." Boogey giggles.

"With all the money you spend playing, you could have had that rust bucket back on the road by now!" Winton exclaims, holding two dollars tightly and causing Boogey to tug lightly to get it free.

"Ah, quit your whining! You sound like a nagging old housewife. Just loosen your old, decrepit Speedos and man up, dude!"

"Man up? Naw..., you man up..., and man up on this!" Winton playfully grabs his crotch. "And walk home!" Winton yells, forgetting his drink when skidding off fast.

Over at the rehabilitation center, Dale, Boogey's grandfather, sits, taking six of his daily fifteen pills.

The nurse hands him a juice, checking that he swallowed when Dale stands, walking off.

Dale stops and continually pulls something invisible off his skin and throws it to the floor. His eyes stay glued to the far end of the hallway until his imaginary friend appears, approaching from out of nowhere.

"What are you doing, Dale?" his friend asks in a commanding tone.

"What? Do you see this?" Dale declares, clutching another handful of nothing. "Come on! Come on! I'll kick the crap, oucha, too! What? What? I wish the heck you would..., I'll kick the crap oucha too! Come on!" Dale utters, standing alone and playfully looking around with his fist balled, tightly.

Other residents roll into the lounge when the television suddenly blares, almost peeking the volume out.

Seconds later, Dale eases into the lounge, staring at a female across from him. "Huh," he says, looking at his imaginary friend. "Yeah, she does have a knotty-tail head..., huh?" Dale declares in deep laughter. He bursts out, repeating his comments until uncontrollably laughing.

In Mundson, outside the club, the low-rider sports car from the mill park in front of a convenience store, and the guys take turns hitting off the fifth when the young guy from the mill lights up a joint, putting it in rotation.

Everyone in the car spots a stranger walking up until veering off.

The strange man, wearing a toboggan and trench coat, paces, and they watch, soon spotting a shotgun when the wind blows the windbreaker open, slightly.

"Hey, hey, hey," the young guy from the mill whispers in excitement, patting the headrest and pointing.

The stranger paces longer until the convenience store door swings open, and an old lady and a little girl walk out.

The three watches until the driver nervously pulls away, making a U-turn, and parking in front of the club.

The stranger ducks beside an ice machine, slipping on a mask when drawing his gun and backing the clerk inside as he is walking out. "Get inside! Get in there and clean out the tiller!" he yells to the clerk with the gun to his head.

The stocky clerk backs up, looking at the stranger's powdery lips and dark-ringed eyes.

"Get going, I say!" the crackhead says, still backing the clerk up with baby steps.

The guys sit staring, excited, until the man's legs fade from the glass door into the darkroom when the joint burns down to the driver's fingers, and he unknowingly drops it.

"The tiller..., now, not next week! Are you clueless? Don't make me drop a hot ball in ya (you)!" the crackhead shrieks, waving the gun over the clerk's body when taking a step forward with the clerk backing, and trembling.

"Ok, ok...," the clerk says, pissed from having the gun trained on him. We can work this out. "What..., big bills..., small?" the clerk asks with a tight fist, even more pissed. "What..., fives, tens, quennies (twenties), or fidies (fifties)? What? What?" He slightly backs the crackhead up from aggression.

"What? Ah man, just give me my money before I blow you to kingdom come!" he says, shaking when his hand wipes his white, foamed lips.

The driver looks down; sniffs then looks, buzzing while looking at his friend next to him with empty hands. "Y'all smell something burning?" He looks over his shoulder at the guy's empty hand.

"Ah, man, it's probably that pulpwood from my clothes," the stoned guy from the mill sarcastically says, laughing.

The clerk sizes up the crackhead, finally realizing that he has been backing him up when using more aggression.

"Take another step, clown, and your momma will be having church services this Wednesday, son!" the crackhead utters with wide eyes, shoving the gun forward.

The clerk's eyes wander over the barrel and then the trigger, noticing there's no trigger when becoming confident, leaning his shoulders back and sticking out his chest. "Ok..., now that you put it that way, for you; I'll clean out the register, safe, and jewels safe," he responds with a smirk.

"What? Jewels? You mean you got jewels back there, too, son?" he excitedly whispers, scratching the side of his white lips and coming up on his tiptoes, looking over the clerk's shoulder toward the pitch-dark, back room.

"Oh yeah, yeah..., lots of freakin' gold jewels, man! The owner owns a mine," the clerk says, slow-walking the crackhead toward the back. "So what..., quennies (twenties), fidies (fifties), hundards (hundreds), how you want it, bro?" the clerk asks with a big smirk when almost bursting with laughter.

All heads in the low rider begin bobbing around. "Man, what's this dude doing, packing up the whole store?" the driver whispers.

"No way, I would be gone by now," the guy from the mill says, wiping his heavy breathing from the steamy window.

The crackhead goes into a daze, not answering but taking baby steps as the clerk slows. "Are you freakin' serious? Heck, hundreds..., hundreds!" he declares, excited. The crackhead sees something glittery fall from the clerk's hand and strains, finding the now shiny object bouncing and rolling before the new quarter falls flat.

"Heads or tails?" the clerk confidently shouts with his back still to him when jumping, grabbing the barrel, and bringing it straight up with his other big hand around the crackhead's neck.

The crackhead tries to free the tight grip, to breathe when yanking the gun with all his strength when his feet rise off the floor.

"Man screw this! Those guys are probably doing the job together to make it look like a robbery," the driver says, waving a hand as if he's had enough.

The clerk squints, discovering the quarter on tails. "Tails it is!" he yells, swinging and sliding the robber halfway down an aisle. "Ok, hundreds!" he utters, sprinting up and kicking him while he's crawling away. "What..., what! Five hundred..., six?" he screams, throwing the gun back, and stomping the stranger every time he inches up, until at thirteen. "Gone point a gun at me!" the clerk screams, kicking him again.

"Oh snap, son, the car's on fire..., on fire, dude!" the driver screams with wide, wandering eyes when expressly opening the door and accidentally slamming his feet in the door jam, hopping on one foot.

Outside, the other two sit high and are somewhat frightened when the guy in the back bursts into a peal of crazy laughter.

Inside, the crackhead moves swiftly, scurrying down several aisles, pulling products and loose shelving down to distance himself.

The clerk doubles back on an aisle, kicking him in the butt and knocking him down. "Naw, take the rest of what you got coming..., gone try and punk me?" the clerk yells, walking up to the crackhead who takes off, screaming and barreling down another aisle.

Outside, the driver stands fanning the floorboard fast. "What! Y'all just gone let my whip (car) burn up?" the driver yells, pissed. "Get your hind parts out..., get out, right now!" he yells, motioning them out.

Inside, the crackhead runs fast, cutting behind the clerk, and slamming into the counter. He takes off even fast this time, closing his eyes when bursting through the glass door, shattering it.

Across the street, the guys outside the car and several bouncers jump, spotting glass flying everywhere as if there was a mini-explosion.

The crackhead burst into the street, veering further into traffic until paralleling a car, and overtaking it until veering off into the woods like a cruise missile, screaming while plowing into thick tree limbs for seconds until clothes hung by a low branch; lying there and moaning in pain.

The guys lean into the car, laughing, and giving high fives. They look again, finding the clerk at the door with the weapon when turning, hearing the bouncers laughing and falling into each other.

The rear bouncer finally gains his composure, doing a double-take, and shakes his head in disbelief when finding the three staggering fools, approaching. "Twenty dollar cover-charge, gents," he says, pointing for his partner to frisk the first guy.

The first bouncer frisks the young man from the mill off to the side, turning him and squatting to wand his shoes when speedily and heavily pushing him forward and into another bouncer, who catches him and stands him back up just as the young boy from the mill swings.

The other bouncer almost cold cocks him but instead backs up laughing. "My bad, I almost lost my balance," he says, returning and approaching as the guy calms down.

The rear bouncer bursts into heavier laughter, noticing the guy's smeared drawers when five women walk up, and one girl instantly notices the nice-looking young man from the mill.

She steps to the side, looking at him with bashful eyes. "Hey handsome, are you waiting on me?" she asks, winking when another girl makes a nice comment about the guy blushing when he takes a few steps toward them.

"Keep it moving; you can holler inside," the bouncer who pushed him says.

His friends fade through the open door, but the young man tries to act cool and show off his swagger when turning and reaching for the door.

"Uggghhhh! Are you serious?" the sexiest girl shrieks, bursting into laughter and crazily falling back into her girlfriends.

The guy from the mill looks back, finding their faces frowned, but he's too drunk to realize they're laughing at and talking about him when entering.

The door closes, and the bouncers fall into each other laughing and the women laugh until it tapers off when the women walk up to the door and go inside.

The girl who made the first comment heads down the steps, finding the young guy from the mill waiting for her. She steps off the last step and the young guy reaches, with her fans him away with nervous flapping hands; trying to make sure he doesn't touch her.

"Hey..., what's up? I thought you wanted to holla!" he declares, coolly leaning back against the wall to support his high and drunken stance.

"Is that weed I'm smelling? Uh, uh naw..., see, my baby daddy is a weed head, so I'm not even about to put up with that mess, again," she says, making up a quick lie before walking off, swiftly.

"Girl, you're too stupid!" her girlfriend whispers, walking up, laughing. "Your baby daddy, huh? Like you got a baby," she utters, laughing even harder.

"Girl, please…, how is he gonna step to somebody with those stank drawers on, looking like he's been slipping and sliding on a freakin' chocolate bar," she says, bursting into the loudest scream of laughter.

The young guy follows the girl until she turns one last time, coming off loud and rude with him. He veers off, stands by himself for a few, and then heads for the bar, walking up behind the last guy.

One of the bouncers rushes in and over to the DJ's booth, telling him about the guy, and instantly, dim lights draw darker, and a fast-growing floodlight slowly makes its way toward the bar, stopping inches behind the guy from the mill.

The DJ adjusts the mic when the last song ends. "We have minutes before the comedy, but…," he says, waving for the comedian to come over.

"Sup, man?" the comedian asks, reaching for the mic being held out to him.

"Follow the spotlight and interview this dude under the lights," the DJ says, laughing so hard that he spills his drink over his hand.

The comedian heads over, and a bomb beat bleeds out of quality speakers when he performs a special step to get a few folks laughing. He still can't figure out why he's there until a guy who has his back to the guy from the mill walks out of line.

The comedian's eyes grow wide, spotting the heavily smudged drawers when pouncing past the young man and coming up beside him yet standing clear. "Hey! Hey! I've got one right here, Mr. DJ!" he yells, whispering in the young man's ear when his drunken face lights up, and he follows the comedian to the empty dance floor.

The guy's two friends stand in the corner talking to two women when the driver looks back, hearing the comedian announce their friend's name while guiding and showcasing him in a circle before the huge crowd, showing off the stain.

The driver soon gets the other friend's attention, and they head for the dance floor. "Hey!" the driver shrieks, finally getting his friend's attention by pointing at his butt and then back to his friend on the dance floor.

The young guy from the mill looks at his friend's gesture, confused until finally looking back, pulling his shorts and finding the thick, brown stain. His face turns bright red as he lunges forward, running at top speed, tackling the heavy-leaning, over-exaggerated, laughing driver when the two begin brawling, and causing patrons to disperse.

Two bouncers immediately intervene, escorting the three out. Still, the fight spills into the street until a cop pulls up, diffusing the situation and not running them in when getting a gist of what happened.

The young guy from the mill stands by the cruiser, swaying while the crowd disperses. "Excuse me, sir, but can I get a courtesy ride?" He reaches for the door.

"Car Four Eight Seven," the cop fakes in responding, when pressing his earpiece closer. "Sorry, sir, I have another emergent call," he says, pointing to the bouncers. "Hey! Can you call him a cab, please!" the officer yells to the bouncers, sliding inside, turning the lights on, speeding off, and swerving as if drunk from laughing so hard.

Twenty minutes later, a cab pulls up, and a foreign guy comes around, opening the door. "My friend! Where to..., my friend?" He closely trails behind until spotting the heavy stains when his hands go to the saw mill worker's shoulder, backing him up fast. "Hey! What is this? What is this on your butt..., my friend? No, no, no..., not good! No good..., this is not good for me," he says, slamming the door fast and brushing off both hands fast before holding them out to the man to keep him from advancing.

"Come on..., I'll pay double the fare..., no problem," the young guy utters, staring into the foreigner's face.

"No problem? Doo-doo, yes, doo-doo is a very big problem for me, my friend. I have excellent customers and can't have them smelling doo-doo all night, so it's a huge problem, for me!" The cab driver stands in deep thought when a smile comes as if a light has come on when he eases out a pen. "Here, for you, my friend, come..., come...," he says, pulling out a business card to his competitor. "You pull up your pants and call; no..., I'll call," he exclaims, snatching his cellphone back, dialing, and then handing him the phone and jerking it back stealthily. "You no-touch..., I hold for you, ok..., ok?" he declares, frowning slightly.

The cabbie jumps in, hitting the locks. He heads down the street, cutting off the in-service light and headlights, making a U-turn, and parking. He calls his co-workers and a few buddies informing them about the transfer, and before long, there are several cabs lined up a ways from the club with the slew of cabs slowly backing down with flashers on when finding the young man walking toward them.

Within minutes, five more cabbies converge across the street with lights out, watching the competitor cabbie pull up slowly, honking and waving.

Several cabbies sit on their hoods talking or smoking but all watching the heavyset and mean-looking cabbie throw on his flashers while curiously looking at all his competitors when easing out, scratching his head, confused. The new foreign cabbie opens the door, rushing the young man who climbs in fast, then slowly turns, gazing at over 20 cabs, and staring at them with confused hand motions when walking off.

The competitor cabbie climbs in, sitting and still looking at the other cabbies until finally pulling off slowly and in deep thought, still looking at some through the rearview and then as far ahead down the road as he can see. His eyes wander into several competitor cab finding fast-waving hands and bright smiles; still in deep thought until speeding off, and growing more curious.

The cabbie slows, adjusting the rearview and bringing the young man's half-closed eyes into view. "Hey, hey, hey..., what's going on, here?" he asks, turning at the corner and pulling over. His eyes shoot over his shoulder with a mean stare. "Why didn't you catch one of those cabs across the street..., about the slew of cabs along the stretch?" he asks, finding the young guy half passed out.

The cab driver calls out to the young man again, not getting an answer when pulling off and coming up to forty-five when his dispatcher chimes in: "Car Ten..., come in..., please disregard the nightclub pickup; I just got word that that boy done messed his drawers," she says, laughing hard and giggling when releasing the transmitter.

Without hesitation, the cab driver's feet go high; both kneecaps almost in his chest, when both feet slam on the brake, abruptly lunging the young man forward and over the headrest with his skid-marked butt jerking in place, inches from the cabbie's face when the cabbie screams, jumping back into the driver's door. He huffs and puffs, pulling hard on the handle until breaking it off and throwing the door open. He shoots out almost as if invisible and dances around in circles with a torn-up face, flapping disgusted hands.

Out of nowhere, a loud horn comes with a car swerving and barely missing him and the door when the cabbie comes to his senses; rushing to the trunk, pulling plastic, and somewhat quickly wrapping his behind. He pulls the young man out and over to the curb, patting him down for valuables, then snatches his gold herringbone chain.

Seconds later, a fast-moving, eighteen-wheeler comes out of the curve and blows, still barreling toward the cab.

The cabbie looks back fast, throwing other items of no value from the young man back at him when running and diving inside the cab when another truck's flashing high and low beams appear.

The first tractor-trailer veers across the yellow line and then back in his lane, avoiding a head-on collision when in a flash, spotting the cabbie coming up, adjusting in the seat with both hands at his head.

The cabbie screams, jumping and nervously looking while the truck bears down, faster when his mind somewhat clears, and he expressly reaches for the missing door handle and jumps back when the eighteen-wheeler rips the door from the frame, knocking it fifty feet from the front bumper.

The cabbie screams, crying out loud and banging the steering wheel, still hearing a fast-fading horn blaring when looking through the rearview, finding two more eighteen-wheelers side-by-side.

The cabbie's fat hand shoots forward, churning on the ignition and listening to the whine when slamming the cab into drive, losing control and fishtailing when brushing against the sidewalk's concrete wall. The cabby's eyes instantly widen, seeing bright, sparks from scraping the concrete bridge until slightly swerving away and stopping, still skidding over 10 feet.

Seconds later, a car rolls up, blowing its horn, causing the young man to awaken and slowly shuffle around while staggering to stand when pulling off.

The guy from the mill staggers more until leaning against the bridge with bloodshot eyes, finding the cab on the curb and the door in the middle of the road.

The young man takes several steps toward the cab, waving high until squinting and noticing the cabbie is holding up a tightly-balled fist. He stops, leaning forward, to make out what the cabbie is yelling then strains over a few more fast passing cars.

"You! You! I'm freakin' going to bash your bird brain in, you..., ooooh!" the cabbie screams, side-stepping and taking off in a sprint toward the young man.

The young man takes one last step forward, then a few unassured and unintentional steps forward when backing up fast, then going backward faster, while maintaining his distance.

The cabbie's feet slap hard against the pavement, slowing until stopping and veering around then back to his car.

The young man takes faster steps backward with eyes constantly on the cabbie until discovering him at the trunk, patting down his pants pockets until running to the driver's side, clutching his keys, and hurrying back to the trunk then to the passenger side.

The young man hysterically turns, staggering, and instantly hears loud shots; a few rounds cruising past when the cabby stops, wide-legged, steadying his aim. He ducks taking cover behind a pole, and soon peeks out with his back against the post.

There is silence, then more shots with the phone post wood crumbling with the cab driver still wide-legged with a steady aim.

The young man's mind goes haywire until he is somewhat clever when pulling off his belt. He wraps the belt tightly around his fist, holding it out and drawing it back when the cabbie's eyes widen, and he takes cover behind a pole as well.

The young man finds the big cabbie sticking out on both sides of the pole when his drunken mind causes him to chuckle. "Don't make me shoot!" he yells, taking off fast, distancing himself more, and not looking back for a while when turning and slamming into a telephone pole, staggering and dropping down.

More shots ring out when the cabbie takes off for the next pole, peeking out at the young boy who staggers when his belt buckle unravels, falling to the ground.

A car slows, then stops, spotting the young man staggering. The driver rolls down his window quickly, pushing the door open, expeditiously.

The young man staggers to the open door, and multiple shots ring out, some spraying the door when the concerned driver guns the engine, swerving to gain control until eye-to-eye with the cabbie when shooting past him.

The driver looks back through the rearview mirror, finding the young man fading off to the side of the road when gunning the engine harder, flying over the hill, pulling over, and swiftly dialing 911.

The young man looks through the concrete beams, finding lit apartments down an embankment. He barely hears another clip loaded when rushing off and jumping over the low-cut ledge, rolling downward in tall grass for minutes until drunkenly slamming against a log. The young man's eyes expressly go up the hill when rolling fast to take cover behind a truck when more shots ring out, pinging off tires and doors when he finds the cabbie leaning over the hand railing aimlessly waving the gun.

Distant sirens blare out of nowhere when the young man looks up, finding the cabbie running away.

On the other side of town, Rev ends his Bible study with a prayer, and people continue talking amongst one another.

Tony, a fifteen-year-old, watches a shy girl who finally stares at him and winks when looking over, finding his grandmother's evil stare.

The grandmother's fist balls tight and then relaxes after discovering another woman's hateful gesture toward her.

"Get over here!" she says under her breath with a half frown, noticing the woman still staring when her hand rests on his shoulder, and she pinches him hard.

"Ouch!" he shouts, pulling away with a frown.

"Oh, did I hurt you? Go..., wait in the car," she says, looking as if she could kill him right then and there. She walks over, talking to another friend, until finding the hot-tail little girl wandering from her mother and slipping through the door.

The grandmother talks longer, eagerly watching the door, expecting the girl to come in until anxiously rocking. "Wait," she utters, briskly walking away. She eases out front and finds the two of them holding hands. "Aww..., two little kiddies sitting in a tree, K_I_S_S_I_N_G!" she lowly sings with an evil, weak, trembling eye when her fist clenches so tight that it sounds like manila ropes under pressure.

Their hands instantly untangle, and the boy steps back when the girl walks toward his grandmother and in a quick fake move, dashes off and vanishes at the corner.

"Yeah, get your puny, hot-tail inside with your stuck-up mama! And you..., you little hardhead mother...," she begins to say when her hand connects with his head, and he flies backward over bushes with feet sticking out and frozen in place, moaning.

She spins, hearing fast footsteps, finding Rev walking up when turning and intercepting him.

"Is everything alright, Sistah?" he asks, intentionally easing to the corner.

"Yeah, I had to get out for some fresh air..., you know; and by the way..., do your folks have a cat or something because I feel my allergies coming on?" she says, in a sigh of relief, finally seeing the bushes swaying.

"No, no pets here," he says, stepping past her when hearing a light moan. What in the...," Rev says with a hand over his mouth and wide eyes when rushing up to the bushes. "Are you alright, son?" he asks, helping the young lad up.

"Boy, what are you doing playing around these folks' house? I told you to sit in the car," she says, frowning then straightening her face as Rev looks back, puzzled.

"What are you doing back here, anyway?" Rev asks.

The boy looks at his grandmother's hand, which she swipes past her lips for him to zip it, then across the throat to let him know she is serious.

"Uh..., uh..., looking for my rubber band," he says, stepping onto the sidewalk, jerking his arms and covering his head when her arm moves fast, grasping her slipping purse at the shoulder.

"Boy, what's wrong with you? Out here acting like somebody gone knock your head off your shoulder, I reckon," she utters, cutting her eyes at Rev when her grandson staggers off in a rush.

"Sistah, you are right to discipline, but don't abuse him. Spare the rod, and you spoil that child," Rev whispers when looking at the boy's slight then heavy stagger before he vanishes. Rev sees her off and then waits for his brother and sister-in-law to come off the porch.

"That was a good session," his brother says. "I still think you have a calling, but understand you have to wait on God," he says, shaking Rev's hand with pride.

The following morning, Boogey and Nattie get up early.

Boogey takes a stroll to Sam's house while Nattie prepares breakfast. Afterward, he sneakily makes his way to the store, buying lottery tickets, and comes up on the front porch, finding Nattie easing from the door, and shaking her head in disbelief.

"You're a lottery fanatic! You'll sell your Soul to the devil to hit, wouldn't you?" she says in a weak tone when wandering off and into the kitchen.

"Huh? You lost your cotton-picking mind woman, talking 'bout somebody selling their Soul; women get for real…, please! How in the world did we get from playing a simple number to selling a Soul?"

They dress after breakfast and sit in the living room until a cab blows.

Later, Winton stops by Boogey's, knocking, and then sits tinkering with the dash molding until seeing a foreign couple at their trunk when loud music blares from a car speeding into the foreigner's yard. He watches five bandana-wearing foreigners who continually sit, looking around until an old foreign woman climbs out wearing a bandana, throwing up a gang sign and seizing her crotch.

A tall, young foreign guy runs up on the porch, lifting the old lady, hugging her, and then walks over to the couple, hugging them.

The old lady throws up a different sign, pointing her index finger and moving it forward as if shooting, and then sticks her finger in her pant pockets like she's cool.

The young foreign guy jumps back in, revving the engine, before backing out and stopping when a guy in the back touches the driver's shoulder.

The four foreign guys look over, staring at Winton, who finds an Uzi in a tight, gripped fist alongside the car's body.

The foreign couple wave, and the car's engine revs, spinning wheels, kicking up dust, until skidding wheels across the asphalt on the road.

The old woman walks inside cool-like, letting the door slam hard.

The young foreign woman finally looks off and finds Winton staring at her hourglass figure when her husband cuts his eyes back in a mean stare. The wife stares longer, and Winton does not break his stare, so she throws up a middle finger, patting her butt in disgust when going inside, slamming the door.

Winton is distracted when a big truck turns into the adjoining driveway, backing onto the main road and pulling in front of the foreigner's house. He cranks up, pulling off, still staring at the truck until he stops halfway in the adjoining driveway.

Two men jump out, one with a clipboard, the other lowering the tailgate.

Winton sees the men fading around front and then sees house windows closing, quickly. "Well, I'll be a monkey's uncle," he says to himself, smiling when hearing a loud knock.

"Knock harder! They're in there!" Winton screams, giggling when stopping at the road. He sneakily stares until hearing another knock when pulling onto the road and easing past the truck's front bumper, when stopping.

The short man knocks harder. "Mr. and Mrs. Cho, we're here for the couch, three big screens, etc...., three bedrooms, refrigerator, kitchen table, living room, etc. Come on, sir; your neighbor just told us that you're in there!" the truck driver says, pissed and shaking his head.

The Cho's take turns peeking, fierce that Winton had dimed them out.

Mr. Cho gets madder until walking in circles, chanting mixed curse words in crystalline English and his native tongue, while his wife continually quiets him.

"Awe..., come on! Knock harder!" Winton shouts, provoking the tall, mad delivery man until he bounces on the balls of his feet, finding the couple's heads peeking through stained glass over the door before scurrying away.

The tall driver motions his partner closer, whispering then balancing on one foot when the short co-worker drops to his knees and hands.

"Yeah, get that fine, thick-bottom hammer (woman) out here, so I can get a good look at her fine foreign bootwau (booty)!" Winton yells, leaning over to see what the tall man is doing when his second foot lifts onto his co-worker's back, balancing.

Mr. Cho stops dead in his tracks, finally registering Winton's sexist remarks when walking in circles again like an idiot and cursing when his wife hits him, quieting him as his voice grows louder.

The tall driver peeks in again and begins walking his hand upward against the door to maintain balance.

Mrs. Cho looks back at her husband, who is stomping in circles with his hands over his head, cursing when finding the driver's long shadow extending across the hall floor.

Granny glances down at the movement spotting the shadow when her eyes grow wider behind thick trifocals. She backs into her room, intentionally doing some silly version of the robot to get a laugh when closing the door.

Mr. Cho's wife finally sees the top of the man's head coming into view when shuffling and diving into her husband, pushing him into the room, tumbling.

The tall driver's eyes gaze through the glass. His forehead presses hard against the window, discovering the couple's shadow extending across the hallway floor when side-stepping and leaving his co-worker's belly bowed, heavily.

"Look..., enough! Enough!" the short guy utters with both arms trembling.

"Knock harder and get that fine hammer (woman) out here, wit hu (with her) fine self!" Winton yells, looking wide-eyed through the rear-view when finding a speeding car swerving and laying into the horn.

Mr. Cho storms out with his wife hot on his trail and stops in his tracks, when hearing Winton's irritating voice again. He heads for a backroom, ravaging through several boxes, and his wife tries quieting him when his hand goes back, and he points, apoplectic when another one of Winton's harassing comments comes. His face turns candy-apple red, and his eyes cross with his mouth foaming a thick, white substance.

The tall delivery man takes one foot down balancing against the door.

Mrs. Cho steps back, staring when her husband pulls out a short, thick baseball bat. She quietly pleads with him, taking backward steps until locking the door when he fades through the adjacent door, rushing into the hallway.

Granny peeks again, staring at her son-in-law, shaking her head while doing the robot again, until easing her door shut but slipping in her satin socks and falling face-first into the door, slamming it shut.

Out of nowhere, Mr. Cho's wife hears the front door slam against the house.

Mr. Cho looks angrily past the delivery guys, finding Winton with eyes still in the rearview. He lunges, jostling into the short man, shoving the tall one aside when springing from the top step, taking seven long, fast, and almost invisible leaps toward Winton's car.

Winton gets sidetracked, finding someone crossing behind his car when rising in the seat, looking at a woman's plump, round bottom until frantically waving to a fast-closing car with hand out the window.

Mr. Cho takes a final leap; one foot through the rolled-down window and inches from Winton's face as Winton turns, frozen, feeling the wind from the sole then seeing it materialize when jumping, screaming and finally hearing a delayed loud thump from his thigh against the door's frame.

In slow motion, Winton's face instantly frowns when the stench of funky feet gets funkier with him looking away fast and then turning back, finding the trembling little kung-fu shoe with dust spraying off it. "Ahh!" Winton shrieks in a delayed, high-pitch.

Black smoke rises fast when Winton guns the engine, spinning Mr. Cho around fast.

Winton instantly swerves into oncoming traffic, barely missing a truck that burns rubber, stopping to avoid hitting Winton.

Mr. Cho continually spins fast like a ballerina until spinning one last time when wobbling and staggering off into the grass.

The tall driver rushes up to Mr. Cho with a mean face. "Mr. Cho, we're here to pick up your rentals!" the tall man yells, shoving a clipboard deep in his chest while Mr. Cho's continues resting on elbows while shaking off the dizziness.

# CHAPTER THREE

**China In The Express**

Later, just before dark, over at Boogey and Nattie's home, Nattie hears a horn and looks, slowly lifting her dangling glasses from the dingy shoestring around her neck. She stares at the high dusty trail as an old, war-torn battlewagon swiftly closes; following it while its heading straight for the porch. "Ahhh!" Nattie screams with wide eyes while expressly backing away from the door.

"Ahhh!" Bud shrieks, finally seeing the rusty grill emblem closing fast.

Davillier, Nattie's soon-to-be son-in-law, screams, straining and fighting the non-powered steering wheel, slightly veering off and barely missing the steps by inches when slamming on brakes with dust rising high.

The basketball tread, worn down tires slides continually until finally bringing the car to an abrupt stop; thrusting thick dust forward and higher until the car is no longer visible.

Nattie and Bud ease forward, with both heads finally appearing until slowly glancing around the doorframe when hearing several squeaky doors opening.

Melissa, Nattie and Boogey's daughter; thirty-four, and Davillier; forty, and their kids: Rebecca, sixteen, and Elizabeth, eleven, climb out, fanning.

Davillier sprints for the back door, flinging it open when Melissa pulls out seven-month-old Cameron from a makeshift bolted down wooden and pillow covered car seat. Davillier leans forward pulling hard on his sun-dried, Sunday belt that's holding the baby snug then walks off, rushing to the hood, raising it and unlatching a set of vice grips from the battery.

Instantly, bright arks flash, thrusting the metal cable gashing Davillier's head and knocking him back when he cusses, swaying his words when cutting eyes back at Nattie. He yelps and stumbles alongside the house with blood running down his forehead.

Davillier's pointy-toe, worn boots kick up dust until forcefully falling back, in a turn and accidentally twisting his ankle when falling into a trough filled with slop.

Nattie and Bud hear the loud splash and freeze, slowly looking at each other with quiet, jumping shoulders until abruptly going into a burst of loud and uncontrollable laughter.

Nattie's hands fly over her mouth, fighting back the tears, but Bud is still loud as ever.

Bud's cage rocks and his wing covers his face, quieting yet giggling and trying to be as quiet as Nattie when bursting into a silly laugh that makes even the kids laugh.

Nattie finally composes herself, easing onto the porch, fanning mild dust.

The kids rush up the steps laughing and greeting Nattie, who grabs the baby, walking off the porch and onto the edge of the last step.

Melissa slowly approaches Davillier with her nose pinched tight, trying to diminish the overwhelming smell of mule patties all over the yard. She cautiously steps over several dunghills, accidentally stepping in a steep pile covered in dust, when her face frowns and her feet nippily shuffle in a thick patch of tall grass.

Davillier lies there in disbelief until getting his thoughts together when wiggling his boots, with thick clumps of dung falling and releasing an even bolder smell.

"Whooo wee!" Melissa shouts, backing away fast with her hands out, leaving smears in the grass when looking at her shoes again, almost blowing chunks.

"Help!" Davillier finally whines, squirming to gain his balance with one limp wrist.

Melissa cleans her shoe more and walks over to him, taking a step forward, and then two back; about to toss her cookies.

Nattie finally peeks alongside the house, finding Davillier's boots, face-up when gently shoving the baby into the oldest child's arms; falling instantly forward and grasping her knees, laughing silently.

Melissa makes several more attempts to help with one hand over her mouth with shoulders heavily jerking with her churning stomach when even the kids burst into deep laughter again. "Uh, uh, Davillier, I can't do it, babe! I just can't," Melissa shrieks, gagging and about to lose it.

Davillier kicks his boots harder, pissed, until sliding to the foot, getting a hold of the mounting post, and slowly pulling upward.

Melissa finds him almost on his feet when she takes off in a wide-legged stride, jumping over more dunghills and running until letting off a scream of laughter.

Davillier slumps over, in shame, drenched with flies swarming while taking baby steps with a brown, murky liquefied substance heavily dripping from head to toe.

Nattie's laughter fades into a smile, eyeing Davillier as he slowly walks past. "Go on out back and hose yourself down; I'll have Lissa bring you a change of clothes."

Davillier stops and then turns, walking back over, pulling the battery out, still staring at Melissa under eyed. "Can you at least do something right and ensure the battery gets in the fridge?" he says, frowning while staring at Melissa's cherry, red face.

Melissa continually tries composing herself; wiping the smile away until silently giggling when he turns away then cuts the giggling short each time he looks back at her.

Davillier takes more baby steps, looking back at intervals when Melissa finally straightens her face, still heavily giggling when he vanishes around the house.

Melissa flops down on the last step, crying in laughter when the kids and Nattie join in, in a loud outburst when Davillier stops and shakes his head.

Minutes later, the heavy laughter tapers off and the five head inside.

The kids rush to play with Bud and Nattie rushes for a change of clothing.

Melissa comes to the back door, finding Davillier with his back to her.

Nattie walks up a few seconds later holding out an old, dingy T-shirt and a pair of oversized dungarees, not realizing its Boogey's favorite shirt, turned inside out.

Melissa opens the back door, easing Boogey's funky brogans over to the edge of the porch with her foot. She passes Davillier the clothing when a slight hint of manure from Boogey's boots rises to an even stronger stench.

"Dag..., dang!" Davillier yells, jumping back and being nosy when leaning into the boot, inch-by-inch when the stench grabs and slaps him around, and his head jerks when flopping around more, gasping for air. "Hot..., diggity dog, what the...?" he asks, forming his mouth in an 'ah...,' when his eyes widen, letting Nattie know the word almost slipped.

The skies darken suddenly, and a flash of distant lightning appears when fast sprinkles turn into a torrential downpour.

Nattie takes one step back. "No need to bale water, just stand out yonder (there) in the rain," she says pointing out in the field when walking onto the porch, easing her hand out in the rain before going back inside to get a towel and bar of lye soap.

Melissa turns seconds later, clutching the hygiene items and passing them to him.

Nattie shakes her head in disbelief, eyeing the slop still dripping from his clothing and hair. "Go on! Go out there behind the old oak and clean up, then wrap yourself up and come to the porch and get dressed." Nattie heads to the bedroom for extra slippers.

Melissa turns within seconds, grabbing the slipper, easing them down, and closing the screen door.

Davillier rushes toward the oak when the rain thickens, and most of the slop begins falling off, but a few big chunks cling to him. He strips, thoroughly washing and peeking until noticing the makeshift hunting stand, mounted ten feet in the side of the tree. He soaps down quickly, easing from the tree into the heavy rain, and drapes the towel at his waist when his stomach begins bubbling. He looks back at the outhouse, walking through mud, until flinging the door open, falling back and clenching his nose tight, from the funk.

His eyes widened, finding turd heavily smeared over the seat when grabbing tissue and dodging behind the outhouse. He squats, and when almost done, he hears a twig loudly snap; and looks back; eye-to-eye with the largest copperhead ever seen, coiled and ready to strike when he screams over the loud downpour. His adrenaline shoots him forward and he high steps with knees almost touching his chest.

The snake strikes a few times then maneuvers quickly, grasping the towel, twisting it as if it has its prey.

Davillier takes a fearful leap, tripping and tumbling forward then low-crawling and swiftly slithering until on his feet again, in stealth mode. Both feet pound the wet ground when taking longer strides until lunging, missing the first three steps and rushing up two more. Davillier's body slams into the screen door and sounds like a heavy jolt of thunder, startling everyone inside when a strange squawk comes.

"Ugh, oh!" Bud says mildly, leaning heavily with his neck stretched to maximum capacity when looking toward the kitchen.

Melissa sprints for the door, staring into Davillier's eager eyes.

Davillier presses hard against the screen, stark-naked. He trembles with eyes peeled back and locked onto the slow-twirling dirty towel when nervously and heavily pulling and rattling the flimsy, locked screen.

Melissa finally realizes the door is locked when unlatching, and Davillier flings the door open, rushing inside, taking deep breaths. He stares into her excited eyes with eyes open wide and then looks back at the slow twisting towel, completely covered in mud.

Melissa stays eye-to-eye with her mouth torn open from his, even more, express movements, finding him still a mess and naked. "What! Get out of mama's kitchen with no clothes on!" Melissa excitedly murmurs, looking over her shoulder for Nattie.

Nattie rushes in, looking back at the kids then the television. "Oh shucks!" Nattie shouts, quickly covering her eyes with both hands. "Davillier, if you don't get your naked tail out of here, you better!" Nattie yells, reaching for the broom handle until hearing the baby's cry and rushing off.

Davillier hesitantly pushes the screen door open, jumping out while Melissa blocks his body as he moves against the wall, sticking his head near the door. "Lissa, get me some tissues," he says, realizing he cut his business too short.

"What? Davillier..., now I know you're not going to drop a stinking load here!" She peeks and finds him looking alongside the house. "You better bring your trifling behind inside and act civilized. Come in and use the bathroom after you get dress!"

Davillier looks near the clothes, finding newspaper flapping slightly in the winds until increasingly flapping from the velocity and sudden shift. "Oh, never mind..., girl, you know I was just messing."

"Ugh huh...," she exclaims, rolling her eyes. "Whateva!" She walks away.

Davillier pulls the door shut, inching over to the edge of the porch, grabbing the newspaper. He twists the paper, softening several pieces until he has enough then grabs the paper and clothes, tiptoeing, and nervously looking around while proceeding alongside the porch.

Out of nowhere, lightning strikes a transformer, knocking out the power and the community goes pitch-black.

Davillier eases the paper down, feeling for the corner beam of the porch when leaning back, straining. Suddenly, he jumps, hearing heavy breathing when looking back quick, finding the dog inching up, and sniffing his butt. "Get! Get, I say!" he whispers, kicking backward a few times when the dog runs off and he goes back to handling business.

In a flash, he feels the dog's nose hairs at his butt when a long wet tongue licks one tight clenched cheek.

Davillier lets off a loud, muffled scream, drawing forward fast when kicking the dog and running him off. He stands for seconds then grabs a piece of firewood, throwing it in the dark toward the grown and mild barks.

Minutes pass, and the store's generator kicks in, lighting up the store, part of the field, and alongside the house.

Davillier slowly adjusts his sight from the darkness when the newspaper becomes mildly visible. He tries to wrap things up when straining again, but nothing until finally straining so hard that he's sweating. His eyes instantly turn bloodshot when a loud strain from under his breath blurts out.

"What was that?" Melissa fearfully asks, stumbling in the dark for the back door, throwing it open, and staring into pure darkness. "Davillier...! Dee!" she whispers.

Out of nowhere, a strange man who makes it his unauthorized business to help himself to Boogey's moonshine daily, drifts through the path. He freezes, spotting Davillier's dark silhouette when dropping down in the tall weeds, giggling and watching closely from a distance.

"Go back inside; I'm almost dressed," Davillier whispers, still slumped and clinging to the post so she can't see him when the half-rotten beam lightly yawns and then cracks from his heavyweight.

"Davillier!" she whispers. "What was that? What in the heck are you doing? Where are you?" she whispers as the wind slightly picks up again.

"Not sure..., but it sounded like hunters; now go on, and I'll be in, in a few!"

Melissa backs away slowly, stumbling into the living room which is now lit by candles.

Davillier finishes and reaches for the newspaper, which slowly wobble then slides out of reach when a gust of wind blows it farther then off the porch and into a mud puddle. "I will be, damn!" he declares in a low tone.

Seconds later, Boogey and Winton pull up outside the general store.

Boogey sprints inside, finding that the machine is down so he buys a scratch ticket then rushes out, climbing back inside.

Winton continues talking to an old man sitting on the bench until the conversation dwindles, with the man telling more tales that Winton and Boogey knows are lies.

The old man instantly goes into another story and there is no break in the last lie when Winton cuts him off, laughing, waving, and slowly pulling away. He turns into Boogey's driveway, spotting Davillier's reflective taillights.

Davillier's glistening eyes stare at the T-shirt for seconds. He shakes his head in deep thought until looking upward in a smirk when leaning forward, clutching it, and taking a few good swipes. His bright, white eyes look around until leaning, looking under the house, and flinging the shirt as hard as he can, giggling senselessly.

Winton sees something low and fast run past the front of the car when flipping on the high beams, shining bright lights on the house. Winton rises high, finally veering off to one side, missing a scampering cat, and fights the wheel until the bright lights are now shining alongside the house.

"What the..., hell!" Boogey shrieks, looking into Davillier's shiny then glowing eyes and then over at Winton when the engine revs high.

Davillier stares into the bright, fast-moving lights, clenching his cheeks tightly as he hurries to the other side of the porch out of view. He scrambles, seizing the pants, and dances around, hopping on one leg, trying to get them on when the man in the weeds falls back quietly giggling in a fetal position.

Winton veers and brings the car to a screeching halt with dust flying high.

Boogey jumps out overly excited, and Winton eases out excited and fanning.

Boogey rushes for the porch. "Nattie! Get me my smoke pole (gun)! Nattie! Nattie!" he repeatedly cries out in a loud, echoing yet whiny voice.

"Uh, oh!" Bud declares, whistling. "Boogey gone smoke some hind parts! Boogey gone smoke some hind parts!" he sings as if in a cartoon song.

"Oh, hush that noise up, Bud!" Nattie yells, flinging the door open and staring at the bright lights and then Boogey's shadow when rushing up and over towering her.

"My smoke pole! Where is it?" he asks with eyes quickly scaling over her body.

"What is it, Boogey?" she asks, calmly staring into his shadowy face when he eases her to one side, rushing in and reaching behind the door.

"There's a naked Peeping Tom out back," he yells, gripping the gun and frightening the kids.

Nattie laughs out loud, and everyone inside finally calms before joining in laughter. She reaches, holding a tight grip on the gun, refusing to let go. "Oh, shucks..., that's nobody but that crazy tail Davillier!" Nattie declares, still laughing. "Poor boy fell in the trough earlier and had to change out back."

Winton and Boogey instantly make eye contact, keeping near straight faces to keep from laughing when bursting into a loud laugh when hearing Nattie tune-up again.

Soon, everyone inside joins in, and minutes later, the laughter finally dies down.

Davillier springs forward when a quick whipping sound comes, echoing from the steel rake slamming into his forehead, and raising a rapid swelling knot and reopening the wound. "OUCH!" Davillier hesitantly screams, staggering and slightly dizzy when falling into the side of the house. He grabs his forehead, wobbling more until finally stepping out from the side of the house. His hand comes from his head, wiping the thin trail of blood and wiping more until there's just a smear.

"What was that whipping and smacking sound?" Boogey asks, stepping off the step.

"Oh nothing," Davillier says, preventing more laughter at his own expense.

Winton slides past Boogey, walking up to Nattie, hugging her when Melissa slides a hand alongside the door's frame, unnoticeably latching it.

"How was your day, cousin?" Winton asks Nattie, releasing her and looking over at Melissa in the doorway. "Howdy, cousin," he utters, looking into Melissa's pretty eyes when gently tugging on the handle.

"Just fine, Winton; how are you? Tell Nelle I said hello."

"I'll be sure to do that, cousin." Winton backs up to the edge of the porch.

Boogey points and they all look up the road, finding bright, yellow warning lights appearing when utility trucks slow and veer off the road.

"Look ou…," Boogey begins the shout when Winton stumbles over the battery, falling backward from the top step.

Winton's backside hits the dust and a dust cloud rises, shielding the headlights when the porch grows dim with dust reflections mirroring against the house. Winton jumps up quick, embarrassed, and dusting himself off as loud laughter grows.

"What's so damn funny? Man! I almost broke my darn neck!" Winton says, rubbing his neck.

Davillier's loud laugh grows over everyone else's, and Winton finally looks back at him with a mean stare.

"What? Are you serious? This ain't even funny…, I could have killed myself!" Winton shouts with a slow balling, tight fist.

Davillier keeps pointing at Winton, unable to stop laughing.

Soon, everyone except Winton is in tears when Melissa cuts her smile short, finally becoming aware of Winton's aggression when finding his fist tight and him slowly inching toward Davillier.

Melissa stares at Winton, remembering how he steals on folks when catching them off guard, so she reaches for the aluminum bat, quietly unlatching the door.

Winton takes a few more sly steps until, within striking distance when looking down and throwing his head back in a sarcastic laugh. "Laugh all you like, but I'm not the one with dung between my toes!" Winton laughs harder until finally walking away.

Davillier's eye goes to his feet, wiggling mushy toes when frowning and shaking the thick dung loose.

Boogey, Nattie, and Melissa, swiftly slither to the edge of the porch; all eyes on Davillier's feet when giggling and fighting back their laughs when Winton's irritating laugh rings out even louder.

Boogey composes himself and vanishes to the back but on the grassy side of the yard.

Winton climbs in the car and pulls alongside the steps, tooting the horn. "Later there, crappy toes," Winton yells when intentionally spinning wheels and a few doughnuts, leaving Davillier in a cloud of thick dust with the others rushing off or inside.

"You stupid son of a...," Davillier yells, cutting the cussing short when recalling that Nattie and Boogey are there when taking steps, trailing behind the car with a tight fist until veering out of the dust.

Boogey, Melissa and Nattie back away from the door, easing it shut when finding dust drifting inside.

Davillier eases over to the worn-down steps, shifting his feet in the sandy dirt, removing more dung, and from time to time, he bobs forward or backs up, fighting to keep from throwing up when his hands shoot to his nose, pinching it, tight.

The door eases opens and Melissa and Nattie look at him trying to figure out what Davillier is doing. They stare eye-to-eye, backing deep into the living room, knocking over things while holding their laughs until bursting out in tears.

Boogey reappears with a foot pail, old rags, and lye soap. "Here, make sure you get that crap off, good before you come inside," he says with a frown while backing away from the stench and covering his nose.

Davillier grabs the pail, sliding it closer to the step.

Boogey feels around in the water for the rag and soap. "Here, this will do you well," he says, handing it to Davillier. "Oh yeah..., deep freezer?" Boogey declares, grasping the battery in a tight grip and running off.

"Yeah, thanks; I thought Lissa would have had it in there by now," Davillier says, looking back at the dark screen door.

Boogey steps inside, greeted by his daughter and grandkids, when looking around the dimly-lit room. "Where's the baby?" he asks.

"Over there, Daddy," Melissa utters, pointing near Bud's cage.

"Shucks, I can hardly see in the light, more or less the dark," he says, stumbling.

"I can't tell, as nosy as your tail is!" Nattie utters under her breath, walking off.

Boogey stops and rolls his eyes, playing down the comment when briefly talking to the other kids before rushing off. He steps on the back porch, adjusting his eyes to the dim light that shines alongside the house from the store. He takes a few steps, and the freezer finally comes into view when creeping over, bracing the house. Boogey flings the freezer door open, feeling around for his battery when shoving it aside and easing Davillier's down.

Out of nowhere, the strange man finally wanders back into Boogey's yard from the woods still in tears, finding an even more giant shadow on the back porch when freezing with his arms spread out like a scarecrow.

Boogey braces the wall, making his way to the door, and looks off, trying to make out the T-shaped, distant object when fearfully slipping inside. He locks the screen and stands for seconds, trying to make out what it is until slamming and locking the door.

Boogey's dog unknowingly trots alongside the house. He comes into the yard, stopping when finally spotting the unfamiliar T-silhouette, as well. The dog trots away, continually keeping his eyes on the shadow until taking off at top speed when the man's arms tirelessly drop. The dog comes up over by the back door, sniffing and anxiously wagging its tail until barking and howling at distant sirens that race down the highway until other dogs join in; all soon sounding well-orchestrated.

Boogey fumbles around in the dark bedroom for a flashlight, and the light flickers then steadies when Boogey enters the living room and sees Davillier walking inside.

"Where's the shirt?" Melissa asks when Nattie looks up at his bare chest with surprised eyes.

"Shirt? What shirt? I didn't see a shirt."

"Davillier, there was a shirt right on top," Nattie says, intervening.

"Lissa, look…, I'm telling you there wasn't a shirt unless you dropped it," he responds, nervously cutting his eyes over to Boogey.

Boogey goes into the bedroom again, bringing out a shirt that he's outgrown.

"Never mind, I'll look for it in the morning," Nattie says.

"Keep that one; it's too small for me anyway." Boogey throws the shirt to Davillier and Davillier slips into the shirt, brushing his permed hair back down, quickly.

A growl, then several loud growls come from the youngest daughter's stomach. "I'm hungry and thirsty," the youngest daughter says.

"Come to think of it, I am too," Melissa utters, looking at Davillier. "I'm so hungry; it feels like my stomach is about to touch my spine," Melissa says, taking deep breaths of the now overwhelmingly scented possum casserole.

"What do you all have a taste for? The possum casserole and green beans should be done by now. I also have a big pot of leftover muskrat stew," she exclaims, staring into their dim, shocked faces.

Rebecca's head jerks, cringing and Davillier, being from the city, looks at Melissa, giving her a secret sign with fingers and the clearing of his voice, letting her know that it's time to go.

"That sure does sound tasty, Mama, but you know these kids ain't even eating that stuff, but you can fix me a plate, to go." Melissa playfully licks her lips.

Davillier straightens his face after finding Nattie staring out of the corner of her eyes.

"How about you, Davillier?"

"Uh..., no..., no, ma'am, I ate already, but add a little on Lissa's plate because I may want to try it later," he says, cringing.

"Lie, lie, lie, lie...! Dee..., I don't know who lies better, you or that gal who lied her way off death row, but now that I think on it; I think you got her beat for some reason!" Nattie says, smiling.

Boogey plays with his grandkids and then takes a seat when the lights go off again and instantly flicker then stay on.

Boogey's eyes brighten, and his feet shuffle when turning on the seventeen-inch black-and-white television, flipping through channels.

Nattie walks off and prepares the food, and minutes later, stand stuffing Styrofoam plates and plastic grocery bags, then a bag for Davillier's wet clothes.

Everyone soon converges on the porch, with Melissa holding the bags and the kids looking around to make sure they aren't going to slip through the wide cracked planks on the porch and steps. The family reaches the bottom step, and Melissa looks over at Davillier, motioning to him that he's forgotten something.

"What?" he responds, clueless.

"Dauh..., the battery?"

"Oh yeah!" he declares, surprised when looking back, finding Boogey holding up a finger for them to wait.

Boogey marches off and through the house, flinging the door open to find the dog wagging its tail until Boogey steps out. His eyes go immediately to the scarecrow-looking object, finding it no longer there. He looks around, then down when the dog jumps up with muddy paws, landing on Boogey's thighs and pawing until almost at his shoulder, leaving smeared paws marks until rushing off. Boogey snatches the battery and before he makes it to the front, the dog is there barking at everyone.

Davillier sees Boogey and pops the hood, grabbing and slamming the battery in the half-rotted-out compartment, then takes his time reconnecting old, twisted wires when the interior light flickers. He leans further, tweaking the wires a few more times, before applying the vice grips when slamming the hood shut. Davillier grabs the bag with his clothes, buckling the baby back in the seat then slams the door, rushing for the driver's side, sliding inside and cranking up. He allows the car to idle while Melissa gets her hugs, grabs the food, and jumps in when throwing the car in reverse.

"Hey, hold on a minute!" Boogey hollers, frantically waving when both brake lights flicker, and one goes out. Boogey disappears around the house and rushes back up to the car minutes later with a small jar of his famous moonshine. "Davillier, I've been promising you this for some time now," Boogey utters, rubbing dust from the greasy-looking jar, when accidentally passing him a jar full of kerosene and water left by the thief.

Boogey slightly turns, raising it to the light from the back of the store. "I think she's well fermented," he says, slightly in a turn when turning back to the light, holding it with a concerned look when finally seeing unfamiliar grease swirls.

Davillier notices minuscule particles of dross and grease around the top. "What the…?" he mumbles, breaking off the curse word. "Is that trash or dirt?"

"Hell naw…, the hell you say! That ain't neither…, shiiiii…, that's the stunt in it, son!" Boogey declares, cutting off the cuss word when the girls lean forward to get an earful, bursting into laughter.

"Stunt! What in the world is a stunt?" Davillier asks with wondering eyes, finding Nattie a ways off.

"Boy…, you 'bout as dumb as a freakin' possum. Where do you think they get the word stunt hole from?" Boogey asks, looking at Davillier as if he's stupid.

"Oh…, yeah, oh, yeah, I almost forgot," Davillier exclaims so that he doesn't look like a total idiot.

"Now, this hea (here) batch might be stronger than usual. Trust me, too much of this hea (here) will have you pissing in the wind and barking at a half-moon, thinking it's a full moon," Boogey says with a sneaky grin.

"Yeah, I'll be sure to remember that when I tap this baby open," Davillier says, tooting the horn once more while Boogey is backing away.

Davillier leans in, turning up the radio, chuckling.

"What? What's so funny?" Melissa asks, throwing a hand out the window, waving when Davillier slows, putting on the turn signal when banging hard against the steering wheel, laughing loud and as if half crazy.

"What? What?" Melissa asks again, smiling before her shoulders go up and down heavily in laughter.

"Your silly tail, dad, with that 'pissing in the wind and barking at the moon crap'. Where does he get those country sayings? And oh, by the way, the possum ain't so dumb if he knows the stump hole from the stunt," he says, bursting into a burst of deep laughter that draws the girls into laughter when the baby heavily and continually giggles in the background.

"That's just my daddy! Most of the stuff he makes up off the top of his head. What a character," Melissa utters, running her hands through her long hair.

Boogey and Nattie watch the car pull into the road, picking up speed when another car comes up fast from behind and almost rear ends them.

The driver lays into the horn when Davillier's arm shoots out; waving until giving them what looks like the middle finger when the other car is passing him under a streetlight.

Boogey shakes his head, and they turn, walking inside with the television flashing the headline news, talking about the possible murder and missing person's case before mentioning the cops having a few leads.

Davillier punches the gas with the country store fading in the background when lifting the jar, leaning it toward Melissa, who backs off of it. "Smells like rocky mountain oyster juice and looks like it's mixed with kerosene," Davillier says, sniffing and giggling when tossing it high, barely hearing it burst when flooring the gas pedal.

Later that evening, at Rev's brother's house, Rev walks up the sidewalk steadily, rushing in and immediately going into prayer. "Ok, the Book of John, tonight," he mumbles, rapidly flipping through a few pages.

Thirty minutes later, he flips to Revelations, explaining verses when noticing many of them in awe. "Ok, now I want everyone to close your books," he says, laying his Bible down. "I want everyone to close your eyes as tightly as possible," he says, waiting and finding a few peeking before following his instructions.

The room soon gets totally quiet, and he reads more of Revelations and the horrible things to come.

"Now listen...; what I'm about to do require your full participation, so just meditate on what I say to get the true meaning and experience. Just relax..., let yourself go and imagine you're in a dark place; the darkest place ever and unlike no other. Now imagine things upon this Earth that you fear. Yeah..., just let your imagination go..., yeah, like that..., now imagine something lowly growling, or how about things crawling all over you, and you don't know what they are. Now..., imagine a warm breath slightly sniffing at your flesh..., a sudden lick at your flesh," he exclaims, quieting. "Just keep your eyes closed tight and meditate on this pure horror and evil," he says in a mild tone. "Can you see it? Pure darkness and so much evil around you until hearing close and distant screams," he says, discovering them well relaxed, as if hypnotized.

Rev walks around with his voice echoing through the closely held mic until making strange animal and sometimes unheard-of sounds, when finding a few smiling faces. He makes his way over near the light switch and then passes back by it, with the microphone as close as he can get it to his mouth when flipping the lights off. "Arrrrhh!!!" he growls, then screams, barking immediately and deep like a vicious mastiff or pit bull with the room trembling.

Everyone instantly jumps, screeching in total darkness, with their adrenaline kicking in, when bucking their eyes in and unable to see when the rumbling comes.

Some bump their heads together, run into others or fall until the lights reappear with several folks lying on the floor, or some reaching for the door, but one man sits in the back without a care, smiling.

"Alright! Alright! That wasn't so funny after all, huh?" Rev sees a few in pains when laughing, and can't stop but manages to stop when not finding many smiles.

The old man stays in an uncontrollable laughter. "Girl, I tell yah (you), you were moving some furniture up in here..., you hear me!" the old man says to the oldest lady, who stands nervously trying to unindent her head print from the busted drywall.

"Huh, you can sit there all you want, my mind was deep into it, and when I opened my eyes, I was still in darkness, huh...," she says, losing her train of thought when shaking her head.

"I'm truly sorry, but something told me to do that, but I'm glad you all were able to experience true horror, even if for a second. Now take that experience and multiply it a hundred times over, especially for those who will end up in Hades if your life ain't right," he says, clearing his mind when looking over at his brother and sister-in-law, confirming there are no significant issues with the damages when Rev motions that he will handle the repairs.

"If that is a fraction of the end, I need to get my life right because my heart just left my body," another elderly lady says, running her hand across her fluttering heart and then a knot on her forehead.

"So many people act tough, but I tell you, there's not a man alive that's not scared of something; a snake, alligator, wild bear, boxes etc. Some people fear the silliest things, like balloons, spiders, caterpillars, mice, etc.," he exclaims, making his way to the center of the room.

"Well, let me end here..., look, everything is coming to life, or should I say reality. Sodom and Gomorrah were destroyed for the very things the world is into today, which are an abomination to Almighty God. Has God changed so that he doesn't despise these things? No..., of course not..., God forbid! For our, God is steadfast, firm, and unchanging.

Life is about choices, so look..., think, and choose wisely. You only have one life, one Soul; save one..., and let it be your Soul. What will you say before the throne of Almighty God when he asks: 'My child, I have given you a perfect life, and you were the apple of my eye when I formed you; no matter how I formed you, I formed you perfect and with love, so tell me, what have you done with this perfect life?' What will you say? Of course, you will faint if the Word is not with you, for every knee shall bend and mouth shall confess before HIM. Before anyone says something silly..., some perceive their response to be; like Lord, you did not show me a sign. Well, to that, I say, look around you..., the whole Earth and everything in it is a sign, so that is one excuse you won't be able to use," Rev says, motioning everyone to stand.

Hours later, Rev reaches the outskirts of town when heavy rain starts to pour, so he stops at a café, hurrying inside and gazing over the lengthy menu. "Yes, ham and cheese, large chef salad with oil and vinegar and a sandwich made the same. Oh, and grape juice, please," he utters, hearing the door slam when slightly turning, finding a young, drenched couple rushing inside.

A set of eyes outside stay glued on Rev, nippily fading when he looks back, not seeing the silhouette.

Rev grabs a newspaper, pays minutes later, and exits with the paper over his head. He waits for a car, then another to pass when running toward the car. He throws things in the seat, eases in and shakes off the excess water then jumps. "Oh shiii...!" he yells, cutting the cuss word short when a high beam from a passing car reveals movement in the backseat and his eyes shoot back, finding a body tucked in the passenger side corner.

"Rev, huh?" the irritating feminine then manly altering voice lowly says. "You let words like that come out of the same mouth you praise with?" the waitress, Tamika, from the restaurant, asks, licking her pretty, plump, red, glossy lips. "No worries; I won't condemn you," she says, spreading her trench coat open and running hands over her curvaceous, red, teddy-covered body.

Rev's eyes wander over her firm, sexy body, running up and down her curves, until finally embarrassed and looking off. He's drawn into her when her eyes transition to black marbles and he stares again as her hand floats to her firm, cupped, raised breast, then down to her thin waist, then double-jointed hips, which look like the smoothest of butter pecan, tan complexion. He tries but can't keep his eyes off her bodacious figure but briefly looks away, deep in temptation, when slumping down, closing his eyes tight and whispering a silent prayer for strength.

Tamika floats forward into a thin ray of streetlight with hands gently caressing the back of his head before running along the side of his face. He her index finger withdraws from her soft, warm, wet, perfect lips, coming to his, leaving them soft, warm and wet.

Rev's mouth slowly parts open, taking the tip of her finger deep inside until gaining his strength when snatching her hand away after recalling a scripture which he meditates on: "Get ye from me Satan or his demons," he shrieks when she leans back from the low-level lighting, into darkness with her face transforming into pure evil. "I rebuke thee..., flee ye from me," he says in a weak voice, glimpsing to find the evil face transforming back into Tamika's natural beauty when his voice grows louder, repeating the phrases.

Tamika falls back in total silence, and Rev finds her pulling her coat around her and tightening it. "I'm hungry..., hey, do you have money so I can get myself something to eat?" she asks in a low voice.

Rev's hand hesitantly moves toward the sandwich. "Here..., I'm not sure what made me buy this anyway because the only thing I wanted was a salad," he says, handing it to her and passing the juice. "Maybe it's a sign that you would be here, needing it," he exclaims, finally brazen enough to look back into her lovely face. "Well, it's raining pretty hard out, so is there somewhere I can drop you?" he asks, looking back with his eyes briefly wandering over her hot body, when starting the engine.

"I have nowhere to go," she utters in a sad voice. "I managed to lose my job, apartment, kids, and car; all in one month, so what do I have to live for?" She sits in deep thought, meditating. "Well, that is..., no place to live unless I can stay with you for a while," she says, transforming again when a demon briefly takes control.

"I don't have accommodation but money for one night; a hotel, maybe," he says, slowly pulling into mild traffic. "Any special hotel," he asks, stopping at the red light near a streetlight, looking at her smile through the rearview, and noticing her eyes when they instantly turn black and shiny, like glass, but beady like snake eyes.

"The Beltmore," she responds, choosing the most expensive hotel she can think of, hoping he would change his mind and invite her to his place.

"Ok..., ok, the Beltmore it is," he says, entering the expressway and picking up speed and continually making small talk, while keeping her in view, through the rearview.

She continues eating and continually tries seducing him from time to time.

Minutes later, she takes the last bite, dropping the wrapper in the bag, and sips until the dry sound grows long and irritating when trying to gain his attention.

Twenty minutes or so later, the rain stops for a few minutes, then starts lightly drizzling when they pull into the hotel's packed parking lot.

Rev sits for seconds, trying to break the strange feeling of being drawn into her when finally meditating on his last session and snapping out of it. He unlocks the door, grabs his umbrella, and rushes around, opening her door.

Tamika sits, intentionally unraveling the thin belt to her coat, then steps out, leaving her coat wide open, revealing her beautiful body and luscious thighs.

Rev freezes, stunned at her beauty with eyes wandering over her until pulling her coat closed and slowly retying her belt when grasping the umbrella, and shielding her.

They walk off, and she slides her arms through his, appearing to be a couple when walking through the double doors. They pass a bellboy who overly stares at her beauty, not giving Rev any respect until he breaks his stare when looking over, finding his manager's mean stare.

The female desk clerk continues dusting until finally looking back, surprised to find them standing there. "Oh, sorry..., welcome to the Beltmore. How can I accommodate you two?" she asks, admiring Tamika's beauty, though her head is somewhat torn up. "I love your hair," the questionable clerk says, beaming.

"Yeah, right!" the bellboy mumbles when looking over at guys at the bar with their backs turned.

The female clerk looks over at the bellboy, transitioning instantly to a cheerful smile when looking back at Rev and Tamika. "So can I interest you in a single, double..., or king?" she asks, looking at Tamika's lovely face again with eyes running over Tamika's thick, luscious lips, in a daze and unintentionally seductively licking her lips. Her eyes wandered over Tamika's curvy body as Tamika stretches the tightly closed coat tighter to show more curves.

"Yes, umm...," Rev hesitantly says, watching Tamika comb her hair down with her worn-down painted fingernails.

"Single," Tamika utters, blushing when looking into Rev's eyes with a bright smile and black beady eyes that he fails to recognize when looking away.

The clerk processes them, running his bank card, and hands him two electronic keys.

"Thanks..., we'll only need one." He slides one key back, grabbing the other when walking off and over to the elevator with the clerk's eyes swarming over Tamika hot body in a heat of lust.

Tamika stares at Rev until making him blush when a big smile comes, and she reaches for his hand hearing the elevator bell rings.

Rev eases from her grip, placing the key in her hand.

They ride up in silence, with her continually looking at him with fast transitioning eyes, subconsciously making him weak until startled by the bell with the spell breaking.

Rev playfully bows her out but she stays, leaning back, refusing to get off.

Rev's mouth drops open, staring into her lovely face when she winks, and he flinches, instantly weaker again. "Hey..., this is as far as I'm going, so have a blessed night, beautiful. Trust me..., I will not let Satan trap me in a night of folly and cost me my life. Take this as a new start, and think about where you are and where you need to be in your life. You are just off track right now, but it will all come together in due time.

God has a great purpose for your life, but right now, he has you on this road to get redirected. Well, that's my thinking," he says, when the buzzer sounds and the door closes fast.

Rev nervously looks up, noticing they had passed her floor and were now on the 41st floor, not giving it a second thought when closing his eyes. He whispers a silent prayer when the elevator buzzer rings again, causing him to pause and look at the number again, noticing it is the 52nd floor, not giving it much thought when continuing higher.

The lights flicker with the car bouncing when Rev nervously grabs her hand, hears screeching when the cables begin yawning heavily, with several cables loudly snapping when the elevator trembles and then drops dead-weight.

Rev's heart rapidly beats when glancing at her with his mouth torn open, finding Tamika's eyes bleeding red tears. His eyes wander over her shoulder, finding the elevator numbers dropping steadily until unreadable when screaming for Jesus three times, at the top of his lungs with his grip even tighter."

Instantly, the bell rings, and the doors slowly open.

Rev's tight grip releases her and she rubs her hand to get her circulation back when he grips the key and her hand, tightly.

They step off, and he releases her, backing away fast. "Good night, my sister." He passes the key, shaking her hand, quickly.

"It's Tamika," she answers, looking at the key's number, then the row of doors before slowly striking out. She seductively twists her hips, unraveling her coat's belt until slipping the coat off, looking back, winking and blowing kisses while dragging the coat along the plush, carpeted floor.

Rev stands in lust with eyes swarming over cheeks, extending below the extent of her thin teddy, watching the most beautiful woman he has ever seen walk away. His eyes continually rush over her curvy body, barely covered in lace, with thick thighs, wearing high heels.

A man and his wife walk out ahead of her, heading in the opposite direction.

The man looks back and Tamika winks with beady eyes, controlling him and making him look back from time to time, eyeing her each time she winks.

His wife is also put under the spell of jealousy, eyeing him and turning where the hall ends when he slams into the wall and looks back at Tamika, with his wife's hand extended from the adjacent wall, slapping him and making him stagger.

Tamika's index finger extends outward to Rev, motioning him to come a few times; the other hand running under her bra strap, loosening it from her shoulder so that her breasts show from the side when her eyes transition and he grows weaker.

Rev continues watching until one foot shoots forward and he instantly buckles at his knees, yet his head shakes in disbelief, and his index finger unknowingly comes to his lips when he bites down, gently. He musters up all that is in him, resisting temptation until turning, looking for the stairwell, which he swiftly exits through.

Across town, Winton leaves home to get the kids some milk and pulls up at the store twenty minutes later with a familiar hooker running up. "What! What! Girl, what do you want, now? One thing a man ain't going to pay for is a yellow-teeth, pissy-tail nightrider!" he says, rolling up the window before stepping out, giggling senselessly at his quick and degrading joke. "And by all means, lose some freakin' weight! You got the nerve to have a Santa belt around that big gut. Do you even know that belly is about to pop?" he declares, bursting into even deeper laughter from the earlier weed and liquor.

"Yeah, yeah, yeah, well, all that jaw flapping ain't putting no money in my hand," she says, looking off and over at five male teens at a distance yet approaching.

"Just in..., and trust me..., breaking news!" Winton laughs. "I ain't putting nothing in your crusty ole hands," he utters with keen eyes.

The hooker's eyes slowly drift over Winton. "Ain't you got a nerve, with that big beer belly? Santa ain't got nothing on you, honey! What is that anyway?" She sticks a sturdy finger deep into his belly, giggling. "Is this a seat or headrest for your son?" she asks, chuckling when the teens walk closer, and all of them burst into laughter from the comment.

"You busted, seventies trick!" Winton declares, seeing the boys bumping into each other from laughing so hard.

"Busted? I wasn't so busted when you were all over this, and I had you crying like a newborn baby; telling me this is the bestest (best)!" she says with a somewhat convincing face when the boys stop in their tracks, looking back and patiently awaiting a response. "Oh..., I see..., so you still pissed because I didn't give you back your used wrapper or fifty? Well, get over it, sucker, because what was in it is in this swollen belly now, and that fifty and more has gone into prenatal pills, so this belt is cuddling your soon-to-be new baby," she screams, giggling senselessly.

Winton's mouth drops open in shock, and his face turns bright red. "Ahh!" Winton screams, lunging with both hands going for her neck with the boys instantly restraining him.

She backs up in fear. "Either you gone start paying for this baby, or I'll see you in court, sucker!" she yells, sticking up both fighting fists, and standing her ground while backing away a few more feet. She keeps staring into his mean face, laughing, and still backing up until half a block away when shooting Winton the middle finger.

Winton continually cusses, wrestling to be free until the last guy releases him, falling back in laughter, seeing Winton run after her as she fades around a house.

They soon hear heels clicking when looking back, finding Winton's heels sparking as he runs past them and up to his car.

Winton jumps in, turning fast, and skidding wheels until slowing when advancing near several houses.

The hooker peeks out from around a house further up the road, and Winton spins off, slamming on brakes and looking around that house.

The teens observe until Winton's tail lights flicker near another house when they find the woman peeking out again.

Winton's tires squeal and he floors the gas when the car hits the sidewalk hard, closing in on her when she dodges into a dark alley.

The tires skid a few feet when Winton jumps out then back in quick, finding the car rocking a little. He springs out, almost slipping when taking off and cutting through another alley, looking both ways.

Winton searches longer then comes from between houses, heading for his car.

Something hits a trash can, causing him to jump and take a step back before looking up when a two-by-four slams into his face, knocking him out cold.

The woman's heels anxiously click against partially paved asphalt until she staggers to one side, dropping the wood. She bends over, snatching his fake gold chain, and counts off the seventeen dollars he has on him. She quickly stuffs the loot in her loose bra, stepping over Winton and walks away fast, giggling as if she's high or stoned on something.

Ten minutes or so later, Winton comes to, finding a mangy mutt licking his face. "Gone! Get! Get your mangy as...!" he shouts, cutting it short when finding a house window light up.

The dog rushes back up to Winton while he is coming up, licking his face again when Winton shoves the dog off, kicking in a silent mumble until he's standing and swaying from still being dizzy.

Winton staggers toward the street, stopping and leaning heavily into a house.

Suddenly, thick curtains fly open with bright eyes and a wide, screaming mouth when a young girl come eye-to-eye with Winton.

Winton backs away fast, staggering until turning, zigzagging when loud, unrelated gunfire rings out. He floods into the street for the car, digging in both pant pockets when his keys fly up, landing on the hood, leaving Winton dancing around with shaking hands and scrambling for the keys.

He barely stares back at the window quickly, finding manly hands and a mean face pressed against the seamy window when the curtains drop. Winton jumps inside with a trembling hand, fumbling around to get the key in the ignition. He revs the engine skidding wheels and burning rubber when peeking through the rearview, finding the dark silhouettes of a big and smaller man taking aim under the bright streetlight.

Winton's heavily zigzags more, throwing off their aim when swerving and barely making a sharp turn when a blaze of continuous gunfire breaks out with bullets hitting the taillight and busting the back, passenger-side window in a sharp turn. He finally hits the straightway at top speed, clearing the housing area, when piercing bright lights close in swiftly out of nowhere. Winton guns the engine, cutting off his lights when turning into the yard of an abandoned house. He floats through that yard and comes up on another street alongside another abandoned house, listening for the car when hearing his heart racing.

Before long, a car turns the corner and comes slowly down the same street when Winton slumps in the seat with eyes barely peeking over the dashboard.

The car slowly creeps by, and he sees an old lady driver with what looks like a joint hanging from her lips while a tall, mean man hangs out the passenger window, cautiously looking around.

Winton squints, following them closely until they stop, back up, and turn on another side street. Within minutes, Winton sees them patrolling another street when their headlights go off, so he waits longer, finally finding them at the top of the hill when putting the car into gear.

Winton feels the trunk dip and looks around then nervously looks in the rearview, discovering a floating red dot. He squints, finding a man's big, white eyeballs, then the outline of his face when noticing him puffing a cigarette and leaning over the trunk, nosily peeking inside.

"Ahh!" Winton shrieks, stepping into the gas and leaving the drunk's hands moving forward then wind-milling even faster until falling flat on his face, screaming. Winton cuts the wheel hard, shooting out on the half-empty road, barely missing a few parked cars by inches when picking up speed.

The drunk comes to his knees fast, staring in disbelief while brushing off mud when staggering a few feet, and stepping over low-cut shrubs.

Winton hits a back road and speeds until almost home when reaching a service road where he slows down. He begins driving even slower with his face torn up and growing more pissed when turning on his parking lights after making a turn, remaining undetected. He makes the last turn onto a pitch-dark road, slowly coming around a curve, and finds movement when slamming on brakes and energizing his high beams. Winton veers off with lights shining in a dingy-looking man face, sitting Indian style with his eyes to the ground. "What the hell!" Winton shouts, easing beside him. "Have you lost your cotton-picking mind, man? You can get killed out here on this dark road! Hell, I could have killed you!" he yells, staring at the top of the man's tilted, narrow head.

"Leave me alone! Let me be, I tell yah (you)!" the mad man yells, fanning Winton off with fast-moving hands. "Just let me be…, I tell yah (you); let me be!" he screams again, looking off to the side and then back down.

"Oh, so you want to kill yourself, huh? Winton declares, still pissed about the hooker and being shot at.

"Leave me be! Just mind your own freakin' business, punk!" he yells, waving Winton off again but more snappily.

"Naw, see…, when you sit out here and make it so that I could have hit you and ran my insurance high as hell; you made it my business. You look a hea (here); you brought the business, pal!" Winton yells in a high pitch, pissed when slinging the door open fast and stepping out even faster.

The man uses his peripheral vision, finding Winton's fast-moving shadow.

"Naw! Come on! You want to end your life? Then I'm going to help you!" Winton yells, seizing the frail man by the arm, lifting him, and pulling him off to the side of the road and in the tall weeds, with the man fighting with all the strength he can muster.

The man digs his feet into the grass, snatching tall weeds, trying to break his stride, but Winton is too strong for him and keeps pulling him deeper into the taller grass. "Come on, daggonit! Come on! You want to kill yourself, then uma (I am going to) take you over here in these woods and peel that cap (head) back!"

The man throws his head back, letting off a death squawk, but Winton keeps a tight tug, dragging him further. Without warning, the man hauls off, kicking Winton in the shin, finally breaking loose when popping up tall, and high-stepping.

Winton jumps around on one foot for seconds, in agonizing pain until limping then finally gives chase seconds later until he's almost out of breath. He stops, leaning with hands on his knees, taking deep breaths, and gaining control of his breathing. Winton comes up on his tiptoes a few times; the last time finding the man leaping across a ditch and striking out through the trees until fading into a dark cornfield.

Winton bends forward again, catching his breath until uncontrollably chuckling with heavy jumping shoulders. Out of nowhere, he screams with laughter at the top of his voice when the man drops down in fear, low-crawling through mud and dipping into a swamp. Winton soon lowers his voice, still giggling, when stepping off and easing by the car's rear door. He makes it to the hood, leaning onto it and breathing hard for minutes before finally getting in and pulling off.

Across town, Boogey stands, covering the bird's cage while peeking at the store, then Nattie when finds her nodding. He slips out the back, cutting into the cornfield, and minutes later, enters the store's back door, walking up behind the third person in the line, drenched in sweat.

Boogey's eyes wander to the window, doing a double-take; thinking he sees Nattie's face until a passing car's headlight soon confirms no one is there. He slips the clerk the dollar, backing away fast, and then looks at the window again, grabs the ticket, and exits. He returns home, coming up on the side of the house, loudly rattling around mason jars until pulling one out, blowing into it until holding it under the camouflaged faucet, filling it with chilled shine. He eases up on the back porch, stomping, so Nattie hears him and whistles while walking inside.

Boogey stands in the doorway, listening to her snore before creeping into the bedroom in a cheerful mood. He reaches over, pulling out his guns when easing to the edge of the bed, cleaning the first one.

Boogey finishes the last sip of shine an hour or so later, heavily swaying while putting the gun back together. He accidentally slides off the foot of the bed, sitting back up and straightening up when loading a clip. He grabs the next clip, pulling it even closer with eyes wandering up and down between his favorite television show and the guns when turning up the jar, finally realizing it's empty.

Boogey lays the trigger to one side, staggering to the head of the bed, pulling out a flask and turning it up until down to the last drop. He jumps, thinking he hears Nattie coming when staggering to the foot, watching the remainder of a show.

Boogey is three sheets to the wind within another hour when swaying with his eyes crossed from being sleepy and close to passing out when a new commercial comes on, excitedly catching his attention. He sits, tensed, and when it ends then stands, stepping on a switch that changes the channel to one of his favorite shooting galleries with targets continually running across the screen.

Boogey slides off the mattress, and his hand goes to his side, balancing with a gun slid under his hand when his mind swiftly shifts to the game, feeling around for what he thinks is the gun for the game. His hand comes up with the loaded gun, and out of nowhere, three shouts ring out, causing him to duck and drop the gun.

"Ahh!" Nattie yells, hitting the floor with Bud cussing, and looking around.

There is silence for minutes until Nattie finally sees the hole in the wall when bursting through the door, finding Boogey looking at the gun as if it's a foreign object.

Boogey looks over at the demolished, heavily smoking television.

"You…, idiot! You…, drunkard! You're about the stupidest…," she mumbles, backing out and slamming the bedroom door.

Later, Boogey paces around in the kitchen, listening to food frying while waiting for her to walk out so he can sneak another mason jar. On his fifth stroll through, he finds the back door open, so he grabs a pint jar, slips it in the back of his coverall pocket, and expressly turns, stepping into her.

"Ain't this a darn shame…, sneakin' around your own house!" She frowns in a stare. "You're pathetic," she says, ranting and raving to strongly carry her point forward.

"I ain't got to sneak nothing! I was just trying to figure out if I really wanted it," Boogey says, nervously squeezing between her and the countertop.

Nattie waits until he tries to pass and shoves him, causing him to stumble a few feet when his brogans slap the floor hard while regaining his footing. She slips on the thick, dusty mittens, seizing the black, hot, cast iron skillet to flip over the meat.

"You need to go on with that mess before I put this upside that grape (head) of yours," he says, balling his fist tight in a playful yet joking mood.

"Oh yeah, and it will be somethin' to tell the captain, baby!" She shakes water from the two-prong fork into the hot grease so that it sizzles louder.

Instantly, Boogey's eyes grow big, hearing the loud popping when taking a big swallow, picking up his pace unnoticeably to give her some space.

"You know what? You're starting to be the lyingness (the most lying) man I know," she says, looking over her shoulder before hearing the screen door slam.

Boogey makes his way around the house, draining another nice cool glass of shine. He shuts off the secret spout, holding the glass to the light, twirling it around, and testing that it is good when minuscule bubbles speedily vanish. He pulls the glass to his lips, taking big gulps and leaves less than a gulp. 'Ahh…, ugh, ugh, ugh…, now that there's some good shine if I have to say so myself, Mr. Boogey!' he says in a whisper, when bursting into a silly, quiet laugh.

Boogey makes his way back to the front, sitting on the step, looking at his watch until feeling brave when getting up for another round, but he only gets enough for a few swallows.

An hour later, Boogey is still sitting when hearing the soft but loud rubber bottoms from Nattie's slippers when looking over his shoulder, discovering her still quiet as she stares out into space.

"Is this all you've resorted to, a drunkard and gambling fool?" she asks, staring at the back of his head when turning up her shot and slipping the shot glass in her apron.

"Go on wit that bull, Nattie, cause I ain't feeling it right now; I tell yah (you)!" He stares toward the main road when taking the last swallow.

"Well, you gonna feel it yah (you) two-time loser! You got that! I said…, you got that?" she screams, slurring without him noticing. "I don't know why I married your sorry tail! My mama said you would never mount to nothing but a wannabe punk!"

"Look!" he declares, cross-eyed and in a stale stare into space. "Gone wit (with) that, Natt, and on another note; the hell wit (with) you and your raggedy-tail mama…, a buncha gold diggers! That's all you two are…, a bunch of deep, gold diggers!" he exclaims, looking at the jar as if hoping it would refill itself.

"Gold dia gger?" she drunkenly stutters. "Listen here, boo-boo, if gold…, then where the hell is it at? You sho (sure) ain't got it, boo-boo! Now that lottery…, hell, you wish you could hit," she says, quieting for a minute, in deep thought. "Well, breaking news, Champ! Crap in one hand and wish in the other, and see which comes first, Jack!" she yells in a drunken and uncontrollable laugh, for minutes.

Boogey drifts into deep thoughts, accidentally biting his tongue and his drunken face instantly transforms with his eyes crossing worse when his shoulders shrug while he huffs and puffs to calm down.

There is total silence for some time until Nattie continues ranting and raving.

In a delayed response, Boogey silently mocks her voice, jumping up, staggering. "Oh, and while you on that thought…, oh, I'm gonna hit all right cause Mrs. West said it is in my cards; then what? Boogey this! Boogey that! Boogey! Boogey! Boogey!" he yells, prancing around in the yard in some silly dance until kicking up dust while acting like her and her mom, when they're riding on their high horses.

Nattie's face turns bright red. "Now you look ah here; I ain't gone let you keep talking 'bout (about) my momma! When she is here, you kiss nothing but pure-T butt, and behind her back, you wanna (want to) talk crap! Well, screw you, buddy!"

"Look! Just leave me be, I say…, leave me be!" Boogey yells, even more pissed.

Nattie's moonshine takes over her drunken mind and all sorts of things rush in when a smirk comes. Her eyes dim when stepping through the door, swaying.

Across the lawn, the nosy foreign couple sits on their front porch, hearing distant, fluctuating yet arguing voices.

Mr. Cho turns down the blaring country music on the transistor radio, placing a cold beer bottle next to four cool, empty bottles when leaning and listening harder.

The couple turns to each other with wide eyes when the husband motions her to the door, then the living room, entering with her hot on his trail, and so close that she trips him.

Mr. Cho stumbles forward in a fast trot, headfirst into the couch, when his narrow head slips between the springs with skinny legs furiously kicking.

"Honey! Honey! I'm so sorry, honey!" she whispers with hands over her mouth, fighting back her laugh yet wondering if he's ok.

"Get me out! I can't breathe..., I can't breathe," he shrieks, muffled with both hands on the springs to get more air.

His wife bends forward fast, giggling until hearing him gurgle when halting her laugh and fearfully jumping on the couch, prying the springs apart with foot and hands until his head slips out.

Over at Boogey and Nattie's, the full effect of the moonshine kicks in when Nattie struts over to the dirty, broken-down couch on the front porch. She drops down, unknowingly shifting the high cinder blocks off balance and slightly rocking until letting off a long death cry, when wobbling even heavier when a loud crash comes.

Wood crumbles, bringing Boogey out of deep thought when he jumps up with eyes shooting over his shoulder, catching a glimpse of Nattie's legs flying high and vanishing fast with the end of the couch disappearing even faster. "What in the hell?" he shouts, coming up slightly on tiptoes, finding Nattie rolling continually in the dirt until resting against a tall pile of leaves.

Nattie stays still for seconds, moaning then slowly draws in her knees with her butt high and her panties covered with dirt and mud.

In the foreign couple's house, the husband and wife finish bandaging his neck and rush from the bathroom.

"Come to the window..., the window!" the wife whispers, shoving him until flowing into the bedroom.

The couple drops down, easing the blinds open to find commotion in Boogey's yard when easing the window up, finally hearing the end of Nattie's whiny voice then Nattie screams.

"Booooggeeeyyy! Booooggeeeyyy!" Nattie cries in a delayed, drunken voice.

The foreign couple looks the porch over, not seeing Nattie when the wife looks over the yard, finally spotting Nattie facedown with her butt still in the air.

"There, there," the nosy wife murmurs, chuckling.

Boogey stares longer, still frozen in disbelief, noticing that Nattie is fine when bending, grabbing his knees in a silent laugh while she finally sits with her back to him. His belly uncontrollably shakes as he tries not to blurt out until a loud, uncontrollable laugh comes out of nowhere.

"Booooggeeeyyy! Booooggeeeyyy!" Nattie cries, somewhat lightheaded.

Mrs. Cho's face turns fiery red. "Did he hit her? Did he hit her?" she screams, waking her mother-in-law. "Should I call the sheriff?" Mrs. Cho asks, looking again and finding Nattie kneeling on one knee.

Mr. Cho grips his wife's hand, pulling her down quickly. "Look..., this is no business of ours, Lin Lu," he utters, feeling good after four beers when smiling and winking at her.

Boogey pulls himself together, pretending to be concerned but his belly shakes uncontrollably when he shrieks. "Ahh, uh, uh, ahh...!" He continually laughs, stumbling over.

Mr. Cho pulls a pillow from the bed, motioning his wife for a beer while adjusting the blinds to remain undetected.

Nattie sits, whining more before screaming. "I'm here hurting, and you think it's funny, Boog?" she declares, unnoticeably drawing in two full hands of mingled sand, dirt, and mud.

Mrs. Cho sprints back in with two beers, cuddling next to her husband. "Did I miss anything?" she asks, popping the tops and passing him one.

"No, not a thing; he's just standing there," her husband responds, looking back at the door when hearing his mother moving around in her room.

Boogey laughs uncontrollably, extending one hand forward and leaning further when Nattie's filled hands lunge forward, releasing the sand, dirt, and mud.

Nattie slaps the residual away with her hands quickly.

"Hot doggity dog!" Mr. Cho screams, being the first to see Boogey high-stepping and dancing around like a dancing bear, when kicking up dust.

"Popcorn?" the husband asks, waiting for his wife's response and finding her speechless with her mouth still torn open when looking back at him.

"Your turn..., you go!" she says with a smile, still staring until laughing at Boogey's dancing and fancy footwork.

Mr. Cho peeks from the top of the blinds, takes a few steps away, and rushes back to look once more before fading through the door.

Boogey's eyes wander back and forth, feeling the grit swishing around while fighting to gain balance, yet continually rubbing his eyes.

"Laugh at me, will you! Yah (you) yellow-belly, two-ton baboon!" Nattie yells when springing up, swinging at Boogey's face and missing, from Boogey seeing intermittent visions of her fist cruising inbound, fast.

Other nosy neighbors converge near the store, on porches, or in yards.

"Take this!" Nattie screams, taking yet another forceful swing, and then more swings while Boogey blindly dances back and forth from the instant blinks or sound of each stealthily and windy blow.

Mr. Cho eases a popcorn pan on the stove, turns the knob high, and waits for the oil to heat when accidentally dropping half the amount of kernels, per serving. He eases the glass lid on and rushes back in the room, glancing out of the upper part of the blind.

Seconds later, something catches his attention when he looks down the hallway at the dim light shining into the kitchen from a streetlight, hearing the first pop.

Boogey quiets, hearing her fist sail past his head, still sporadically seeing her when dodging until his eyes are somewhat clear when taking a blunt blow to the gut, bending forward when cracked square in the lips. "Oh..., ho..., ho..., ho!" he yells, finally absorbing another blow to the chest.

A firefighter sits grilling out back at the fire station next to the Cho's house when hearing and seeing the fracas and waving to other firefighters out back.

Boogey's eyes clear fully, and he grabs the next jab, pushing her back. "Look, I don't hit you, so keep your hands off me, or you gonna find yourself sucking soup through a straw the rest of your life, woman!" he yells with a painful look on his drunken face.

The foreign couple and others tenses, wondering if Boogey will beat Nattie down when seeing his fist balled tight.

Nattie squirms while Boogey holds her until she seems calm then finally releases her, and she stands with her face slightly transformed, knowing he's gotten the best of her.

Instantly, burnt popcorn rises in the Cho's nostrils, and the husband's head goes over his shoulder, finding smoke drifting slowly into the bedroom. "Yo, babe! Yo babe..., yo!" Mr. Cho screams, expressly tripping over his wife, who moves even faster when coming to her knees.

The foreign couple begins coughing heavily and feeling their way in the thick, smoky hallway, toward the kitchen, hugging the wall until easing inside. They begin feeling for the kitchen counter, continually coughing heavier when Mr. Cho's hand accidentally drops onto the hot popcorn lit, and he dances around shaking off the burning sting.

Mr. Cho sees the lid through a patch in the smoke and grabs the lid by each handle, dispersing a heavy burst of steam, burning his hands when dropping it, leaving it banging with a loud blast and high-stepping even higher and screaming louder.

The grease catches fire and the curtains go up in a blaze.

One firefighter sits eating and mysteriously stares at the foreign couple's house window when springing up and stepping into the foreign couple's yard, confirming its smoke. He takes off in full stride, screaming to other firefighter while scurrying over for a two-hundred-foot wall attached firehouse hose.

A light scream comes, rising higher when granny low-crawls into the hall with a full-blown, clear garbage bag over her head with duct taped at her neck.

The husband looks back while reaching for the knob, screaming. "Ahhh!" he shrieks when his shirt sleeve catches fire and spreads to another curtain.

Granny passes the kitchen with hands hard upon the wall in the smoky hallway and heat instantly seals the bag when she low-crawls faster until coming to her knees at the door. Her feet fade out of the thick smoke when slithering onto the front porch, springing up, and breathing harder when the bag sucks in and out, sealing tightly, fast. She grows lightheaded, losing oxygen fast when pulling at the plastic. Her hands slide across the dense melted plastic when jumping off the porch and taking off in a stealth sprint. She runs past an intercepting firefighter who grabs her by the arm, slinging her around in circles a few times.

She screams muffled with one hand still pulling at the plastic when growing weak and slipping from him when he trips her, and she bounces back up but a little weaker.

The frantic firefighter grabs her from behind, slinging her around, and on the second turn, pokes two fingers through her wide, screaming mouth, and she unintentionally latches down. His mouth flies open, and his other hand clinches tight when punching her deep in the gut, instantly forcing her mouth open wider.

Inside the couple's house, Mrs. Cho heavily fans her hands, barely able to see her husband when grabbing a towel, swiping fast until the curtain's fire is out.

The couple keeps choking and blinking from the thick smoke, unable to see until their eyes close tight and their hands go for the window; both fighting to get it up.

Mrs. Cho finally gets her hand on the latch first, screaming. "I've got it! I've got it!" She feels her husband's hands still fumbling around when slapping them fast, leaving them stinging when feeling him pull away fast. She fumbles more until churning hard on the latch, and it clicks.

The two lean forward with eyes still closed, thrusting the window upward when the smoke escapes and they look at each other, smiling until fading instantly and falling into the far wall when the high velocity of water from the firefighter's hose hits them square in the chest as the firefighter stands, yelping.

Within minutes, the smoke clears, and the couple hears firefighters call out to them before several firefighters rush in, assessing the scene.

A scream comes from the fire chief when both high-velocity fans kick in, heavily blowing things and the couple sideways.

Boogey walks alongside the house for a shot of moonshine.

Nattie drags herself on the porch, hearing distant screams, seeing the last firefighter running toward the Cho's house, then another running to the fire station when more attentive.

Boogey finally leans into the house, laughing hard, and stops when hearing a door shut, not knowing it's his nosy foreign neighbors. He comes alongside the porch, bending, lifting, and sliding the couch back on the porch and finds Nattie slumped-over in a wooden chair. Boogey staggers around front, not making eye contact for seconds but soon comes up on the top step, forcefully jerking back in a delay when Nattie's tight-balled, little fist swiftly retracts from his head.

Nattie's sharp elbow begins pounding the top of his head. "Laugh at me, will you?" she yells when Boogey pushes her away, pissed. "Oh heck, naw!" Imma (I am going to) have to cutcha (cut you) now!" Nattie says when Boogey rushes slamming the door.

Nattie knocks and kicks the base of the flimsy door non-stop for seconds, then eases into the lopsided couch, lying there for minutes until fast asleep.

An hour later, Nattie is woken by the dog licking her face when springing up sluggishly; swiping fast and running the dog off. She rubs her sleepy eyes and jumps, hearing a loud truck pass when the driver lays deep into the horn near the store. Nattie's eyes wander over the quiet yard and then back, noticing the door is cracked open when taking in a fresh breath of air and quietly easing up then creeping inside.

She latches the door quietly, freezing for a second when hearing Boogey mumbling in a slurred, low tone until his voice tapers off to a soft cry and then weak whine. Nattie stands listening longer then creeps over by the bedroom door, listening closely until easing the door open. She walks in unnoticed, finding him with a gun tight in his hand until he lays it on the bed.

Boogey's head stays down until coming up slow. "Shoot me! Just get it over with, you evil woman! Just put me out of my miseries," he says, with several wet and dry tears tracing his lightly dusty and powdery looking face when easing from the edge of the bed, lowering himself to his knees.

Nattie remembers unloading the gun earlier, so she double-checks, slightly turning it to make sure when slightly training it. She stays quiet for minutes listening to him whining until sniffling, then pretending to cry. She pulls the hammer and trigger, and the click sends chills up Boogey's spine, with a jump and high spring to his feet.

"Woo Wee! Ok, Ok..., let's not try that again," he nervously yells, looking at her bright-eyed and swiftly pulling the gun to his side.

Nattie keeps a poker face and then bursts into a crazy, uncontrollable laugh. "Silly-tail man, I unloaded this gun right after you shot it, like an idiot," she says, walking away laughing and shaking her head.

Deep in the woods, in the wee hours, near surrounding little cities, the sheriff and six deputies furtively close in on a location that is based on very reliable tips that Big Hank was hiding out there.

The officers meet at a fork in the road and then follow in a convoy, heading deeper into the woods until pulling off when signaled.

The sheriff jumps out with a pad in his hand, walking toward the hood. He motions the men over, and they rush over, converging on a map he's already spreading out over his hood with large ammunition rounds holding down the corners.

The shortest deputy pulls out a matching pen, pencil, and penlight, shining it over the hood when the sheriff slides the map further under the light.

The sheriff slips fingers in his shirt pocket, extending an aluminum pointer toward the map when giving instructions on their unplanned and unrehearsed attack. "Here, this is where we'll enter: here, here, and here, and double up on the front and back," he says, pointing out who should be where and when.

"Sheriff, we'll park a car on each road and block the exits!" one officer cleverly exclaims.

The sheriff gets quiet, and his head comes up slowly, gazing deep into each man's face as they make eye contact, confirming he has their undivided attention. "Hell..., shoot to kill if you have to, and we'll doctor up the freakin' reports; am I clear," the nasty sheriff utters, folding the map and looking into their dimly-lit faces and positive affirming heads. The sheriff gets sidetracked when looking at one sleepy-eyed, snotty-nosed deputy. "Look..., you better get the sleep out of those eyes before I slap it out. You gonna (are going to) mess around and get one of us killed. Pay attention, Slick!" he yells in a thunderous voice with stealth eyes still glued on the deputy; when the deputy's eyes widen. The deputy accidentally wipes the thick wad of snot on his shirt sleeve then spits a wad of tobacco accidentally on his round belly, leaving the heavily stained tobacco smeared. He then wipes more tobacco with his hands, smearing more on his pants.

The officers disperse, parking the first two cars, and those officers jump into other cars, heading for the cottage, deeper in the woods.

Other cars park on the third and back road, where two deputies jump out drawing their guns.

Everyone meets on the high road to get the upper hand and a better, bird's eye view of the scenery. The team of officers jumps out, running toward the sheriff, who points them into positions where they wait for the radio signal before advancing up the hill.

The signal comes minutes later, and they expressly advance almost in unison.

The sheriff is the first at the top, finding thick smoke coming from the chimney of the cabin when it fully comes into view, and each of them drops when in view, low-crawling.

Two deputies pull out binoculars, and begin thoroughly scanning the perimeter.

Suddenly, and out of nowhere, a manly body stumbles alongside the cabin, wrestling to get his pants up when zipping them tight. He shakes off the chill with both hands shooting deep into his pockets when shivering and looking back when hearing a twig from a deer stepping on it when instantly making eye contact. The man keeps his eyes peeled back and takes two steps, stumbling over a raised tree stump, unable to extract his hands from the tight jeans when falling face-first and screaming cuss words while waddling around, still unable to free his hands.

"Hold your positions," the sheriff whispers with eyes wandering over the man's body then around the cabin until spotting another man's head near the window shaking his head in disbelief while on his tiptoes, watching the man still struggling to get his hands free for seconds.

The man in the window shoulders goes up and down in a heavy chuckle, not wanting to laugh out loud and piss Hank off.

Hank sits, drunk off his tail, but stands after a long card game he's been cheating his way through and winning. "Well, let me go in here and squabble (do number two)! Felt like I pulled the last one out my chest." He senselessly giggles when easing from the chair. He takes a step, cocking one leg high and ripping a good one when looking back over his shoulder at the men expressly scrambling from the table.

Hanks looks off in the corner, finding one of his frail guards sitting with teary eyes and a shirt sleeve running across his snotty nose when sniffing again. "Man, you sure you cut out for this hea (here) job because every time I see you, you're crying and plucking on this hea (here) guitar." Hanks leans forward, lifting the guitar, plucking a few out-of-tone strings when passing it back, and watching the man's head lift upward until seeing bloodshot eyes and a sleeve wiping nose.

"Hey Hank, got one for you..., something was weighing heavy on my mind and I gotta (have to) get it out...; I did my time, cared for mine, but there's still doubt," the frail man senselessly rhymes while tuning his guitar strings and clearing his voice. "Now here's one deeply rooted, boys!" he excitedly screams out of nowhere, causing a few to jump and some to reach for their side arms.

"What's the name of this one hea (here), Juke Box?" one country speaking, card player screams, still standing back and waiting for the strong scent to clear.

"Oh, this one? Well, I ain't rightly named it yet but let's call it..., ah, ah..., deadbeat Dad," the frail man giggles wiping his snotty nose with his sleeve again when tuning up the guitar and clearing his throat. "Here we go, boys!"

'A grown child, raised in anger and so much hate,
Honor thy mother and father should be their fate.
If it's all about love, why shorten your life,
All for her hatred and all for her strife.
Did she tell you of the great times, the beginning till the end?
Did she tell you the time we were real good friends
Did she tell you bout the good, tell you bout the bad,
Did she tell you that my title was to be called dad?'

He pauses. "Well, and the chorus would break down a little something like this," the frail man says, shaking his head when going off into another tempo.

'Well, here's this tall, tall tale, and it may seem wild,
So is the dad, and so is the child,
If I'm a deadbeat dad, I damn sho got a deadbeat child.
Did she tell you she's the only one with the right to judge,
Did she tell you what it was I did for her to hold a grudge?
Did she tell you bout the hard times, the things we went through,
Did she tell you of all the times, but how much of it is true?'

"Then the chorus breaks down again," he says, winking when shaking his head with the tempo changing.

'Well, here's this tall, tall tale, and it may seem wild,
So is the father, and so is the child,
If I'm a deadbeat dad, I damn sho got a deadbeat child.
What about the heartache? What about the pain?
What about the situation we just call shame?
Did she mention any of my struggles, my battles never won?
Or did she just praise herself and labeled me a Con?
Did she tell you bout the heartaches, the trials, and the pains?
Did she tell you bout the mess, the bloody heart, and the stains?'

"Well then the chorus breaks again," he says, shaking his head.

'Well, here's this tall, tall tale, and it may seem wild,
So is the father, and so is the child,
If I'm a deadbeat dad, I damn sho got a deadbeat child.
What about the great times you and I could have had,
But I'm just left with just the name of a deadbeat dad.
Oh me? Well, I guess you can say I'm doing mighty fine,
Drinking my whiskey, sometimes drinking my wine!'

Hank's loud laughter breaks out. "Damn, son! I think you got a big hit there, Boi!" Hank yells when a round of applause comes with laughter and hand clapping. "Heck, I can use that for my lame-tail boy! Hank yawns when turning and freezes, looking at his two hookers dressed in garter belts, stockings, and self-altered dresses that are too short to even be called dresses.

Hank finally walks off when another man walks up, finally sniffing in the air like a dog when sliding Hank's chair back and sitting. Hank walks over by the wall, passing the cozy fireplace when kicking his boots off and looking back at the men.

The women rush into the bedroom, flopping onto the bed, high as kites, and looking back at Hank and then each other, bursting into a burst of silly laughter.

"So, this is what my money gets me, huh? A bunch of lazy card hands, for security! Is this what I pay for?" he says, shaking his head in frustration when walking away.

One man stops shuffling the deck and looks at Hank, then the playful hookers in the background until Hank slams the bedroom door.

The three men stare at each other, confused when the number-three lead guy shrugs his shoulders with a sly grin when dealing. "Just chill, Hank! No need to be all tense! This hea (here) place is locked like a hen outside a chicken coop!" he shrieks, riding the chair on hind legs.

Hank's trusted sidekick stands outside, quickening dirt and straw from his face. He comes up on the side of a car, looking in the mirror to ensure his face and hair are clean when lifting the infrared goggles, and walking toward the cabin window.

"We do this on three," the sheriff whispers over the walkie-talkies, staring at each officer's position and giving individual hand signals before looking back at the cabin and Hank's confirmed side-kick.

Instantly, the cabin's front door flies open and bright light stretches outward, across the ground.

"Hold it," the sheriff utters, pulling binoculars from the hand of the deputy next to him.

The women stumble out in hoochie struts, high-stepping like plucked chickens.

One card player finally straggles out behind the women, stuffing his long-barreled gun in the front of his trousers with his chest stuck out.

Hank kicks in the bathroom door, standing in just his pants and a tee-shirt, dropping his pants then drawers and flopping down on the cool toilet with tensed then flapping shoulders to warm up. He pulls out a magazine, flipping through a few pages while letting out loud and obnoxious farts and giggling, senselessly. He knows his men heard it, and they all frown as he begins chuckling real hard with other loud and uncontrollable farts following each laughable bounce; until he's a laughing and bouncing fool.

Hank's sidekick adjusts his infrared harness over his head, watching the man and two women jump in the car. He rushes for the driver's side, passing the driver a long black bag when the engine cranks, revving a few times.

The car rolls forward then stops with loud, vibrating music when the motion sensor- infrared goggles light up, still over Hank's sidekick's head.

The officer's earpieces click and then energize when the sheriff keys up. "Ted and Ed, stand down and proceed to the car to give chase, if need be," the sheriff whispers, motioning to the two closest officers.

One deputy backs down the steep hill, tripping over a stump and yelling in a muffled tone while falling backward. "Ahh!" he shrieks, his voice echoing and fading while continually rolling faster and farther.

Hank's sidekick jerks forward quickly, and the goggles drop over his eyes as he scans the hills, seeing several red eyes and silhouettes that spring up fast. "Po-Po!" he shrieks at the top of his lungs, banging against the car door when tires kick up dirt with the car taking off like a jet; the driver laying continually into the horn.

The man and women scream, and gunfire erupts; several rounds penetrate the car's body, shattering the window, with the three ducking low while the car fishtails with a few more long honks.

Hank and the others hit the floor, with the men aiming for the front door.

Hank's sidekick dodges around objects, diving alongside Hank's shiny Cadillac, which shakes when riddled with bullets as he fires back. He throws the car door open, shielded and staying low when slithering to the cabin door, knocking hard with his tightly-balled fist. "It's me; it's me! Open up..., quick..., open up!" he yells, finally seeing the door cracked when pushing and expressly, low-crawling inside.

Hank lies still, but his mind goes haywire until slowly low-crawling with his face frowned from the strong stench. He rolls onto his back, reaching for some tissue, when bullets fly through the window, causing him to struggle to get his pants up.

"Hank! Hank! Man..., we gotta get out of here, pronto, Homie! Hank..., fast, brotha (brother)!" his sidekick yells when the other two open a secret door in the floor, climbing inside while non-stop gunfire rages through the roof, walls, door, and windows, continually pouring into the bathroom, and keeping Hank pinned down.

The getaway driver jets over the hill, discovering a deputy's blue lights when throwing the steering wheel hard and swerving off the dirt road. The car jack-knifes high, barreling through the woods, as the professional, ex-race car driver maneuvers, ducking and dodging thick trees.

The sheriff and his men rush to the cabin, taking cover and slowly walking up, blazing when all the lights go out except one, and there's total silence for minutes.

Hank turns slow and in fear until fixated on the plunger when seizing it, and slowly pushing it back with sticky, stinky hands, when his face frowns as he wipes them on his pants fast, using the plunger to flip the lights off.

More gunfire comes, bursting the lights and shattering the switch.

Two more deputies rush up on the sheriff's car, jumping in, skidding wheels until coming up on the parked deputy car blocking the road when backing down, fast.

The getaway driver slows, cutting on the lights when easing onto a graveled, quarter-mile of well-hidden road. He cuts the wheel hard, coming off the gravel and heading for a mini-power station door built into the side of the hill.

The sheriff motions a few men into view, who motion others on the opposite side of the cabin, gathering until feet apart with guns drawn at eye level.

The secret door inside slowly eases shut until cracked, with fast, white eyes still scrolling around the dark living room.

A set of bright white eyes stare upward at the backside of Hank's sidekick until he looks down, making eye contact before looking out again and calling out to Hank, who stays silent; not giving away his position or letting them know he's even there.

Hank's sidekick waits a few more minutes, looking down again. "Go! Go! Let's get out of here! Hank isn't coming; he must be shot!" Hank's sidekick shouts, still not getting a response when turning, grasping the shiny firehouse-type pole, and clinging to it when sliding through the hole, and dropping twelve feet into the tunnel. His feet slam onto the dusty ground just as the last man rushes off, and he looks as far ahead as possible, finding a thick cloud of dust from the other two when calling out to them and heavily fanning when trotting until high stepping, even faster, with eyes glued back over his shoulder at times.

The other two continually beat down the dusty trail until finally hearing a faint voice that grows strong when Hank's sidekick high-steps, double-timing to catch up.

The cabin's front door eases open and stays open for minutes.

The sheriff tiptoes inside, training his gun about the darkroom until backing deep into a dark corner.

There is total silence for minutes until the bathroom door, then seconds later, the bedroom door eases open; at squeaky intervals.

Hank's eyes wander over the darkroom as he stays in a prone position then kneels, nervously rocking in anticipation of running but decides to drop down; low-crawling until grabbing the handle to the secret door, and entering headfirst with the door stopping him at the hip until he is finally freed with an ear full of screaming.

"I got me a big fish! Big fish!" the sheriff transmits over the headsets with a wide hand deep in Hank's back; at the collar. Big John's right-hand jerks Hank's trousers, seizing him at the belt, jerking hard again, and his firm hand grips Hank's corpulent butt, holding him while his feet furiously kicks.

Hank shrieks like a whiney brat when the front door bursts open.

A deputy rushes in, grabbing Hank's other side, and they pull him high until thrashing him to the dusty floor with Hank rolling over fast, looking in mean faces.

The sheriff's big gun stealthily flies into Hank's wide, whiny mouth. "Well, well, well! It looks like we caught a biggon (big one), fellas!" the sheriff shouts, shoving the barrel further until it looks like Hank is sucking on it. "If I didn't know any better, I'd think you like this big ole gun, just like your hooker like big thangs!"

Hank gags a little, so the sheriff eases the barrel out, then pulls it out, wiping it with Hank's shirt when the smell of human waste rises, and he frowns. "Uhh!" the sheriff mumbles, rushing off, and staring at a third deputy when he draws on Hank, and backs down, getting a nose full.

The deputy backs off even faster, still forcing Hank over with loud commands, when Hank rolls over, facedown when the sheriff's foot presses deep in his upper back.

Hank's men burst through the secret steel door, jumping back quickly, seeing fast-moving headlights but keep the door cracked, easing it back until they recognize the car and run out. They pile in when the headlights come on with the driver making his way down a secret passage with several asking questions about Hank.

The sheriff eases his hand to his face again, frowning when the deputy copies his action, and both frown harder, expressly breaking for the kitchen sink.

"I think you done made ole, big man mess his britches, sheriff!" a deputy says, holding his gun to Hank's head with his nose clenched tight while angrily grabbing Hank at the back of his collar, pulling him up with one hand.

Hank wobbles, coming low and close when grabbing the deputy's gun and slapped silly, and kicked. He stumbles, double-timing to break his fall when slamming into the backs of the sheriff and deputy, who are drying their hands.

Hank expressly reaches, seizing the sheriff's holster with him pressed hard into the counter and pulling until the sheriff elbows him in the head, knocking him up and back into another deputy when a great outburst of laughter comes.

The other deputy pushes Hank forward, into another deputy who slaps him, knocking him into another deputy, who slaps him, then another, until caught up in a slapping frenzy until heading for the sheriff, who jumps, drop kicking him in the chest.

Hank double-timing feet go backward until flying backward and expressly sliding across the floor backward, taking out chairs until slamming into the wall. Hank freezes, still lying on his back with a swollen, red face and blood trickling from his mouth. His tears mingle with blood as he slowly rolls over, looking around, whining. He eases up, frowning from the funk while sitting with his hands over his head as a deputy swiftly closes in, knocking him out with a fat fist to his face.

The sheriff and deputies freeze, looking back at the front door when hearing brakes squeal. One deputy creeps over to the window, pulling back the curtains to find two cruisers with doors flying open.

"Get this filth out of my sight!" the sheriff angrily shouts, looking at the top of Hank's big, fat, lifeless swaying head before turning away.

Two new deputies rush up, cuffing Hank, and heavily frown while escorting him to the door, with even heavier frowned faces, while looking around for something to wrap him in.

The sheriff looks back at the trap door. "What about those other hoodlums?" the sheriff asks, looking away then back at the floor when motioning two officers to check the escape route.

"They got away! Tricks! They vanished like ghosts in the night..., I mean stankin' thieves in the night!" He pushes Hank in the back harder, causing him to stumble and then stagger over to the open trunk of the cruiser.

The two deputies man handle Hank over by the trunk near the deputy with the 12-guage who slams the butt of the gun in Hank's face, dropping him into the truck and wrestling to get his busty boots inside.

Over at Boogey and Nattie's, Boogey walks inside with a loaf of bread and a secretly played number.

Nattie sits, rocking, until eventually nodding off, and from time to time, she takes sips of her spiked iced tea and stares at the television until nodding off again.

Boogey continually cuts his eyes over at her and then the clock, anxiously patting his foot. "Natt, gone (go) to bed before you fall out that there chair." He stares. "Up in here looking like a helicopter doing touch and goes," he says, giggling.

She opens her eyes for a minute, cutting her eyes over at him. "Oh yeah..., well, it can't be any worse than the touch and goes you be doing in those drawers, leaving burn marks..., during vertical takes-offs..., I reckon," she says, laughing to herself with fast jumping shoulders until gagging and looking over, finding his mean stare.

Nattie sits longer, yawning, and then eases up, walking toward the kitchen. She backs up, picking up his tea jar, still half-filled with shine. "Make sure you cut the lights out," she says, yawning and dragging her feet. The kitchen lights finally go out, and she walks over with his tea. "We're almost out of tea, but I'll fix another batch in the morning," she exclaims, yawning and walking to the bedroom.

Boogey watches her fade into the room and then sits rocking for minutes, but stops when hearing Nattie snoring. He lifts his cool glass, takes a few sips, and then stirs it until the ice rattles. Boogey turns down the volume, hearing Nattie's light snore, which grows until sounding like an eighteen-wheeler downshifting. He walks into the kitchen, mixing another batch of tea when adding his arcane sleep remedy before stirring it. He eases into the bedroom, setting the jar on her nightstand. "Natt, I fixed a little tea in case you want more in the middle of the night," he exclaims, pointing when turning and walking out.

Nattie's head slowly rises, drowsily looking and falling deep into the pillow.

Boogey pulls the door halfway shut, listening to her snore go deeper until she jerks in her sleep, getting off-rhythm when smiling. He grabs his boots, and like clockwork, two bright lights flash at the end of the driveway and then go out.

Bud being nosy, peeks through the shredded sheet at the clock and then out at the too-familiar car.

Boogey glimpses back and then creeps onto the porch, easing down the steps in a mad dash with eyes looking back at the windows and door a few times.

"Man, you got that sleepyhead tonic down like a mad science, huh?" Winton declares, watching Boogey ease the door shut.

"No..., like a mad scientist!" Boogey slicks his hair back over his ears.

Winton turns slowly, stopping when facing the foreign couple's bedroom window, seeing Mrs. Cho walk past through thin, sheer curtains in sexy, red lingerie.

Mrs. Cho stares at her husband, who is lying in his boxers. She blows kisses, seductively twirling her hips in a wonton fashion when easing into an Egyptian dance until slowly squatting and lifting.

Boogey and Winton sit with their eyes wide, eye-to-eye at times and smiling until something flies past, slamming into the window screen; splashing water into the room and back against the car's windshield.

Mrs. Cho screams bloody murder, dropping to the floor, low-crawling.

Winton's eyes speedily look into the rearview, finding a tall, manly silhouette that ducks fast and fade into darkness.

Tom, the town's crackhead, ducks lower, running faster and managing to pull off his notorious water balloon pranks without being identified.

Winton's eyes fly forward fast when Boogey's fast-moving hand pats his shoulder rapidly.

Mr. Cho nervously crawls to the window and his tiny head eases into the screen with bulging eyes growing, finding Winton's head and an unidentified person slumped over.

Delayed tail lights light up, and tires dig deep, kicking up a cloud of dust until the house vanishes and headlights come on, shining against a wall of dust.

Winton steps into the gas, losing his balance when spinning in continual circles until stopping and nippily gaining his bearings by the light from the general store when rapidly aligning with the driveway.

Mr. Cho's loud shrieks grow, and his body fades in from the thick dust, landing on Winton's hood, screaming with wide eyes and his mouth torn wide open. One hand slides in the crease near the windshield; the other brandishes a cannon-like gun when rising high and letting go of the windshield and balancing to cock it.

Winton stares down the barrel, screaming, and then steps into the gas, forcing him face-first into the windshield when slamming on the brakes, sending him rolling off the hood and onto the ground. He backs down expressly and then swerves hard, going forward and missing Mr. Cho by inches when barreling for the main road.

The car jack-knife where the dirt meets the concrete and Winton swerves into the street, paralleling a car, speeding past, and cutting in front when increasing his speed, hearing several loud gunshots echoing.

Boogey and Winton grow excited until tears of laughter burst out when eye-to-eye at times, with surprising stares, laughing until reaching the city limits. They pull up outside the comedy club, still laughing.

Over at the jail, the sheriff props his pointy-toe boots on the desk, riding on the chair's hind legs.

Outside, the door to the sheriff's cruiser eases shut, and several feet shuffle away quickly with blue light flashing and siren blaring, causing the sheriff to fall flat on his back. He struggles to stand, rushing to the window, finding the door open and flashing lights. "What the hell?" the sheriff shouts, swinging the 911 operator's door open. "Betty!" he screams, rushing out, and flinging the front door of the jailhouse open when stepping out with a cool barrel easing slowly to the back of his head.

Dallas, Hank's mean brother's deep, calm, peaceful voice, rises in Big John's ear. "You got my peeps (people) up in there, Sheriff?" he asks, chewing a long stem of hay while pressing the barrel tighter to his skull while Dallas' partner removes the sheriff's gun and valuables, patting him down. "One wrong move and your bird brains will be scattered all over this hea (here) cruiser," a hooded Dallas says.

Dallas shoves the sheriff inside, and instantly headlights veer around the corner with a ten-gallon-cowboy-hat wearing, nosy woman slowing with eagle eyes pierced on the lighted cruiser until finding a tobogganed, hooded man climbing out of the sheriff's car toting a shotgun.

The lady rolls slower, spotting the man stopping and looking back, eye-to-eye when gunning the engine and burning rubber until fishtailing.

The sheriff is cuffed quickly and begins to resist when inside when dropping to the floor, not willing to go anywhere near the cells when dancing left and right with his boots scuffing the floor when fighting to stand. He instantly freezes in place, spotting something blue in the corner when the 911 operator flies forward, forced into her chair by a long-haired blonde.

"Give me the keys!" Dallas shrieks, pushing the sheriff into a swivel chair. "Get up out of them there clothes and boots; down to your drawers, and make it snappy, buddy," Dallas utters, slowly fanning his two-shooter over the sheriff's face.

The sheriff stares into Dallas' hooded face with one eyebrow cocked.

"If you don't get up out of them clothes, Sheriff, I'm going to cuff you to this door and beat you up out of them!" he yells, raising his voice.

The sheriff resists longer until the barrel presses against his lips and an almost invisible hand slaps him silly, leaving snot and drool mixed with a trail of blood on his lips. The sheriff springs up, and within seconds, he is down to a T-shirt and pants when he stops, nervously staring at Dallas, eye to eye with teary eyes.

"Either you think this is a dream you're going to wake up from, or you're an idiot," Dallas exclaims, watching the sheriff grip his trousers and not move until slowly squirming out of them.

There is a strange outburst of laughter then a flood of laughter for seconds, discovering the sheriff's cartoon-colored drawers with superheroes painted over them and a turd looking stain in the middle of one character.

Three hoodlums bend over in tears until Dallas jumps back, drawing his gun on the sheriff when finding him in a pouncing position.

One hoodlum eases up from behind the sheriff, pulling his drawers up high and prying him forward until finally releasing him with a well-stretched wedgy when the elastic pops, sounding like a firecracker, leaving his flimsy drawers five times bigger.

The blonde hooker points her gun at the 911 operator, making her undress.

Dallas' sidekick shatters a glass case with his gun, grabbing the keys, and rushing to the door leading to the cells. He flings the door open, hearing shouts as he rushes through the long, narrow corridor to the last cell, finding Hank with his sweaty face pressed through the bars, tensed with bright scrolling eyes, looking confused. "Dallas is out front! We're here to bust you out, buddy!" he says, adjusting his mask before rattling the bundle of keys and trying several in the lock until it clicks and the door swings open.

Hank and the man make their way up the narrow corridor when a hand grabs Hank's arm, holding him tight until he looks down in the cell in the face of a super drip, jerry curl, jacked-up teeth, thick coke-bottle glasses, and Planet-of-the-Ape faced man. "What about us, Hank? Come on, brotha, can you spare some time, a dime, or a glass of wine?" he asks with sad, drunken eyes.

Hank grabs the key from Dallas' sidekick, throwing them in the man's cell. "Listen and don't come out until we're gone," Hank utters with a serious stare.

On the back roads, the old lady throws back her ten-gallon hat, barreling down the highway with the speedometer needle dropping off the scale.

Smoke trust from dual pipes until the woman reappears from behind a thick tree line and slowly exits onto another road.

Back at the jail, Hank bursts through the door, falling joyfully into his brother's arms, while Dallas' sidekick trains the gun on the sheriff.

Big smiles grow on Dallas and Hank's faces as they continue embracing. "Glad to see you, little brother," Dallas whispers, pushing him slightly away and looking in his face when gladly embracing him again.

Hanks backs away and his eyes go straight to Big John's mean face. "Man, you are just in time because ole Big John was planning on taking me out back when his boys get back to teach me a thing or two, but look..., we've got to get the heck out of here before this place is swarming with deputies!" Hank fearfully says.

The old woman's speedometer needle drops off the scale again until slowing when making another turn on an even darker road.

At the ten-gallon hat-wearing woman's house, on her front porch, glows a red, bright dot from a cigar being puffed by her husband until it dims and then brightens. The rattle of a cool jar of stump-hole liquor comes up from the dark porch, stirred until tilted back to old, dry lips.

Back at the jail, Hank stands shaking his head when seeing the sheriff's draws. He ravages through shelves until grasping a handful of cuffs, throwing them over the table, and motioning to the 911 operator, who is down to her bra and panties.

The sheriff's eager eyes wander over the young operator's soft skin and then her entire body, getting a woody, which he tries covering in a constant, forward lean.

"Stand up, Big Boi," Hank says, looking in the sheriff's mean face when smiling and motioning Dallas and his people over in a corner, whispering with all eyes and smiling faces looking back at the sheriff in intervals.

Hank turns, walking up to the sheriff with glistening and keen eyes. "Sheriff, before we go, I'd like to play a favorite game that is too familiar to you and your dirty men." Hank snatches him up by the neck, backing him up in the middle of the floor with Dallas' people spreading around in a circle when two more of Dallas's men rush inside, immediately motioned into positions.

Hank walks up to the sheriff, and stands eye-to-eye.

The sheriff watches Hank close in with an eyebrow rising when he's slapped silly with the long hair slightly over his eyes shifted sideways.

Hank pushes the sheriff hard in the chest and snatches him back by the shoulder, spinning him and lunging him forward and into another man who slaps him, knocking him into another man, who slaps him, then the blonde who slaps him so loud that it sounds like a firecracker when the sheriff is caught up in a too familiar slapping frenzy and heading for Hank a second time when dropkicked.

The sheriff double-times backward to gain balance when slamming expressly backward into the wall with the windowpane deeply bruising his back.

Three men rush up to the sheriff, holding him when Hank backs up with a balled tight fist, swiftly closing in on the sheriff, knocking him out and leaving him in a slight snore.

Hank turns, murmuring to Dallas' sidekick, then walks near the phone, running his hand over the panel for the sheriff's home number when looking back, hearing the sheriff moaning and scuffing the floor to stand.

The sheriff takes his time standing and turns sideways so they can't see that he's still excited by the operator.

Hank pulls the blonde hooker to one side, whispering until her smile grows on her serious face, and she bursts into laughter.

The blonde walks over, gagging the 911 operator, then attempts to gag the sheriff when he tries to bite her, but she draws back, quick, and with all her strength, punches him in the face then head butts him, leaving a bloody nose.

The sheriff staggers for seconds, screaming through the pain until losing his balance and falling back in the chair.

Dallas rushes up, snatching the sheriff in his chest, shaking him, and notices the sheriff's shrinking woody. "What you got up in there, a number-two pencil, Sheriff?" Dallas asks, bursting into laughter. "I think you got the hots for ole Sally rotten crotch, here, huh?" he says, slightly moving the 911 operator's hair to one side and from over her eye with the tip of his gun.

At the house, the old woman's husband gazes into darkness on the back road, slightly leaning forward when finding light moving fast along the road. He leans further, tapping his feet until his boots go off rhythm, and his mouth drops open when his feet stop.

The headlights slow, almost coming to a stop when turning down the long, dirt trail leading to the house, when high beams flash in his eyes and stay on as the car comes up to top speed, still smoking.

The old man becomes almost mesmerized when looking at the jar of shine, then back at the car, shielding his eyes until the car is twenty-five feet away when he shrieks, diving over the bushes in a roll.

The car abruptly stops inches from the porch with dust rising high until swarming over the car and front of the house.

The husband's eyes pierce from the thick bushes, nervously staring at the bumper for seconds before slowly climbing to his knees and shaking his head.

The wife continues frantically fighting to open the door but keeps nervously hitting the locks, until finally opening the door while still buckled in and snatched back; clothes hung, gagged, and in shock until fighting to get free and finally unlatching.

Over at the jail, the blonde whispers to Dallas' sidekick.

They approach the sheriff and operator, backing up seconds later with the operator bent over, and the Sherriff hog-tied in an intimate position.

Everyone stares when Dallas bursts out, making everyone laugh harder.

Hank motions the blonde over, chuckling when the phone rings.

Everyone's eyes stay peeled on the flashing light until they laugh so hard that Hank and the Blonde can't lift the receiver, but they try to clear their minds of the devilish plot when the phone stops ringing.

Instantly, the sheriff's pager, which is in his pants on the floor, buzzes and vibrates and then stops.

# CHAPTER FOUR

### Cat And Mousey

Back at the old couple's house, the wife runs for the door and then back to the car for her keys. "Quick! Quick! Some hooded folks got the sheriff at gunpoint, down at the jailhouse!" she shrieks.

"What! Have you lost every red sense in that nugget (head) of yours?" her husband yells, confused. "Shoot! Done made me spill a good darn drink! You done (have) messed up my high! What the heck's gotten into yah (you)?" The husband steps over bushes, gaining his footing and rushes inside, finding her on the couch and a nervous wreck with the phone at her shoulder and ear.

Over at the jail, the lights on the 911 operator's headset light up when the phone rings, causing everyone to stop and look.

The drunk husband shakes nervously, at the old couple's house, supporting his weight with the doorframe. "Now, what did you say is going on?" he nervously asks, looking at her trembling hands as she reaches over the table for her smokes, spanking the pack fast and hard.

"Someone's got the sheriff at gunpoint, dagnabit!" She pushes the phone closer, and it slips with eyes widened when hanging up, and calling back. "Jeb, dagnabit..., do something! The whole town may be under siege by all these non-Americans that helped build this great country!" she exclaims, staring at his drunken face.

The husband sways, balancing when a hand comes up in a clueless gesture.

The wife runs, throwing herself on the bed in tears, then lye there, thinking when springing up, without warning, running off and rummaging through the closet in another room. She pulls out guns, holsters, and leggings, throwing them to the bed.

Her husband walks in, and his eyes follow her hands as she puts out the cigarette, passing him his holster and two guns while stepping into tall, leather boots when slightly balancing against the wall.

The 911 operator station lights up and soon there's a direct light indicator from the sheriff's home again.

"Hello, Operator 911..., breaker, breaker, good buddy!" the blonde playfully says while giggling and easing into a chair. She adjusts her mask to uncover her full, glossy lips, licking them and making them look freshly glossed when answering, more professionally. "911," she utters in a soft, sexy voice, looking at Hank and winking.

"Hello, Betty, is the sheriff there? Have you seen him?" his wife asks worriedly.

"Oh, yeah, but he's a little busy! Girl, please..., we're up in here handling some business right now, so just call back later," she says in an even sexier voice.

"Well, I don't care how busy he is, you just put him on right this minute; do you hear me?" his wife frantically screams.

The blonde pulls the phone back and lightly moans when Hank lifts her, pushing her into the wall with heavy breathing in the mouthpiece. She moans deep, and a scream comes through the earpiece when the phone goes dead.

Hank releases the button and backs away, looking at the steaming sheriff, who is as red as fire.

The woman and her staggering husband rush down a long hallway which is plastered with black and white, Bonnie and Clyde-style photos, at the old couple's house. They step onto the porch, strapped at both hips with their shadows reflecting over the lawn while drunkenly posing in different positions.

At the jail, the phone rings again, and the sheriff's house button lights up and then goes off and on again until his pager activates between switchboard calls.

The car's tail lights grow bright in the old couple's yard until white backup lights steadily glow. The car jerks with tires digging deep in the dirt when the car jerks back, then lunges forward in a swift U-turn, lighting up the tree line while the wife swerves to align the car along the dirt trail. The car speeds to the paved highway and stops with dust rising high when looking both ways then shooting out and uncontrollably swerving. The car comes up on a four-way intersection fast and the husband's drunken eyes notice white lights converging at the crossing.

The husband's mouth drops open in a scream when his wife slows, pumping brakes fast when swerving halfway into the road, barely missing the T-bone crash.

The other car comes to a screeching halt, and the driver's hand goes hard on the horn, non-stop for seconds.

His wife brings the car up to top speed, flying under an overpass, and making a sharp turn when gunning the engine with the odometer needle dropping from the dash and the tailpipe burning red hot until smoking black.

The husband's gun-loaded hand grips against the door and a pissy drunk smile glows as he watches the dashed highway lines turn solid when going even faster.

Another call comes from the sheriff's house when Hank and the blonde pick up instantly moaning and then breathing harder again with the sheriff's muffled and gagged screams in the background until the dial tone blares in the sheriff's wife's ear.

The sheriff's face turns red, and he screams in an even higher, muffled tone.

Dallas steps off and pulls back the curtains, looking out along the quiet street where there is complete silence for a long time. Dallas drops the curtains and motions to Hank when they walk off, standing in the corner, whispering a plan.

The door to the cells opens, slowly.

Hank turns immediately, motioning the five men out, and the men walk by giggling, seeing the sheriff's looney tune drawers and his red, angry, jerking face, and stern eyes which closely follows them as they pass.

The sheriff finally screams muffled words, motioning the jailbirds to do something, but they quickly exit and go about their business.

"Well..., let's get out of here!" Dallas says, rumbling through cabinets until finding the sheriff's secret stash of moonshine when pulling out two shot glasses and booze; staining one with the blonde's lips and setting both highly visible near the front door. Dallas cut off certain lights, making the room romantic and cozy.

Hank locks the door, and they take off, cutting between two vacant buildings.

A car's tires squeal out of nowhere, and an engine revs as a car straightens and slides, burning a long rubber trail when stopping in front of the jail and behind the sheriff's car.

The sheriff's wife's watery eyes wander over the dark jailhouse windows with fast swiping hands continuously wiping tears. She blows for a spell then flings the door open, pulling out a custom-made shotgun. She blows again, donning her little hunter's cap; adjusting her oversized plaid shirt, shoulder strap, and suspenders supporting her manly jeans when loading two shells. She slowly approaches the back of the sheriff's car and stops, hearing mild car tires squealing when Dallas' car breaks out from a dark alley several buildings away. She ducks alongside the sheriff's car when Dallas' turns deep with his hubcap popping off when swerving on the straightaway.

The sheriff's wife peeks out spotting fast fading tail lights, and stays down, listening longer. Her head finally pops up, then drops down, hearing more distant tires squealing until coming up, creeping to the front door, pulling on the handle, and finding it locked. She peeks in the window, finding the switchboard unmanned with lights flashing when a loud ring comes, and her eyes wander to the counter, discovering the liquor, two half-filled shot glasses, and one heavily stained with red lipstick.

The sheriff maneuvers when seeing the top of her cap with her big wig sticking out on both sides when it hugely projects a shadow on the wall. Her forehead presses into the window and he screams in a muffled voice below the loud ringing phone.

The sheriff's wife presses her ear to the window, hearing what sounds like moans when drawing closer but immediately backs away. She soon hears tire squealing and a high-speed engine when finally seeing bright white headlights veering around the corner.

The gun toting couple's car comes into view, with the front raised as if high on hydraulics.

The sheriff's wife backs up, easing closer to the side of the jail when a loud and crazy, bird call comes.

The old woman sits with a steady aim, firing a delayed shot near the corner of the building where the wife's body had just vanished. She takes another unsteady aim when blazing on automatic alongside the jail, barely missing the sheriff's wife when she dives, low-crawl against the building and into a deep indentation.

The old couple's car speeds off, going several buildings away when tires squeal as the car slings around, and wheels spin fast when coming up on the jail, with the wife yelling for her husband to blaze.

The sheriff's wife listens to the loud engine then backs further into the structure. She takes cover, listening to more gunfire, and then squeals when seeing concrete spray from the stoned architecture into a cloud of dust and mist. She leans down and then drops off in the high grass, firing two cannon-like booms when accidentally flipping the gun on safety and sliding it to her side.

The old couple's car increases speed, going further while screaming and looking over their shoulder when the car slings around and she pulls over to the curb where they sit, senselessly laughing while reloading. "Just like old-time television, Bonnie and Clyde, hey Jeb?" the wife hollers, almost cross-eyed.

The sheriff's wife backs up, reloading and dropping one shell in the grass when coming up on the side window near the sheriff's desk.

The old man watches his wife reload her last round while pulling out his premium chewing tobacco and stuffing his gums.

"Hittem and gettem, Babe!" the wife shrieks, spinning the loader and accidentally kissing the hot barrel, and screaming while backing off the mildly sizzling steel, and expressly fanning. "I'm gonna get me some butt for real now..., done made me burn my darn lips!" she shrieks with a not-too-happy face.

The husband turns, chuckling and trying hard not to laugh at her. "Let's get em', Babe!" he finally yells, spitting and smearing tobacco juice over the back passenger window and alongside the door as she steps into the gas.

The sheriff's wife's vision clears, and she finally sees the operator bent over with her husband behind her when slamming the barrel against the window, going numb.

Tires continually squeal with everything the engine has to offer.

The phone rings in the jailhouse, but the sheriff's wife is still in a trance with the ringing falling on deaf ears, and hearing nothing when slamming the barrel against the window frame again when the phone stops ringing.

The sheriff and operator wiggle hard and manage to turn with wide, glowing eyes when staring down the barrel, watching the wife's face transform with a murderous scream when shaking.

The sheriff's wife presses hard on the trigger, but nothing, when the sheriff's eyes expressly wander to the safety latch. Her eyes drop to the safety with her thumb removing it when taking another aim when distracted by a fast revved then slow running engine when tires squeal and bright, white lights flood the alley.

Guns stick out from both car windows, and then two more stick out when the couple leans halfway out, screaming for her to drop her weapon.

The sheriff's wife waves the gun high, releasing it, and drops down when the gun prematurely fires. She scoots under the car, quickly gripping the bumper with both hands, and without warning, the couple responds with more blazing until their hammers continually click on empty, in the smoked-out alley.

The sheriff's wife's hands come high over the hood, trembling.

The couple's shaky hands point their guns with frowns until finally recognizing her big hair when her cap falls off.

The old man eases out with the empty gun drawn until lowering it.

The sheriff's wife grips her gun and runs to the window, pressing the trigger while screaming and the trigger loudly and continually clicks.

The old woman's husband drops onto the hood, stoned, and slowly slides off.

The old woman sprints to the window, peeking inside. "They got the sheriff and Betty tied up! I told you those non-American masked men were here!" she happily shrieks, looking over the grim-looking yet cozy office until finally spotting the drinks.

On Friday, after dinner, Boogey and Nattie watch television until nodding off, but a soft ring turns loud, bringing them out of their sleep.

Boogey's run-down boots shuffle across the grit-covered run-down wood floor, fighting to stand on long legs after coming out of the deep-sunken, busted spring couch, which has his circulation cut off.

Nattie leans forward in the crooked chair, staring at the clock with a frown.

Boogey grasps the phone, pushing it tight. "Yello (hello)!" he sluggishly answers.

A deep, manly voice mumbles for minutes then rattles on for minutes.

Boogey flips on a dim light, scrambling over the table for a pen, and then seizes a sealed envelope, scribbling. "Ok, call it to me, again," he says, going quiet when meditating on what he had scribbled. "And you think it's a good one, huh?" he asks, writing the last number more legibly. He leans back, looking at the dusty clock, and the phone drops, realizing he only has ten minutes before the lottery closes out.

The phone bounces on the long cord until banging lightly against the wall and dangling inches from the floor.

The busted screen door flies open, loudly banging against the house before retracting halfway on rusty, stretched springs when Boogey's boots leap from the top step, hitting the dusty trail.

"Ole fool!" Nattie shrieks, walking to the screen door and finding a trail of dust rising while shutting it and then rushing to the phone. "Wint! Wint!" she shrieks. "Hello! Who da (the) heck is it?"

Winton quietly giggles, refraining from answering.

"I know this ain't nobody but yo (your) trifling behind, Wint! Speak up like you got a pair!" she shrieks, intimidating him.

Winton holds the phone longer, covering the mouthpiece tighter and senselessly giggling when Nattie tears him a new one until he slams the phone down.

Nattie covers Bud's cage, enraged when sitting and breathing hard. Her foot anxiously pats as she thinks back on all the debt when rushing off, looking in the cupboard, finding the last five-dollar bill gone.

Nattie settles in the chair, ruffling through stacks of bills bundled with rubber bands when patting down the cluttered desk for the old calculator. She walks to the refrigerator, pulls out two AA batteries, inserts them, and begins adding up the bills.

Minutes later, she sees Boogey and hears his boots slapping against the steps.

Boogey slowly opens the door and peeks inside, finding Nattie punching furiously at the numbers.

"What are you doing, Ma?" he asks in a soft tone to calm her.

"What da heck do you think Imma (I'm) doing?" she asks, frowning. "Trying to make these dollars make some sense," she says, sarcastically.

Boogey bursts into laughter. "Oh…, you mean, make cents make dollars, right?"

"Ohh!" she shrieks. "No…, like I said…, make these dollars…, these dollars…, makes sense because the money we have and don't have, make no sense with what we owe," she says, cutting her eyes back over at Boogey.

Boogey looks dumbfounded as hidden, silent tear drops. "Our day will come soon. I can feel it because it's promised…, we're going to hit, and you can have the world."

"Listen at you…, your brain is full of malarkey! Yeah…, you and a million other dreamers out there are going right down the tubes behind a darn lottry (lottery) dream. Y'all dreaming of hitting while spending your last on an unreachable dream; living day-to-day to make a dollar out of ten cents."

The room goes silent for seconds. "Ma, I tell you, this lottery thing…," Boogey says, turning from her in deep thought.

Nattie stares at the back of his head, covering her ears and closing her eyes. "La la la, la la la, la la la, la la la," she continually exclaims as if it is a long, joyful song.

"Ok…, I see…, so you wanna be rude, huh?" Boogey screams, raising his voice even louder when looking back.

"La la la, la la la, la la la," she continually exclaims even louder until totally tuning him out when he grows pissed, walking out and slamming the screen door.

Boogey goes around the house, pours a small mason jar of moonshine, and then comes around to the front, easing onto the steps.

Nattie grows even more pissed when finding him drinking. She walks to the screen door undetected and stays quiet while steaming until unable to keep quiet. "Look…, my life was easy until you: A-1 credit, apartment, car…, hell, I had it all, and look at me now! I moved into this run-down shack because of what; a dream? A dream you planted in my head so long ago; a dream of a big house with a white picket fence and a little dog. Well, heck, even the dog is mangy; the fence well, it's busted all to hell with only two good pegs left, and the house…, let's not even discuss that, shall we? I'm almost convinced…, you can't do anything right, Boog!"

Over at Winton's, Winton sits at home in the dark, anxiously patting his foot while waiting for Nelle to bring the car back.

Soon, headlights shine on the house, and he slumps, pretending to be asleep.

The door flies open, and the kids run in, hurrying past as if he isn't even there.

Nelle eases two bags on the counter and takes off her coat, putting things away. She eventually drops onto the couch beside him when his eyes shoot open, yawning, until sitting and looking at his watch, when he begins lacing his boots. "I thought you were in for the night," Nelle says, reaching for the television remote.

Winton sits clueless for seconds. "Oh..., I'm out of smokes." He reaches for the keys, kisses her and heads for the door. He swings by the store and then the junkyard to talk to a friend who works a double shift as a crush operator. Winton pulls up minutes later, blows, flashes his bright lights, and pulls into the junkyard.

Suddenly, two coverall covered bodies secretly cross behind Winton's car, and they run as swiftly as they can by the crusher.

One hides behind a pile of crushed cars, and the other climbs into the operator's booth.

Winton blows and then makes his way by the crusher, where he sometimes finds his friend when making his way down a narrow path. He turns near another pile of crushed cars, and then proceeds to the crusher, not knowing he's directly under the staged giant magnet crane.

The loud crusher engine grows in Winton's ears when his window comes down, and he looks around until leaning into the horn again.

Winton's friend stays kneeled, moving levers until the magnet is dead-center when lowering the magnet and stopping it when the cables make a whiny noise.

The wide plate lowers more until inches from Winton's roof while the operator waits for Winton to look away, but he doesn't, so he invisibly throws a metal bar against a few closely stacked cars.

Winton looks in the direction of the bang, and his body slumps and shakes as the magnet attaches and lifts the car, stealthily, startling Winton. "Ahhh!" Winton shrieks, peering over the door with tears filling his eyes as he continually looks down, screaming louder. "Ahhh!" he continually shrieks for as long as possible when refilling his lungs and letting off another continual, loud cry.

The guy brings the car up fifty more feet until it lunges forward, slightly swings in circles around the crane's base, three good, complete turns, then rocks back and forth and side to side for minutes until almost stable.

Winton finally hears a scream and wipes his teary eye, finding his friend standing in the booth, waving and laughing.

Winton's balled fist extends out the window, followed by his middle finger until a big smile grows upon realizing he is now only five feet high.

The tires barely touch the ground, and Winton finds his friend climbing out of the chair when the car fully rests on its shocks.

Winton follows his friend, jumping when hearing a different sound and immediately finding the high metal wall coming up over the doors when trying to open the door. He spots his friend in a mad dash and playfully screaming until fading behind the wall.

The main operator motions his coworker to start the crusher then runs to the crusher, pulling out a disposable camera before climbing up the ladder, well hidden.

The loud, hydraulic doors jerk and a loud audible alarm sounds.

Winton finds the big steel doors closer and tries to open the door again but can't when screaming with his face torn up with more tears when screaming louder.

The double doors fold, and the operator bends, laughing until pulling himself together, then lowers the crusher more until it touches the roof and jerks the car.

Winton's face fills with tears, and a murderous scream comes with Winton's face torn up more.

A second flash of light causes him to straighten his face when finding his friend shooting a roll of disposable film and giggling half-stoned.

The alarm stops, and the machine slowly unfolds, then shuts down as laughter loudly grows.

The men climb up on the platform, in view as the two crusher doors fold completely open.

Winton sits shaking his head, continually wiping his tears when cranking the engine fast, hitting the gas, and speeding out, leaving the men on their knees in laughter and a plume of dust.

In Fikesville, winds begin to pick up within the hour, and rain pours hard until almost blowing sideways.

Boogey sits with more pleasant things and good times with Nattie on his mind until giggling. Fearful of thunder and lightning unless drunk, Boogey goes into a deep trance, thinking about her heart-thrashing comments when shaking his head.

A sudden burst of thunder causes him to spring for the bedroom door, breaking his neck to get through the door after two quick and sharp flashes of lightning.

Nattie cuddles near the headboard when a second hit startles her and causes her to clench the pillow tight.

Boogey's heart races as he stands with his back against the bedroom door as more bright flashes come with heavy thunder. "Man! I forgot to get soap," Boogey says, looking up at the clock when another bright flash comes.

"As bad as that thunder and lightning are right now; just wait until morning," she says, scared to be alone when curling up tighter and peeking over at the clock.

"Who's to say it won't be worse then?" Boogey says, jumping when the sudden, sharp lightning and thunder come again. He stares at the clock, realizing he has twenty minutes before the lottery closes.

"Well, wait to see if it slacks up," she says, fearfully giggling. "You have twenty minutes, huh?" She intentionally glances at the clock longer, shaking her head.

"There you go again…, always thinking someone wants to play a daggone number!" he says, picking up the wad of cash from the dresser.

Her eyes follow the money, which he balls tightly in his fist and pushes deep into his pocket. "If you're not playing, then take just enough for the soap and leave the rest," she says, peeking and then jumping when lightning flashes again.

"You ain't said nothing but a thang, butta (butter) bean!" he senselessly exclaims, reaching in his pocket and secretly peeling off a few extra dollars. "Ok…, here it is…, soap is three, so one, two, three, and four with taxes," he exclaims, leaving the rest.

"Huh…, I know it is killing you." She quickly puts her head under the covers when a mild flash and a heavy boom come. Nattie hears him enter and walk by the bedroom door twenty minutes later.

Boogey listens to see if she is still awake when calling out to her but gets no answer, so he tiptoes and then staggers into the kitchen, trying to keep from hearing Nattie's mouth about eating late and being low on cash for groceries.

Nattie lies there listening to each light squeaky floorboard until he slows near the worst boards which she knows are by the refrigerator.

Boogey stands with his hand over the switch, leaving the lights off, noticing the kitchen's night light still on.

"Boogey, you know good and well that you don't need to be eating late! You always complaining about your weight!" she yells, lowering her head and listening.

"Well, forget that!" he says, listening to his stomach continually growl.

Nattie jumps up, tying her robe tightly and peeking out. "Yeah, forget that when you're fat as a champ!" she says standing behind the door, swaying and mocking how he would look overweight when poking out her jowls and moving her arms from side to side as if wobbling.

The phone startles Boogey, and he answers to find Winton begging for money. "What? A hundard (hundred) dollars!" Boogey says loud, then again in a whisper and slurred tone. "Hell, man…, I ain't got no cash on me like that!" he whispers, looking swiftly over his shoulder.

Winton continually pleads, until realizing Boogey isn't breaking when ending the call.

Instantly, Boogey's mind drifts back to the sandwich, when pulling out peanut butter and opening the fridge for jelly. He makes a thick, sloppy sandwich and then slaps the bread together, laying the sandwich on the table and pulling out a chair.

Boogey quietly opens the refrigerator, looking over his shoulder, accidentally pulling out the expired milk Nattie left for buttermilk biscuits. He pours a glass then opens the freezer, pulls out the ice tray and twists and turns until a few cubes drop, then places the milk in the fridge, settling down. He smiles at the hearty sandwich, winking and playfully whispering to it when lighting into it, and minutes later, licking his fingers before the last bite. He leans the chair on both hind legs, relaxing, and stares at the ice-cold glass with thick condensation and dense spots on the ice.

Boogey hears Nattie again, so he swiftly grabs the glass, gulping half down with jowls instantly filled when leaning forward, blowing chunks across the table, and tilting the chair back, falling against a low-cut cabinet.

A thick, wooden, rolling pin drops from the cabinet, rolling under the table and to the other side when Boogey braces his fall, losing his grip, but falls flat on his back, kicking and waddling fast.

Boogey stands, and lightning and thunder hit so hard that he stumbles, losing balance. He falls forward with fingers slipping down, inside the toaster, and his weight presses down when letting off a loud scream from the heat at his fingers.

Boogey's other hand accidentally flies out, hitting the stove's pilot knob, turning a burner on high, when his hand goes over his head and against a cabinet, causing him to lose his drunken balance. He slams against the unstable wall cabinet, and the left frame unleashes glasses and dishes, which roll-off, smashing to the floor, one at a time, as leftover grease in the skillet on the stove heats faster.

Boogey staggers, turning on his heels until dancing fast on the rolling pin, one heel after another until falling back into another flimsy cabinet and then flat on his back. He immediately freezes, tensed when staring up at the bag of flour rocking for seconds when speedily falling and bursting in his face. "Shucks!" he shrieks.

The bedroom door flies open, and Nattie rushes in with big, green rollers and cream smeared over her face; one hand holding up busted elastic drawers. "Ahh!" she shrieks, looking at the debris and white mess all over the floor and Boogey's face. Her eyes wander to the lopsided wall rack and then her deceased grandmother's China, sprawled in pieces over the floor, finally realizing the room is filling with smoke.

Boogey's slurred speech mumbles a few unknown words as he fights to stand when the bubbling cast-iron skillet pops with water and dish detergent Nattie had put in earlier to dissolve the grease burst, and a fireball springs upward.

"Ahh!" they scream, jumping back when Boogey springs into action.

Nattie stands screaming while Bud mocks her with his cage excitedly bouncing.

Boogey thinks quickly, grabbing a kitchen towel when inching to the stove, and backing off several times, screaming like a female. He sees the fire die down a little and rush up, reaching for the metal handle with bare hands; a towel unknowingly draped over his arm when lifting it with searing heat setting in. "Ahhh!" he finally shrieks with a fast growing painful face when dashing the skillet forward with grease splashing in the windowsill and on the curtains; setting them ablaze.

Nattie runs for the bathroom, holding her drawers tight in one hand while straddling and returns, dashing a pail of water in the window. She expressly makes each trip with her drawers, working their way down until running out of them and standing, kicking them off.

Boogey's hand throbs while nippily wrapping it in a towel and seizing the handle while the fire is still blazing hot. He flings the door open, kicking the screen wide and lunging grease accidentally on the dog that lets off a pained, aching yelp 'Arrp..., Arrp!' and runs off. "Oops!" Boogey groans covering his mouth with wide gazing eyes trailing the dog until he vanishes in tall weeds.

Nattie runs to the door, breathing harder than ever when taking deep breaths after seeing everything is under control when frowning. She stays in total silence and Boogey in total embarrassment.

There is even more silence as they look the kitchen over and begin cleaning up as much as possible without a single word.

Afterward, Nattie heads for the bedroom, locking the door.

Boogey climbs on the sofa, curling up and grabbing a throw.

The following morning, Boogey and Nattie sleep in, but Nattie is the first to start moving around while Boogey embarrassingly pretends to be asleep with his back turned and eyes open, listening attentively.

Boogey soon hears the door open and squints with one eye closed tight.

The phone rings, and Nattie answers in a deep voice on the third ring. "Hello!"

"Yes, Tom's Rental, for John or Nattie," the bill collector utters in a nasty tone.

"Who? Ron and who?" she asks, faking a hearing problem.

"No, ma'am, John or Nattie," he says, pressing the phone tighter.

"Ugh..., Ron and Maple? Ah..., ah..., ah..., you have the wrong number," she says, chuckling.

"Hugh...," he responds with squinty eyes and a slightly tilted head, listening more carefully until hearing the too familiar bird whispering in the background until repeating Nattie's last comment like a broken record. "Well you look here..., this is Eddie Hauser, so stop playing on the phone, Mrs. Johnson! We need payment by close of business today, or we will pick up that black-and-white set come Monday...!" he rattles on before going quiet. "We thought you two were honest people when you came up in here for credit," he says, recalling knowing Nattie since she was a child and her honest parents. "So tell me..., what freakin' part of the game is that?" he shrieks, apoplectic before making more degrading comments, including an even more degrading one about her mother, when slamming the phone down.

Nattie's face turns fire-engine red when blasting back with words worse than a seasoned Sailor; cursing and getting all her slanderous remarks out about the man's entire family when taking a deep breath and finally noticing the dial tone growing louder.

Over at Rev's brother's house, Rev walk in and everyone grows quiet. He stares and then leads into a prayer. "Ok, the Book of John," He rapidly runs his finger over a few verses when questions come back-to-back as he folds his hands.

"Now, some think they're spiritual if their Bibles are tagged or color-coded. Some get success, and it seems instant. Take an athlete who starts as a kid; motivated by self-motivation or pushed by others who have a strong influence or personal gain.

Some get fame sooner than others because some of us are like those in the Bible. What could have taken a very short time sometime end up taking years. Many of us try to do it on our own and others with God first; trusting that HE will bring it to us or take us through it. Some do the same thing and depend on different results, but most of all, people always want things fast, but anything received fast goes fast.

You have to pay attention to your fleshy body because it's trying to cooperate with the enemy who has one goal, and that's to kill you. The flesh..., well, it wants and feels; sometimes it wants to stay up when you should be asleep, or vice versa. Oh yeah, Satan has a full workday of distractions if you submit to him.

Satan wants to destroy us as little children when we're the weakest vessel. Some things he even gets us tied up in aren't our doing, but people perceive they are, and later in life Satan finds a way to confirm a lie from your youth to bind you. Think about when bad things happen to people; the first thing they want to do is blame God. I mean, come on, people! This is Almighty God! We are not even worthy of questioning HIM, because we're nothing but dust from which we shall return.

God is not a puppet that every time Satan leads one of your loved ones astray, HE should run, putting out fires. Besides, if that were the case, HE would be a fireman and a laborer of Satan. Then again, there are some who rise to the occasion of trying to play God, but God is God alone! Oh, let's not forget the senseless gangbanging. One thing they fail to forget is the possibility that they may kill one of God's anointed! Woe to that man! Also, when one sheds blood on this Earth, the Earth shall require their blood," Rev utters, finding several bright eyes.

And there is one more thing..., everyone claims to want to go to Heaven when they die, but no one is willing to make preparations. Fact..., your day will come, so stop making the internet your insurance plan. Burial insurance is only pennies a day so stop leaving this burden on your loved ones.

And hear me on this one..., learn to apply the gift God blessed you with; your brain. Stop living off of fleshly desires and assess what those fleshly desires have brought you thus far; pain, grief, and if it hasn't yet, it's coming.

Have you considered life's processes? It all seems to be geared around making the cut; job, sports, store closures, relationships, college entry, college exits, the list is endless, and it even seems that way with getting into the Pearly Gates."

Rev eyes a kid in the back staring into space. "And finally, for the life of me..., I don't know why people look for signs when God said there will be no more signs. Have you ever thought about why? Maybe, because all his creation is a sign and it's right before your eyes; all you have to do is open your eyes and ears..., yeah, it's just that simple, but you resist even something as simple as that...; well until the doctor tell you that you only have so much time left on HIS green Earth.

Take Ecclesiastes 8:6 - because there is time and judgment; therefore, man's misery is great upon him. Hey..., you are going to have some misery! What about the evil, good if any? You have either been going through something for sure or it is to come. Was it from this or that in the past? You thought you got through without judgment over time? God's wrath we can't stand and can't endure, so HE...; now this is just my thinking so don't quote me..., but HE issues it a little at a time, having Mercy on us. So, as a youth, do the things you do with caution because there will come a day that HE will judge every action. Let everyone stand!"

Over at Boogey and Nattie's, Nattie deflects more bill collectors.

Suddenly, Boogey is awakened, hearing the bird cage-rattling when lying there smelling hickory-smoked bacon.

Nattie removes the cage's cover then heads for the room, closing the door and tapping Boogey's shoulder. "Your food is on the stove," she exclaims, tightening her robe and walking away.

Boogey sits, looking around before dressing and dragging his feet toward the kitchen. His eyes wander over the gloomy kitchen, fixating on the burnt curtains and soot-covered roof. He eases into his chair, thoroughly inspecting the food until sniffing, then holding the plate up and lightly tilting it toward the light when looking back, making sure Nattie isn't standing there. He digs into the piping hot meal until hearing something at the door, finding the sad dog with large sections of singed hair.

Boogey looks for minutes with sad eyes, until carrying over a plate, and unlatching the door, but the dog turns, fearfully looking back and sprinting when Boogey swings the door open. Boogey's eyes follow the dog off into the tall weeds, when he sits, finishing his meal until chomping down on the last bite of bacon when a horn blows. He leans the chair on hind legs past the door frame, dropping forward fast then stands, pushing his chair under the table when shuffling for the door.

Nattie eases from the bed, pressing her ear to the door.

Boogey squints, trying to figure out who it is, until unlatching the screen and easing out on the porch, listening when the mild music lowers.

"Hot dog! If it ain't ole Boogey Johnson!" the medium-built man says, easing out of the passenger side and brushing down fresh, new threads before tilting his slick brim.

"That sho (sure) is a nice set of wheels you got there, mister!" Boogey says, trying to make out the guy when Winton and two other men jump out, laughing.

"It's me..., Melley..., Mell from the Daily Free Press, Babe!"

"Ahh man! Show me some love, babe! Man, it's been years since I've seen your ole trifling tail!" Boogey wobbles down the steps to greet him while thinking back on the dirty prank he had played on Melley to make them break friendship.

"Boogey, did you put money on the numbers last night?" Winton anxiously asks, standing next to Melley and the other two neatly dressed gentlemen.

"Don't be a fool, Wint! If you gave it to me, and I played it! You used to be the dunce in school, but hell..., don't be the last man standing with the dunce hat on, main (man)," Boogey says, making the others laugh with his jive talk.

"Well, did you?" Winton asks again but with more nervous excitement.

"Heeellll yeah! Did you?" Boogey asks, growing a little more excited when finding a camera in the car and overly excited when Winton reveals a newspaper out of nowhere, anxiously flapping it open and fanning it in Boogey's face.

"Ugh, ugh..., see, Nelle's silly behind had left with the car, so by the time I got there, the lottery was closed, but if you played, then we're rich, Babe!" Winton yells with a sly grin when hesitantly rocking back and forth then lunging into Boogey's arms with his arm around his neck.

Boogey bows heavily forward from his weight, letting him slip until Winton's arms flop tighter around Boogey's neck. Boogey strains harder to support Winton's weight until his arms go forward, releasing him flat on his butt. "Oh, sorry, Wint!" he cheerily declares when leaning forward to help him up when Winton frowns and the three men burst into great laughter.

They continually stare down at Winton, pointing and still grinning while sipping on the moonshine being passed around in a flask.

Winton springs up and the four smile and continually glow as if up to something, but Boogey is too excited to catch on.

Everyone except the driver heavily sways and somehow freely stands until swiftly leaning into the car.

Boogey's heart races, and he feels he's about to explode, but remains calm.

Winton flashes the newspaper again, and the low up-tempo beat from the car's radio drifts into Boogey's ear when he looks at Winton, embracing him in the semi-cradle position, dancing up dust like a pure fool.

Nattie hears the fracas and eases into the recliner near the door to get an earful when finally able to make out what they are saying when smiling. Her heart fills with joy, and she daydreams of things she wants when turning on the television, adjusting it just below their loud voices.

Boogey releases Winton, reaching for the newspaper and opening it. His eyes ogle across the line of zeroes when breaking off, dancing the jig and a few other unfamiliar dances that leave the men in tears.

"How about a story for the paper, Boogey?" Melley, his rival-turned-instant friend today, utters.

"Sure thing, main (man)!" Boogey declares with the biggest smile ever.

Melley interviews Boogey, taking a couple of pictures, and then recaps his words on a notepad. "Tell me, $5,000,000..., what will you do with it, Boog?" Melley asks, mischievously smiling.

Boogey first mentions the bill collectors and cars until rattling on for minutes, naming a laundry list of the first things that come to mind.

The men ease over to the step, listening and drinking as much as possible while Boogey talks up a storm before Melley mentions having a dinner to attend.

Within thirty minutes, they soon load up and bid Boogey a farewell.

"Sucker!" Melley mumbles as the car began to turn near the porch. Melley looks through the side-view mirror, adjusts it, and brings Boogey's happy feet and dancing body into view, and the three join in the laughter but Winton's heart drops, knowing he has betrayed family and his best friend; his first cousin.

The car stops at the road, and everyone looks back, finding Boogey waving and still doing some ridiculous dance when the four hands rise; two on each side, waving as they burst into heavier laughter, but Winton sits, looking sad.

"Remember our agreement, Wint! Not a word of this or you'll owe me double!" Melley whispers, looking back at Winton while taking puffs to relight his cigar.

"Scout's honor, but you know I'm no scout!" Winton declares, unconvincingly.

"Wint! Now you look ah, here! A deal..., is a darn deal, so don't go wimping out on me now!" Melley yells with his eyes cut back until grabbing another ten to seal the deal and put a smile on Winton's face.

Boogey keeps his eyes on the car until it flies past the general store and fades behind the tree line.

"Sucker, remember our deal! Sucker, remember our deal!" Bud repeats over ten times, but it falls on deaf ears because Nattie and Boogey are too excited. Bud stays quiet longer then whispers. "Sucker, remember our damn deal!"

Nattie finally hears Bud curse and rushes up, slipping soap in his mouth, when catching him off guard while he's still looking at Boogey in a daze.

"Plu! Plu!" Bud sounds off, trying to get the unpleasant soap taste out. "Plu! Plu! Plu!" Bud continues when scarfing up seeds and downing most of the water.

Boogey locks the door and turns.

"We're rich!" Nattie screams, lunging into Boogey's arms as they fall back into the rocking chair, crumbling it and lying there laughing until Nattie stands and extends her hand to help Boogey up.

Boogey jumps up, hearing a favorite jingle on television, and breaks out in the Pee-Wee Herman looking dance and a few other awkward dances as Nattie dances and does the stinky leg dance and a few other dances that didn't look too familiar.

They continue dancing, then slap high fives and do other arcane handshakes and then do whatever dance they like, worry-free and as hard as possible.

Nattie bends over, and Boogey inches from behind, working his butt as if intimate when easing closer and spanking her butt when Nattie assumes the football hiking stance with her booty moving fast. There comes a loud slap when Boogey slaps her hard this time, and it stings.

Bud looks over on the next smack, and his eyes brighten. "Ooh! Naw! Naw! Naw! Heck naw! Didn't I tell you before? That's just plain nasty!"

Boogey and Nattie freeze, then fall in each other's arms, laughing, hugging, kissing, and jumping around.

Nattie grabs a handful of bills from the table, ripping and throwing them high in the air.

Boogey joins in, easing over to the door, dancing around until seizing a baseball bat, and taking a few Louisville slugs at the television until it is demolished. In their folly, everything they owe money on, they smash beyond recognition. "We'll show those bill collector's whose boss!" Boogey says, laughing when slamming the bat down so hard that the coffee table breaks in half. He continually swings on things until he's almost out of breath when throwing the bat to the floor, shuffling over to the kitchen and a seat.

They sit at the table, pulling out a pen, paper, and calculator, and get serious, when figuring out future purchases and expenses. They begin listing everything they want or want to do, and when done, figure they will still have over two million left.

"Yeah, that's good," Boogey utters, looking over the hundred-page list. "We need to save some for our little future nest, and let's not forget Bud; it's about time we get him a little playmate, you know a companion," he says, walking to the cage. "Look at my little Bud! You want a lover too, huh, Bud?" Boogey says, looking at Bud excitedly shaking his head 'yes' before whistling.

Boogey and Nattie ease back down, adding a few other things, then a few estimated costs for trips, before noting that Bud needs a companion and a new cage.

Nattie wanders out and back into the kitchen.

Boogey sits longer, repeatedly going over the sheets.

Nattie pulls out her secret stash from a mason jar, unraveling wadded bills and adding them up; coming up with five hundred dollars put away for hard times.

Before long, they sit, planning what to do for the evening, when Nattie goes into deep thought. "Hey, let's get the best room at that new bed and breakfast near I-99 and show them how bigwigs do it up; la vida loco, babe!" she says, letting down her long hair and pinning it in a way that gets Boogey hot and bothered.

They rush to get dressed in their best attire, which looks like it's been run through the mill, then pack a few things and call a taxi to take them to the thrift store.

They cover the cage and, within the hour, grab their things, hearing the taxi.

"We'll see you later, little buddy," Boogey says, waving to Bud.

"Man, screw you! Sucker..., remember our deal! Remember our deal!" Bud shouts even louder.

"Yes, I will remember our deal, little buddy," Boogey utters, thinking only of the promised companion and new cage.

"Horny-tail bird!" Nattie softly whispers, picking up a smashed, black purse.

"Horny bird..., horny bird.., yak, yak..., yo (your) nappy-head mama!" Bud shouts.

Nattie's head turns, staring at Bud with a weak, trembling eye until Boogey's hand comes to her shoulder, easing her to the door.

Over at Winton's house, Winton finishes smoking a cigarette when looking over at his neighbor's house, discovering him looking back through the screen when Winton jumps with his back to the door. Winton peeks again, finding his begging neighbor walking up when easing the door shut, scrambling to hide his good liquor and leaving the cheap stuff out in the open.

A knock comes, then a too-familiar knock, followed by heavy pounding when the door flies open, with Winton holding the knob tightly with a serious face. "Man! You tryna (trying to) tear the door down?" Winton asks with a more serious frown.

"Hey, man, can I borrow your toothbrush? Naw..., I'm just kidding, but can I get a hit of that liquor?" he asks, pulling a cup from his windbreaker jacket.

"Man, I can't support your habits! Pops always said don't start no habits you can't afford, and it looks like you're definitely a dependent." Winton walks out.

"Dependent? Man, all I asked for is a little liquor, and you take me over the forest and through the freakin' woods over that? See..., I would never do you like that," he responds, clenching the cup even tighter.

"Never do who like that? Man, ever since I've known you, you've been drinking for free. Most grown-tail men at least pitch in but let the fellas come over and pitch in on a drink. Hell..., you walk off like the word money is a damn plague," Winton says, bursting into laughter.

"Ah, man, go on with that crap! Man, you know I'm good for it," John utters, holding out the cup again.

"Look..., this is it! I'm telling you; no more of this free crap! Either you put out or get the hell out!" Winton steps inside and grabs a cheap bottle of booze.

"Aw..., naw..., naw..., hell naw, dude! Man, I ain't drinking that cheap crap! That stuff will make your head bad! Mess around and get a headache you can't get rid of, dude. Shoot! I want the good stuff..., that good, good!" he says, looking at Winton under-eyed and repeating the word 'good' several more times until it sounds like a song when John sways, almost dancing to the words. "Oh yeah..., then take it or leave it!" Winton says, stepping inside and putting the bottle on the counter.

"Come on! Just this last time, I promise," John says, staring through the screen.

Winton stares with a mean look with sweat popping on his forehead. "Look! I am out of the good stuff! I was on my way to restock while out, so you stroll on home, scrape up some change, and have it ready when I get back, Jack!" Winton utters, stepping out and locking the door. He heads for the car, watching his neighbor sadly drag his feet. "Hey, look..., when my wife gets home, tell her I'll be right back!"

Winton eases in the car, pulling away, and stares through the rearview, finding his neighbor peeking, then fading behind a tree and drifting back into Winton's yard. Winton slows and tries to make a U-turn; but instead makes a five-point turn, speeding up, to find his neighbor peeking then jumping in excitement. "Yo! Yo! Yo! What's up with you main (man)?" Winton yells, leaning halfway out the window.

John looks down for seconds then slowly looks up. "Uh, uh, uh..., oh man, I dropped my contact," John says, finally kicking dirt to one side as if looking for something.

"Yeah..., but how are you going to wear contacts and glasses simultaneously?" he asks, looking at the glasses over the head. "Look..., who do you think I am; Sam Sausage Head?" Winton yells, cutting the wheel fast and pulling up in the yard.

"Sho (sure, you are) right, sho right, I almost forgot," he says, finally lifting his glasses and letting them rest on his head again.

Winton watches him walk away, then eases up and parks, walking back inside.

An hour later, a car pulls up, and Winton finds Nelle climbing out of her girlfriend's car.

Nelle walks in, and Winton hugs her, heading for the door.

Nelle looks back disgusted, shaking her head with her hands on her hips. "Winton, where are you going, now? I come in..., you go out, or vice versa," she utters, shaking her head in disbelief again.

"Oh, woman, get off my back..., you straight tripping! Ain't no mess like that going on!" he says, walking out and closing the screen door. Winton stops at the edge of the porch, looks for John, then climbs into the car, tooting the horn.

Nelle soon opens the door peeking out until finding him motioning her over.

He smiles as she approaches. "Hey, look…, keep your eye on that slick ass cat next door," Winton says, pointing at John's house. "I had to turn around just before you got home because he was prowling around like he was casing the joint or going to break into our house."

Nelle looks over her shoulder with a mean stare. "Oh, ok…, I'll stay here until the kids get in from school, then my girl is taking me to get my hair fixed," she says, running her fingers through her knotty hair.

Winton waves Nelle off, pulling forward into the yard, then alongside the house; heading through the backyard, and veering down a dirt path toward a paved road.

An hour later, the kids arrive.

Over at John's, he sits watching television, and his head shoots over his shoulder fast, hearing a horn and finding Nelle's girlfriend's car pulling off. He eases out, rushing across Winton's yard, knocking for seconds until the door finally swings open. He turns from looking behind him, hearing a car pass when staring into Winton's daughter's smiling face. "Hey, hey…, look, your dad told me to stop by for a bottle of liquor, so can you get it for me?" John asks, staring with bloodshot eyes.

Winton's fifteen-year-old daughter coughs, backing away. "Dag…, that smoke sure is strong!" she says, fanning and frowning until up against the cabinet. She turns, looking over the counter, finding the cheap bottle of booze, grabbing it to turn.

John turns back to her with eyes stealthily flowing down until spotting the cheap booze and slowly then expressly shaking. "No, no, no…, I mean…, that is not the right bottle!" he utters, with his forehead pressed tighter against the screen.

Winton's daughter steps away and fades behind the door, reappearing with a half-bottle of top-shelf. "Is this the one you were referring to?" she asks, shocked when hearing him swallow hard.

"Yeah, yeah, baby girl…, now you're talking!" John says, excited. "Exactly…, you hit the nail right on the head…, hey, thanks!" he says, pulling on the screen.

"Psych!" Mama said you would be coming," she yells, laughing and slamming the door. She steps back to the door fast, watching him through the glass until she finally hears him whining with his head down while walking away. The daughter steps to the counter, reach for a cup, then looks again, opening the door, and calling him back. She pours a drink and looks out, watching him sadly dragging himself to the door, reaching for the half-full paper cup. She looks away then leans to shut the door, finding the empty cup stretched forward. "One more and I'll go," he says, staring at her sarcastically rolling eyes when she turns to pour another.

Winton enters the next city, stopping at a red light. He sits humming and anxiously comes out of his seat when spotting the white van and driver who smashed his car. He squints, reading the tags, and turns after the light changes, closely following the swerving van for miles until it turns into a driveway. Winton comes to a perpendicular standstill watching the van vanish down the dirt path and in a bend.

Boogey and Nattie arrive home in a taxi on the other side of town, rushing inside, changing into something nicer.

Hours later, the same taxi pulls up, blowing a few times.

Boogey watches the evening news mysterious disappearance case when the horn comes again and the cabbie leans, looking until seeing movement at the door.

Nattie turns off the television, checking on Bud and covering the cage and then steps onto the porch, and Boogey steps out with their bags, locking up the door.

The heavyset cabbie squeezes out, loading their things while they climb in, then squeezes back inside, looking back with a big smile.

Boogey stares over at the general store when the cabbie pulls up to the street, and his feet start tapping fast until tapping the cabbie's shoulder. "Hey..., pull over so that I can get...!" Boogey starts to say.

"Lottery, right?" the cabbie responds when Nattie shakes her head, laughing.

The cab pulls up at the immaculate bed and breakfast thirty minutes later and Boogey passes him a huge tip, demanding he keeps the fifty-cents change.

Boogey and Nattie step out, staring at the high-rise, fabulous architecture as if they have never seen it before. They gather their luggage and walk up to the electronic doors, greeted by bell boys.

Boogey leads Nattie to the desk, looking at the male clerk's back until he slowly turns, finally recognizing them standing there.

"Afternoon, sir.., ma'am..., how may I help you?" the clerk asks, cheerfully beaming.

"Afternoon, Davillier," Boogey utters, gazing over his shiny nameplate.

"Excuse me, but it's pronounced Da-vil-i-a," the clerk responds, slowly running fingers over each pronounced letter on the tag.

"Oh really? Well, it's spelled D-A-V-I-L-L-I-E-R, so Da-vil-li-er," Boogey responds, smiling. "So, look..., we have a Davillier in the family, so don't you think I know how it is pernounced (pronounced)?"

"Da-vil-i-a..., but anyway, how can I help you, sir?" he responds in a nasty tone, and a sarcastic stare with a genuine hotel welcoming smile.

"A room, Mr. De-Vill-lii-errr," Boogey utters, jokingly dragging out the name just for the hell of it.

The bell boy comes around the corner, reaching for their bags, carrying them to their room while they head over to eat with the bigwigs (wealthy folks).

Boogie and Nattie scroll up to the seating podium, and the hostess turns up her nose as if they are not there; hoping they will go away until looking past them again.

Boogey clears his throat with a nasty stare.

Out of nowhere, another hostess scrolls up, points them to the entrance, and they follow, looking around at folks with their noses up and as if they are peasants.

Boogey and Nattie ease into the plush seats, looking over the menu and ordering the most expensive meals and high-end drinks.

An hour later, Boogey gets loud, then louder after the tenth, strong drink, and becomes belligerent; banging his fork against fine crystal until it shatters. "Hear ye, hear ye, the soon to be the richest man in Fikesville speaketh!" Boogie babbles.

The room grows quiet instantly, and folks lean into each other or other tables, whispering, until gazing at their dingy attire and sluggish postures.

The lead hostess rushes into the huge room from out of nowhere with wide eyes and fast-moving feet. "Excuse me, sir! If you keep this nonsense up, I will have to ask you and your lady friend, here, to leave."

Boogey looks up almost cross-eyed. "Lady, what...? Lady what...? Lady, friend...? Say, wwwhhhaaattt! I beg your pardon, but this hea (here) is my wiiiffeee! And what's your name, sir? Hmm..., let me tell you something..., I'll buy this place next week and have you looking for new employment, you silly trick!" Boogey yells with drunken eyes and one eyebrow cocked.

Nattie sluggishly shrugs her shoulder, adjusting her bosom when somewhat straightening her smashed, dingy hat. "La, la, la, la, la, la...," Nattie continually yells at the top of her voice.

The head hostess's eyes widen, and his face turns blood-shot red. "Please don't be rude, ma'am!" he says in a pleasant tone, trying to get control of the uncontrollable situation.

"La, la, la, la, la, la!" Nattie repeats but even more audible, tuning him out until he points, then waves for other waiters to remove their settings.

Boogey's eyes grow wider in disbelief. "Fine then...! Next week you'll be working for me, sonny boy, or you'll be on hoes row..., or was that skid row? So expect to get hired and fired on the first day!" Boogey pulls out a few dollars, throwing them in the man's face when he balances to stand.

Boogey and Nattie grow into some silly laugh, pointing at folks staring or swaying to chat or looking at them like they are on cheap drugs.

"Impertinent for no reason!" an older gentleman yells with dignity and then leans, whispering to guest at his table.

Boogey rolls up both sleeves, and a loud slap rings out of nowhere when his hand slaps his fast-moving upward arm. "Up your nose with a rubber hose, buddy!" Boogey yells, slamming his hand into his fast-moving arm a second time.

Winton, Nelle, and the kids sit outside Boogey and Nattie's early on Sunday morning, blowing until the dog runs from alongside the house, stopping when he hears Winton slam the flimsy front door.

Winton calls to them when the dog barks and approaches under-eyed, out of view.

The kids whistle then scream when finally seeing the mangy dog running up.

Winton spots the horrifying four-legged creature and runs on the porch in fear, screaming and pounding on the door; causing the dog to run off. He peeks as far as he can alongside the house and keeps his eyes peeled on Nelle and the kids waiting for them to signal or scream. He fearfully leaps off the top step, hitting the dust, almost out of breath, pulling on the door so hard that the handle pops, partially dangling. "What the hell?" he screams, almost breaking his legs, getting inside when hearing an even closer bark with his eyes peeled back to find the dog on the other side of the house and coming up on the car's trunk fast.

Over at the bed and breakfast, sunshine shines through the sheers, and thick, parted, decorative curtains with sweat rolling off Boogey and Nattie's bodies; waking them in heavily soaked, outlined satin sheets.

Boogey eases up, groggy, stumbling over, and turning up the ice bucket of warm water; licking his tongue out while running his hand down the shaft of his neck. "Man, Natt..., it is hotter than Hell up in here!"

"Pour me a glass," Nattie moans, sticking her cotton-mouth dry tongue out while looking at her cheap but expensive-looking broken watch.

"What time is it?" Boogey asks, pouring hers then pulling the bucket to his lips, draining it dry when flipping the air conditioning switch to the coldest setting.

Nattie stares at her watch again, tapping its face and bursting into laughter. "Hell..., this watch hasn't worked in years, but it keeps great time at least two times a day," she utters, laughing, lying her head down and rolling over.

Boogey turns on the television, and the time displays.

Nattie finally notices the clock on the nightstand. "Duh!" She points, smiling and they get a good hangover laugh and then reach for their clothes strewn over the room until they are dressed.

Boogey eases into the chair and calls Winton's house but gets no answer.

They store the rest of their things, call a taxi for church, and arrive an hour late for morning service. Boogey and Nattie ease inside, glowering over the congregation until finding Winton and Nelle in the seventh row and in the middle. They work their way over as close as possible when finding Winton and his family, smiling and nodding while still making it to their seat.

Several people back off with heavy frowns and stares, smelling the strong, old liquor stench.

Others look back and around when getting a hint of the stale odor and frown, shaking their heads in disbelief.

An evil, trembling eye follows the two of them close. "They ought to be ashamed!" an old, senile man sitting behind them says, so many can hear it without disturbing the service. "Been on that stuff all night, now crawling in here to save their worthless Souls!" the old, senile man says louder when looking over at his daughter until jerking; from her shoving and quieting him.

Thirty minutes or so later, the service ends, and everyone watches the pastor make his way to the front door with a deep frown when passing Boogey and Nattie's row.

The second pastor motions folks to stand, and they single-fill out by rows.

Boogey and Nattie finally shuffle up until about fifteen folks away from the pastor, when someone loudly comments on the stench and others frown, looking back with some breaking away from the horrible smell.

Boogey finally takes notice at the commotion and grips Nattie's hand, pulling her out of line and backing up, expeditiously. They rush to the end of the long line.

A female usher waves them back to their spot when Boogey points, pretending they need to go to the restroom. The usher waves again and her pleasant smile turns mean when sharply motioning again with a firm hand until taking off in a mad dash after them.

Boogey and Nattie notice her aggression, walking fast until in a sprint, along the outside aisle. They drift into the back hallway, finding the female in a lean for the door when Boogie pushes it shut, locking it.

A heavy pounding comes; the usher distracting folks who look back with some being nosy when forming more gaps in the line.

Boogey and Nattie rush out the back door, coming around front fast and almost in a jog, finding Winton, Nelle, and the kids loading up. They intercept them with eyes still glued to the front door.

"Hey, you guys!" Winton yells out.

"We came by earlier but got no answer," Nelle says, buckling in their youngest child.

"Where are the other brats?" Boogey asks, finally looking back and finding the pastor pointing and deacons wrestling with the furious female usher until finally getting her in a headlock while she's still throwing jabs and kicking.

"Home being grown," Nelle responds, finally hearing the usher shouting something when the door opens, and she's instantly elbowed and pushed inside by another male usher.

"You missed us because we were out celebrating our new wealth," Boogey utters, smiling with his chest proudly stuck out.

"What? Say again..., new..., what?" Nelle asks when Winton nervously interrupts, secretly shoving her in the back and causing her to bite the tip of her tongue and start licking it to ease the sting.

"You forgot, honey!" Winton says, turning to Nelle, winking to cut her off.

"Oh..., oh...! That wealth..., oh, I see," she responds, pretending to be cheery. "So..., how much?" Nelle anxiously asks without a clue.

"What? About..., hey..., let's talk about this over lunch," Winton says, nervously interrupting again when swallowing hard and staring at the cross on the church's roof, fearing telling a lie on church grounds.

They pile in, and Winton pulls onto the main road leading to the interstate.

Nelle's curious mind goes haywire when anxiously quieting the kids. "So really, how much?" she asks again, looking over the headrest with inquisitive eyes.

"What..., five-million, huh, Boogey?" Winton nervously says with tightly clenched teeth and a heavy chest when swerving back across the yellow line when hearing a horn and seeing a middle finger extend out the window of a long, horn-blowing, passing driver.

"So we hit, too, right, Wint? I mean, you call Boogey nightly with numbers..., right?" Nelle anxiously asks.

Winton unnoticeably grips and squeezes Nelle's hand, winking.

"You can't blame ole Wint here, Nelle. Hell, had you not gone with the car, he would have made it to the sto (store) in time..., I reckon."

"Gone?" she begins to say when Winton pinches her thigh and then strokes it, calming and comforting her.

Later, in town, Rev walks around the supermarket, mixing and matching meals, until distracted when finding three women, family members of a well-known young, punk, gang member, rushing up in tears, when Rev does a double-take.

"Hi Rev," the slain boy's oldest sister says. "Hey..., mama needs a big favor. You see..., Pastor Moore left town right after we left word for him that we needed him for my brother's funeral service, and now we can't find anyone to preach the sermon. Mama asked about every pastor in the phone book, and each of their secretaries claimed their pastor was on vacation. I had no clue that they all went on vacation simultaneously. It must be some kind of retreat or something," she says, looking back to find her mother a ways off and closing slowly with teary eyes.

"Well, there seem to be two problems; one, there are no conferences until next month, nor are there retreats until two months from now, but on the other hand, I'm not ordained; I just teach," he says, putting a can of spinach back. He turns slowly, hearing the mother's sniffle when looking into their fast growing watery eyes.

Rev feels that he needs to speak with the mother one-on-one out of respect, so he pats the daughter's arm. "Excuse me, but may I have a few words with your mother alone?" Rev leads the mother further down the aisle before stopping. "Now, Miss Bliss, out of all respect, ma'am, I pulled you to the side because you seem to be a very reasonable woman," he whispers, patting her hand and looking back at now; two sisters converging and whispering. "First, let me say this..., now you know your son's lifestyle and know he was far from a Saint. Ecclesiastes 8:3 says, 'Be not hasty to go out of HIS sight: stand not in an evil thing; for HE doeth whatsoever pleaseth him. So now, just meditate on that for a second, would you? Now..., with that said..., it would be an honor to speak, but please know that I'm not like some of the others. I will speak only the truth and will not lie."

The mother's eyes widen, immediately and her mouth slowly drops open in shock; speechless for seconds. "Well, I'llllll be...!" she finally says in a mild tone, death stare and a slow, tight balling fist.

The nosy stock clerk stands dusting and minding his business, but the long, drawn-out 'I'llllll be' resonates when looking, moving closer, and making it his best to find out what's going on. He turns his back to them and inches back a few feet, well within a clear listening distance, when turning and finding the woman's crazy stare then heavy frown.

"Absent from the Earth is present with the Lord, but at the Seventh Trumpet; those who haven't labored in the Lord, HE will not know. Now, being a humble man, I said this to say that if you need me, I'm here for you, but I will not dare lie and try and put your son in Heaven," he utters, patting her shoulder when suddenly noticing her over flaring and almost alternating nostrils, and fast changing demeanor when taking a nervous step back.

Miss Bliss's eyes turn fiery red and her fist balls even tighter; sounding like rope under pressure when coming down by her side. Her fingers stretch wide and she tenses, staring deeper into his eyes until cockeyed and looking as if looking through him.

Rev hears another woman talking to her little girl when passing and turns, looking for Miss Bliss's daughters.

The mother's widespread hands lunges as if in a quick draw, sailing forward almost invisible and whistling loud.

The clerk who's looking for job merits in becoming a manager, grabs Miss Bliss firecracker-sounding fist, inches from Rev's face, sounding like a fast softball slammed into a glove. His hand flexes back as if he just caught a professional pitch when shaking off the sting with his mouth torn wide open when slightly dancing around, screaming then moaning.

Rev goes immediately into some crazy move that looks almost like the guy in the movie 'Matrix' when coming up low, then backing off fast when she recoils, veering off this time and driving with all force, tearing through over twenty bags of white flour and going expressly into the cornmeal.

"You heathen! You son of a so-and-so! You ain't no better than my boy! No damn better!" she screams, raising her voice as high as she can when cocking back another white, flour-covered fist to tear off Rev's head.

The daughters rush up, flummoxed yet overly excited, and breathing heavy. "What's going on? What's going on, Ma!" the youngest asks with a hand in her purse and quickly brandishing a knife at her side.

"Calm down, ladies, please calm down..., there just seems to be a little misunderstanding. Now, I apologize if I insulted you in the least, Miss Bliss," Rev says, finding the other daughter gripping a pistol still openly held in her purse.

The clerk hyperventilates and is too excited to see the immediate danger but takes the least resistance when happily directing Rev out of the store.

Back over, at the bed and breakfast, Boogey and Nattie invite Winton and Nelle in for lunch, allowing them to order until their heart's content.

Winton excitedly waits for the right chance to pull Boogey aside and tell him that he found out where the van driver hangs out or lives.

Meanwhile, Nelle sits eating like a starved horse, and the kids mess through more food than the law allows.

The patrons get disgusted at their appearance and how they are carrying on when some excuse themselves and leave or begin talking about them until pointing.

On the other hand, Winton sits so long that he continually thinks about the prank until getting the bubble guts and getting fidgety.

Boogey and Nattie grow more jovial, inviting them to the room and they accept.

Within minutes, the room door flies open and Nelle hits the first three shots heavy and back-to-back, until feeling real good. She begins feeling herself after the fifth when questioning the money again when Winton tenses and suggests leaving.

Boogey grows over-excited. "What..., leave? The day is still young, and the night is ahead. Hey, let's head down to the comedy club," Boogey excitedly suggests, and keeps begging until convincing them.

Later, they head over to the other side of town to drop the two younger kids off and stay there for some time, drinking more.

Hours later, Winton pulls up half a block from the club, jumping out with the door still open. "Hey..., I'll see if they have any seats because it looks pretty packed tonight," Winton says, staring into Nelle's numb and tipsy face.

Winton steps inside minutes later and sees one bouncer; then another he has never seen before and feels relieved, so he heads back to the car. "Hey, they said I have to pay to look inside but assured me there are more than enough seats," he says, lying when looking into Boogey's curious, smiling face.

The four make it through a security checkpoint with no issues.

Nattie and Nelle rush, making their way to the crowded restroom, slightly bumping into one another to get to the mirror.

Minutes later, Nelle steps out of the stall when the cross-dressing bouncer with the hots for Winton drunkenly walks up to the mirror.

The female restroom door swings open, and a young girl sprints up beside the bouncer. "Girl, you're not gonna (going to) believe who just came in...; your, succumbs!" she whispers to the cross-dressed bouncer, who looks in the mirror, beaming. "Honey, see..., I told you he just couldn't resist staying away from all this, and I ain't even given him the eleven-inch sugar cane yet!" he says, smiling when making a crazy hump move with one leg lifted high behind and almost kicking a woman walking by the stall.

Winton and Boogey wait in the second hallway until a mean-looking bouncer motions them into the main room.

The door to the main hall opens, and loud laughter pours out, causing people in line to look toward the door.

Nattie waits for a stall, but the cross-dressing bouncer skips in line, walking past her and Nelle, sticking his nose up.

Nattie giggles and turns, hearing the stall door open. "What's that clown dressing chump doing up in the ladies' room? He needs to be in there taking a piss in the urinal, like a real man," Nattie whispers, giggling slightly over the moderate music.

Nelle goes into tears of laughter. "I know, right? Shucks, now you got to go in here and wipe that brown ball stamp off the seat," she whispers, laughing when Nattie walks into another vacant stall.

The cross-dressing bouncer rushes out, entering the ballroom with his three-girl posse following. He spots Winton, rushing up and grabbing a handful of booty, instantly blowing in Winton's ear and slipping a tongue inside before Winton can turn around.

Winton tenses, nervously looking over the bouncer's shoulder with eyes frantically searching for Nelle and Nattie. "Hey, my family up in here tonight, so lay low, or there's gone (going to) be some shooting up in this mother!"

Sadly, the bouncer looks deeply into Winton's eyes when Winton nods to let him know Boogey is there as well, but Boogey is in deep laughter and heavily swaying from a recent joke.

Boogey is so tipsy that he feels numb, so he can't hear that good and never looks back.

On the stage, the comedian sits on a stool, laughing. "Yall know what I mean, Mundson?" the heavy set white comedian says, waiting for confirmation when more incredible laughter comes.

The cross-dressing bouncer spanks Winton's butt hard and then palms it again, winking when walking off. He spreads his hands wide, playfully pretending to grab a hand full of Boogey's behind when looking back to see if Winton is watching when trying to make him jealous, and finds Winton's hand clenched together with a fast, 'no', headshaking gestures; knowing Boogey would turn the place out.

Boogey notices the bouncer's shoulder-length glossy hair when he passes, and Boogey's eyes wander down to his hourglass shape as he seductively twists. Boogey looks for their women, and then back quickly, getting Winton's attention cautiously, when nudging Winton to get a look when looking again and finally noticing the bouncer's too familiar tattoo. "Uh, uh, uh," Boogey says with his face torn up and a big head shaking off the thought.

The comedian goes on: "Take, for instance, my wife, a fine chocolate bunny, yeah, that's right! You brohams (brothers) can hate all you want, 'cause I'm putting it to a phyne sistah!" His voice fades in the background with laughter from the audience.

Nattie and Nelle walk into the main room, and Nelle nudges Winton, causing him to jump, then nudges Boogey when they drift to the opposite side of the room and find a nice candle-lit table.

The comedian is in tears. "Now, tell me this! Why is it that when a nice-looking woman comes around, my girl's gotta size them up like they're a threat or something?" he says, fading into the background and going on until his theme song comes on, and the commentator comes out, laughing and going on with the show.

They are there a good two hours when Nelle points to her watch, motioning to Winton that it's time to leave.

An hour later, they arrive at the bed and breakfast, where Boogey and Nattie convince them to come in for a nightcap; and they do, sitting and drinking a while longer until Nelle taps Winton, but he keeps talking.

Another hour goes by when Nelle motions and Boogey and Nattie walk them out and bid them a farewell.

Winton pulls off, and Nelle holds her peace for a spell until without warning, hits him square in the chest with a firm backhand fist. "What! They hit, and you forgot to play?" she anxiously asks, confused.

"What? Hit! Hellz (hell) no..., please..., those fools didn't hit anything but a small pot! It's just a debt paid to get us out of a sling with Melley. You know..., the two thousand we borrowed for eight months' rent when we were in a tight."

Nelle instantly reminisces on how uppity Nattie was acting, like a bigshot when her drunken smile turns into a silly laugh, and Winton fights back his laugh, bursting out and weaving over the road.

Boogey and Nattie wake early the following morning, heading for breakfast, and then lounge around, looking over future purchases to see what they missed.

An hour later, Nattie calls for a taxi and the cab drops them at the general store later.

Boogey and Nattie rush inside and up to the register, where the female cashier anxiously runs his ticket, but the ticket flashes a non-winner across the screen.

"Naw..., naw! Rerun it..., rerun it! There must be a glitch or something," Boogey anxiously says with a fast-beating heart sounding in his ears.

The cashier reruns it, but nothing, so she eases it to the counter, and Boogey becomes furious, snatching it and grabbing Nattie's hand, storming out to pay the fare before they cut through the path, walking home.

A strange, black, shiny car pulls up on the main road outside the general store, and two neatly dressed gentlemen sit, watching them.

The cashier hears the machine beep, instantly noticing the network is off-line when rushing outside, and walking to the edge of the store. She sees Boogey and Nattie's front door close and becomes distracted when another customer approaches.

Boogey rushes for the bedroom, pulling out the ticket and matching it with the newspaper Winton had left, as directed by Melley. "I don't understand," he whines, passing the ticket to Nattie.

"Maybe the machine did have a little glitchy, glitch," Nattie playfully responds, trying to reassure him and get him in a more cheerful mood.

Confident with the newspaper article, Boogey leads her to the street, waving down another taxi and asking for a drop off at Kinston Motors.

"Are you sure? Do you want to go to Kinston or Goldsboro?" Nattie asks.

"Definitely Kinston, because Goldsboro has the sucker commercials with the man dressed down in the crazy attire, using his kids to promote business or acting a fool; like that's going to sell cars!" Boogey utters 'non-winners' when getting a good laugh from the cabbie.

Forty minutes later, they pull into the lot, and several associates rush out like a swarm of bees. "May I help you, sir…, ma'am?" two ask simultaneously with other hungry salesmen still approaching in a mad dash.

The strange black, shiny car pulls in, swarmed by sales associates when waving them off.

The driver steps into the gas, speeding off through the over inventoried lot with several associates still barreling through the lot after the car until it shoots out of the lot.

Boogey eyes the black car at the light for seconds in deep thought, trying to recall where he had seen it when digging deep in his pockets, paying the cab fare. He turns to the sales associates with the biggest, cheesiest, and friendliest smile. "We're just looking, but we'll purchase after collecting our lottery winnings."

The more serious-looking salesman does a double-take. "Lottery? My good friend, did you just say…?"

"Yep…, yes I did, and the biggone (big one)," Boogey says, waving the deceptive newspaper and tight-fisted balled ticket.

"Well, I'll be…, now, if that's a fact, you can ride today because we get' er done here at Kinston Motors!"

"Can you, really?" Nattie asks, staring back and over the plush showcase.

"Sure, at Kinston Motors, there's no deal we can turn down!" he recites from a commercial when walking them to the owners' office. He takes them inside and asks them to sit while he goes in and explains to his boss.

Within seconds, the salesman and owner rush out, shaking Boogey and Nattie's hands, speedily congratulating them and asking for credentials.

After validating the newspaper and number, the owner approves the deal, giving them a firm shake, unlimited buying power and turning them over to the salesman.

Boogey and Nattie rush forward with the salesman hot in tow, and within the hour, the salesman catches up, almost out of breath. "What shall it be?" the salesman asks, anxiously rubbing his hands when Boogey and Nattie take off, walking the entire lot again until he catches up, breathless, and they decide.

The salesman pulls the dealer's tags, and they take turns chauffeuring.

The three soon return and head for the office, where Boogey cautiously watches the man fill out the forms when slightly leaning, and overhearing giggling. He leans slightly forward, nosy, when finding a young girl and guy leaning into each other, whispering and then senselessly giggling until distracting their salesman, whose frown turns into an uneasy smile.

"Who is Westland?" Boogey cautiously asks in deep thought.

"Oh, he's the head honcho, well after the boss!" the salesman says, pointing to the huge glass window, across the wide showcase and up a level.

Boogey and Nattie sit cheery when the girl and guy's laughter grows, and Boogey finds the girl on her knees laughing while the guy dances, acting a fool.

Boogey leans again, staring hard until making out the phone handle lowering over and into the cubicle where the two teens are giggling their heads off. Boogey looks off and smiles at another girl peeking over the cubicle and then at Westland's office when Westland's phone suddenly rings and he stands, picking it up.

Boogey's eyes go between the offices until staring at Mr. Westland's face when it turns fiery red as he listens to slanderous remarks from the two mocking him.

Mr. Westland clears his throat loudly, motioning to the girl hanging over the cubicle to pass the phone, when the girl and guy stare at each other surprised when the phone base comes into view at the top of the cubicle and goes to speakerphone.

"Pack it up! There are new boxes out back!" Westland says calmly with Boogey and Nattie softly giggling.

Boogey and Nattie leave the dealership within the hour and ride by several neighborhoods, honking and showing off their new rides.

Boogey grows anxious, wanting to get to Winton's house when taking the lead and turning before Winton's street; stopping to pick up one of Winton's friends.

"Hey, Amp, you need a ride?" Boogey proudly asks, slowing in excitement.

"Hey, Boogey, nice wheels, main (man)! Naw main, I'm right here!" he says, pointing to a house a few feet away.

"Ok, well, have a good one!" Boogey says, pulling off when looking up the road and tapping the brakes. "Hey, ain't that Winton's wife's cousin?" he asks Amp, pointing to the staggering drunk.

The drunk man stops, shielding sunlight for seconds, then bursts into a drunken laugh when doing some sill dance to get the people on the porch laughing.

Amp stares until shaking his head in disbelief. "Main (man), yeah, that's that clown, but hey..., you don't want to pick that dude up; he'll be up in your new truck pop whiteheads all over your dash and windshield, all the way down the road," he utters, laughing harder and waving Boogey off when bending to his knees, laughing.

"Whiteheads? You mean freakin' zits?" Boogey asks, smiling and then bursting into a deep laugh with a sudden, serious stare.

Out of nowhere, the same strange, black, shiny car sits half a block away from the back of Nattie's car, filming them until slowly moving forward with them.

Boogey slows, quieting the engine and cringing when quietly passing when a hand taps on the windowsill. "Hey, Boog!" Winton's wife's cousin shouts, beaming with yellow, butter-churned-looking teeth.

Boogey stops and stares while Nelle's cousin rattles on, then shakes his head with a smile and slight frown while looking closer at the polluted, yellow, filled indentations in his teeth; not a crease anywhere in sight, but smooth and buttery.

"Now you got yourself some nice wheels main (man)! Hot diggety dog!" the cousin excitedly yells, slapping his hands and laughing more until waving when seeing Nattie not too far behind. "Good googlamaloogala!" he exclaims, throwing up two thumbs and staggering back a few feet in a peal of deeper laughter. "Man! Not one but two damn new rides! Man y'all must done (have) hit that lottry (lottery)!" he yells, sticking his head inside the window with Boogey leaning back, frowning from the overpowering, stale liquor smell.

Boogey frowns, leaning farther away yet trying to be courteous by pretending to be reaching for the radio when smelling sour breath mingled with old liquor when the engine shuts off, and a speaker energizes. 'Mr. Johnson, the monitoring system detects alcohol! Sir, you cannot start the engine for fifteen minutes. If you are in a dangerous area, push the green button, and we'll dispatch a tow truck. Thank you, and drive safely,' the automated voice responds with a series of loud beeps.

Boogey stares, pissed, and then looks at his watch and back at Nelle's cousin. "Man, back the hell up! Damn…! Done got my truck shut down, and I'm the one driving. I was going to give you a ride, but hell…, if so, the truck might not ever crank!" Boogey yells, opening the door quickly and backing him away with a mean, look.

Boogey walks up to Nattie and talks for minutes until looking back, finding the man's head inside again. "Get! Gone! Get, now! I done told you to get!" Boogey screams, jumping at him and about to run after him when a big outburst of laughter comes from the crowd sitting on the porch and standing in the yard.

Nelle's cousin jumps, and a smile grows when he becomes meddlesome and hops from side to side, continually touching the truck and standing as if he is about to take off running.

"Look! I'm not playing with you clown! I said get…, sucker!" Boogey yells, jumping until taking two swift steps when one-foot slips, and he drops to the ground, shuffling, balancing and screaming when skinning the palms of his hands with laughter in the background.

The cousin laughs even louder, and more nosy folks come out into their yards.

The men in the strange car burst into tears; one zooming in for closer shots.

Boogey runs to the curb picking up a handful of rocks, slinging them when the cousin takes off, then stops and does an old, drunk dance that has everyone hollering in laughter. Boogey's mean face turns calm when making his way to the truck, looking at his watch. He throws a thumb up to Nattie with two minutes to spare when climbing inside, turning on the radio, and bobbing his head for seconds until churning on the key, when the engine sounds off. Boogey floors it a few times to proudly make it dip to one side when showing off the mean horsepower.

Nattie stares at where the man vanished and freezes with eyes dead set on the drunk, who reappears drifting into the road with a busted box, somewhat slumped over.

The men in the strange car are in tears as they point to the drunk and continue filming more.

The drunk leans down in slow motions, digs deep, and then leans way back, looking up like he's about to fall backward.

Nattie sees something sailing high until she loses sight of it at the top of the windshield when suddenly, something splatters over the street and lands about ten feet from the front of Boogey's truck. Her mouth drops open after the second splatter when laying into the horn, realizing they are huge rocks, when the third rock crumbles into pieces, rolling alongside Boogey's truck, and alongside her car.

Boogey finally lowers the music, registering Nattie's loud blaring horn, and jumps, looking through the back window, finding Nattie waving as mini boulders lunge forward. He hears wheels squeal and sees her drift backward, fast, through a thin trail of black smoke.

Instantly, the strange, black, shiny car driver revs his engine, accidentally dropping into neutral when Nattie is about to plow into them.

Their laughter ceases, and their faces turn red when the transmission thumps, and their tires burn rubber, backing down, and paralleling Nattie until she slows.

Boogey finally sees something disintegrate right before the hood. "Ahh..., Ahh!" Boogey screams, throwing the truck into reverse in stealth mode, backing and burning rubber when seeing more small boulders landing in the spot where the truck just was parked.

The strange car slows, and the men's hearts race as they look in excitement.

Boogey slows, swerving and coming up on the side of Nattie. "What in the world is up with that damn idiot? Let's get the hell out of here before that nut chunks more rocks," Boogey utters, turning around to make the drunk think they are leaving the area and won't end over up at Winton and Nelle's place.

Boogey and Nattie's horn sounds off almost simultaneously near Winton's house within minutes. They pull up to find Winton and Nelle on the front porch, swinging, and the youngest kids playing on the other side of the porch.

Winton and Nelle walk out to greet them, but only Nelle acts surprised.

"Cheer up, Wint, before long, you can put that rust bucket of yours to rest," Boogey says, pointing and making fun of Winton's ride.

"Hey, Boogey, man...," Winton says when Nelle shoves him and intentionally interrupts.

"Man, those rides are fly!" Nelle yells in fear of going back under Melley's debt.

Winton and Nelle play as if interested in looking the car and truck over when out of the blue Nelle mentions them having to run out to get groceries.

"Well..., we can take you," Nattie says, proudly smiling. "It'll be great!" she says, even more convincingly.

Winton walks past the back of Nattie's car, noticing the too familiar-looking shiny car with heads quickly ducking. He grips Nelle's hand and holds her back. "We'll ride later," Winton says, cutting his eyes over to find one man waving his hand and sliding it back and forth at his throat, frightening Winton.

Boogey and Nattie hang around a little longer and then follow each out of the neighborhood in a different direction, heading home.

Later, the strange car pulls up near the general store, watching Nattie climb into Boogey's truck.

Instantly, hard rap music blares from Boogey's speakers with dust kicking up and Boogey's head bobbing when heading for the main road.

The men in the black car duck when the Boogey's chrome hood faces their car, and they ease up, looking back.

Nattie stares over her shoulder, about to comment about the curious men, when out of nowhere, Boogey blasts the bass louder.

Nattie and Boogey's heads begin to bop as hard rap goes higher when Boogey hits the amplifier switch, punching the gas and bringing the truck up to top speed.

Before long, Boogey and Nattie reach the next city, where they plot the next shops to hit, and as with the dealer, the managers offer them the world after they provide proof of hitting the lottery.

Hours later, Boogey and Nattie have spent well over twenty thousand more, to include appliances and other things held with a future delivery, in good faith, before leaving the last little city furthest from their house when heading toward Mundson.

On the straightaway, Boogey slows, coming up on a stoplight that turns yellow when looking in the rearview in fear of being hit by the strange car, when punching the accelerator, and making the light before it turns red.

The strange car revs its engine, skidding wheels, and causes the sheriff to stop writing a ticket when more horns blow as the strange car burns rubber, blasting through the red light and swerving to avoid a collision.

Boogey stares through the rearview and finally sees blue lights in the curve of a side road when his heart races.

Sheriff Big John runs to his car, throwing the clipboard inside and jumps in, throwing the cruiser in gear with blue lights still continuously flashing. He vanishes around a building then rushes up on the strange car's bumper and hits the siren again.

"Are you guys strapped?" the strange car's driver nervously asks.

"Yeah," the man in the back utters, slouching behind dark-tinted windows, hiding his .25 in the crease of the seat and confirming it is hidden.

The car finally slows in a bend and pulls over on a dusty road.

The sheriff eases up and sits, running the tags and his eyes brighten after the dispatcher cautions danger. He speedily slides the door handle back with dusty boots pressing hard against the door when jumping out with his shotgun at eye level. The sheriff approaches slowly, pressing the key on his shoulder-mounted walkie-talkie, requesting backup. He keeps his eyes on the car, focusing through the illegally tinted windows while approaching wide-legged.

In seconds, a mild, then loud siren blares as dust flies high on the opposite side of the road when a deputy jumps out with his shotgun drawn.

A set of eyes gaze from a dirty house window, staring at the car and then the cruiser's flashing lights when the old, fatigue bottom, veteran hippie notices the sheriff's gun drawn. The drunk runs to the bedroom in a mad dash and quietly gears up in his fatigue top. He kneels in a prone position in the dirty screen window with his muzzle aimed at the strange car with three heads heavily bobbing inside.

The deputy approaches, and the veteran repositions, stepping on a beer bottle, slipping and accidentally firing on automatic, taking out the sheriff's blue light, and busting his own truck's windshield.

The sheriff and deputy drop to the dusty ground, scrambling when taking cover.

The three men duck, and the black car's engine revs high when the strange car's transmission drops into gear when thrust forward in front of another car, almost rear-ended.

The strange car fishtails as the men duck when a barrage of fire hits the back window, shattering it.

The driver revs the souped-up engine, stealthily hitting the familiar back streets at top speed.

The sheriff and deputy converge on the road, checking each other over then rush to their cruisers with loud sirens blaring when shooting off.

The overly intoxicated war veteran runs, yelping through the house like a lunatic. His combat boots slapped against the hardwood when he dashes down the hall with his gun high and mouth torn open, yelling.

His wife steps a foot into the hallway with a crying baby, and he almost knocks her over when shooting past and bursting through the screen door sideways. He loses his balance, stumbling to the dusty ground when springing forward for his pickup. He jumps in, fighting to get the key in the ignition until jamming the key in, flooring the gas, kicking up dust. His truck shoots alongside the house, coming out on the other side when he stops, and dust heavily swarms over the truck, spilling into the street and causing cars to swerve and some to crash.

The truck carelessly shoots out across the street and spins around in an open field, kicking up more dust until swerving back onto the highway.

The drunk veteran maneuvers around confused drivers and comes up on the straightway, heading in the direction of the deputy's car with blue lights fading over the hill.

The sheriff and deputy lose sight of the car but depend on folks alongside the road to guide them until they finally find a glimpse of the car's tail lights.

The sheriff steps into the gas, and the deputy closes in swiftly.

The getaway driver hits a switch under the dash, disconnecting the taillights when slamming on the brakes. He turns, bringing the car back up to top speed with a cloud of black smoke rises high as the sheriff blazes through it before realizing it is tire smoke and burning rubber when both his dusty boots rise high as he cuts the wheel hard, slamming on the brakes, throwing the car into a sideways slide.

The deputy looks in the rearview, finally spotting the veteran closing rapidly with the sheriff's car still sideways. He slams on the brakes, excitedly watching the veteran slam into his rear end when a shot fires, prematurely piercing the truck's firewall, with the truck plunging the deputy's vehicle into a deep ditch.

The sheriff completes the turn, pulling alongside the deputy. "Hey..., are you alright?" the sheriff shouts, drawing his gun, counting bullets before slamming the barrel into alignment.

"Yeah! Yeah!" the deputy shouts, holding the door open with his foot and grabbing his rifle. "How about you?" the deputy yells when looking over at the old vet who sits holding his ribs then away and back at him, finally looking over at the veteran's grey beard and dingy fatigues.

"Yeah, daggonit!" the veteran yells, with his rifle lodged between the seat and dash.

The deputy limps over, climbing inside with the sheriff when he punches the accelerator and then brakes, turning hard to make the sharp turn.

The getaway car reaches a dead end and backs up into tall weeds. The men anxiously stare in fear before the driver comes up with a clever idea, which he meditates on and then discloses.

Without warning, the front passenger's door pops open and he runs to the top of a hill, discovering a high trail of dust approaching as the sheriff gives it more gas.

The sheriff floors the engine once more, unknowingly several hundred yards from a low cliff when the man on the hill raises his hand, and the strange car's engine revs up, almost shaking.

The driver watches the man on the hill closely when he clenches his fist tighter, nervously anticipating the plan's quick execution.

The sheriff sees the turn ahead and begins to slow but not overcompensate when the cruiser is twenty-five feet away.

A tight balled fist spreads open, and the getaway driver slams his foot on the gas, letting off the brakes, and a cloud of smoke rises from the rear tires when the car fishtails, hitting the rear end of the sheriff's car and putting it in a fast tailspin.

The sheriff and deputy's eyes and mouth grow wide when the deputy's feet rise to the dash.

The sheriff's hands fight for control until the car jackknifes, and they lean back as if bronco riding until the nose levels out and everything goes into slow motion as they descend into an even steeper nosedive. Their mouths open wider, staring eye-to-eye, when letting off an even louder scream when slamming into murky water, partially submerged.

The deputy lunges forward, fearful of what lurks in the waters, and instantly comes up on the hood quickly and the roof even quicker, screaming before the car settles.

The sheriff sits with a mean, soaked face. He swings the door open and dips, wading in the water at chest level until hearing a loud splash. Upon looking back at the deputy, who points, speechless with fast flapping wet hands, the sheriff sees the biggest alligator ever, cruising in like a missile.

The sheriff screams a death cry, reaching high for the roof's busted light bracket with boots constantly scuffing the car's rear panel; fighting to get out of the water.

The deputy's eyes grow wider, watching the alligator sail in like a high-speed boat when finally grabbing the sheriff by the collar, giving him more leverage when he springs up, screaming and watching as the huge jaws of death swim by, inches from his boots, taking out the floodlight and side mirror.

The getaway driver makes several attempts to start the stalled vehicle, and on the third attempt, the engine revs up.

The lookout man rushes up, jumping in, and the car fishtails on the dirt trail in the opposite direction.

At the pond, the ripples in the water soon settle when new, minuscule ripples form as more crocs, tree-trunk-sized snakes, and then gators swarm around the tilted cruiser.

The sheriff leans into the door for the radio when a large gator swims by, so he backs up, remembering his shoulder radio, which he uses to call for assistance.

The getaway car reaches the paved road, and the driver sits, quickly deciding which way to go; when distracted, finding a man slowly pulling a shotgun from a ditched, blue truck while doing a double-take.

The wounded, war-veteran trembles, nervously reaching for shells then screams, taking off in a drunken, wide-legged sprint, with his dusty boots slamming the pavement as he closes in on the car, fast. "Freeze!" the old war veteran screams, stopping to load and then coming up in a standing, prone position.

The driver cuts the wheel hard and floors the engine, leaving black skid marks when a shot fires, driving a hole into the trunk.

The men duck, and the car swerves more as they approach a sharp curve.

The second round shatters the back window, taking out the rearview mirror with all heads down and the driver driving blindly and swerving.

The vet screams as the driver leans hard into the turn.

The driver floors it, taking several back roads and cutting through property lines and private roads until reaching Melley's other cottage, deep in the woods, hours later. The car pulls around by the porch, and they find Melley sitting, chewing tobacco.

Melley cuts his eyes over his reading glasses, finding the front frame torn out, windows shattered, and the hood askewed. He leans, spitting tobacco when his eyebrows lift to one side, and his face frowns when slowly standing, and hacking up cold then spitting. His corduroy sleeve slides across his snotty nose, until wiping excess snot away with his bare hand when creeping off the porch and up to the car when it stops.

Melley stares at the driver with raised eyebrows. "What the hell have you done to Dallas' wheels!" he screams with a weak, trembling eye with both fists tight.

"It was Big John!" the driver nervously says, hyperventilating. "He got after us near Tilton's pond," the driver says, nervously and excitedly cutting his eyes at the others.

"Well, forget that! When Dallas sees his baby busted up like this, you gonna (are going to) wish the sheriff did get hold of you, son," he yells, snatching the driver by the collar through the window and releasing him when intentionally rubbing his snotty hands on the driver's shirt.

The next day, on the eve, on the other side of town, Rev says a closing speech and then looks at his watch, grabbing his Bible. "I hate to rush, but I have a few errands to run, so be careful going home," he says, rushing out. He climbs into his SUV, staring into space until his hand slides over the sun visor, pulling out a thick, gold envelope. His eyes wander over the scribbled words when he starts the truck.

A knock, mumble then a clear voice comes as he rolls down the window.

"Is everything alright?" the old lady asks, staring.

"Yes, everything is fine, sister," he responds, looking at her and the others, who stare with concern when he waves and eases onto the road.

# CHAPTER FIVE

**Fools Without The Gold**

    Rev drives twenty minutes before reaching the first stoplight, where he puts on his signal, patiently waiting. He goes into deep meditation when the light turns green and he's startled when a horn blows as the light turns yellow when shooting through it. He sits at the next light, and another horn blows, bringing him out of a mild trance when pulling away. He pulls out a cd single, sliding it into the player when a mild and pleasant male's voice tunes up.

> *'Our eyes are to the hill, from where our strength come,*
> *though somewhat broken, HE sustains us all as one.*
> *The potter will put us back together again,*
> *So we see this as trial with a victorious end.*
> *No never forget the KING and HIS army that sustains,*
> *For HE fights for us, through hail and through rain.*
> *Understand though not thou WHO is for me?*
> *Disregard not when HE says how it will be.*
> *Once again Satan comes to destroy God's fans,*
> *Yes, humanity this time, no longer just lands.*
> *Please hear me now, man woman boy and girl,*
> *We are here only a short time in this place, this world*
> *For we won't give up, we won't give in,*
> *We will fight with all our strength until the end*
> *For we won't give up, we will defend,*
> *We will fight with all our heart and we will win!*
> *Before great pride stands a great fall,*
> *truly a sight to see, come one, come all.*
> *Jealousy and pride is crueler than the grave,*
> *But we'll keep on fighting, never to be your slave.*
> *You removed some from home, some from land,*
> *But we stand in unity, yes that is how we stand.*
> *Though you begin to kill us the end is far away,*
> *And those taken now have a better place to stay.*
> *Their love an memories, never to be erased,*
> *A love so dear that it can never be replaced.*
> *For my love for them is stronger than their deaths,*

*So I'll keep fighting until just one last breathe.*
*For we won't give up, we won't give in,*
*We will fight with all our strength until the end*
*For we won't give up, we will defend,*
*We will fight with all our heart and we will win!*
*I sleep but my heart wakes me in tears,*
*And HE revives me, so there are no fears.*
*Their knocks, comes to my heart's door, in a swirl,*
*HE who is for us is greater than any in this world.*
*Yes, look for your rest, but it shall never come,*
*And though none give chase, you'll run, yes you'll run!*
*For it ain't over even when you think it really is,*
*For the end result is not ours but always HIS.*
*So press on my enemy and far from righteousness,*
*But know that this trail will only be another test.*
*Though you brought the business but surely we'll bring the end,*
*That's what we'll tell our children, our family, and our friend*
*For we won't give up, we won't give in,*
*We will fight with all our strength until the end*
*For we won't give up, we will defend,*
*We will fight with all our heart and we will win!*

Rev repeats the chorus line, nodding when entering the expressway. He drives slower and cars zoom by so fast that it looks like he's driving in reverse. He goes into more profound thoughts, and out of nowhere, an eighteen-wheeler rolls up on his bumper, continually blowing until Rev nervously veers out of the passing lane.

Minutes later, he exits an off-ramp, coming into a rough, war-torn area when easing to the stop sign. He comes to an abrupt stop with the turn signal on, and goes into a semi-trance; pushing play with the song playing gently in the background.

Bam, bam, bam! A heavy knock comes at the window; when he looks, finding a homeless man's face disfigured from his overshadowing hoodie.

Rev jumps, fearfully jetting into the street and swerving to miss a bag lady. He slows on the straightway, still looking in the rearview, and spots the same man under a bright streetlight with his balled fist still raised high and screaming something.

Rev taps the brakes then eases into the gas, continuing down the dark street until turning down an even darker, balled-grass, narrower trail. He flashes his high beams, spotting two men waving him forward as they come into view but further down the alley. Rev passes them slowly, staring under-eyed while watching their movement in the side and rear view mirror until they fade as he comes up over a slight incline. He dims his headlights, pulling into a lot where two other men direct him to park alongside a black, shiny, classic car.

The back window of the old, classic, stretched car rolls down when a heavy cloud of weed smoke rolls out and Rev smells a slight hint of the stench through his vents.

Rev sits, easing up the volume when the cd gets to the chorus line again, turning it up a few notches, then a little more when the break, then chorus flows in again.

*'For we won't give up, we won't give in,*
*We will fight with all our strength until the end*
*For we won't give up, we will defend,*
*We will fight with all our hearts, and we will win!'*

Rev continues looking for seconds then slowly rolls down his window with a burst of loud clamorous laughter rising when turning the song to a whisper, then off. His eyes wandered slightly behind him and over to the two shady men who directed him into the spot then slowly into the car's front and back seat.

"You're late! Well..., actually, I didn't think you were going to show. I hope you got my money, and don't come trying to fill me up with these talks about evil doings," the tall, chubby man in the back utters, sipping on cognac and tilting the glass for his sexy woman to pour another.

"Yeah, whatever, Mack! You know good and well that this is nothing less than classic blackmail!" Rev says leaning for the glove compartment and retrieving the thick, gold, double rubber-band-wrapped envelope.

"Wrong as always, but you just remember you weren't always the so-called perfect man that everyone perceives you to be," Mack says, leaning forward under the thin trail of streetlight and then back, slowly opening his mouth when the woman slides a Cuban cigar to his lips, lighting it.

"So when..., when does it end?" Rev asks, finding the two men in the front looking over their shoulders with mean stares. "What's next? One of these clowns comes after me for the same thing, money for silence?" Rev squeezes the envelope's edges until it creases.

"I'm about my word, Jack!" Mack leans forward then eases back, blowing a ring of smoke in Rev's direction.

"Your word doesn't mean, Jack, or we wouldn't be here right now!" Rev responds, furiously. "Look..., I was young and dumb back then. My only mistake was allowing you fools to convince me to get caught in that gang mess, and look where it got me! Let me answer if for you..., nowhere! And you called it what, back then..., family? Huh? Well..., family won't use things to keep you down in life. You guys were nothing but a bunch of bullies, nobodies, and look at you now; you're still just a bunch of old fools who still haven't accomplished anything in life, and on this course, you never will. You ain't nothing, and you ain't ever gone be nothing until you change your wickedness. So…, tell me…, how many more people have you framed since me? Yeah, I heard about the millions y'all got out of Timmy, who finally made it to the top, but where is he now? Let me answer that as well…, dead, and all from your selfish greed!" Rev screams, livid.

Mack sits in deep thought until one eye closes, burning from the cigar smoke. "Hell, man! Timmy was dealing with his own damn demons. All he had to do was make my payments, and he would have been good…, you hear me!"

"Yeah…, and that's garbage, and you know it! I was with him two days before he killed himself, and I was supposed to meet him the night he hung himself. You guys were threatening to tell the cops about the house he blacked out from those folks snitching about that botched heist back then. He warned me that you guys would be coming for me next since y'all think I have it going on. What? A truck, a decent job, and a one-bedroom apartment? What is that, huh? Man, I wish someone would have been told me the real deal about this senseless so-called gang crap back then," he utters, enraged.

"Well, too late for that, Jack, so just hand over my greenbacks and keep doing as I say, or there will be another blackout, and someone else will be driving that nice SUV. Mack slightly rises, looking at the extended version SUV. "Huh…, extra edition, too, huh…? Well, I'm sure that cost you a pretty penny, but hey…, it sure would look good in my collection," he says, looking at the SUV's shiny, extended version emblem this time.

"All in a day's work, but I can see you're still doing the same with what little money you're scavenging: smoking and drinking, that is. Look at you…, still hanging around with the same knuckleheads from Pre-K and elementary school. Like I said, you were never nothing, and will never be nothing, but Hell awaits your evil deeds."

Mack's driver's door swings open abruptly, and he shoots out, rushing around the front, putting a gun to Rev's head when snatching the money. He moves the gun against Rev's nose snappily. "I should have killed you before we offered to let you in, so don't go talking like you're better than us!" the driver yells, griping Rev tight at the collar with Rev's hands nervously rising.

The front passenger, Reggie, eases out and walks behind the driver, cooling him down, until gripping his wrist, and easing the gun from Rev's sweaty and trembling face. Reggie's hand comes to the driver's shoulder, easing him back more until motioning him over to the car while calming him. Reggie turns back to Rev slowly and winks before walking away.

The driver gazes at Rev. "You just remember this, sucker. There's no statute of limitations on murder, so there's still a lot of years in your life to spend in that new cell. You just remember who put you there when you're in a pink thong, and Big Bubba got you hanging curtains and tossing his nasty salad," the driver says, staring under-eyed when looking over at Rev while standing at the driver's door, still pissed.

Rev sits with unnoticeable tears, looking ahead until more tears flow. He looks away, wiping tears fast then looks back at Mack, shaking his head, disgusted. "I'll live with taking that old man's life for the rest of my life, but you know what? It would be better if you just go on and put that gun to my head and do me right here and now!" Rev says mildly and in somewhat of a trance, slightly trembling.

"All this fear injected over something I did back then, and now I'm too afraid to be close to someone..., afraid to marry or have children because I know all of that can be taken by someone that I roughed up back then or one of you clowns. There's no end..., there's just no end for me! I'm living in Hell every day, all because I made that one mistake of following people who were never going to be anything in life. A gang..., man, please! We were nothing but a bunch of young punks, cowards, and now we're older and still cowards, hiding behind guns, still running in packs, and too scared to be alone.

Well, at least I have one thing going; I can walk these streets alone, though I have to look over my shoulder. God has given me peace from that fear, too, and deep in my heart, I know HE will make all my wrongs right because HE is a loving and merciful God. I will not fear what man can do to me, with God, so let it soak into your pea brain when it sobers."

Mack looks at Rev in a long, deep thought. "Man, crank up, and let's get out of here before this fool converts us in this hea (here) parking lot!" Mack screams from the words cutting like a knife until feeling all eyes on him when his middle finger comes up as the car cranks up with the thrust mufflers mildly rumbling.

The driver's face frowns, looking over his shoulder, staring at Rev with his hand still on his gun, at his waist when passing Mack the envelope and staring at Rev's mean again.

Mack takes off his glasses, opens the envelope, and stares at the crisp, thick wad of hundreds.

Reggie smiles and winks at Rev again, then climbs back in the passenger seat.

Rev stares at Mack longer. "Looking at those bags under your eyes, I would say you're not sleeping too well these days," Rev calmly says, looking at the driver then away before staring at Mack again.

"You just keep paying me, sucker, and next time, less talking and more passing," Mack utters, cheery when the woman snuggles, kissing

Mack with her index finger brushing over the hundreds until fanning them out.

"How about next time you come alone? How about that?" Rev says, finding the driver fidgety when cranking up and flipping the cd volume high again and just when the chorus is about to chime in again.

*For we won't give up, we won't give in,*
*We will fight with all our strength until the end*
*For we won't give up, we will defend,*
*We will fight with all our hearts, and we will win!*

Rev throws the truck in gear fast, skidding wheels and kicking up a patch of skimpy grass. He turns in the alley and steps on the gas upon seeing the two men again, causing them to scatter until waving their guns high, pissed.

Boogey stop at the red light and turns toward another side of town. He comes upon a country store and cuts his eyes at Nattie and then at the store slowing down.

"What you looking at me for, wit (with) yo (your) ugly self?" Nattie giggles at their favorite phrase; staring at the store while he turns into the lot, running inside.

Boogey jumps back within minutes, driving a little further when seeing the lottery headquarters sign from a distance. He gazes at the clock on the dash, rushing into the lot to find a man at the door with his back to them.

"See? Greed! We would have made it if you had not stopped at all those stores, for tickets," Nattie says, staring at him and shaking her head.

Boogey revs the engine more, racing faster across the parking lot.

The director happens to hear the revved engine when looking back, and turning the key with bulged eyes, finding the truck bearing down on him. He continually stares until releasing the key, throwing up his briefcase and trench coat, screaming when diving into a flower bed; tucking, and rolling. The director expressly climbs to one knee, within seconds, brushing dirt from his clothes when finally hearing tires squealing.

Boogey throws the vehicle into park, hurrying over to help the old man up.

"Heck! What were you planning to do, reconstruct the dang building?" The old man shakes his head, kneeling and slowly standing when reaching for Boogey's hand.

"Oh hellz naw, I had a handle on thangs (things). I was just trying to catch you before you left so that I can cash in this big, mega, Jackpot winner!" Boogey excitedly says when reaching into the bottom pocket of his overalls.

"Winning ticket?" he exclaims with a flummoxed look when dusting off one shoulder.

"Why, yes, the biggon…, the big jackpot, right here!" Boogey says, finally patting down and then unbuttoning his shirt pocket, for the ticket.

Nattie stares in the man's face and then Boogey's to get a reaction.

"Well, you'll have to come back tomorrow because it takes two officials to validate a winner." He reaches for his briefcase and coat, dusting them off.

"Man! You can't call no one back in?" Boogey asks in a little friendlier tone.

"Nope! Office policy…, besides, we close early on Mondays, so Mrs. Gigglesworth can audit the books with the auditor. You'll just have to come between 7 AM and 5 PM, tomorrow. What's another day going to hurt? No worries, right!" the director says, reaching for the keys and locking the door. "Well…, that's if you have a winner!"

Boogey drops his head and drags himself to the vehicle, climbing inside delivering the bad news.

Forty minutes later; in the vicinity of another major town, Boogey slowly strolls past a long stretch of stores on the main drag of Dover Street. He makes it his business to park in front of the finance office and across from the rental center when rushing out, opening Nattie's door, then turning, talking to a man. Boogey indulges in senseless chatter, looking off from time to time until spotting a finance worker frantically pointing him out through the big picture window.

The finance manager, Sean, bust through the door, rushing into the busy street, running over, and staring at Nattie, who cuts her eye back at him. "You two…, just who I've been looking for! Are you here to settle your debt on the car?" he asks, angrily looking at Boogey and then curiously at the new wheels.

Boogey ignores him until Sean shouts Boogey's last name; before he can answer when Boogey finally looks back, ignoring Sean longer.

Sean impatiently listens to them go on about nothing with folded arms and fast tapping feet going faster. "Ok, look…, enough of this senselessness; are you here to pay your delinquent debt?"

"Oh, Seen!" Boogey finally says, pretending to be surprised when turning and smiling.

"Seen? It's Sean (Shawn)," the man yells, frowning

"Well, your name tag spells S_e_a_n: Sean. Let's see, g_l_e_a_n, glean, c_l_e_a_n, clean, so s_e_a_n, Seen," Boogey meddlesomely says, beaming when seeing Sean getting really pissed.

"Well, I sorry you're illiterate and all, but it's Sean (Shawn), for your edumication (education), and since you're so special, and all."

"Man! Why do people waste time making up their names? Use the name your mammy gave you, even if they thought they were naming you something else," Boogey says, smiling.

Boogey turns red, pissed that Sean would blurt out his business. He turns to the old man again, smiling. Without warning, he swiftly jerks grabbing Sean in the collar, swinging him around, and throwing him on top of a woman's car as she stops and throws it into park.

The old woman nervously screams when Boogey lift and slams Sean on the hood again with more body slams following until denting the hood, and almost knocking Sean out.

The woman screams with eyes scrolling over the huge dents when her head begins going in circles until fainting with folks running up to assist her.

Boogey jumps back fast, spinning out and coming down with a hard, professional wrestler-style elbow which throws him into a spin when sinking his elbow deep in Sean's chest. Boogey bounces back and goes in for the last spin, which goes out of control when he lands between the car tire and sidewalk, screaming in agonizing pain.

Sean's eyes spring open. "Help me! Help me! Somebody call the sheriff; this man just assaulted me!" Sean screams, finally sliding off the hood when his trousers sunk deep into the crease of his butt. His pants happen to go even higher when he bends forward and wobbles back to his office with higher than high water cuffs.

Boogey rolls, crawls, stands, and dusts off his clothes, slowly reaching for his keys with skinned knuckles.

The owner of the rental center runs out, crossing the street, apoplectic. "Hey..., hey..., hey..., now Nattie, I've called you a hundred times, and I'm sick and tired of you playing on the phone. Now, you need to turn that black-and-white television set in, or I'll see you in court!"

Boogey leans against the vehicle, cheery, out of breath and shaking his head.

Nattie stares at the man's serious face with a bright smile. "Oh..., that set? Do you mean the one Boogey took the Louisville slugger? Oh yeah, sure..., come on by and get it, but bring a few boxes and trash bags," Nattie says in a crazy snicker.

"Yeah..., you can bet your bottom dollar we'll be there, and it better be in excellent condition, and I do mean not a scratch, or you'll pay top dollar in court," he utters, looking both ways when stepping swiftly into the street.

"Top dollar?" Boogey exclaims with great sarcasm.

"What was that?" the man says, turning and staring at Boogey's smiling face.

"I said top dollar..., hell, why not the bottom? Is it because it's easier to bet the top?"

"Ohh..., you and that trashy-tail mouth! If I weren't a perfect gentleman and Christian, I'd let the whole town watch me mop your butt up and down these hea (here) streets, as if you were in a Super Bowl parade!"

Boogey slowly stands, walking up to him eye-to-eye, until shoes and boots touch. "Well, there's nothing but air and freakin' opportunity betweenxt (between) us!" Boogey yells, sucking in deep. "Ah...! Now there's just an opportunity, babe!" Boogey shouts, stepping on one shoe when taking his back-in-the-day fighting stance. One leg goes forward, riding back on the other, rocking while rolling up sleeves and holding both fists tight before the man's face.

A crowd grows fast, some instigating until the street is gridlocked.

The big guy wiggles his foot slowly then fast, trying to free his foot when Boogey smiles, taking a quick, playful jerk when his fist intentionally flies past the man's fathead, and the man drops to one side, ducking and then drawing in both big fists.

"Daddy! No, Daddy!" the man's young daughter screams, running from her mother's tight grip. She rushes fearfully up to her father, pulling on his fat hand when he jerks his foot back hard, stepping back and away with her.

"Yeah, go on with your little girl before you get the snot knocked outcha!" Boogey yells with his chest proudly stuck out.

The man slams his fist in his hands a few times with firm, beady eyes as his daughter leans deeper into him. "You just wait 'til the sheriff gets wind of this; you just wait!" the man screams, frowning. "My little girl just saved him a whipping of a lifetime, Jack!" the man proudly screams to bystanders, pointing to his daughter and looking back at his wife, totally embarrassed to have stepped down.

Back in the woods, near Tilton's pond, the sun rises as a tow truck, animal control, and other deputies wrap up the rescue effort.

The sheriff drives another deputy's car to the road, looking both ways before heading for Fikesville.

Like clockwork, Boogey calls in sick on a day they start work late.

Later, Boogey and Nattie sit outside the lottery office talking when the director rushes to the door.

Over at Winton's house, Winton tries reaching Boogey several times by phone, feeling worse than ever, but gets no answer, so he pulls up at Boogey's house twenty minutes later. He knocks but gets no answer. Winton looks over at Nattie's car, listening for the dog, and then heads for the back, hoping to find the truck until rushing, realizing the time and that he will be late. He dashes for the car; skidding his wheels and kicking up dust.

Boogey and Nattie patiently wait while the lottery official sets up, and when they finally see the open sign light up, they rush inside, wide-eyed and bushy-tailed, with the doorbell ringing loudly.

Boogey fights, tearing through several pockets until pulling out the ticket.

The director looks again. "Sir, we're still waiting for the machine to link with the satellite," the director utters, punching in more security codes. He excitedly looks over his spectacles, smiling when eyeing his assistant walking in, greeting them and vanishing into the back room then coming out.

A retired naval officer, Commander Smithy Gigglesworth, steps inside. "Top of the morning, my chickadees!" she senselessly says, followed by the craziest laugh that tapers off like the sound of bumblebees.

Boogey laughs, beaming, and then giggles at her annoying laugh.

Her phone soon rings, and everyone listens to her talking until several buzzing laughs come again when Boogey playfully swats his face fast as if it's a joke.

The next round of bee laughter comes when Nattie, Boogey, and the director playfully swat until the commander looks back when the laughter gets louder.

Nattie stops horse playing when in tears then quiets, giggling while waiting for Boogey and the director to react.

The director holds his laugh until bursting out in a peal of loud, crazy laughter.

The retired commander rolls her eyes and then laughs when everyone is in tears until it tapers off when she hangs up, finding them staring at her, one at a time.

The director reaches for Boogey's ticket, which he anxiously passes, gracefully. He instantly releases the ticket in the slot, and bells and whistles sound off almost instantaneously, indicating a winner. The director smiles and then sticks out his hand, congratulating him. "Congratulations, you are indeed a winner, folks!"

Nattie springs from her seat about three feet high, clicking her heels.

Boogey jumps around, and the two soon join hands, dancing in circles of joy.

The nosy commander sits staring at them when her phone rings again.

The director looks over at his assistant, smiling. "Oh, Mrs. Gigglesworth, can you please figure out the tax deductions and type out their check?" the director says, looking at Boogey, who smiles and shakes his head when whispering the assistant's name to Nattie in a funny tone and fighting to hold his laugh.

Mrs. Gigglesworth walks out, looks at the amount when smiling, and bursts into laughter, which sounds like a loud diesel engine cranking.

Boogey giggles then turns so he can't see the funny-looking woman with her ridiculous hat cocked sideways when the nosy commander leans.

Mrs. Gigglesworth drunkenly tiptoes and somewhat staggers, disappearing and reappearing minutes later, finding Nattie and Boogey humming the new lottery television jingle. She stamps the check with a seal and hands off the certified check to the director.

Boogey kisses the check, bowing when passing it to Nattie and twirling like a seasoned ballerina for minutes, with eyes closed until peeking, and finding Nattie's troubled face.

"What! Five thousand? I don't understand! What!" Nattie screams in tears.

Boogey snatches the check with bulging eyes. "Is this some sort of sick prank? This is wrong..., dead wrong!" he screams. "We hit the biggon (big one) I tell yah (you)! Mega..., not damn thousands!" Boogey screams even more confused.

"No, but you're wrong, sir. The big one hit over in another state, but please, please tell us what made you think you hit it big? Maybe I can help you get down to the bottom of this mess," he says with a smirk while folding his hands behind his back.

Boogey freezes in deep thought. "Nattie, quick..., the newspaper?" Boogey says, excited again.

Nattie springs from the chair and sprints to the counter in a jiffy, pulling the heavily wrinkled newspaper from her purse, and flipping it open to the cover, fast.

The director leans back, rummages over several old pages when turning around, flipping through several more papers until lifting the two, and comparing them.

The nosy commander hangs up, hurrying over to all the fussing.

"Hmm...," the director says with curiously rising eye browse, noticing there's no date on Boogey's copy when smiling. "You've been conned, duked, samsnoozled and any other word for pranked..., and big time, I might add, my dear, sir. You mean you didn't notice there's no bloody date in this newspaper?" the director asks, bursting into laughter and then swatting past his head when the commander bursts out in a loud laugh.

"Winton! Melley! Winton! Melley! Dang! I should have known!" Boogey screams in rage, continually slapping his fist in the palm of his hand until it turns red along with his eyes.

Nattie sees red-tinted tears roll from his cheeks.

Boogey drops in the seat, slumped over crying when Nattie strokes his back, comforting him. "Imma kill em'!" Boogey screams, trembling and standing slowly and embracing Nattie at the waist when turning to walk out.

"Excuse me..., you have to sign," the director says, watching the door swing shut then open slowly with them sadly returning and signing.

They sit in the vehicle, numb and empty, and then sit longer until an hour passes when Boogey cranks up and makes the long drive home.

They pull into the yard in silence, and when Boogey parks, they sit, looking out into space as the beautiful weeping willow gracefully blows peacefully.

Boogey's mind continually fills with more horrible thoughts until he jumps out.

Nattie follows him closely inside, thinking of something comforting to say, when Boogey suddenly reaches behind the chair for his shotgun.

Nattie stretches forward fast, and her hands guide the gun back behind the chair. "No, it's not even worth it!" She releases the gun to the floor, hugging him.

Boogey holds her tight and soon breaks down in more tears until he pulls away and heads for the bathroom.

Nattie uncovers Bud's cage and plays with the bird until she hears the toilet flush.

Boogey passes her, walks out, and sits on the top step, staring out into space, teary-eyed until looking over at the new vehicles; thinking back on all the drama he caused in town. "I'm heading in to work, Natt; I just hope I don't lose my job, messing with these scoundrels," Boogey utters, handing Nattie the check, climbing in, numb until pulling off and kicking up a long, high, feather-trail of dust. He makes the drive, and from time to time, finds himself well below the speed limit when mediating on revenge. Boogey arrives at the mill and sits for a while, trying to calm down.

Several folks see Boogey coming with his chest stuck out, already warned of the prank by one man at Boogey's house the day of the prank.

Winton and the man who was at Boogey's stand shooting craps in the back, on their ten minute break as usual. Winton grabs the dice, furiously shaking them, and by chance looks up to find Boogey barreling down with a freshly-treated, heavily-splintered two-by-four when Winton screams, and the two run into each other, scrambling to get away. Winton ducks around some logs hides behind a stack of pallets for minutes until fearfully breaking out for the office.

Old Man Anderson instantly spots the chase and steps out, stopping Boogey and trying to reason with him. He patiently listens to Boogey tell the horrific ordeal and sympathizes when convincing Boogey to hand over the two-by-four finally.

Boogey assures the boss that he's cool then walks past the boss, taking off in a fast sprint after Winton again.

Winton ducks through the door and runs around the big office, knocking things over until stealthily running back into the yard.

Old Man Anderson finally gets fed up, and sprints to the hallway, seizing Boogey by the arm, pulling him to one side, trying to talk sense into him again until realizing it is useless, so he motions his son to call the cops.

Within minutes, the police arrive, escorting Boogey off the premises, and the boss calls for Winton, laying him off, indefinitely.

Boogey drives to the park to cool off then immediately heads over to Winton's house, where he waits for hours after Winton is off. He finally grows restive, climbing out, confronting Nelle, who sticks to her story of not knowing a thing.

Nelle almost convinces him and he recalls the incident at the bed & breakfast, where she was clueless, when assuring him that she knows nothing.

Boogey sits longer then finally cranks up, leaving when the sun sets but returns later, parking in front of Winton's friend's house, barely seeing Winton's house. He pulls out a flask from the glove compartment, taking a few swigs, and suddenly sees bright headlights as a car slowly drives past Winton's house and turns at the end of the road.

The phone rings at Winton's house an hour later, and the curtains pull back with Nelle staring into Boogey's white eyes as he sits on the porch, smoking a cigar.

Around midnight, Boogey stomps, putting out his last cigar, and then tramples through the yard.

The dog next door barks loud and then louder until finally quitting.

Boogey gets in driving away slowly, and sees headlights, so he slowly approaches the car that has been ridden by several times. His eyes stare deep through the slightly rolled-down, tinted window, but he doesn't recognize anyone, so he speeds off and leaves the neighborhood.

The car turns and follows Boogey until he enters the ramp that leads to the highway when Winton's head pops up with him senseless giggling.

Boogey exits at the next off-ramp, stopping to get a bite; a beer, a pint of liquor, and a lottery ticket. He sits, staring into space, when his mind wanders over the course of the day.

An hour later, Boogey is drunker than Tucket ManNucket when he eases the key into the ignition and spots a deputy cruising through the area. He excitedly watches the deputy make his rounds down by the elementary school and cautiously pulls away in the opposite direction. He heads to Winton's house again, pulling up in the backyard this time with the lights off. He eases out, tiptoeing and looking for the neighbor's dog, which he hears inside until his barks grow louder. Boogey's drunken eyes scramble over the dim, moon-lit ground, then at a trash pile finding a heap of trash and a busted dog muzzle and wire.

Out of nowhere, the friendly dog runs up on Boogey, barking until soothed by light whistles, chirps, and the leftover sandwich from the dash while happily wagging his tail.

The dog leans forward to eat when Boogey nippily leans in, slipping an old, dried muzzle on the dog that does not fit when reaching back for the chicken wire, easing it over the dog's mouth and tightly adjusting it.

Inside Winton's house, Nelle fusses at her daughter about not hanging the clothes on the line and then walks into the master bedroom sifting through Winton's clean clothes. She puts Winton's favorite jersey on then swirls her hair, slipping on one of Winton's duo-rags.

Winton sits on the phone giggling about Boogey until hearing something out back when easing the blinds open, unknowingly staring through a reflected window and deep into Boogey's bright white eyes.

Boogey closely stares, not blinking, when a tear falls just as Winton walks away. He parallels Winton through the house, peeking into each room until looking in Winton's bedroom, seeing Nelle silhouette with the covers thrown over her head. Boogey anxiously waits for Winton to undress and suddenly hears the radio flipping through several stations as Winton tunes in his favorite station, turns down the volume a notch, and begins singing.

Winton soon wanders into the bathroom, dropping his boxers, removing his shirt, and adjusting the water to his desired setting.

The moon soon fades behind thick, dark clouds, and Boogey maneuvers by the shed, searching for Winton's stash of rubber bungee cords, which he slips in his pockets before heading for the front door. He comes alongside the house, ripping the phone cord out of the junction box while Winton's daughter is hanging up from talking to a friend.

Winton sings louder, skipping over most of the words he just doesn't know.

Boogey's hand runs alongside the chair on the front porch, slightly shifting it to one side when feeling around for the kids' spare key.

Winton's nosy neighbor glances out but then drops down, continually peeking when finding the man's frame broader than Winton's but recalling Boogey's stature when walking away and going back to his favorite television show.

Boogey slowly slides the key in the lock, turning it in intervals until the door eases open. He slips inside, pulling the door tight until it lightly clicks then creeps down the hallway, gazing around until the baby boy walks out, half-dazed. Boogey kneels quieting the kid, then motions him to the bathroom. He takes a few more quiet steps when his big hand slides over Winton's bedroom door, turning it slowly when Winton tunes up to another song, then stops, quietly listening while lathering up more, and then listens again, until slowly humming then stopping.

Boogey freezes, wondering if Winton is in the bedroom or bathroom.

Nelle eases out of bed groggy and leaning forward when feeling her necklace fall. She bends over deeper to pick it up at the same time that Boogey eases into the darkroom with a tightly balled fist.

The door squeaks and Boogey sees movement; his eyes speedily roll over the slightly raised flat bedspread, thinking Winton is there when spotting the duo rag and coming down hard on the top of what he thinks is Winton's corpulent head.

Nelle heavily staggers and Boogey leaves Nelle flopping lifelessly backward; her feet flying high until her body bounces on the edge of the mattress, flipping head first when sliding off and to the floor, settling, yet sitting in the corner.

Boogey's face transforms into sorrow, hearing the light feminine snoring while squinting in shock, staring at her peacefully sleeping. He shakes his head in disbelief, swiftly refocusing and taking more silent steps toward the bathroom, easing inside, waiting for Winton to hit another high tune when easing the door shut, and quietly locking it. Boogey closes his fat, balled, tight fist even tighter, drawing back with all that is in him, when it sails through thin, plastic curtains and into Winton's shadowy head, knocking him out cold.

Winton's body drops dead weight, bringing Nelle out of her snoring.

Nelle screams, grabbing her throbbing head, wobbling until springing up, lightheaded, and running into walls then scrambling for the bathroom door.

Boogey's head shifts and his raised, evil eyes gaze toward the door where Nelle's continual screams crying out for Winton then pulls on the door, twisting the knob, continually calling out to Winton.

"Now, Nelle!" Boogey says in a deep, loud voice.

"Open this door right now, Boogey!" she screams, banging with her fist.

"Now, Nelle, look..., I just need to talk, Ok! I just need to talk to ole Wint! Now, I'm sorry for hitting you, but it was an accident because I thought you were Wint!" he says, staring back at Winton to find a tear dropping.

Boogey eases down until sitting on the toilet with his head in his hands, feeling bad.

"You can talk all you want, but open this door, Boog!" she yells, pulling hard on the knob until her hand slips off.

"Now I'm telling you, Nelle..., this here is grown man business! So, see your way out of it, and it will be over soon," Boogey says, pulling off his wide, rhinestone studded belt when hearing Winton's moans and seeing him moving, sluggishly.

Nelle picks up the phone, clicking the receiver, but nothing. She sprints for the wall checking the cord then the inside junction box, finding it intact when checking the receiver again but nothing.

The bedroom door opens, and her youngest son walks in, rubbing teary eyes.

Boogey snatches Winton up by the neck, punching Winton in the face then throws the belt on the counter, tying Winton's hands with the bungee cord. Boogey rises, securing the bungee cord laced hands to the showerhead, then flips the nozzle upward so Winton can't slip off. He turns Winton to the wall, sitting down, waiting for Winton to come to when hearing him groaning again.

Winton moans heavier and Nelle continually begs until banging and kicking the door. "Open this door right now, you...!" Nelle screams, causing her son to cry.

Boogey slides the curtain back more, turning on the water until it's mildly hot and trickling evenly over Winton's body. He grabs the shampoo from the tub's edge, squirting over and around his feet.

"Nelle!" Boogey yells again but in a more demanding voice.

"Open this door right now, Boog!" she screams in tears, waking the other kids.

"I just need to talk, now. I just need to talk, and then I'm out of here!" Boogey yells out, taking a seat on the edge of the tub.

Winton's vision becomes somewhat blurry when Boogey's mean face focuses, and Winton yelps and struggles to get free.

"Why, Winton?" Boogey cries. "Why would you do us like this after all we have done for this family?"

"It was Melley, Boog! Ok, ok, ok, look..., I owed him big time, Boog, and he was about to put his goons on me," Winton whimpers, continually twirling, slipping, and falling while trying to stand.

"Melley...? We're first cousins, main (man)! Wez (we are) blood, main (man)! You out here making a fool out of Nat and me is one thing, but you could have warned us, but nooo...! Well, let me be the first to tell you..., there's a painful price to pay, pal!" Boogey utters, with a crazy smile then sturdy face, when grabbing his wide, leather, studded belt with the buckle in hand. He begins rolling it tightly around his fat fist with tears falling, and his face frowns until turning into the purest of evil.

The almost invisible first lash comes out of nowhere, sounding like gunfire when Nelle and the kid duck, hitting the floor.

Winton screams loud with each forceful blow of leather and stud tearing through flesh, stinging from the lashes and trickling hot water.

Nelle and the kids scream out loud, jumping after each lash, until the other children draw close to their room doors, listening fearfully.

Boogey's head falls back with his mouth torn wide open; when a death cry comes. He goes into suicide mode tearing into Winton's naked flesh when swinging in any and every angle, and as hard and as fast as possible with the belt almost invisible.

Winton continually screams a dreadful cry, fighting to get free when turning, sometimes hit in the face and every other exposed part; even his feet. At times, the wet leather sounds like tiny blasts of M80s, sometimes sticking to his wet flesh, slowly twirling his body while sliding off slowly when Boogey tugs to free it and swing again.

Boogey's tears are somewhat clear, and finally, he starts to have pity; seeing Winton's swollen and blood-striped body. He sees a trail of blood running in a steady stream down the drain when unraveling the belt; letting off another scream, which echoes around neighboring houses, causing more nosy neighbors to peek or come out and look down toward Winton's house.

Some of Winton's neighbors nosily wander out into their yards.

Boogey stares longer in tears then finally turns, opening the door, and looking down while glowering over the darkroom of whiny voices.

His eyes somewhat focus, finding Nelle with an aluminum bat drawn high over her shoulder, rocking as if on home plate and ready to hit a home run.

Boogey's hand rapidly spreads. "Now, Nelle, I'm gonna have to ask you to put that bat down right now," Boogey says in a mild tone, stepping forward when she leans back, riding high for leverage.

"Come closer, and it's on!" she screams. "Who do you think you are? So, you think you can just come up in here and whip my man like a stankin' dog in front of me and our kids?" she screams, hearing Winton's cry in the background when the baby boy trembles, fearfully holding onto her garment tighter when crying louder.

"Now you look here Nelle..., that whipping was nothing compared to what I felt like giving him, so just consider him lucky because he could have counted himself dead!" Boogey says, taking sideways baby steps when safely clearing the door. He steps into the hallway when something catches his attention, discovering Winton's daughter wheeling a thick, shiny butcher's knife.

Boogey stares under-eyed and then focuses on the shifty blade. "Now you listen, here lil missy..., you can just put that down, little lady, before you get tore the hell out the damn frame!" Boogey turns backing then begins strolling down the hall, sadly with eyes continually looking back at her standing there in tears. He stops, shakes his head, then turns to look back then away, hearing something slam into the wall hard. He throws his head back, finding Winton's wet, bloody, limp, half-naked body coming off the wall, staggering. Boogey squints, seeing something long in Winton's hand when leaning forward, lunging, then running and diving off to the side and out of the narrow hallway.

Immediately, buckshot blasts down the hall, shredding the walls and busting the sixty-inch television screen head-on. The next shot sends couch stuffing flying high with bird feathers floating and falling slowly.

Boogey comes from behind the small kitchen island, diving behind the couch, low-crawling until over by the window.

Winton struggles to stand on blistered feet and then hops a few feet, waving the gun while trying to see through swollen eyelids.

"Over by the couch!" Nelle screams, guiding Winton and directing his aim when buckshot sprays by the couch, missing Boogey by inches when more feathers float high, falling slowly as Boogey draws in his feet.

Boogey lies on his side, listening to the two fighting to get the gun reloaded when springing up and bursting through the interior garage door.

The stock realigns with the barrel, and Boogey cringes to the loud sound of the click when sheetrock crumbles with Winton getting off a potshot along the wall leading to the garage door.

Boogey grips the garage door lever, full of adrenaline when pulling, but can't get it open. He looks back, hearing someone when grabbing a long futon pillow, backing up to the door. Boogey takes off, quickly diving and closing his eyes when bursting through the glass window, hearing someone kick the door in when loud shots ring out. Boogey's body slams to the ground, and he rolls, springing up as if never down when taking off in long strides.

Winton and his wife quietly listen until crying in laughter when out of nowhere, they hear Boogey stumbling over tires, hubcaps, and buckets in the backyard.

Nelle reloads, but lays the shotgun down and hands Winton the .45.

Winton strains to see when easing up to the kitchen window peeking with hands slowly running over the door knob. He listens for Boogey a second longer then nervously rocks, bursting through the door and running in the yard, firing back-to-back shots into darkness.

"Whoo wee!" Boogey nervously murmurs, fighting to get to the keys which fly out of his pocket and slide under the truck when he expressly drops, following them. He grabs the keys, kicking fast while backing out when a few un-aimed rounds land close with one passing inches from his head.

"You die tonight, American! You die tonight!" Winton screams in well-rehearsed foreign accent when one round hits Boogey's tailgate and the second shatters the back window.

"Let's just call it even right here, Wint!" Boogey yells when taking off, running toward the thick woods.

"You should have thought about that before you made me look like a fool in front of my family!" Winton hollers when a third-round hits the rear of Boogey's truck, piercing the gas tank, with a sudden blast then fireball going twenty feet high, leaving the truck engulfed.

"You'll pay for this, Wintoooonnnn!" Boogey yells, scurrying through the dirt path leading to the mini-mart and ice cream parlor.

Things stay quiet for minutes, and after a longer spell, the neighbors swarm the street; many rushing to the big flame when blue, cruiser lights cover the street.

Winton quickly rushes to his back door, passing the gun to Nelle, who runs inside, hiding both.

Two deputy's cars swerve into Winton's backyard, finding Winton un-muzzling and playing with the neighbor's dogs, with hands rising slowly as they approach.

"Winton! Was that you out here doing all that shooting?" the deputy asks with his gun still drawn until finding his hand empty.

"No, sau (sir), I suppose some kids ran through gang banging. They even set this truck here on fire; yes, they sure did, sir!" Winton backs deeper into the dark yard, evading questioning and keeping Boogey from being arrested because he wanted to kill him.

A deputy asks about his bloody bruises, but Winton lies about falling from a tree stand while hunting earlier.

One deputy calls for a fire truck, while the other shine lights around the dark yard, with both clearing the scene when more nosy neighbors rush up.

More deputies roll in, wandering around, trying to get more leads, but nothing, so they hang around until most folks peel off and leave shortly after the fire trucks.

Boogey finally reaches the mini-mart, nervously fumbling through his pockets for change while nervously looking around until hearing a car door slam and jumping. His eyes pierce into the darkness toward a row of trailers where he finds a man and woman going inside. Boogey nervously looks along the creepy, winding trail leading to Winton's neighborhood when slowly dropping quarters in the payphone and dialing while nervously looking around from time to time.

Nattie answers on the fourth ring, and Boogey whispers, telling her some of what transpired and where she should pick him up then hangs up.

He scurries alongside a building, seeing a car near the corner and hearing the moderate then blaring music. His heart races fast when backing deeper into a dark, shadowy area with only white eyes showing.

At Rev's brother's house, Rev walks in, and everyone grows quiet with all eyes following him until he leads off with a prayer for the sick.

"Ok, the Book of Timothy," he says, looking into confused faces. "You see, the apostles taught us how to walk, meaning, how to live. Your pastor can't just tell you how to please Almighty God; he has to teach you." He folds his hands behind his back, walking around then raises the Bible high. "You notice how every product you buy comes with instructions? Well, this Bible is our instruction for our life here on Earth and our Soul into eternity. It tells us how we should live to get the fullest of days now, in the end and the new Kingdom but unlike man-made products, we get the endless reward...; eternal life whereas with products you get longer product life." He smiles, looking around at exciting faces to the new revelation.

Over at Boogey and Nattie's, Nattie slips on the last shoe and grips her coat from the pile of clothes and boxes. She rushes out, warming the car, dimming the headlights, and backing up.

A short, manly figure pops up from the hillside, veering until wandering toward the back of Boogey and Nattie's house when her bright lights shine on him, unnoticed, when he ducks quick, veering more until fading behind their house.

At the mini-mart, a car pulls in, slowly shining bright light alongside the building, so Boogey scurries behind a trailer home. He hears the car squeal wheels, backing down, and then sees the car fly past when he reaches the fourth trailer, where he stops, catching his breath until high beams rush up on him.

"What the...!" a young, jealous boyfriend screams out the window, finding Boogey bent over near his girlfriend's backdoor. "Kattie! Kattie! There's a damn Peeping Tom out here! Quick..., call the law..., get my gun..., get my heater!" the man screams springing out and finding Boogey sprinting around other trailers while heading for his girlfriend's front door.

Boogey shoots past the last trailer, dodging into tall weeds.

The boyfriend bangs harder, finally waking his girlfriend, when hollering at the top of his lungs then letting off a hunting then mating cry to the wild when running around banging on other trailer walls before running back and banging on his girlfriend's again.

Boogey cuts through the woods, cutting down a dirt path leading to the road where Nattie would meet him. He picks up his pace, closing in on the paved road, when dodging into higher bushes, kneeling.

Out of nowhere, come low mumbling voices then shouts from several angry men, followed by loud barking hounds that flood in as hunters swarm the patch of woods, shining flashlights, and strobe lights.

High beams flash high overhead where Boogey is sitting when he rolls fast, hits the dirt, face-first, low-crawling. Boogey slides into a ditch and continues moving further away until slithering out alongside the road them coming up slow when diving fast at the sight of headlights. He begins low-crawling faster, then freezes with hands over his head, surrendering when a vehicle approaches at a high rate and slams on the brakes with bright lights shining directly on him.

"Get your tail in this car, Boogey!" Nattie screams. "What do you think you're doing out here, this time of night!" Nattie's high-pitched voice furiously echoes.

A smile comes to Boogey's face, but it leaves quickly, hearing the men and dogs getting louder until screaming voices call him all kinds of obscene and embarrassing names over the loud barks.

Boogey sprints past the back of the car, gripping the body and scurrying around for the door handle. "Go! Go! Go!" he screams, jumping in and pressing her kneecap down with legs still barely hanging out; causing the car to fishtail while coming up to sixty miles per hour.

Nattie eases off the pedal, slowing down to make a sharp curve, still fussing then guns the engine when completing another turn; heading for the highway. She slows to fifty-five miles per hour, entering the highway when getting quiet. "What's going on, Boogey? And where's your truck?"

Boogey sadly looks over with crossed, drunken eyes until his frown becomes a big, bright smile, and then a brighter, drunken smile when bursting into a peal of non-stop, loud laughter.

"Your truck..., well? And what's this that Nelle is talking about on the answering machine? Something about you whipping Winton naked in the shower and punching her in the freakin' head?"

Boogey tries gaining his composure when laughing harder until in tears.

Nattie looks at him, frowning until cracking a smile and joining in the laughter. "You're one crazy-tail man!"

Boogey catches his breath and begins telling her everything that transpired until they are in tears as they ride, recklessly swerving down the dark highway.

They finally arrive home and Boogey sprints inside, pulling out weapons, loading all of them, and strategically placing them in various rooms.

Nattie sits curiously watching him run around like a lunatic, shaking her head before heading for the bedroom.

Boogey walks in minutes later, climbing behind her, snuggling. He lies there with his eyes open for hours before finally dozing off, just as the rooster tunes up to crow.

The alarm blares an hour or so later, and Boogey falls back asleep, feeling secure that Nattie is up and about.

Later that morning, Boogey awakens to a drip outside and lays there for a long spell listening until slipping into his trousers. He eases alongside the house and then sprints inside for the phone, grabbing the phone book while easing into the chair.

"Stone's plumbing," the old, grey-haired gentleman says in a frail, scratchy voice.

"Yeah, yeah..., look ah here..., I have a leak, I reckon; well, I can hear it and see a wet spot against the house. Now look ah here..., I need it fixed real soon because I can't afford to have my water bill run-up like it was before; about two hundred or more, which I had to pay."

"Alright, sir, well, we're a little tied up. I've got guys working a few things here and two out in the field, I reckon so it'll cost more for emergency services. So tell me..., are you classifying this hea (here) as an emergency?" the old man asks, with the trembling pencil held anxiously over the emergency block on the work order.

"You daaammnn skippy, it's an emergency, but last I checked, you were one man deep, so who did you say was in the field and busy with these other jobs?" Boogey asks, pressing the phone closer when listening to the quiet background.

"Oh, naw, I'm fully staffed as of this week. I know you can hear all the racket they are making," the old man says, immediately slamming doors and rattling different tools or electric tools until muffling the phone and throwing his voice; making it sound like a conversation is going on in the background. He pretends to be talking to people until asking Boogey to hold while looking over the empty office. He soon ends the call and sits in the quiet office, staring before opening the register with two dollars inside.

Boogey looks up the dirt path over and hour later, finding a white, war-torn service truck slowly turning in the yard when cutting his eyes back at Nattie, and backing away from the dusty screen. "Here come this lying-tail man; talking about his office is fully staffed just to make an extra buck," Boogey says, dragging his feet.

The dingy truck pulls alongside the porch, and before Boogey can reach the door, the truck door flies open, and a high-water pant leg slowly extends to the ground.

Boogey makes his way into the yard and dust rise high as his size elevens slam down hard into the dust. He stares at the man's dusty boots, and his eyes wander to his overly ashy ankles when his belly begins giggling, from silently laughing so hard. He laughs even harder, seeing the man's ashy knuckles holding the door as the old man tries leveraging himself.

"Ever heard of lotion, petroleum..., or what Southerners call petro?" Boogey asks, with his mouth open, in a frowned laugh, when staring at the man's knuckles again and spotting one area whiter than snow.

"What?" the old man asks, in a mean tone, adjusting his coke bottle glasses and hearing aid at the same time.

"Lotion..., petro..., you know..., the stuff that turns dry skin into smooth flesh. You know..., like bringing it from death to life!" Boogey says, beaming.

"Oh, hush your darn nonsense trap! I've been using lotion since you were an itch in your pappy's pants, a brown stain in your parent's dingy, banana boat mattress," the man responds, frowning when looking, then leaning back, reaching for his rusty and heavily dented toolbox.

"Then maybe you need to reacquaint yourself with it...; walking around here with hands looking like you've been punching a ten-pound bag of fine, self-rising flour," Boogey utters, laughing even harder.

"Aww, quit all that yapping and talking that nonsense, man! I'm short-staffed, as is, so I had to come out and handle this hea (here) emergency myself so there could be an upcharge on that emergency. Well, anyways..., what seems to be the problem?" the plumber asks, looking at the side of the heavily painted, peeled house.

"Well, when I woke this morning, I heard a continual stream of water, and it seems to be coming from this side of the house. I know there's a pipe running along that inner wall, and there's a big water spot right there, but I'm not sure how to get to it.

"Ok, well, let's have a look," the plumber says, walking alongside the house and stepping over fresh potholes and dung patties. "Hmm..., there's the dang problem; there is a leak right there!" the plumber says, excitedly pointing at the same big spot that Boogey had shown him.

"Well, I'll be dang..., you are damn good! I mean, the spot is as big as day, and come to think of it..., I showed it to you. Well, I sho (sure) hope you don't charge me for figuring that one out," Boogey says, shaking his head in disbelief.

The plumber leans, running a hand over the wet spot. "Yeah, it's wet, alright," he says, looking back at Boogey, smiling as if it's his discovery.

"Look..., tell me this..., when does the clock start ticking for service, because you've been here for what, about fifteen minutes already, and haven't done a dang blasted thang!"

"Fifteen, you say, huh? Well, tell me this..., how long was it before you saw my truck over against the tree line before turn in the driveway?"

"About five minutes," Boogey cluelessly responds, looking at his watch.

"So, twenty plus the ten-minute drive; keep adding, son; keep on..., you've almost got it!" the plumber says, smiling when cheerfully stepping back and looking at the side of the house again.

"Drive? You expect me to pay that? Have you done lost a few screws or marbles? Yeah those coke bottles must be frying your brain in this hea (here) hot sun," Boogey mumbles under his breath.

"Hey..., what did you say?" the plumber asks, looking over his shoulder while walking back up to the wall and pressing his ear to it.

"Just fix it and make it lickety-split, Jack," Boogey utters, sticking his hands in his pocket and walking over to the man.

"Well, I don't hear anything here," the plumber says, continually hitting the house with the ball of his fist.

"Figures..., then maybe you should try banging it with your head," Boogey sarcastically says when shaking his head and then anxiously and nervously looking at his watch again.

"This sound..., what did you say it sounded like?"

Boogey makes several attempts to replicate the drip, but the plumber cannot figure it out, so he keeps asking Boogey to make more sounds, sometimes replicating Boogey's sounds until Boogey is just about fed up.

The plumber asks a few more times and then makes the sounds that Boogey had just made sound even more comical when Boogey grows furious. "Hey..., I'll tell you what..., wait right here in this spot, right here," he points. "I think I have the right thing to replicate it," Boogey says with a sly grin when taking off around the house fast and gone for well over five minutes.

The plumber scratches his head, then runs his fingers over his forehead, feeling a mist, then sprinkle then solid stream when backing up, blinded by the solid stream of water when spotting a shadow on the roof. He backs up a few feet, limping fast until taking off faster, running in circles, screaming in a high-pitched, frail voice with hands over his head. He slows and turns around again, looking up, finding an even heavier stream sailing downward and spiraling when picking up and dropping his feet as fast as possible, until backing up and falling into the trough.

Boogey's loud laugh gets even louder then echoes while standing with his boots planted on each side of the roof's pitch, pissing even harder and moving his hips in circles, swirling his piss in a design on the ground until it looks like a professional logo when smiling and waving. "Yee-haw!" Boogey yells, moving his head and butt as if broncoing.

The plumber frantically kicks and then kicks harder to get out when springing up. He dashes for his truck, drenched, when running almost sideways. He swings the passenger side door open, pulling out his hunting rifle from the back window, fighting to load two shells.

Boogey drops to the roof, hanging on with death-gripped fingers, slowly peeking over the ledge when seeing the plumber slap the barrel in alignment and aim.

'Blam!' the first round echoes.

Boogey heavily slips, screaming when rolling off the roof, landing face down, in the backyard, in a plume of high rising dust.

'Blam!' the second round comes, tearing a hole in the roof's edge.

Nattie's wide eyes pierce through the curtains, and she screams with feet expressly scrambling across the gritty floor.

The plumber comes around back, in stealth mode, with his gun pointing up at the roof, until finally spotting Boogey facedown and moaning about back pains. "I'll teach you to piss on me, you stupid sucka (sucker)!" the old man yells with a frown.

Boogey rolls over, covered in dust and still moaning in distress when finally feeling more pain in his ribcage when tears come with him fighting through the pain, with his sight slightly blurry.

The plumber aims, aligned with Boogey's head, when the back door slams suddenly, and he doesn't register it. He cocks his head to take aim but instead finds himself staring down the long, trembling barrel that eases from his temple.

Nattie tightens her grip, cocking her head, slowly. "You get one chance to go for that trigger then I'll blow your sweet little tail to smithereens!" Nattie presses the barrel forward and harder, slightly shifting the man's head to one side with his eye cocked.

The plumber begins slowly raises his gun and hands high when turning and backing up a few inches; noticing her shaky finger in the trigger well. "This bastard pissed on me!" the plumber whines in a girlish pitch when sniffing about his shoulders and frowning from the strong, stale moonshine-smelling piss.

"I don't want to hear it..., get your crap and get the hell off my property before I have your family dressed in black by the end of the week!" Nattie screams with one eye cocked with the gun still at his face.

The plumber trembles, turning bright red. "You all are a bunch of whackos!" he yells, slowly backing up with his gun at his side yet continually looking back, and finding her head still cocked and aiming. The plumber expressly walks to the truck, throws the gun in, and climbs in, spotting her then Boogey coming into view.

He turns, stopping with a sneaky grin, and then without warning guns the engine, raising a high dust cloud while plowing several deep doughnuts in the yard until the dust becomes so thick that Nattie and Boogey can hardly see each other or the plumber's truck.

He stops, waiting for the dust to settle a little then gets his bearings, kicking up more heavy dust. The plumber veers off several feet from the dirt path, intentionally taking out their mailbox before hitting the paved road, burning rubber.

Nattie shakes her head, turning and finding Boogey standing and holding his ribs. "What was that all about?" Nattie asks, lowering the gun. "Got me caught up in your mess, again! You gone (are going to) make me unintentionally smoke some fool one day, Boog!" She angrily shoves the gun in Boogey's chest when walking off.

Boogey shields his eyes from the bright sun, looking up at the long roof drop. He makes his way to the front, finding that the few strands of good grass he had are now scattered or smeared over the lawn. Boogey heads inside, scheduling another plumber then limps to the bed, where he falls and lies there until fast asleep.

Around noon, Boogey rises to the smell of road-killed Muskrat. He lay there, stretching, wiggling his toes through torn, mismatched socks, before sitting up and getting dressed. Boogey slips his feet in rundown, lopsided moccasins, pulls his coverall straps up, and stops at the kitchen door in deep thought when turning, collecting the staged weapons but leaving the shotgun at the front door.

Nattie steps inside with an empty clothes basket. "About time your drunk tail got up! There are lots of chores needing tending to since you're not going in today," she says, dragging her feet.

Boogey eases in the chair, eating when the phone rings and he answers on the fourth ring.

"Boogey, this is Rev."

"Oh, good morning, Rev, and top of the day. So tell me…, what can I do for you or get out of ya (you)?"

"Well, I'm calling because Sistah Mitchelle stopped by Sistah Nelle's, and she told her all about you and Winton tussling and all and the shooting and carrying on. Do I need to come over and pray for you?"

"Naw Rev, sometimes boys just gonna be boys, main (man). Me and ole Wint are first cousins, but it's all good; it's all about love, babe!" Boogey bites his bottom lip to keep from bursting into laughter when thinking back on Winton's old-fashioned beating.

"Well, I'm gonna swing by later anyways while I'm out making my rounds, so let's say 4 PM, if not earlier.

"That'll be just fine, Rev. I'll have Nattie put on some of that homemade apple or tatta pie that you like so much," Boogey says, looking over at Nattie, who sticks up her middle finger, frowning.

"That would be just grand, buddy. Well, I'll see you then, and until then, keep the peace, brudda (brother)," Rev says, running fingers down a list of phone numbers.

The two of them rattle on longer until the call ends.

Boogey sits a little longer until Nattie sits up with the lottery check in her hand, staring at it. "We have to figure out a way to clean up this mess we've gotten into with the car, truck, clothes, pending deliveries, confrontations, and all the stuff we selfishly busted up," she says, sadly staring over the check again.

Boogey pulls out a calculator, crunching numbers for hours, until devising a plan.

Later, Winton calls Boogey, and they argue for quite a spell before calling a truce.

Boogey feels that he has Winton's undivided attention, so he informs him of his plan to report the truck vandalized, so neither would have to pay for the damages or spend time in jail.

Later, Boogey and Nattie figure out how to diffuse the rest of the mess; laying out a plan to close the loop on everything and still have a thousand or so in cash left over.

Nattie gets up and cleans, then dresses for the bank and DMV.

They arrive at the DMV, and find five customers seated and three at the counter.

Boogey takes a number and reaches for the registration forms and they take a seat. He gazes over at a medium-built female making her way to the counter with five different hair shades.

The woman dressed in a white and black swirled outfit walks up to the counter, heavily smacking gum. "Uh..., yes, I would like personalized plates with the words D_I_V_A," the square-bottomed, booty woman, whose bottom cheeks form in the shape of a downward arrow, loudly and proudly says; swinging long, colorful hair to one side and acting proper.

The receptionist continues filing her nails and then leans forward, looking the woman over, from head to hips, then stands, leaning over the counter, looking down a dingy bedroom slipper-covered feet. "Ugh ugh, see..., we ain't got none! You can have D_E_B_A, DEBA, or ZEBRA, but we're fresh out of anything that even looks like DIVA," she utters, smacking and popping gum when filing her nails more.

The woman eases her head down slowly, scribbling down other names, which the receptionist types in and declines, though the computer says they are available. "Girl, look, I have other customers, so either take a seat and come up with more names, or go home and come back, or go with the DEBA tags; shoot, DEBA is what's hitting anyway," the receptionist says, winking at the male coworker next to her.

"Shoot, aight (all right)..., give me DEBA," she mumbles, frustrated.

Out of nowhere, a loud, manly voice breaks out in the testing area. "Oh..., hellz naw! Forget that! Somebody better explain to me why I can't get my license today!" the tall, no-lens, black rimmed, glass wearing guy yells with his face torn all up when told he missed the test by several questions this time.

"Now, calm down, sir! Get a hold of yourself because we can't have these loud outbursts in public places," the supervisor says, walking behind the issuing officer and waving off security. "What seems to be the problem?" she asks, looking over the screen and then at the issuing officer's fresh, manicured fingernails, which point to the top, slowly scrolling down.

"He has been in here seven times in the last two months, and each time, he scores worse," the issuing officer responds, running her fingers over the screen again at the horrible test scores and fifty percent of the missed signs.

The man's face frown the worst. "Well, obviously, y'all write these exams so hard that people can't pass them…, but I'm just saying!" the man utters in a loud tone, frowning more when seeing the supervisor's demeanor change.

"Bull Sh…!" the supervisor blurts out in a fake cough, excusing herself. She leans forward, fading under the counter, snickering until coming up almost a minute later, with a bright red face and red eyes, pretending to sneeze again.

"Well, y'all (you all) need to figure it out and get me my license…, today! Hell, I'd have to be dumb as hell to flunk a test nine times in a row!" the man exclaims, noticing them smiling. "I'm a freakin' genius! I have a degree from DIT, CID, PPIP, and TFT. I'm smarter than the both of you put together. So you tell me what the problem is, boo-boo!" he says, watching the supervisor fight back her laugh until she's calm when asking him to lower his voice again.

"Well, for one thing, we have to update your education on your registration for sure sir, if you have all those degrees," she says, looking at the city's certified school validation bold checkmark next to fifth-grade dropout.

"Well, if it ain't in there, that's another problem y'all gotta fix, now ain't it?"

"Sir, I think you need to take your time and read the questions the next time," she responds, passing him a sheet of paper from the printer with the big word, 'FAILED' stamped on it.

"I still say y'all need to review those questions before I come back," he says, dumbfounded.

"Well, I don't know about that because just last week, I saw on television where they gave the exam to third graders who got them all right with one week of studying," she says, laughing and then straightening her face when looking back at him.

"Word? Shoot! Snotty-nose little suckers must have been cheating!" he says, grabbing his personal documents and walking away, mad.

Boogey and Nattie sneakily eye the man as he turns and approaches with a red face, holding in laughter and busting a gut, laughing and falling into each other when the door closes and their number is called.

After leaving, Boogey and Nattie drive around for hours, renegotiating debts, and then return the car, explaining things to the manager, who is understanding while assuring them that the dealer's assets are covered fully through the dealer's insurance.

They catch a cab and the cabbie stops them by the auto store, where Boogey purchases a new alternator and battery, and then they return home with over nine hundred left.

Nattie puts five hundred in the jar, but the four hundred and change they agree to put in the bank.

The phone rings. "Hello?" Nattie utters with the phone at her shoulder, still counting money.

"Is Boogey in?" the frail, too-familiar female voice asks, coughing up phlegm.

Nattie frowns, holding the phone tight to her chest and muffled.

"Who is it?" Boogey asks, frowning with shrugged shoulders.

"It's your ugly-tail mammi," Nattie responds, covering the phone until stretching the long cord and pushing it heavily into Boogey's chest.

"Mama? Hello!" Boogey responds, smiling.

"Boooooggggeyyy, babe!" she says in a long whining voice. "How does your weekend look? Your daddy wanted me to let you know we are coming up, Baby!"

Boogey cuts his eyes back at nosy Nattie, finding her pretending not to be looking when looking back. "Oh, Ma, this might not be a good weekend because Nattie has plans for us to go to Stony Brook Park with the grandkids," Boogey says, cringing from the lie with surprised eyes.

"Oh really, Baby?" she says gracefully. "Well..., cancel it!" she says in a nasty and stern voice. "Baby, you never know when the last time will be that you'll see your mama and daddy, Baby," his mother says, taking another deep puff and plucking ashes in her hand and then on the carpeted floor.

Boogey nervously looks over his shoulder, staring deep into Nattie's eyes. "We'll see, Mama, but I know the kids are looking forward to it," Boogey responds, feeling really bad for lying. "But if we can cancel, will it just be you and Dad?"

"Hmm..., naw..., your brother, his girlfriend, and probly (probably) their kids," his mother responds, walking to the door, hacking up more phlegm, and spitting it toward the ground when it lands on the front porch railing, dripping off the ledge.

"Mama, you do still know we only have one bedroom, right? You complained about how tight sleeping quarters were with just you and dad the last time," Boogey utters, hoping she would cancel.

"Well, your brother and his girlfriend and her kids can stay at the hotel, for all I care; that's even if they bring their kids. I just hope that raggedy car of yours is able to get us back and forth," she says, popping the top off an ice, cold beer.

"What..., Betsy? Oh she'll be up and running later today," Boogey proudly says, in deep and questionable thought. "Shucks..., ole Betsy will be up and running like a champ!"

"Then pick us up at the station, Friday around six," she says, coughing again.

"Like I said, Ma..., we'll see, but I'll call back to confirm," he says, looking at Nattie's mean frown.

Deep in the heart of the county of Fikesville, at the sacred Fraternal Order of Police, special hunting club, the sheriff rallies up crooked local deputies and other distant sheriffs, police officers and deputies who are club members. Most bring food, beer, and moonshine, but a few come empty-handed.

Everyone indulges, and when Big John introduces a plan, everyone feels proud to be a part of the illegal outfit.

The room grows dark when photos of all the outlaws including the jail breakers they want behind bars flash across the projector screen for various unlawful reasons.

Later, a younger sheriff shuffles mug shots of Dallas and Hank on a dartboard.

Big John, whom everyone is afraid of walks over, placing more pictures up, and then places Dallas and Hank in the center. "There!" he exclaims, lighting his illegal Cuban cigar and acting mischievously cheery. "We'll do this by the numbers, boys!" he says, opening his gold dart case and asking the men to draw their darts when setting the bets by throwing down a hand full of crumbled bills.

Many of the crooked officials lean forward with the bills piling up fast until the last bill is thrown down.

The deputy in the swamp with Big John throws his dart first, hitting a bulls-eye on Hank and then Big John, the best thrower, hits Dallas, dead center, on his nose.

Other deputies' darts land either on the board, on the outer wheel or the wall until all darts land, pinpointing them all.

The deputy, with a notepad, begins numbering the photos, and another deputy, runs copies, passing them out while others lean collecting their distributed shares of the pot.

Big John pulls out the first five hundred dollars, laying it on the table.

Those without money write promissory notes, but two deputies don't participate due to hardship and are asked to leave.

"Well, there it is, gents, various dollars on each head, and the top dollar on these two clowns with an additional five hundred per head, from me, to any man that catches them tonight; dead or alive!" Big John utters, pointing to Dallas and Hank with a vicious stare.

The men end their meeting and are about to disperse when Big John calls the jail and puts out an All Point Bulletin (APB) on all ten.

Everyone disburses but three deputies stay behind, shooting pool.

The shortest deputy walks to the refrigerator, and grabs a foil-covered plate, sitting it on the counter. His nose runs closely over the edge sniffing until drawing back fast from an unfamiliar stench that rises. He uncovers the plate and his fork digs into what looks like a light layer of mold, removing and disposing of that section in the trash when walking to the microwave. He re-seals the plate with aluminum, sets it inside, and then sets the timer, dropping the fork on the stove and causing the other two to look back when walking away.

"Hit the freakin' deck!" the tallest deputy screams with wide eyes, diving into the deputy in front of him.

The three hit the deck, two drawing guns when the tallest deputy points to the microwave, and the three rush over then drop, finding the foil sparking.

'Kaboomaloomaloom!' The loud explosion echoes, blowing off the microwave door as they low-crawling with the shattered plate and door hurling across the room, with metal and glass fragments stuck in the wall.

They come up quickly in the smoke-filled room, and the shortest deputy rushes over, and open the front door.

Another deputy runs off, pulling a fan from the closet, cutting it on high, de-smoking the room, and the third one opens a few windows.

The three walk around shaking their heads, and turn to find the breaking news of an approaching hurricane.

Deep in the woods, another county over, Big Hank sits in his recliner, leaning and tuning up the stolen police scanner brought from a crackhead, and immediately hears his name. He tenses in fear, hearing the APB rebroadcast, knowing Big John and his men are coming, and there is no stopping them. Big Hank listens closely, hearing charges of racketeering, pimping, kidnapping, and a laundry list of other erroneous, illegal activities, when a sly grin comes, causing him to burst into a silly, delayed laughter.

A hooker walks out of the kitchen, bringing Hanks a cold beer on a serving tray.

Big Hank settles down, turning up the hockey game. He grips the walkie-talkie, switching channels, and warns his men of a possible raid, in code then flips through television channels, stopping on the missing body case. "Hell..., that body is probably in Davey Jones' locker by now!" He laughs.

"Davey, who?" a hired gunman asks, clueless when scratching his sleepy head.

"Oh, never mind, you would have to have been in the Navy to know what that means," Big Hank proudly responds easing his sleeve back and proudly staring at his tattoo when popping the bottle top of another ice-cold beer just passed to him from another hooker.

Around rural communities, a team of lawmen kicks in folk's doors, putting pressure on several folks known to frequent Hank and Dallas hideouts.

Big John drives in deep thought until cutting the wheel hard, slamming on the brakes, and slinging the car around in the middle of the road when heading for Fikeville's Free Press. He radios to a few deputies, mentioning his plan when stepping into the gas with black smoke and then fire shooting from the dual barrels.

Ten minutes later, Big John speeds into the Free Press lot, parking alongside the building, with the other cruisers out of sight. He eases his door open, rushing up to the wall with the others, with his back pressed against the cinderblocks. Big John gives a hand signal, and they begin sliding sideways until near the side door.

Big John slips through the door, with the others hot on his trail until peeking into the press room. Big John eases the gun in his holster, motioning the deputies to another door. He holds up three, two, and then one finger, and they burst into the room through both doors almost simultaneously, finding Dallas and Hank's baby brother, Melley hitting the last button on the print machine, when shutting it down.

"Get down!" Big John screams wide-eyed and almost cock-eyed. He pushes Melley backward hard guiding him to the floor and flipping him then pressing his huge cowboy boots in the crease of his back, holding him still until Melley's wiggling like a worm.

Melley screams non-stop until the pointed-toe boot presses even deeper, and he's almost out of breath, sounding almost like a high-pitch cartoon character.

"Shut your freaking pie hole! Just shut your trap right, now!" Big John yells, releasing the pressure but still resting his big boot on his back.

"Ohh..., I have a bad back..., a bad back!" Melley hollers.

Big John applies more pressure and begins rocking his big foot, exerting more pressure and pain. "Son..., you have yet to start feeling the real pain! Now tell me right now, where can I find your punk brothers and their goons who ran into my cruiser and hogtied me and my dispatcher?"

"My brother? What? Hell…, everyone 'round here knows Dallas is in rehabilitation, in Maysville, and has been for weeks. And Hank…, well, I have not seen him in months. Goons…, what goons?" Melley screams, still squirming to ease the pain.

"The people he frequent with, you idiot!" the sheriff screams, snatching Melley up by the collar. "Where the heck are they? I want to know and right now!" The sheriff snatches him up and shoves him face-first into the wall when the new deputies repositions to get a better view.

"I see…, hmm…, well, I'm trying to recall if they have any friends. Hmm…, no…, I'm still trying, but it just ain't hitting me just yet," Melley says, almost out of breath, still lying to keep from dealing with his brothers, who are three times tougher and more notorious than Big John.

"Malarkey…! Well, let me tell you this; it ain't the thinking that you gone (are going to) have to worry about hitting you if you don't start spitting names, pal!" Big John yells when shoving Melley back into a seat, slightly leaving him swiveling when motioning his men when Melley wiggles to shake off the pain and swiftly falls to the floor. Big John walks up, kicking Melley deep in the side, almost lifting Melley inches off the floor.

"Ahhh!" Melley screams in a high pitch like a female in distress.

Big John stomps Melley, trying to hold him still but loses his balance when Melley low-crawls halfway under the steps.

The two deputies reach forward fast, pulling him out by his feet, holding him upside down with change and a crumbled dollar falling from his pockets.

The deputies raise him higher and a silver dollar finally rolls over near Big John, and he stomps it flat, picking it and the other money up and slipping it into his pockets.

The deputies hold Melley longer, still looking at the sheriff, and acknowledging his nod when dropping Melley on his head and pulling him up by the collar, then flinging him in a sturdy seat, cuffing him.

"Ahhh!" Melley screams like a female again seeing then feeling the wind when Big John's wide hand sprung back to slap him.

"So it still ain't hit, huh?" the sheriff yells, staring at Melley when making some ridiculous-looking move that looks like the Texas two-step. He does faster, fancy leg work, then hauls off, slapping his tightly balled fist in his hand before slapping Melley with it sounding like gunfire.

Two deputies, not paying attention, jump, reaching for their guns and come up slow, easing their hands down, looking around, and feeling foolish when backing up.

Melley's coworker walks several feet in the press room, reading a document and not paying attention until opening his mouth to say something when freezing. He backs up and finds Big John's hand coming up with fingers to his lips to silence the man, and the man halts with eyes slowly gazing over at the deputies.

"Get the hell out of here, and don't come back!" Big John yells and frowns when turning back to Melley in a rush. "Listen here, either you tell me where they are, or I'll run your trifling tail through this here paper press, and your blood will be on everyone's porch come next run," Big John utters, stepping from the desk with a paperclip in his hand and running it under his dirty nails, in deep thought.

Melley sticks out his chest, deceptively toughening up like his brothers when finding his coworker still glancing through the breath steamed glass of the door's window.

"Oh, so you want to puff up like big bird..., maybe a rooster of some sort, hey?" Big John utters, drawing back hard and thrusting his fist deep in Melley's chest causing him to yell out some strange noise with most of the air knocked out of him.

Melley manages to take the first few stealth blows like a real man, holding it in until his chest feels like it's caving in when letting off a loud cry out of nowhere and then screaming in a high-pitched voice, higher than before.

Melley's coworker swallows hard, backing away and hurrying to the main office.

The sheriff does more fancy legwork, then leans forward, hauling back and slapping Melley's face as hard as he can with an open hand, and blood instantly rushes from his nose and ears over his shirt.

"Hot..., damn! Hot, digetty dog!" the youngest, newest deputy screams in an out-of-body experience, seeing Big John in rare form for the first time. Big John hauls off with an even louder slap, sending his ten-gallon sheriff hat flying to the floor. "I will be..., dayyaamm!" the youngest deputy utters, cringing from the firecracker sound and the sight of blood gushing out even faster when Melley's head twirls to one side as if he's about to go into an exorcism.

The door swings wide open, and the deputies look back fast, spotting a tall, six-foot-one, gray-haired, ten gallon hat wearing, old, pale-looking white, business-looking gentleman in his sixties. Melley's boss heavily wobbles down the steep steps fast. The owner runs up to the sheriff, who is drawing back swiftly, catching the sheriff's fully cocked hand as she releases it toward Melley's face, throwing the sheriff slightly off balance.

Melley's boss holds the sheriff in a tight grip, straining with all he has in him. "Stop it! Stop it! This is absurd! Look..., you can do your dirt elsewhere, but not on my watch!" he utters, staring down the sheriff, eye-to-eye. His nose begins flaring before feeling the sheriff's tension mellow out, then tense when the sheriff snatches away.

The sheriff brushes down his shirt before bringing his arms down to his side.

Un-cuff him or charge him, but no more of this nonsense, or I'll call the judge and mayor!" the old man utters, staring eye-to-eye with the sheriff without flinching.

The sheriff keeps staring at the man until slowly turning and motioning the old deputy to un-cuff Melley when turning and leaning into Melley, under-eyed. "You damn better well hope your bother is in rehab, because if not, when I come back, you'll be needing some rehab, and a lot of it because you're going to be in for a world of hurt, boi. I'm going to whip you so badly that your nappy head mammy won't recognize you," the sheriff utters, pissed and trembling with almost crossed eyes.

"Sheriff!" the grey-haired man screams again, stepping forward and pressing his hand deep in the sheriff's chest when slowly backing him away.

The sheriff licks his lips, reaching to the floor for his hat when nodding to the deputies as they single-file out behind Big John.

Melley's boss follows them to the lot, making sure all of them leave.

Melley's coworker's forehead soon presses against the window again with flared nostrils forming steam against the glass as he stands, giggling.

The door finally flies open and the coworker barges in fast, laughing so hard that he bumps into chairs and tips over a few things. "Man..., dat..., dat..., dat..., dat..., there sheriff...," he stutters. "Dat..., dat..., dat..., dat..., there sheriff had your bu..., bu..., bu..., butt cheeks so tight I be..., be..., be..., bet they were about to br..., br..., br..., br..., break!" he utters, laughing even harder.

Dale pisses off a feminine male orderly over at the rehabilitation center while on the phone with his lover when the conversation transitions into a whisper. He goes on to tell how Dale is hospitalized for an injury and how Dale is half-crazy from him switching Dale's prescription to Vellitrixal, a hallucinogen.

Dale walks past, whispering until talking crazy. "If there's a skeeter on your peter, pluck it off! If there's a skeeter on your peter, pluck it off!" he playfully sings, cutting his eyes at the orderly. "Hey there, skeeter!" Dale utters, closing the orderly and backing away when seeing the guy's fat fist.

After a late dinner, Dale dresses in his thrift store military fatigues. He stands before the mirror, turning and looking his uniform over until grabbing his combat boots and giving them a spit shine.

Dale's imaginary friend Colonel Bigsby appears out of nowhere in an all-white uniform with medals dangling. "Man up, Soldier!" the colonel yells, leaning forward and into Dale's ear when Dale snaps to attention with boots held tight in hand; his other hand giving a snappy salute.

"Get dressed, you lifeless slime ball! How dare you eat rations this late, you disgusting piece of blubber! Drop and givvvveeeee meeee twenty!" the colonel screams, staring eye-to-eye with his nose pressed hard upon Dale's nose.

Dale drops, pumping out twenty push-ups like nobody's business. "Permission to recover, sir!" Dale shouts, with his hands hard against the cool floor with eyes swarming over a few folks peeking out of room doors and fading back inside fast from his delusions.

"Recover…, you slime ball!"

Dale pops up, and his feet taps until doing a partial moonwalk, then turns quickly, expressly walking to where he hears music with the Colonel fading in the background.

The perfect beat grows louder as Dale approaches his best friend's room, easing up to the door, and peeking inside.

The music stops, and the beat starts over when the old man's (whose room it is) twenty-seven-year-old grandson rewinds the beat, and his two friends bob their heads when the beat comes on again.

The grandson, a famous rapper, balls his fist, rapping through the song, and then motions his friend to start the beat when he messes up. The famous rapper takes hits from a flask pulled from his jacket and then raps again but keeps messing up from being so high.

Dale peeks inside and leans back, running to the housekeeping station for a broom handle.

The music starts again, and Dale waits until the frustrated rapper stops the beat, takes another sip, and motions to his friend. "Take it from the top!" the rapper yells, frowning while gripping his fist tightly. The beat comes again, and before the rapper opens his mouth, Dale slides in, rapping and making up words to make it comical.

Everyone in the room is in tears, hearing his perfect yet unrehearsed words.

Dale raps the whole beat, putting his own little twist on the end, when loud laughter rises and hands pat him on the back with some giving high fives or clapping.

At Boogey's, around noon, the phone rings, and he answers on the third ring.

"Hey, Daddy! Davillier got off early and wants to know if you can go with him over to Mundson to pay a speeding ticket," Boogey's daughter asks.

"Sure, but I need to shower right (real) quick." Boogey looks back at the clock. "Have him get on over here now because we don't have much time," he says, kicking his boots off.

Nattie walks into the bedroom, looking around for something for Boogey to wear. She soon paces by the door, hearing the shower running then the curtains slide shut. She waits longer until she can no longer wait when slipping inside quietly, easing onto the toilet. She hears a second stream of heavy water and leans slightly forward peeking through the crease in the shower curtains.

She releases her strong urination, instantly noticing something dark, and almost fluorescent flowing in a solid stream; channeling toward the drain when her eyes widen. "Oooh! Ya (you) common buzzer! In here pissing in the bathtub like you ain't got no home training and sense!" Nattie screams, loudly releasing herself and frowning.

"What the...!" Boogey utters, slamming the curtain seam shut. "Damn! I can't even use the bathroom in private! What is this world coming to?" Boogey utters, even more embarrassed.

"What's wrong with you, Boog? What type of man does that? Name one man that does that, crap!" She lets off a loud and obnoxious fart, then an even more solid stream of urination that lasts for well over two minutes.

"What man? Hell..., what woman sneaks in the bathroom and stank it up while talking a bunch of crap and pisses for what..., three minutes? Only men piss that long! Now that's some real gangsta (gangster) stuff right there! What woman did you say..., huh?" Boogey asks waiting for an answer when there is total silence then mumbling.

Nattie grows quiet, senselessly and quietly giggling with a few more accidental bouncing farts. She holds her laugh back until bursting into laughter while flushing.

"Ouwah!" Boogey yelps, bowing backward and flinching from the unstable, fluctuating ice cold then hot water beating off his chest. "Nattie!" he screams, balling his fist tight, and piercing his fist through the curtain in a sharp, professional boxing jab as she passes and ducks fast.

He sprints out fast minutes later and is almost dressed when hearing Davillier blow before parking. Boogey listens for Nattie when sneaking a deep-throat swallow of moonshine and reloading his flask. He steps onto the porch, finding Davillier easing out of his truck. "Perfect timing, Davillier. You drive." Boogey walks around to the passenger side.

They jump in, and Davillier pulls away, slowly. He comes up to the main road, waits for a huge farm tractor to pass, and then pulls behind it, swerving around and speeding off in front of it.

In record time, they reach the outskirts of Fikesville, running into a little traffic due to a lot of farm equipment moving amongst fields.

Boogey nervously sits, looking around, and then pulls out his flask, taking a hit.

"Oh, snap, let me get a hit!" Davillier utters with his hand out.

"Not while you're driving, me, you won't!" Boogey utters, looking off as if Davillier is crazy as heck.

Traffic clears, and Davillier looks at his watch, increasing speed. He closes within miles of the court, trying to beat a red light when flying through it, in front of a deputy's car as it eases out on the green and then slams on the brakes.

Blue lights flash, and the deputy skids wheels through the intersection, barely missing another car.

Boogey and Davillier's eyes drift to the rear and then side mirrors when blue lights appear around a sharp bend in the road.

Davillier pulls over, and the cruiser pulls up on his bumper.

The deputy jumps out, rushing up to the driver's door. His heart races fast and his hand goes to his hip, over his gun. "What the hell was that move you pulled back there, numb nuts?" the deputy yells with a mean stare.

"What?" Davillier asks, looking into the deputy's red face, dumbfounded.

"Ugh! Driver's license and registration! Driver's license and registration, now!" the deputy yells with his shaking finger in Davillier's face.

Boogey reaches for the glove compartment, pulling out the registration, while Davillier leans to one side, pulling his wallet out.

The deputy snatches the license and then other documents.

Boogey pulls out his ID when asked, and playfully drifts back and forth each time the officer reaches until giving it to him after the fourth, frustrating attempt.

The deputy stares at Boogey, frowning and rolls his eyes but keeps his eyes on him, backing away and fading alongside the truck, climbing into his cruiser. The deputy reappears minutes later. "So why did you speed through that red light? I don't see red paint, emergency symbols, or flashing lights on this here vehicle, so slow it down! Besides, you have a ticket in the system already."

"Yeah, yes, sir, I was trying to make it there to pay the speeding ticket before they close," Davillier utters, thinking the deputy is a little friendlier.

"Yeah, well, just slow it down, and this will remind you of that lead foot in the future," he says handing him the documents and small clipboard. "Just press down hard, son; you're making three copies!" the deputy utters, carefully pointing the box and watching him sign. He grips the board, rips the copy off, and passes it to Davillier along with his documents.

"Thanks a lot, Dick! I mean, Derek!" Davillier says, doing a double-take on his name tag.

The deputy nods his ten-gallon hat, walking to his cruiser when his eyes grow wide, looking up and twisting hard, sideways until pressed up against the cruiser.

Davillier throws the truck in gear, looking through the side mirror at the deputy, hearing his dreadful scream until seeing an eighteen-wheeler blast past.

Strong winds from the fast-moving trailer blow the deputy up against the cruiser and fling his hat over the hood, to the ground, slightly leaving the vehicle rocking.

The deputy throws the door open quick, jumps in and swerves into traffic, causing drivers to slam on brakes, avoiding a rear-end collision.

Boogey jumps out quickly and grabs the hat, dusting it off then shines the dusty badge with his shirt sleeve, slipping it on, quickly. "I say, boy..., boy, let's get this here stagecoach, ah moving, boy!" Boogey shouts pointing at Davillier in an imitated cartoon voice and laughing when climbing back in.

Davillier uncontrollably giggles, pulling away and comes around the third sharp curve, finding the deputy standing outside the eighteen-wheeler, pointing upward, screaming, and motioning the driver down with his gun drawn.

Boogey smiles, waving when speedily snatching the hat off before in clear view. He waves to the deputy, and Davillier lays into the horn a long spell as they pass.

The deputy throws up a middle finger at them, snatching the driver down by his big belt buckle as his feet hit the first step on the big rig.

Davillier pulls up at the clerk's office, passes a few metered parking spots, and then swerves into handicapped parking, jumping out and scurrying inside.

Boogey adjusts the radio, finding something to his liking, when his head begins bobbing and his feet continually tap. He lifts the hat, reading the badge when feeling someone walking up, causing him to jump and slam the hat in the crease of the door. He looks off, finding a meter maid at the back of the truck. "No, no, no, no..., he just ran in for a minute." Boogey yells nervously opening the door, and reaching back in to hide the hat.

"Well, your friend didn't look handicapped to me!" the female utters, tearing off the yellow slip.

"Man, you people are over this place like flies on a hairy pair of bull's gonads (nuts)!" Boogey utters, rolling his eyes and snatching the ticket.

"You have a good day, sir, and remember, I'm just doing my job just like you have a job to do, but I have to do my job to the best of my ability," she utters, strutting off and over to the next car parked in handicap without a sticker.

Davillier jumps in, and looks at Boogey when he hands him the too-familiar colored slip. "What's this?" Davillier asks, dumbfounded, looking into Boogey's eyes.

"Take a guess, but you only get one chance to get it right," Boogey utters, shaking his head. Boogey's eyes glaze over at the other car, then the men's heads bobbing while they sit, talking, joking, and flirting with the meter maid. "Forget this! Just pull up alongside them," Boogey screams, enraged. "Hey, you...! I've got a bone to pick..., how you (are you) gonna (going to) ticket us and not these damn clowns?" he asks with a mean face when Davillier tries calming him.

The meter maid slowly turns, motioning the men to wait when taking a few steps up to Boogey's door, but stands a ways back, looking through at Davillier. "Now, sir, I'm going to have to ask you to move because you're in handicap and no-standing zone."

"Oh yeah? Well, stand on this!" Boogey makes a ring hole with his index finger and thumb, shoving his middle finger in and out repeatedly while in a silly laugh.

The woman looks away, then back at the meter machine, checking the tag number and mashing the number five when the machine spits out five tickets back-to-back. She rushes to the passenger-side window. "Let's see how much these will cost your driver," she utters, throwing each ticket in the window.

"Hit the gas, Dee! Hit the damn gas! This trick is crazy as hell!" Boogey yells when Davillier speeds off and comes to a stop sign. He turns, burning rubber across light sand and gravel until the tires smoke as he slows.

Sirens ring out, and blue lights flash when a different cruiser closes in fast. "Dang, son! You (you are) shooting bad, main (man). After this, let me take the wheel before you end up in jail with all these tickets," Boogey utters, pissed and shaking his head in disbelief.

The trooper jumps out, mounting his hat and staring at the vehicle as Boogey moves around, trying to hide the deputy's hat. The trooper steps back, nervously drawing his weapon. "Engine off..., and hand on the dash!" The trooper shouts adjusts his shades.

Boogey continues moving until cramming the hat alongside the seat.

"What the...!" the deputy screams. "Shut it down! Shut it down, now!" he nervously screams, looking at Davillier until the engine shuts off. The deputy sprints to the passenger side, curious about Boogey's excessive movement. "What are you over here hiding, you slick son of a gun?" the deputy screams, slipping his gun in the holder and pulling out a fluorescent stun gun.

Boogey makes one last shove and packs the hat against the seat and door. "My hemorrhoids..., my hemorrhoids were acting up; you know, itching and all?" he utters, faking it when moving more and lightly squirming.

"Yeah, Ok..., well, we'll see about that!" the deputy utters, adjusting his ten-gallon hat and pulling at the door handle until it swings open and the wrinkled deputy hat flies out with the badge facedown. The deputy jumps back, aiming at Boogey's side when Boogey's right hands rise to the roof as he begins to slide out.

The deputy screams for him to get back in when a different eighteen-wheeler overcomes his voice when he points to the bright, shiny badge on his hat. He stares at the smashed hat when another eighteen-wheeler's winds, roll the hat, face up.

The deputy's confused face turn mean when finding Davillier in laughter.

Boogey's face turns stale when the stun gun discharges, un-aimed, barely missing Boogey and hitting Davillier and throwing him into convulsions from holding it too long.

Boogey looks back at the Davillier, laughing so hard that his hands hit the open door's windowsill, fast when the nervous deputy quickly retracts the leads. Boogey shoots out, picks up the hat, dons it, and dances around slowly, like a true drunk.

The deputy immediately fires again, hitting Boogey and holding the charge until he stands stiff as a board and falls face-first in the grass, continually jerking with his body bowed and his feet curled up in the air.

The deputy drops the stun gun and goes for his weapon when another trooper who just passed slings the car around swiftly, sliding sideways and burning rubber until pulling up behind the other cruiser.

The other deputy jumps out, drawing on Davillier. He slings the door open and slams him face down in the narrow, dusty trail between the truck and road.

They speedily put them in cuffs and sit them on the ground, questioning the possession of the hat when Boogey tells the drawn-out story and then mentions looking for someplace to return it.

The short trooper walks off a few feet, calls the other deputy on his handheld, confirms the story, and then un-cuffs them. He writes Davillier a ticket for skidding wheels and then allows them to leave.

They clear Mundson's city limit when Boogey motions Davillier to pull over to a store that has a lottery sign in the window.

Boogey opens the door for a female and stares at her hourglass figure.

Davillier finally looks up to find Boogie stuck on stupid when the female sprints to the van, and a big man stands pointing at Boogey in anger. Davillier hears the female talking the man down and getting the man to get back in when she jumps in, and the two doors close with them pulling away fast.

Boogey finally reappears minutes later, opening the front door of the store, and screaming. "Fire in the hole!" he staggers out and finds Davillier staring, slumped over, laughing like a crazy man when spotting a female rushing behind Boogey, then a line of people: all vigorously fanning.

The first lady, the store owner keeps her shoulder against the door, pinching her nose with her other hand pointing at Boogey, cussing up a storm.

Boogey climbs in with a silly laugh, and his eyes dimming from overindulging.

Davillier's eyes almost cross when falling to one side, rolling down the window fast and gasping for air. He expressly slings the door open, scurrying away from the truck, heavily fanning, and walking up minutes afterward, then rushing off again, fanning even harder. After several more attempts to make sure the stench is gone, Davillier approaches sniffing then eases inside, staring in Boogey's red laughing face then pass him and at the store owner flipping Boogey the bird.

"Hey, swing me by Sweet Briar Convalescent Home so I can see my grand pappy before we head back," Boogey utters, sweating profusely.

Within thirty minutes, Davillier pulls up at the rehabilitation center and finds Dale hiding in the bushes, attempting to sneak up on a female in a wheelchair.

Boogey stands looking at Dale, shaking his head, when Dale creeps within feet of the woman, reaches forward, furtively unleashing her brakes. He leans back as far as possible and pushes her chair down a long, deep ramp with her hollering at the top of her lungs.

Boogey yells to him and Dale jumps, looking around.

The woman continues hollering, looking backward while rapidly rolling down the incline, trying to get hold of the fast-spinning wheels.

Boogey takes off in a wide-legged sprint when the woman grips one wheel slinging around fast and forward, wobbling when Boogey intercepts the chair with the metal footrest deep in his shins. "Ahhhhh!" Boogey screams, hopping when the chair veers off and stops. Boogey jumps around longer, holding more screams for as long as he can when letting off a loud cry while dancing to ease the excruciating pain.

The woman sits breathing hard and cutting her eyes over at Dale until her tight fist rises when looking for Boogey. "Thank you, young man, you're a gentleman and a scholar," she utters, still frowning until looking back at Boogey, smiling.

Davillier jumps from the bushes still bent over laughing. He wipes away the smile and walks up to Boogey, staring at Boogey's painful frown.

Boogey, Davillier, and Dale walk inside and down to the administrator's office.

Boogey approached the counter, swaying while signing Dale out.

Davillier backs into a corner, laughing at the administrator's frown as she backs away from the stale liquor stench.

A city away from Fikesville, Boogey taps Davillier's shoulder when coming up on a convenience store and veering off.

Within minutes, the doorbell jingles when the door swings open, and the three walk inside.

Dale brings up the rear, wandering off to the back, near the beer cooler and comes up alongside, finding the door cracked open when slithering inside.

Another man walks in dressed almost like Dale and heads to the cooler with eyes wander until closing the door and moving to another door. He holds the door open even wider, looking for his brand until hearing commotion inside. The man peeks around a few stacked beer boxes, finding Dale laid back, popping cold beers, back-to-back. He looks over his shoulder toward the register and then back into the cooler, laughing in disbelief until pulling another door slightly open, hearing empty beer cans hitting the floor one after another at very slow intervals.

Boogey's eyes wander around, finding the man he perceives to be Dale when moving up in the line.

Dale cracks open the tenth beer, leaning over, sizing up the 40 oz. Malt liquors when downing a couple of swallows. He tries standing but staggers back a few feet into ten boxes of bottled beers, stacked eight levels high, creating a loud domino effect with the ten other stacks.

Everyone in the store instantly turns or looks back at the cooler, hearing the continual crashing with a few patrons looking at the door thinking its thunder.

The owner freezes, looking over everyone's heads then the door but slowly ringing people up until curiously looking toward the cooler from time to time.

Dale leans to pick up an open box, and while still bent over, he looks back to find the Korean-looking man staring through the glass door before turning and walking away. Dale freezes, anxiously looking around until hyperventilating when scavenging through boxes, loading his coat and pants pockets with beer bottles with an additional four cool bottles stuck down his pants.

Boogey looks over his shoulder, finding the back of the man's head, who he thinks is Dale, noticing his shoulders moving up and down, giggling. Boogey pays quick, looking longer when motioning Davillier over to the other side of the adjoining store for a submarine sandwich.

The store's front door swings open, and twelve teens walk in looking suspicious. They separate and go down different aisles when the clerk motions to the man in the side office and then nods in the direction of the kids.

The other clerk tilts and zooms the camera, watching the kids, and then hits the alarm when one grabs a handful of items and the others follow suit, scattering and busting through the front and side door.

The side door of the cooler soon flies open, and Dale slips out. "Inbound!" Dale screams, pulling a bottle from his pocket, twisting the cap off with his teeth, and throwing the bottle high toward the counter at the Korean man who had just had donned his big straw hat, when covering his ears with both hands.

Everyone at the register takes cover, immediately spotting the high twirling bottle and watching it until it bounces from the front of the counter, bursting. They all come up slow, immediately locked onto two more bottles sailing high when dropping and hearing one burst, with the other falling short, and hitting the front of the register, bursting.

Dale falls back into the wall as if in the war, pretending to be staggering like a wounded Soldier in battle when his hand comes up high, and he leans back, lunging two more bottles as patrons scatter out the front door, screaming.

"Inbound!" Dale screams again, discovering several cans of dog food coming back at him when covering his head and ducking down fast.

The lead clerk stealthily lunges several more cans, ducking while pointing to get the owner's attention.

The other clerk and owner bend over behind the counter until the owner pulls out his twelve-gauge sawed-off pump, checking to ensure it is loaded and leaving it bent.

The other clerk screams in his native tongue, and Dale takes cover at the end of an aisle well-hidden and peeks back at them.

The Korean customer kneels, cutting down an aisle, staying low while making his way toward the front door, looking back when yelping in his native tongue. He grabs a few bottles of orange drink, firing them off, with the drink splattering at the top shelf of the potato chip rack.

Dale drops down with his back against the rack, pulling a cold beer bottle to his lips, peeling off the cap. He flings two more over his head at the counter when Boogey and Davillier's head pops up of nowhere peeking from around the corner.

Boogey leans forward and motions for Davillier to follow him then bends over, peeking down one aisle.

Dale low-crawls alongside the cooler's side door and come up around the back where he sees light and exits through a cracked open door.

Boogey looks back, hearing the gun latch when finding two men stepping down from the platform with mean stares. He slowly makes his way over the first aisle, peeking around the next aisle and then the next, when telling Davillier to get to the vehicle and pull around the corner. Boogey looks toward the wall alongside the store and sees a ray of sunlight shine against the wall when he turns, calming the man with the gun. "Let me go first," Boogey utters, making his way down the aisle and motioning the owner to hold his position, then motioning him closer a little at a time.

Boogey moves further down at an even slower pace, cutting his eyes out the door's glass, finding the truck still parked with the back door easing shut.

Dale sits up high, glances out the windshield, and jumps when the front door flies open, and the vehicle shifts to one side when Davillier jumps in and speeds off.

Davillier turns at the light and looks over his shoulder for traffic when spotting movement when swerving and screaming.

Boogey stares longer. "What the hell? He must have gotten out through the back door," Boogey utters, looking over his shoulder at the man, surprised.

The clerk and owner move fast, passing Boogey.

The owner trains the gun in the cooler's side door when flinging it open and going in as if a trained officer with surprised eyes when stepping in an inch of beer, and high stepping.

Boogey waits until the man comes out and then follows him out the side door, where they stand looking around the perimeter.

Loud sirens and blue flashing lights roll into the lot, and a few pedestrians run up, pointing down the street in the direction Davillier took off in, still pointing with others walking up.

Minutes later, more sirens are heard when two more cars pull up. The two cruisers disperse, combing a few streets until returning, taking more statements.

Davillier goes home to drop off his vehicle and gets the other vehicle, heading back to fetch Boogey. He pulls up an hour later, spotting Boogey sitting on a bench across the street when swerving into the lot, tooting the horn.

Boogey makes sure he is clear of the deputies when walking over and climbing in, looking back at Dale, who is drunk off his tail and in tears of laughter.

Davillier pulls off, coming up on a stoplight, slowing down, and stopping.

Boogey looks over his shoulder when feeling a cool breeze rush up the back of his neck from Dale's window going down fast.

A car pulls alongside with two, six, or seven-year-old kids in the back, staring at Dale, who stares back until one kid makes silly faces.

The kid behind the driver seat gets the attention of his friend, pointing when his friend flips Dale the middle finger and laughs, senselessly.

Dale motions for the boy in a friendly manner, convincing the closest kid to roll down the window while digging deep in his pockets.

The mothers look around, and the driver looks at Boogey, turning her nose up.

The kid finally gets the window down when both lean to see if they can hear or make out what Dale is saying while moving his lips saying nothing while pulling a lighter out.

Davillier and Boogey look back, hearing a light sizzle when smelling a hint of sulfur. "Dale!" Davillier screams, looking at the fully expanded slingshot with the cherry X bomb attached to an M80 style stick when it releases.

The firework hits the far side of the car's door and rolls under the seat.

The woman driver looks over her shoulder, hearing the boys making a lot of noise and using a few selective cuss words when unbuckling and stomping. "Hey, watch your mouths, you two! Calm down and put your seat belts back on!" the driver screams when the other mother looks back, motioning to her that the light has changed.

The boys keep stomping the too-familiar-looking fireworks when the cherry bomb explodes first, and they draw their feet back, bracing for the blast. The kids scream for their mother's friend to pull over, but she eases into the gas pedal, rolling through the intersection, looking back, and screaming when finding the car filling with red smoke quickly, with the boys vanishing fast.

The driver quickly makes her way to the shoulder and veers back into the road seeing the road's shoulder disappear when several honking cars speed by, swerving.

Everyone in the woman's car screams when the car swerves in both outer lanes, causing Davillier and other cars to vector in and out to avoid hitting her.

Davillier drops back a little, and their eyes fill with tears, watching the stuck-up woman swerve before slamming on the brakes and rolling the windows down fast.

'Kaboom!' The loud sound comes, shooting red smoke out of all four windows, when the car shoots off like a rocket, traveling over a hundred feet when the smoke clears from the car's stealth movement.

The woman makes her way to the side of the road, slamming on the brakes.

Davillier makes a left at the intersection, racing the engine to distance them.

Boogey sits, looking over his shoulder at Dale when tapping Davillier on the shoulder. "Ain't no way I'm getting a drop of sleep with gramps in this condition. Turn around, and let's drop him back off at the center," Boogey utters, looking once more to find Dale slumped down with a sad face.

Dale grows pissed hearing he's going back, so he stays quiet the entire trip.

Boogey makes mild conversation but never gets a response from Dale, who sits staring into the rearview mirror at Davillier's face.

When Davillier isn't looking, Dale playfully sticks out his tongue and uses hand gestures to make silly faces or sticks his middle finger up at him or Boogey until caught by Boogey a few times.

They arrive at the center and sign Dale back in, then turn to find folks coming out of the cafeteria when Boogey asks for a plate for Dale.

Boogey spots another late eater rolling in and up to a table.

The senile old man stares at the ceiling, and then around while the old female orderly pulls up a chair to feed him.

Dale sits next to the man, curiously staring at the woman and then the man until cutting his eyes over at Davillier and Boogey, who are now standing off in a corner.

A female from the kitchen appears with two sandwiches and a carton of juice, setting it before Dale, who stares at it, then smashes the sandwich and forcefully pushes it away when pouring the juice over the table.

The senile man shakes his head and then looks away from Dale, pissed. He takes a few hearty mouthfuls and, before long, motions when done. The senile man eases back into the wheelchair, sticking his chest out, looking at Dale, whose eyes are crossed from the serious hangover.

"I've dined, and I'm sufficient," the senile man utters, beaming while rubbing his tight stomach.

"You say you went fishing?" Dale asks, looking over with intent.

"Poor ole soul," the man mutters, shaking his head.

"You say you broke your pole?" Dale responds excitedly with drunken eyes.

"That meal sure was nice!" he utters, looking at the ceiling, shaking his head that Dale is such an idiot for not knowing it's an old saying from some unknown person.

"You say you broke it twice?" Dale responds, waiting for the man to mysteriously talk more about fishing.

# CHAPTER SIX

### Fun With The Drama

Boogey and Nattie sit in the house in the cool of the day, both slightly leaning forward, when spotting Rev's truck coming down the dusty driveway.

Nattie eases up, checking on dinner, while Boogey eases to his feet, adjusting his trousers until pulling a hand full of sticky draws out then smelling his hands.

Rev barely spots Boogey at the screen door, waving when slightly veering off to the side of the porch. He climbs out, adjusting his tie, and then slips on his thin jacket. "Nice day, huh, Boog?" he utters, nervously walking up the flimsy, half-rotted, wood steps; with several boards missing.

"Mighty fine day, Rev..., mighty fine!" Boogey looks over Rev's shoulders toward the main strip spotting the sheriff's car zooming by with its flashing blue lights but no siren. "Come on in, Rev..., glad you could finally make it on this end," Boogey mutters sarcastically.

Rev steps inside, freezing in place when looking around the junky living room.

Bud opens his mouth to greet Rev but squints instead, finding a fat cat easing up on the bottom step; licking its sharp paws.

Rev's eyes go back over his shoulder, finding Boogey in a sideways stare when taking a few more hesitant steps. His eyes scroll through the room and then over the dirty couch, finally finding the cleanest spot that appears to be close to suitable for his clean threads. "You know..., I'm sorry I couldn't get by sooner, Boog," he says, unknowingly looking around in disbelief with excited eyes as his mouth slightly drops open when scanning more and finding the bedroom even worst and filthier.

Nattie enters, and Rev springs up like a perfect gentleman; walking over and shaking her hand. "Top of the day to you, Mrs. Natt," Rev utters, making it known that the house is a hot mess with excited and slow, wandering eyes.

Rev gazes over several dust-covered pictures on the wall as he takes a few steps around the junky room. He walks off and heads to another wall with Melissa's perceived K-12 school pictures which are all stamped 'PROOFs' or 'SAMPLEs'. "Hmm..., lovely pictures, but did yawl (you all) ever give it any thought on buying them?" Rev asks, cutting his squinty eyes back at Nattie who looks away fast and then over at Boogey when his eyes go straight to the ceiling.

"Yep! Sure did..., oh yeah, we did a lot of thinking, but the money was kinda funny..., we'll you know what I mean," Boogey utters, cutting his eyes over at Nattie's embarrassed, shaking head.

Rev makes his way back over, easing into the cleanest spot with both hands at his side to readjust when looking down, noticing a greasy then bugger-looking smear on each side when cautiously drawing his hands in his lap.

Boogey locks eyes with Rev immediately, finding his eyes still wandering until stealthily locking onto the busted television that he obviously missed when passing it. Boogey's eyes trail over the table and onto the broken television glass then a pile of glass swept in a heap in the corner. "Shii..., I mean, shoot..., that thing fell the other night when the power went out, and I tripped over the cord and almost broke my neck," Boogey utters, cutting his eye over to see if Rev is buying off on the little white lie, especially after spotting the baseball bat next to the television with a few glass shards sticking out.

Rev's curious eyes and swift mind puts one and one together when slowly looking back over at Boogey. "Well, you be careful now because I don't want to lose any up-and-coming members," Rev utters, looking over the junky table, apparent gunshot hole in the wall and then down at the big hole in the bottom of the screen door.

Nattie finally eases back up to the kitchen door, smiling and blushing, but wipes the smile away when finding Boogey staring with a jealous frown. "Will you be staying for dinner?" Nattie asks, being mannish, just to get Boogey jealous when unraveling her thick, braided ponytail and shaking out her long hair.

Rev takes another look at her radiant glow and wavy hair. "I thought you'd never ask, but on another note, I do have to be going, so I'll take a rain check; but I sure would love to have some good ole tata (potato) pie," Rev utters, getting nauseated after meditating on having ever eaten anything out of their nasty house when the aroma of the warm pie rises deep in his nostrils.

Nattie nods with a smile, drifting back into the kitchen.

Rev keeps looking around until noticing Boogey's frown when thinking quickly and striking up a conversation about his services.

Minutes later, Rev changes the conversation to keep the momentum but becomes distracted when an unfamiliar sound rises in Rev's ear. He looks near the recliner, finding a fat cat pulling its flexible body through the big, busted screen opening.

Boogey springs forward. "Where have you been, little fella?" Boogey asks when the cat stops; looks at Boogey, up at the birdcage, and then sits licking its paws with a long stare at the bird which now looks like a statue; too afraid to make a move.

Bud remains still, speechless, with not a word, peck or blink. His eyes stay straight as the cat looks at him then out of the corner of his eyes each time the cat looks away, swallowing hard with sweat dripping onto newspaper at the bottom of the cage.

On the last look, the cat stops and looks back in an even longer stare, licking its paws even longer.

Nattie rushes through the kitchen, tending to dinner, then walks in view of Rev, setting the pie on a low-cut cabinet, before walking out the back door without a clue that the cat is even inside.

Boogey hears the back door slam and leans forward, not seeing the cat but assuming that Nattie took the cat out.

Boogey and Rev keep talking until Rev spots the cat with its back arched.

Rev leans further, finding the cat fading out of view until pouncing on a chair, and with another leap, the cat lands on a low shelf, climbing onto the low-cut cabinet with its hind parts and tail waving over the pie.

The cat stoops fast and its bottom drops on the rim of the pie, slowly easing up when spotting Nattie walking past the door. He licks his paws a few times cutting its head back at the bird, and Bud looks ahead and freezes.

The cat licks at Rev, with its sharp teeth showing; its head jerking and looking like he's laughing and winking when one eye closes and opens fast. The cat turns, eases up on the pie, licking the pretty, golden brown crusted rim then licks its paws, its butt and the pie again.

Rev feels weak after several attempts to clear his mind when looking away, then back, finding the cat with a humpback and its tail curiously waving over the pie for minutes again. "Ugh!" he says under his breath.

The cat is distracted by something in the kitchen when freezing and focusing with wondering eyes and pointy ears. It turns its head further as if looking out the back door when sitting and leaving a deeper butt print on the edge of the pie. It comes up fast, hearing Nattie's feet beating down the steps in a slow trot.

Instantly, the back door slams and Nattie's feet nippily shuffles across the gritty, war-torn, linoleum floor.

"Ugh....," Rev utters under his breath again and louder than expected this time, in disbelief. He looks away then looks up real slow, making eye contact with Nattie, who stares and then smiles, putting her back to Rev, and sheltering the cat.

Boogey stares at Rev with jealous eyes slowly drifting toward the kitchen and the floor, looking for Nattie's shadow when leaning more and then easing back when not seeing her shadow fade.

The backdoor springs loudly yawns when the door flies wide open with the cat being thrown high; letting off a loud scream, followed by instant heavy, long hissing when landing on all four.

Boogey's embarrassed eyes float over to Rev. "So Rev, does it look like the financing will come through on the lease?" Boogey picks up a butter knife from the coffee table, digging deep under black, dirty nails when un-cautiously looking over and finding Rev turning his head in a frown until shaking his head in disbelief.

Nattie pops through the kitchen door within minutes, handing a cool glass of lemonade to Rev, then one to Boogey, and he thanks Nattie, smiling while looking the glass over.

Rev notices a pair of red lip stains on the edge and looks more, finding something black, like a pellet floating on the surface when sticking a finger inside and pulling out a dead baby fly. "Woohoo..., you folks are too hospitable, but I ate earlier, and had my fill of dining; I'm as full as a tick with deep claws," he utters, passing the heavily condensated glass to Boogey. "Here..., now look ah here..., I can't waste you folks' hard-earned money," Rev anxiously utters, cheery.

Boogey grasps the glass, staring at another floating dot, finding a fly then another black object that had just floated to the top when plunging his finger in when Rev turns to look over the house, mentioning the pie to Nattie again. Boogey downs half the glass, easing Rev's cool glass down on the table, and starts sipping on his glass again.

Nattie notices Rev inching further to the edge of the couch. "Well, let me get you a piece of sweet, hot tata (potato) pie." Nattie walks past Boogey, grabbing the butter knife Boogey cleaned his nails with from the table.

Rev finally looks out the door then back at his glass, noticing Boogey had already emptied it when in a hiccup motion, almost blowing chunks but quickly gaining his composure, when poking out his washboard abs. "Yall might as well put a halt on the pie, too! Does it look like I can get another thing inside this here belly?" Rev utters, playfully holding his belly out again until he can't any longer. "Ok..., ok..., Mrs. Nattie, just cut me a nice piece and wrap it up," Rev utters, sitting back a little and leaning forward fast, watching her cut into the hot pie with Boogey's nail cleaning knife.

"Aw, come on, Rev..., one slice right here and now ain't gone hurt nothing," Boogey utters, offended when his mind wanders to the street where he sees the sheriff's car fly past in the opposite direction; just lights and finally the siren.

"No way, bud..., I know my limits, so I'll just take it and enjoy it right before bed, with an ice, cold glass of milk," Rev utters, swallowing hard when thinking about the cat lickings and pressed rump serving.

Nattie steps on the back porch, accidentally slamming the door, loudly.

Boogey leans to one side, then the other, and can't unstick his drawers when leaning hard and away from Rev, grabbing a handful. He eases to the edge of the chair, sliding sideways to get them unbundled when leaning heavy to one side again.

Rev's eyes drift down to the deep crease in Boogey's hairy butt, finding his hand when Rev's head goes forward with shoulder raised high, trying to keep from gagging with several unnoticed shoulder jerks.

Nattie comes back in and finally shows back up at the living room door.

"Nattie, how 'bout wrapping Rev a hearty serving of that there good ole tata (potato) pie for his journey," Boogey utters, chomping down on dingy a toothpick he had just picked up from the floor.

Nattie turns and has the pie wrapped in clear plastic within seconds, passing it to Boogey, who uses the same hand to dig in his butt, to grab the pie.

"Here you go, Rev; I'm so glad you came by," Boogey utters, beaming.

"My first time, but it's always a pleasure; yes, always when it comes to new members; Boogey and Mrs. Natt," Rev utters, looking down at the pretty texture of the warm pie when remembering the cat, the knife, and Boogey's turdy hands when gathering his final thoughts.

"Well, Boogey, you know we kind of got sidetracked there, but I'll call you so we can talk about you and ole Winton's ordeal," Rev utters, looking at the pie again to find what looks like several cat hairs with the edge heavily sunken in deep. Rev shakes his head but straightens his face quickly, discovering Boogey looking with a slight frown and evil squint.

Boogey and Nattie walk Rev out and say their goodbyes. They stay on the porch watching Rev make what looks like an incomplete three-point turn until Rev is pulling away from the house.

Boogey smiles looking at Nattie and finding her looking in his eyes. "You know, Nattie, I got a strange feeling that ole Rev didn't want to eat your food for some reason, I reckon." Boogey looks at the taillight when the turn signal comes on.

"Hmm..., I can understand why..., shucks, you let that ole, ugly cat in the house. When I came back in, the cat was on the counter. I'm not sure if he messed in the pie, but I wonder if ole Rev saw him in it," Nattie utters, folding her arms and leaning against Boogey's arm.

Over at the convalescent home, Dale walks into the facility, takes a few puffs off his cigarette, and stares at the receptionist while putting the cigarette butt out in a flower pot. All of a sudden, he jumps when hearing faint music in the rapper's grandfather's room. He freezes in excitement, listening.

The grandson and two of his friends sit, drinking and bobbing their heads as before when a new dope beat comes on.

The grandson balls his fist, rapping through the beat then motions his friend to restart the beat while taking hits from his flask when rapping and messing up again.

Dale waits until the frustrated rapper stops and motions for his friend to restart the beat.

"Take it from the top, dude!" the rapper says, frowning when gripping his fist tighter. He opens his mouth to rap when Dale slides in with a tightly held broomstick; rapping like before with everyone bursting into tears of laughter, hearing Dale rap the whole song through. Out of nowhere, more loud laughter rises, and soon hands begin clapping.

The rapper and his friend hang around longer then wrap things up.

Dale and the grandfather follow the guys out front, standing off, watching them load up in the shiny, grey, and decked-out SUV. The two wave then head back inside, stopping at the main door, and watching people converge around the television when making their way to the front of the main event room.

Dale rudely shoves folks until coming up on the tallest man, being instantly mushed at the top of his head; back into the crowd.

The television displays a colorful weather forecast map as the newscaster walks back into view, pointing with a laser, speaking about an approaching hurricane.

Dale finally works his way to the big screen from another side, laughing. "Scared, huh? Scared ain't cha (you)? Eyes are glued to that tube like it's a million bucks! The weatherman tells you a storm is coming or the world will end on a certain date, and what do you do? I'll tell ya (you) exactly what you folks do: you run and get your water, smokes, tissues, or stock the house up with candy, sardines, potted meat, condoms, and tampons.

No one ever prays and asks for the storm to turn through faith. Even if it's a direct, forecasted hit; you pack up and get ready to go, but always..., always pray first, so you don't run smack dead into the storm or another unpredictable storm," Dale utters, looking into all of the quiet and concerned faces that are still glued on the television but nosily listening.

All of a sudden, a deep voice comes. "Ah, Dale, sit your decrepit tail down and quit running your flytrap! Hell..., during the last storm, I saw you balled up under your bed like you were in a room full of demons," the tallest man utters, laughing out loud and looking around at others who don't laugh but laughs when the tall man gives an evil round of stares until almost everyone is faking laughing.

"Man, you be crippin' (trippin'), you ain't never seant (seen) me balled up in nothing but those sheets with your nappy-head mama!" Dale nervously utters, staring into the man's shocked face, which turns red with jowls dropping and a slow, tight fist balling. Dale gives him a 'don't care' look, and then continues. "You see..., our thinking process is all screwed up!" Dale utters with wandering eyes that stay tuned to the tall, mean man. "Someone talks storm or Armageddon, and you overreact, but the Bible warns us of the World coming to an end one day, and we do nothing to change and act as if nothing has ever been mentioned."

Dale stares over at the tall man until he finishes then looks away then back finding the man shoving people aside when making his way over to Dale with a frowned face and a tighter, big fist.

"I'll show you a storm; you poodle-hair-wearing fool! How dare you talk about my mama!" the man screams with his face torn up in frustration from people not moving fast enough. The tall man continually lunges forward, mushing more folks in the face and shoving them to one side with eyes stealthily glued on Dale.

Dale stays there with a smirk on his face, yet cuts his eyes down at the edge of the chair, waiting for the man to get closer.

The man takes a few more steps, and Dale grabs the back of the chair, flinging it in front of the man, causing him to stumble, face-first when rapidly recovering like a precision Soldier when giving chase.

Friday morning, Boogey and Nattie arise to the loud sound of the alarm clock.

Boogey sluggishly hits snooze, rolling over and falling back to sleep.

Nattie lies there, slightly rocking, in deep thoughts until the fourth snooze comes when finally getting up and starting breakfast.

Later on, Boogey stumbles into the kitchen, for the phone, thinking to call work and apologize to old man Anderson for his insubordinate behavior, and he does.

The two talk until finally, old man Anderson accepts his apology, and the conversation transitions into company business, new policies and procedures.

After the call, Boogey does a few chores and then wanders into the yard, working on his car.

Nattie comes out later, leaning against the old heap while Boogey is underneath, and suddenly, he feels the car slightly shift when stealthily looking at the busted jack, which is leaking fluids faster than ever. "Whoa..., whoa..., whoa..., Nattie!" Boogey utters, steadying then looking over at the gushing hydraulic leak again. "This here jack is not steady at all, and she's busted a leak!" Boogey utters, frowning when Nattie eases her weight off, backing away slowly with nervous hands stretched toward the car.

"Well..., I'm going inside to make lemonade..., care for a glass?"

"Naw..., no time for that; I need to get this hea (here) job done, first."

Nattie goes inside and goes about her chores, then sits at the table an hour or so later, shucking a bucket of corn, when the phone rings.

The call comes a second time breaking her concentration, and soon speedily brings her deep into laughter while talking to her best friend.

Boogey moans a few times, then strains, taking a few more turns on the vice grips when holding it, tightly. He hears a car rush up and sees a cloud of dust shoot over and under his car while fanning with eyes glued to the jack.

Boogey hears fast-moving feet, cutting his eyes over, finding a pair of size thirteen or lager, dust-covered boots just behind the front driver's side tire. Boogey wiggles, coming out quickly when the jack drops even faster until the frame pins Boogey, and Boogey screams at the top of his lungs. Boogey looks alongside the engine block, then through wires, finally finding Sheriff Big John staring down with a slick grin.

"My..., my..., my..., what in the hell do we have here, Boog?" the sheriff utters, tightening the lock on the jack, yet still holding a firm grip.

"What the..., now you let me up out of here, you crooked son-of-a-gun!" Boogey screams, staring into the sheriff's quick squinting eyes when one eye clinches tight from the steady stream of cigarette smoke.

"Now you just settle down, you crusty old sucker! Settle down, I say! I'm the one doing the damn talking here, so shut your pie hole and listen to me, dagnabbit! Now, I'm going to ask you one question, and I don't want a lot of clueless jaw-jacking..., you got it, Jack? Now, where's that low-life cousin of yours..., Winton?"

"Wint? Man, get the hell of here with that mess! It ain't my job to watch him because if it was, he would be six feet under right now. So let me make this easy for you..., that's no business of mine and probably none of yours either; well, from a legal and lawful perspective, that is," Boogey sarcastically utters with sweat beading over his face.

"Oh yeah? Well, you don't say, do you? Well, you listen here, you better make it your damn business and quick, and that's what I say..., do you understand me?" Big John screams, dropping the car down half an inch until Boogey feels warm metal pressed harder in his chest when taking strained breaths.

The sheriff leans even deeper into the car, trying to get a better look at Boogey's face when the sheriff's head dips slightly forward, instantly feeling a cool piece of metal pressed hard against his neck until pressed harder.

The metal slides upward at the base of the sheriff's skull when the sheriff's hand eases from the jack; both hands rising slowly.

"One wrong move, and I'll blow your brains all over this hea (here) yard, chump!" Nattie utters in an imitated, deep, manly voice. "Now get that there darn jack up, skippy!" Nattie utters in an even deeper voice when pushing the barrel forward until the sheriff's head slightly bows.

Big John makes eye contact again, slowly then boldly smiling at Boogey, until his face transforms into something more sinister.

"The hell with that! Don't let him touch that ja…," Boogey begins to scream when interrupted.

"Now what!" the sheriff confidently utters, jerking with a firm grip on the jack's handle again. "Hmm…, you ain't bold enough to shoot a sheriff, now are you? Uh-huh…, last I checked, capital murder equals the electric chair for shooting a man in the back, in cold blood. So go on now, just take a second to think about all of Fikesville's electricity on the grid, shooting through your frail body with your head so hot you can fry an egg and sausage on it. Those eyes…, well, those beady eyes will be bulged for seconds before popping out of that smoking little gourd of yours," the sheriff sternly utters, still anxiously staring at the jack's handle.

The sheriff flinches a little to gain balance and then slowly cuts his eyes back to see who has him at gunpoint. "Now drop it or this fat joker is as good as squashed roadkill," the sheriff utters, looking further over his shoulder to find the shadow of a manlier figure swiftly coming up behind the unidentified first shadow.

"Easy," the masked man utters, cocking his rifle hard when the sheriff cringes from the man's confidence.

The sheriff's eyes wander, trying to figure out the somewhat familiar and then unfamiliar voices.

Nattie trembling hands swiftly lowers her rifle, backing away slowly when jumping out of the way.

The man passes fast, coming up on the sheriff with the barrel pressing even tighter and faster to the back of the sheriff's head. "I dare you to even think about going after that there sidearm. One wrong gesture and there will be red all over this hea (here) car," the man firmly yells, slightly altering his voice when pressing the rifle harder and unlatching the sheriff's gun, emptying it with one hand, and throwing it behind them.

The sheriff swallows hard, slowly raising his hands, and easing them forward as if bowing when moving down to this side. "Show yourself, you freakin' cowardly bastard! This here is none of your business, obviously! You're interfering with the dang law, I tell yah (you)!" Big John shouts, slightly turning when the butt of the rifle flings upward, almost transparent, thrashing him in the head and dropping him to the ground.

"Here!" old gray-haired Sam utters, handing Nattie his rifle until quickly laying it against the car. He removes his mask when his hand falls forward, swiftly raising the jack off Boogey's chest.

Boogey wiggles out fast with boots kicking up dust and fearing the jack's hydraulics will burst from the sudden pressure. He clears the car fast; rolling to one side, kneeling then standing and breathing rapidly. Boogey's eyes open wide with hands trembling with great fear when sticking them out, and looking at how bad they are shaking.

Boogey stares over at Sam with big tears in his eyes. "I don't know how I can ever repay you, Sam," Boogey utters, grasping and shaking Sam's hand and then grabbing the shotgun from Nattie. "Thanks for the quick response, Natt!" Boogey utters, embracing her when a tear rolls down his cheek.

Sam retrieves the sheriff's gun and bullets reloading them then sticking the gun in the back of his belt before reaching for the sheriff's boots. "Give me a hand putting him in his car!"

Boogey turns fast, gripping the upper body, struggling to place him on the cruiser's passenger side.

Sam sloppily places the sheriff's wide hat on his narrow head, posing him in some ridiculous looking fashion when jumping; finding the sheriff groggy. Sam gets nervous, turning in circles until leaning forward, swiftly drawing back, and releasing a devastating blow. He jumps back excited and more nervous, finding the sheriff shaking off the punch when throwing another jab, but harder and with sound, knocking him out.

Sam jumps back, high stepping, trying to shake off the throbbing pain then pulls off the sheriff's sweaty rimmed hat, flinging it inside. "I will be!" He yells, wiping the sweaty, funky smell from his hand on his pants. "Uh, uh, uh..., quick..., somebody get me a funnel, duct tape, and a short hose! And get me some of that moonshine, Boogey," Sam mutters, looking around for anything else useful.

Boogey rushes off while Nattie runs to the open trunk for duct tape and a funnel and then turns, picking up a hose from the ground when walking back up to Sam.

Sam grasps the tape and funnel, attaching the hose to it, then holds the funnel out when Boogey is coming; motioning Boogey to pour.

Boogey sprints up, pouring moonshine until Sam motions him to pour slower.

A couple of minutes or so later, they manage to get a third of the shine down.

"There, he won't remember a thing," drunk-looking, Sam utters, giggling. "Get out of here for a few hours in case this cat wakes up pissed and drive back by your house. I've got some horse medicine I can shoot him up with. Heck, with that alone, he won't remember his own name when he comes to," Sam utters when giggling like a mad scientist. "We need to shift things around to distort his memory." Sam points to Boogey's car, snapping his fingers at the car and pointing to the woods.

Boogey pulls the jack out of the way, throwing it in the trunk and slamming the trunk. He leans forward, helping Sam push his car, when Sam jumps in, steering.

They throw other things in the yard around or turn them over to alter the scene.

"There, that should do it!" Sam utters, picking up the edge of the trough and turning it to one side. He looks around and then out to the highway, noticing there is not much traffic, so he waits for the last car to pass and jumps in the cruiser. Sam throws the cruiser in neutral, rolling and then coasting a ways off until clearing Boogey's car when popping the clutch and cranking up.

He steps into the gas, heading down the long dirt and grassy patch trail that leads a few miles through the woods and connects with another highway. Sam veers, angling the car halfway off the road until the tire settles in a burrow and rocks when the sheriff's head rocks as if he's dead.

The driver-side door flies open, and Sam's rugged brogans hit the dust when he leans forward, taking off, staggering through the long path and coming alongside his house when scurrying into the barn.

Sam appears minutes later with a long needle filled with a milky, caramel substance. He eases up on the passenger side, rolling up the sheriff's sleeved arm, hanging out the window. He taps a time or two, looking for a good vein, then sits the needle down, pulling off the sheriff's belt, wrapping his arm tight, when tapping again.

Sam's drunken hand holds the long needle tight, sliding it in the sheriff's now bulging vein, and he jerks, passing back out. He pulls the needle out slowly, applying more pressure, and then slaps the sheriff's arm hard, jumping back, staring. Sam creeps up, slapping the sheriff's arm again, then jumps back, staring with one eyebrow raised until slowly drawing his hand closer.

He stares at the sheriff's arm and then the needle bruise marks. Sam's face frowns, and he squints, finally reading the fine print when noticing he has used the wrong medicine. "Dagdangit! Wrong freakin' syringe!" he utters, shaking his head when rechecking the sheriff's pulse.

The sheriff's right, blurry, eagle-eye slightly cracks open and wanders around, fast. His hand flexes, springing forward, tightly seizing Sam at the collar and pulling him closer.

Sam comes slightly off the ground with legs dangling when letting off a loud, long, ridiculous scream with his hands furiously beating the sheriff in the chest.

"Halt..., who goes there?" the sheriff screams with his vision even more blurry when his body jerks, and he screams at the top of his lungs, shaking in fear.

Sam continues to free himself when his hand pushes the handle, accidentally unlatching the door, and Sam falls backward, pulling the sheriff up and out.

The sheriff rise high, stands tall, and releases Sam to keep from falling face first. He balances quickly, strutting around like a spring chicken and does fancy footwork. He stops then does more fancy footwork in a comical dance when high-stepping. His neck goes back and forth until kicking up a high trail of dust until looking like he's doing some unseen ritual dance.

The sheriff's feet stop and he freezes as if quietly listening for something then jumps, kicking up more dust as if in a different ritual dance. He continues until kicking up an even bigger cloud until vanishing as stiff as a board when falling face-first into the tall weeds.

Sam scours the ground, looking around and crawling a few feet near a bale of hay, covering the sheriff's body with fast and nervous hands. He moves frantically, dropping more hay until dropping the last handful over the sheriff's head. Sam backs up, standing somewhat sober from fear; watching the sheriff's feet stretch out and then jerk a time or two before looking lifeless.

At Boogey's house, Boogey lifts the hood and finishes the repairs, nippily twisting bolts and tweaking things until jumping inside, and starting the engine.

Nattie steps on the back porch, smiling and clapping with joy before rushing back inside.

Boogey makes more adjustments with the carburetor until hearing a backfire.

Nattie jumps, trembling and hitting the floor, low-crawling until easing up, running to the door and finding Boogey backing slowly away from under the hood.

Nattie stares until knowing he is alright when Boogey turns, staggering, and she sees his black, soot-covered face when backing inside, laughing uncontrollably.

Boogey shakes off the numbness, and out of nowhere, he feels a gust of wind when cutting his eyes at the porch, finding something flapping back and forth under the house. He rushes over, kneeling on one knee, looking closer until squinting and finding his favorite shirt.

Boogey shoots up, sprinting for the steelyard rake, flinging it under the house and makes a few attempts to hook the shirt and finally hooks it. He drags it out slowly with a mean frown until clenching his nose fast when getting a whiff of the overpowering funk. He slowly reaches, clenching a piece of the material and spreading it out against the porch. He slowly flips it to one side, jumping back and throwing it to the ground, when spotting the deep, black streaks down the middle and more steaks along the shoulder.

Boogey's eyes wander over the porch for a stick, frowning when picking the shirt up with the stick when the heavy stench rises in his nostrils just when the mild wind kicks back up. "I will be…!" Boogey screams, disgusted when sniffing the shirt again and confirming it's indeed turd smears when looking for a clean piece of the material, and lifting the shirt.

He angrily loops it around until slinging it high and releasing it with it falling expressly onto his shoulder when the wind blows it back. "Ah…!" Boogey cries in a loud scream, dancing fast in circles and screaming even louder when fanning faster to get it off. Boogey's eyes flow downward fast, then to his shoulder when frowning, and highly pissed. His mind instantly thinks back on Davillier being naked and in the backyard, under the bright headlights. "That sorry son of a…," Boogey begins to say, hearing the screen door open and seeing Nattie walk out.

"What? What is all this hollering and carrying on about?" Nattie screams, looking around until finding the heavily stained shirt when freezing in confusion. "Isn't that your favorite shirt?" she asks, surprised, not thinking about giving it to Davillier.

"Yah think?" Boogey sarcastically asks when bending over and lifting the rake. He throws the rake's teeth into the shirt, almost punching holes in it this time.

"What are you doing? Put it on the porch so I can wash it," Nattie utters, frowning when the stench rushes up and slaps her as she backs off fast, pinching her nose.

Boogey finally lifts the shirt with the rake, turning it to Nattie as she steps off the last step with the black, long streak floating in her face.

Nattie screams, then ducks, throwing up both fists in a rocking fashion. She rocks even harder but manages to keep her distance. "Mother…," Nattie utters.

Boogey guides the rack from her for a second, and Nattie swings at Boogey's face, taking a few stealth jabs, barely missing. She takes a few steps back, bracing in another stance, pissed even more than ever when eye-to-eye with Boogey.

Boogey finally sees her aggression and drops the rake, bending over and uncontrollably laughing harder with one hand slapping his knee. "What? You said to put it on the porch," he utters, laughing.

"I don't play that bull, Boog! Come one…, Come on!" Nattie shrieks, shuffling her feet more until she can hardly see Boogey through the thick cloud of high rising dust.

Boogey wanders off, picking up the rack, lifting the shirt again, taking it over to the burn piles; and laying it on top. "Hell, you out here swinging on me..., you need to swing on that nasty tail Davillier! Why would you give him my favorite shirt, Natt?" Boogey asks, shaking his head, pissed.

"Had I known it was your good shirt, I wouldn't have; look, the lights were out but anyway, that's irrelevant. I gave it to him to put on, not wipe his butt!" Nattie utters, shaking her head in disbelief.

"Oh, you just wait until I get my hands on that sorry-tail sucker!" Boogey utters, highly pissed, with one eye slightly closed and the other squinted.

Boogey and Nattie stay in the yard a spell longer and then go inside, clean up, and grab money from the dresser and a few dollars from the jar.

Boogey locks up and holds the passenger door open, playfully bowing and waiting for her to climb inside. He sprints to the driver's side, cranking up and slowly revving the engine. "Woo..., she sounds like she did the day we got her," Boogey utters, looking at Nattie, smiling when throwing the car in drive and heading for the road.

Boogey stops at the paved road, watching a car pass when turning onto Main Street, bringing the car up to top speed, and tooting the horn at a couple of folks when passing the general store. "Cauto Mighty, No (heck, naw)! She runs like a champ!" Boogey mumbles, smiling when clearing the line of other dilapidated and closed-down stores.

Boogey drives further with a big grin, approaching the tree line. Out of nowhere comes a loud backfire when Boogey and Nattie's eyes go back, finding a large mushroom cloud of black smoke.

Their eyes stay peeled in the rearview and side view mirrors, following the continual flow of black smoke from the exhaust.

"Uh-huh..., well, I guess the damn champ isn't doing so good these days, huh?" Nattie utters, looking at him then out of the side mirror again until the smoke disappears.

"Shucks, Nattie! She just needs to blow off a little steam..., or smoke, I should say, that's all," Boogey utters, slowing then easing back up to the speed limit.

They come into the next city thirty minutes later, pulling up to a red light, alongside a car with four, mixed-race young men wearing gold-and-blue head bandanas.

The young driver turns up his loud rap music which bangs from the power amplified speakers, slightly vibrating Boogey's car.

The passenger looks at Boogey and instantly feels offended by Boogey's mean stare and how he shakes his head in disapproval when the volume lowers. "What the hell you looking at, old head?" the front passenger utters in an intimidating voice.

"Now you listen hea (here), young blood; you need to learn to respect your elders. Now go ahead (on) and calm down with that bull!" Boogey utters, sticking his head further in hopes of intimidation.

"Look, clown, I'll smoke you…, you old fool!" the guy in the passenger seat utters, riding high against the back of the seat and reaching deep in his pants.

Boogey's eyes grow wide, seeing the nozzle of the Uzi-type gun as it passes the window's ledge when he steps into the gas pedal, burning rubber. Boogey's car backfires again, covering them in black smoke and causing the driver and his friends to duck with wide, frightening eyes and scream like little girls until the driver punches the gas pedal, and clears the smoke.

The driver dips down a side street, and the car immediately swerves to one side when the young man in the backseat turns sideways, firing at the rear of Boogey's car.

"Ah…!" Nattie shrieks, slouching down and pressing Boogey's leg down hard on the gas pedal, which hits the floor, sticking.

The passenger takes a steady aim, and a few rounds whistle past the taillights, hitting a building and shattering windows.

Boogey swerves on the straightaway, fighting with his foot to get the pedal unstuck and he does. He comes up to seventy and then eighty miles per hour for minutes until reaching the next town's red light, where he comes to a screeching halt, dipping into a snack bar's parking lot. He inches up and then turns, coming around the building to find a deputy's car parked when parking with the engine running.

Boogey and Nattie sit with their hearts racing. For seconds, they stay quiet and soon hear the loud music blasting from the thug's speakers when the decked-out vintage car lowers on hydraulics.

The gangbangers pull into the lot, hiding their weapons when spotting the deputy near the building, and the car veers; circles back and comes up on the other side of the building.

Boogey comes eye-to-eye with the four, confident that the young punks wouldn't do anything with the law there when raising his middle finger and giggling.

The guys sit steaming until slightly rising and smiling when Boogey and Nattie's heads turn slowly, looking over their shoulders to find the deputy's car vanishing around the building.

The young man in the back seat smiles harder than others when slowly bringing a sawed-off shotgun into view. His fast wandering eyes stay peeled to where the deputy's car had faded when riding high on the backrest.

Boogey and Nattie's eyes bulge until the driver's hand covers the muzzle; bringing it down when nodding at the deputy's car as it comes into view again.

"We'll deal with you later, old head!" the guy in the back yells, frowning and throwing up a gang sign.

The vintage car continually heads toward Boogey, and Nattie then pulls away in a rush; meeting the deputy's curious, wandering eyes near the other side of the store.

Boogey and Nattie arrive in Mundson; the third city from Fikesville, thirty minutes later, where they park near the front door, backing in and sitting for a spell. Their eyes continually wander over the parking lot and main road for the hoodlums until getting out and going inside a clothing store.

The doorbell chimes as they walk in and quietly stop when greeted by a petite and very friendly saleslady. "What can I help you with, sir, ma'am?"

"Work clothes for him." Nattie slightly pulls up her skirt when Boogey sees the knots tied in the back of her stockings and whispers to her when she leans again, readjusting the skirt.

"So..., what are you, sir..., maybe forty-five in the waist?" the saleslady asks, accurately judging his round, pop belly within a centimeter of an inch.

"What! No way, I'm what, Natt..., twenty-nine, and ah..., ah..., ah..., the shirts, ah..., ah..., ah..., sixteen, so a two X, extra-long shirt."

The saleslady leans off and around a mannequin, trying to hold her laugh, and manages to muster up a straight face when coming back in view. She looks from the corner of her eye, spotting and reaching for a measuring tape, stretching it as wide as possible, smiling.

Boogey's eyes wander to the ceiling with his mind going fast. "No need for that..., I've worn the same size practically all my life, so it is just a waste of time," Boogey utters, placing a hand on each hip and sucking in hard, unable to alter his circumference at all until rocking back and forth and holding his breath until he turns red.

"Well..., the customer is always right, sir." the saleslady says, smiling cheerfully when guiding them from the big and short section through big and tall then over to regular menswear. She thumbs through the top layer of pants, neatly folded, picking out various colors, and laying them to one side.

Boogey flips the pants over, looking at the prices and sizes. Minutes later, he picks out his favorite styles, close to company colors then looks at everyday wear.

"I really do recommend trying these on, sir, because different makers have different cuts depending on the quality of the fabric," the saleslady utters, looking at his Santa belly pressed tight in his pants and shirt.

"She does have a great point, Boogey," Nattie finally utters, smiling.

"Alright then...," Boogey grabs the top pair of pants and a work shirt, entering the men's room, undressing, and sweating profusely until huffing and puffing. He fights with all his might until his fingers are sore trying to get the pants buttoned when taking a breather. A few seconds later, he fights longer with sore fingers and thumbs then numb hands until finally buttoning the pants. He tucks the long shirt inside and strains, pulling the excess material down through the open zipper.

Boogey stays inhaled, still sucking in air, and the pants feel somewhat comfortable at first, though well below his belly, and a bright smile grows. He eases out some air, then sucks in his gut and holds it until turning red again from straining and getting the shirt button in the last hole. He looks in the mirror from the side, finally releasing his breath, and frowns when the pain at the waist creeps in. Boogey stands longer and the pain mellows as the pants stretch a little, but the button's nylon threads slightly yawn when he bends to zip the pants.

Boogey stands and bends when the stretched material retracts fast with his body heat as Boogey flings the door open.

Nattie and the saleslady look Boogey over with fast, wandering eyes when hearing a light whining.

They immediately look at the pants button under pressure then nervously look at each other until Nattie finally sees the saleslady's fast-motioning hand when they slowly sidestep behind the clothes rack, ducking and taking cover, fast.

Boogey takes one more step, and the pant button pops like a firecracker and flies like a bullet, knocking over a few mannequins, smashing a mirror, and barely clearing another mannequin while still traveling in stealth mode.

An old lady steps aside, holding the external door open, hearing a mild incoming whistle when ducking with the door handle still in hand and her big hair duo sheared down the center. The button flies into the parking lot, hitting a car window and activating the car alarm system.

Nattie and the saleslady's heads finally come up slow peeking at the shirt that is now under pressure.

"Twenty-nine, huh, sir?" the saleslady utters, trying to recall his claimed measurements when grabbing Nattie's hand and ducking speedily again.

Instantly, the first button explodes, followed by a delay, then three more sporadic pops, sounding like popped bubble wrap when hitting hanging clothes and making the clothes rack shift.

Nattie and the women lunge into tears of non-stop laughter when Boogey walks off embarrassed.

The women come up slow, laughing, and find Boogey, when walking fast to catch him and lead him to the bigger selections where the women begin gathering larger sizes.

Within the hour, Nattie and Boogey leave that store, heading to a department store in hopes of purchasing a cheap twenty-seven-inch color television. They walk around a bit until stumbling upon the television section, seeing twenty versions of the weatherman appearing across all screens, forecasting severe weather.

Boogey reaches for a remote on the counter, flipping one big screen to a comedy channel, and finds a comedian joking about U.S. foreign policy. The comedian goes deeper into his skit until Boogey is almost to his knees in tears. Boogey turns up the volume with a few folks running off with their kids when hearing the first cuss word.

The comedian says a few more funny lines that even have Nattie in tears when the comedian screams through the mic in a deep, imitated voice, and Boogey bursts out even louder with more adult patrons wandering over.

A manager soon rushes up, turning down the volume with a mean stare, when Boogey and Nattie walk off and over to a register where they finally make a purchase and leave.

Boogey and Nattie drive down the back road, arriving in Fikesville just before dark with Boogey clutching the steering wheel, tightly. His eyes drift to his watch when stopping at a red light, under a lamppost before speeding off, trying to make it to the general store before it's crowded.

Boogey parks, sitting and looking at a group of men shooting dice on a concrete pad alongside the store. He rushes to the door and inside, getting his numbers and a cold beer, then walks outside, finding the guys laughing and swatting mosquitoes from time to time.

Two men stand off to the side, whispering when finding Boogey peeking around the corner, turning up the beer.

"Man, you're joking, right?" a young guy screams to the tall guy in laughter.

"If I'm lying..., then guess what..., I'm flying, right? Right or Right, Wrong or Wrong," the tall guy senselessly utters in tears reciting something someone senselessly had made up at some time or another when leaning against the wall with one hand. "Well, look hea (here)..., Champ and the boys told me that a man had Lil Reggie up in that shed yelping last night, like a little biatchhhh!"

"Oh man, don't act like that's new! Lil Reggie's been into men since high school. Hell..., by the way he switches, you can tell that he's about it, 'bout it, but hay, it's all desire and free will, Baby! It's the way of the

Gentile, the other Nations that we are not to follow, if we are true Christians!" the man utters, laughing with excited big white eyes.

"Just last week, his boyfriend beat him in the middle of the street over a crack pipe," the other guy says, digging deep in his pocket, and counting off a few more singles.

Boogey listens for a few and then waves for Nattie to go on to the house then watches Nattie climb behind the wheel and pull off until the bright taillights fade and the mosquitoes begin biting. Boogey swats a few times, then fans until bitten in the hand and thigh. He smacks himself more and walks back into the store, buying another cold, tall beer.

Boogey walks out, pulling the brown paper bag sleeve down, taking a deep swig, and swirling it around a few times before taking another hit. He looks down the street and then walks off alongside the store, leaning against the wall, watching them gamble. Boogey swats a few more times, smashing a few big mosquitoes that swarm by, sounding like gnats.

Soon, more sweaty bodies converge when a few sweaty ballers walk up joking when everyone starts fanning and smacking their arms and legs.

The younger guy holding the dice slaps his ears, shakes the dice hard, and throws them to the ground. "Snake eyes!" the young guy jokingly yells, laughing when actually rolling a three and four and everyone breaks out laughing at the young guy dancing before he stops to pick up the dice.

The next guy steps up, rolling, and then slaps his bare arm. "Man, these mosquitoes are off the chain tonight!" He fans his face. "But hey, I got nothing but time and money, Babe!" the guy utters, rolling the dice and then stepping to the side. "Time is nothing but money, and I got plenty of cash, but all y'all are going home broke tonight, Jack! Baby needs a pacifier, and Mama..., well, Mama needs a new hairdo because that kitchen (neck area) is ate all up, Jack!" The guy fans his face faster, then rubs the dice together, instantly jumping for joy upon winning the pot.

Everyone reaches into their pockets, pulling out more dollars for the next round.

At the same time, the tallest guy that was talking about Reggie counts his money until leaning, peeking through the darkness, cutting his eyes, and slightly bending. He bends further, looking into the field near the dim barn light. "Hey, man, ain't that..., hey..., ain't that, ah..., ah..., ah..., Reggie?" he asks, looking at the guys' surprised faces as they come from alongside the building, looking toward where he's pointing.

"Whatttt? Hell yeah..., that's Reggie, alright!" the shortest guy yells, picking up his five wrinkled dollar bills and shoving it deep in his pocket.

"Man, there are too many mosquitoes out to be messing around with Reggie tonight! I'm out of here, Jack!" the tall guy utters, slipping alongside the store and fading into pure darkness.

The others disperse and Boogey looks back, finding Reggie in a slow trot, so he walks into the store, making his way to the side door with eyes on Lil Reggie as he enters the front door.

Boogey exits, running fast and wide-legged for his house with heavy material swishing at his thighs.

Winton pulls up at the general store minutes later, gazing into darkness when looking at Boogey's house, and finding the front porch light on. He pulls over to the curb and goes into the store, purchasing a tall beer and a pack of smokes. Winton's eyes wander over the folks in the store, hearing someone in the back telling jokes when expressly making his way to the bathroom. He stops by the water cooler looking around for seconds to make sure no one is watching when turning the knob, and finding the door locked. Winton rushes outside, instantly swatting mosquitoes, until easing further back on the bench.

The bathroom door finally slams open, and Lil Reggie walks out, making his way to the front and out of the door. He eases onto the bench next to Winton and sits looking at the condensation dripping off Winton's beer can when taking a deep swallow. Lil Reggie looks away and then back at the can, quickly. "I sure wouldn't mind having a sip of that cold one," Reggie utters, looking at Winton puffing on his cigarette and blowing hard when waving off a few mosquitoes.

Winton cracks a smile and shakes his head in disbelief while pretending not to have heard him. He looks down, kicking the side of a rock that barely sticks out of the ground. Winton's hand comes up, fanning more mosquitos when he sees a shadow and finds a guy standing on the side of the store, curiously peeking out.

"I sure wouldn't mind having a sip of that," Reggie says again when a car pulls up, and a man breaks out from the side of the store in a mad, staggering dash.

"Sup, Lil Reg!" the guy yells, rushing for the door handle and motioning for his girlfriend to roll up the windows quickly; when all four windows come up, instantly.

"Sup, Blue! Hey Blue..., you got any spare change?" Lil Reggie yells, swishing his hips when running to the car, seeing the door slam fast and hearing the car skidding wheels. Reggie looks back at Winton to find a disgusting look on Winton's face as Winton's cigarette nervously drops from his mouth and his shoulders lower.

"Lil Reggie? Lil..., Reggie..., you mean, McMannis? Reggie McMannis from down by the train tracks?" Winton nervously asks, easing up and backing up, slowly.

"Yeah..., and? That's my name, so don't wear it out, Daddy!" Reggie utters, swerving his index finger forward in a diva fashion.

"Oh, hellz naw!" Winton screams, fanning the mosquitoes faster and backing up to the bench until falling backward. He springs up and runs to his car fast. Winton's engine revs with smoke coming from the tires, leaving the burning smell of rubber.

Reggie rushes over, grabs the cold can and begins sipping on the tall can of beer.

Everyone grows quiet over at Rev's brother's house when Rev takes a seat out front, leading off with a lengthy prayer. "Book of Luke tonight," he utters, looking over his small audience while reading a few verses.

"Now, whatever you do, don't get caught up in all these worldly things. Yeah, God wants you to have the things you desire in your heart, but not so that you worship them. It's not the nice car that you drive, but the God that drives you, not the pretty, big house you live in, but the God that lives in you, not the fancy purse or new wallet, but the God who gave you that job so you can put money in it," Rev utters, gawking into the eyes of his attentive audience. "Storms..., huh? God already knows it's coming before your storm brews because he knows everything. HE sees the storm and jumps right into it with you, so HE does not need you to avoid the storms of your life because they will come, and HE will cover you and bring you through them then restore you. HE will make you better than before, but there is a lesson to be learned in every storm, so live and learn or learn and burn!" Rev utters, drifting into deep thoughts about the blackmailing he's going through before continuing.

On the other side of town, Winton drives slower, rocking his head to the music, still a ways from home, remembering the drugs when slowing, and making a U-turn.

Twenty minutes pass when the general store comes into view again and Winton slows. He squints, finding Reggie still sitting out front, sipping on something, until finally remembering it's his ice cold beer that Reggie is sucking down. Winton parks a ways off, turning off the headlights while listening to mellow music.

Twenty minutes later, headlights pierce from the tree line.

The car finally pulls up, and Reggie stands, turning up the last swig when ditching the can and climbing inside with the car heading toward Winton when he ducks as it shoots past.

Winton cranks up, cruising by the store, staring in and around it before making another slow U-turn. He makes another pass before pulling over across the street, where he sits longer, observing his surroundings.

After some time, Winton gazes at his watch when easing out and scurrying across the street with beady eyes following his movement. He slips alongside the store, entering through the side door with eyes wandering fast until discovering the clerk reading a comic book and the butcher shutting off a few lights in the back.

Winton looks at the clock, and with only twenty minutes left before closing, he struts down an aisle to the back and down another aisle, rushing for the bathroom.

Silent feet shuffle when a set of eyes peer inside through a mirrored door, following Winton closely when he slips inside the bathroom.

The front door abruptly flies open within seconds, and Lil' Bobby stands wide-legged with his cigar hanging from his lips. His eyes shoot over the store, gazing at the bathroom sign when gripping the bat tighter. Lil Bobby makes his way down the backside, waving to the butcher and motioning him over. "Hey..., get the sheriff over here quick!" Lil' Bob whispers with bloodshot, red eyes while chewing on the tip of the cigar and walking off fast.

The bathroom door bursts wide open, and Lil' Bobby finds Winton on the edge of the toilet seat, on tiptoes, reaching high in the overhead. "Is this what you want, you low-down dirty dog, sorry bastard? How dare you bring this crap in my darn establishment!" Lil' Bob screams, waving the clear plastic bag of dope, almost cockeyed when the cigar falls to his coverall and then the floor.

Winton's eyes grow wide, frozen in time until getting it together when hopping down and falling backward from Lil' Bobby's tightly balled fist, slamming deep into his chest. He knocks Winton backward and into the stall door and onto the heavily manure-smeared toilet seat with stains heavily smeared on his backside.

Lil' Bobby slams the dope back in his pocket, gripping the bat tight when taking a stealth swing but missing and busting the porcelain sink open. He re-cocks fast, and the next devastating swing slams into the urinal, taking it halfway off the wall with water shooting high.

Lil' Bob screams, leaning forward and snatching Winton in the collar with one hand, pulling him forward when underestimating Winton's height when falling back, and releasing Winton. Lil' Bob kicks to gain his balance when Winton shoves him harder and sprints out, staggering into a few shelves until steadying.

Winton comes up the back aisle, ducking and dodging when faking out the butcher, who lunges for a tackle but falls into a rack of can goods, knocking over a display. He comes up the main aisle, ducking when seeing the broom handle held tightly in the clerk's hand when the nice swing misses him, slamming into a shelf with a plume of self-rising flower clouding around the clerk until invisible.

Winton turns a sharp corner, slamming a knee into a metal cooler, hopping for the side door when spotting Lil' Bobby on the back aisle. Winton runs, limping to his car with his hands nervously digging in his pockets until holding the keys tight. He pulls on the jammed door with no success when crawling through the window with legs dangling and kicking until Lil' Bobby grabs him, with an instant frowned face from the toilet seat smeared stench when pulling hard while Winton kicks and screams.

Lil' Bobby drops one hand, pulling off his belt, and pulls on Winton until at his waist when laying into him with four good, hard whacks when screams come.

Winton kicks harder, screaming louder when wiggling, turning sideways, and focusing on getting the key in the ignition. Tears heavily pour until Winton sounds like a newborn baby screaming for a bottle after more whacks come. He hears and feels the engine turn over when a hand drops to the gear shift and his other hand drops to the gas pedal with tires squealing and smoke rising, burning rubber while swerving with Lil' Bobby being drugged a few feet, on kneecaps, alongside the wobbling car before letting go.

Lil' Bobby strings up, jumping around from the road burns when staggering and falling into the tall grass screaming and rolling. "Aii, Yii, Yii!"

The butcher and clerk stand looking at Lil' Bobby in disbelief then take off in a mad dash over to where he is lying.

Winton's car keeps swerving erratically until it suddenly veers off into a cornfield and comes to a stop. Winton's head pokes up, nervously scanning the area when springing up in the seat, backing quickly onto the road, and taking off fast, finally hearing Lil' Bobby's gun fire with distant sirens closing fast.

The next day, just before noon, the sheriff kicks a few times and then sits in the heat of the day, buzzing off the strong drugs. His hands flop about his face, knocking away the hay and fanning flies while trying to regain consciousness; heavily drugged and drunker than Shooter Smith when easing up. He kneels quickly, continually losing his balance.

He stands, swaying until doing some crazy-looking drunk walk when stumbling back over to the car and swinging the door open. The sheriff plops down in the passenger seat, pulls the door shut, and then lays his head out the window, breathing even heavier when the wind begins blowing lightly. He feels a breeze, remaining still until finally dozing off again.

Sam leaves home with a fishing pole, tackle box, and a cooler of ice-cold water, walking down the long trail. He veers off, heading down another trail leading to the sheriff's car, whistling a loud, mellow tune. Sam swings his hands, approaching and pretending to be surprised in case the sheriff is looking. He stops, acting surprised when dropping his gear, scurrying over then limping, screaming. "Sheriff! Sheriff! Are you alright?" He yells, wiping away the cheesy grin before reaching for the sheriff and shaking him a little. He pulls on his arm again until releasing him. "Sheriff! Sheriff!"

Sam nervously grabs him again vigorously shaking him then throws a few jabs to his jaw. He thrusts the sheriff in the head a third time when the sheriff glances out of the corner of his eye, catching the fourth inbound, low and stealth fist in the palm of his hand when the loud slap sounds off like a firecracker.

"Alright, already!" the sheriff sluggishly utters, shoving Sam's tightly balled fist back as hard as he can when rubbing his pained face, and slightly rotating his aching jaw.

"Are you alright, Sheriff?" Sam asks, with concern when looking into his bloodshot eyes.

"I'm well to do, I reckon," the sheriff slowly responds, sitting up and looking at his eyes through the rearview mirror and then looking outside the car while pushing his calloused hands against his blistered, sunbaked lips.

Sam looks around. "Well, I thought I heard something loud run-up in these here weeds real fast late yesterday, but I thought my ears were playing tricks on me."

"How long ago? I can't remember a thing," the sheriff utters, rotating his head slowly, clockwise, and then counterclockwise, ad easing the stiffness.

"Oh, hell! I would say about a good two maybe three hours, but no telling," Sam says, sidetracked when looking back at his water cooler and fishing rod in the path, realizing he had unintentionally changed from a day to hours. "Can I get you a cool drink of spring water?" he says fast, trying to throw the sheriff off the conversation.

The sheriff sits again and then slumps over, almost passing out when sticking one foot out and then the other. He pulls heavily against the door, standing and swaying in a drunken stance when falling back into the car. "Yeah, I reckon I'll have that water after all," the sheriff utters, licking his tongue through scorched lips.

Sam rushes over, returning with the cooler and funnel-shaped paper cups, peeling off a cup and handing it to the sheriff when nervously leaning against the car door.

The sheriff holds out the cup for another round, and Sam turns the cooler up, nervously spilling water all over his hand, which severely trembles from the sheriff being so stoned.

Early the following morning, Nattie enters the kitchen pulling together a hearty breakfast for her expectant kinfolks.

Boogey wakes to the smell of the bacon sizzling in a large, cast-iron skillet. He sits up, yawning and stretching, before finally wandering into the bathroom, and washing up. He walks in by the time Nattie is done uncovering Bud's cage. Boogey slips into the kitchen, and his aftershave sinks deep in her nostrils when Boogey comes up behind Nattie, kissing her on the neck.

Nattie grows weak with slow closing eyes when Boogey presses against her, playfully swaying as if slow dancing. "Umm..., you keep this up, and your folks will have to wait." Nattie says, smiling, bending back deeper, and following his lead.

Boogey smiles and pulls her in closer. "If that's the case, you should've stayed in bed longer," he utters, looking over her shoulder and out of the kitchen window before burying his head deep in the nape of her neck.

"For what, so you can snore in my ear?"

"Snore? Yeah..., I would have been snoring, alright. Huh..., I would've been in there moving some damn furniture around in that mother...," Boogey utters, heavily laughing in her ear.

Nattie looks over her shoulder and slightly turns, looking in his eyes, beaming. "You know you're out of your get-right pills, right? So I can't see you moving anything around except your jewels by hand. Heck, it's been a minute since you've even moved your legs in bed." Nattie laughs, getting a good, unexpected joke in.

"What? Now don't play me..., because you know I can shut it down, Natt! Don't play me, now!" Boogey whispers with a smile when slightly daydreaming about how he used to put her to sleep after each session.

"Are you serious? Well, I must admit you had it going on back in the day. Come to think of it, when is the last time you saw, little fella?" Nattie takes a few side steps over to the oven, releasing his extended hand that still rests on her shoulder.

Boogey snatches his hand back and draws hot quick with Nattie bringing him down; knowing he has impotent moments for some unknown medical reason; possibly diabetes. "Well, that ain't my fault, and even the doctors don't know what's wrong. They just say it'll come and go, but I still think it's from that vasectomy during my four-month Army tour. On the other hand, I think it's just psycooligical (psychological) by now," Boogey utters, staring out into space before breaking his concentration.

"A psycho what? Man, please! Seems mighty funny how your trousers bust at the seams when ole Sally Rotten Snatch comes around."

"Sally Rau..., who?" Boogey asks, somewhat frowning with a flummoxed look.

"You know who! Hank's hoes (whores)!" Nattie thinks back on catching him looking at the girl in the general store, in Daisy Dukes and low-cut tops.

"Hank..., Sally? What on earth are you talking about, Natt? Do you have the slightest inkling of an idea, Gal? Sometimes I think your cheese is done plum slid off your cracker..., Whoo wee! The lights are on, but nobody's home," Boogey says, throwing both hands up and wiggling his fingers at his ear to insinuate she's crazy.

"Something's gonna be sliding off alright, and if you keep running your trap, it's gone (going to) be this hot pot of grit sliding off yo (your) narrow tail!" Nattie utters, feeling insulted. "You think you got all the sense in the world..., look at you: a lottery junkie! You live and sleep lottery! Heck, if it wasn't for me pinching dollars off your paycheck and saving money, we'd be living in a cardboard box or a chicken coop by now," Nattie says, rolling her eyes.

"Yeah..., well, who's the breadwinner? Yeah, you make a few dollars here and there stitching up a thing or two for those folks who come ah (a) calling, but dat (that) there is nothing but chicken feed!" Boogey shrieks, staring with a frown. "I pay the freaking bills here, so you can just stomp dat (that) fire out and quit blowing up like you're doing something big by pinching a few dollars! I don't see you pinching dollars off those crumbs you're bringing in," Boogey says, quickly cutting his eyes over at her.

Nattie stays quiet for a spell with silent tears dripping. "Forget you, Boogey! You think you can just say anything, and I'm supposed to take your bullcrap lying down?"

"Well, you brought the business, so deal with it!" Boogie screams, leaning forward and pouring a cup of coffee from the hot kettle when setting it back on the table.

Nattie's tears unnoticeably flow when lifting the plate, fixing it in silence then sliding it in front of him. She takes her time fixing her plate and sits at the far end of the table.

"Natt, how 'bout passing me the butter?" Boogey utters seconds later, feeling guilty.

"Man...! I can't even eat for having to do this and that, yet you gonna (are going to) sit here and tell me how worthless I am!" Nattie says, enraged and thinking back on his hateful comments.

"Hell, I'll just get it myself! For the life of me..., I don't know why I don't just leave so you can just go shack up with that stankin' tail Freddy!" Boogey eases up slowly with eyes set on her while grabbing the butter and sitting.

Nattie slams her fork down without warning, swiftly leaning forward. "I'm tired of you throwing Freddy in my face! It's always Freddy this and Freddy that! If I want Freddy, I can have him now, so how do those apples grab you?" Nattie screams, pointing her index finger toward Boogey until its trembling.

Boogey flinches and his face turns bright red. His hand eases to the plate and the silverware drops when the plate skyrockets against the cabinet, shattering with hot grits slowly sliding down the wall, and the rest of the food lying scattered over the floor. "Forget a Freddy! You can go to him right now if you got it like that!" Boogey utters with boots digging deep in the floor when pushing away from the table. The left chair leg digs deep into the wood, snagging on a raised notch when Boogey twists and turns, losing his balance and rolling to the floor. He climbs up quickly, embarrassed, and scurries through the living room, rubbing his throbbing hip when entering the bedroom, grabbing his brim.

Nattie burst into a silent laugh and then an uncontrollable giggle.

Boogey shoots out, heading for the door, and he pulls the door shut hard and then slams the screen door, causing Nattie to cringe.

Bud's head turns slightly to one side. "Hey, punk! Easy on that damn door! Easy!" Bud yells, flapping downward from a ledge and swinging on the swing with his head still tilted to one side.

Nattie cleans the mess mediating on his words and begins crying when hearing the engine rev a few times then fade.

Boogey heads up to the main street fast, spinning wheels and kicking up a long trail of dust. He lays into the gas pedal, spinning wheels and burning rubber when speeding past the general store. He makes it a few miles and then pulls into the first lottery store he sees. He arrives at the bus station with half an hour to spare. He sits a spell with eyes wandering until climbing out, heading for the ticket window, and making sure his folks are on schedule. He takes a seat inside, looking at people walking in and out for a while until gaping over the backside of a female passing by who turns up her nose when she finds him looking.

Thirty minutes later, his relatives' bus pulls in, and the announcement blares over the PA system.

Boogey watches everyone through the station's picture frame window and then the door where other folk exits, when finally spotting his people still sitting.

Within minutes, Boogey's mother exits, leaving the luggage with her husband. She swings her fake mink over a shoulder, walking like a proud peacock.

One of Nattie's old schoolmates comes out of the bathroom, standing near the door and looking around before noticing the back of Boogey's head.

Boogey turns looking around until daydreaming.

"Well, hell..., if it ain't Boogey, hitting it just right, Johnson! How the heck are you doing, man? Where's Nattie?" the woman curiously asks, looking around. Are you two still together?" she knowingly asks when stepping back and looking him over.

"Well hell…, I'll be a monkey sitting next to the monkey…, Sweet Bea! How the hell are you doing there, Guul (Girl)?" Boogey asks, holding out his hand when without warning, Sweet Bea rushes deep into his arms like a horny toad.

Boogey's mother strains to see who she thinks is Boogey until pulling her eyeglasses from the dangling gold chain around her neck, refocusing quickly.

"You better show a Sistah some love, lover boy!" Bea whispers, holding Boogey tighter with a hand dropping quickly, to his bottom. She slides his hands down around her waist and then down to her big butt when Boogey's eyes spread wide in excitement. "What's up with this handshaking stuff, man?" Sweat Bea asks, looking around for Nattie again before getting even fresher. "Where's Nattie?" Sweet Bea nervously asks, looking around yet again.

Boogey's mom swiftly walks up, angry at their flamboyancy. "Boogey!" she screams, startling him and stopping him dead in her tracks. "Boogey 'Long head' Johnson! Who the heck is this skeezer, tramp, trick you all hugged up wit (with)?" Boogey's mother shouts with all the breath in her with bulged eyes.

The loud station instantly grows to a whisper.

Boogey remains in shock when backing up and almost pushing Bea to the floor, but he catches her quickly, helping her balance.

"Ugh, ugh…, see, you don't know who you're messing wit (with)!" Bea utters with her index finger extended until inches from Boogey's mother's face.

Boogey puts his hands together in his mother's face, pleading when turning to Bea, speechless, and then nervously turning to his mother begging her to be quiet.

"You had better keep your orangutan's paws off my Boogey before I punch you in the face and have you looking like a raccoon up in this mother!" Boogey's mother yells, dropping her coat and reaching for her purse; pulling out a big jar of petroleum jelly. "Don't nobody put their hands on my Boogey! Boogey, you should be ashamed, messing with this filthy, outdated trash!" his mom utters, dipping a finger or two in the petroleum, greasing her knuckles, and dropping the plastic jar back in her purse.

A crowd converges in a semicircle, which forms an even larger circle when people waiting in line for tickets disperse from the line.

Boogey thinks twice, trying to calm his mother, knowing Bea is short a few screws, eccentric, and very explosive.

"Oh, chick, you done flipped your wig! You don't know who you're messing wit (with), cause the queen Bea will pop a cap in yo (your) tail before you can count to one." Bea looks around a few people's smiling and frantic faces, for her luggage.

"Count what? Oh pleases...! Cap and count this!" Boogey's mom screams, stealthily lunging a right hook and barely missing when her ring tangles in Bea's big wig. Boogey's mom grabs a handful of the wig with plaited hair, swinging Bea around in two to three full circles, releasing Bea into the crowd that expressly pushes her back toward Boogey's mom.

Bea catches her balance, somewhat bent forward. "Boogey! Who is this crazy tail hef...?" Bea begins to say when Boogey's mom's small but powerful fist tears through Bea's forehead, knocking her over a bench where her feet rest, sticking straight up and not moving.

Boogey cringes and his hand covers his eyes in fear of looking back.

Bea lies there for seconds until a bystander rushes up, checking her pulse when her toes wiggles in flip flops and her feet jerk with her head slowly shaking off the pain.

"Mama, Mama, Mama..., woo..., Mama, Mama!" Boogey fearfully shrieks, picking up his mother's coat and bag then whizzing her out the door. He looks back to find a few folks helping Bea up and releasing her when she staggers with her wig crooked and halfway off her head. He looks over the loading area quickly, waving to his folks when looking back and quickening his mom to the car.

Boogey's brother's fiancée comes up on the other side of the car, drops the luggage, then backs up a few feet in terror, finding a stray dog frozen in his tracks and staring at her with its nose cringed until showing teeth.

The dog rushes to the luggage sniffing when she screams.

Boogey's brother comes up from behind her, and the dog comes into view. "Quick, get the bags!" the brother yells, shoving past her when the dog cocks up one leg high, growling to keep them at bay while pissing on the luggage. "Get! Get, you!" the brother shrieks, looking over the roof to find Boogey motioning them to hurry and get in when looking back at the main entrance.

"What's the rush, son?" the father asks, finally limping up fast.

"Daddy..., Mama..., Mama knocked a crazy lady out inside the station!" Boogey nervously screams with fast shaking hands, motioning them to get in, with fast scanning eyes hoping for the sheriff or deputies. Boogey looks back to make sure Bea is not coming when his mind flashes back to her notorious record for shooting folks back in the day. He sprints, throwing their luggage in the trunk, then motions to his slow-moving father.

The brother, father, and fiancée enter from the driver's side, while the mother proudly takes her time coming around and climbing in on the front passenger side, with her chest still stuck out.

"Come on, Mama! Hurry up! Hurry!" Boogey nervously yells, slipping her feet in and then rushing the others while continually looking back and waiting for Bea to bust through the door, blazing at any moment.

"Don't you ever rush yo (your) Mama from a fight! I can handle my own, and ain't no heffa gone talk that ying-yang to me!" Boogey's mother utters with one leg still hanging out. Her tight close-knitted fist throws forward, professional style jabs when Boogey eyes her and backs the car down fast with his mother's feet sliding when she screams, dragging her foot inside, quickly. "You're trying to kill your mama, boy!" his mother screams, punching him in the side of his gut with a mean stare.

Boogey shakes his head 'no' in a quick response, hearing the door slam when revving the engine and taking off like a jet with dust high rising fast. He fights the wheel to clear a few cars and luggage carriers before coming past the front of the building and station's exit. He steps into the gas pedal on the straightway, looking through the rearview to find Bea standing wide-legged, pointing, more than likely, her favorite, two six-shooters.

Boogey confirms it's definitely Bea with a double-take, turning hard when executing his zigzag plan and throwing everyone from side to side continually until executing six more sharp turns.

"Hold on, boots!" his father shouts, grasping a dry rotted leather strap on the side of the door, and breaking it off when forcefully falling into Boogey's brother.

Instantly, bullets blaze past the car, one hitting the passenger side mirror and shattering it. "What the...," his mother screams, seeing the mirror hanging from a wire." What kind of crazy hoochies you've been messing around with, boy?" his mother screams, ducking fast with her head shooting deep into Boogey's lap.

Boogey's mouth drops wide open, and his eyes grow wide when leaning forward, looking down. His eyes instantly float over the back seat finding everyone's head leaning forward, over the seat, and down with wide excited eyes. He hits another straightway when everyone settles down, and the car swerves fast when Boogey's mom's head pops up, and her hand accidentally extends between his legs, slightly clawing under his butt while reaching for her dentures. "Ah..., Ugh!" Boogey shrieks, feeling her hands fiddling around his family jewels.

This time, all heads go further forward, following her arm, which extends between Boogey's thighs with no hands in sight.

His mom looks back with a big, peaceful smile. "I'm just trying to get my dentures, that's all," Boogey's mother says, with a crooked smile, giggling.

Boogey swerves, finally lifting high, and she seizes the dentures. He drops down, punching the accelerator with the metal pedal slightly breaking through the rusted floor board.

Other shots hit a stop sign when Bea cuts through two adjacent buildings, straddling and almost out of breath when Boogey's car jets by, gaining distance.

Boogey turns onto another road behind the station, spotting Bea running toward her car. His mind instantly goes into overdrive, and he fears going straight home and being confronted by Bea.

Upon entering the city, he makes a sudden last-minute turn, taking his family to a town a few miles away for sightseeing and afterward, he takes them over to spend time with the grandfather.

Upon exiting the facility an hour later, Boogey's mother mentions a restaurant where a best friend's friend is cooking when talking about how good the woman cooks.

Boogey searches for the place for minutes until finally asking a couple and pulls up within minutes looking at the small establishment, when rushing everyone out.

The tiny doorbell tingles as they enter with eyes swarming around a few sporadically seated people when rushing up to the counter.

"Yes, buffet for five, please," Boogey says looking off then back when hearing the waitress quickly banging out the register's numbers, and joyfully adding the tab before they can change their minds.

Boogey leans back in whispers as they huddle close. "Hmm..., are you sure this food is good because I'm a little leery about restaurants where you pay before you play..., I mean eat."

His mother's face frowns. "Boy, go on and pay! Earlene said Johnnie May is the best cook in these parts of town.

Boogey comes up on his tiptoes looking over at the buffet and can only see the stacked, golden fried chicken when settling down, looking at the smiling waitress when pulling out cash, and paying.

Another smiling waitress comes over and guides them, pointing to their table, when taking their drink orders, and rushing off.

Boogey is the first to stand then the other as they single file over to the head of the buffet, walking past the food slowly with wandering eyes slowly looking back and forth at each other with some giggling.

They continue down the line, staring over everything that looks like mixed, colorful pans of puree until getting to the dessert that looks just as bad with some desserts unidentifiable.

Boogey giggles and whispers. "Johnnie, May, huh? Well, Ms. May must be deep into making baby food these days because other than the chicken, corn, and soggy looking green beans she must have just bought a new blender."

Everyone burst into laughter except his mother who is too embarrassed to claim making the mistake of suggesting the place.

They grab plates and load up on what they think is good, and the mother makes several trips until sitting with three plates, championing her recommendation and still bragging.

Boogey reaches for everyone's hand and they join when he leads into a lengthy payer that ends in a smile.

They all dig in with little talking, but everyone tastes this and that when the head waitress comes up looking over the full plates with only the mother still joyfully chomping.

Twenty minutes later the head waitress comes by filling drinks for the fourth time with eyes wandering over the full plates when walking off.

Boogey looks up and over near the kitchen finding about ten heads peeking out with curious gazes and ducking down quickly when finding everyone at the table looking back then off or up at the ceiling.

Minutes later and throughout their stay, they keep finding folks in the kitchen curiously peeking out and rushing off when spotted.

The mother's head stays down until she finally comes up for air. "This is some good food, to me!" she says with wondering eyes over each full plate with everyone sitting down drinks at the same time.

Boogey gazes at her. "Mama..., chicken? Even the chicken is busted. I mean who messes up fried chicken? All this stuff is mush! And..., at fifteen dollars, a plate?"

Boogey's mother slows her chomping, looking over their stacked plates with single bites and fork indentations when shamefully pushing her plates forward. "Ugh, you right..., this food ain't that good, is it?" she asks, finally taking sips with curious eyes. "What was that seventy-five with taxes?"

The head waitress finally pops back up. "How is everything?" she asks gazing over four barely touched plates.

"Fine," everyone mumbles, lying when smiling.

"Ok, well if there is anything I can get you just let me know," she says, looking away and waving at another couple when looking down, finding all the plates pushed to the edge of the table in front of her when staring, curiously. She takes a few un-stackable plates to the kitchen and several shocked heads pop up, looking back over at the table with some vanishing until the waitress returns for more un-stackable plates.

Boogey looks at his mother. "Ma..., you know the best thing about this place?"

She shamefully looks over at him, curiously.

"It's this ice cold water," Boogey says laughing when everyone joins in with laughter, with a few nosy folks looking over at them, smiling when they stand.

They exit and see a man in an apron with the business logo embroidered on his shirt, proudly walking up as if he's the owner and could have been. "Yall have a great day and come back and see us now, hear?" he says with a cheery smile, confirming he's the owner while holding the door for a couple and cheerfully looking back at the four and Boogey's mother.

Boogey's mother slings her door open making eye contact with Boogey then the owner. "Ah..., kiss me tail!" she says far enough away that the owner doesn't her but joyfully waves to them.

Everyone burst into laughter and sits continually laughing until it tapers off and Boogey cranks up.

They make the thirty-minute ride home, arriving well after noon with Boogey pulling in the yard, with all eyes watching the winds pick up as limbs from the weeping willow gracefully swaying in a gentle breeze. Boogey pulls closer to the porch, intentionally backing in, so the car points out, in case he has to give chase to Bea.

Everyone eases out and stands, looking at the yard and then surroundings to see how much it has changed. Their eyes soon wander to the deep, run-down tire tracks made by the plumber's truck, shaking their heads, but no one asks questions but curiously cut their eyes at each other. They all look back when hearing the busted screen yawn from being stretched wide, and Nattie extends it even wider when they turn, grabbing their things and heading up the steps.

"Hey, Mrs. Johnson," Nattie utters with a fake smile when Boogey's mother looks up.

"Evening, Mrs. Johnson," his mother responds in an unwelcoming voice.

They all wave as they greet Nattie with hugs as they walk up. They wander inside to find Bud excited when he breaks out, talking up a storm while everyone settles down with the conversation finally tapering off shortly thereafter.

"Aperitifs, anyone?"

"Sure, Nattie," all of the voices murmurs.

"What do you have?" the father asks, looking at his cracked watch face.

"Lemonade, tea, juice, moonshine, and prune juice," she utters, standing near the kitchen door with a hand on her hip.

Boogey turns on the news to find a lawyer's personal injury commercial when the fiancée leans forward, meditating on the commercial as if in a trance.

She anxiously pulls out a pen and piece of paper, writing down the number as it flashes across the screen a second time.

Her fiancé looks at her strangely, when suddenly other eyes wander over at her.

Boogey's mother shakes her head, rolling her eyes, and then leans back, shaking her head again.

Nattie opens the cupboard, pulls out a box of minuscule laxatives, easing them into a spoon, and then puts another spoon on top, crushing the pills.

Another commercial comes when Nattie walks in with a serving tray loaded with drinks, including the prune juice that her father-in-law loves. Everyone stares at the television, hearing a new jingle for a dating game. They grab drinks, loading up on snacks before the next commercial, which advertises a credit card; the American dream.

Boogey glares intently at the screen before giggling. "Now, ain't that an oxymoron?"

"What? I just got a credit card last week. It is truly the American dream," the fiancé mutters, looking at Boogey's brother, cheery.

Boogey goes into a daze. "Yeah, it's a dream…, for a moron. Hell, give me the cash any day. You know…, there is something about paying some clown not just the money I owe but interest every month, especially after maxing the credit out…, it's just crazy if you ask me…, just crazy! That just don't make no-sense whatsoever. If that is your American dream, then you're just pitiful," Boogey utters, blindly reaching behind the chair for his wrinkled dunce hat purchased as a prank gift. He leans hard, giggling and almost falling off the chair when passing his brother the hat and then nodding for him to pass it to his fiancé.

"Man! Where did you get his mess?" His brother laughs hard, stretching out the wrinkles and slipping the hat on his fiancés head when she looks toward the kitchen.

"Something I picked up for Boogey to wear when he makes a fool of himself!" Nattie says in laughter while holding her side when everyone joins in the laughter.

A loud alarm sounds and warnings flash across the television screen, warning of a hurricane a few days out.

Boogey's mother turns up her glass, takes a deep swig, and then holds her blown-out jaws before slowly swallowing and looking at her husband while passing him the rest. "Uh, uh, uh…, this here be (is) for you," she utters, shaking her head with a frown and swishing her mouth around when trying to get rid of the nasty prune taste.

Nattie stares with a mean look, which she manages to clean up by shaking her head in disbelief, but knows Boogey's mother will reach for another glass to wash down the taste, so she turns the tray, positioning the glass of spiked sweet tea.

"Yes, child, yes! Now, this here be (is) some good ole country tea," the mother utters, easing to the edge of the chair as Nattie sits beside her. Boogey's mother downs the tea fast, rattling the glass for a refill.

"Boogey, you're closer; how about refilling her drink?" Nattie utters, nodding.

The mother has a second drink and her stomach churns within the hour. She twitches until it's unbearable when gracefully walking to the bathroom and slowly shutting the door. She flips on the fan and light, tiptoeing, with her cheeks tight until her hand cups her butt, taking baby steps. Her stomach bubbles but it sounds like a lion's roar when she feels something move stealthily and furiously. Boogey's mother eases onto the seat, accidentally letting out a loud fart while wiggling.

The television show ends, and before the next commercial, they hear a monstrous noise when she has no choice but to let it rip, uncontrollably.

Boogey's mother sits, giggling, and can't stop laughing when other farts sound off while trying to maintain her composure.

Boogey gets embarrassed and turns up the volume while Nattie sits snickering as if she's on laughing gas.

The fiancée looks surprised and as if she's seen a ghost. "I didn't know you had elephants here," the fiancée fearfully utters with a flummoxed look that leaves them in tears.

The mother hears the volume go up a second time, so she snickers, easing out loud back-to-back farts. She stays in the bathroom a while after she is done, removing her dentures, placing them in a cup, and pouring a solution over them. She sits the cup on the edge of the counter and rejoins them.

Nattie stands, asking the fiancée to join her in the kitchen when everyone is well into the show so they can prepare the meal.

Like clockwork, the father finishes the prune juice and sprints for the bathroom. He forgets to flush, and washes his hands, then reaches for a paper towel, which almost falls over when swatting hard to prevent it, and accidentally knocking the dentures into the unflushed toilet. "I will be da…!" he lowly exclaims, looking for something to fish the dentures out of the brown, murky water when yelling for Boogey after not find anything.

Boogey knocks, and his father peeks out, motioning Boogey inside, when Boogey backs off with a pinched nose, viciously shaking his head 'no.'

"Boy, get in here and hurry before your mother comes! I've smelt more of your poop than the law allows!" he whispers in a mean stare.

Boogey takes a deep breath, rushing in, and grabbing the spray.

The father rushes past Boogey, locking the door, and before he can turn, Boogey lets off a longer blast of bathroom spray that lasts so long that his father fades into the smog then fades back into view seconds later, looking at the can, surprised that it's still spraying. Boogey hits one more blasts and covers his nose while fanning hard.

The father nervously backs up until Boogey's mouth drops open and his eyes widen, looking in the toilet and faintly seeing the teeth in the background.

They stare at the dentures longer until Boogey bursts into laughter. "Man, better you than me!" Boogey whispers, looking at his nervous father whose hand covers his mouth with wide eyes and a red face when bursting into a soft laugh, to muffle the sound.

"Nattie!" Boogey shouts.

"Look, man!" she responds, dropping the spoon in the glass mixing bowl and swiftly sliding it over to the fiancée.

The mother hears Boogey and her husband laughing, so she grows curious when easing to the edge of the couch.

Nattie passes through the living room, and the mother jumps up, trailing behind Nattie, and stands with her ears glued to the bedroom wall when the door shuts.

Nattie knocks then steps back from the light hint of the stench.

Boogey eases the door open and asks Nattie for a wire clothes hanger.

Nattie steps off, looking through the closet until pulling out a clothes hanger, and then eases inside to find them with their backs to her.

The mother slips into the bedroom, tiptoeing over and putting her head to the bathroom door, listening. She turns to her better ear when the door flings open, and she catches the edge of the door, dead center of her forehead when Nattie rushes out to check on the food. "Oh my…, my…, my…!" the mother whispers, feeling a little dizzy and rubbing her head at the tiny indentation.

"I'm so sorry, Mother Johnson." Nattie says, passing and lightly rubbing her shoulder.

Under loud, uncontrollable laughter and them bumping into each other, Boogey's mother grabs the doorknob and slowly opens it without them noticing.

Boogey and his father quietly lean into each other again, slowly falling to their knees in tears.

Boogey's mother gently tiptoes, leaning over them, bracing the countertop, and looking into the toilet bowl then Boogey's heavy jerking hands and the shifting hanger.

Mother Johnson's eyes grow wide when her dentures pass the brown-filled rim, gripping her stomach; feeling sick, and almost puking in the sink. She turns the water on high and leans forward with her heavy weight balancing on the nozzle.

Boogey and his father's eyes grow wide, hearing the pipes yawn from her weight. "Look out!" Boogey yells, diving from the sink and pulling his mother back when water shoots up and before she gets her weight off.

The faucet's head instantly slams into the ceiling with water continuously flowing in a solid stream.

The mother falls back and the father dives into the tub and Boogey low-crawls under the cabinet, with his legs sticking out, kicking while getting drenched.

The steady, pressurized waterfall begins to slowly drop then turns cold, fast, when Boogey turns off the hot, then cold.

Boogey's father looks back, and his eyes widen, seeing his wife's mean frown.

Boogey climbs out leaning over the toilet, fishing again then lifts her teeth, guiding them to the sink, clinging together.

"Woouut!" the mother growls to keep from puking. "Woouut!" she growls again, rushing for the living room, flopping on the couch with her legs sprawled out, about to pass out or go into shock.

Nattie shoots into the bathroom, smiling and looking over her father-in-law's shoulder to find Boogey leaning in the tub, running scalding hot water over the dentures. She reaches for the dentures with a few tissues, and then stands at the door, dangling them at her mother-in-law, whose face is torn up. "Honey, don't even worry, I'll boil them in bleach, and they'll be like new," Nattie utters, staring at her brother-in-law, who looks over at her, clueless. Nattie rushes into the kitchen, leaning into the fiancée, whispering when the fiancée bends over in silent tears of laughter.

An hour or so later, Boogey steps on the back porch, pulling two sun-dried, old, wooden chairs inside and sliding them under the table, before walking to the other side.

Nattie bends over to tend to the hot, buttery rolls in the oven.

As Boogey squeezes past Nattie, his eyes wander over his shoulder and he sees his brother's fiancé walking out. His hands ease to her hips, playfully humping her on the sly before looking back to find his dad shaking his head and smiling when Boogey rapidly releases Nattie and acts as if he's trying to get by.

"My boy!" his dad whispers in passing while patting Boogey's shoulder and shaking his head.

Nattie eases the rolls back inside with a mischievous smile. "You want it?" Nattie utters, poking her butt out and backing up until looking back, embarrassed when finding her father-in-law looking with Boogey nowhere in sight. Nattie rubs her hip and limps, downplaying her naughtiness.

Everyone takes turns wandering into the bathroom minutes later, to wash their hands while Boogey and Nattie wash theirs in the kitchen sink.

The mother finally drifts into the kitchen, and Nattie pulls her dentures from a jar with a fork. The mother stares with a mean look, daring Nattie to laugh, and then snatches them, squirting denture cream while continually shaking her head and slowly opening her mouth wide and closing when they are inches away. She shakes her head more, slowly bringing them to her mouth until closing her eyes. "Woouut!" she growls. "Wouut! Ugh ugh! I can't; I just can't!" Boogey's mother utters until weak.

"Now, you know you gone need them their teeth to eat this fine meal Nattie's been slaving over all afternoon, Mama," her husband utters with a slick grin which he wipes away when she looks back at him with a hand on her hip.

Boogey's mother stares at the breathtaking food, pulling the dentures close and shaking her head. "Woouut!" she growls. "Woouut!" she growls again. "Uh, uh, I can't...! I tell yah; I just can't. No way am I putting these nasty teeth in my mouth," she utters, wrapping them in a paper towel.

Nattie reaches into the cabinet, pours straight bleach into a pot, sterilizes the dentures then prepares a few plates while the fiancé stands, helping.

They join hands, and Boogey leads off in a lengthy prayer when everyone reaches, partaking in the hearty meal and passing the bowls.

Boogey looks at his mother, gumming a buttery roll and peas while rolling her eyes, pissed.

"Chicken or beef, Ma?" Boogey asks, holding the basket of crispy, fried chicken close to her.

She stares over the golden, brown chicken as her mouth waters then takes a few deep breaths, swallowing hard before her eyes drift to the teeth being laid on the table. "Woouut!" she growls, flipping the napkin over her teeth. "Here, get this mess out of my face," she utters, passing the teeth to her husband.

"Oh shush, woman, as much as your breath be smelling like fresh hog chittlins (chitterling)! You better put those teeth in and hush that fuss! Heck, you eat hog turds all the time but can't stand the sight of your teeth in a little brown water," Boogey's father utters, frowning in frustration.

His wife gives him the evil eye, and her tight fist slams onto the edge of the table. "Breath? I know you ain't talking wit (with) that halitosis breath you got!" she shrieks, frowning.

Everyone keeps quiet but stares at her, trying not to laugh.

Later, Boogey watches the clock, motioning to his dad and brother that he has to run to the store when the three strike out, laughing and joking there and back.

The phone rings at 9:35PM, and Boogey answers on the third ring. "Hello?" he utters in a relaxed voice, slightly pulling the phone away.

"Bita boom, bita bang!" the loud and obnoxious drunken female voice shrieks out against the high volume of the background music and loud, drunken voices.

"Who is this?" Boogey knowingly asks, easing the phone closer.

"Bita boom, bita bang!" the drunken female voice yells again, with her voice going into a burst of long and crazy laughter. "Sam I am, Sam I am!" Bea shrieks.

"Who?" Boogey asks, looking at Nattie, pretending to be clueless when shrugging his shoulders.

"The Queen Bea! You better recognize or ask somebody, sucker! You know good and damn well who! Yeah..., I started to drive by and black that joint out on my way over to the juke joint, tonight," Bea utters in a drunken, whining voice when downing another shot of liquor and chasing it with a tall, quality brand beer.

"Gone wit (with) that crazy stuff, Bea! You were wrong, and you know it!" Boogey utters with his back turned to everyone.

"Right or wrong, wrong or right?" she shrieks faster. "Right or wrong, right or wrong!" she senselessly shrieks repeatedly until messing up the old saying.

"What?"

"You heard me: right or right, wrong or wrong?" she utters, faster and more slurred.

"Like I said gone wit (with) that craziness!" Boogey utters, finding Nattie easing to the edge of the couch, listening, yet pretending to be into the television show.

Nattie leans more until his mother slightly leans Nattie to the opposite side. "Man, you nosy!" the mother utters, giggling, and lightly shoving Nattie again to get a smile.

Boogey lets her rattle on but keeps politely telling her bye; trying not to be impertinent but wanting to end the call on a peaceful note.

Bea goes on and gets louder. "Sam I am! Sam I am! Bita-bing! Bita-bang!" she utters faster but even more slurred.

"You must be drunk out of your damn mind, calling here this time of night with all this B.S!" Boogey utters with a mean look when growing tired of the senseless comments.

"Sam I am, Sam I am," she utters, continually.

"You're a grown woman, Bea, so stop playing on my damn phone!" Boogey finally utters, totally irritated.

"Playing, my foot! You think this is playing? Just wait until I leave this joint! I'm gonna roll through and smoke everybody up in that mother! Consider it an MF blackout there tonight, trick!" Bea says, looking at a man walking up when turning her butt and grinding on him. "You just tell that old heffa to eat her last supper light, so she doesn't weigh too much up in that coffin!" she shrieks, senselessly giggling while backing up deeper into her lover, who kisses deep in the nape of her neck.

"Keep talking stupid," Boogey utters, deepening his voice while stretching the cord to take a seat. "You come here messing around if you want, and I can promise you, you ain't gone like the outcome: six pallbearers, naw, make it eight for your big tail! You might want to designate a few before leaving that juke joint tonight," he utters, leveling the playing field, yet nervously swallowing hard then looking at the clock and swallowing even harder.

"Oh yeah? Well, tell your nappy-head Mama that she's gonna (is going to) be the first to go, so pick out one of Nattie's pretty dresses, and don't worry 'bout making up her ugly face because Imma blow her freakin' head slam off!" Bea utters, seriously, until continually and playfully purring like a cat.

Boogey's mother grows mad, staring at him from time to time. "Now you look hea…, (here) that there is my doggone (darn) business!" Boogey's mother finally moans, overhearing her loud voice when she proudly sits up, looking like a prize-winning chicken.

Nattie eases onto the edge of the chair again. "Maybe, but naw, cause this hea (here) is my house, and ain't no hooker gone call here talking to Boog about a bunch of knickknacks!"

Boogey listens to more derogatory comments when slowly walks to the phone base on the wall.

"Sleep light, suckers!" Bea shrieks when Boogey slams the phone down.

"What the heck happened to Bea, Boogey?" Nattie finally asks, easing back and curious.

Boogey eases in a seat and starts telling Nattie all that had transpired leaving out Bea's flirtatious gestures.

Boogey's mother joins in on the best part, telling how mad she was, and then gives a play-by-play, slow-motion episode, while keeping the room in an uproar of laughter.

Nattie intervenes in a fearful look. "Look hea (here)." The laughter tapers off when she gets even more serious, leading into Bea's rambunctious past. She goes on, mentioning how crazy Bea is and how even the police are afraid of her when the room grows so quiet that they hear one of Bud's feathers slowly hit the bottom of the cage, and jump. "Boogey, you remember Bea choking a female out with one hand, right?" Nattie says with a serious face.

"Oh yeah, Natt, how can I forget that? Especially after seeing her body slam the chick on the table, then elbow her in the gut to bring her to, like in that legendary comedy movie!" Boogey utters, shaking his head and swallowing hard.

"Shush!" Boogey's father says, hearing the back door lightly slamming from the wind.

"Oh, that ain't nothing but the wind, Pops," Boogey says, but not too convincing.

Everyone's eyes nervously gaze about the room, at the window and doors.

Boogey's mom reaches for her tea with her lips easing onto the edge of the glass when her side teeth lightly rattle against the glass as she takes a nervous sip.

Everyone grows quiet again, listening.

"What was that?" the fiancée asks with her head slightly turning to see if she can make out a sudden noise.

"Boo!" Nattie shouts, causing the mother to spill tea over her skirt.

"Forget you, Nattie!" she utters, frowning with her hands running over her clothes, brushing off beads of tea. "I could have choked," she utters, frowning and laughing senselessly.

"Don't worry about choking because Bea will be here soon enough to choke you 'til you tap out," Nattie utters, making everyone laugh and feel at ease.

Within the hour, a car's headlights shine upon the house, and feet shuffle across the floor with everyone dropping, taking cover, and quiet, until Nattie bursts into a crazy laugh and gets everyone snickering while trying to be quiet.

Boogey reaches for his rifle, and Nattie cuts off the television, peeling back the curtain, when Boogey peeks out, spotting someone getting out. The interior lights go off immediately, and Boogey is unable to make out who it is but keeps looking until fogging the widows and backing off in fear.

The tall, dark silhouette vanishes into pure darkness as the car backs out quickly and slows down.

"Hit the lights..., someone's coming!" Boogey utters, looking over his shoulder and then back out the window. His eyes scan over the yard, jumping when losing sight of the tall figure that passes through the yard and keeps walking.

Nattie reaches into the dusty bookcase bringing out candles and lighting them.

Boogey fears killing someone, so he pulls out the orange box, unloading the shells and loading rock salt but leaves the gun unlatched.

There is a long spell of silence until the fiancée knocks over a candle, scrambling for the corner to retrieve it.

"Shh...," Boogey whispers, listening to their heavy breathing when the clock grows loud.

Boogey's heart beats fast until hearing it, when suddenly they hear the loud sound of something drug alongside the house, kinda like a dog chain being yanked, until it quiets. "Anybody out there better leave damn skippy, or Imma (I am going to) light this yard up with buckshot!" Boogey shrieks in a frightened voice.

Boogey's dad leans forward, about to bust a gut to prevent him from laughing so hard at Boogey's imitated voice but tenses, hearing the chain again when his wife silences him.

Bright white eyes gaze inside through the bedroom window, until ducking down fast.

The dog finally yelps, rushes off the back porch when hearing footsteps, and slowly runs when seeing the black-silhouetted shadow extend across the yard. He barks, taking off at top speed, running toward the cornfield with all that is in him.

"Daddy..., back door, quick!" Boogey whispers, taking aim as his father closes in quick and Boogey turns, whispering the plan, which is for his dad to open the door so he can shoot.

The manly body swings a long, black object held tightly in his hand as he climbs the steps slowly, listening when gently applying five distinctive knocks then two.

Nattie cringes, jerking when realizing the too-familiar special coded knocks.

Boogey presses his ear to the door and thinks he hears whispering voices when freezing. "Three..., two..., one!" Boogey shrieks as quickly as possible with the gun snapped into alignment with his finger tight on the trigger.

The tall man turns and jumps high off the porch with arms swinging until wind milling with feet in motion before hitting the ground.

His dad unlatches the deadbolt fast.

The tall man's pointy boots dig deep into the dirt, and his hand go to his head, catching and holding his ten-gallon cowboy hat as he cruises into the cornfield.

Boogey sprints out, firing off a few high, un-aimed shots where the light-colored shirt vanishes and then takes aim a few feet ahead and lower, firing.

"Ouwooh!" the loud, high-pitched voice yells when the man grabs his buttocks and upper back thigh, limping at a fast and then even faster pace while constantly looking back.

Within minutes, tires burn rubber on the asphalted back road as the car swiftly backs down and comes up to speed.

Boogey and his father run to the back corner of the yard, finding the car going around a sharp curve before the taillight comes on when skidding more wheels. The two stand watching until the car vanishes, then look back to find the women holding back the curtains and piercing their eyes through the living room window into pure darkness.

The women's nervous voices squawk when out of nowhere, Boogey and his father shoot past the window, and they drop in fear, listening as they shuffle up onto the front porch. "Did you see who it was?" Nattie very nervously asks, leaning on the young girl's shoulder.

"Don't know, but I got some salt up in him, so he won't be lying too comfortable for a few days!" Boogey excitedly says while fumbling in his pocket and reloading and holding the gun at his side.

A car turns on the main road and the headlights appear a few hundred yards away from the car parking.

Everyone inside the house or on the porch watches until finally seeing a body lunge from the thick row of corn. The manly figure slightly limps, under the streetlight, toward the car when the car's signal light comes on, and the car makes a U-turn, picking up speed.

Boogey and his dad look over the yard and then close at a few slow, passing cars.

His brother emerges through the front door, sitting in the sun-dried, wooden chair. "Man, y'all got some wild, wild West crap going on 'round (around) here! Hell, the only thing missing is damn horses." The brother says, tensing when looking at his mother until nervously staring into pure darkness.

"I'm just glad y'all were here because this is normally the night I shoot craps or play bingo." Boogey looks at the ground in deep thought. "I heard last week that these roguish, wannabe gang members busted people's lights out, cut on their water faucets, and waited for them to come out then ambush em' (them) or ran them up in the house and put them facedown," Boogey nervously utters, looking around.

"What? These country tail boys?" his brother utters, laughing.

"What..., are you surprised?" Boogey curiously asks.

"Well, sorta..., I mean, you hear about silly stuff like that in the city, but not in the boonies." The brother rides the chair on hind legs until the back rests against the wall.

"They need to get tough on the laws. The world got worse when they took prayer out of schools and threatened folks about spanking their kids," the mother utters.

"I don't think they said you can't spank them, but don't abuse them, Ma," the fiancée utters.

The conversation tapers off minutes later when they stagger inside.

Shortly after midnight, the heater burns too hot from the brother accidentally adding a log too many, so they walk outside and talk longer until in tears of laughter.

Boogey looks at his watch, realizing the juke joint is about to close but wants to stay outside longer for early warning, so he strikes up several more conversations.

Mosquitoes gather in full bloom an hour later, so they wander inside and watch television while taking turns changing into their sleeping attire.

Boogey walks into the living room, feeling fresh. "Nattie, how about serving up some of that fine hot tea?" Boogey utters, looking over at Nattie beaming while listening to the fiancée talk until Nattie breaks the girl's train of thought.

"Man..., I've been on my feet all day!" Nattie eases to the edge of her seat.

Boogey's mother assumes that Nattie spiked the other drink, so she stands, waiting for Nattie. "I'll help," the mother curiously says, looking out of the corner of her eyes.

Boogey flips through a few channels and then flips through more, slowly. "How about helping them?" Boogey utters, nodding to his brother's fiancée, who stands swiftly and walks toward the kitchen, taking a seat at the head of the table.

The channels flash speedily to a porn channel where strippers work it out on the pole when the up-tempo rap music's volume nippily goes down.

Nattie pulls out a kettle, rinsing it before turning to the stove.

Boogey gawks at his brother and father, who are all smiles, while his eyes drift between the kitchen and the television.

Boogey's mother notices it is quiet, so she backs up, barely seeing nude flesh then swiftly walks up behind Nattie, leaning into her and turning the knob to ease the heat. "If you took care of him at home, my son wouldn't watch that filth," the mother utters with a disgusted look until eye to eye.

Nattie tenses and her temperature boil from harsh words when eye to eye and inching back up on Boogey's mother.. "Well, I can say the same since your husband is in there, but I won't since you can rush to judgement, and you run such a tight ship," Nattie utters with a smirk.

The mother walks into view, pretending to close the cabinet then slams it and doesn't look back.

Boogey expressly presses buttons, changing channels, but nothing happens when he furiously presses several more and then nervously hits the power button.

Boogey's mother finally looks back, noticing the room is pitch-black when easing to the door with eyes swarming over fidgety, dark silhouettes. "Why are you all sitting in the dark?"

"I don't know…; the TV just blanked out for some reason," Boogey utters, pretending to punch more buttons.

The mother rolls here eye at Boogey, letting him know she knows he is lying then grabs a coffee cup, turning again and making eye contact with her husband to give her disapproval, before walking out of sight.

The kettle soon whistles loudly, and Nattie places it on a wooden coaster and then begins filling the cups that her mother-in-law is placing on the table.

After tea time, everyone stays up talking until 3AM when both parents yawn.

"I'm sleepy!" Boogey's mother says when yawning and causing her husband to yawn again.

"Sleeping arrangements?" Boogey's brother asks Nattie when she approaches.

"Boogey brought blow-up mattresses, so we can put one in the kitchen and one in the living room and close the curtains for privacy, if needed."

The mother looks at her husband and then Boogey's brother, who looks surprised that they would not offer their bedroom to their parents.

Boogey's brother motions him to the kitchen. "Man…, I can't believe you gone let them sleep on the floor, on a blow up. Man, you done lost your mind?" the brother asks, concerned.

"Uh-huh…, so, you think I should give them the bed, huh? Well…, ok, you know what? What was I ever thinking? You're so right!" Boogey walks into the living room, looking at his parents, who slowly stand in anticipation of change. "Mom, would you and dad like to take the bedroom?" Boogey asks.

A big smile comes upon their faces, and they look at one another, surprised.

Nattie frowns until a mischievous smile comes. "Give me a minute to straighten my things," Nattie utters, entering the bedroom and shutting the door. She lifts the side of the mattress, shifting the support boards so they'll have a rough night's sleep then alters the clock to intentionally wake them very early. Her feet quietly shuffle across the floor when she sprints into the bathroom, squirting Boogey's rotten-egg-smelling aftershave on a rag and smears it under the pillowcase on the mother-in-law's side.

Nattie opens the door, and Boogey walks into the closet, pulling out the two new double-decker inflatable sleepers.

The mother and father stand looking until the beds are fully inflated.

Boogey's mother's eyes drift into the grim-looking bedroom and her heart drops when her eye skirts alongside the lopsided, banana-boat-looking mattress.

Nattie takes her time making both beds with fresh, crisp, new, three-hundred-thread-count linen.

Boogey's mother swallows hard with her head leaning to one side, imagining how comfortable it would be to dive into the inflatable lap of luxury.

Nattie makes the last bed, diving onto it and snuggling with a pillow.

"They look so comfortable," the mother says, walking past the foot of the closest one.

"Here…, sit, Mother Johnson," Nattie utters, patting the edge when sliding over.

Boogey's mother eases onto the edge, gently rubbing back and forth until lying back when her tense body melts into the mattress, which grabs her firmly, holding her tight. "Umm…, this is so nice. I wish we had one," the mother utters, looking at Nattie, who ignores her, and then Boogey's brother, who turns his head when his fiancée squeezes his hand hard, secretly kicking him and giving him a serious look.

"Come on, Daddy!" Nattie says, looking at Boogey, who removes his flip flops and sits.

The lights go out, and the only light is a dim television when an emergency alert signal dances across the bottom of the screen again, causing them to look at the hurricane warning.

The volume goes up a little when the reporter reports that the hurricane is a day or so out and tracking as close as fifty miles east of Fikesville.

"Do you think it is going to hit here, Boogey?" his mother asks, very concerned.

"Why worry? Mama, with faith you used to pray away storms." Boogey smiles.

"That was home, and we never get weather like that there, but I still have faith," she utters, grabbing his hands, and looking around until everyone stands, joining hands when she prays, and then backs away, looking at Boogey, cheery.

"That's my mama!" Boogey smiles at his daddy, who proudly sticks his chest out.

# CHAPTER SEVEN

### Big Mama's Knockout And Take Down

An hour or so later; Bea pulls alongside the main road, turning off the headlights in front of the Asian couple's house. She guzzles a few beers, patiently sucking down two four-piece fried chicken wing dinners, then wipes her greasy mouth. She guzzles down two more cold, forty-ounce beers then lets off the most prolonged belch ever, until sounding like several people belching back-to-back.

Her belly starts to hurt so she pops the glove compartment open, popping four antacids and instantly she leans heavy to one side with a long, loud, and obnoxious fart that leaves her breathless and with the ugliest frown ever when fanning fast. Her eyes instantly shoot over her shoulder into the back seat; fighting to get to the can of air freshener when her face looks even worst when grabbing it and spraying non-stop.

A drunk rides up on the rear of Bea's car, staring inside hard when finding her swaying and bouncing around with uncontrollable looking arms until fading into the thick mist. He scrolls close alongside the car amazed with bright eyes and floats by with eyes still peeled over his shoulder and in the foggy windshield giggling. He stares, still looking back and so long this time that he veers off, slamming into the side of a parked car and running off in the tall weeds, screaming.

The thick fog soon thins out and Bea sits looking around for minute before wrapping up the bones, slinging extra, empty beer bottles out the window and into the Asian couple's yard.

Bea eases out, pulling a wrinkled, damp bag that once contained the cold beers from the front seat, staggering to the rear where cautiously looks around, sticking the key inside. She eases the trunk up, leaning into the junky trunk, giggling so hard that she almost falls in but backs out fast with a thick tissue roll. She walks back to the driver's side, sticking her hand inside the open door, pulling out a cigarette lighter, when easing back slowly until the door shuts and the light go out.

Boogey wiggles his toes inside the house until an unfamiliar funk lightly rises when quickly pulling a pillow from the couch; placing it over his flip flops, and somewhat muffling the unearthly smell.

"Woo wee...! Hooooottt..., damn! Is that your feet smelling like cheese popcorn up in here, Boogey?" his brother asks, finally getting a good whiff and holding his breath with his nose pinched tight.

Nattie bursts out giggling, and the fiancée joins in, laughing and trying to stop until each is bursting out in laughter, which lasts for minutes.

An hour or so later, everyone settles in, but a couple of them twist and turn; getting comfortable yet still attentive to the slightest sounds.

Bea staggers past the country store coming up alongside it until fading off and drunkenly stumbling into Boogey's yard. She immediately thinks she sees movement in a window when veering off and into the cornfield where she stays a long spell until reappearing not too far from Boogey's porch.

She soon stumbles out with the damp bag, holding it an arm's length away with a mean frown while quietly staggering toward the porch. She walks up beside the steps, leaning as far as possible, when easing the bag down in a stern frown. Bea pats down her blouse until flicking a lighter a few times and then freezes with it burning; thinking she hears footsteps when backing up slowly and alongside the house with heavy, uncontrollable jumping shoulders.

Boogey rolls over, and his head pops up fast in the dim, television-lit room listening when Nattie's head pops up as well, with both staring at the front door then back into each other's nervous bright, white wandering eyes.

Bea springs forward and leans in again; lighting two edges, when going into a deeper, muffled, and drunken laugh when swiftly falling back, expressly executing a wide turn, and running zigzag, as if stoned out of her mind. Bea runs until ten feet or so away; jerking when stopping by a pile of bricks, cutting her eyes back over her shoulder when seizing the one with a big clump of mortar attached. She strains to lift it then leans way back, slinging it with great force towards Boogey's house like a javelin when bursting into an echoing, drunk laughter.

Boogey and Nattie's heads spring up simultaneously, listening with the brick still silently gliding high, as if in slow motion from her drunkenness. It fades into darkness until reappearing in the light from the back of the general store; its shadow reflecting against the house in a flash. "Kaboomaloomaloomaloom!" The brick tumbles shattering with broken mortar spraying all over the place and sounding like a barrage of shrapnel.

Everyone else shoots straight up from their pillows, screaming, and trembling, until nervously listening to a non-stop, deranged, and echoing giggle.

Boogey jumps back, flipping the television off when loud laughter rises again then gently fades into a whisper when another brick slams into the house, heavily bouncing across the porch. He sprints for the window with white eyes roving over the dark yard when the brother pops up in the next window with only scary, white eye balls showing.

The third unforeseen brick soon comes, slamming into the front of the house, and vibrating so hard that a few pictures fall from the wall, causing them to jump and scatter about in fear.

"Everyone stay low in case there's some shooting!" Boogey yells with fast roving eyes.

Everyone stays low, waiting for a sudden barrage of gun fire.

Boogey keeps looking until nervously lunging for his shotgun, when hearing tires peeling rubber minutes later and before he can get to it. He flings the front door open, instantly waving off the thick, red, cherry bomb cloud of smoke, when finding the high, flame burning bag. Boogey expressly turns the gun upright, leaning low and forward, when slamming the butt into the bag, and striking the porch.

'Blam!' The weapons sound off, discharging rock salt, which tears through the brittle wooden roofing, leaving a gaping hole and almost blowing his head off when everyone hits the floor.

"Forget it, Boogey! Forget it..., you're gonna (going to) kill your damn self!" Nattie shrieks, rushing for the open screen door with wide eyes and everyone close in tow.

Boogey smells a light hint of manure, which grows stronger as the paper burns down but brighter when the thick wad of tissue flares up.

The women grip their noses and chests in fear, nervously backing inside until bumping into Boogey's brother as the door slams shut.

The door immediately flies open, slamming against the house.

Boogey's brother's hand comes to his shoulder as he rises high, as if in slow motion, screaming a war cry with tight slippers on when Boogey looks over his shoulder, finding him in midair and going higher.

"Nooooo!" Boogey shrieks when his brother's hand lightens from him, still going higher, until coming down and stomping the burning bag hard and fast; the fifth through seventh stomp coming even faster, when the strongest scent of manure rises.

"Boogey, Boogey, Boogey, Boogey!" Bud shrieks, shaking off the strongest scent ever, when a shift in light winds causes it to float inside.

Boogey frowns, closing his eyes tight and slowly looking up, shaking his head in disbelief when slowly glancing down at his brother's loose, mud-covered slippers. He pulls the butt of the rifle close, jerking it away, fast with an even bolder stank look. "I'm gonna (going to) kill that biiii...," Boogey shrieks, refraining from cursing when looking back and through the screen, deep into his mother's eyes.

Boogey's brother's face frowns without delay, realizing he's been stomping poop when frowning worse while wind-milling until holding Boogey's shoulder when hopping, and trying to pull off his tight socks.

He hops in circles until his fiancée rushes up, gagging and hurrying to the far side of the porch with a weak stomach.

"I wish y'all wouldn't have messed with that crazy-tail woman!" Nattie says, shaking her head; knowing it's just the beginning of the madness. "That woman ain't wrapped too tight, I tell you. Bea is the daughter of Satan in disguise!" Nattie yells, unsettled and trembling in fear.

Boogey stares back at Nattie. "She can play psycho all she wants and make me break some da..., foot off in her fat tail!" Boogey utters, trying to refrain from cursing when staring at his mother, who is in total fear and doesn't hear him.

The fiancé eases into Boogey's brother. "Hold still if you want me to get the flip-flop and sock off!" She bends over with the brother bracing her back and finally manages to get the funky sock off, throwing it to the ground when he balances on his heel with brown and black smeared toes.

The brother stands balancing against the house while the fiancé walks back in, meeting Nattie midway in the living room with a bucket of lye soap and old rags.

The fiancé eases out, sitting the bucket down, throwing the rags off to the side, and passing the soap quick.

The brother eases into the sun-dried seat, taking his time cleaning up and then takes another shower.

Boogey continues looking around until seeing something waving off to the side when turning, reaching for the rag Nattie is handing him. He squeezes some of the suds off, wiping the butt of his rifle and continually takes distant whiffs until it is somewhat clean.

Boogey's brother comes out and finds them reclining; three on one inflatable bed and two on the other, giggling about the incident with distant stares.

"Son, do you have another gun; because I'm not going to get any sleep with all this non-sense and commotion," Boogey's father utters, nervously staring deep into his eyes.

"Yeah, a peashooter under the mattress, on my side," Boogey utters, walking into the bedroom.

"Under the mattress? What are you trying to do, kill us? You know I'm afraid of guns, and you have the nerve to have one under the mattress? What if I would have sat down or kicked the mattress too hard?" Boogey's mom says with deep concern.

"Aight, Mama, no need to go and get yourself in a knot because it has the safety on," Boogey utters, looking away when his father cringes, seeing Boogey's mother's trembling, slow opening hand when her left eye goes weak.

'Kapowyow!' The slap comes without warning.

"Ouch! What did you hit me for?" Boogey asks, rubbing his red face.

"I raised you better, Boogey! Don't ever sass me, boy!" she utters, frowning, teary-eyed.

Nattie's fist balls tight, easing to her side when the fiancée sees it, smiles, and begins gently patting her arm to calm her.

"I'm sorry, Boogey, but you know I raised you better," Boogey's mother utters, gently rubbing his face.

An hour later, everyone is comfortable and soon falls fast asleep, one at a time, but Boogey is the last to go.

Two hours later, the alarm sounds, waking the parents who lie then sit, tired and worn down.

The mother eases up, yawning and stretching until her hand comes down past her face when she jumps back, holding her hands out in disgust.

"What?" her husband asks, looking back when a light sulfuric scent drifts by then grows stronger.

"Did you mess yourself and get it on my arms?" Boogey's mother asks, carefully looking her arms over and cutting her eyes back over at her husband.

"Heck no…, what foolishness are you talking, woman?" Boogey's father utters, popping his lips.

Nattie accidentally barges through the door, finding their matching adult diapers lying side-by-side on the floor, and backs up with a disgusted look.

"Nattie! Nattie!" the mother shrieks, staring eye-to-eye.

Nattie backs out quickly, slamming the door shut fast when falling on the mattress, and lying there, smiling until quietly giggling.

"Nattie! Nattie!" the mother shrieks, staring at the doorway.

Nattie keeps quiet, ignoring her for minutes.

Boogey sits wiggling his toes until finally standing, and then walks over to the door, knocking when opening the door. "What, Mama?" he asks when the aroma rises. "Is that my shaving cream I smell?" Boogey asks with a confused look.

"Ugh, ugh, ugh!" Boogey's mother shrieks, rushing into the bathroom.

Boogey's father shakes his head and smiles. "Girls will be girls." The father eases back on the pillow, rubbing his bald head. "Nattie is as bad as Bea when it comes to guessing if she's off her rocker, huh?" Boogey's dad utters, giggling.

"What's up for today, Pops?" Boogey excitedly asks, frowning when seeing the open diapers.

"Boogey, Boogey, Boogey!" his father whispers, slipping on his diaper under the long t-shirt then walking up to him. "Hmm…, we were thinking about seeing pops, but son, this is too much for me and your mama; all this fighting, shooting and carrying on," the father utters, yawning.

"What? Fighting? Shooting? Come on, Pops..., Mom started this! If she had not knocked Bea out, none of this would be happening," Boogey utters, livid when picking up a few things from the junky floor.

Boogey finally walks out, falling into the mattress, waking Nattie from a catnap when she turns over, lying on her back. Boogey lye there longer in deep thought then rolls over, resting on the end with the air release plug, unknowingly. He runs his hands back and forth for minutes until playfully fiddling with something protruding outward until intentionally pulling the plug when realizing what it is, releasing the air. He jumps up quickly looking at Nattie's frown when she begins fighting to get up but can't, before it collapse.

Nattie comes up high and fast, about to swing but deflects, when hearing the bedroom door knob jiggle; playing it down when floating into the kitchen with the fiancée following to help prepare breakfast.

The mother soon eases into the kitchen, sitting and grabbing a cup from the table when the fiancée pours coffee and then sets the kettle back on the stove.

Nattie gazes over the refrigerator, finally realizing they are out of fresh country ham and bacon when calling out, to Boogey.

"Yeah?" Boogey finally utters, walking in, and running fingers through his wet, permed hair.

"We're out of bacon and country ham, so can you run to the store?" Nattie reaches in her bra, pulling out a twenty.

Boogey's father stands a few feet behind as Boogey turns, sprinting to the front door and pulling the door shut until it clicks.

Boogey finally lightens onto the sidewalk and instantly frowns, finding Bea's car parked across the street from the general store when picking up his pace. He enters quickly, stopping when finding no one in line, so he runs up, purchasing a lottery ticket. He backs away from the counter slowly, looking over the store and then back along the meat counter, finally sighting Bea in bright, fluorescent hair rollers when she springs up, from reaching a bottom shelf.

The store's door swings open, and Boogey's father enters, coming up behind Boogey and clearing his throat when Boogey looks back at him.

The father looks the store over then takes off behind Boogey, until seeing him stop several feet away from Bea when recognizing her hairdo and instantly veers down another aisle.

Boogey steps up even closer behind Bea, clearing his throat.

Bea keeps her eyes on the meats in deep thought while licking her thick lips until noticing a reflection from behind, through the meat case glass when finally turning and looking back with raccoon-circled eyes.

"Bea?" Boogey utters, looking deep into her eyes then closer when frowning. "Damn..., I mean, what happened to you?" Boogey asks with a concerned look.

"Look..., you know good and damn well what happened! Don't play dumb, Boogey, damnait!" she screams, looking dead into his eyes until bursting into laughter.

"What? What's so funny?" Boogey asks, confused and nervously nodding at an old lady who passes.

"When we gonna (going to) do this thang, Boogey?" Bea asks, winking.

"Now..., Bea, you know I'm a married man, so there's no messing around in my cards," Boogey responds, staring firmly.

"Well then..., you need to relook those damn cards or die an old fool," Bea utters, looking over her shoulder and finding his nosy father peeking then ducking with fearful, wandering eyes.

"Ole fool? Why? Because I'm not creeping like most of these clowns around here?"

"Look! You're a good man, Boogey," Bea utters, teary-eyed.

"Thank you, but why are you crying?" Boogey asks, reaching for a napkin near the cheese sample tray and passing it to her.

"You're just a good man, period!" Bea utters in a delayed smile. "Just please open your eyes, man!" she screams, teary-eyed, when turning away, grabbing the wrapped package of smoked sausage from the butcher.

"What's that supposed to mean, Bea?" Boogey asks, even more confused.

"Wow..., you really don't have a clue, do you? Poor Baby," she says, looking into his eyes, pitifully. "Your little flower has withered, been deflowered, and oh, let me think of a few other choice words for that stank trick," Bea utters, raising her voice and frowning when thinking about her own man whom she loves so much.

Boogey's face frowns and his fist balls tight.

His father cringes at the disgusting comments while still peeking through large bags of chips.

A few patrons pretend to be waiting on the butcher while attentively listening.

"Now, Bea, I've always treated you like family and never said anything to degrade you or your family, and I ain't gone let you talk about my Nattie like a dog!" Boogey utters when huffing and puffing.

Bea gets louder and then laughs pointing a thick index finger in his face until he turns red and a vein pops in the middle of his forehead.

"Enough of this crap, Bea," Boogey whispers in anger, with his fist still balled tightly. "I've never laid a hand on a female, but if you don't stop this nonsense, I'm going to knock you back into your first day of birth, even as far as conception!" Boogey utters, looking deep into her dark ringed eyes. He stares even harder then decides to take a step back when something blubbery pushes hard against Boogey's back with Bea's eyes going high over Boogey's head when Bea's grandson, a six-foot-three, four-hundred-sixty-pound, husky fella, stuffs his pockets with stolen gum and jostles Boogey again; no smile, just a mean, killer stare.

Boogey slowly turns, looking at his belly then slowly upward with his head thrown way back when looking into stale eyes and a mean face.

"Is this something I need to handle, Granny? What! What, punk?" the grandson yells, jerking fast and making Boogey flinch. "Man, I'll fold you like a piece of paper!" he shouts, looking down at Boogey while cracking each knuckle in unison.

Boogey swallows hard; feeling overwhelmingly intimidated and does not want any part of this young sasquatch-looking dude.

Boogey's father sees the boy's corpulent tight fist cocked back when the father slips down, low-crawling around another aisle quickly, and ducking down. He comes up attentively and tiptoes away and then turns down another aisle, distancing more when cringes, yet nervously and attentively listening for the first shot, slap, or punch.

"I got this (hea) here, Junior!" Bea slips her hand into her purse.

The butcher abruptly backs up, slipping inside the cooler and the cashier ducks behind the counter while others disperse as if never there, yet still peeking from behind things.

"Come on, Bea, why are you doing this? I mean really..., do you really have to do this? Hell..., we're family, Baby! We go way back like two peas in a freakin' pod, like a jack with the rabbit, a bunny on the rabbit!" Boogey ridiculously and nervously utters, looking for his father while trying to swiftly diffuse the situation; knowing good and well the Bea and her grandson could mop him up all over that store without a second thought.

"Shut up punk! You ain't no family of mine, chump!" the grandson yells with a torn-up face, when pushing up on Boogey with hot breath at the top of Boogey's head while looking down.

A knife flies to Boogey's neck, with Bea's hand trembling while staring deep into Boogey's eyes, smelling rotisserie chicken when her nose goes high, throwing her in a trance, and causing her to look back over her shoulder a few times then back away with eyes dead set on the deli while licking lips.

The grandson soon looks away and over at the deli, rubbing his round belly until altering his stare at the food and Boogey

Beads of sweat rush over Boogey's forehead, and his heartbeat drifts in his ears when the grandson steps even closer, almost forgetting about Boogey when moving toward the deli.

Boogey fearfully inches back by the continual force of his belly. "Now look, Bea, you need to get your grandson because I ain't gone have him disrespect me," Boogey utters, nervously looking at him from the corner of his eye.

"Gone, Junior!" Bea finally yells, easing the knife in her bag, picking up her orders, and then moving aside to where the glazed ham is still turning and glistening.

The grandson soon steps off, heading down another aisle, joyfully stuffing his pockets with eyes glued on the butcher and clerk from time to time.

Boogey stares at the back of Bea's head, then turns.

Bea grabs the last package, puts it in her cart, and slowly trails behind Boogey.

Boogey nervously turns off down an aisle to get her from behind him, then stops, looking over the store for his father. Boogey screams, "Come on, Pops!" and finally notices his father's head nervously peeking over the potato chip rack with hands gliding over the chips as if searching for a particular brand before walking away like he's cool, calm, and collected.

"So tell me..., how long you (are you) gonna (going to) keep letting Freddy sleep in your bed while you're out nights shooting crap and playing bingo?"

"What! What did you say?" Boogey asks making sure her grandson isn't near when stepping to her.

"You heard me, you ole fool! Come on; you can't be that dumb, Boogey! You're intelligent, so you have to have known, or are you just that wrapped up into Nattie foolishness that you can't see the forest for the trees?" Bea says, looking back to find Boogey's father being nosy with his eyes nervously wandering around until looking off and whistling.

Boogey eases to one side, with curious eyes, listening to Bea, and the more she talks, the clearer it becomes when his frown turns calm and tears begin dropping. He thinks back on unexplained times when things seemed out of place or when he smelled unfamiliar smoke on the back porch or in the house. Boogey begins to sweat, feeling faint when easing into a rocking chair, wiping more tears when his mind drifts on to shooting at the tall figure running from the porch.

Bea begins to pity Boogey. "Hell..., now I'm sorry I even said anything," Bea utters, running her hand over his head and sliding his greasy hair back when seeing more tears roll down his cheeks. She stares longer and then waves to her grandson, who stuffs more stolen candy in his pocket, unnoticed. Bea plays a number, pays for the groceries and meets her grandson at the door.

Boogey sits in deep thought before feeling someone standing near him, when looking up, finding his father quickly wiping tears. "Where were you just a minute ago, Pops? Did you hear all that crap? I ought to kill em' (them)!" Boogey utters, balling a tight fist when pulling his weak body up on weak, trembling legs.

"Who…, me? Oh, yeah…, I was over yonder, looking for some can sausage, then chips; why? Anyway, let's get this meat and get back to the house," his father utters real quick before Boogey thinks to ask again. "Look son…, you have to find out for sure before you do something you'll bemoan, son," his father nervously goes on to say.

Boogey thinks long and hard, then heads over to the butcher's counter and gets in line.

Boogey's father tries to get things off Boogey's mind and even cracks a few very stale jokes, but it doesn't work.

They approach the register and buy more tickets, but Boogey pays. Along the way, his father makes him promise he will not mention a thing until he's sure.

Nattie is observant of Boogey's stale face as soon as he walks in and throughout breakfast. Afterward, they clean up and load the family's things into the car.

Nattie remains observant, realizing he's upset, but she's not sure why when she tries to persuade his family to stay longer.

The father rushes back inside and calls to see if there is room on an earlier bus and receives confirmation. "Well, we're set for six. We won't see Pops again this trip, so let's go to Munson and get some last-minute shopping done."

The father looks at Boogey to remind him of their agreement when Boogey stares, then smiles, until nodding. His father attempts to get the pressure off by bringing up the upcoming family reunion when going on about the planning and scheduling for when they come back when the father motions to Boogey's brother to try and brighten Boogey up.

"Hey, Boogey, I almost forgot; I brought one of my new inventions that you have to check out, man," the brother utters, walking to the door.

The dad rushes, motioning Boogey outside; discovering the brother pulling things from the trunk and throwing them on the ground.

"Hey man, I think I have a winner here!" Boogey's brother excitedly utters.

"What in the world is this contraption?" Boogey asks, coming out of a daze and watching him don the harness while the dad pulls out thin, used looking long, cylindrical bottles; mounting them inside the two nylon pockets in the back.

"Alright, Daddy," Boogey's brother utters. "Set the timer and let her rip!" he utters, even more excited.

Boogey backs up when the father turns the dial and then backs up even slower and farther.

Boogey's brother slides the protective sunglasses down like a superhero, about to launch into space. "Stand back!" he shrieks loudly, looking down as accustomed, in his previous field testing.

A mist simultaneously flows from the tanks when a blast of smoke magically thrusts downward, jerking him and forcing leaves around when blowing a whirlwind of dust. The ground shakes with more dust when Boogey's brother disappears in a cloud, and the jet sound stealthily vanishes.

The dust slowly clears, and they look at each other, dumbfounded.

Boogey's brother head goes forward attentive and as if listing for something until he jumps. His head drops back with eyes peeled to the sky with a light then quickly mild whistling sound grows causing him to stare longer until with hands shielding the sun with his smiling face soon changing into disbelief.

"That's it?" Boogey asks, bursting into a burst of deep, silly laughter when looking up and around for the bottles.

"Run for your freakin' lives!" Boogey's brother shrieks, finally seeing both cylinders inbound like cruise missiles and growing louder as they scramble; taking cover on the porch. The brother gazes from the edge of the gunshot hole in the roof, backing against the house with his arms spread wide with Boogey and the father doing the same, when one cylinder and then the other explodes through the porch's roof, startling them.

"Dang, Dad! You forgot to strap the bottles down," Boogey's brother utters, frustrated when appearing from the porch filled smoke, when coming off the wall pissed.

"Forget that!" Boogey utters, leaning and peeking up into the even larger roof hole as smoke drifts to one side. "What about my freakin' roof..., you idiot!" Boogey screams, continually peeking through the gaping hole when the women frantically rush up to the door.

What the heck is going on out here?" Nattie fearfully yells, looking at Boogey's beaming face when he looks up at the even bigger hole in the roof and the fresh hole in the porch as his face continually frowns.

"Ah man, don't even trip; that roof needed replacing years ago, not to mention the gunshot blast. Heck, just send me a bill for some surplus wood," the brother utters, kneeling when picking up the somewhat sunken bottles from the hole in the busted porch.

"I'll show you how it's done this time, buddy!" Boogey's brother utters, rushing to the car for two more new release pins and more bottles.

"Are you serious? You mean to tell me you're seriously going to try this again after failing; no retesting like most professionals or mad scientists?" Boogey utters, shaking his head in disbelief but watching from a greater distance.

Boogey and the women watch him carefully check the straps when the dad pulls out two more thin and long cylinders, mounting them in the two nylon pockets before strapping them in tight.

"Alright, Daddy!" Boogey's brother shrieks. "Set the timer again and really let her rip!" the brother shrieks, throwing up two thumbs.

The women wander into the yard where Boogey is backing up, when the father bent over, turning the valve to a setting on the dial and backing up fast.

Boogey's brother slides his protective sunglasses down, standing in the same wide-legged stance. "Stand back, Daddy!" the brother screams, staring at the ground.

A mist simultaneously flows from the tanks when a blast of smoke thrusts to the ground, blowing a whirlwind of dust. The ground shakes a little and Boogey's brother loses balance, falling forward to his face and struggling to stand.

A blast comes out of nowhere, then a sonic boom when the brother takes off like a human missile; his head driving forward into thick dust and sand at a high rate of speed until creating what looks like a funnel.

The missile sound rises high then higher, with Boogey's brother's body vanishing yet leaving a trail of dust that slowly disappears.

The women scream, and everyone runs toward the thick trail of neatly plowed ground, screaming more until dipping into the trench where it looks like his body finally came out, near a tall bale of hay strewn all over the place. They call to him several times, until nervously and fearfully screeching his name as they creep up on the bale, in total silence.

The women burst into tears, not hearing anything until seeing hay at the far end of the field rising high and then staggering with him looking like a straw man as the hay falls away slowly and the brother become visible.

Everyone stands in disbelief, staring at him, wobbling about and falling several times until slowly turning when hearing a strange sound.

All heads turn back, finding Boogey with his head thrown back, stomach giggling, but nothing clear comes out. His eyes fill with tears when a scream comes from deep within, and Boogey bends to his knees, endlessly laughing until everyone joins in with teary eyes; watching the blurry body stagger toward them.

Later that afternoon, Bea puts a lid on the warm deep fryer at her house and turns, guzzling a forty-ounce beer when slipping a hand into a bag of pork skins, gobbling down a handful. She turns up the radio, striking an unfamiliar pose and replicating a few fancy moves as seen on television, at cookouts, or at the juke joint. Bea closes her eyes, working her body hard until sweating and fearfully jumping when finding her grandson laughing.

"Granny! What the…?" he says, uncontrollably laughing.

"The same thing the young'uns (young folks) are doing at the juke joint." Bea turns, playfully backing up until her bouncing, big, butt backs into him.

"Ah…, gross!" the grandson screams, pushing her back to stop her when falling back in the chair, laughing. "Ugh! That is against the law, for real, though!" he mutters, shaking his head and bursting into a hilarious laugh.

"Boy, you just mad cause your granny got it going on!" Bea utters, almost out of breath. She grips her belly, leans forward after the last crazy dance which has shaken up the beer and pork rinds that now have her stomach in an uproar.

Her grandson finally gets control of his crazy laugh and walks out front.

Bea leans from the counter, sweating, and steps toward the hall bathroom, sprinting and bursting through the door. She grabs her nose, backing out from the strong stench of booty gas. "Junior! Daggonit, boy! It smells like something crawled up your tail and died in hea (here)!" Bea shrieks, flipping the fan on, quickly.

Junior sits rocking and laughing until his belly jiggles.

Bea turns, expressly making her way to her bedroom, pushing the door open with sweltering heat swarming over her as she makes her way. She throws the lid back, drops her pants, drops down, and cuts loose in a series of weird farts with giggles after each new sound. Bea handles her business and then looks at her top, which is only wet from the top to midway.

The room grows quiet when Bea freezes, thinking she hears a baby's rattler. The sound comes again, and Bea looks at the ceiling and then stares in the corner at the exhaust fan when her mind wanders to the stove. She leans forward, listening for the deep fryer's popping grease when pulling up her panties and leaving her sweat suit pants still around her ankles to cool off while flushing.

Bea eases the seat down, sitting when feeling a hot flash and fans her face with a magazine; jumping when hearing metal rattling against the floor. Bea leans past the vanity toward the hidden vent near the tub when the noise grows louder. She bends further until almost off the toilet when a snake's arrow-shaped head shoots out. "Ah…, Junior! Junior!" Bea shrieks, losing her balance when springing up, tripping in her sweat pants, and falling flat on her belly, low-crawling as fast as possible.

The long, yellow, and orange snake coils with its head slightly tilted before looking as if shaking its head in disbelief until dropping back and shooting back through the vent. "Junior! June Bug! Junie!" Bea screams louder, finally kicking the pants off and low-crawling through the bedroom. She kicks one last time, and one leg frees when she swiftly comes to her knees, slamming into the adjacent wall and shooting down the hallway.

Junior surprisingly steps into the hallway, and Bea bulldozes him, and bursts through the front door, screaming and tripping over Junior's radio cord as she lunges off the top step in a spin, her feet hitting the ground, unbalanced. Her hands swirl wind milling fast then faster as she fights to balance until falling into the leaf-covered, murky, kiddy pool.

She stays in shock for well over a minute, until shaking her head for seconds with fast wandering eyes when thinking back on the snake; screaming and expressly backing out.

Junior sprints up and for the door, finding her shaking leaves off and crying. "What! What happened? What was it?" Junior asks, rushing to help and giggling when she isn't watching.

"Boy! There's a snake in the damn house!" Bea utters, pushing his hand away. "Get your tail in there and get that snake out of my house, right now…, and I mean right now!"

"Yeah, right! The hell with that shii…," Junior begins to say when Bea's face grows grim and her balled fist swings past his face, almost taking off his head.

"Don't cus me, boy! And you better not run from me!" Bea utters, backing him up when advancing and taking another swing but missing when he ducks and falls backward giggling while running.

Junior burst into laughter until turning and finding his cousin Tom, who isn't afraid of snakes, walking up.

The two teens head inside, looking until hearing a light rattle when finding the vent open. They see the fluctuating light shining in the dark hole until growing darker until the light stays bright.

The cousin closes the vent and rushes out and around the house, finding the snake a foot from the trailer in tall weeds.

They come from around the trailer looking for Bea, and find her at the door with a crazy, scary look.

"Auntie, is this it?" the nephew asks, laughing while holding the snake close to her and a ways from the back of its head.

Bea's face transforms until she looks deranged with water still dripping from her hair when she jerks her hand upward with her gun pointing at the nephew's head, until quickly training and shooting the snake's head off.

He jumps back, shaking his numb hand, yelping from the vibration and discharge, which stuns him. "Ya crazy aa...," he begins to say, shutting it down when Bea slaps him and knocks him backward, and he falls backward into the murky pool, moaning in pain.

"Yeah? Now run along and tell that, will you!" Bea shrieks. "Boy! As long as you live, you had better not ever put a snake in my face." Her eyes stay glued on him while he pulls himself together and slowly stands. "Hell, I raised your puny tail!" Bea utters, finding Junior laughing hard and pointing at his cousin.

Over at Boogey's house, he and his family make the final rounds to ensure they haven't left anything, then load more things and climb inside the car.

Boogey turns onto the main road, barely waving back to people leaving the general store while remaining silent as he imagines Nattie having sex with the vile Freddy.

They stop over in the next town, and go window shopping, then have dinner at a drive-in before Boogey arrives at the station ten minutes before their scheduled departure.

The father heads inside for the tickets.

Boogey's mother looks at him through the rearview mirror as they quietly wait. "You sure are quiet, Boogey," his mother utters, staring with a comforting smile.

"Just got a lot on my mind, Ma..., work and all..., well, you know." Boogey looks at her and then speedily out the window to keep her from seeing a tear form when sniffing hard a few times. He unnoticeably wipes a few tears, creating a fake sneeze with several whispers of blessing when wiping with his shirt sleeve.

Later, over at Rev's brother's house, everyone stares at Rev as he turns to the Book of Proverbs, reads Word for Word, and then explains in detail.

Minutes later, the door slowly squeaks while opening when the girl from the café, the old lady she insulted, and Boogey and Nattie take a seat in the back. "They are being led astray because of false teaching," Rev continues. "Take, for example..., you, you, you, and you come up," he utters, looking at the chosen few.

Rev lines them up, whispering to one to have them relay the message, only to find that it has been altered several times before reaching the last person. "You see! This also holds true with different teachers, one teaching this way, another that way, etc.; so you see why people are flummoxed. So read your Bible daily, meditate on the Word, Word for Word, so you can keep from the deception of those who know just enough about the Bible to be dangerous.

If you truthfully want to know God, spend some quality time in this Book and HE will show up and show you HE's real and teach you the way to walk. That is the beauty of HIS love, spending time together to come to know our GOD, LORD and or SAVIOR Jesus Christ.

God says, upon this Rock! Upon this Rock, I build my church! This Rock! HE is the Rock! Now look..., sometimes you run from this church to that church, following those pulpit pastors who change the tone in their voices when doing nothing but babbling, and not feeding the flock! Those pulpit clowns! They're nothing but modern-day entertainers and actors hiding behind smoke and mirrors. If you're gonna (going to) preach, then do as it was done in the Bible and set an example for us! Those men were firm and weren't driven by church persuasions but by the Word only.

Most pastors can't preach the truth because they're paid off, paid too well or living too well! They have become fattened off the flock. Then you have a lot of what I call church hustlers," who use Jesus' name to get money. Let's not forget those big pastors who are too big to preach to small crowds or charge a big fee for the Word! Come on, people; if they're bringing the Word and you can't afford to buy the ticket, who profits and whose Soul is saved? The Word from God is for everyone, not just those who can afford it..., it is entirely free!

To show up at these big ticket events is pride on your behalf and a lack of common sense because there should be nothing that that man can say that you can't already read in the Bible for yourself. Please don't let this destruction bring you to nothing because the Bible clearly tells us that before pride stands a fall; meaning all pride that people finds themselves into.

Almighty God has the resources to all the money in the world, so stop getting hooked on these pastors, who you know are only in it for the dollars; charging you for a fifty, a hundred, five-hundred or five-thousand dollar blessing, or whatever amount for the blessing they're promising. Now, don't get me wrong! It is great and a blessing to give to the church and to give wholeheartedly, but as I have said many times before, the blessings from the Almighty are free!

Plant a seed in the mud, the heart, or the solid ground, and through HIS blessings, it grows and brings forth something wholesome and free." Rev grows quiet yet stares around at a few faces. "If there's anyone who wants to give their life to Christ tonight, please come forward so this brother can take your name." Rev continues watching over the group until watching an old couple stand, when leading off with a hymn.

The following morning, Boogey wakes up early, stretching and yawning while listening to Nattie snore lightly when checking the time. He stands, looking for car keys, quietly slipping into the bedroom, when grabbing a new work outfit, and putting it on.

Nattie turns over and lye there listening until rolling over, looking at the clock. She quietly turns, pressing harder into the squeaky bedsprings, until facing the door.

Seconds later, she hears the car's engine turn over, and rev a few times with a few tears slightly soak the pillowcase when her tightly balled fist pounds hard upon the mattress until she springs upward. She heads for the kitchen, looking into the piercing dawn in deep thought, trying to figure out what went wrong.

Later, after work, Boogey leaves with a sad face, making his way to his car when he hears Winton and finds Winton's used, run-down car when it pulls up.

Boogey sees dark marks on Winton and feels ashamed. "So, will they let you stay on?" Boogey asks, throwing gear in his car's backseat and walks up to Winton's car.

"I spoke with the big boss, and he assured me that they will look into things. I can work tomorrow until my admin hearing, but I have to be on time between now and then and my points have to go through review before they make a final decision." Winton's hand slides between his legs, rattling a paper bag until he pulls out a mason jar of moonshine. "Man, you gotta try this hea (here); I think they might have yours beat," Winton utters, showing Boogey the state-certified seal when easing the jar closer.

"Shiiiii..., are you kidding me? Man, I've had that crap before, and it's not even close. Besides, I have a new additive so maybe you should come by this weekend, and we can crack that puppy open." Boogey says, giggling when passing the jar back.

"Jump in," Winton utters, patting the hooptie's leather, worn-down seats.

"So, is this what you picked up with your insurance money?" Boogey asks, laughing at the car that looks worse than the first and reminds him of a first production model run of the Gremlin.

"Yeah, my buddy at the strap yard put it together and only charged a few hundred, so we pocketed the rest." Winton smiles. "Hey, they just opened this new bar and grill." Winton unlocks the door and watches Boogey jump inside.

They ride around joking until it's Boogey's turn, when he draws quiet, and tears roll down his cheek. Boogey wipes, thinking the tears have gone unnoticed.

"Hey, are you alright?" Winton asks, swerving into a vacant lot.

Boogey breaks down and manages to cut it short. "Hey, let's go! Yeah..., yeah, I'm fine..., just got a lot on my mind." Boogey wipes his face then cracks a dry joke then a better one to get things rolling again.

They pull into the bar's lot and get out.

Immediately, four young men intercept them, slightly bumping into them and rudely scurrying inside. The young men walk around briefly, asking folks questions, and then walk off until finally making their way to Boogey and Winton, asking if they have seen Steve; the missing guy when flashing his picture. The four gang members linger for a while before breaking off and intercepting others before leaving.

Boogey and Winton overindulge before the full effects of the shots and chasers kick in.

Boogey's vision blurs and his speech slurs severely when stumbling to the bathroom. He stops at the payphone on the way out, letting Nattie know where he is and that she should pack his supper for lunch then informs her that he's heading to bingo.

Boogey drinks more and soon realizes that he's too drunk for bingo, so he rides home with Winton, who is even drunker and swaying all over the road. "Here, pull over here!" Boogey yells, anxiously looking at his watch. "Drop me at the general store," Boogey utters, realizing it's time to confront Nattie's demons.

Winton becomes alert and feels a little sober when diligently looking for the store owner and employees while leaning into the car door and talking for a few minutes.

Boogey finally eases out and stays kneeled, staring past a truck, when seeing a car approach then turn into his driveway with the lights going out, instantly. He talks longer and finally decides on a time for Winton to pick him up, when adjusting to an earlier time when waving Winton off and walking into the store.

Boogey slips down a few aisles quickly, slipping out the side door and creeps alongside the store. He peeks out with eyes gazing through pitch darkness, discovering a familiar looking car barely tucked nicely away in the back yard.

Bea finally pulls up, and her lights go out; sitting and looking at Boogey's familiar silhouette, wondering what he's up to, when Boogey lunges forward, trotting alongside the cornfield. She stares toward his house for some time until her eyes drift, finding the tail end of Freddy's car lights.

Tears come to Bea's eyes, and her heart grows heavy. She eases from the car, standing on tiptoes to get a better view then eases on top of the hood.

Boogey veers through the cornfield, popping out near his neighbor's barn where he stumbles through more scattered corn, running into several stalks, and breaking them off.

Bea sees Boogey's head plowing through more rows then fading.

Hurtful tears fall from Bea's eyes when she slides down, easing inside the car.

Boogey soon exits, creeping up on Freddy's car fast, looking inside, finding a deflated clown suit when stumbling to the shed, quietly shuffling through his toolbox for a screwdriver. He slips over to the car, seizing a steel-prong rake, laying it under the back tire then flattens the passenger side front and back tire, before standing in the dark, angrily looking around.

Boogey reaches for a brick, holding it tight until lunging it toward the windshield but slowly curving it off and down then lowering it to his side and easing it to the ground. He walks to the side window, glimpsing through sheer curtains to find their shadows moving across the living room floor. Boogey hears the loud television blaring and the weatherman forecasting a delay in the storm. He feels a light wind briskly blow across the back of his neck as if someone ran a finger across it, and nervously jumps with wide, excited eyes.

At the general store, a short female walks out and sits on the bench, talking to a tall female who stirs at the ground with a thick stick, scribbling in the dirt. The short woman leans, looking up the street to find a young girl strutting up.

The girl soon drifts from the dark, into dim lights until the bright light shines from the side of the store; shining on her.

The short woman's face frowns with eyes wandering over the girl's body.

"Girl, what you looking at that girl like that fau (for)?" the tall woman asks, seeing her still leaning in the same direction.

"What? Shucks, looking at how petty she is..., out here in her funky PJs. Now that's straight trifling. What man wants a female who's too lazy to wash her stankin' tail then gone be in the streets in something she is obviously too lazy to change out of? So lazy and stank. I mean, who presses PJs? Just petty," the short woman utters, looking at her friend, who leans past the post, staring.

The tall woman leans back and then forward, still drawing in the dirt until finding the girl closer and at a moderate pace. "She's either special, lazy, dirty, or a few other things. For sure, she's slow on the uptake or just too crazy to understand it's not attractive at all!" the tall woman utters, smiling. "A three-year-old got more common sense than to come out in PJs!"

The girl walks up to find them with their noses turned up, so she takes a few more steps, accidentally dropping the stick she's carrying. She bends to pick it up then stands, grabbing a handful of gathered, sticky material from her butt, when pulling it out of the deep crease.

"Whoo-hoo…, hoo…, hoo!" exclaims the short woman, standing and screaming, before bursting into a strong laugh as the tall woman shakes her head in delight.

"It's called a nice, clean swipe with tissue, maybe moisture wipes if it's that sticky," The tall woman says, standing and staring at the girl, who looks back in a mean stare. "WTB…, WTB…, WTB!" the tall woman shrieks.

The girl stares at them with a mean look. "Are you speaking to me?"

"WTB…, WTB…, Wash that butt! Wash that butt!" the short woman yells as if it's a song when easing up and doing some silly dance while repeatedly singing until doing another silly dance when stopping, and dropping it like it's hot. She stands eye-to-eye in a mean stare with her chest sticking out until the girl backs down and walks away.

At the convalescent center, Dale's special friend and the rapper's grandfather stand at the door, peeking inside Dale's room until turning around, simultaneously.

The grandfather takes a few steps away and then returns when his grandson, the famous rapper, shoves him into the room.

Dale lies in bed, dazed from the extra meds the mean orderly pumped into him.

Dale's roommate glances over, peeking from under covers, and being nosy.

"Dale!" his friend murmurs, looking at Dale's eyes rolling in his head while half cracked open and staring at the roof.

"Dale! Dale!" the invisible friend whispers, with his voice growing louder.

Out of nowhere, Dale jumps, letting out a short burst of snoring until throwing a few unexpected jabs, and causing everyone to jump back.

The rapper makes a sound and then be-bops a dope beat when the rapper's drunk friend walks up and join in, beating on the door and then the stool.

Dale drowsily sits, rocking while easing up and doing some crazy-looking dance.

"That's my boy," Dale's friend, the rapper's grandfather, utters, patting Dale on the shoulder when Dale's invisible friend walks off, vanishing into thin air. "Man, get dressed. My grandson is gonna (going to) take us over to his mansion for drinks," the rapper's grandfather utters, walking out in the hallway behind his grandson.

Dale sluggishly takes his time dressing and meets in the lobby, slipping out of the facility with his friend and imaginary friend, who walks alongside the building and vanishes again.

The rapper and his friend distract the receptionist and then walk out, finding the grandfather and Dale on the front bench, anxiously looking at their watches.

The grandson, the rapper, walks off with the three in tow and climbs into the SUV, eases off with Dale and the grandfather's feet from the truck when the receptionist bursts through the front door, screaming.

Dale and the grandfather look back, screaming while sprinting to catch up with the shiny SUV that is still rolling and slowing to come to the stop sign. Dale and the grandfather throw both doors open; diving in with legs dangling while screaming for the grandson to hit the gas.

They arrive at the mansion forty-five minutes later, pulling around the long stretch of yard as Dale's eyes glisten at the bright lights and fine architecture.

Dale's smile grows brighter when gazing over other SUVs and super sports cars that look like they're still sitting in a showcase.

The grandson walks them to the door and flings it open. "Welcome, Gramps, and you as well, Dale," the rapper utters, walking in behind Dale.

Dale's proud shoulders come up, and his whole attitude changes as if it's his house from his strut and confidence.

The grandfather grows jealous until everywhere Dale goes the grandfather follows at a distance, keeping an eye on him until finding Dale looking mischievous.

The grandson drifts down a corridor, coming back minutes later on his cellular phone, holding up a vintage bottle of wine. He motions everyone to the kitchen, where he sets the bottle on the island bar, pulling out wine and liquor glasses.

The four sit around drinking for a while until the doorbell rings once, and like magic; the house is swarming with plenty of young and old people when the party starts as if well-rehearsed with more people pouring in and the noise growing.

Before long, Dale walks up to a beautiful older woman and begins talking intelligibly, as if a well-educated scholar or professor; sticking his hands in his pocket but pulling them out quickly when a finger slips in a hole.

Later, Dale watches the rapper's grandfather nod and jump from time-to-time until Dale finds him fast asleep.

The grandfather nods more and Dale rushes to the kitchen, where he discovers two guys chasing moonshine in shot glasses. "Let me get in on this! I hear that, that right there is so smooth it'll make you slap your pappy silly," Dale utters, taking the first straight shot to the head.

"Hey..., hey...! Easy there, ole fella; the night is still young," one boy says, looking at his friend and giggling until fighting to bring the bottle from Dale's lips when finding out quickly that Dale's too strong for him.

Dale drains the bottle and soon finds the rapper sitting another bottle down.

"Dale, you aight (all right) wit (with) me!" the rapper utters. "Drink up and be merry, man! There's plenty more where that came from!" the rapper says, patting Dale on the back and walking off.

Dale waits for the two guys to leave and mixes four different white and brown liquors in a glass, topping it off with one-hundred-eighty proof liquor and dropping in four, fast-melting ice cubes. He draws a more oversized glass, walking past the rapper's grandfather sitting on another couch, but well out of the grandfather's sight.

The rapper's grandfather's head swivels forward a few times, then drops all the way back when he goes into a deep snore and wakes to find his neck stiff. His hands shoot up fast, grabbing his head as if holding a wobbling pumpkin until able to move it freely again. Instantly, he sits up, looks over the room, and then stands, looking around for Dale.

Dale peeks, looking at the sleepy-looking grandfather until giggling. "Aw man, sit your drunk-tail down; up in here watching me like a damn hawk!" Dale lightly yells over the music before standing and instantly staggering into two young girls who look at him, disgusted. "You think I'm gone steal something?" Dale asks the grandfather; standing on the other side of the partition, and slipping expensive crystal figurines into his pant pockets.

"Man, go head (on) with that crazy mess, ain't nobody watching your ugly-tail!" The grandfather turns up his drink and sways when taking his seat. "Heck, I'm watching these phat hammers (thick women) up in here!" the grandfather utters, crossing his legs with faster wandering eyes.

Dale goes into another room, mingling with the same woman until pouring her a drink then continues in conversation while looking at the rapper's grandfather, whose head is thrown back again. Dale eases away from the lady, coming up on a door near the bathroom where he backs up, when finding the rapper in his office with a well-dressed gentleman. He watches the rapper reach for a key, open a vault, and pull out one of many demo CDs from the stack when handing one to the man.

Instantly, the rapper looks through the seam of the door, noticing movement, and walks over, but before he can reach the door, Dale vanishes into a dark closet, backing up until nothing is visible but the whites of his big eyes until closed.

Minutes later, the rapper opens the office door.

Dale closes his eyes, peeking then closes them when the rapper and the man's voice get louder, then fades. Dale inches out and finds the rapper walking outside when sprinting to the rapper's office. He rushes in, shuts the door, and moves like a whirlwind; overstuffing his pockets with valuables. Dales freezes, hearing voices, then moves even faster, grabbing a CD, a wad of cash, change, and a lucky penny from a try before it hits the floor.

Back over at Boogey's house, Boogey remains on a stump, quietly crying until pausing when slowly standing in a daze. He back slowly into a dark corner of the yard in deep thought, listening to their joyful laughter while Freddy unknowingly stands in the bedroom helping Nattie fix the television's reception.

Boogey moves closer to the window and sees shadows dancing across the floor.

"Naw, Nattie…, you got to hold it like this…, yeah, Baby…, just like that!" Freddy utters in somewhat of a sexy tone, impressing her. "Now, does that look good, or what?" Freddy asks, staring into the now somewhat crystalline television screen. "I know you ain't never had it this good!"

Bud leans forward, listening to the too familiar voice. "Nattie, is that cousin Wintonel visiting again? Hello Wintonel…, it that you, cousin Wintonel?" Bud asks, properly calling out to Freddie but using the fictitious name Nattie has introduced him as that sounded more like Winton.

"Yeah, you know that sho (sure) does look pretty," Nattie utters, looking over the partially rubbed-out channel numbers displayed in the corner. "Hey, look…, is it okay to move it around a little, like this?" Nattie asks, moving the rabbit ear antennas around a little more.

Boogey remains on his tiptoes, peeking and quietly crying until pausing and listening when drawn into a daze.

"Oh yeah, Punkin', you still have that magic touch, girl!" Freddy utters, looking into the screen and at her slow-moving hands, when turning the antennae as the thin, light static lines fade away.

"Yeah, Boogey could never get it like this," Nattie utters in a sexy voice.

"Yeah, I heard that, Buttercup! Well, look ah hea (here); don't you want to put it in now and try it out?" Freddy reaches for a dusty VHS tape, passing it to her.

"You know I do, big boy!" she giggles. "I can hardly wait to see how it's going to respond when it gets inside because before, it was tearing something up mighty bad," Nattie says, grasping the VHS tape.

"Girl, please…, if it acts up this time, I'll pull it out fast…, I promise. You can trust me to pull it out quick…, okay," Freddy giggles with a hand cautiously in front of the VCR.

Bud leans forward more, listening to the too-familiar voice again. "Nattie, is that cousin Wintonel visiting? Hello Wintonel..., it that you, cousin Wintonel?"

Boogey remains on tiptoes, peeking and quietly crying until pausing and listening when drawn into a daze again.

"I will take your word and trust you to do as you say now, Freddy."

There is a moment of silence while they both watch the VHS with Freddy's hands at the front of the VHS player with Nattie standing with exciting eyes on the screen until her mouth drops open.

"Wow, Freddie..., look at it; it's like it's pulsating again," Nattie utters, looking at the screen, which seems to be pulsating with more static.

The screen blanks out, and Freddy reaches for the cord, accidentally shorting out the frayed cord. "What is that all about?" Freddy asks, backing up a few feet.

Nattie stands back, then goes forward and stays bent over, laughing. "I think you pulled it out too quick," Nattie utters, giggling.

"Pulled it out? I didn't even know it came out," Freddy utters, stumbling on the cord when the end falls completely out of the outlet. "Nattie, turn it around and sit it right here. Yeah, let's try that and see if it's any better," Freddy utters, moving a few things around so that she can turn the television a little.

Boogey remains on tiptoes, peeking and quietly crying until pausing and listening when drawn into a daze with even heavier tears pouring.

"Look at you..., now you done pulled it all the way out of the hole," Nattie says, looking at the other end of the plug, giggling.

"Never mind that here..., just stick it back in, but slower this time," Freddy utters, slowly turning the television around.

"Which hole you suppose I should put it in this time?" Nattie asks, bent over while he stands watching her lean toward the outlet.

Their shadows continually sway across the floor more and in different positions until in a position that looks as if he's close behind her.

"That's up to you, but maybe you should go ahead and put it in the bottom hole so I can put this in the other whole," Freddy utters, holding the other extension cord when his hand then shadow extends outward across the floor and Boogey's eyes shut tight with more tears dropping.

Boogey remains on tiptoes, peeking and quietly crying and listening when drawn into a daze when taking a few steps back, shaking his head in disbelief.

"Oh yeah! Right there..., right there, don't do anything else! That is perfect!" Nattie excitedly screams as they stumble backward and fade out of view with excited eyes on the clear picture, smiling.

Bea grows impatient until looking at her watch. She begins looking around before cranking up and anxiously looking at Boogey's house, the yard, and the cornfield.

Boogey grows sick, listening to the slow music mingled with Nattie's sexy, whining voice with tears continually swelling until climbing on a crate, looking for their shadow. He barely sees them until unable to watch any longer when stepping down. He falls back when the crate bursts, and shifts forward fast, when flinging hard against the house.

'Bamalam!' The loud bang comes, startling them and causing them to freeze, with Boogey bent forward, in the darkness, looking like a statue.

Nattie accidentally rushes for a kitchen window, opposite from the one where Boogey is, pressing her forehead against the cool glass with fast scanning eyes that widen when glowering at the clothes line, and seeing a shirt that she mistaken for Boogey.

Boogey backs alongside the house, pulls out a sharp knife, and jumps back in a stance, making moves as if he's training for a combat mission or stabbing someone. He makes a few more silly combative moves before stopping, shaking his head, and thinking it's not the right way to deal with Freddy when looking for a big stick.

Boogey walks the yard quickly, finding a stick just right when pulling the thick, stubby branch tightly into his hand. He steps forward fast, thrusting the stick forward as if it's a sharp sword, swinging really fast until slamming it down as if clobbering someone or something, until stands in deep thought, shaking his head as if it wasn't the right way.

Boogey creeps to the front, freezing, when spotting a thick, manly figure holding a gun as his shadow moves over the ground with the thick tree branch behind him mingled in his shadow. He also sees a thick branch that has fallen and is stuck in the ground, thinking it too is another slim man from the casted shadow when jumping and putting both hands overhead. He quietly drops to his knees, begging in a whisper, until finally looking down and finding the branch shadow further off.

Boogey cuts his eyes over at what he thinks is a man as well, taking a few bolstering swings, jabbing, and then kicking the stick and swaying. He kicks, rushes the stick, and misses one last time, falling in the dust and rapidly crawling to his feet. He tiptoes up the front porch, turning the knob, finding the door locked, when snapping fingers downward when backing up and easing off the porch. He draws alongside the house again, reaching in a wooden trunk, pouring shine, turning it up, and taking several swigs while frowning through distastefulness until he's had his fill.

Nattie stands longer, still looking the entire backyard over, then slowly backs away, assured that things are okay. She turns, pulling Freddy closer, caressing him when he grips her by the hand, leading her to the kitchen.

Boogey comes around back again and hears laughter then perceived moans, followed by furniture banging against the wall as Freddy helps pull the heavy furniture from the wall to get something that fell.

They rock the furniture a few times trying to get it aligned with the wall when more tears roll down Boogey's face.

Freddy grabs her at the waist and Nattie slightly pushes him back when thinking she hears Boogey crying. Unsure and no longer concerned, she pulls Freddy close, and he lifts her in his arms.

Nattie's legs lock around his waist and he walks her into the bedroom, playfully wrestling in dingy sheets until exhausted.

Boogey eases alongside the oak tree and then kneels, crying harder for minutes when sprinting, and then expressly bursting into the cornfield and walking alongside the store minutes later. He pukes then pukes again, reaching in his pocket for a handkerchief. Boogey finally turns, finding Freddy's headlights pop on, and stares at the dark figure outside the car leaning, in the driver's window, apparently kissing though talking.

Nattie pulls away, then leans further inside, getting a final kiss, when pulling away, looking around the dimly lit yard before coming close again.

Freddy grabs a handful of one thick cheek, and Nattie giggles, playfully pulling away, cheery. She walks past the hood, and Freddy's eyes follow her bottom with scurrying eyes floating alongside the store, catching a glimpse of a dark, manly silhouette; the stature of Boogey.

Freddy squints to make out the person, but Boogey vanishes immediately through the store's side door before the high beams flash. He revs the engine, barely moving when lighting a cigarette while putting the car in reverse, then rolls forward, puncturing a tire with the rake loudly banging against the bumper. Freddy stops, then rolls forward a few feet before finally realizing the tire is flat when his eyes grow wide as he jumps out. He runs to the other side as Nattie runs off the porch. "Man!" Freddie yells, kicking the rear flat and looking at the flat, front tire.

Nattie's head tilts back and she looks through the screen at the kitchen clock as her heartbeat quickens as she turns her gaze to both flats, finally spotting the rake. "What are we gone do, now, Freddie?" Nattie asks, panicking.

"Quick! We've got to get this car into the woods," Freddie utters, pulling off his windbreaker and throwing it through the window. "Here! Get in! You've got to show me the back way out!" Freddie nervously utters, staring back over near the store with fast, wandering eyes.

"What? That road goes to a neighbor's locked gate, and these other two may be too muddy with all the rain and all. The best you can do is drive deep in the woods and pick up the car tomorrow when Boogey goes to work," Nattie utters in her deceptive but quick thinking; out of fear of being caught.

Boogey saunters, passing the front of the store, and bright car lights from across the street, shine in his face as he shields his eyes until the lights go off, when finding Bea's car tucked away.

Bea's park lights come on, and the horn blows when she waves over the roof.

Embarrassed, Boogey wipes his face with his snot rag, walking to the driver's door.

They talk a spell until she has him tricked into a night of revenge when he reached for the door and slips inside.

The drive over is filled with foreplay; Bea getting him all hot and bother from her talk and constant rubbing of his legs until letting go when cutting the wheel hard and turning in the yard.

Bea rushes off for the door and Boogey enters, looks over the trailer and how immaculate it is. "Thanks for inviting me over," Boogey utters, looking at her approaching and extending the glass to him.

An hour later, a blue, beaten-up van pulls up at the general store, blowing.

Freddy sprints out of the cornfield and jumps in on the driver's side while the young boy slides over. He steps in the gas, squealing wheels and swerving before gaining control. Freddy reaches the boy's house, getting out, to be greeted by the boy's mother when he pulls the woman into his arms, French kissing before going inside and kicking up his heels at the kitchen table with an ice-cold beer.

Over at Bea's, Boogey downs the third glass when Bea dips two fingers deep inside, stirring his drink, licking her fingers, and bringing them to his lips with him licking the residue. She sits on the other end of the couch, turning sideways, and slides one foot behind him when the other comes upon his thigh, stroking until his eyes widen in excitement.

Boogey reclines, continually indulging in conversation about old classmates, well over two hours, which leads to her making more advances and playfully running her feet along his inner thigh, instantly arousing him.

Before long, Boogey forgets all his troubles and his drunken mind fully accepts her sexual advances. He places his drink on the coaster when she leans forward, grabbing him in the collar, pulling him closer while leaning back on the chair arm. Boogey slightly turns, standing with one knee on the sofa's edge, repositioning until lying between soft, thick thighs.

Bea's feet lock behind his legs as she opens her deep mouth, and her tongue slips deep inside his hot mouth.

Before long, Bea begins moans until her long, loud moans turn into shrieks when heavily screaming his name while burying her mouth deep into his neck. Her last screech grows even louder, and in a higher-pitch as she calls Boogey's name again when wiggling and slipping out of the tight spandex until down to just a top and G-string.

Boogey unzips his pants, easing to his knees and reaching down for his drawers, when out of nowhere; a rough, knife-cutting callused hand slaps the back of Boogey's collar, yanking him up and choking him. Boogey's body shoots straight up on the next yank, slung around, and then let loose, when stumbling hard into the coffee table, breaking it.

Bea's drunken, horny mind is deep in lust still twirling her hips harder, and puckering up until opening her eyes, screaming. "Stop it! Stop it!" Bea shrieks in terror, looking at the dark, manly, broad-shouldered silhouette.

A tight fist strikes Boogey in the face, almost knocking him out.

"Stop it! You're out there doing your dirt, so why worry about what I'm doing?" Bea shrieks with teary eyes when jumping and swinging at the dark, manly figure while loud thumps and smacks grow louder and faster as he administers continual, swift, devastating blows to Boogey's drunken body and loud screaming mouth.

A loud, unfamiliar long sound comes from the man's quick unbuckling and what sounded like endless pulling on his worn-down, long, thick leather belt until unleashing several loud whipping lashes.

Boogey immediately sounds off, screaming like a female on the second lick, while quickly low-crawling away when let go until drug by his feet; kicking and stomping.

"Stay right there..., don't you go nowhere because you're next," the man's deep voice shrieks in anger, pointing at Bea with a mean face and trembling finger.

"Stop you! Fight him, Boogey..., fight him!" Bea cries, bouncing back and forth in a stance then hurrying to the back room with the long phone cord. She locks the door with the cord stretched under the door until it falls from her hand when snatched. She scrambles for the phone on knees, backing into the corner on a beanbag, dialing again when the phone flies away, slamming into the door with the cord severed.

"Fight him, Boogey! Fight him, Boogey!" Bea screams even louder yet somewhat muffled.

Deep footsteps fade as the man heads back to the kitchen and presses his wide, cowboy boots on Boogey's butt when he comes to his knees and tries to stand.

Boogey falls forward, low-crawling fast when the man grips his heels, dragging him back a few feet from under the table. The man's feet go way back, and high, kicking Boogey in the ribs. He grabs Boogey fast, lifting him and slamming him into the kitchen table and then into two dim-nightlights, sticking out of an outlet.

The dark figure twists the front doorknob, flinging the door wide open when drawing the belt back as hard as possible and continually slapping Boogey across his back. The fourth strike draws blood, and the fifth split Boogey's shirt down the middle. The man keeps quiet but continually throws fierce blows until Boogey screams, crying and begging for mercy. "Cisco (Let's go) buddy, cisco (let's go)!" the man tongue tardily screams with each swing until up to the eleventh fierce lick; breathless and breathing harder.

A few nosy people walk past, or rush up, hearing the loud, manly voice giving commands, mingled with Boogey's womanly, high-pitched shrieks; thinking it's Bea's.

Boogey shoots up and draws back quicker to get one good and clear, slow-motion swing when the man dropkicks Boogey through the front door before his hands go forward.

The man hears a window break and sprints down to the bedroom with his belt wrapped tightly around his fist. He churns on the locked door then leans back against the wall, kicking in the door, with shattered lock parts everywhere.

He bursts through the door, and stops, staring at the busted window pane and mangled screen, finding Bea's feet fading as she drops to the ground. She feverishly rolls under the trailer with bright, white, bucked eyes feverishly looking around for snakes.

The mad man bursts out of the bedroom, drunkenly running into the yard, stomping Boogey a few more times, when finding him still low-crawling. He takes off fast, running wide-legged into the backyard, screaming Bea's name at the top of his drunken lungs with neighbors rushing off; whispering when thinking they say a gun.

Boogey sees a minuscule light through his swollen eyes and braces against a tree to get his second wind when running with all that's left in him.

The man gazes over the dark yard for minutes with tears falling then runs to the front, looking for Boogey again.

Bea lightly sniffles, continually gazing out from the doghouse, from behind the dog while holding the low growling dog in place. She cautiously looks toward the bright light, following Freddy's stealthy movement when looking off to the side, and finding Boogey ducking down beside the neighbor's water pump.

Bea closes her eyes and then peeks again and sees Freddy walking to the van when crawling out and running into the high weeds; ducking behind a tree. She glances back at Boogey, wiping her teary eyes and quietly listening until her heart beats loudly while she cries, until out of nowhere, she begins laughing hard with heavy jumping shoulders, knowing she's made Freddy very jealous for the first time.

The van's lights finally come on, and Freddy revs the engine a few times when backing up, and shining the high beams around the yard, in the field, and between the trailers until backing out and driving up and down the road, slowly looking for Boogey again before speeding off.

Bea fears going inside and doesn't want to see Boogey, so she takes off in the opposite direction, walking miles on a backroad journey to her cousin's house.

Boogey strains, watching several vehicles pass and taking deeper cover each time he sees different lights. He finally sees the van again and keeps his eyes on it until the van picks up speed, fading around a steep curve. Boogey then waits, well-hidden, for over an hour before peeking out again.

After midnight, Boogey feels somewhat sober but is deeply hurt and embarrassed when wobbling to stand. He cuts through a path, walks to the edge of the road, looks back when seeing headlights approaching, and jumps into a deep ditch, peeking out until noticing it is a pickup.

Boogey rushes out into the road without warning, throwing both hands high, waving down the small, old-timey pickup, which swerves until it is about to run him over and then passes before veering onto the shoulder.

"What the hell you trying to do..., kill your damn self?"

"Naw..., I just seriously need a lift," Boogey moans.

"Where you are heading, buddy?" the old, drunken man asks, slowly grinding gears with bulging, bloodshot, red eyes while staring into Boogey's heavily bruised face and bloody clothes. "Dang, son! It looks like someone whipped you with a dang ugly stick!" the old man hollers with a silly-sounding giggle when halfway passing out.

"Thanks for stopping..., Fikesville," Boogey utters, leaning into the seat with his face frowned when sweat begin burning deeper in the cuts and whelps.

The stoned, drunk looks at Boogey with glassy, beady eyes when flooring the pedal with their bodies jerking from the transmission, slipping and leaking fluid.

"Hey, hey, hey!" Boogey screams several times during the quiet drive, trying to keep the man awake and on the road with nervous eyes while easing one hand to the wheel whenever the man nods off.

The long drive home has them continually all over the road, sometimes having to swerve hard to miss oncoming cars, but ten minutes later the general store's lights come into view.

Boogey quickly lets go of the wheel, happily nudging the man, and waking him again. "Hey, buddy..., we're here!" He says with a final nudge at the wheel, one last time to keep from side swiping a passing car.

The man pulls over with eyes barely open; nodding and then smiling while looking straight ahead with half-open, stale eyes.

Boogey looks at the man with sad eyes. "Hey, you sure you don't want to park in my yard and sleep off this high? Come on, main (man) sleep that booze of..., how about parking in my yard at least until the booze wears off?"

"Yack, yack, yack, yack..., just like that nagging little wife of mine!" the drunk, old man says when licking his tongue at Boogey and making his denture grossly flap until a drunk smile comes with heavily dimmed eyes again.

Boogey takes several steps away when the truck backfires, causing him to dive and roll in the tall weeds with his head coming up fast, looking around until finding a plume of smoke behind the old truck, when shaking his head with a smile.

The old man leans toward the passenger side and pops up a middle finger in Boogey's face when the gear grinds heavily, and the truck eases off slow on the shotty first gear.

Around 1 AM Boogey creeps up on his pitch-dark porch.

Nattie hears the door quietly shut and pretends to be asleep with squinty eyes.

Boogey's face frowns when he finally feels a deep burn run down the middle of his spine. His hand goes to his back, and he frowns, then slowly moves his hand up and down the shirt to find it shredded.

Bud whistles and then quiets as he peeks through the busted sheet, quietly following Boogey around the room. "Uncle Wintonel was here..., Uncle Wintonel! Wintoneeelll!" Bud yells, dragging out the name the last time when Nattie cringes.

Boogey heads for the bathroom, stumbling in the dark before cutting on the lights. He turns to the mirror, and his eyes drift over his bloody back, then into dark-ringed, swollen eyes and his face, when tears swell and run down his cheeks.

Boogey hears Bud yell something that he can't make out when cracking the door and hearing him whistle lightly. Boogey turns the water on high when Bud begins repeating sexual comments and moans that Nattie and Freddy made, then a few oldies he had heard coming from the radio, but Boogey doesn't hear them because of the fast running water.

Nattie tenses, covering her ears until hearing the shower running when Bud quiets.

Boogey undresses, cringing when stepping inside and washing swiftly. He exits, drying off and gently smears on ointment to cover the whips and cuts, yet frowning, quietly moaning, and cringing from the pain of touching his body. Boogey shaves and then slicks his hair back when more tears fall in a whisper. He walks into the living room, closes the bedroom door, and drops his new clothes on the couch, walking into the kitchen.

Boogey stands in one spot staring at the old, low-cut cabinet Freddy and Nattie were grooving on when grabbing the corner, shifting then straightening it.

Nattie hears the cabinet leg slide and thinks about other things left out of place. She stares into space and then looks over at the clock, discovering it's almost 3 AM while lying there listening for minutes until nodding off.

Boogey's eyes curiously scroll until he eases back with his face torn up, flipping on the television. He falls asleep, awakened hours later by a horn blowing out alongside Main Street. Boogey sits up with a hangover, realizing that Winton should be there soon, when looking at the closed bedroom door, quietly dresses while yawning and stretching.

Nattie awakens from the sound of two, long distant trucks passing along the main road and blowing minutes later. She lies listening while Boogey creeps to and fro until the front door flies open and slams when the sound of an engine grows loud when Winton revs the engine again.

"Woo wee..., your face looks as bad as mine; Nattie must have put something on you last night from running that mouth. Good for ya (you!)," Winton mumbles with Boogey at the door

"Yea, right..., Sam's tractor was stuck and he needed help. I was doing the driving and not paying attention when running into some thick limbs before I could get to the brakes." Boogey cuts his eyes over to see if Winton brought off on his quick lie.

Nattie's tears drip while she sits and slides her feet into her slippers. She walks to the kitchen, replaying the last two days in her mind, continuously trying to figure out what happened to have gotten Boogey in a different mood.

At the convalescent center, Dale awakes, pulling out the stolen CD. He slips it into the player, slips on headphones, and his head begins to bob to a dope beat while quietly moving his lips. Dale reaches for the nightstand, pulls out a paper pad, writes down the lyrics to some of the tracks then flips through the tracks, thinking of a few new dance steps.

Dale's roommate lies with his back turned and a handheld mirror in his tight grip, continually eyeing Dale for hours.

Miles from work, Boogey taps Winton's shoulder, and Winton veers into the store's lot.

They get on the road, and minutes later, Winton sees thick smoke billowing from the plant until a huge plume bursts from the back of the mill near the river.

Winton looks ahead, noticing the road is backed up, and gets creative as his eyes cut over at Boogey. "Hell, man, we ain't gonna get to the job for at least thirty minutes at best. I am going to stop off at Mom and Pop's store and get me a sausage and egg sammage (sandwich)," Winton utters, looking over at Boogey.

"Are you serious, dude?" Boogey utters, shaking his head in disbelief. "You really think these people are playing, don't you? Winton, Old Man Anderson is looking for a reason to fire you..., you dummy!" Boogey utters, looking out the window and then into Winton's eyes with a serious face.

"Old Man Anderson, Old Man Anderson! Well, the hell with him! You can sell out to the man if you want, but right now, Old Man Anderson can kiss these..., these..., these..., grape nuts!" Winton utters in a crazy laugh.

"Grape..., grape what?" Boogey asks, dumbfounded.

"These..., nuts!" Winton yells in a silly laugh when groping his groin.

"You know you ain't got a bit of red sense (brains)!" Boogey shrieks, bursting into a long, silly laugh. "You're a grown tail man, so do you; besides, my points are low, but you, on the other hand, are always late whenever you drive to work alone, so tell me, why is that?" Boogey asks in deep thought, wondering himself when the car takes a hard turn, heading to Mom and Pop's place.

They arrive at work to find a news team interviewing bystanders.

Boogey steps out and sees Old Man Anderson and his son near the office.

Old Man Anderson looks at his watch, whispers to his son, and then walks into the office. "Two points, Boog!" The son looks at Boogey as he quickly passes.

Winton sprints and tries to squeeze past when Young Anderson puts his hand on Winton's chest. "Winton Moe (Moore), you can just turn yourself right around and gone on home now! We gone (are going to) dock your pay, and you can come back tomorrow for your inquiry as to whether we keep you on or not."

"What? Man..., we were stuck in traffic; tell em' Boogey!" Winton shrieks, looking at Boogey fiddle around for his time card while trying to get past the son, who continually holds him back with his hand even deeper in his chest.

Boogey finally shakes his head 'yes' and clocks in, easing his time card back in the slot. He takes small steps, looking back over his shoulder until fading around the corner.

Young Anderson curses and Winton stares mean, flying hot. "You bleep! Bleep! Bleep! How the bleep you gone tell me what to bleeping do? What I ought to do is kick your bleeping bleep. You can't tell me what to bleeping do because your bleeping dad brought me on this bleeping contract!" Winton shrieks, not using one curse word which he knew would cost him his job.

"I won't have you curse me; it's insubordination," Young Anderson utters.

"Curse you? You're the one who cursing! I have been bleeping, so how is bleeping, cursing?" Winton asks, looking half-crazy with his permed hair sticking up in the back like a rooster's tail.

"You were thinking it, so it's just like cursing," Young Anderson utters with one eyebrow slightly raised with his finger inches from Winton's nose.

"Well, bleep you and your bleep bleeping dad," Winton utters, pissed when turning and heading down the breezeway when Young Anderson reaches in his pocket. "I need to talk to Old Man Anderson 'bout this bull!" Winton shrieks when Young Anderson pulls out a switchblade.

Winton backs up a few feet fast hearing Young Anderson shout.

"Gone, get! Get, I say!" Young Anderson shrieks, looking at the news team on the other side of the van. Young Anderson picks up a few stones, slinging them at Winton when Winton advances fast, distancing himself even faster.

Winton jerks when a bigger stone lands near his foot; the second big one hitting his steel toe boots, and causing him to quickly dance around and back up even faster.

Young Anderson picks up more rocks, chucking them, until one hits Winton in the chest, then another in the back when he falls in a turn, ducking when cutting a corner.

Winton rushes to his car, pissed, and then stands with hands buried in the bottom of his pockets for keys when a tap comes upon his shoulder, causing him to jump and flex in a boxing stance. "Whoa! Whoa! Man, you almost caught the damn business, and it ain't even your business!" Winton says, looking into the face of the sexy female reporter and straightening up after noticing the camera is on him. He quickly brushes down his frayed uniform to look presentable and then his greasy hair, pulling his comb out and running it through with one swoop.

"Sir, I see that you work here," the beautiful woman reporter utters, looking at the shirt's company logo.

"Yeah..., been 'bout fifteen years, now," Winton utters, staring over her shoulder at Old Man Anderson, who continually waves Winton off through the office window to get him away from the cameras, quick.

"Can you shed any light on what could have caused this explosion?" she asks, handing Winton the microphone and whispering in the cameraman's ear. "Make sure you get a close-up of his hair and clothes," the reporter utters to the cameraman, giggling.

"What explosion?" Winton asks, dumbfounded.

"Oh..., ok, so you mean you don't know?" she asks, seizing the microphone, quickly.

"I'm just getting here, but I can tell you what probably happened is these clowns are still stowing propane bottles out back. For years, I've been telling them they can't stow those bottles near the furnace," Winton responds, finding the administration office curtain pulled back and closing fast when the cameraman zooms toward the window.

"Oh..., I see. Well, do you think this is an OSHA incident? Do you think we need to get OSHA involved?" she asks, looking him square in the eyes while patiently awaiting a response.

"OSHA? Huh? I don't know nothing about no OSHA, lady," Winton utters, looking very confused.

"Oh..., so you're telling me you have not had OSHA training and have not read the brochures?" the reporter asks, handing Winton the too familiar-looking brochure.

"Oh..., that!" Winton utters with a stupid laugh. "I thought you were saying Oceans! Oh, yeah..., I've had that training plenty of times..., almost annually," he utters, making her think he knows what she's talking about when gazing at the waving booklet in her hand.

"Then read this third paragraph about disclosure in the case of an incident," the reporter utters, pointing and then looking into his nervous eyes.

Winton's eyes glimpse over a few big words when the camera zooms in on him and then his mouth as his lips slowly part without a word.

The most profound and heaviest laugh comes out of nowhere, which is uncontrollable and growing louder until finally tapering off. "Of Shucks, woman, you don't know, Jack..., ole Winton here can't read a damn lick!" the deep, manly voice yells out when the mild running van engine floods over the chatter.

"What? What simple-minded chump said that?" Winton screams with fast, wandering eyes until finding Freddy parked in a partial chicken suit, puffing heavily on a stogie and blowing circles.

What? I can to read; It's just that I don't have my ah..., ah..., ah..., glasses," Winton utters, patting his clothes down quickly as if looking for glasses.

Freddy goes from neutral to park quick and jumps out. "Here, let me get them their glasses for you because I got to see this hea (here) reading for myself. I think I have a spare set."

Winton cocks his eyes and head to one side, pointing to Freddy. "I'm sick of you! I'm sick of you, ole boy!" Winton yells in a real high and long pitch.

The reporter leans into the cameraman. "Are you getting this, chicken man?" the reporter whispers, pushing the cameraman's arm to ensure he gets a good shot.

"I got it, I got it!" the cameraman whispers as the camera continually jumps from laughing so hard until the camera steadies when speedily mounted on a tripod.

"Ok, let your friend get some glasses, but I have one more question while we're waiting," the reporter utters, taking a deep swallow.

"What's that?" Winton utters with the keys clenched tightly in his pocket while his hand continues nervously stirring around.

"Come on, I ain't got all day; I've got to get to work!" Freddy looks at his watch, and tightens the glasses in his grip until holding them out to Winton.

"What can you tell me about the owners? There have been rumors that the plant has had a lot of infractions over the last few years. So, do you think the owners are law-abiding citizens?" the reporter asks, looking away and back at Freddy, drenched in the hot suit with sweaty palms still held out.

"Old Man Anderson..., that prick? Well, he and his son are some crooked some (sons of)...!" Winton utters, cutting the profanity short and unsure if he will be getting his job back after provoking the knife and rock incident.

Everyone jumps, hearing a loud boom from the re-flash then other re-flashes, which causes the news team to run to the chain-link fence, filming the huge mushroom cloud.

Instantly, Freddy looks down, hearing jingling keys in Winton's hand when Freddy takes off, hurrying to the fence and looking in the sky with others at the even larger mushroom cloud. Freddy briefly looks back, beaming when finding a minuscule plume of dust in the gravel and the faint taillights of Winton's car merging into traffic. "See! I told y'all, Winton's can't read a damn lick!" Freddy blurts out, laughing when looking at his watch again then sprinting to his vehicle and taking off.

Later that night, the general store closes early, and four hours before the brunt of the storm is to reach the closet point.

Fikesville becomes a ghost town when everyone retreats as dark clouds roll in and light to moderate flashes of lightning display miles away, lighting up the skyline.

Winton leaves an illegal card game and is on his way home when passing Boogey's house. He toots the horn and cuts on his high beams when hearing a loud crack of thunder. He shakes his head with a smile, knowing how frightened Boogey and Nattie must be when a bigger smile grows, and then laughter comes when he pulls over, makes a U-turn, and thinks more about his playful plot. Winton turns off the headlights, turns into Boogey's driveway, and parks further from the house, turning the car off when a torrential downpour comes out of nowhere. He reaches in the backseat for his rain gear, dressing out then exits the vehicle with a crowbar in hand.

Another heavy clap of thunder comes just when Boogey sits on the bed and jumps back in fear, then jumps again when Nattie tears through the bedroom door, diving on the bed with her hair sticking up.

Winton eases up on their power panel, waiting for the next thrash of thunder. His bare hand grips the metal lever tight when hearing a small crack of thunder that leads to the loud thrashing when he flips the switch down, securing their power.

Boogey closes his eyes tight, playing tough.

Nattie curls up tight and lies with her back to him until a bright flash of lightning lights up the room, followed by a loud crack of thunder; the closets ever when they back up, jostling into each other out of fear.

Winton silently giggles, waiting for lightning or thunder, when a stealth streak drops from the sky, slamming into the crowbar and shooting it through the bedroom window, shattering glass over the floor. "Yeeelp!" Winton sounds of shaking like a leaf with lightning flowing through his body until busting his boots.

"What the...!" Boogey shrieks when Nattie springs up, frightened.

Winton stands as stiff as a board for seconds until falling back like a log, in a deep splash; paralyzed and lightly moaning under the heavy rain. His hair and boots continually smoke when the downpour comes even heavier. Winton begins slowly moving his lips as if praying for recovery from the pain and paralysis.

Boogey creeps over to the window, hearing a low, moaning voice.

Winton moves his lips and uses his damaged vocal cords until he's speechless. 'Man..., what in the world possessed me to do such a stupid thing? If I can just get through this one, I will never do such a foolish thing ever again. I hope I still have my strength, my legs, arms, feet, and anything else I might have forgotten to mention.' Winton mumbles, with water refilling the new puddles around his face.

He cuts his eyes to one side, seeing the water rising when jerking and crying. Winton soon get creative when turning his head slightly and drinking water to keep from drowning; sometimes taking in dung patties and spitting it out fast.

Boogey backs away from the window, inches from seeing Winton's head.

Winton moans in a world of hurt, realizing he only has motion in one leg and arm when closing his eyes, whispering a prayer when out of nowhere, the rain trickles and soon stops.

Winton lye there until 4:30 AM and becomes somewhat mobile when the feeling comes back. He lies a little longer, nervously cutting his eyes around with the flooded yard outlining his body and face; just his mouth and nose, sticking out. His head rises slightly and then slams backward when taking in a mouthful of floating horse patty and quietly spitting it out when shooting upward in a quiet gag.

Around 6:30AM, Boogey leaves the house.

Nattie makes her way to the general store later, entering and finding a few women who work there looking at her, disgusted. She frowns back and then looks around to see if it's just those two with attitudes or others.

"What can I get for you, Mrs. Nattie?" the young butcher asks, putting fresh hotlinks in the cooler's window before shutting the rear door.

"Jimmy, you got a minute?" Nattie asks, finding no one waiting.

"Anything, Mrs. Nattie," Jimmy utters, coming to the counter's edge.

"Jimmy, were you here the other morning when Boogey and his father came in?" Nattie asks, glimpsing over her shoulder when hearing the bell on the door ring.

He hesitantly looks over at the cashier, who motions for him not to talk to her. "How many pounds of those fresh links can I get for you, Mrs. Nattie?" Jimmie loudly asks when winking, then looking at the cashier who has her back slightly to them with eyes cut over her shoulder, watching and listening.

"Just a pound," Nattie utters, catching his hint before he turns to walk back behind the counter.

He unravels the wrapping paper, scribbles, wraps the meat, and slips the message inside the fold.

Nattie grasps the meat and pulls it to her chest with a sad look when shaking his hand. She rushes to the counter, reaching in her bra, pulling out a ten, and paying.

The front door flies open and Nattie bumps into a man, apologizing before rushing off. She unravels the paper reaching for the note with the meat tucked under her arms. Her eyes glance across chicken scratch, making out keywords when tripping in a pothole, wobbling, and fainting in the tall grass.

She gains consciousness almost an hour later when something wet licks her face. Nattie smells a hint of sausage; when springing up, shewing the dog away with sausage links drug by the dog through the grass. Her mind drifts on the note again until engraved in her mind when imagining looking over the note again, which reads:

'Yes, they were here." Bea told him all about your affair with Freddy. Sorry…!'

Nattie slowly crawls, picking up the empty meat wrapper and note. She looks around, spotting the dog chomping down when reaching back down fast, throwing a rock at the dog. She wobbles up the steps, weak, and walks around looking over the things they had collected, accomplished, and worked for over the years.

Nattie stops, staring at the bed, slipping into a trance when envisioning Boogey cuddling until hearing soft love-making music, and the room then house filled with playful laughter. Her thoughts quickly transform to Freddy with her legs wrapped around his hard, masculine body when the beat to the music turns hardcore.

Later that night, a few cities over, in an apartment complex not far from the mill, a tall, big boned female, Rebecca, stands fussing with her short husband, Bill.

Bill gets the best of her, degrading her dress code until she's in tears.

"You know what..., I should have listened to my mama. She said you didn't care and that you were just after one thing!" Rebecca says, backing away from him.

"Well, tell your trifling-tail mama she's right! You two are the biggest gold-diggers I've ever seen! Money, money, money; that's y'alls song! Never do I hear the song - can I help!"

"Look! You ain't gone talk 'bout (about) my mama, and she ain't here to defend herself!" Rebecca forcefully yells, walking up to him and backing him up a few feet.

"Well, call that heffa on over here so I can tell her to her face, again. This isn't the first time she's heard it, and it sho ain't gone (going to) be her last. Shucks, I should have listened to your daddy when he told me to run for the darn hills and run like hell!" Bill mutters, walking away.

Rebecca finally bursts into tears, walking into the bathroom to make up her face and get dressed.

Bill eases onto the couch, huffing, and puffing while staring at the bathroom door until Rebecca opens it and walks out.

"I need some money." Rebecca throws her long, multicolored hair to one side.

Bill sits shaking his head when pulling out a few dollars; throwing them on the end table.

"See, you ain't even funny. This ain't even enough to get gas..., more or less get in the club or buy drinks," Rebecca utters, snapping her fingers in a circular motion.

"Ah...! Look Delicious, it's always money! You better get one of those slick cats in the joint to pay your way in and buy you drinks. Babe, need shoes, clothes, and Pampers 'round this mug, so you best to get to stepping!" Bill angrily says, rolling his eyes and walking off.

Tears drop as Rebecca watches him vanish into the kitchen to check on the food baking in the oven. She reaches for his wallet, quickly pulling out a couple of twenties then runs out the door, still in tears but laughing.

The kids stand in shock against the wall with their mouths torn wide open, still staring at the half-drained wallet lying sideways.

Bill struts back in, in a flash, hearing the engine rev and finds the kids with their mouths dropped open and in frozen stares. He looks at the disfigured wallet then the cracked open door and runs out, yelping, with his bare feet slamming loudly against the pavement while drifting into the street. Bill stops when seeing the car's taillights fade around the corner, shaking his head in disappointment.

# CHAPTER EIGHT

### Big Bust and Beat Down

Boogey finds people mysteriously wandering over and looking at his bruises at the mill, but due to his mean stare; they only snicker when out of sight and don't dare confront him or laugh in his face.

Boogey walks out after work, sad; kicking up a few rocks, until hearing and then seeing Winton's car easing up. "Man! You look worse than you did the last time I saw you. You need to come clean..., who you done (have you) ran into that whipped the snot oucha? (out of you) Whooo!" Winton utters, frowning then smiling.

"Yeah, right, I already told you about Sam' tractor," Boogey utters, quickly deflecting. "I wasn't paying attention," he says, running a hand over a few bruises.

"Ugh, ugh, ugh," Winton utters in an unconvincing tone; rolling his eyes to insinuate he's not buying that lie. "Right..., more like the brunt of Freddy's big, fat fist that you managed to fall into, repeatedly." Winton yells, falling back, and laughing.

"Ah..., hellz naw! Man, you are crazier than a damn bedbug! Ain't no way Freddy is ever gonna (going to) step to this!" Boogey shouts, sticking his chest out and flexing one arm to show off his little muscles.

"Man, I done herdt (have heard) rumors of how Freddy mopped Boogey all over Bea's place, like a rag doll. Bea's neighbor even herdt (heard) you screaming; so come on..., fess up! Freddy whipped that butt in a damn chicken suit, didn't he?" Winton screams, bursting into a burst of even louder laughter.

"Look here, main (man)! Have you dunt (done) lost your rabid-tail mind? Freddy ain't man enough to ever step to this hea (here)!" Boogey responds, livid and in a crazy laugh, to keep Winton laughing and throw off his beliefs. Boogey walks off and over to his car before Winton can reflect on his and his wife's whipping.

Winton walks up to Boogey. "Hey, Boog, what do you say about us swinging by the pool hall for a couple of games before heading home?"

"Naw, main (man), I got to get home." Boogey spots a beer truck passing. "Wow, they sure do know how to make those beer ads tempting. Hell, come on..., I can stand to whip your tail and send you home crying like a little baby," Boogey responds, tensing after mentioning crying when thinking of Winton crying during the beating in the shower.

"Now, that's my boy!" Winton pulls out a fifth of liquor from his back pocket.

Boogey walks over and climbs in, cracking open the bottle and taking a few hits.

They begin passing the bottle until Winton holds it up with just a healthy corner left when pulling over in a vacant lot, polishing it off.

"Hurry up, main (man); we could have been there by now!" Boogey reaches for a new bottle barely extended from under the newspaper in the front seat, spanking the bottom.

"Yeah, right. How…; goose necking down the road like we're crazy as hell?"

Winton pulls off, easing into the intersection, staring at a fast passing car's personalized tags when drifting in thought. "B_A_U…, Boo!" Winton shouts out in a slurred speech, laughing with his eyes somewhat crossed. He steps into the gas, pulling alongside the car; finding a female with a chicken-looking hairdo and dark rings around her eyes, with an index finger in her nose, and almost up to the second joint, churning away.

Winton bursts into laughter, with the woman snatching her hand down quickly and cutting her eyes over at them. He leans, staring, and inches up until she smiles with teeth torn up; and maybe two or three good teeth left. "BOO!" Winton shrieks, with wide eyes, laughing and straightening his face when he sees how jacked up her teeth really are when she smiles even harder.

Boogey inches up a little until slowly peeking past Winton. "BOO? B_A_U…, you should have said B_A_U, as in butt ass ugly!" Boogey drunkenly yells when the woman's smile vanishes and her extremely long middle finger waves when easing up to the red light out of view.

Winton and Boogey sit in deep laughter when the woman looks over once more, finding them in tears when flooring the gas pedal and laying into the horn as the light changes, green.

Winton sprints off, past a few more cars and slows when coming up on another car. "H_O_T_W_O_N…, Hot One!" Winton blurts out fast in his drunken voice as he slows down, paralleling the car through a yellow light.

They look over quickly, finding a little old lady glancing over the dash and then slowly over at them.

"Hot one?" Winton utters in laughter. "Yeah right…, more like…, not one!" he utters, giggling as Boogey gets another look when they pass again, rushing past a few more cars.

"There…, there's another one!" Boogey shouts, pointing to the far center lane.

Winton throws on the signal light, maneuvering over. "That is a good one, huh?" he excitedly yells, squinting.

They stare for seconds until Boogey grows excited. "D_L_S_H_U_Z..., Delicious!" Boogey anxiously shouts, finding Winton's eyes somewhat closed. "Hey! Man, what else have you been drinking cause you're toe (torn) slam up!" Boogey looks past Winton when they finally catch up and come alongside the car.

Winton slows at the intersection as the light turns red then eases up, and the woman inches up as well to avoid them staring. Winton inches up more to get a good look and almost taps another car's bumper when Boogey's hand shoots to his shoulder with Winton tapping the brakes with the car jerking a few times.

They gaze over and Winton inches up as the car in front moves, discovering the female with tree trunk arms in her oversized, flimsy jacket. Her hair and makeup look as if it's been sprayed with paintballs that match her colorful clothing.

"Delicious! Hey, Delicious!" Winton playfully screams and hollers, laughing, pointing, and staring until she; smiles, winks, and points for him to pull over.

Winton anxiously points to the side of the road and waits for her to cross over in front when Boogey stares in her overly made-up face, pounding Winton's thigh, and Winton bursts into laughter, speeding off like a jet.

The woman slows and watches them jet by when frowning, cutting the wheel hard and fast. She steps into the gas pedal with tires squealing; leaving a plume of black dust.

Boogey looks in the side view, finding the car dust veering off and the car gaining, quickly. "Here..., here, slow down at the light and take it before it turns red!" Boogey utters excitedly while uncontrollably laughing and looking at the light and the woman's car in anticipation.

Winton barely makes the light, and the woman barrels through it, flooring the gas pedal and pulling alongside on a narrow, two-lane bridge and then the over path.

The woman heavily swerves, rummaging through her purse; wide-eyed and mad, with tears dripping.

Winton continually looks at her and the road, laughing and pointing while going even faster.

"Hey, floor it then bank a hard right at the off-ramp right beyond the bridge," Boogey eagerly utters, looking past Winton until staring down the barrel of the woman's heavily waving big gun. "She's got heat! She's got heat!" Boogey screams, slumping down and pulling Winton over by the shoulder when the car swerves close to the sidewalk with Winton fighting to keep his eyes above the dashboard.

"Man, what the hell are you doing?" Winton sluggishly shrieks in a slurred speech, not registering the word 'heat' but still trying to sit straight, when the woman's car drops back, and a loud blast comes; shattering Winton's back window. "Oh…, ho, ho, ho, man!" Winton shrieks, dropping lower but going even faster.

The woman swerves, barely missing a few oncoming cars, when speeding up until alongside Winton's rear quarter when firing and busting out the rest of the back window. She swerves behind them as another car ahead passes, then steadily lays into the horn. The woman floors the pedal at the top of the hill, when not seeing a car ahead.

Winton's eyes stay glued to the end of the bridge and exit sign, then her car when making some distance, as he closes in on the end of the bridge faster.

The woman steps into the pedal, coming alongside Winton's rear quarter again until almost alongside when her gun comes to eye level just as the exit sign flashes past.

Winton veers hard, shooting down a ramp, and coming up on a very high hill; airborne with sparks flying out from the front of Winton's undercarriage until airborne again when the roof takes out a low-hanging street sign, leaving bright sparks.

The woman skids wheels until black smoke rises high then spins in reverse, backing through a plume of darkness with cars swerving and wheels squealing to miss rear-ending her.

Winton slams on the brakes, coming over another hill, finding traffic stopped, when his wheels squeal; sliding inches from a car's bumper with tires smoking.

The woman hits her flashers, rocking the car while holding the windowsill. She shoots out then leans back inside for her gun. Her sprints off, heels expressly clicking loudly, as she hustles to the edge of the second bridge, looking down the steep hill. She gazes over bright lights, finally spotting Winton's car when backing up, wide-legged. She cries, wiping away tears and pointing along a row of cars when the traffic slowly moves. The woman's jacket tightens as she takes aim and her hands come together, ripping the jacket down the middle when she transforms into a muscle-bound beast. "This or that, this or that…!" she senselessly whispers with one eye closed tightly and her tongue clenched to one side when the first shot ring out.

The round hit Winton's driver-side door panel when Winton and Boogey screams.

Winton cuts the wheel sharply into oncoming traffic and continually blows; flashing headlights while still hearing more muffled shots when merging back into traffic and cutting a car off.

Boogey looks back full of fear with eyes swarming in the background; looking for the woman, and out of nowhere, Winton bursts into a crazy, drunken laugh.

"Man, no more of that crazy car tags mess! That crazy heffa could have smoked us!" Boogey yells almost cross-eyed when looking in the side mirror, feeling uneasy.

"Oh man, no worries..., heck..., that was fun!" Winton utters, looking even drunker.

Minutes later, Winton pulls into the pool hall, slamming on the brakes when he sees what he thinks is the crazy woman's car backing in, ahead. He goes expressly into reverse and slams on the breaks, finding a car on his bumper, then looks ahead again when the car ahead bright lights come on while slowly moving forward and slowly approaching.

Boogey and Winton frown with torn-up faces, skittishly embracing. "I love you, big cuz!" Winton murmurs, whining with chattering teeth and a few tears falling while eye-to-eye with Boogey then back at the car's dark interior.

"I love you too, little cousin. We've had some great times, main (man)," Boogey utters with a drunken tear dripping when looking back over, finding Winton's face covered in tears as he looks at Boogey again.

"I guess now is a better time than any to tell you..., but when we were kids, I had a crush on you; you know, seeing you running around in those cute, little animal drawers," Winton whispers, staring into Boogey's watery eyes.

Boogey's face somewhat straightens up with a raised eyebrow. "Man, gone (go on) with that craziness! I always knew you were a little fruity, but man, that's just plain nasty," Boogey utters, finding the woman's perceived headlights come on then go to bright lights as the car cuts over and pulls ahead.

The car behind Winton blows. "Hey! You freakin' idiots, get a hotel room!" the old, grey-haired man screams, leaning out the window when swerving around Winton and coming alongside, finding them slightly ducking in the center.

Boogey and Winton's heads come up slowly, looking around then behind, finding the perceived woman's car parked again with a family getting out.

Winton shamefully cut his eyes over at the driver throwing up double barreled, middle fingers.

Winton stares then Boogey leans staring as the car goes to park with two old men easing out.

The men stick out their chests, walking back toward Winton's car while rolling up sleeves when both jump back, finding the two old men throwing up fists to rumble.

Another car blows for the two old men to move and they do, turning and heading back; walking cool when jumping in and easing forward.

Winton catches Boogey still staring when throwing on the flashers and bursting into laughter when slapping the back of the seat. "Gotcha!" Winton utters, looking at Boogey, laughing.

"Gotcha…, gotcha, nothing! That was indeed a true confession," Boogey utters, easing back into the corner of the door, and staring with amazed eyes.

"Man, you crazy as Hell! I was trying to get a good laugh because you looked like you were about to have a heart attack," Winton says, trying to convince him.

"Yeah, right…, the only thing hard is your thoughts of me as a kid. Huh…, besides, you already confirmed your fruitiology at the club with the bouncer. What…, you got a ten-pound bag of sugar up in yah (you), huh?" Boogey utters with an evil eye. "You're just a little frosted flake dressed up like a cornflake!"

"What, so you want to get all raw, now, huh? Man, we used to joke about anything under the sun but all of a sudden we can't?" Winton utters in a serious sense with a stale stare to get Boogey's mind off the ordeal.

Boogey looks off, finding two dark, slow, staggering figures coming toward the car with sticks and chains. "Man…, will we ever get a break?" Boogey asks, squinting and then doing a double-take.

Winton squints, throwing his hand over the seat, backing down fast.

The tall, old men scream something obscene out of the blue and pointing when about twenty distant bikers take off, charging Winton's car.

They all run faster but fade into darkness just before Winton slows down.

A beer bottle careens high, fading into pure darkness until it reflects off another car's headlight before hitting Winton's windshield and cracking it at the base.

"Enough of this bull!" Winton shrieks, pulling on the door handle and flinging the door open when Boogey grips him by the arm.

"Posse!" Boogey yells in a muffle after clearing his throat from a swallow of liquor. "Posseeeee!" he screams more clearly when Winton slides in quickly, stepping into the gas, stealthily backing down fast.

Winton exit the lot fast and drives for miles until reaching another billiard.

A couple of hours later, Winton head to the mill, and when twenty minutes away, Boogey nods off. He steadily watches Boogey until slowing down, turning down a dark road, and driving past a narrow entrance. Winton slows again and then turns when Boogey comes to, with curious, sleepy eyes.

"Winton..., where the Hell are we, main (man)? We should have been back by now," Boogey utters, looking at his watch as the car creeps under a dim streetlight.

"Trust me..., you've got to see this, Boog!" Winton slows, turning the lights out.

Boogey nervously eases to the edge of the seat, anxiously looking around while slowly tapping his fingers on the side mirror. "Man, you better not get me jammed up in no mess, or I'm going to whip that butt, good fashion," Boogey utters, tensed, when cutting his white eyes over at Winton's narrow head, feeling bad when thinking back on Winton's whipping.

Winton's bright white eyes stay peeled on the dirt trail as they slow down and then draw slowly around a sharp curve. He squints until something white appears through thick bushes when cutting the wheel sharp and parking near a bunch of junk cars. Winton steps out quick, hurrying to the trunk with wide and excited, roving eyes.

Boogey sits in suspense, looking over the junky yard and then at the run-down house fully lit up with bright lights.

Winton rushes to the driver's window. "Man, come on!" he whispers, giggling.

Boogey nervously looks around again then slowly climbs out, easing the door shut before creeping toward the back of Winton's car.

Winton slings a heavy bag over his shoulder, easing the trunk down, and then gently lays the bag on the trunk, feeling around until the sound of the zipper grows louder. He maneuvers until the streetlight provides more lighting, then pulls out fireworks and two stun guns.

"Winton, this might be fun and all to you, but what are we doing here?" Boogey utters with a confused look when cautiously picking up a stun gun, and looking it over.

"The van..., the white van with stickers..., remember?" Winton responds, slipping the big bag back into the trunk.

"What freakin' van, Wint? You been hitting that crack again?" Boogey whispers. "Main (Man), on the real..., I think you've been drinking too damn much tonight!" Boogey utters, flipping the stun gun in different angles to figure out how it works.

"Ah man, just slip it in your pocket," Winton mutters excitedly.

Boogey grows frustrated, easing the stun gun in his pocket when stepping forward in a pothole; dipping and accidentally hitting the trigger, when discharging the gun, and jerking as he goes straight down; sounding like something fizzing out.

Winton closes the trunk, looking around, confused. "Boogey! Boogey! Shoot man! Look..., this ain't no damn time to be playing hide-and-seek!" Winton whispers, skittishly jumping in fear when seeing his body on the ground, thinking it's a dog, and accidentally stunning Boogey in the thigh. "Get your tail up..., what are you doing down there?" Winton mumbles with fearful eyes coming up and looking around, quickly.

Boogey kicks again, going in circles until Winton finally takes his nervous finger off the trigger.

"Oh..., oh..., my bad!"

Boogey lies there for minutes until slowly moving one leg then lye longer until sitting, and finding Winton bent over in deep, silent laughter. "Figures..., ke, ke, ke! Always laughing like a hype hyena!" Boogey whispers with a frown then fearful, swarming eyes.

Winton giggles nonstop until finally straightening his face, then giggles more until his laughter gets out of control.

Boogey slowly kneels then springs up, gripping Winton tight in the collar, shoving him into the car. "Speak the plan now before someone busts a real cap in our tails!" Boogey murmurs in anger.

Winton straightens his face quick, whispering when a smile expressly grows on Boogey's face until giggling. "Here, this is how you use the gun," he utters, flipping his gun toward the dim light and quickly showing Boogey the neat little features. Winton pulls out stocking caps from his pocket, passing one to Boogey when pulling his tight until his eyes slant.

Boogey dons his with the butt part, sliding down tight with eyes shut tight and stuck closed. He takes a step, running into Winton, and backing off fast while adjusting the cap, and staring cross-eyed with his face torn up. "Man, Wint! What is that awful tail smell? Did you just cut one?" Boogey asks, frowning even harder.

Winton leads the way over near the house, finding the van when taking off at a slow pace, coming up around a few broken-down vehicles.

They come up to the back of the van when Boogey's favorite song grows louder.

Boogey stops and starts grooving in a crazy dance then twirl. His fist goes to his mouth as if it's a mic when he turns, finding Winton gone and ducks quickly, cautiously looking around.

Winton comes up on the driver's side, kneeling.

Boogey stops, still heavily sniffing in the air again then takes off and comes up on the passenger side, kneeling.

The front door of the dilapidated house swings wide open, and the big man's woman steps out, calling out to him for seconds, then goes back inside.

"Yeah, yeah, yeah! I'm coming!" the monstrous beast shrieks, turning up the volume and rocking his head to a new tune when turning up the moonshine and bringing it down fast. Suddenly, the music stops, and he flings the door open with Winton stepping forward with the man in the crosshairs.

"What the…!" the man begins to say, shoving the door hard and knocking the stun gun out of Winton's hand. He shoves Winton back and down, diving for the stun gun but drops; shaking when Boogey hits him in the butt with continual full charges.

The man continually shakes, bearing all his weight on Winton, who strains and kicks; breathing hard to catch his breath, until taking another deep breath, when straining and rolling the big man to one side.

Winton grabs his stun gun, springing up and reaching through the door, hitting the charge just for the Hell of it, bringing the man inches off the ground with each playful, frequent charge.

"What now?" Boogey asks, still sniffing for the uncanny smell while coming from the back and rushing up on Winton.

Winton senselessly laughs, still hitting the man with a full charge until watching him rise completely off the ground, foaming at the mouth.

"What now? Well, for one, we gone (are going to) take his hea (here) van," Winton utters, digging deep in his pocket and passing Boogey his car keys.

Boogey rubs his forehead, and his hand slowly drops with his face frowning worst. His hand flies back up, sniffing with eyes growing wide and both hands clawing stealthily against the stocking when the stun gun prematurely discharges at his temple, dropping him.

Winton draws a foot back, swiftly kicking the big man in the butt, and then jumps in the van. He eases the door shut and hangs out the window laughing when hitting the man again with more voltages. Winton reaches for the keys in the ignition, looking through the side mirror, finally discovering Boogey climbing slowly to his feet. He watches Boogey making his way to the car when the van cranks. Winton revs the engine a few good times and then retracts the stun gun leads by the wires.

The big man turns over slowly, finding Winton's red tongue piercing against the stocking with a hand at his ear, making flapping comical motions when the man frowns, inhaling deep until squawking some awful, unheard of sound, with it echoing.

A loud bang echoes when the front door of the house flies open, slamming into the side of the house.

The woman steps out with a baby tight in her arms, at her shoulder when her mouth falls open, finding her man on the ground, and the van's dim taillights when Winton completes the U-turn and takes his feet off the brake.

The man takes another deep breath, letting off another painful call to the wild when the girlfriend rushes the baby inside, shuffling through a closet for the rifle.

Boogey speedily leads the way with Winton hot on his trail until reaching the edge of the winding road, at a distance but alongside the house.

Winton turns and slows down to adjust the mirror.

The man's woman with a petite upper figure and broad, double-jointed hips, dressed in spandex, lunges from a path, grabbing Winton at the neck with a lanyard, pulling him out of the window.

Boogey looks through the rearview, finding the girl hanging from the side with feet pulled in tight.

Winton's left-hand drops low fast, grabbing a handful of plump, soft, round bottom, excitedly palming it while gagging and senselessly giggling. He slightly leans in, then inward harder, pushing in the cigarette lighter while gasping for air and turning red.

A light pop soon rings out when Winton pulls out the lighter, holding it on the nylon rope until it snaps.

The woman manages to ease her feet down, instantly in a fast sprint when Boogey speeds forward then Winton, and she screams running until veering off and rolling down a slight embankment into tall, thick weeds.

Winton floors it and overtakes Boogey.

They travel above the speed limit for a while then slow down, turning into the junkyard's back gate, fifteen minutes later, furiously blowing and pointing his friend to the crusher.

Winton pulls the van's passenger side against the crusher's wall, squeezing out.

His friend swings the magnet, lowering it then steps from the magnet winch, coming up on Winton fast. "Hey man…, I've been looking for a work van," his friend says.

"Ah hellz naw…, man, trust me…, you don't want no parts of this one because the people it belongs to don't live too far from here, and they'll beat the bricks off your bony behind!" Winton utters, laughing.

Several hours later, Winton checks his voicemail at home, confirming his appointment for his administrative panel review the following day.

Around 10:30PM, at Boogey's house, the phone rings, and Winton's voice rises in laughter.

"What's up, Wint?" Boogey asks, taking a seat in the recliner.

"Oh nothing…, got a few numbers for ya (you)," Winton says, rattling off two sets.

"Oh yeah? By the way, what did Young Anderson say?" Boogey asks.

"Oh, they left a message that my inquiry is tomorrow. What I ought to do is go in there and put my pistol in the son's mouth and make him suck on this cool barrel! Sucker gone pull a knife on me and throw rocks like he's a plum fool!" Winton utters, rubbing his bungee-cord, bruised neck.

Boogey holds his laugh. "Hold on a second." He covers the mouthpiece, bursting into an uncontrollable laugh when pulling the phone to his ear, giggling.

"I know you ain't laughing 'bout that crap, Boog!" Winton utters, concerned.

"Naw, naw, I was laughing at Bud's crazy behind," Boogey utters with his stomach still jumping from Winton's jive talk. "Well, let me get on over here to this sto (store)," Boogey utters, looking at the clock and ending call, when bursting through the front door.

Within minutes, Boogey rushes under the store's shelter, smiling when finding no one in line. He pulls out his money, throwing it and the paper with the numbers scribbled on the counter, asking for an extra easy pick ticket.

The cashier puts the ticket in Boogey's hand, and Boogey instantly smiles when a chill runs down his spine, causing him to stop and kind of shake it off, in somewhat of a little, playful dance.

Boogey pays, folding the ticket and sticking it in his pocket when walking off looking for personal hygiene items. He clenches the ticket when a strange feeling comes over him again and a bright smile comes when Boogey sees a man he has never spoken to walk through the door. "Have a good night, sir," Boogey utters, watching the man tilt his hat forward with a surprised but happy look.

Boogey eases outside, flipping through the tickets, and when touching the last one, a light wind spikes the hairs on the back of his neck. He feels giddy, smiling when striking out and soon staring at his front door. Boogey looks up, finding a shooting star when making a wish and when he opens his eyes, he stares for a while finding a cluster of stars appearing to be aligned in the number seven which vanishes quickly.

He rushes home, stopping at the top step, turning, sitting, and looking around at the stars longer for other numbers but now through the hole in the porch's roof until heading inside. Boogey undresses and sits, watching television until turning it off and reaching under the chair, flipping on his CB radio.

Deep in the wilderness, Melley and his brother Dallas walk past a guard and burst through the cabin's door, freezing in their tracks. The listen closer, hearing and finding; 5' 9", scrawny, greasy-headed Juke Box, dressed in dirty coveralls, tuning up the guitar.

Dallas shakes his head in disbelief. "Hell, Juke Box..., with all the writing you are doing, you better make me rich one day, boi, because you're always composing, as if on my dime." Dallas smiles then looks away with a 'yeah right' stare.

"One day for sure..., Dall, but yall check this one..., hot off the press!" he responds, wiping a tear when continually motioning until the last man walks over.

Dallas walks past followed by Melley and another man, heading over by the fridge for a cold beer.

The four turn with all eyes on Juke Box when he looks up with a silly grin while slinging his long slick hair back to one side.

"This one hea (here), I wrote when bumping into Sheriff Big John's mother at the general store the other day. Now, there's no bigger racist in Fikesville than that poor ole sole. I'm sure his trifling pappy was the same way for it to be instilled so deep in Ole Big John..., now, it's called..., My Mom, My Dad. Now it starts out with Big John's friend talking..., well, you know..., anyway, it goes a little something like this...,"

'Saw a long-time friend just the other day,
I had a chat to see just what he had to say,
He told me he was doing just..., fine.
Then I sat him down to wine and dine.
He stared at me..., and oh so long,
Then he just tore into this touching song..., he said.'

"Now right here is when the tone changes, like this..., Chorus."

'Here's my mom..., and here's my dad...,
Thought they were the greatest thing I ever had.'

"Then the tone changes," he says with excites, wandering eyes.

'Now when I was a child, I did good on my own,
They led me from good..., to doing wrong.
Embedded hatred of race is what they did,
And I was just a friendly, loving..., little kid.
Race cards played..., across all races,'

"Then the beat changes, like..., [doom, doom, doom, doom du, du du doom] beat."

'And you can't go..., by these smiling faces.'

"Beat again..., [doom, doom, doom, doom du, du du doom] beat," Juke box repeats.

'And you can't say..., who is who,
Cause they are sure enough gonna turn on you.'

"Again, the Chorus," Juke Box says proudly, looking up at their smiling faces.

'I have to thank my mom and thank my dad,
Cause they gave the worst advice I ever had.'

"Now then the tone goes back down, like this," Juke Box says, leaning a certain way when putting his heart into the song.

'Well, shame on mom and shame on dad,
Could've chose good, but you chose bad.

Well, don't poison my boy..., or my girl,
So they can grow to be special in this world.
Racism across every nation,'
"Then the..., [doom, doom, doom, doom du, du du doom] beat," he says smiling at several smiling faces.
'And we all have our share.'
"Then! [doom, doom, doom, doom du, du du doom] beat," he says, grinning.
'Deep-rooted through generations.
And somehow, we just don't even seem to care.'
"Now back to the..., ah..., ah..., ah..., chorus."
'Well, now pray for my mom and pray for dad,
Cause this life..., they portray it's been oh so sad.'
"Then down..., you know, like before!"
'Lying here..., on my dying bed,
Look away, my friend, and don't you dread.
And it all seems matter of fact,
Cause in the end, all flesh turns black.
Hell bound seems late to rearrange,
For them..., tell Satan nothing's changed.
Their stagecoach..., will soon arrive for Hell,'
"Then the! [doom, doom, doom, doom du, du du doom] beat," he says smiling even harder.
So I guess they, sure enough, won't be making bail.'
"Then! [doom, doom, doom, doom du, du du doom] beat. Now the last part is when Big John's friend floats back in..., you know, talking but sounding like he's singing. The ah..., ah..., ah..., the narrator..., and he says,"
'Now there's a place call Hell in the end,
These are the words from my long, lost friend.
Thanks to his mom, thanks to his dad!
Cause life doesn't have to end like this, it never has!
Are you that mom..., Ooooh!
Are you that dad...,
It's just so sad. Ooooh! It's just so sad.'
"Then the music kinda fades off," Juke Box says, smiling when the room goes hay-wire in laughter.

Dallas smiles the hardest, rubbing his fat hands together to insinuate a big payday coming soon. "Well, I'll be a skunk's musk..., I think you done wrote yourself into a good one right there, JB!"

"Why, thank you, thank you very much," Juke Box responds, sounding almost like the near-perfect Elvis impersonation when tilting his ten-gallon cowboy hat.

The five indulge in beer and liquor for well over an hour until one man breaks out the poker chips.

The sheriff and two deputies pull alongside a dirt trail in the same woods along a dark country road, near the cabin. They draw their guns, rushing until coming to the top of a hill where the sheriff points them to each side of the little, log cabin.

Walkie-talkies key up with a Morse coding going on and then stops and keys up again.

The sheriff creeps over by the black, shiny Cadillac parked under a lamppost.

One deputy reaches for his walkie-talkie. "Sheriff, nothing on this side." He looks through the pitch-black cabin window and a face unnoticeably backs away with the tip of the gun's barrel slowly fading from the window, yet still pointing upward.

A whisper comes and a hand inside the dark cabin rubs over the main power panel switch, pulling it down slowly when the rest of the cabin grows darker.

The sheriff flinches with his eyes upward, looking around when hearing movement in the forest.

"Ahii...," a deputy screams on one side of the cabin when his voice slightly fades but continually shrieks.

The other deputy runs around back, coming up on the other side. "Oh, man!" he shrieks, with wide eyes and his voice slightly fading but continually screeching. "Ahii..., Ahii!"

The sheriff runs wide-legged to the other side, looking around for them and then up, finally seeing something swinging, when their yelping voices grow louder. He stops in his tracks, shaking his head then spreads his arms, balancing and taking backward, baby steps until flung off-balanced and rapidly swinging. The sheriff's arms continually spin express windmills until stepping to one side, whisked high into the air as well, in the net, next to the last deputy.

Curtains from two dark windows slowly pull back with big, white eyes looking around them up when one man's concerned look turns into a bright smile with bright, white teeth, shining.

The front door slowly squeaks when Melley and his brother Dallas walk out, followed by others with guns drawn and attentive eyes on the hilltop and around thick trees.

Dallas slips two fingers against his tongue, whistling in code and instantly, two more men appear from high in the trees, camouflaged and almost transparent.

The men's infrared goggle stay charged over their eyes for minutes until pulled back over their heads, still energized.

"Drop em' fellas!" Dallas quickly utters, raising and pointing the sawed-off shotgun up at the sheriff and deputies, who have their hands on their weapons but can't draw them from their weight and the net being too tight.

Minutes later, the sheriff and deputies' guns slowly fall into the dust like clockwork.

The men rush over to the tree, loosening the ropes and lowering them until they are in arms' reach.

The tall camouflaged man pulls out a flask, turning it up. His bloodshot eyes glimpse over at the swinging nets when he breaks out in a crazy laugh that echoes.

The sheriff looks at them with a mean stare and then cusses, continually calling Melley and Dallas all kinds of nasty names.

The short camouflaged man screams, expressly staggering and seizing the sheriff's net, running in a drunken zigzag until releasing it, and leaving it swinging high. He replicates the same motions with both deputies and then stands back, giggling.

The sheriff and the deputies scream at the top of their lungs, kicking as their bodies come close to colliding over and over again.

The short man waits until they settle and then repeats the same drill but swings them even higher with more creative twists and turns that bring them even closer together until slamming together.

"Ok, men..., it's time for a little round-robin," Dallas yells out, when stopping the sheriff's net when it slows and holding it while backing down, slowly.

Melley, Dallas, and the short man hold the nets as far back as possible, turning and running in a fast clockwise motion, yelling with drunken and coked-out minds.

"Three..., two..., one!" Dallas screams when they release the nets, which twirl clockwise with the ropes twisting, and their bodies clashing hard together like a bag of old, crusty bones when dust shakes from the ropes as the bodies slow in momentum and swing low.

After a few more smash drills, the men wrestle with the officers, hog-tying them and quickly backing away.

The sheriff continually yells derogatory things at Dallas after being told to shut up several times until Dallas takes the butt of his shotgun and slams it into his knee. The sheriff's death-cry echoes, causing a family up the road to stop eating and carefully listen, for minutes.

"It's probably just the winds howling," the grandfather finally utters, reaching for the big bowl of buttery butter beans and ham hocks.

Melley grabs the sheriff's walkie-talkie. "I always wanted one of these! Breaker, breaker, good buddy..., come back!" Melley broadcasts in his looney-tune voice, giggling in his well-known laugh.

Boogey's sleepy left eye peeks open, at his house, slowly staring around the dark, grim room.

"I said, breaker, breaker, good buddy…, come back, on the ten-four, nine eighteen!" Melley senselessly yells when giggling and broadcasting again until senselessly and uncontrollably giggling.

Boogey's feet shuffle with knuckles scraping the gritty floor when softly moaning in pain, and shaking off the burning abrasions.

The birdcage bounces when Boogey springs up, hitting its bottom with his shoulder. He brings his knuckles up, discovering blood spots when shaking his hand with a pained look when reaching for his CB as Melley's voice rises again.

Boogey stands, and his feet anxiously tap, then slows until stopping and shuffling quickly. He rushes for the couch, rumbling through piles of clothes. "Nattie, where's that big black bag with the outfits?" he asks, throwing things over the overly junky room.

Nattie stays quiet for a spell until he calls her again. "Man, please!" Nattie utters, turning over, lying there listening to him tear through things until finally quiet.

Boogey spots the bag's string, shuffling for it when gathering a few things. He plops down in the chair quickly, unlacing his boots and then dressing into a black clown bottom and ninja top before putting on a headband and face shield.

Nattie creeps to the door, easing it open until finding him with his back to her. She giggles, leaning against the wall in tears when he turns, staring in the mirror at the ridiculous-looking outfit; not noticing her.

Boogey cuts off all of the light with the lights from the back of the store shining through the front windows when expressly stepping off and rushing past the bedroom and onto the porch, slamming the door.

Nattie stumbles from the room and rushes to the couch, plopping down in a crazy laugh with the curtains slightly pulled back and only white, possum-looking teeth showing.

Boogey freezes, hearing her hee-hawing, then looks back and sprints off. He jumps in the car, revving the engine, then kicks up dust, and heavily swerves until straightening the wheel. His hand rubs over the face of the CB receiver, flipping knobs when shooting past the general store. Boogey fades behind the tree line, turning up the volume when hearing more profanity and laughter with several, different shrieks in the background.

The 911 operator finally intervenes to cease the racket when hearing a voice scream that sounds like the sheriff's.

Boogey passes the old lumber yard, doing seventy in a fifty-five mile-per-hour zone, hoping to corner Melley at his house.

A different deputy sits parked deep in the woods, listening to Melley and more screams while curiously puffing a joint, and looking up fast, seeing Boogey's white lights jet past. He accidentally drops the joint in his lap, rising and fanning until knocking the joint to the floor, expressly stomping in a dance to put it out. The deputy's hand drop to the seat belt, with his body moving fast, to free himself while stomping faster when smelling burnt carpet, and finally seeing a small flame.

His hands nervously yet continuously fiddles with the seat belt when a flash of smoke, then more flames rise higher when the deputy screams, kicking faster until the seat belt comes loose and the door flies open. The deputy snatches his ten-gallon hat, fanning smoke until his boots slip inside, stomping faster, in a Texas five-step dance, if there is such a thing, until securing the fire.

A hot seed finally burns through his pants, hitting his thigh when he hollers and it echoes when dancing and unbuckling his trousers, shaking off the hot seed.

Boogey overshoots his turn, finding the minuscule blue flashing light at a great distance and closing fast. He continues around the curve with his eyes set on the lights until they fade when hitting the brakes, cutting off his lights, and making a U-turn.

The deputy floors the pedal, hitting the turbo switch when the needle drops. He wrestled for his seat belt for minutes until losing his grip and reaching again.

Boogey veers back onto the road fast, cutting on lights when entering the curve, finding blue flashing lights inbound like a cruise missile. He speeds out of the curve and sees the deputy's face and waving hands when he almost invisibly shoots past.

The deputy's hand remains tangled in the seat belt, uncontrollably keeping straight into a field and cutting down low-cut tobacco leaves for a quarter of a mile.

Within minutes, the deputy heads for the highway and overshoots it, crossing the highway into another field filled with corn, plowing for seconds until finally swerving out and onto the road seconds later. He floors it until slowly pulling behind Boogey at forty-five miles per hour then off the road under a bright street light.

The deputy kicks the door open with his dusty boots, leaning to one side, when grabs his shotgun, and jumping back, pointing the gun in a scream. "Let me see your freakin' hands, now, you idiot!" the young, freckle-faced rookie shrieks with deep tobacco stains and smudges on his shirt.

Boogey slowly rolls down the window with one cartoon-looking gloved-covered hand extended out, then the other.

"Cut the engine and open the door, slowly! Let me see your freakin' hands at all times," the nervous deputy yells.

"Look! Make up your freakin' mind! You want me to cut off the engine, open the door, or keep my hands visible; which one is it?" Boogey yells, frowning.

"Now you look here! I'll do all the darn talking, and I say..., all of the above, and don't mimic me!" the deputy yells, slowly raising then jerking the gun to eye level.

Boogey's head slightly veers around the steering wheel with hands still out the window, fighting to turn off the ignition with his teeth when the engine shuts down. He follows other commands and eases the door open, slide-out, and back up against his car, then slides over near the back door. He keeps trained eyes dead set on the nervous, gun-holding young deputy's frightened face.

There is instant silence as the deputy's face transforms to confusion when eying Boogey from head to toe until jerking as if having a seizure when breaking out in a silly laugh, as high as a kite, and he can't stop laughing. He falls forward into Boogey's trunk and then the cruiser's hood, laughing even harder.

Boogey stands staring until slowly easing his hands down, shaking his head, pissed when looking longer until waving his hand, blowing the deputy off. He climbs inside, still looking at the laughing deputy through the side mirror, finding him with his shotgun over the cab of his cruiser and his head down, senselessly laughing.

Boogey cranks up peeling off when instantly hearing a shotgun blast, when ducking and swerving slightly off the road. Boogey's eyes nervously drift back into the side view mirror again, finding the deputy's shotgun on the ground with him still up against the cruiser. He goes to the rearview, spotting the deputy skittishly and expressly drawing his sidearm and firing toward the woods.

The deputy stands wide-legged, bent over the cruiser in a stance, continually firing into the woods, round-after-delayed round when firing back at each of his own gun's echoes.

Boogey slows watching the deputy fade into darkness with sparks from his gun finally fading then catches a glimpse of him swiftly reloading and disappearing when in a steep curve.

Boogey drives for ten minutes, turning down a narrow driveway enclosed on both sides by high weeds. He clears a curve, and a house neatly tucked away in the woods slowly comes into view. Boogey backs along the driveway, looking over his shoulder when turning around in tall weeds when the house vanishes and he makes a U-turn, backing down.

He climbs out, opening the moonlit trunk, feeling around until pulling out the end of a thick, industrial-strength rubber band. He pulls the band tight, dropping the bitter end and allowing it to snake out while holding it by the other bitter end. He glances out along the trail and then crosses over the dusty path, securing the band to a thick tree.

He grasps the other end, pulling it over to another tree, wrapping it around a stubby but firm oak when securing the other end to his rusty tow-hitch. Boogey puts the car in reverse, easing back slightly with eyes glued on the band until it comes off the ground, lifts high, and draws very tight. He cuts the engine, sitting and listening, and before long, he nods off.

Back in the woods, Melley, Dallas, and the men stand off to the side of the three tired swinging bodies, still drinking and acting crazy.

Dallas pulls one of the men to the side, whispering then climbs in his car, and Melley climbs on his motorcycle, both looking at each other with a smile, then over at the sheriff and deputy, winking when pulling away.

Melley enters the expressway, drunkenly swerving from lane to lane, until increasing speeds beyond eighty miles per hour in a fifty-five zone. He slows down when going through the city and comes up to the last intersection, cranking up to ninety when exiting the city limits when his driving worsens.

His eyes continually dim as the cycle guides on the white line, swerving heavier from time to time until approaching the intersection leading to his house. Melley turns, and instantly, bright lights shine from an eighteen-wheeler on a collision course, somewhat blinding him.

The truck's loud horn blares, waking Boogey, who sits up quick, anxiously looking around, and Melley, who comes out of a heavy nod. The truck slightly swerves, with the driver laying into the horn again, watching the motorcycle veer from the head-on when almost sideswiping the truck.

The motorcycle's engine rises with Melley's delayed screaming when leaning hard with eyes finally peeled over his shoulders, staring back at the truck's bright taillights flicking through a heavy trail of black burning tire rubber.

The truck veers more, barely crossing the white line when it slams on brakes, stopping for the red light but running into the intersection with heavy smoking tires.

The light sound of a heavily raised motorcycle engine with muffler thrusting rises in Boogey's ears like sweet music when Boogey cranks up.

Boogey's reverse lights come on with the brake lights blinking while Boogey pats the brake pedal. His eyes lock stealthy onto the entrance of the driveway in excited anticipation when grinning.

Out of nowhere, the motorcycle lights veer fast, brightly lighting up the drive when Melley floors the engine and speeds through the invisible band, which grips him in the chest, with a scream, catapulting and sending him flying backward in a continual high pitch, and somewhat sober scream.

The loud motorcycle crash follows with a slightly fading yelp when Melley's body flings to the ground, almost lifelessly.

Melley lay unresponsive for minutes until kicking and rolling from his back to his side and slowly climbing to his knees.

Boogey remains standing behind Melley, adjusting his face mask until lifting his feet high, smashing Melley's butt forward until Melley falls face-first in the tall weeds.

A tight balled fist goes to Melley's head, knocking him out.

Melley drops to his knees with one knee instantly thrusted into Melley's back.

Boogey's hand shoots deep in his pocket, digging until pulling out the black, thick tape when partially wrapping Melley's face, then his body, and dragging Melley by his feet.

Melley finally comes to, kicking and heavily moaning with heels digging deep in the dirt, resisting being drug when kicking harder and almost loose.

Boogey let's go, grabbing him at the belt loop, dragging him to the dirt-covered driveway, dropping him face-down when sticking a short, hollow pipe to his head, pretending it's a gun. "Listen! Pipe down before I put a round in ya (you)!" Boogey yells, pressing his feet deep into his back.

Without warning, Boogey runs toward the car, jumping in, and retrieving the band, throwing it in the trunk. He turns the wheel hard, paralleling the trail then ease out, approaching slowly when almost in reach of Melley, and Melley is almost to his knees.

Melley springs up, nippily running in circles until accidentally stumbling and drifting toward Boogey when Boogey draws back a wide hand and slaps Melley silly, making his walk backward then sideways before falling on his back.

Boogey walks up staring at his crossed eyes when Melley springs up, stumbles toward him again when following up with an upper-cut, knocking Melley high and backward with the bottom of his boots showing. "I'll teach you to make a fool out of me!" Boogey utters, turning and walking away.

He reaches into the front seat, backing out fast, pulling out a manila rope, and tying it to a tree. Boogey grabs Melley, dragging him over and tying him then pulls off his thick studded leather belt. "I'm going to give you something I should have given you a long time ago!" Boogey screams, tightening the long belt around his hand, a few turns.

Melley looks back, begging and pleading with tied hands to his face, trembling when a light swirl and quick whistle grows and fades repetitively and fast with Boogey in a belt-whipping frenzy.

Boogey becomes breathless taking a quick breather then begins twirling the belt high until bringing it low fast, striking Melley across his half exposed butt with the powerful licks now sounding like firecrackers, with screams after each lashing.

Mellow dog barks come from out of nowhere then fades off.

The lashes and screams get louder then cease.

Melley falls, kicking when more lashes come with screams when slapping Melley's legs and thighs, shredding his clothing.

Boogey takes another breather, allowing Melley to stretch back out then gives him even heavier lashes until Melley's clothes spot with droplets of blood. Boogey bends over, catching his breath again when finally getting a closer look at him.

Melley slowly comes to his knees, digging his stubby fingernails at his mouth, slightly unraveling the tape when balling up in a fetal position crying, and tensed, with a hand moving faster to hold Boogey back.

Boogey walks off, looking back, and then shakes his head while taking a few deep breaths to slow his heart rate.

Low level, muffled barks come again, fading off when the winds pick up.

Boogey turns, taking a few steps toward the car when Melley's left hand falls free, and he speedily reaches for his front pocket.

Melley cranks down hard on the key remote, activating the double garage doors, and a loud whistle comes from out of nowhere, causing Boogey to jump and look back when hearing a light bark followed by several different barks.

Boogey takes off fast and falls in a pothole, twisting his ankle when thrown to his knees and coming up quickly, limping around the front of the car. His hand grips the hood, supporting his turn when briefly looking down the dim path at three big-headed mastiffs charging as if in slow motion but in full stride.

Boogey's footwear slams onto the front bumper, denting the hood as he climbs onto the roof; his foot barely missing the wide jaws of the first mastiff that lunges past the car.

The second dog leaps onto the trunk, coming up on the roof when clown shoes slam into his face, forcing him off, backward, and onto his back, yelping.

"Attack...! Attack! Kill..., kill!" Melley shrieks at the top of his lungs, still pulling tape away as fast as possible while coming to his feet, fighting to uncover his eyes.

"Call off the dogs! Call off the dogs, or I'll shoot you deader than a doorknob!" Boogey shrieks in a frightening tone when finding the biggest dog on the trail and walking into sight as if he's a man or lion.

"We gone see if you can handle this whipping I'm going to put on you when I get my hands on you..., you!" Melley screams, still trying to remove the thick tape from over his eyes.

"Put your hands down, or I'll shoot!" Boogey points the hollow pipe at Melley.

Melley keeps trying to free the tape when Boogey bangs metal against the roof, making it sound like he's locking and loading.

"I hope these dogs don't mean nothing to you because I'm going to shoot all of them and then kill you!" Boogey yells in a more convincing voice though nervous a heck.

"No…! No…! Not my babies!" Melley whines. "Not my babies! My babies!" he screams, freezing as he slowly raises hands over his head. "Here, boys, here…!" Melley screams, kneeling when he feels a heavy dog paw pressed deep into his leg.

Boogey keeps his eyes on the dogs, nervously looking for more when finding the biggest one staring him down until finally breaking his concentration and walking over to Melley. Boogey extends a hand for the handle, opening the door. He looks again and jumps down, hopping inside and slamming the door shut.

Boogey rolls the window up, seeing a shadow on the ground when a fourth dog springs high in the air past the window in a deep growl that seems almost in slow motion. He floors the pedal, throwing the car in drive, kicking up a high trail of dirt and dust when fighting the wheel, trying to straighten up on the narrow drive.

Later that night, across town, Dallas and his posse hide outside the train station, peeking out from parked rail cars. He keeps looking at his watch, then down the dark train track, anxiously sipping on a narrow flask of Sekif's cognac. "Dang, where in the hell is Mel?" Dallas utters, looking at six of his men when one gets Dallas' attention, pointing to fast moving headlights afar off before they go out.

The car's passenger door soon flies open, and Melley jumps out, limping alongside the front fender with a thick backpack in hand. His other hand hits the hood when lights come on, and the car pulls away, turning at the end of the street and parking in a vacant lot.

Like clockwork, a too familiar, distant sound comes at a whisper until the train's engine then whistle blares faintly when stealthily closing on the station.

Bright, fast headlights shine along the distant highway closing in until blue, flashing lights, glow, brightly. White, bright, cruiser headlights pass a car when the blue lights go off and the cruiser soon passes the car in the lot, slowing at the train station entrance.

Other vehicles' lights expressly appear, rushing toward the lot when two deputies appear, teaming up with the sheriff, in separate cars, and cruising the train station parking lot with eyes heavily wandering over and around the station.

The shortest deputy looks over his shoulder, backing into a parking spot, and cutting off all lights.

The sheriff speeds behind the building, shooting out on the other side, heading for the highway.

Melley's driver looks anxiously at his watch, then over at the passenger, who finally pulls out a gun, slowly screwing on a silencer with trembling hands.

The train's whistle blow heavily a few times as it slows, making its way past the station when applying heavy shrilling brakes.

Dallas, Melley, and the gang wait patiently, looking between the train and cruisers. They visually trail the train longer as it loops around the wide turn in an open field, stopping as the crew begins connecting forty more cars.

The train worker works diligently, making the connections, and then checks the connection for well over twenty minutes when the train begins rolling forward. The tracks switch, with the train finally pulling past the station minutes later.

The train's whistle blows one long blast as it slowly moves forward, picking up momentum when passing the cruiser; when the cruiser's headlights come on, and one deputy jumps out, hurrying to the train, kneeling to find several feet running fast toward the train.

The deputy draws his weapon, looking more aggressively between more cars and running even faster, without looking ahead. His boots slam heavily against the concrete, then over unstable rocky gravel, running off the sidewalk and expressly into a high, dirt mound, screaming when hitting a low-cut post.

Instantly, the other deputy and the two men in the car burst into a loud outburst of laughter, with both vehicles heavily rocking from side to side.

The second deputy in the cruiser continues laughing non-stop until somewhat calm when the dual barrels blow black smoke. He swerves out of the lot over to the end of the sidewalk, throwing the car in park and laughing even hard while trying to get a straight face. He finally gets himself together, heavily teary-eyed, when jumping from the cruiser, rushing over to assist his partner.

The two hoodlums continue giggling when the passenger opens the glove compartment, easing the gun back inside, still wiping his teary eyes.

The last of Dallas' men's feet dangle from the train for seconds until another hoodlum's fat hands snatches him by the collar and he springs up high, still in the tight-fisted grip until released and brushing his threads down fast when he and the man that pulled him up turn slowly.

They lean, finding others staring into the faces of two old, white hobos sitting in a thin beam of light shining in from the half-moon.

Dallas looks away from the two men, back at the two old white hobos with a meaner almost red face. "Well, as I was saying, this train hea (here) ain't big enough for all of us, so you guys had better get to stepping!" Dallas utters, stepping to one side when his men take a few steps back to make a clear path for the hobos to the door.

Out of nowhere, a third and the biggest, muscle-bound hobo leans forward, fading in from pure darkness, towering three feet over everyone on the train.

Dallas, his men, and Melley's eyes go upward slow until all are with heads thrown way back until finally looking into the tall, black man's face.

"As you were saying," the black man voice rumbles when looking over their shoulder and out the door at fast passing trees, big, light-tinted cornfields, other colored fields then mixed, shaded fields. More colorful fields soon pass, with a few men looking off at the fast passing then almost invisible vegetation as the train picks up momentum.

Everyone continually eyes each other with mean stares, not a one cracking a smile, but all looking timid, or looking away.

The train whistle sounds off loudly, coming up to its minimum cruise speed, and soon crossing a high trestle when increasing speed with black soot shooting alongside the cars with a lot of smoke drifting into the car until everyone is invisible. The whistle blows again, coming up on a railroad crossing with pulsating lights and a squawking, train warning alarm, blaring.

The smoke somewhat soon clears, escaping through the other seamlessly cracked open door when all faces drift into view again. "Well..., the way I see it..., you guys are outnumbered, so here is what I'm willing to do just this one time, and please..., gentlemen, consider me most generous in my offer," Dallas yells over the loud squeaky wheels with a cheesy grin that brightens when drawing his gun and everyone drawing, almost simultaneously.

"Now..., now! Numbers..., remember!" Dallas screams with a fast index finger waving past his mean-looking men. "Now, hear me out..., here's my proposition. When the train reaches the other side of this hea (here) next trestle, you can jump off in the hay fields to safety and just move along little donkeys."

The tall, black man fakes being afraid when breaking out in a loud and thunderous laugh that leaves Dallas, Melley, and Dallas' men a little uneasy. The tall man laughs even harder until a confused looks comes across Dallas's face. "Yeah..., well, for a minute there, I thought we were outnumbered as well," the tall, black man utters, whistling loudly when a few tall bales of hay fall forward with eight other men appearing out of the darkness with hand tight Uzis' already drawn at eye level.

Melley's empty, shaking hand comes up fast when taking a few steps forward, then backward even faster until on Dallas' toe when heavily pushed into the tall black man and shoved back into one of Dallas' men who stops Melley and balance him. "Hmm..., well, well..., now look ah here, gentlemen. There has to be some way we can handle this like real gentlemen," Dallas skittishly utters with bright eyes when slowly holding one empty hand higher and easing his gun into his holster.

"Drop em (them) and drop em fast!" the big, black man utters, laughing as if stoned on cheap drugs when another man steps out of the darkness with three muzzled, vicious-looking pit bulls, which he unmuzzles then says some foreign word when the vicious barks begin echoing.

Two hobos raise their guns to Melley's head when two more appear from the dark behind Dallas and his gang, and one sticks a gun to the back of Dallas' head, slightly shoving him forward.

Dallas' hands go even higher when a hand suddenly slides in Dallas' holster, pulling his other gun out when the man smiles, gazing over Dallas' new pearl-handled gun, anxiously shoving it deep inside his waistband. Dallas opens his nervous, trembling lips with fast shuffling eyes scanning about the car.

"Now look hea (here)..., let's all be men about this, shall we? On second thought, and now that I've looked at the sitiation (situation), I think this car will suit us all just fine," Dallas mildly utters, expressly reconsidering when looking up at the tall, black man, who motions him to direct his men to drop their weapons, with head nods.

Dallas stares deeper in the tall black man's eyes when seeing his demeanor change even rougher. "Ok..., ok, ok..., drop em' (them) fellas!" Dallas nervously utters, looking at his men, and nodding to each as the metal begins banging back-to-back with Dallas' men raising their hands high, almost simultaneously.

The view outside turns from water to big fields of a lighter tan color when the tallest man advances; kicking the guns to one side, near the door. He points to Dallas, allowing him time to grab his gun, then grabs him deep in the collar as he comes up, slinging him out into the cornfield, hearing his sharp, jerking scream fade off to a whisper, until he hits the ground and rolls over twenty feet or more before breaking his fall, jumping up and running until slowing and dusting off, limping.

Melley follows the same profile, picking up his gun when thrown.

The tall man takes one step at a time, going through the men as if they are rag dolls. He throws the last man, Juke Box, off, dusting off his hands when turning, watching his friends fade slowly into the darkness with serious faces, with the one man re-muzzling the dogs.

Juke Box's scream comes, the loudest of them all continually tumbling the longest until somehow coming up on a high roll to his feet, running until veering toward the men and passing them when slowing. "Hey, fellas! I gotta new one! I think it's going to be a hit! It's called..., 'being thrown from a freakin' train.'

Dallas takes a few steps back, pissed and slapping his thick balled fist into this other hand. "Better yet..., I have one..., and it's going to be called..., 'your face thrown into this fat fist, non-stop with no breaks and no time off!..., or better yet..., why does my face hurt so bad!'

Boogey awakens early the next morning, yawning and stretching while looking at the clock on the wall. He hears Nattie lightly snoring when getting dressed and notices when she suddenly draws quiet.

Nattie turns over, hearing Boogey jostle into something, and then rush off.

Boogey dresses, slipping on his boots faster when reaching for the doorknob.

Nattie hears the screen door spring open, then the door shut, fast.

Boogey's car engine comes next, turning over a few times with thrust mufflers mildly humming when pulling away. He pulls up at the general store, rushing inside to buy a ticket, and pulls the other tickets out, looking at the numbers for seconds.

He puts the easy pick on top, sticking the tickets back in his pants pocket, slowly turning in deep thought. He rushes for the door, climbing back in, tuning the radio to his favorite station when speeding off and up, so he has time to park and listen to the previous night's winning numbers before going into the mill.

Boogey soon pulls into the lot beside a few coworkers who sit listening to sports replays. He waves, backing in next to a car in the middle of the first row. Boogey's radio volume comes up, and he pulls out the tickets, closely listening. His eyes glance over the three tickets, which he holds side by side in excitement.

Boogey turns the volume higher when the announcer calls out the first number. His eyes roll and stop on the easy pick ticket's second number, then the third, dropping the others when the fourth is announced. Boogey's heart drops on the fifth when the announcer delays, making the show sound even more interesting.

The radio reception fades when the man calls the last number, and Boogey mistaken the number, assuming he has all of them. He closes his eyes, growing anxious when clenching the ticket and jumping out dancing with the door still open.

The guys roll up their window fast, trying to hear the sports commentator while pointing and laughing at Boogey's out-of-date dances.

Boogey jumps back in, pulling off with the door barely closed when rolling over by the office, waving through the window at the secretary, who finally notices him when vanishing from the big picture window and rushing into the breezeway.

"Hey, Sandy, put me in for a sick day; I forgot my medical appointment was today," Boogey screams, lying while waiting for her acknowledgement when speeding off.

Winton turns on Mills Road, immediately staring at Boogey's car closing in fast until staring at Boogey's bouncing body, bright eyes, and smiling face as he shoots past. He continually looks over his shoulder, flummoxed, then curiously in the rearview and side mirror until Boogey fades in a deep turn.

Winton's eyes shoot forward, finding a driver with a big cowboy hat pulling away fast then banking right. His bright, white eyes shoot open, barreling down on a car stopped in the middle of the road with what looks like ten cowboy-hat, covered heads or more inside. Winton yells loudly, with knees high and deep into his chest, when both feet forcefully slam on the brake, busting the pedal through the rusted-out floor.

The car's tires burn heavy rubber, leaving deep, black tire marks stretching over twenty-five feet long, with Winton's tires overlapping the car's deep, asphalt, burned in tracks.

Winton's bumper surges a little, stopping centimeters from the car's bumper, and all heads sit still, waiting for the pre-planned rear-end crash. He stays wide-eyed with butt cheeks tightening, and a death grip on the steering wheel, with finger impressions heavily stamping the foam as his face turns fierce red when his door flies open. He jumps out, shifting his weight, and the bumper jerks forward, barely touching the other bumper when everyone fall out or slumps forward, screaming at the top of their lungs.

Winton gets hysterical seeing their delayed reaction when jumping back inside, hearing loud tires squealing, several horns, and fast passing cars. He check traffic in both mirrors, springing out, grabbing his head, walking swiftly in circles until screaming in a delayed response, as if a lunatic. He makes a few more ridiculous turns when stomping.

Winton stops, looking across the street, finding a deputy parked alongside a building with wide eyes, shaking his head in disbelief. Winton frantically runs in front of oncoming traffic, barely missed by a fast-moving, non-stop horn blowing car when closing in on the cruiser. "Officer! Officer! Did you see that? Did you?" Did you?" Winton shrieks, almost out of breath.

"Yeah…, yeah…, yeah…, every second of that BS!" the old, coke-bottle-glass-wearing deputy utters, flipping on his blue lights when keying up the mic. "Nice try, ladies…, but no dice! Now get your sweet little britches up and get the hell out of here before I haul all of you away!" the deputy calmly says, shaking his head again.

The men remain sprawled out until the driver mumbles something in a native tongue, and they jump up like precision Soldiers, loading up and fleeing the scene.

Winton wipes sweat from his forehead, bidding the officer a good day when cautiously returning to his car. He pulls off and stops at the red light, discovering a female in tight, white, stretch jeans. Winton's eyes stay glued on her hourglass shape as each cheek goes up and down until almost mesmerized. He flies past her and pulls into the driveway in front of her, watching her until realizing that he knows her.

Debbie smiles, swaying her hips more while approaching and walks up, leaning over with her arms folded over the roof and her forehead resting on her arms.

Winton's glistening eyes swarm over her hot body.

"Hey, Wint, where have you been, man? I haven't seen you in a long time, dude," she utters, cheery, trying to look sexy when accidentally showing her jacked-up teeth.

"Dang! I mean, dang…, you looking good, girl," Winton utters with a diminishing stank look that he cleans up, quickly.

"I guess I messed you up the last time we were together, huh? I mean…, well, you know…, with me letting all that freak out on you without giving you any warning," Debbie says, slightly beaming.

"Girl, quit playing! You know that won't no freak!" Winton says. "The funk," Winton mumbles unheard when a loud truck passes with the truck driver swerving with his head thrown back, with eyes dead-set on her gorgeous body.

The driver stares out the side, and then rearview mirror, unknowingly crossing the yellow line until a longhorn blows.

"Man, you crazy! That was sho nough (sure was) some freak coming out of me!" She laughs. "All I know is you went downtown and rolled over like a dead bug. Shucks, I really thought you were dead," she says, smelling and waving off her stinky breath faster and playing it off when looking around as if fanning a few flies.

"Dang! Ugh! I mean…, wow…, and you put on some weight girl, but it looks good on you," Winton utters, looking at her broad hips when she backs away, turning in a seductive dance with his eyes glued on her thick bottom.

"Thanks, Wint, but hey…, it makes you wanna go another round, huh?" She turns and jumps from leg to leg like a horse jockey to make her butt heavily bounce.

"Uh, uh, uh…, well, hey, I'm running late; but I'll get with you later," Winton utters, slowly backing down into the street and turning into the mill's lot shortly after that, finding a man vanishing into the breezeway.

The secretary's heels fade around the corner when she knocks on Old Man Anderson's door, then knocks again when a light, frail voice whispers again. "Wait a minute!" Old Man Anderson utters, pulling up his trousers. "Ok! You can come in, but turn around until I get my britches secured!" he lowly utters, laughing.

The secretary backs inside, taking the last bite of the glazed doughnut, still backing close to his desk when her pen drops. She finds him still looking down after dropping to her knees, fumbling around for the pen when the office door flies open.

Winton finds Old Man Anderson with his back to the door, adjusting his trousers and looking over his shoulder when looking off to the side, finding the secretary on her knees, looking up with shiny lips and a light, creamy crust at the corner of her mouth.

She drops her mouth open surprised, finally seeing his zipper still open. "Winton, have a seat near my desk," the secretary utters, looking more suspicious when springing up, walking Winton into the main office, where he sits, as she heads for the conference room. She opens the door seconds later, motioning Winton inside.

Winton stands neatly brushing his wrinkled clothes down while entering, finding a panel of five staring at him, with not too friendly faces.

The side door opens, and Old Man Anderson and his son enter.

Winton happens to see the news on, quickly taking a seat, and nervously staring at the floor when he sees his interview with the reporter flash across the screen, as the next topic. "Nice day, huh?" Winton mumbles, trying to distract the panel.

Old man Anderson sits gazing over a long list of documents for seconds until clearing his voice. "So, Mr. Moore…, in a review of your record, for the past fifteen years, it seems as though you started out as an excellent worker, but the last two years have been straight crappy," the old man utters, thumbing through Winton's thick file until his eyebrows rise, when spotting something that stands out.

"What's that, my admin record?" Winton blurts out sarcastically. "Sir, if we're to continue, can you be so kind as to turn off the television because I can't concentrate," Winton skittishly utters, finding a commercial on the quiet screen.

Young Anderson cuts off the television just when "breaking news" scrolls across the screen.

The ole man stares at Winton, still in deep thought. "No..., not your admin record, but being concerned, I took the liberty to have your police record updated per the contract. Now, I'll be darned if it wasn't sent on disc; now that's a first," the old man says when he chuckles and slams his fist on the table, drawing it back, fast, and shaking off the pain.

They go on for over an hour with the interview and then get quiet, when beginning to recalculate Winton's points.

The short, foreign woman who smells like a light hint of weed, whom Winton despises rattles on about her previous employment, and her story lasts a good while.

Winton's eyes wander over all of the frowned faces that try to comprehend at least one sentence and make sense of it all when Winton bursts into laughter but quickly contains himself. His mind drifts, and his head turns sideways, trying to comprehend and seem professionally interested.

Old man Anderson grows bored and interrupts the woman. "Son, I want to know what's going on in your life to cause these drastic changes because this is a reputable business. We need people who are prompt, honest, and hardworking," the old man utters, with a friendly, reassuring smile when sarcastically looking at the ceiling.

The room grows quiet as the clock's ticking grows louder.

Old Man Anderson sits in deep thought longer. "We are willing to give you a second chance, only if you'll start with points and you know how the point system works, so consider this a six-month evaluation and your very last straw, here."

There comes a knock when the secretary sticks her head inside, motioning Young Anderson over, and he exits quickly. Another knock soon comes, and young Anderson sticks his head inside, motioning his dad out.

The panel anxiously sits, wondering what is going on, until quieting when the door slowly opens.

Winton sits up, proud to have his job back. His shoulders shrug back further and proudly when the owners enter with his paycheck they had on hold and admin papers that Winton has become accustomed to signing.

Old man Anderson eases to the edge of his seat with raised eye browse. "Hmm..., well, there's just one more little thing before we seal this deal," the ole man utters, nodding to young Anderson, who pulls the remote from his back, flipping on the television.

Everyone turns their chairs to get a good view when Winton's soft tapping feet tap faster with sweat instantly shining on his forehead.

A commercial comes to its end with cameras swaying over the mill then the big blaze, with fire trucks rolling onto the scene when the son turns up the volume.

Winton feels a knot in his stomach with more sweat shining until drenched with the top of his shirt wet around the collar and sweat visibly draining down evenly until halfway through the shirt.

The news rerun switches to the news team talking to bystanders and then switches to Winton's face, which is bright red.

The old man pulls out matches, sliding his pipe into his mouth. His jaws tense, listening to all of the nasty things Winton has to say about his family and business.

Winton looks around at everyone's unbelieving frowns, as they stare between the television, Winton, and sweet, little Old Man Anderson, who manages to look even more pitiful until making his eyes droop more.

Winton swallows harder with eyes locked on the hardwood floor, counting floorboards in his mind until distracted, when hearing the old man clear his throat and shakes the matchbox, loudly. "I'm sorry, sir," Winton utters in a pitiful, weak voice.

"Hell..., I know good and darn well you're sorry, son! Tell me something I don't know. Shucks..., you've been sorry all your darn life, more than likely!" the old man mutters, leaning back, even more pissed.

Winton finally gets brazen and looks at Young Anderson and his father, finding them whispering with red faces when looking at the screen hearing Freddy's insulting comments finally coming, about Winton not being able to read.

The room grows even quieter with heavy jumping shoulders while everyone fights, holding back their laughter until they hear and see Freddy trying to get some glasses so Winton can read the OSHA brochure.

Winton looks around, then up into their quiet yet laughing faces when a thunderous roar of laughter breaks out, leaving him feeling minuscule. His eyes cut over to Old Man Anderson, who laughs himself almost out of his chair.

Old Man Anderson soon gets control of his laughter and lights his cigar, firmly holding the burning match while glowering at Winton under-eyed. "You're fired!" he screams, throwing a match at Winton, then match after struck match, until Winton's mind finally catches up and comprehends what is happening.

Instantly, Winton's eyes follow the last match down when finding a match in his pant cuffs, and burning out.

The last match catches Winton's pant cuff again, lighting up the dried cotton as Winton shoots up, dancing around for seconds to put out the fire.

Young Anderson patiently waits then shoves Winton down fast, jumping, and stomping his leg, until intentionally kicking him in the shins until the fire is smoldering.

Across town, in the lottery office, the director allows the lotto machine to warm up. He happens to turn and look out the window and finds Boogey's car speeding toward the building. He keeps a nervous and tight gripped hand on the counter, hesitantly rocking as if about to run when the car slows and comes to a screeching halt.

Boogey jumps out and almost slips until balancing against the door.

The front door flies open, with Boogey rushing inside.

"Mr. Johnson, correct?" the director utters, motioning his assistant out as Boogey makes his way to the counter with his chest stuck out. He smiles, pulling out the ticket and hands it over, pulling his fist to his mouth, slightly biting the knuckle of his index finger in excitement.

The director reaches, slipping the ticket into the machine, and the bells and whistles sound off, unlike before.

Boogey screams, joyfully dancing until behind the counter, waltzing a round or two, in circles, with the director and then his assistant.

They jump around, happy for him, especially knowing about the dirty prank.

Boogey dances until almost out of breath when easing into a lobby seat.

The director leans over the counter, looking for Nattie. "Mr. Johnson, we can start the paperwork now, sir, but we need your wife here as well, for the signing."

"What? You mean she has to be here if I purchased the ticket myself?" Boogey devilishly asks when his mind replays Nattie and Freddy's heated encounter in the house.

"Well..., the law is the law, and we're to abide, sir," the director utters, looking over his shoulder and ensuring that his assistant is in the other office when whispering. "Now, for a healthy fee, I can tell you how to get around sharing if that's your choice," the director utters, winking and twisting his long, wax-tipped mustache.

"How much?" Boogey asks, leaning into the counter; ear-to-lips.

"Let's say ten percent, but that's a small price to pay for a one-hundred-and-fifty-thousand dollar pot of gold, after taxes," the director utters, pulling out his business card with his cell number already scribbled on the back.

"A hundred plus after taxes? I thought I hit the jackpot, dag doggit!" Boogey finally notices the winning display screen for two hundred thousand.

"Not quite, sir. You missed it by one number, though, so you should be proud."

"I'll be damn...! Well, anyway, let me think this through and I'll let you know," Boogey utters, slightly frustrated when signing the back of the ticket. He sticks around longer for proof documents, and then bids him a farewell.

Boogey arrives home late, backing in and sitting a spell, watching the sunset.

Nattie sits in the living room glowering at him through the dusty screen door until finally getting up enough nerve to walk onto the porch.

Boogey glowers at her, and silent tears run down his cheek; then more tears when she walks off the porch, alongside the passenger's side door, unnoticed.

Nattie's tears heavily flow when turning her back to the door, crying harder but quietly.

Boogey wipes his tears, quick and unnoticed, when finding her there.

There is total silence for a long spell until Nattie licks and wipes the last trail of tears.

"Excuse me," Boogey utters, slightly motioning Nattie back when leaning and rolling up the window. He turns off the radio, easing out slowly.

Nattie meets him in front of the car, sticking her hand out and gripping him at the wrist when he snatches away. She bursts into tears, walking behind him until draping over his back when he turns, gently pulling away. "So you gonna (are going to) pull away from me and treat me like this, Boog?" she cries, playing dumb when grabbing him at the waist again and slinging him to one side. "What, you think you better than me now!" she shouts with her voice slightly echoing.

"Screw this! Just go, Natt! Go on with Freddy since you're so in love and have to creep around and sleep with him in our bed and have him in our home. Hell, it's all around town that you've been creeping and sleeping around for quite some time now! So just gone now; let me be!" Boogey shrieks, heavily waving her off with both hands.

Nattie trails closely behind and into the house, crying until pulling on his clothes. "Oh, so you want me to leave, huh? For what, so you can be with ole, stank-butt, Bea? Oh..., you can look down on me, huh, but you ain't got no mess with you, right?" Nattie utters, pushing him deep in the chest.

"Bea?" he utters, intentionally raising one eyebrow and playing dumb.

"Yeah! What..., you didn't think I would find out about your little, stankin', tramp, hoe (whore)?" Nattie utters, putting her finger in his face when he shoves it away.

"Ahh..., that is nothing. Bea just caught me off guard after discovering my wife and her lover bent over the kitchen counter, going at it, butter-ball naked!" he shrieks, walking away.

"That's not what I heard," Nattie utters, finally shoving Boogey deep in the chest with her index finger. "You're no better; you just didn't get caught up!" she utters, watching him turn when shoving him in the back hard when really getting pissed, from him confirming that he was with Bea.

"Look, keep your hands to yourself! I have never put my hands on you, so keep your hands to yourself! I am not going to tell you again!" Boogey yells, pointing a firm index finger in her face.

"Or what? What!" Nattie shrieks, poking him and backing him up while provoking him to hit her, so she does not feel so bad about him knowing.

Boogey draws a backhand high, holding it until trembling.

Nattie instantly draws back, fearful of his aggression, when backing down and falling onto the sofa in tears, with her face torn all up.

Boogey slowly lowers his hand, walking into the kitchen, where he sits glowering until a smile grows when thinking about the winnings.

Nattie soon wanders into the kitchen, and Boogey's smile fades, but he continues fiddling with the toothpick dispenser.

Nattie puts the kettle on the stove, turns the knob to high, and walks to the sink with Boogey nervously watching; thinking she will do something crazy.

Within minutes, the kettle starts to whistle at a high pitch and Bogey sits fidgety longer and then walks to the refrigerator. He pulls out the water jug. "I'll talk to an attorney about a divorce, tomorrow," he utters in deep thought.

"Huh! Over my dead body, dangit!" Nattie shrieks, grabbing the steaming kettle, which immediately quiets. She holds it in her tight grip. "If I can't have you, nobody will," she utters, with the kettle sprung back as if ready to dash it.

Boogey stares into her bloodshot, watery eyes, chuckling until in a stream of teary laughter. "Hell, I would have believed that bull until the other night, but now…, your words are just horse manure!" he utters. "Huh! Seriously…," he says, pointing to the steaming kettle. "I probably wouldn't even feel it as numb as I am right now," Boogey utters doubtfully while still pointing and staring at her uneasy hand.

"Oh really? Hmm…, now I'm curious as to whether we should test that lame, numb theory of yours," Nattie utters with the pot stealthily in motion when she swings it away to shift the flow of fluids and not spill a drop.

Boogey instantly yelps, when cringing and trembling in a low, trailing moan with anticipated pain with hands rubbing over his body quickly as if to brush hot water off fast until realizing that she's called his bluff.

Nattie falls back into a deep laugh, making him look stupid when he looks down, trying to proudly stick his chest out and play tough.

Her distasteful words continually fly out until Boogey staggers into the living room with her following.

Later, around 10:30 PM, Boogey's eyes excitedly drift between the phone, clock, and television as he waits for his routine call, and like clockwork, Winton calls. He lets the phone ring a time or two then takes his time getting up. "Yellow (Hello)?"

"Sup, Boogey?"

"Oh, nothing Wint, just taking it easy, but hey; will they let you come back?"

"Nothing final, and if bad news, I will have to break down and tell Nelle. Huh..., I can hear her mouth, now," Winton utters, swallowing hard when lying about still being on the contract.

"So, what's your backup plan?"

"Any ole job will do, but I'm thinking one of those high, top-paying IT jobs."

"You say and I..., what?" Boogey asks in deep thought.

"IT..., Intro Techniligical (Technological)," Winton boldly utters.

"Man, have you lost what little brain you had? Hell..., you can't even spell IT, more or less, pronounce it or work on it."

"Oh, ye of little faith," Winton skittishly responds.

"Little what..., faith? Man, you need to get off those cheap drugs because you must done (have) lost your mind up in here if you think for one minute that you can go into IT. Hell! You don't even have a certificate saying you can even cut on a computer, more or less operate or run one," Boogey utters, senselessly giggling and straightening his face when Nattie looks back at him in a mean stare.

"Well, I can get a certificate from a neighbor and alter it with this new editing software he's been bragging about. He said he could hook up the credentials, and give thirty minute of training, just enough skills to get in the door, for fifty bucks," Winton utters with a serious face.

Boogey's shoulders heavily jump up and down in silence, and out of nowhere, he bursts into the craziest laugh ever with alternating sounds that even have Nattie silently chuckling. "Yeah, he'll get you through the front door alright, and they'll throw your stupid butt out the back door and on top of that big, fat head," Boogey utters, laughing even louder and quieting when seeing Nattie staring over at him then off fast with heavy jerking shoulders.

"You'll see, Boog! Stop hating..., and don't get jealous when I'm making top dollar..., one hundred big ones a year, dawg! Don't hold out your hand, ah (and) beg for nothing, not even a ticket."

"Oh, Yeah? Well, don't be ashamed to come and tell me you made a plumb fool of yourself," Boogey hesitantly utters, taking a deep breath when Nattie passes, heading for the kitchen. "And on the other hand, actually, I won't need to beg because I hit the biggon (big one), dawg!" Boogey whispers, looking over his shoulder to ensure Nattie is not eavesdropping when looking for her shadow.

"In your dreams," Winton utters, laughing while sitting and pulling a boot off.

"Ok, then watch the late-night news, dude; we hit and after taxes about a hundred-fifty," Boogey says when the phone clicks off before he can say a thousand.

Winton immediately calls Boogey back while walking into the bedroom, nervously looking over at Nelle.

Boogey clicks the receiver and gets nothing.

"What is it, Winton?" Nelle asks, looking at his stale, blush face and then quickly back at the television.

"Hey..., Boogey said they hit for a hundred million," Winton utters in a slow, shocked voice.

"Yeah..., right..., they wish." Nelle laughs, nervously flipping through more channels.

Boogey flips to the news, which broadcasts the lottery but the biggest only. He gets comfortable, pulls out his wallet, and sits looking at the non-winning numbers, shaking his head after each number drops in the display window after being called by the sponsor.

Nattie eases into her chair without him knowing, watching him cringe while balling paper tightly and shoving it deep in his coverall pocket, when giggling and rolling her eyes. "Dang fool! You 'bout the dumbest dodo bird I know; spend all your hard-earned money on that crazy lottery," she utters, laughing loudly to degrade him more.

"Yeah, but if I hit, what would you do? Spend your share on getting Freddy out of that chicken suit, probably?" Boogey vengefully responds, glowering over at her.

"Forget a Freddy; I would still be with my husband and take care of my family, but what's the use of dreaming? Heck, you've been dreaming since we met. If I had the lotto money you threw away, we would be rich already," she says, sarcastically.

"Woman, you 'bout as crazy than a damn bedbug! Ain't no way you can be rich off that little money I done (I've) played! Well, anyway, it's good for the Soul to dream because you just never know. It's just less thinking to do later," Boogey utters, smiling when looking back at the television.

The room grows quiet until Nattie's heavy breathing kicks in, followed by light then heavy breathing until heavily snoring.

Boogey quietly stands, accidentally dropping the remote, and startling her.

Nattie sits, looks around then yawns before pulling herself together and walking into the bedroom. She showers and, afterward, climbs into bed.

Boogey remains in the living room watching a game show then flips through channels, adjusting the volume when Nattie begins sounding like she's sawing trees.

Friday morning, a few minutes after midnight, Boogey leans forward, turning the television's volume up, just as he spots bright lights shining upon the house. He swiftly turns the volume down, easing his hands on his rifle, while slightly pulling the curtains back. He stares longer, finally recognizing Milton Wiggins's hood ornament then Milton when he jumps out limping until running up on the porch.

Boogey shoves the gun in the corner, reaching for the remote, adjusting the volume up and then quietly makes his way to the door. "Sup, Milt?" Boogey asks, slowly opening the screen door and easing it shut while stepping onto the porch.

"Sup, Boogey? What have you been up to lately, man? I haven't seen you in shoot..., what..., months if not more? Look..., do you need to be tapped off wit (with) some moonshine? I got a whole truckload that I need to deliver, but I can tap off your drum for a little of nothing later."

"Aight, later, but I need to have the drum checked for a leak because ain't no way I've drunk that much in that little time," Boogey utters, scratching his head in deep thought.

"It doesn't make no, never mind, man. I'll still top you off at fifty percent off, until you get it patched, if you make this run with me over to LeeLeeville, tonight," Milton utters when staring back at the neatly loaded, squared off, covered truck.

"Whatttt? For real?" Boogey looks back then into Milt's bucked, white eyes.

"Yeah, man, my shotgun partner got caught up in some mess with that crooked tail sheriff the other night; something about walking out of jail, unauthorized. Now how in the heck do you just walk up out of jail..., but that beats me. So look, anyway, I need a second set of eyes," Milton utters, looking back toward the main road when hearing an eighteen-wheeler's horn blare twice.

"Man, I don't know..., Nattie already turned in for the night, so I had better call it a night as well," Boogey utters, rubbing his belly and scratching his head.

"Come on, Boog! It ain't gonna (going to) take but a few hours. Shucks, I'll have you back way before Natt even knows you're gone, I reckon. Aight, look it..., there's some money in it for you as well, and I know you can use some extra lottery money," Milton utters when Boogey lights up with a smile.

"Well, you do drive a hard bargain dea (there), Mr. Milt; you surely do, sir!" Boogey jokingly utters in an imitated voice, looking over his shoulder for Nattie.

"You…, you…, you…; jive-tail, sucker! I knew you wanted to go all along! You were just holding out until the stakes got higher," Milton mutters, shaking his head in laughter.

Boogey slips inside, seizing his jacket and cap. He steps into the bedroom, pulling his pistol from the closet, then tiptoes into the living room, dropping in the seat, and tying his boots. He makes his way quietly to the door, locking the deadbolt.

They mount up in the old, model-T converted truck, which looks souped-up.

Milton operates a makeshift panel on the dash, refreshing Boogey's memory on which deceptive lighting buttons to work.

They climb out, walking from the front to back, making sure the decoy lights properly work when Milton cranks up, and pulls away, slowly.

Milton comes alongside Boogey's house, cutting through a path in the cornfield, taking various roads to avoid the law. He takes his time, working the CB and police scanner at each junction they approach, as professionally accustomed.

They reach the LeeLeeville's city limit thirty minutes later, when Milton brings the truck to a slow creep when passing a little vacant, rundown house alongside the road. Milton stops, throwing the truck in reverse, looking over his shoulder while backing alongside the house. He cuts out the lights, and they sit looking and listening to the crisp, tuned-in CB and scanner for minutes.

Twenty minutes past and a loud duck call come with Boogey nervously ducking and shuffling for his weapons.

"What the hell…?" They whisper, simultaneously.

Milton leans on Boogey's kneecap for the glove compartment while Boogey leans hard in the corner, looking around and in the side mirror.

A Donald Duck character's voice comes.

"What the…?" Boogey says with fast scanning eyes peeled back then into the mirror with Milt aimlessly looking around.

They hear a mild chuckle along with other playful, looney tunes voices and then there's silence and other weird sounds rushing in, and causing them to tense.

There is more silence until the sounds come again but sound more distant when fading off in a whisper.

"Damn! What the hell was that? What the hell are we sitting here for, main (man)? I thought you just had to make a drop and then head back," Boogey skittishly utters, staring over into Milton's scary, white eyes.

"I know…, right, but this is a big shipment for a prominent businessman," Milton utters, slipping his gun in his holster when Boogey grips his even tighter, holding it out the window with his elbow pressed tightly against the side of the door.

They sit longer, listening closely to more strange, loud, unfamiliar, and distant sounds that soon tapper off with loud crickets cheering up.

Out of nowhere, two shotgun barrels unknowingly ease up to the back of Boogey and Milton's heads, simultaneously.

The weird faced, masked men ease forward with guns pointing in a more direct aim when crunchy leaves lightly grow in everyone's ears.

Milt's hands shoots to his holster, and Boogey hands tense.

"Ott, ott, ott! You ladies don't want that bad luck on yah (you)?" the tall man utters, coming in view when shoving the barrel deep in Milt's cheek.

A gun barrel presses deep in the side of Boogey's cheek, almost making him look like he's smiling on one side.

"One wrong move, ladies, and we'll blow your sweet bottoms to smithereens!" The tall man eases the barrel slightly under Milt's chin. "As a matter of fact, you can just throw those firearms out, slowly." The tall man spits out the wad of tobacco through the small, stitched mouth opening, slightly smearing it over the white mask and his shirt.

Boogey and Milt lean slowly away from each other as directed with guns hitting the tall grass when the door flies open on the driver's side.

"Out and on your knees…, my Sweet Baby!" the tall man shrieks, kicking Milt's gun further away and into deeper grass.

The short, stocky-built man motions Boogey out at gunpoint.

Boogey eases one leg out, unbalanced, when the short man slings him around with a fast, almost invisible leg out, tripping Boogey face first to the fresh cut ground.

The tall man shoves Milt to the passenger side, sticking out his foot, tripping Milt over Boogey's body and dropping him on the soft, wet grass.

"Watch 'em (them) while I see what these here boys brought us, tonight" the tall, slender man, Skeeter utters, slinging his shotgun over his shoulder by the frail, worn down leather strap. He steps up on the indented foot ledge, popping strings from the tarp with a sharp knife, throwing back the canvas fast with excited eyes and a big smile.

"Well, I'll be! I'll be a monkey's uncle, sitting next to the uncle and the other money's uncle! Woo…, wee! I think we done (just) hit the mother load tonight, boy!" bucked-tooth Skeeter yells, smiling then spitting another wad of tobacco juice out, when smearing the mask more while his partner, Junior, keeps the gun on them with eyes frequently glaring over at the fully stocked truck.

"We are set for a long time, Skeeter," the short guy utters, smiling until finding Boogey's fat hand reaching slowly for his gun. "You looking for this hea (here), boy?" Junior utter showing Boogey the shiny gun under the moonlight when moving his big, worn-down, boot back. "One more stunt like that boy, and I'll have you out here polishing my monkey with those pretty lips!" Junior shrieks, rubbing his busted, zippered inseam until zipping it up and down really fast until halfway off the track.

Boogey's eyes grow wide and stale fast when swallowing hard.

Junior takes a step over to Skeeter, who has his eyes on Milt and Boogey, and they discuss what they will do with them when Junior smiles, overly-whispering of hog-tying and sodomizing them; causing Boogey and Milt to swallow hard with teary, bucked eyes. Junior takes steps toward Boogey with sensual eyes roving from head to toe. "Maybe a little deliverance tonight..., my Sweet, Little Darlings," he says in a girlish tone when reaching to caress Boogey's face when Boogey snatches away. "Maybe a little tuning of those sweet, little vocals will mellow you out."

Boogey shivers intensely to shake off the gross gesture when looking off mean and as if ignoring Junior.

A quick cocking of sawed-off shotguns rings out with Skeeter and Junior freezing while staring eye-to-eye with arms going high, slowly.

One gun is snatched away and the other cut away from Skeeter's back with a sharp blade when snatched.

"On your faces..., ladies!" Two tall, mean men dressed in expensive-looking Sekif suits utters.

Sketter and Junior tremble, easing to their knees and then scary faces and whiney voices.

"Milt!" one of the tall men utters.

Boogey and Milt roll over with their faces and perms covered in grass blades.

Boogey spits out fresh-cut grass, brushing off his face and then hair while sitting up.

"Ahh!" Boogey screams when a fist hits him square in the back of his collar, with the tallest men pulling Boogey up slightly and unintentionally gagging him.

Milt is pulled up seconds later, dusting off his clean threads.

"Sorry we're late, buddy, but the boss had an emergency with his kid," one of the tall guys utters, directing them to the edge of the dark road.

A new, shiny Rolls Royce slowly pulls up with the back window slowly lowering with smoke heavily billowing out.

Boogey squints, trying to make out the man in the back, in the cut, through the thick electronic generated smoke.

"Evening Milt!" the commanding voice resonates.

"Yessum (Yes sir), boss..., got the load just like you asked, boss!" Milt utters, leaning and looking into the gapped, tinted windows.

"Great..., follow us, and we'll get you unloaded quickly, fellas. I have a few guys at the club who can expedite getting you out of here, fast," the mob boss utters. "The car back there will follow you from a distance, and if there's trouble, just pull over and keep your head down low while he handles the situation," the boss utters, pointing back down the even darker road and toward a dim street light.

Milt squints, finding a cop's cruiser in the cut, when a hand lifts from the window, saluting. "Sure thing, boss..., got it, boss!" Milt utters, shaking the boss' hand when the window lowers when receiving the thick envelope, and tucking it in his back pocket.

"Hey, boss..., what do you want to do with these two goons?" one of the tall men asks, looking back at the two men who are still lying face down, whispering and still whining.

"Count to ten, and if they're still around, blast the hell out of em'!" the boss utters in a mobster tone when taking another hit off a Columbian cigar.

The tall, clean-shaven man walks over, whispering to his partner, then walks over into the grass. "Ok ladies, here is the deal..., ten..., nine...!"

When the tall man gets to eight, Skeeter turns back for his partner, who is slow on the uptake and doesn't get it. The tall, clean-shaven man gets to four, and the two countrymen are in full stride, digging boots deep, and kicking up dirt and dust.

The other tall man, who is bearded unloads real buckshot, and loads salt buckshot when handing a few to the tall, clean-shaven man, who slips them in his pocket, retrieving his favorite choice of weapon when the shotgun and AK loudly click.

'Blam! Kiya! Kiya! Kiya! Blam! Kiya! Kiya! Kiya! Blam! Kiya! Kiya! Kiya!' the guns repeatedly sound off, non-stop with smoke filling the air.

"Ouch! Ouuuch!" Junior shrieks, turning and cutting around a bend at the end of the cornfield.

Skeeter tears through eight-foot corn stalks at top speed, and like nobody's business with his head thrown back and his boots kicking his butt with mud on his back and head.

The two gunmen finally cease shooting and stand covered in a thick smoke cloud that slowly drifts into them then passes, slowly covering giggling Boogey and Milton with the two mob men soon laughing.

Later, over at the club, the mob boss has them unloaded as promised and the police car follows them to the city limits, turning under a bright streetlight.

Within minutes, Boogey and Milt are deep in laughs and jokes. They get a good laugh out of each other concerning the near robbery, sodomy, and how they were acting when the goons had guns on them. The laughter grows louder when Milt brings up the sodomy again, which throws Boogey into a crazy uncontrollable laugh when he brings up the way Milt kissed up to the mob boss, like an old slave hand.

Before long, Milton leans forward, and the radio rocks with them, doing their best at seat dancing.

They come up on a four-way and Milt veers off before the four-way, cutting through a path, still an hour from Boogey's house.

"What the heck now, Milt?"

"Oh, I thought I told you I had a pickup as well," Milton utters, cutting his big white eyes and smiley face over at Boogey's not so friendly stare.

"How long will this take, man? You said I'd be back before Nattie realizes that I was gone. Damn main (man), you lie like a doggone rug!" Boogey shrieks over the music with a frown.

Milt slows, leaning in the glove box, handing Boogey a hundred-dollar bill.

"Hot diggety dog! Now you're talking my kind of music!" Boogey screams, tapping his feet and bobbing to the music while turning up the volume. Boogey soon sees a lottery sign lit up in a window when they come over a hill and pats Milt on the shoulder, pointing. "Here, here! It will only take a minute!" Boogey yells, gazing back into Milt's white eyes as the truck slows then swerves off the road.

"Man, hurry the hell up! I got to get down to this place before they start running the next batch, or it'll take all morning to get loaded!" Milt utters, looking at his watch and then back at Boogey rushing up to the front door.

Boogey flings the door open, finding an Arab man with a turban staring back while speaking in Arabic on his cellular phone. "Yes, one..., Powerrrrrball..., one..., Meeegggaaa..., Millionnnnn," Boogey utters in a slow, long, drawn-out speech. One..., Powerrrrrball..., one..., Meeegggaa..., Millionnnnn," Boogey utters again, but even louder and slower.

The Arab man slows his fast-chewing toothpick and sucks his teeth in slightly while shaking his head. "Hey... where you from, man?" the Arab asks in very clear English, still shaking his head and laughing.

Boogey looks dumbfounded, pointing at him with his index finger and laughing while throwing the money on the counter when they go into greater laugh.

Boogey rushes, jumping inside, leaning to slip the ticket in his wallet.

Milt drives for about twenty minutes or so and comes up on a little house where a man runs out to meet them.

The man turns and walks in front of the truck through a path that ends at a fence guarded by two men who come out of nowhere through tall weeds with guns drawn.

Milt waits for the gate to open, then nervously nods when passing.

Boogey's eyes wander all over the place until looking through the side mirror, finding the electronic gate shutting slowly.

Milt heads for a building that looks like a small oil refinery, pulling up alongside and coming up on the backside, backing into the low-cut loading dock. "This will only take a minute," Milt utters, looking at his watch and then over at Boogey while pulling out the envelope, counting off dollars from a thick wad of bills.

A big, tall man rolls the first cart of shine out, then other men start rolling cases out, and within forty minutes, they are fully loaded.

"See, like clockwork! I told you it wouldn't take long," Milt utters, standing outside the truck, watching one man neatly cover the booze and tightly strap it down then back away when Milt climbs in, waiting for the signal to move the truck.

The drive back is quiet and relaxed when Boogey and Milt are crossing Mundson's city limits. They continually creep, about to cross into another county when Milton's eyes drift to the speedometer, realizing he's speeding.

Out of nowhere, blue lights light up, like a Christmas extravaganza; reflecting off a long line of trees and street signs.

"What the…?" Milt screams, looking over his shoulder and then through the side mirror when the cruiser pulls up on his bumper and the loud PA system keys up.

"Pull over!" the deputy yells, rising and pretending to be looking at the taillights.

"Oh, damn, Milt! What we gone do?" Boogey anxiously says in a trembling voice. "What we gone do! What we gone do?" Boogey nervously asks again, in tears.

"Oh, hush up with that racket, numb nuts, before you give us away! Hell…, I get stopped all the time; besides, they have to have probable cause to search," Milt utters, looking at the deputy who is walking up, shining a light over the truck's sleek body and neatly canvased covered bed.

"Evening, gentlemen, license and registration, please," the deputy politely utters, looking over the tight straps, and illegally plucking one with a tightly gripped index finger, hoping it would unravel when Milt jumps, cutting his eyes back.

Milt's gazes through the wide side-view mirror, cautiously following the officer's hands again when he makes another illegal attempt to pop the string.

"Can I ask why you stopped me, officer?" Milt asks, reaching into the glove compartment when the officer shines the light inside the cab and into their faces.

"Your tail light is out, and you were just starting to come up over the limit until I stopped you," the deputy utters, secretly reaching in his pocket, pulling out a pocketknife and easing it open until it clicks.

Milt jumps at the sound of the blade, looking toward the officer when the flashlight goes out, and the truck becomes well illuminated by moonlight. He eases up against the seat, fumbling in his wallet, hearing the spring-loaded canvas strap snap; tearing open the canvas. Milton's eyes shoot to the side mirror, seeing the glistening knife blade.

The deputy expressly flips the canvas back with a foot on the step, coming up high with excited eyes. "You dirty son of a gun!" he yells, cross-eyed when the engine shrieks with the truck heavily swaying to one side with one tire burning rubber on asphalt and the deputy in a tail spin.

The deputy screams still twirling when falling against the asphalt, fighting to put the knife away. He pulls out his gun, nippily crawling to his feet seeing the brake lights come on at the intersection when steadily aiming and firing two shots. He runs at top speed with a slight limp to his cruiser, jumping inside and burning rubber while reaching for his walkie-talkie, radioing for help.

Boogey's eyes buck and move all over the road while bouncing around, rapidly piercing his eyes behind when a speck of blue lights appears from a distance.

The chase on the main stretch is a good ten-mile run when Milt slows down.

"More speed…, more speed! This ain't the time to be slowing down, Bubba!" Boogey screams, seeing the cruiser gaining like a cruise missile.

Milt keeps his eyes on the cruiser, speeding up a little until slowing when coming into a veering into the steep curve with blue lights vanishing. He slows faster, coming to a dead stop when timing, then flipping light switches so the taillights look like headlights and the front end looks like the tail end. Milt swiftly drifts into the other lane and slows again, cutting on the bright flood lights and then lowering them.

The deputy sees the light appear in the curve when coming to top speed but not overdoing it, knowing a sharp curve is ahead. He slows, seeing headlights then swerves, avoiding what he thinks is an oncoming car, instantly seeing it's a truck when holding the wheel tightly yet swerving hard to keep from going off the road when blinded by the instant, bright floodlights. The deputy sits adjusting his eyes when flooring the gas pedal, bringing the cruiser up to eighty miles per hour.

Milt switches lanes when spotting bright, oncoming lights ahead.

The officer ascends a steep hill, looking back and finding the lights switching back over when both feet go to the brake and the cruiser skids slightly off the road.

The tires stop then spin around fast in the opposite direction, kicking up dirt, gravel, and grass as the car sways back onto the road.

The deputy hits the straightway, killing his lights when noticing the truck's lights have reversed again by accident while Boogey is checking as another car passes.

The deputy closes in on the truck within minutes as if he never lost sight of it, pulling right up on the bumper when hitting the siren and so close that it looks like the blue lights are mounted in the truck's bed.

Boogey screams with hands pressed hard on the dashboard when Milt reaches under the seat, pulling out a nitrogen bottle. "Here, screw that in that hole, right there in the middle of the dash," Milt utters, slowing when speeding up.

A shot rings out, shattering the truck's back window, and they duck.

"Here! Here! Turn here and hit the city line. He can't follow you into another jurisdiction," Boogey yells staying low, and still fumbling around to match the bottle's treads.

"What the hell are you doing, Boog? I need that nitrogen now, not next week, man!" Milt shrieks, looking out the side view, finding the deputy aiming the twelve gauge out the window when Milt begins swerving then zigzagging to throw off any unexpected shots.

The nitrogen seats in the chamber, and Boogey slaps the securing strap down when the transition throttle sounds off, becoming sweet music to Milt's ears.

"Sweet babe, baabbeee!" Milt sings with a big smile, sounding like a famous rapper when leaning forward, pressing the pedal to the floor, and bringing the needle to eighty, and then slowing down in a curve. His hand eases over the activation switch, patiently waiting until the straightway before flipping it up, pulling away from the cruiser as if it were standing still.

Instantly, fire flashes out of both exhausts pipes turning them fiery red when Milt flips the switch again.

"Almost there! One more mile, and he'll have to stop," Boogey shrieks with a big smile and sigh of relief when looking back at the last city limit sign fly by; almost invisible.

They stare into the rear and side views, waiting for the deputy to slow down or stop, but he blows through the sign as if it isn't even there.

Milt looks for the scanner, finally pulling it from under his jacket lying in the seat. "Here… turn up the volume of the scanner! There has to be some reason why he's still following!" Milt shrieks, looking back at the dim-looking blue light as the car fades.

They are within half a mile of the next curve when they pick up speed and hear a deputy screech over the scanner, sounding like he's crying.

"Free at last, free at last!" Milt screams, swerving around the sharp, pitch-black curve when the road lights up with twenty cruisers and the road completely covered with blue flashing lights.

The unfamiliar-looking, short, mean sheriff of that county stands out front with both guns pointing straight ahead; biting down on his cigar with an even meaner frown.

"Ahii…!" Boogey and Milt shriek, looking aimlessly at one another with bright, white eyes while the truck barrels forward, faster.

"Light 'em (them) up, boys!" the mean sheriff yells over the loud PA when more blue lights light up along the shoulder with the barrier, double-stacked by cruisers.

Milt concentrates on the solid, yellow line until seeing a break, cutting the wheel hard when flying through a wide, rocky driveway leading into a huge cornfield.

Milt and Boogey yell at the top of their lungs, blinded by large tobacco leaves.

"Ugh, ugh, ugh!" the sheriff shrieks, running wide-legged for his cruiser while other cruisers fly past, dismantling the barrier as they head for the field's entrance.

Several cars make the turn, but a couple turns too early or too late, flipping in the deep trench.

Boogey's head hangs out the window, looking back then ahead with wet leaves slapping his sweaty face, turning it dark brown until he focuses on a windmill ahead when navigating Milt to a back road he has been familiar with since he was a kid.

Cop cars run all through the field, and two cars meet head-on, and crash. The remaining four cars increase their speed. The cruisers are hot on each other's trail when the deputy in the lead swerves, thinking he sees a man walking, then running, when the other two cars keep straight, with the lead car running into a tree.

Boogey's eyes fill with excitement when noticing they are close to the main road.

Several other cruiser turn away, barreling down to the cut over where they turn to find detour signs and turn anyway from the direction arrows. They barrel forward, at high speed, until a mile down the closed road when finding the road blocked with yellow machinery. They veer off road and continue forward, ignoring all warning signs, even the one with the bridge being removed for new construction when pressing forward and faster.

The four cars stay back to back then two by two, swerving around signs and equipment until airborne, with all mouths wide open in screams until splashing into the water and sinking fast.

The last cruiser burns rubber, coming to a screeching halt with the deputy staring at the other side of the road for seconds. Without warning, he floors it, dropping the needle from the dash when the cruiser veers hard, dodging signs and other equipment until heading for the dirt mound. The cruiser dips then shoots straight up and high with the officer screaming in victory as his eyes drift down then back clearing land and hollering 'land-ho'. His eyes slowly drift forward when slamming into the replacement bridge with the car bursting into flames.

"Here, here..., slow down..., slow down! Make this sharp turn, now, now, now!" Boogey shrieks, anxiously pointing when the truck comes about swiftly with tires riding inches from the edge of the deep reservoir.

The sheriff closes in on the two remaining cars, tearing down more leaves when shooting past and taking the lead. He increases speed in excess of eighty miles per hour, clearing the cornfield and coming up on a hill. The sheriff turns hard, running into a stack of hay, and the other two cars shoot ten feet, side-by-side upward; the four deputies squawking as if in slow motion while descending into the reservoir with loud splashes and high water swells seconds later.

The sheriff spins his wheels, rocking until freeing the car then pulls up to the reservoir, watching the deputies swim to the side. He turns off his lights, jumps out, and stands, shaking his head, pissed. The sheriff looks around, discovering Milt's truck making the farm's main gate and exiting onto the highway when stomping and slamming his hat to the ground. "You two have to be the stupidest chumps I know!" the sheriff screams, looking at them climbing out, slowly. "How the hell didn't you know that the reservoir was here? Dangait, I break right, you break right, but noooo...! You turkey were gonna (going to) do what, try and jump the damn reservoir?" the sheriff utters, picking up his hat and dancing around, pissed, before throwing his ten-gallon hat to the ground again, stomping on it.

"Heck, Sheriff P, I thought we could make it!" one country-talking deputy shrieks, looking back at how close they were to the other side.

"Well, the only thing that counts when it comes to close is damn horseshoes and hand grenades, and you have neither!" the sheriff utters with his hands on his hip.

Out of nowhere, a mild tractor engine grows louder.

The sheriff reaches down, pulling the first deputy up the steep embankment.

The tractor drives closer and then pulls alongside a dirt intersection. The driver jumps out with a high-powered rifle, staring at the white lights shining from the sheriff's headlights when finding men messing around in the reservoir. He takes a steady aim, firing off a round, blowing out a headlight.

The sheriff and the deputies drop to the ground or along the bank, staying low when another headlight bursts.

The men in the reservoir hug the side closer, screaming that they are the law.

The sheriff and the other two draw weapons, firing in the air when the sheriff's windshield shatters. "Hold your fire! Hold your fire!" the sheriff shrieks, low-crawling to his hat, waving it when another bullet pierces through the windshield.

A short deputy low-crawls to the sheriff's car fast, flipping on the blue lights.

The gunfire ceases, and there is total silence for minutes when a door slams loudly and the tractor's engine revs up until bright, tractor overhead lights shine along the road as the driver makes his way around the dirt trail.

"Help!" One deputy shrieks, sliding down the steep slope until a deputy rushes over, giving them a hand.

The tractor makes one last turn, and bright lights light up the side of the sheriff's car.

The sheriff and another deputy shield their faces with wet, wrinkled ten-gallon-cowboy hats slightly leaned back on their heads.

The tractor slows, and the bright overhead lights go out with the regular headlights on when the driver stops, swings the door open, and stands at the fender. "What in the name of Jed Tuckett are you doing out here this time of the morning?" the mean, heavyset man yells over the idled engine, until reaching inside to cut it off.

"Evening, Billy! Sorry to have to come to the reservoir..., yada, yada, yada! Any damages the city will settle, but hoodlums run amuck through here, and we were in hot pursuit until losing them."

"Losing them?" Billy hee-haws. "Lost my butt!" He looks over the reservoir and sees the tips of two cruisers' blue lights sticking out and spits out a thick wad of tobacco, with spit rubbed into his chin and shirt sleeve. His hand slides into his back pocket, pulling out a can of tobacco when packing more tobacco in his jaws, climbing down. "I guess you gonna want their cars pulled out, huh?" Billy utters, walking up and looking at Sheriff Preston and then the drenched, muddy deputies.

"I've always said you were about as sharp as a bowling ball, Billy, and I'll be damn if you don't confirm that theory every time we talk," Sheriff Preston utters, shaking his head in disbelief. "Look here! You pull their cars out later in the morning, and I'll send ole' Kooter down with the flatbed to pick em' (them) up."

Billy holds a hand out for money, and the sheriff slaps his palm, walking off. "You'll get your costs at the treasurer's office when you come to town. I'll submit the claim when you call in the bill and keep it reasonable," the sheriff says, smiling.

Boogey and Milt slow down when a quarter-mile from Boogey's house and Boogey suddenly motions for him to slow down more and turn down a side road up ahead.

"Where dis here (does this) road lead to, Boog?" Milt asks, looking over at Boogey with white eyes shining from the dashboard lights.

"Just turn here..., this road will bring us up behind my neighbor's farm," Boogey utters, motioning for him to slow down some more.

Milt pulls up in Boogey's backyard, swerves around the outhouse, and comes around Boogey's car alongside the house.

Boogey climbs out, easing the door shut while looking over his shoulder at the dark house. "It's been fun, Milt, but I ain't never..., and I mean never stepping foot back in this hea (here) truck..., main (man), ever! You hear me, Jack!" Boogey skittishly says, giggling while holding out his hand for more money. "Pay me like you owe me, chump!"

Milt counts off a few twenties. "Ah, man, this is a daily run-of-the-mill for me, Boog. Man, I miss my partner," Milt utters, inching up and slowly pulling away.

Boogey gazes over the house and then out the windows for any indication as to whether Nattie is up. He holds his watch to his face, tapping the face to see if it works, then creeps onto the porch, working the key around until opening the door.

Hours later, and before the rooster crows, Boogey eases out of bed and into the kitchen, pulling a mug from the cupboard. He heads out the back door and walks alongside the house, filling it with cool moonshine. He glows, going into the greatest mood after the first shot, then stands, looking around, happy to have made it home safely. He takes another hit, slowly sipping, then looks off into space, taking the last swig before heading inside to prepare breakfast, something he has done only once before when hitting the lottery for eighty dollars.

There is a minuscule crack in the bedroom door at Winton's house when Winton eases it open, slipping out with his clothes in hand and rushing to the living room, to dress. He opens the front door, staring into the heavy fog until he hears a loud slap and roll sound, then shortly thereafter another slap. He eases the door shut, peeking through the window, focusing on the bicycle, then the newspaper boy, until he passes. He inches the door open, cutting his eyes over at the neighbor's house, then eases out, reaching for the damp pillow on the porch's couch. Winton sprints into his neighbor's yard, throwing the pillow over the paper and picking it up.

Instantly, the neighbor's porch light comes on, and the door slowly creeps open when the old lady curiously peeking out. "Hmm…, Monin (Morning), Wint! Hmm…, have you seen my paper?" she nastily asks, creeping onto the porch, and looking around a few bushes.

"Nu…, nu…, no ma'am, Ms. Yongtu," Winton utters, pushing the pillow tighter to his chest and backing away.

"Hmm…, well, what your sorry tail doing in my yard this time of the morning, anyway?" She raises a curious eyebrow and squint her even more curious eyes.

"Uh, uh, uh…, the kids left this here pillow in your yard, so I decided to get it because I know you don't like things in your yard, Ms. Yongtu," Winton utters, loosening the grip when hearing the paper's plastic covering crinkle a little.

"Yeah…, well, not just the pillow, because one of those things just happens to be your sorry tail too, Wint, so get your tail to steppin', and don't step on my freakin' flowers, or I'll smoke your ole raggedy tail! Lemme (let me) find out you had something to do with my paper coming up missing," Ms. Yongtu utters, sticking her hand deep in her robe pocket when Winton backs up and almost falls backward.

Winton keeps an eye on her until she fades into the yard and around a bush when rushing inside and glimpsing back out when hearing her chamber a quick round. He throws the dewy, damp pillow to the floor, rushing to the kitchen table and spreading the paper open. Winton's eyes glance over the classified ads, the job section.

His fingers run over minuscule ads, stumbling across big words that he tries to pronounce, then bigger and bigger ads with banners for walk-in IT hires. Winton spots a shadow against the wall and throws the paper to the floor, finding the top of Ms. Yongtu's head at the edge of his window seal then her beady eyes peeking inside when quickly lifts the youngest child's coloring book and pretends to be reading.

"Ugh…, in there pretending to be reading when everyone knows you can't read a lick, sucker! Let me find out that my paper is in there, Wint! We gone (will) be doing some one-on-one remodeling up in that mother…," she mumbles just enough for him to have to strain to hear her when cutting his eyes back at the window.

# CHAPTER NINE

### The Shakers, Makers And Takers

At Boogey and Nattie's, Nattie awakens to pans rattling, instantly smelling until hearing sausage frying. She slightly lifts from the pillow then lies in pleasant thoughts, getting her mind off the argument when shaking her curious head.

Boogey begins whistling until lightly singing something accustomed to the few times he has cooked.

Nattie sits, resting on elbows when wondering what has gotten into him, to have his demeanor suddenly changed.

Boogey pulls out a plastic serving tray, drunkenly stumbling into the table when lifting a Styrofoam plate and stepping off slowly, and stumbling a few times.

Nattie finally hears him coming and sits with a curious stare, and then smile when the door eases opens. "Well…, well…, well…; to what do I owe this bedside service?" she asks.

"Oh…, it's nothing! Well hell.., it's the least I can do for my soon-to-be-ex." Boogey exclaims, beaming in a slurred speech. He turns, easing the door shut, and then stumbles on an unleveled floorboard, accidentally falling forward with food all over her. He springs up quickly, lifting her maple syrup, covered, sticky hair in fear.

"You…, you…, you…! You're 'bout (about) the clumsiest man…! Heck, you're clumsier than your simple-tail mama!" Nattie shrills, pushing him off when he drops down, and she begins wiping the sticky residue away with hands then the sheets, until finally springing from the bed.

Boogey stays low, watching her with amused, drunken eyes until she fades into the bathroom and slams the door shut.

Boogey grabs the bedspread, springing up, when drunkenly stumbling with feet stuck in the covers when wind-milling until spinning. He fights to get free then stands, slightly swaying until grabbing the side of the wall, balancing when hearing the bathroom knob jiggle a few times and then fly open.

Nattie rushes up to him with her hand held tight behind her back until something black and yellow flashes and draws back fast, when the plunger mushes and instantly seals over his face. "I'll teach you to drop crap on me!" Nattie shouts, pulling and pushing on the plunger with great force until slinging him around fast and with heavy jerks.

Boogey continually mumbles until grasping the base, pulling hard to get it loose when rocking, sucking in, and sealing it tighter with each deep inhale.

Nattie furiously slings his around more, pushing hard each time she finds the indentation in the rubber vanish; creating a tighter seal when backing up fast. She slings the door open with one hand and drags Boogey out and through the living room, quickly.

Boogey drunkenly stumbles to his knees a few times coming up fast and breaking his stride when Nattie pulls even harder until his boots are sliding across the gritty floor. He reaches for the door frame, with quick short breaths, fighting hard to disconnect when bracing the kitchen doorframe again. Boogey's hands go down and up fast, trying to get the plunger off while slowly sliding into the kitchen with full resistance.

Nattie furiously shakes the plunger, and then slings him to one side; pulling hard again, until looking up to find crocodile tears when Boogey draws weak from loss of oxygen.

Boogey's heart rate goes even faster when swinging his first at her as Nattie continually grows stronger, dragging and then flinging Boogey onto the porch.

Nattie uses all her strength, flinging the plunger once more, while straining out loud when throwing Boogey around and down the dilapidated steps. She comes up high, and stands with her chest stuck out, huffing and puffing until dropping the plunger. Nattie stands in a mean stare, proudly slapping and dusting her hands off before storming inside, and slamming the bedroom door. Her eyes immediately swarm over the messy room when starting to clean.

Boogey stays stretched out on the ground longer with eyes glued to the sky, which soon starts spinning. His hand goes to his stomach, rubbing until his tummy jiggles from laughing so hard, until slightly frowning through pain. Boogey's knee then foots slowly rises until he's on his feet, stomping while senselessly trying to stop the spinning while gawking at the sky.

He soon gets the spinning settled when wobbling around, and then sits on the step, dusting himself off. He stands again, stumbling up the steps and swaying while nervously peeking through the screen; looking for Nattie's next deceptive plot. Boogey eases inside the kitchen and then leans into the doorway, finding the bedroom door shut and surprisingly jumps when the phone rings. He continues to stare at the bedroom door then stumbles inside after the next ring; and over the chair, overcompensating, and expressly heading for the floor when slamming onto it.

Nattie picks up the phone while Boogey staggers to his feet.

Boogey stands still, staring at the phone, then lifts it when he thinks he hears it ringing again; but listening to it being hung up.

The loud ring soon comes again, and before he can figure out that it's from the television, he slams the receiver down, lifting it and leaving it on the countertop.

Nattie struts out with a tray full of food and paper towels, stopping a few feet from Boogey; staring with a mean look. "As long as you're living on God's green Earth, you had better not ever try that mess again, Boog!" she says, under-eyed and with a single tear dropping.

"Oh, woman, hush that noise! All you do is complain..., just complain all the freakin' time! Your jowls just be ah, jabbing, nonstop, for no reason! Now..., now...; wasn't none of that going on when you were up in here with Freddy, getting your groove on! Huh..., but look a hea (here)..., you can best believe you were doing some moaning!" Boogey exclaims, laughing in pain when a serious, painfully produced tear falls.

"Man, let that mess go..., let it go because it ain't gone do nothing but kill ya (you)! Ok, so you saw him here, so now, what? You ain't going nowhere..., and you ain't going to do nothing about it, so why even bring it up? Like you're gone do something," Nattie boldly blurts out, staring with one fist balled tightly. She shoves the tray down on the table, easing into her favorite fighting stance, with both fists tightly loaded while slowly rocking and bouncing back and forth like a seasoned, professional boxer.

"Just consider yourself lucky is all I can say!" Boogey declares, looking under-eyed longer, without blinking.

"What's luck got to do wit (with) it, boo-boo!? Ok..., like I said, you caught me, and nothing happened, so just shut that trap of yours! Shoulda (should have), woulda (would have), coulda (could have)! You won't gone (going to) do nothing up in here because Freddy would have whipped the dog snot outcha (out of you), in your own darn house; just like he did over at Bea's! Heck, the whole town knows he whipped you like a stankin' dog! Huh..., rumor even has it that he whipped you so bad that your screams were heard miles away, even as far over as Johnston County...; what thirty miles or so, I reckon," Nattie affirms, sarcastically naming the farthest city when smiling and shaking her head.

Boogey concentrates long and hard on the incident, until shoving past her and heading for the living room, where he sits in the recliner in even deeper thoughts.

Nattie stays in the kitchen, quiet until moving a couple of things around.

Boogey goes into a slight daze, listening until something falls, startling him out of a deep meditation. "What..., Freddy beat me, huh? Freddy..., beat me? Wow, I mean Freddy, Freddy..., really? Naw..., not Freddy," Boogey whispers, still in a slight daze when trying to convince her otherwise when tensed, until able to draw in a frown. He lowly laughs, in sarcasm, knowing full well that Freddy had given him the worst whipping of his life.

Nattie reappears, maneuvering around the junky living room through what looks like narrow walkways. She walks through the front door heading for the store and, within minutes, finds a lot of activity out front when rushing up fast, and being nosy. Nattie looks at the owner, then the news team posting a twenty-thousand-dollar reward poster for information on the big shooting and kidnapping case.

Crackhead Tom appears as if out of thin air, strutting by Nattie. He walks fast with eyes swiftly glimpsing over the poster, then the dollar value, until ten feet past when stopping. Tom speedily turns with one leg sprung forward in a sharp spin, slinging his body around when running back and staring at the poster until curiously watching Nattie enter the store.

In the heart of Mundson, around noon, Winton eases from his car, amazed at the towering skyscrapers in the heart of town. He rechecks the paper for the IT firm's address, and instantly; two guys rush by when looking over his shoulder, finding a few others rushing up. Winton scrambles inside behind the first two, slightly holding the door for the next man.

"Please take a number and fill out this form and I'll be with you shortly," the petite receptionist announces, finding three more guys rushing inside. She steps out and comes back, retrieving a few clipboards, and then directs the first two into separate rooms when turning back to Winton. "Ok, I see you are here for IT as well, so when the first guy comes out, feel free to go right inside, sir," the receptionist asserts, placing new sheets on the clipboards for other candidates.

The double door opens thirty minutes later, and a guy comes out, cheery, with his fist balled, gesturing that he has the job and the guy's friend rushes out before Winton can stand with almost the same expression.

The two continually give each other high fives until handshakes come and instantly taper off with some unknown hand slap then hand signs which leave Winton curiously staring.

"Man…, they're doing some serious hiring up in there! The process is so easy…, they offered me like what…, ninety-five K, to start," the first candidate announces, passing Winton and heading over to the receptionist's desk with a sheet containing the company's letterhead.

Winton wobbles, almost passing out until nervously sprinting through the double door, hallways, and into the conference room, nervously looking around to find five smiling faces staring back.

The woman in the middle points for Winton to take a seat, and he turns, pulling the door shut. "Winton, is it, sir?" she asks, sliding the sheet of paper with Winton's credentials to the man on her left.

"Yes, ma'am," Winton skittishly declares, taking a seat while watching the paper being passed along, then back to the woman in the middle and then to others on her right.

"So, you're here for one of the fifty Express IT positions we're hiring for..., huh; that's great, and we welcome you, sir," she utters, looking at his outdated clothes then back at the worst resume ever.

"So, I've got the job?" Winton blurts out, motioning a high-raised thumb as if he really does have the job.

"Well, it's not that easy, sir."

One man giggles a little, composing himself quickly when the woman in the middle looks with a firm stare. "My apologies, sir, but is that double knit?" the man irresistibly asks, smiling.

"Why yes...; and the finest I might add," Winton asserts, dusting off his double-knit and tweed threads; leaving a slight dusting of dry-rotting material floating or dropping to the floor.

"Whhhaaattt! Now, that's what's up! I heard it existed but never seen it before," the man utters, laughing with the others, quickly chiming in, in laughter but cutting it short.

"Well, I'm bringing it back, so you can bet it's coming back, Jack!" Winton exclaims, smiling.

"Ok, so let's all focus, people," the lead woman says with a serious stare. "Sir, just for familiarization with the standard hiring process; the protocol here is we ask questions, and you answer to the best of your ability."

"Oh..., ok...; sure thing, because I'm an IT guru," Winton declares, uncomfortably easing back and quickly leaning forward. He nervously grips the edge of the seat, rocking a little more, and nervously.

"Ok..., so, tell me about POP and its relationship to e-mails?" the lead woman asks, smiling.

"Oh, that's an easy one! Well, you see..., you don't want to get any pop on your keyboard, causing the computer to blow up; you know, like a microwave with aluminum foil. Now, some also relate to it, like, umm..., banging on it, though some call it popping," Winton seriously responds.

The interviewers mouths drop open and they are so stunned by the outrageous answer that they hold back for as long as possible until burst into laughter.

"Ok..., this is good to know," the lead woman asserts, looking to her right, winking, and then to her left when putting a big, fat, red X in the box. She looks up, covering the paper, when finding Winton raised high and leaning forward to see what was written.

Everyone stares at each other, then Winton's reaction when he shrugs his shoulders like he has done something spectacular.

"Next question: What do you do if you can't publish your certificates to the GAL?" the lead utters, sipping then taking in a full mouth of water and unintentionally holding while awaiting Winton's response.

"Oh, snap…, even easier! Look…, you have to give me something harder. Ok, Ok…, well, in that case, you publish to the DUDE; you know, a gal, a dude…; total opposites…, well, you know" Winton nervously yet seriously responds, smiling when water shoots from the woman's mouth, across the table at Winton as the room bursts into laughter.

Winton sits shocked then joins in laughter, slowly wiping his face.

"Excuse the water, sir," the lead utters, pulling a few tissues from a tissue box and wiping up the water when another interviewer grabs a few. "Ok, Ok," the lead whispers, still laughing until finally getting control. "How does .pst relate to e-mail or system transfer files?" she asks, easing to the edge of her chair while the others lean forward in great anticipation.

Winton sits in deep thought for seconds, then minutes.

"Any minute now, sir," the lead says when peeking at her watch while holding a hand firmly to her abs, skittishly waiting for a response.

"That's a hard one, but I'll say…, let's see…, now .pst…, the (st) is surely for system transfer; yeah, I remember that one like yesterday," Winton utters, easing back.

The panel continues smiling, trying to hold their laughs when bursting into laughter, and Winton smiles with a good feeling inside.

Minutes later, everyone quiets but giggles when the lead scribbles the initials DCUWWCY in bold letters across the paper and then stands with a welcoming and extended hand. "Well, it's been a pleasure, sir," she utters, passing Winton a sheet of paper.

"Well? So when do I start?" Winton asks, beaming in excitement.

"Please see the receptionist," the lead says, leaning again when shaking his hand.

The panel stands smiling and watching as Winton exits, then waits for the lock to click, when they fall heavily into each other, laughing hard and waving for the next candidate to go back out.

The door springs open when the candidate exits and Winton peeks back inside with the interviewing team's laughter instantly silenced as if in an online, silence challenge.

Winton looks around, over the floor then begins backing out while nervously staring in bright red faces until the door clicks and an outburst of laughter comes again. He makes it to the desk fast, somewhat excited but looking confused.

"Hey…, hey…, what's going on in there?" the nosy receptionist asks, slowly reaching for Winton's paper with her head glued in the direction of the uproar.

"Well, you know…, the interview of the century," Winton utters, brushing splintered nails against the double knit when one nail catches, and he fights for seconds to get it free. He looks back up surprised at her wide eyes. "I was literally in there killing them…, as in a killer interview!"

The receptionist finally looks at him until in a slight daze, then back at the conference door. She anxiously takes a step from the desk in the direction of the room and slows when anxiously looking down at his paper and coming back to the desk.

"So when do I start, and how much? I'm told that IT pays ninety to a hundred with a degree," Winton utters, pulling out a manila envelope and slipping out a fake college degree, when expressly shoving it toward her.

"We'll call you, so Don't Call Us, We Will Call You, alright?" The receptionist says, still looking down at the DCUWWCY bold letters. "Oh, and you sir…, may want to contact SUKR (Sucker) University…, I mean Stratfordville, to correct the spelling of Stratfordville. Hmm…, but before you go, let me search the web to double-check my thoughts," she utters, cheery.

Winton snatches the fake degree and documents, pissed. "Now you look ah here…, I'll be waiting on that call," he exclaims when turning, and hearing her giggling.

A car with five men pulls alongside the road, in front of the general store.

The front seat passenger leans out. "Hey, Sammy; do you know Steve?"

"Sammy? Who are you talking to, fool? I'm Tom. Steve who…, fool? Steve Shriner, Steven McNugget, Steve Train, Steve Turdstain?" Tom sarcastically responds keeping his back to them but looking over his shoulder, staring until one man mumbles something obscene.

The front passenger frowns when hearing his friend in the back laughing.

The door swings open, and the passenger stares at a shiny knife slowly protruding downward from Tom's left side, held tightly.

"Imma (I am a) head slaya (slayer), I'll cut a head off, Imma head slaya!" Tommy senselessly repeats, still staring at the guy over his shoulder that's now standing rigid and wide-legged.

"Well, here's a little well-known advice…; never bring a knife to a gunfight, sucker!" the mean guy utters, pulling his wife-beater shirt up, brandishing a chrome platted handle gun when his friend taps him, whispering that a cop car is coming. "Consider this your lucky day, chump!" the mean man utters, looking at the cruiser pull over to the far side of the road.

The driver looks around. "Man, this fool gonna (is going to) get us caught up!" he declares when looking at Tom, who smiles when looking at the deputy, who is putting his hat on and standing.

The men in the front seat quickly pass their guns back to the guy sitting behind the driver, who stuffs them in a secret compartment with trunk access.

"What you say!" Tom blurts out, still looking at the cop while slipping the knife back into his shirt pocket. "What? You gone shoot who?" Tom shouts louder to get the officer's attention. "Excuse me, Mr. Officer, but did you hear this guy threaten me?" Tom asserts, fully turning toward the car, smiling.

"Man, stop tripping! We were sitting here just joking a minute ago," the front passenger utters, looking at the deputy, nodding while walking around the front of the car with his neck slumped forward.

The deputy's eyes cautiously pierce through the light tint at the top of the windshield.

"Oh..., so, we're playing all of a sudden, huh? I outta (should) punch you in your freakin' face, punk!" Tom whispers, eye to eye with the deputy when boldly yet playfully stepping closer to the car.

The deputy walks to the door, looking back one last time then straight ahead while entering.

Tom leans forward fast, sucker punching the mean-looking guy, and instantly hears the store's door slam. His head falls back over his shoulders with one eyebrow slightly rising from pure adrenaline.

Instantly, a tight, balled fist grabs Tom tight in the chest, pulling him halfway through the window.

Tom's eyes buck, and he kicks until lowered when the car rolls, then expressly pulls away with Tom's feet double-timing.

The mean guy head butts Tom twice when quickly and heavily shoving him away from the car.

Tom yells high stepping in a stride until stumbling and wobbling. He spins out into a roll, to the side of the road, in tall weeds and rolls for seconds, until breaking the roll when stopping and rocking.

He turns fast, expressly low-crawling to the road's edge, as if carefree listening to crickets. His face finally shoots out of even taller weeds, looking both ways when finally spitting out a mouthful of dry weeds. Tom stays belly down, listening to the faint, fast-fading engine, then stands, falling back and stumbling more. He finally composes himself and makes his way to the store, stumbling under the makeshift shelter where he sits, trying to make out the poster's fine print again.

"What dat (that) there mean, little man?" Tom finally asks a short man.

"Little man? Now you listen here, boy!" the short man utters with fiery eyes.

"Boy? Hell..., boy played on Tarzan, and Chitah quit, so if you don't know my name, don't call me, Chit (shit)!" the man utters some old saying he heard as a kid when laughing at his old, elementary, dry, incorrectly and mispronounced joke.

"Chit? Ya (you) tongue-tired fool! All you are is crap!"

"Speak English, you babbling fool!" the short man utters, pulling out a knife when Tom reaches for his, finding his shirt pocket empty, when backing away fast, and sprinting until seen seconds later, vanishing between two houses.

At Boogey's house, Nattie stands on the back porch putting meat in the deep freezer when the phone rings.

Boogey jumps out of a deep sleep and loud snore. His stale eyes drift into deep thoughts, staring over his shoulder when hearing Nattie come in when the ringing stops. Boogey eases to his feet and steps off, opening the refrigerator, spotting a beer. His rough, callused hands grip the cold can, popping the top and turning it up; downing the beer in one swallow with a big smile. Boogey slams the can down hard on the edge of the table, trying to crush it, and frowns when it does not budge.

An agonizing pain grows in his hand, and he jumps back, shaking it off, when the phone rings again.

Boogey shuffles, turning, leaning forward, and grabbing the phone. "Yellow (Hello)?" He pulls it to his shoulder and ear when it slips with him leaning further to catch it; immediately falling headfirst and putting a huge dent in the sheetrock.

"Hey, Boogey!" the deep, firm voice hesitantly utters while Boogey takes a step back, shaking off the pain.

"Sup, Rev, what can I do out of, main (man)?" Boogey asks, rubbing his head.

"Oh nothing, just calling to let you know I postponed studies tonight; well delayed it, so it'll be an hour later in case you guys are planning on coming."

"Thanks, Rev," Boogey utters, rattling on until hanging up. Boogey instantly clicks over, dialing and listening to an automated recording. He presses his ear closer when asked for account information, which he provides in a slurred speech, repeatedly.

After the fifth request, he begins cursing and talking back until madly banging the phone against the wall, screaming until slamming the phone down.

Before noon the next day, Boogey hears a backfire, expressly diving for the floor and peeks out the screen door, finding Melissa's car rushing up with a high trail of dust in tow. Boogey comes up slow, stepping to the door, somewhat confused.

The car slows, barely stopping when his daughter springs out, scurrying up the steps. "Hi, Daddy!" Melissa blurts out, slowly making her way forward.

Boogey stands off, staring under-eyed at Davillier until his frown grows deeper.

Melissa slows her pace, staring deep into Boogey's eyes, finally noticing that he's tanked when easing past, and quickening inside.

Davillier sits nervously, staring at Boogey's frown and drunken stare for minutes. He finally eases out, taking small steps, then eases back against the porch's beam when feeling Boogey's uneasy and even meaner frown.

"Hey main (man)," Boogey utters, slightly sucking through his teeth while looking out of the corner of his eye. "What the hell did you do wit (with) my shirt the other night?"

"Shirt? Shirt? What shirt?" Davillier skittishly responds, finally spotting Boogey's tightly balled fist and now, no eye contact.

Boogey turns, tightening his fist until his dry hand sounds like stretched, manila ropes when jumping, drawing back, and swinging with all his strength but feeling like he's almost in slow motion.

Davillier ducks to the slow, triggering response when Boogey's powerhouse fist drives through the dry, rotted wooden beam, breaking the post in two and causing the roof to cave in a few feet on one side.

"I..., yi, yi, yi!" Boogey screams at the top of his drunken voice, dancing around in circles while heavily shaking off the unbearable pain.

"What the...!" Nattie shouts, hearing the loud, continual crashing of dry-rotted wood.

Nattie and Melissa run to the screen door, discovering the roof bobbing with the attached post but heavily dangling.

"Boogey! What in the world is going on out here?" Nattie screams.

Nattie and Melissa step out and onto the porch quickly, with wandering eyes until looking alongside the house, finding Boogey a ways off before fading alongside the house in a wild chase.

The women rush inside and through the house then out back, looking and not seeing anyone until seeing a flash when Davillier stealthily runs out of the cornfield.

Boogey burst out of the field faintly screaming, and hot on his trail, reaching for Davillier with a finger barely touching the tip of Davillier's collar when Davillier's eyes go over his shoulders hollering louder.

Davillier steps up his speed, banking right and dipping under the clothesline, when Boogey closes in with his neck caught up in the line, flinging feet forward and high above his head with his body high before slamming to the ground.

Boogey lies motionless, slowly disappearing in a thin shield of high rising dust.

Davillier slows down in shock, turning slowly to find Nattie and Melissa with their silent mouths torn open.

There is silence longer while watching Boogey move slowly until moaning. He rolls over slowly and climbs to his knees slower, in excruciating pain. Boogey comes to his feet, shaking off the pain and turning upon hearing great laughter growing from the three. He takes a step, turning, finding Nattie and Melissa bent to their knees laughing and Davillier resting his back on Boogey's hood, giggling.

"Laugh! Laugh! Laugh!" Boogey shouts. "Laugh! Laugh! Laugh!" he shouts again, running his hand around his bruised neck and slightly indented Adam's apple.

The three can't stop laughing, but the women briefly stop when Boogey walks past.

Boogey heads inside, shutting the door when the snickering, then an outburst of laughter comes from the three but even louder.

The women finally get a break from the laughter when trying to get to the bottom of the incident but can't from Davillier still laughing so hard.

Nattie soon catches her breath, looking at Davillier's red face as he walks to the edge of the steps with a fast growing frown. She looks at the metal washtub with the lid halfway covering it. "Davillier, can you run me to the market?" Nattie asks, still wiping away heavy tears.

"Sure thing," Davillier responds, slightly lifting the lid and stirring the pot with a long, paddle-like fork while grabbing his nose when a strong turd stench rushes into his nostrils. His curious mind takes over when he folds the lid halfway back, and stirs until a few meatballs-looking circles float up. "What the…!" he says, cutting the profanity short.

"You just come back around dinner time, and I'll show you some good eating, boi!" Nattie utters, running her hands through Melissa's long hair.

"Dinner? Are you serious? There's no way I'm eating anything with turds in it or smelling like a bag of poop!" Davillier utters, closing the lid and wiping his hands on his pants before smelling his hands and frowning.

"Davillier, trust me…; when mom is done with those chitterlings, she's not going to be able to keep you out of that pot."

"Me suckin' (sucking) on turd pipes? I don't think so." Davillier shakes his head.

"Man, please! You know what they say: You can take a man out of the country, but you can't take the country out of the man," Nattie exclaims, giggling.

The screen flies open, shrilling on rusty springs when slamming shut, leaving the three jumping back and looking up in shock.

Boogey floats down the steps, rushing for the side of the porch, slinging a big, frozen turkey and slamming it on the porch with the brand label rocking and slightly spinning. His eyes roll slightly over his shoulder, finding Davillier easing from the pot and making distance when Boogey walks over by the steps. Boogey's fist balls tighter, staring at Nattie and Melissa when easing by the two.

The women giggle, slightly leaning into one another in even deeper but milder laughter.

Boogey reaches under the house, pulling out a deep, rusty pot, shoving the turkey over with it shifting then rocking back and forth. He pulls out the propane gas and then stands, setting it up while looking back at Davillier, Nattie, and Melissa, finding them with big smiles, and whispering.

Boogey leans against the porch's beam, supporting his weight when digging deep in his pocket for matches; pulling out the white tips. He sticks the white tip under his front teeth, popping it forward fast, and finds it unlit when bringing it close, finding it covered with a yellowish, buttery film.

"Ugh, man! You've got enough butter on those damn teeth to butter that whole darn turkey, so what in the world would possess you to think you can strike a match? You're better off using your callused hands!" Nattie screams, looking back at Melissa, laughing. Nattie walks around and then over to the pecan tree, picking up a few pecans, while Davillier and Melissa wander over, helping.

Boogey digs deep again for the matchbox, striking the match with the outer cover this time and giggling when seizing the propane and opening the valve. He adjusts the flame, creating a very light whisper, which causes him to jump back and then rush up, cutting plastic from the turkey and ripping it away. Boogey looks in the deep, dark pot when minuscule bubbles trail to the side, then looks off, finding Davillier creeping up but at a distance, staring. He smiles, hearing grease pop while the condensation quickly burns off. Out of nowhere, Boogey turns fast, nippily hooking the turkey then holds it over the hot, popping grease when bubbles rise from the water dripping.

Nattie finally registers the heavy popping and finds Boogey shielding his face from the grease and heat when dropping the turkey and jumping back, quick, smiling. "Dangit, Boogey! Run for the hills, yawl (you all)! Run for your lives!" Nattie screams with her head over her ears when running with Davillier and Melissa hot on her trail and Boogey finally registers the scream when backing off, fast.

Boogey slows, seeing the bubbles go beneath the edge of the pot's rim, stopping with his hands on his knees, giggling. "Oh, woman, you 'bout (are about) as crazy as a rabid dog," Boogey yells when a high-pitch hissing grows until a loud, fireball explosion erupts. "Well, I'll be!" Boogey shrieks with his head thrown back as turkey parts sail thirty feet high, coming down even faster.

Boogey runs toward Nattie, who shrieks. "Screw you! Screw you, Boogey Johnson! Now, look what you've gone and done!" Nattie yells, looking at the large fire burning the back porch and some of the siding.

The four stealthily close in on the house with the loud sound of turkey parts continually spraying the ground, and splattering everywhere.

Boogey covers his head with turkey parts, continually pounding it then runs to the side of the house, grabbing a metal bucket he thinks is filled with water but is actually filled with a mixture of oil drippings and water.

Nattie rushes over with a semi-charged hose which trickles water when squeezing the nozzle. She pulls it tightly, swinging it, until it replicates like a jump rope when Boogey runs up with the bucket.

Boogey tries to stop but leans forward, leaping and finally jumping ropes to keep from getting tangled.

Nattie pulls the hose tight when a blast of water shoots out, and the hose slaps Boogey in the gut then drops to the ground, and Boogey takes off.

Boogey dashes the mixture toward the house, and the flames burst into a high explosive sound, fully swarming over the porch and wall.

Davillier takes off quickly, scurrying alongside the house, waving high to get the attention of a few firemen out back, washing a fire truck with loud music blaring.

Out of nowhere rises a loud engine when a crop duster flies by, low and fast, going straight up and in a high loop when approaching even lower. The plane clears the roof, dropping hundreds of gallons of water, knocking Boogey and the women down when most of the water washes against the house and shoots back off the porch.

Davillier looks back, discovering Melissa face down, and kicking when turning and running as fast as he can when she sits up, quick, covered in mud. He jumps back, finding Nattie and Boogey face down, kicking to get their faces unstuck from water-filled potholes.

Nattie's hands brush over the ground for the hose, sticking the high-charged nozzle in the ground, and breaking the sealed suction.

Boogey finally slides a finger against his face, breaking the seal as well, when raising his mud-covered face.

The plane's engine grows louder when the retired, acrobat pilot hits the flask again; coming in for another low-level run when Davillier whisks Melissa away.

Davillier rushes from Melissa, waving off the plane, but it stays on course; dropping another load and knocking Nattie and Boogey down again.

Nattie and Boogey crawl to their feet fast, looking around with mud-covered faces.

Boogey grips the hose, working it from the roof down until the fire dies and smoke fades. He looks back fast, hearing a strange smacking sound, finding his mangy dog and another dog lapping up the turkey when spraying them and then dropping the hose in a charge. "Get!" Boogey screams, pissed. "Gone..., get now!" Boogey shrieks, kicking, overcompensating, and falling flat on his back.

Nattie grabs the hose, runs toward Boogey, wetting him, and then holds it to his face while he tries standing.

"Forget you, woman!" Boogey yells, gagging as water fills his mouth as he springs up, chasing Nattie until stepping on the hose, angrily yanking the nozzle away.

The three take off when Boogey turns the nozzle, wetting them while in range.

Boogey's face frowns and he gazes over his muddy clothes when hearing the plane's engine closing fast and low, causing him to run up the steps and inside when the plane makes a pass, not dropping water but veering off.

The three ease over by the back door with cautious eyes on the screen door, wondering if Boogey is up to something devilish. They approach the dirty and ash-covered screen door and run off, thinking they see Boogey in the doorway.

A few minutes later, the women find Boogey sitting in the kitchen, putting on socks, with a towel around his neck and freshwater dripping from his hair.

Nattie and Melissa track mud through the house, making their way to the bedroom.

Boogey hears Davillier out back, dropping a few things on the porch, including the tall frying pot and lid, which rolls around before resting on its handle.

Nattie appears in a robe minutes later and looks through the kitchen drawer, pulling out curlers before heading back into the bedroom.

The women stay in the room a little longer and then appear one at a time.

Melissa sits in the living room tying her shoes when Nattie walks by the kitchen door.

"Boogey..., Melissa and Davillier are taking me to the market," Nattie says, digging through a pile of clothes for her purse. She comes up, grips her wig, shoves her hair under it, then straightens the wig until running a brush through it.

Davillier makes his way alongside the house, coming up on the front.

Boogey hears Davillier out front and slips out the back door.

Davillier reaches for the car door and finds Melissa standing with the screen door handle in hand when nervously looking around for Boogey.

Melissa walks down the steps, making funny faces at Davillier. "You gone chauffer me and Mama, Babe?" Melissa playfully smiles until blowing playful kisses.

Nattie steps onto the porch, pulling several wig strands from her face. "How do I look?" Nattie asks Melissa when playfully putting her hands on her hips. She strikes a pose, cautiously doing some silly runway walk down the flimsy steps; eyes on the rotten holes and loose boards, with hands still on her hips.

Davillier opens the passenger side back and front door for the women then closes them. He rushes for the driver's side, jumping in behind the steering wheel; cranking up, and sticking his head out when looking in the side mirror while slowly backing up.

"Laugh at me, will you!" Boogey screams out of nowhere with something long, wet, white and lifelessly dangling from the end of the green garden hose.

Sprinkles of water splash in Davillier's face until white, light-brown slime pushes forward, slapping Davillier's face gently; followed by a gust of power-house water.

The women duck and scream at the top of their lungs being heavily soaked.

"Boogey! Boogey!" Nattie screams in a high-pitched voice.

Davillier's floors the gas pedal and the car slowly rolls from the busted transmission.

The car lunges forward, until jerking then accidentally thrown in reverse; backing fast in a semicircle a few rounds when the trunk slams into the corner cinderblock of the foundation.

Immediately, the car's back and side windows burst when the porch post caves in on the cab.

Boogey's head instantly drops over his shoulders, finding the roof in shambles when dropping the hose and long chitterling tube; grabbing his head in disbelief. He comes to a stale smile until speedily thinking of the lottery money.

The three-step out in awe and can't believe their eyes while in silence until the phone rings.

Boogey dashes inside, answering on the fourth ring. "Yellow (Hello)?"

"Yes sir, Mr. Johnson…, my kind sir…; lottery director, here. I'm calling to see if you've made a decision…, you know, about hiding the money and all," the director whispers when finding his nosy assistant intentionally scrolling past.

"Oh, no, sir! I'm under the weather, so I won't be in today," Boogey replies, turning when hearing and then seeing Nattie at the door, eavesdropping.

"I'll assume you can't talk right now, but you have my number, so call me before it's too late. You don't want to give that old, windbag half of your earnings so she can spend it all on Freddy, now do you?" the nosy old man utters, laughing.

"Dang…, this mother knows, too!" Boogey says in a whisper when holding the phone away, looking at it, mean. A vein rises in Boogey's forehead when he slams the phone down, dusting off both hands.

Nattie cleans up again, and Melissa goes in afterward, doing the same.

Boogey heads for the screen door, hearing the engine rev when he spots the car pulling slowly away and parting the porch roof from the house. "Whoa, whoa, whoa!" Boogey screams, rushing out and waving until the car stops. "You're about as dumb as a bag of marbles! Now, why in the hell would you move the car, seeing that it's supporting the roof?" Boogey asks, rushing up to the driver's door to find Davillier backing off, sitting in the middle, and fearfully reaching for the other door handle.

Boogey fades off fast, heading out back, and returns minutes later loaded down with chains and pulleys. He makes more trips with Davillier hot in tow, bringing around enough spare materials to patch the damages temporarily when setting up jacks and beams until Boogey realigns the bricks and support beams.

Within an hour, they have the house somewhat patched, but it looks worse than before when the women exit, covering the wet seats before loading back up.

Hours later, Boogey stands pouring warm chitterlings in the sink, when dipping his hand in and around until feeling something hard. He fishes around more until bringing up the last piece, instantly flinching and dropping the tooter in the water, shaking off the weird feeling. He swiftly backs away, frowning with a distasteful look.

"Whoa! Ho, ho, ho!" he utters, shivering and shaking off the awkward feeling more with eyes going back to the water, slightly bouncing until dancing around in circles, still trying to shake the strange feeling.

Boogey shakes his hands more to get rid of the funny feeling until dancing more and then leans forward, rapidly rinsing. He reaches in the fridge, popping a few cold beers back-to-back, while looking over the murky water with each deep swallow. Boogey finally fishes around with a fork, releasing the drain plug, until finally staring down at the heart-shaped pork tooter in the sink.

"Simple-minded bastards!" he says, thinking about the sucker who took the time to perfectly shape the skin around the tooter into a heart. Boogey finally gathers his thoughts, putting the rest of the chitterlings in the pot, seasoning them, and pulling out the greens.

Bud finally wakes up, instantly sniffing and then swinging with his head twitching. "Uh…, uh…, uh…, uh…, uh!" Bud utters, watching Boogey take a seat. "Dang, Boogey! Do you always have to bust your tail in here? Why not the bathroom, man? I mean, come on, you simple-minded chump!" Bud utters, fluffing feathers.

Boogey laughs when Bud's head slightly turns, and he begins mocking Boogey's laughter.

An hour later, the lottery director flips open the keepsake watch, pacing the floor for well over an hour in the lotto office.

A horn blows and Boogey looks, finding Nattie getting out with bags.

"Is there something bothering you, sir?"

"No…, no…, nothing at all," he replies.

"In that case, you need to stop pacing because you're making me nervous," the assistant utters, nervously lighting a cigarette and rattling Boogey's payout sheet.

An hour and a half later, the director skittishly taps the counter, looking up with excited eyes, when finding Boogey's car rushing through the lot. "Ugh!" he utters, breaking the pencil in half when seeing Nattie's big, too familiar hairdo.

"What? What is it, sir?" his assistant asks, looking at his red face and then flared nostrils for seconds when she looks over his shoulder, finding Boogey opening the car door.

Boogey stands proudly, pulling on his suspenders, allowing them to snap back when standing tall.

Nattie straightens her Sunday hat, fanning out her dingy dress when staring at her run-over heels as if she's been a millionaire for years.

The two join hands, taking off in a strut for the door like two proud yard birds.

The director stares under-eyed, pissed, then transitions into a fake smile when discovering his assistant next to him with eyes glued on him.

Nattie smiles, about to burst, but holds her scream, thinking Boogey is playing a prank.

The assistant lays the documents on the counter, and Nattie's eyes fan across the papers and long line of zeroes.

A heatwave swarms over Nattie when she falls back, and Boogey catches her; fanning until finding the assistant handing him a cardboard paddle when retracting it and fanning faster.

Nattie finally comes to and jumps up as if never on the floor, rushing back to the counter, staring at the check again when dancing with Boogey soon joining in.

The two go at it for minutes until finding themselves almost out of breath when they drop into seats and then bounce back up to the counter. "So tell me," what kind of kickback does the lottery pay you guys when someone wins?" Boogey curiously asks with his chest proudly stuck out.

"The store that sold the ticket gets a bonus, not us, sir," the angry director utters with a fake, sad face.

"Well, that's not fair!" Boogey affirms, looking at their shabby attire, then out into the lot at their old, rust-bucket cars. "Hmm...," Boogey says in thought when pulling Nattie aside, whispering until she shakes her head 'no' several times until a smile comes. "How about us giving you two, two thousand dollar a piece..., would that work?" Boogey utters, looking at Nattie, who frowns hearing him double what they agreed on, but smiles when noticing the director and woman's eyes dead set on her.

"Wow..., really..., well if it's your wish, sir, but you'll have to give it to us as a gift because we can't take it out of the winnings."

"Then it's a deal," Boogey utters, shaking their hands.

Nattie pulls her checkbook out, writing two postdated checks.

Boogey begins happily moving until slowly dancing again when making his own, highly hummed tune.

The director and his assistant join in, making a couple of moves, though they are nowhere near in tune with the nice rhythm Boogey has going.

The four continue in an up-tempo dance before looking over toward the door, and finding a small audience.

The director stops dancing in deep thought. "Have you two considered getting an attorney to handle your money and decide what you should do with it?" the director asks with hiring his son in mind. "I have a son who can get you done; he's an excellent attorney," the director utters with a bigger cut in mind.

"What, and give away a third? No sir..., no thank you; I can go to a few investment firms and get free, professional attorney services, and advice; so thanks, but no thanks," Boogey responds, discerningly.

Later, over at the convalescent home, Dale drifts into his room, turning and peeking out before easing the door shut, and glancing inside his nightstand. He pulls out the CD then slides it into the player and begins bobbing his head with his fingers fanning over the volume when turning up the beat. His balled fist pounds on the table when easing down on the side of the bed, into the recliner, beating the chair arm when finding his roommate with his back to him, but his feet in unison with the beat.

Dale stops and the man's foot stops, then moves when the music plays. He switches tracks, and his roommate's feet quickly come in step. Dale works his hand in unison with the beats, rapping through a few songs then restarts each time he messes up. He freezes, then walks over, propping a stick behind the door, then lifts the covers from his mattress, sticking his hand in a slit, and pulling out a flask when the roommate stands, dancing with happy feet.

Dale pours the roommate moonshine and begins rapping but messes up when the music starts over. He stands in a stance, takes a sip, and motions his roommate over. "Hey, can you make that old-school, beatbox sound like the old original rapper?" Dale asks, watching him shake his head 'yes'. "Ok, great!"

Out of nowhere, a hard knock comes at the door, and Dale scrambles, quickly hiding the CD inside a book. "Ok, open it!" Dale whispers with his index finger to his lips, silencing his roommate while dropping in the recliner, pretending to be asleep.

The roommate eases over, removing the stick and the door flies open with the roommate beaming and looking over smiling faces; when looking back, finding Dale slouched in a fake snore.

Boogey stares at Dale with his mouth dropped open as resident folks clap, wandering off.

Dale yawns, tossing and turning until finding Boogey smiling. "Main (Man), where did you learn how to rap like that?" Boogey asks, rushing in.

"Ah shucks, I've been rapping since you were an itch in your daddy's pants." Dale laughs. "I've been working with a friend to make a CD," he utters, looking at the roommate who nervously stares off, afraid to make eye contact with Boogey and confirm a lie.

Boogey stands in deep thought for seconds. "Hey..., we can swing by the pawnshop later for some cheap equipment," Boogey utters, pulling out his grandfather's travel bag. "I came to pick you up and spend some time with you," Boogey utters, rubbing his money-getting hands together, in gesture.

Boogey plays a number on the drive home, and the clerk rushes the sale, misprinting and lying down a two-dollar ticket on the counter. Boogey holds the dollar in his tight grip, expressly patting his pockets for more. "How can you mess up something so simple?" Boogey asks, staring at the ticket when patting another empty pocket.

"Well, you didn't say how many, so I thought you wanted the extra play," the woman nervously responds, staring into Boogey's fiery eyes.

"Well, that's the darn problem then, ain't it? You do more thinking than asking! It's not like I wasn't standing right here," Boogey says, growing more pissed.

"Sir, it's not even that critical," the clerk utters, turning red when looking at others who stand back, quietly staring. "All I have to do is hold the ticket and give it to another person buying lottery..., it's just that simple."

"Oh, yeah..., well, you can forget that, non-sense! Now you look here, you just hold that ticket, and I'll be back fer (for) it. Don't you know its bad luck to pass up on a number? What if it's the biggone (big one)?" Boogey says, swallowing hard with eyes swarming over the lucky-looking printout.

"Ok, ten minutes, and after that, the next buyer gets it," she utters with attitude.

Boogey sprints up to the car, looking for spare change in the ashtray and then on the floor with no success, but finds an old French fry, curiously staring at it when chomping down on it. He rushes Dale out, patting Dale down until both hands are deep in both of Dale's pockets; when Dale's eyes go wide, shoving Boogey back.

Boogey tries bumming money from customers who blow him off, ignore him, or curse him out. He walks by the car, looking at his watch with eight minutes passed, finding an older female standing from her car and taking baby steps when a little kid appears.

His eyes drift to the floor when reaching in, grabbing a beat-up-looking baseball bat, rushing off and up to the kid. "Excuse me, son..., hey look..., I'm desperate..., but look here; how much would you give for a Louisville slugger?"

Boogey eyes glimpse over the bat, and his fingernail runs across the serial numbers, until slightly popping dirt out of two numbers when his eyes drift down again, staring closely. "Hmm..., seven-four-five-eight..., damn..., that's a good number to play," Boogey says, looking at the boy's bright eyes. "So..., how much?" Boogey whispers again, looking at the boy's tight fist clamping down on the thick roll of single bills he had just pulled from his pocket.

"Seeing how it's all old and decrepit, like yourself; I figure a quarter," the kid seriously blurts out.

"Naw..., hellz naw (no), I need at least a dollar, so help an old man out," Boogey utters, discovering the old lady with a handful of lottery play cards closing slowly. "Timing is everything, son...; this is the real McCoy," Boogey says, slightly turning his head cheerily from the quick lie and then turning with a straight face.

"Well then... if it's so real, why would you get rid of it, so cheap?" the boy asks, finally recognizing the partially authentic seal when his smile goes even brighter. "Ok..., one dollar, but that's it," the kid softly murmurs, peeling off a crisp single.

"Here you are!" Boogey utters, passing the bat quickly, snatching the bill in a turn when scurrying past the old lady. He swings the door open, stepping forward, and slamming the door in her face.

"Yah, sorry, no good for nothing...!" the old lady shrieks, cutting it short while raising her cane.

Dale laughs, shaking his head, while watching Boogey run inside.

Boogey sprints to the counter, and waits patiently for the clerk to finish stacking cigar boxes.

The front door swings open. "Hey... thanks for the bat, mister!" the kids sounds off loudly. "It's definitely genuine..., and worth about what; five-thousand, I would say, if I were a betting man," the kid utters, flashing the seal that Boogey has never noticed, covered in mud.

Boogey's eyes scroll over the dollar, then the bat several times when stumbling; a little lightheaded when his hand comes to his sweaty forehead. His eyes slowly follow the bat held over the boy's shoulder until fading down an aisle.

The clerk finally turns, passing Boogey the ticket and taking his money, when something strong and sturdy slaps Boogey in the back of the head and causing him to jump.

The old woman's shaky cane remains high over her head until it's sprung back.

Boogey stumbles a little when cracked in the head again, then in the middle of his back as he backs up, spins, and reaches for the cane several times but misses.

The old woman furiously swings, backing Boogey to the door, when the little boy trips him with the bat wedged in the doorway.

Boogey falls flat on his back, kicking and yelping while sliding back on his hands when more stealth cane whacks heavily drive into his shin.

A loud, scream, then holler follows by laughter when Dale falls into the seat in tears, laughing until the car rocks from growing too excited.

Over at Winton's, Winton rummages through a few hiding places to see how much liquor is left. He stands at the kitchen counter looking over about twenty pints and three half gallons of empty bottles when drifting into a daze, thinking of his neighbor and smiling.

He opens the medicine chest, seizing a red bottle of tablets, drops the pills in one bottle, then pours liquor in an expensive bottle until a third full, and sits it outside.

Winton continually peeks, until finding his neighbor walking out, sitting, and riding a chair on hind legs against the side of the house. He looks at his watch, then at the neighbor, before grabbing the phone and dialing a few numbers. Winton peeks again, finding the chair dropping forward and the man jumping up to answer.

Winton eases out, sitting and drinking ice-cold water, when he spots his neighbor's curtains pulled back and slips the bottle behind the pillow before going inside.

The neighbor rushes through the house with a cup, expressly making his way across Winton's lawn, knocking, then stopping and knocking again.

Winton glances out, finding his neighbor leaning over, peeking inside.

The neighbor fumbles around, grabbing the expensive bottle, taking half of it down when knocking again. He peeks longer, filling his cup again, then walks halfway across the yard when Winton's steps out smiling until putting on a serious face.

"Hey, look, we throwing something on the grill later, so you're free to come back. My boy will be bringing a couple of gallons of liquor," Winton says, throwing up his hand and motioning that he would be right back when fading inside. He falls on the couch, mildly squealing and kicking in laughter, until hearing heavy boots onto the porch when quieting, and finding his neighbor peeking through the screen when he springs to his feet. "Hey! That's a good way to get your stupid tail popped, pal! Man, I have a daughter and wife, so you can't be doing that mess," Winton seriously utters. Winton sees a car pull into the driveway, then another.

"Oh..., my bust..., sorry about that!" the neighbor utters, finally hearing the cars.

An hour later, Winton's three friends and neighbor begin setting up for the cookout when a horn blows, and Winton's family pull up.

The kids run inside, and Nelle walks over, greeting Winton's friends. "I'll start bringing the food out," Nelle utters, beaming while walking away.

Nelle's girlfriend comes up next, friskily making her way over to the men and wastes no time getting fresh with a handsome guy. She bends over, spreading the tablecloth, showing much cleavage when winking and intentionally knocking over napkins to get him to rush over.

Another guy nudges Winton and the others, getting a good look at her sexy bottom while bent over.

"Are you cooking your dish, girl?" Nelle asks when her girlfriend finally stands with wandering eyes gazing back at all the attentive men.

"Everything is done; all cep (except) the chicken," the girlfriend responds in a soft, seductive voice.

The beer-filled mouths of Winton and the guy next to him burst open fast, spraying beer several feet when bursting into a crazy laugh. "All what?" Winton asks, wiping his mouth with his sleeve.

"All cep (except) the chicken," Nelle's girlfriend boldly utters, looking serious when bending over to flip the tablecloth that the wind briskly blows up, back down.

The guys laugh until the guy she likes redirects the conversation.

The girlfriend walks over near Winton's neighbor to tie down the other end of the tablecloth.

Winton's neighbor's eyes continually swarm over her hot body. "Psst..., hey, let me holla at you shawty (shorty)," the neighbor utters, looking over toward his house for his wife when quickly reaching for her hand.

Nelle's girlfriend draws back fast a few times and then holds her hands out, when finally fed up.

"Man, look..., I just wanna holla aight (all right)!" the neighbor utters with eyes wandering over her curvy hips and thick bottom stretched in tight spandex as she turns away.

"Ugh, ugh, ugh..., see..., I don't be talking to no scrums (scrubs)," Nelle's girlfriend responds, pointing at him, when moving her finger in a swaying motion.

Winton's mouthful of beer sprays over a few guys when bursting into laughter until intentionally calmed by the handsome guy who helped her before.

One man nudges Winton, seeing Winton's neighbor staring at Winton's wife's breasts and then her body in a trance.

Winton stares at his neighbor's peeled eyes until looking away when Winton's wife fades into the house. Winton leans into his friend, whispering, when suddenly they burst into mild laughter, breaking the neighbor's concentration.

The neighbor looks at Winton and then down, shamefully.

Another horn blows and three women get out with hands full of cooked dishes.

Nelle appears with another tablecloth and bowl of mac and cheese. "Make sure you leave the food covered," Winton utters to his friends standing near him.

"What are you talking about, Wint? It's too cool for flies," Nelle utters, lifting a dish top when Winton accidentally forces her hand to the hot lid, causing Nelle to jerk back and shake off the burn, fast.

"I'm sorry, babe," Winton says, gently caressing her hands and whispering to her about the pills, when Nelle bursts into tears of laughter.

The neighbor rubs his stomach, easing his cup of liquor down when slithering into a chair, and crossing his legs, tightly. He resists moving when his stomach growls real loud then makes loud channeling noises.

"Man, somebody got a tiger in the tank!" one woman jokingly yells, placing a bowl down and looking over several smiles, until finding Winton nodding at the neighbor.

The neighbor clenches his legs tighter, squirming until bracing the chair on both sides, tightly, when a loud, uncontrollable, long, and hard fart shoots out. His eyes buck, swarming around fast, waiting for someone to point to someone else when folks nippily disperse from him.

"Who the hell was that? Who the hell lit that one off?" one man yells, looking at the other guys, then a female secretly nods her head toward Winton's neighbor who is heavily slouching with heels digging deep in the dirt.

Winton nudges the guy closest to him, who motions others when the neighbor goes into a trance, staring and very concerned about making it home when leaning, and looking at his front door; shaking his head in disbelief and uncertainty.

The neighbor's stomach balls in a knot and he squeezes tighter, farting, cringing, and easing up when everyone looks; frowning and running off, fast.

The kids run out the house, backing down fast from the stench and find the man standing stiff as a board with his hand at his butt; moving snappily and kicking up dust when a loud uproar of laughter comes.

The neighbor advances faster with more loud farts from each step until stopping, then slowly moving until moving faster; in a full stride, screaming for his wife, Betty.

A louder uproar of laughter comes with everyone in tears and laughing even harder when he stops and begins walking wide-legged.

The neighbor's front door slams and everyone listens quietly, hearing a female screaming and fussing for minutes until the front door opens minutes later and a clear bag of material drops; the same colors he was wearing when the door slams.

Nelle walks up to Winton in tears with heavy, jumping shoulders until calm. "Wint, can you run to the store for ice?" Nelle asks, placing a bowl on the table.

Winton motions to his best friend, who walks fast, catching up as Winton walks up to the guy's passenger side door.

Ten minutes or so later, they pull into the grocery store parking lot, discovering a female in tight jeans bent over in her trunk.

The woman soon springs up with her Afro slightly tilted.

Winton stares at her sexy body then throws his head back in shock when noticing her nappy Afro tilted more as if she just climbed out of bed.

Winton's friend continues looking around until finding a closer spot near the front door.

They get out, finding the female making her way past the back of the car.

Winton's eyes follow her closely until she looks back, turning her nose up with Winton getting hot. "Ever thought about combing that nappy head?" Winton yells with eyes still glued to her perfectly-shaped bottom.

"Man, this is all-natural! I'm going natural…, ok…, with your nosy-tail self!" The woman twists her hips harder when seeing an attractive man walk out of the store.

The attractive man gazes, making eye contact with eyes swarming over her lovely shape, then slightly frowns and smiles again when seeing her hair.

The woman stares into the guy's eyes and winks, causing him to straighten his face and blush when passing and looking back at her bodacious figure.

"Must be a knotty natural," Winton finally yells, over a loud, passing delivery truck as it picks up speed. "I'm just saying…, you need to comb that nappy head…, and if not, then you need a natural-born whipping. You know good and well that you've been lying on your back all night and just stepped out of bed," Winton says, very low while still gazing at her.

"Man, just step off! You just a hater with that raggedy darn perm," the woman utters, flipping a middle finger and watching Winton's friend lean forward in a deep laugh and cut down an aisle when noticing Winton turning slowly to look back.

Winton stops in his tracks, looking for his friend, and then breaks off, grabbing a large bag of ice. He drifts down the aisles, still looking for the female, when she crosses over to another aisle a ways off. Winton comes up on the candy aisle, seizing a long pack of gum then walks to the register.

Two young girls stand in front of Winton, behind a young boy with a whacked-out, dry hair duo. The girls begin giggling, until laughing out loud a few times then whispering before cutting their eyes back when finally noticing Winton beady eyes staring at the boy's dry hair.

The girl closest to the young boy pretends she is going to tap his shoulder, and her girlfriend pulls her hand back, giggling. The girl waits a few seconds then holds a hand out; when her girlfriend bumps the girl and she taps him on the shoulder. "Hey, we were just wondering; is that a Lee's curl?" the closet girl asks, smiling.

The boy smiles, blushing. "Ah, yeah," he proudly responds, staring into their cheery faces.

"Right...," the other girl whispers, laughing harder. "It must be the dry version of Lee's," she says louder, when leaning and looking at his over-permed, dry, linty hair.

The boy turns away with a sad face, continually listening to their demeaning jokes until paying and rushes off in tears.

"Did you see that head?" Winton asks, looking at his friend when he walks up behind him. "Damn boy's head is dryer than freakin' tumbleweed...; so dry he can start a forest fire without matches!" Winton utters, looking back for the thick-bottomed woman again. "Do you think that's the natural-hair-wearing woman's boy?" Winton says, beaming when spotting the natural hair wearing female comes out of one aisle and go down another. Winton begins digging deep into both pockets when his friend is playfully motioned aside.

Two short, nubby middle fingers go high, fully sprung back with thumbs when thumping Winton hard in the back of the head, causing him to jump and look back with balled fists.

The short VooDoo lady stands laughing crazily out loud. "Hey Wint! Where is that cheap tail Boogey, Wint? Man..., that Boogey is about as tight and cheap as a two-dollar hoe (whore)."

Winton drunkenly stares into her eyes with a slight frown. "Hell..., your guess is as good as mine," Winton utters, pushing the ice up a few inches on the conveyor before instantly cutting his eyes back.

The VooDoo woman waits for Winton to turn and begins lightly fiddling in his hair for a long strand, until quickly pinching a string and drawing her hand back, quickly.

Winton jumps wide-legged, grabbing her hand; wrestling for minutes until his hand is at her throat and she is bent backward over the moving conveyor and moving forward with him still trying to get his hair back. "Stop playing, now! Stop playing!" Winton screams, startling patrons when his face turns bright red, still trying to free the single strand while expressly jerking his head to her wrist, and growling like a vicious dog.

The VooDoo woman's hand finally fly open, with the strand falling to the floor, and she screams, jumping back and bursting into a deep, crazy laughter.

"You better gone (stop) with that mess!" Winton screams, staring mean yet fearful, when reaching for the strand, and putting it in his pocket.

The woman turns to walk away and then mushes him fast, on the side of the head and stands in a mean stare.

Winton holds his composure then jumps at her when she takes off scurrying down an aisle, loudly laughing like a crazy woman with her voice echoing.

Over at Boogey's, Boogey and Dale watch television a while longer until the phone rings. Boogey drags over, answering. "Boog," he utters, reaching for a kitchen chair, easing down, listening, until slowly hanging up. He remains in deep thought when Nattie walks into the kitchen waving a hand in his face when he snaps him out of the trance, looking up at her.

"Nattie, I gotta go! I gotta get out of here..., I'll be back in a few hours," Boogey utters, heading to the bedroom for his windbreaker.

Within seconds, Boogey sprints out, cranks up, and speeds off.

Boogey clears his mind when crossing into Mundson and pulling into a vacant lot thirty minutes later. He pulls his sleeve back, looks at his watch, then out the rearview when a car pulls up from behind, and the headlights go out. Boogey looks out the window until the car door opens and black boots extend downward.

The dark shadowed man looks around for seconds then rushes to Boogey's passenger side. "Hey, Boog! I didn't mean to get you drug into this, but there's no one else I can turn to," the gang member Reggie utters, nervously looking around again. "I can lose my life doing this, but I have to do it."

"Ok..., well, just put your head down when we get into the city," Boogey utters, looking deeply into bloodshot eyes.

"Come again...! Put what? Put my head down?" Reggie utters, looking between Boogey's thighs to find a tube-like bulge. "Ah, hellz (hell) naw man, I'll get in the back before I do that because I ain't laying my head in no dude's lap."

Boogey bursts into a burst of heavy laughter, watching Reggie fling the door open and climb in the back. "Ok..., so run it down to me again," Boogey utters, turning off the radio and focusing on the long, drawn-out story.

Twenty minutes later, Boogey pulls up at Rev's apartment, sitting and talking, when noticing Rev's living room curtains open and close, quickly.

Boogey and Reggie keep their eyes peeled on the window finding a shadow going to-and-fro, past the thin sheers and stopping each time.

Reggie finally gets to the end of the story, and Boogey sits in disbelief.

Minutes later, the door clicks, swinging open when Boogey jumps out, proceeding to the door, continually replaying the story in his mind. He stands in deep thought, thinking of what to say when finally knocking.

Rev lightly answers, and after the third knock, the door opens slowly. "Boogey..., so tell me..., what do I owe for this sudden visit?" Rev asks, motioning and inviting Boogey inside.

"I need a favor..., I mean a serious favor," Boogey utters, eye-to-eye. "Let me ask you this..., you trust me, right? I mean, you do trust my judgment, right?" Boogey nervously asks, somewhat concerned.

"Huh? I don't know, Boogey..., what is it?" Rev asks, cautiously staring back at him and then over at the door.

"You have to promise you'll give me a few hours of your time, and no questions asked; not even about the person with us," Boogey utters, waiting for Rev's confirmation.

Rev stands in deep thought for seconds then hesitantly nods 'yes'. He turns, grabbing his lightweight jacket when cutting off the light. "I'm going to trust you, Boog, but I have an uneasy feeling about surprises," Rev utters, lightly patting Boogey on the back and guiding him to the door.

They walk up to the car, open the door, and the interior lights come on when Rev backs away fast, staring deep into Reggie's raised eyebrows.

"Listen, we have a deal, remember, so you'll just have to trust me, Rev. I promise you'll see a great outcome," Boogie utters, lightly shoving him forward at the back.

"Yeah?" Rev utters, clenching his teeth when climbing in the front seat with Reggie slouching down deeper.

Boogey cranks up with slow, wandering eyes until easing into the street. He looks over at Rev, finding him somewhat uneasy. "Buckle up," Boogey whispers, looking out the window when it begins drizzling.

They drive thirty minutes then thirty more when Rev becomes very impatient. "Hey, look, I agreed to come, but we have been driving for what..., an hour already?" Rev utters, looking at the dash clock when nervously cutting curious eyes back at Reggie.

"Patience," Boogey utters, looking at Rev then Reggie through the rearview. "Take me in from here, Reg," Boogey utters, looking back through the rearview when passing the first run-down apartment complex.

"Here! Pull into this lot, beside the blue car," Reggie utters, slightly leaning forward with a hand tightly gripping the back of the seat with fast wandering eyes.

Boogey and Rev ease out simultaneously, looking back and waiting for Reggie.

Reggie stands, coming around to the other side fast with eyes wandering around other parked and passing cars.

"Look, I brought you here because a man here needs prayer. Hear him out and then pray over him so he can have some closure," Reggie utters with a serious face.

"That's it? Then why the secret..., because that's what I do," Rev says, proudly sticking his chest out.

Reggie knocks, then knocks heavier when looking back at Boogey and Rev.

"Yeah..., yeah..., yeah...; just hold your freakin' horses! I'm getting there already!" the old man mumbles in a low tone, slightly limping to the door.

They soon hear several locks, then a chain dangling then more locks when the door flies open; stopping at the extent of the longest and third chain.

"Reggie? Reggie, is that you?" the old man excitedly asks, finally recognizing him when the door shuts, and they hear more chains come off when the door swings open. "Reggiieee!" the old man lightly shrieks, smiling and tightly hugging Reggie.

"Hey, look..., these are my friends. This is Boogey and this is the guy I told you I would bring to pray with you," Reggie utters, pointing to Boogey and then Rev when walking past the old man and motioning Boogey and Rev inside.

Rev stands in the middle of the living room, looking around at everyone. "Ok, ok..., so are we joining hands, or is this one-on-one?" Rev curiously asks, skittishly looking over at Reggie.

The old man walks up to Rev. "Thank you, I shole (sure) do preshenate (appreciate) it," the old man utters, looking in Rev's eyes with a weak handshake.

"So what is it you need prayer over, my heavenly brother?" Rev asks.

"Well, there is a lot of hatred in me, so I need you to pray that I get over it. I just think this hatred has gone on long enough, and I want to put it behind me now," the man utters in deep thought.

"Hatred..., well, what kind of hatred? For..., what?"

"Well, I've been harboring bad feelings and hatred for the man who shot me, and I need some relief from it all. I always needed to know..., why me, why he screwed up my life. I just need closure, and there's no better time than now, seeing how I'm only getting older," the old man utters with a tear rolling down both cheeks, fast.

Rev instantly grips the man's hand and Rev's mind instantly flashes back to his own shooting incident when he begins praying and a calm comes over him, and he feels somewhat uplifted.

A smile grows on the man's face when his hands lift from Rev's and Rev ceases praying. The man eases back and slithers in a chair, grabbing tissues when leaning back as if almost out of breath, wiping.

"So, how do you feel, old man?" Boogey asks, looking at the man's big smile.

"For some reason, I feel comforted...; you know, as if something has been delivered to me this very evening," the old man utters, nodding with an even bigger smile. "I just can't say what it is at the moment."

"How about that awesome tea, pops?" Reggie asks, walking up to the old man with an extended hand to help him stand.

"Four cups, coming right up!" the old man utters, smiling when releasing Reggie, limping off and fading around the corner.

The three stand looking through the big picture window into the dark alley then distant city lights. "Boogey, can I have a word with you?" Reggie asks, pointing him to the hallway where they engage in mild chatter when the old man approaches with the first two cups.

Boogey looks back, hearing the man's limp boot hit the floor when he passes again. "Hey Boogey, please grab a few paper towels from the kitchen," Reggie utters.

Boogey squeezing past the old man who approaches and passes with two more cups.

Reggie slightly leans back whispering as the old man passes and instantly, the old man's smile turns serious, then into a deep frown and even more sinister when turning the corner.

The old man limps faster yet continually holding his head down while approaching Rev.

Rev grasps the cup and eases it down, then turns, noticing the old man's reflection through the window. "Thanks...," Rev begins to say when turning with the old man leaning forward expressly and almost transparently driving his knee deep into Rev's private, dropping him straight to his knees in a loud, stray scream. A think vein protrudes at Rev's forehead when on all fours and letting off another loud scream. "What's the fu..., is wrong with you?" Rev screams, cutting the curse word short. "You ole senile foo...!" Rev begins to say when it is cut short when elbowed at the top of his head.

Reggie's hands shoot forward, slamming the glass door shut and removing the key fast.

Boogey breaks his meditation, running down the hallway, shooting past Reggie, trying to open the door. He sees the old man swing at Rev through the glass but missing by centimeters when Rev ducks, still on all fours, low-crawling fast.

"Let it be, let it be!" Reggie screams, brandishing the key and holding Boogey in a bear hug from behind.

The old man's boots come up swiftly, kicking Rev in the face, almost knocking him out. "You screwed up my life..., you!" the old man shouts with a thunderous, echoing voice. He leans forward fast, gripping Rev's leg, swinging him in circles slow then faster until thrashing him heavily into oak furniture. The old man takes advantage of Rev, beating him down until running, bouncing from wall to wall like a professional wrestler, as if working out on the ropes.

Rev's girlish scream sounds off each time the man grabs hold of him, administering more pain, and moans when he lets go. He finally gains some leverage when the man walks off, taking a sip of hot tea and rolling his sleeves tighter. Rev slowly rises to his feet, watching the old man dash for another wall and bounce off it, rushing for Rev when he clothes hang him as he runs past. Rev takes a deep breath, finally regaining his strength and getting the upper hand after somewhat replicating the same punishment to the old man.

The old man shrieks when Rev has him high, ready to give him a backbreaker with scary eyes peeled back at the glass door and into Boogey's and Reggie's wide eyes.

"No! No! Don't, Rev..., stop it!" Boogey screams, pressing his face to the glass when warm breath slightly fogs the window.

Reggie releases Boogey, fumbling to get the key in the lock.

Rev throws his head over his shoulder hearing the door fly open and slam into the wall when losing his footing and staggering off to one side, dropping the man and hearing something loud pops. He leans in a deep turn and angrily lunges forward for the old man when Boogey tackles him at the waist, holding him.

The old man jerks, covering his face, then jerks again, staring into Rev's bruised face with tears. "I ain't ever done you, nothing (no harm)! Do you hear me? I ain't done you, nothing (no harm)! So why did you shoot me?" the old man screams at the top of his voice in deep tears, trembling.

Rev jerks away from Boogey, dropping and crawling off in the corner, in tears. "You? That was you? Look..., I'm so, so, sorry..., I was young and dumb; running around with fools claiming to be family. Look! Look at me! I'm a nervous wreck; always looking over my shoulders; can't have a family because I'm too scared some fool will come after me or my family on day!"

The room grows quiet, and their eyes nervously wander toward each other and then off.

There is total silence when the old man looks up, wiping away the last tear. "For what it's all worth; I forgive you, son. Heck, all the dudes I hung out with back then are dead and gone, so I would have probably been in my grave if this incident had not happened. There's good in all the bad; you just have to look hard for it, sometimes," the old man utters, sitting and then jumping up. "Whoa!!! My limp! My limp..., my limp...; it's gone!" the old man mutters, shaking his leg and then trotting a few steps.

He swiftly moves left then right as if faking and moving on a basketball court, until playfully faking shooting a long and slow three-pointer.

Boogey and Reggie burst into tears laughing when the old man walks over, patting Reggie's shoulder. "You're a good man, Reggie! Thanks for all you've done and for not passing me up on the street the day we met," the old man utters, shaking Reggie's hand even tighter.

Boogey stands over Rev with his hand out while Rev wipes his eyes and then extends his hand upward, springing to his feet. "Didn't I tell you to trust me?" Boogey utters, smiling at Rev and giving him a big hug.

"Thanks, Boogey," Rev utters, looking over at Reggie, who is in the background, and then the old man when he's approaching Rev.

"Thanks for the prayer and helping me free my mind, son," the old man who Rev shot in a dark alley, as a young gang member and assumed was dead, utters, reaching with an open hand, which Rev grabs, shaking joyfully and almost endlessly.

The old man steps back, playfully throwing the old one-two, fast jabs into Rev's ribs, barely touching him. "Now..., that's what you would have gotten had you stepped to me like a man instead of a young punk with a gun," the old man cheerily utters when performing a few more fancy fight moves.

Rev turns to Reggie in a stare when moving his lips; thanking him until closing and embracing.

They stay a little longer talking then greet the old man when leaving.

An hour later, on their ride back, they pass through a small town outside Fikesville, and Reggie happens to look down a side street, finding Mack's girlfriend.

"Hey..., slow down, Boogey! Pull over right here," Reggie utters with one hand on the headrest while leaning and looking back into the window.

Boogey pulls alongside a car, parallel parked when the back door flies open, and Reggie jumps out, running back to the corner.

Boogey and Rev cautiously look out the side and rearview mirrors for minutes. "Man, what's this cat up to, Boogey?" Rev uneasily asks.

"I don't know, but hand me my Betsy," Boogey responds, pointing to the glove box.

Rev continues staring through the side mirror until feeling Boogey tap his knee when reaching for the glove compartment, which flies open. Rev sees the gun neatly tucked away.

"Main (Man), hand me my Betsy!" Boogey says again, unable to reach it with his seat belt tight.

"Huh? Shi..., oooottt," Rev says, cutting the curse word short. "Man, I don't put my hands on people's guns because I don't know how many dead bodies are on it," Rev skittishly responds, swallowing hard and nervously looking away.

Boogey unfastens his seat belt quickly, reaching for a handkerchief, draping it over the gun when pulling it out, and wiping it off while looking at Rev's wide, nervous eyes.

Rev shakes his head in disbelief then looks through the side mirror with a nervous, tapping foot.

Reggie runs faster, waving and screaming at the female with no response.

The woman driver looks through the rearview, finally hearing a loud voice, when her hands lunge for the ignition; fumbling for keys, when recognizing Reggie.

"Girl, what is wrong with you?" the female passenger nervously asks, leaning back with eyes full of excitement before looking back.

The female driver continually freaks out, still fighting to nervously get the key in the ignition when Reggie's hand slams on the roof, and he leans in, staring deep into her teary eyes.

"Ah...!" the driver shrieks, turning sideways and backing up until almost in her girlfriend's lap, skittishly kicking and shaking.

The passenger begins fighting to get her girlfriend off her so she can breathe.

Reggie grasps the window frame, shaking the car to calm her. "Hey, hey, hey..., look..., just calm down! Girl..., I'm not going to hurt!" Reggie utters, looking at her balled fist and keys heavily jingling in the other hand.

Without warning, a huge burst of pepper spray shoots forward; a direct, solid stream splattering between his eyes when Reggie snatches the keychain, yanking it and unintentionally spraying more when stumbling back, temporarily blind.

The women cover their burning eyes when the passenger bangs her girlfriend in the back until getting her off.

The passenger door flies open, and the women fall out; springing up stealthily, recovering, swinging, and screaming in fear while blindly backing away.

Boogey grows uneasy, finally throwing on his turn signal. He pulls off after a car passes and slowly creeps forward, holding the covered gun tightly and letting go of the wheel to roll down the window.

Rev's eyes bulge, jerking into Boogey while grabbing the wheel and swerving back across the yellow line.

Boogey's feet ease on the brakes, slowly pumping them when advancing around the corner.

They circle most of the block and then close in on the corner, leaning into the dash, nervously glancing around the next corner. "What the...?" they say almost instantaneously, finding two women running in circles when the driver runs straight into a telephone pole and falls flat on her back, screaming.

Boogey drops the gun in the seat, turning quickly then skids wheels, pulling up on the female's car fast, and slamming on the brakes.

Reggie flies into the street, up by Boogey's car, out of nowhere, screaming until backing off, fast, and running in a zigzag pattern while swinging.

Boogey and Rev hold their laughs for as long as they can, then burst into laughter, jostling into each other until anxiously jumping out.

Reggie rapidly blinks, licking his finger and sticking them up when taking off running upwind and towards Boogey.

Boogey keeps a steady eye on Reggie, snatching him in the collar and swinging him around until easing him against the car. "Hey, hey, hey, stand here! I've got water in the car!" Boogey shouts.

Boogey runs toward the trunk, finding Rev holding the women and saying something to them. He pulls out paper cups and a gallon jug, rushing over to hand Reggie a cupful and then the women. "What in the hell is going on out here?" Boogey nervously asks, guiding Reggie over to Rev and the women.

"Hell man..., I was trying to stop this nut and talk to her, but she gonna (is going to) mace me!" Reggie shrieks, holding his head back when pouring more water over his eyes.

The three stand upwind, blinking while Boogey and Rev stand behind them quietly, laughing hard and falling into each other, acting silly.

Rev's smile instantly diminishes when expressly tapping Boogey's shoulder when finding flashing blue lights slowly approaching.

The cruiser stops and sits perpendicular with a very old deputy finally and slowly easing the door open. He stands even slower, leaning back inside, grabbing his mangled bifocals. He leans back in the cruiser again, mumbling something and cursing when reaching for his ten-gallon, overly-wrinkled hat.

"Boogey..., the gun?" Rev nervously murmurs when Boogey's face transforms into pure fear.

"What? A freakin' gun?" Reggie whispers, cutting his eyes over at the old deputy who slowly reaches back inside again for his Billy club. Reggie looks at the female driver, walking over to her. "Hey..., give me the mace," Reggie utters, staring into her scary eyes.

"What? Not even!" she sarcastically utters.

"Look..., ole boy got a dirty gun with no telling how many dead bodies on it, and I know you got plenty of dope, so give me the mace, or we're all going to jail for a very, very long time."

Unsure of Reggie's intentions, the female driver finally eases the mace from the key ring, placing it in his hand, when backing away, quickly.

Reggie leans, staring at Boogey's frown. "Is the gun hot?" he asks, watching Boogey nod 'yes'. "Uh-huh..., and ole girl is packing hella (a lot of) uncut dope," Reggie utters, looking at Rev's face go stale. "Follow my lead," Reggie whispers, slowly walking toward Boogey's vehicle.

"Now, you just hold it right there, young feller (fellow)!" the old deputy finally yells; still taking baby steps like a drunk or baby wearing a loaded diaper with his vision ninety percent blurred even with glasses. He finally picks up his pace, easing up on Reggie slowly with a shaky hand over his holster.

Reggie backs from the door, turning when heavily shoved back into the car with the old deputy heavily breathing then wheezing.

The deputy's eyes widen, looking around until seeing Boogey's heat in the front seat. His hands go instantly to his sidearm when a steady blast of mace shoots forward, soaking the old deputy's thick eyebrows and then bifocals, when hearing his old, frail screams.

Reggie continually discharges while holding the gun in the holster, then snatches the gun, wiping it with his shirttail, and throwing it in the tall grass. He grasps the deputy again until releasing the deputy with him screaming louder.

The old deputy high steps faster, screaming until looking like he's continually two stepping. He continually jumps, kicks, and swings, almost in slow motion. He springs for a walkie-talkie which Reggie pulls, then slings the old deputy around by the cord until he falls, kicking, when the walkie-talkie rips from his shirt and Reggie kicks it away. The old deputy's hand comes forward, pulling Reggie's leg forward when biting with the dentures coming out, still clamped and chattering around Reggie's ankle.

"Ah...! Ahh...!" Reggie screams, hopping in circles and then springing forward as if in a sack race when Rev tackles him. Reggie finally sees the teeth in Rev's hand when he calms down, springing up and distancing himself when Rev playfully makes the teeth chomp down and then jumps at Reggie in a playful chase. "Aighhh! Aighhh! Man..., stop..., playing, stop it!" Reggie screams, continually keeping his eyes on Rev when rushing over to Boogey, where they meet between the vehicles.

The old deputy rises high, spotting the walkie-talkie then drops, low-crawling for it.

Reggie walks up, kicking the walkie-talkie with another blast of heavy pepper spray between the deputy's eyes; making him scream and fight harder.

"Follow me close!" Reggie shrieks, scurrying for the girl's car and meeting up with the driver, and wrestling for the door handle while the other female climbs into the front passenger seat. "Let me drive!" Reggie shrieks, pulling her hand until tugging and shoving when the door opens fast, slamming into his shin. "I will be da...!" he shrieks, jumping up and down when motioning Boogey to follow.

The old deputy eyes somewhat clear and he musters up strength, low-crawling with adrenaline, for the walkie-talkie. "Officer down..., officer down..., 34th and Westerly..., on the side road, next to Holden's chicken joint! Ten black men, all with AR-15s, have me at gun point! I repeat..., ten black men!"

The female driver jumps in behind the driver's seat fast and gives her friend a high five with heavy giggling.

Reggie hears sirens closing in fast when cranking, stomping the gas pedal, burning deep rubber, and heading for back roads with Boogey hot on his trail. He puts a great distance between them and the law then slows down, going from county to county on more familiar back roads.

An hour or so later, he drives into a rustic area, proceeding a mile or so until streetlights fade and the road turns pitch black, becoming heavily graveled.

At a distance, a light pops out as they pierce their eyes forward and through total darkness.

Reggie pulls under the streetlight, which lights the corner of an old ball field. He turns off the engine, looking through the rearview, when Boogey pulls up.

"Thanks, Reggie," the female driver utters, sitting up and looking around.

"Not a problem, but you didn't have to mace me." Reggie says, looking in the rearview.

"Well, heck, you shouldn't have bum-rushed me like that. I thought you and your goons were trying to jack me for my car and stash (drugs)!" The female driver giggles.

"Goons? Girl, you tripping! Anyway, I haven't seen you in a day or so..., so what's up with you and Mack?" Reggie asks, watching Boogey's and then Rev's door fly open.

"You mean your old, played-out leader?" the female driver responds, looking at her girlfriend, who smiles. "I got tired of a grown man playing childish games." The female driver opens a pack of gum. "What y'all need to do is step up your game before y'all end up in pine boxes, ok?" She says, unwrapping a stick, and smacking gum.

Boogey and Rev walk up and everyone staggers over by the old, sundried bleachers.

"Hey, I know you." The female driver points to Rev. "The SUV the other night, huh?"

"Yeah, I remember," Rev utters, taking a seat on the third row.

"Man, if I were you, I would leave town..., you hear me?" the female driver utters, staring at Rev with deep concern.

"Oh yeah, and why is that?" Rev curiously asks.

"Because things will only get worse for you. Man, Mack's got a thing for you; I think he's obsessed with you or something. Shucks, he watches you like a hawk and plans to drain you of everything: car, house, bank account," she utters with pity.

"Aight..., enough!" Reggie utters, skittishly interrupting when embarrassingly staring at the ground.

"Well..., well..., is it true?" Rev asks, looking over at Reggie when Boogey walks up on Reggie with a tightly clenched fist.

"Well, is it?" Boogey asks in a mean tone with an even tighter balled fist until staring under-eyed.

"Look, I'm doomed if I do; doomed if I don't," Reggie utters when the female passenger walks over, looking at him with sorrowful eyes while running her fingers through his greasy hair to comfort him as he sits.

"It's ok..., you can tell them," the female passenger utters, stroking Reggie's head and frowning while pretending to massage his shoulders while wiping and cleaning her hands on his shirt with a mushy look.

"Y'all don't know this fool like I do! He's broke as hell, running out of resources, and now, taking roll call to get or stay ahead," Reggie finally says in a concerned tone.

"Oh really..., so why me?" Rev asks staring at Reggie, apoplectic.

"Man, she's right! It's as if it's an obsession. He's dead set on destroying you because of your new walk with Christ and how people respect you. Heck, he studies you like a whore studies a trick, a rat studies cheese, a scientist studies a project, a cop studies a criminal, a snake...," he continues when Boogey boldly interrupts with a frown.

"Enough, already! Yeah, yeah, we get it! We get it, already!" Boogey utters, shaking his head in disbelief that he would go on.

"It's only a matter of time before he snaps, so that's why I brought the business to Boogey and had you meet the old man. Mack doesn't know the old man is alive, or he would kill him and find a way to frame Rev for it," Reggie utters, looking over at Boogey.

"There has to be a way to end this non-sense..., you know; a way bring this clown down!" Boogey utters, pulling his pocketknife from his back pocket, when beginning to clean his nails.

"Well, I don't want no part of that business because he's a plain fool! It's like his brain is fried from corruption and bad drugs," Reggie utters when looking away.

Boogey cleans more dirt from under his nails in even deeper thought.

They talk longer, but only Boogey and Rev are creative in devising plans, which always ends with Reggie drawing Mack into a trap, and Reggie is not fond of that.

"Look, every plan leads to me and this fool! I done (already) told you Mack ain't wrapped too tight, Jack!. Hell, just last week, he shot a man over a nickel bag and the cops know it but too afraid to arrest him, so they turn the other way. He has been diagnosed with things that I can even pronounce. I am telling you…, this dude is a walking, and unexploded ordnance," Reggie utters, drifting deeper into more horrible thoughts of uncanny things he's seen Mack do over the years when growing silent for minutes with more flashes in his mind until distracted.

"Screw it! I'll do it," the female driver utters, looking over at her girlfriend.

"Ah whaaaattt…, girl, are you crazy? That nut put you in the hospital like what, five times, and you're talking about doing it? He just stopped stalking you what…, a day ago, if that so you need to rethink this one!" The girlfriend stares at her girlfriend's thick, makeup-covered bruises.

"Why don't you do it, Boogey?" Reggie utters, laughing as if it's a hilarious joke.

"How? I don't even know the dude," Boogey utters, beaming, knowing he has a good excuse not to get involved. "What about you, Rev? It's your life at stake, or should we draw straws?" Boogey utters, giving Rev an out as well.

Boogey walks away, with his back to them when pulling a handful of tall straws from the ground. He secretly frays one, making it the longest before walking back up, handing them to the female passenger. "Ok, I'll go first," Boogey utters, staring hard at the frayed straw's edge.

"Nope… not so easy there, pal!" Reggie respond, reaches quickly, and touching the frayed one when Boogey feels faint as his eyes close then open slowly, breathing a sigh of relief, when discovering the frayed straw still there. "Ok, now you can go," Reggie utters, backing off, smiling.

Everyone draws, and the girl in the passenger seat is left with the shortest when her mouth falls open. "Oh…, hell naw (no)! I'm not even getting mixed up with this fool! Look, you, you, and you are mixed up in this already, so you better work it out!" she utters, pointing at everyone except Boogey when flicking the straw in Reggie's face.

"Let's just lock him up in a room full of balloons," Mack's ex utters in deep thought.

"What? Are you serious? Naw, a badass like Mack is scared of balloons?" The female passenger utters, looking at Reggie, who bursts into laughter.

"What?" Boogey asks, clueless.

"Do you remember when we were in our twenties, and he ran up in a house to blast this dude who was having a party for his kids?" Reggie asks.

Reggie and Rev stare at each other, holding back their laughs when finally recalling the incident and bursting into laughter while giving several high fives.

"Boogey, you got to hear this one, man! Well..., Reggie and us are sitting in the car, right. Mack's crazy tail runs up to a house with all these balloons and this clown ends up shooting every balloon and not hitting one person," Reggie says, screaming in laughter when drifting off and recalling more of the incident.

Rev joins in happily finishing the story and wraps it up with play-by-play mental pictures when showing how Mack ran out when everyone laughs, in endless tears.

Rev and Reggie wait until the laughter calms down then take turns reenacting more scenes until the laughter grows again and then finally tapers off.

A smile grows on Boogey's face and then grows even brighter.

"What..., what is it?" the female driver asks, being the first to notice Boogey's reaction.

"Here's the plan: The three of you will set it up," Boogey utters, picking up a stick and rubbing his foot across the dirt to smooth the surface when drawing a box. "Here's what we'll do...," Boogey utters, giggling.

Early Sunday, Boogey, and Nattie stop off at the convalescent home, picking up Dale's roommate for Winton's second day of barbecuing.

Boogey pulls onto Winton's street, and his eyes wander over the long row of cars, looking for a parking spot. He pulls in front of Winton's house, and Winton comes out, directing a few people to move their cars further into the backyard. Boogey waits, looking around at the large crowd, and waving to a few people.

Nattie stares over the yard, finding Nelle waving until she looks away, seeing a car's trunk raised, and someone peeking when the man who threw mini boulders at their new vehicle stands, looking around, then digging in a trunk again.

The car in front of Boogey stops, blocking him and another pulls up from behind.

Nattie's eyes grow wide when confirming it is indeed the man when her hand continually pounds hard on Boogey's thigh while speechless yet pointing.

Boogey finally leans past her, spotting the man with a box.

The man levels the box in his arm when slamming the trunk, and then braces it with both hands. He briefly looks in their direction when swiftly lowering the box, until placing it on the ground. His hand comes up, blocking the sun when looking up the road, past Boogey and Nattie, not noticing them when looking back down at the cakes to make sure they didn't shift.

Boogey's eyes grow wide when his taillights come on with the car rolling back fast, slamming into a car's front bumper. He stays on the gas, burning rubber, but only moves a foot or so.

The other frail-looking driver continually holds his brakes to the floor, looking out the window, until leaning out, frowning and screaming with wide eyes.

The carload of passengers continually floats in and out of the thick patch of vape and weed smoke.

Several people flood into the street to see what's going on when Winton rushes up to Boogey's window, fading in from black, tire smoke, in muffled screams while pounding the window hard with his balled fist.

Boogey's wide eyes stare at Winton until he fades back into the black smoke, but the pounding grows harder when raised cylinders finally calm to a dull roar.

"Man, what are you doing? Do you know you just backed into a car?" Winton yells, fading back into view and looking back at the car which is full of neighborhood crackheads who are giving high fives and laughing as if there is no end to laughter.

"What's that dude doing here?" Boogey points at the man who still hadn't seen him but walks up fast to see what's going on when veering off and into the backyard.

"Oh, man, that's Nelle's people; he's just coming back from the sto (store), from picking up the cakes. What do you mean what's he doing here? He's invited just like you and the rest of the neighborhood," Winton utters, leaning back again, to see if the other car has any damages. Winton steps off and a few feet behind Boogey's car to see if there is damage to Boogey's car then comes back.

The stoned driver springs up from the old, rusty battlewagon, skipping between cars and noticing his doesn't even have a scratch, but Boogey's bumper is torn up. "Ugh, ugh, somebody gone (is going to) pay me, boo-boo!"

Boogey slides out, looking around at the few bystanders who instigate and then the stoned driver as he ambles between the cars again. "I will be!" Boogey utters, looking at his mangled bumper, when shaking his head in disbelief.

"Somebody gone (is going to) pay me for this, boo-boo!" the crackhead finally repeats, when slapping his fist in his open hand with each spoken word.

"Hold it a minute," Winton utters. "Look…, there are no damages to your car, only to Boogey's, so why pay you?" Winton utters, walking up a little closer when the strong, stale stench of alcohol, weed and some other unfamiliar smell rises in his nostrils.

"Ugh, ugh, ugh…, I don't even know what kind of damage has been done to my scruts (struts), my shots (shocks), my undacarig (undercarriage), my bakes (breaks), my oils (coils)," the crackhead utters so fast with a twisted mouth that they can't even understand one word.

"Ok…, ok…, we can handle this right here and now," Boogey utters, fed up when digging deep in his pockets and fumbling for his money clip. "So, how much are we talking?" Boogey asks, staring into the crackhead's glassy eyes and then his white lips with white mush in the corners.

The crackhead's snake eyes grow sharper, staring at Boogey's hands, which are still deep in his pockets, while Boogey looks up in deep thought. "At least a thousand…, shoot, next week my neck might hurt, my back, my booty and my…," he begins to sing like the old song, when dancing in rhythm with music blaring.

"Ok, ok, we get it!" Boogey interrupts, thinking a little more when easing his hand out, displaying the thick wad. "Who's your insurance carrier? Give me your policy number," he utters, looking at the guy who eases his narrow, tight butt on the hood.

"Smitty's Insurance," the driver utters after looking over his shoulder at his friend's name tag on his mechanical work shirt when quickly cutting his eyes back at Boogey. He looks back at his friend Smitty who takes another hit off the thickly rolled joint and puts it in rotation as the car fills with smoke until everyone inside vanishes.

Boogey and Winton stare in disbelief then burst into laughter.

"Look, pay me now, or get sued; it's as simple as day!" the crackhead utters, sweating when looking in the car, seeing all the hands fanning when his friends start to reappear, finally.

"Oh yeah? Well, call the cops and let's try recapping: DUI, no license, drugs." Boogey finds a guy with a bagful of rock cocaine held high in a tiny plastic bag. "Hmm…, driving without insurance, distribution…, wait…," Boogey utters, rushing to the window and pointing for Nattie to open the glove box when pointing inside.

Nattie pulls out the old, crusty calculator, looking over her shoulder at Winton.

Boogey eases over to Winton and the crackhead. "So, where were we? Oh, DUI, classes, twenty-five hundred attorney fees, no license, no insurance, another five hundred, drugs, so jail time…, ok, so we're looking at multiplying that cost; plus five to six years per person. Hmm… you may want to ask your friends if they are really hurt because they'll be in a world of hurt to lose the little jobs they may have, if any," Boogey utters, spotting Smith's name tag when slipping the calculator then thick wad back in his pocket.

"Man, you got some mess with you! Aight (alright), five hundred." The crackhead takes a deep swallow and more foam spews from the corner of his mouth the faster he talks.

"How 'bout fifty, but before you make that decision, check with your friends, so we are all on the same page." Boogey looks at Winton, who smiles, shaking his head.

The crackhead slides off the hood, leaning into the driver's window. "Hey, look, this clown only wants to give us fifty. I told him a thousand, but he's threatening to call the cops, and y'all know I can't afford to go back to jail, neither can you, or you, or you, or you, or you," he says, pointing on demand.

"Huh, you take it and let's get the hell out of here before the cops come and block the street. Man, my PO would be knee-deep in me if he knew I was even in this car," the more mouthy guy utters, watching his friend amble over to Winton and Boogey.

"Aight, fifty, yah (you) tight as...," he began to say when Winton interrupts him, pointing to a little kid walking by. "Hey..., there are little kids out here!" Winton yells. "Boogey, pay this clown, and let's get this road cleared," Winton utters, walking away.

Boogey pulls the thick wad out, peeling off a fifty from below several hundreds.

The crackhead's eyes open wide, staring over the big-faced hundreds when grasping the fifty and slowly turning to walk away, discouraged.

Boogey grows frustrated, putting the money in his pocket, when turning.

The crackhead slips a retractable police wand from his pocket, falling in a turn when Nattie sees him in the side mirror and cuts her eyes back, continuously laying into the horn. "Lookout, Boogey!" she shrieks at the top of her trembling voice.

Winton turns, sprinting and jumping between Boogey and the crackhead, blocking and throwing a couple of blows with wind effects, trying to grab the wand.

"Come on, Winton! You know you ain't quick enough to get that wand from a crackhead!" Nelle shrieks, sprinting to the edge of the driveway.

Sirens draw near, and the crackhead screams, jumping toward and from Winton when scrambling for his door.

Boogey jumps in, making a sharp turn in the yard, and pulls behind the trailer.

The crackhead backs down quickly, burning rubber and fading around the corner where tires are heard squealing until blue flashing lights appear, and the cruiser makes a five-point turn, peeling rubber behind the old, smoking, black battle wagon.

Boogey, Nattie, Dale, and his roommate sit watching the chase until it fades around the corner and the sirens fade when they ease out.

DJ Skeet wraps up the last slow song, changing to an up-tempo beat when more folks pack the miniature basketball-looking, cracked concrete pad until almost full.

Dale and his roommate amble around, cautiously looking until fading into the crowd.

Boogey and Nelle's drunk, zip popping cousin meet up at the bar and start talking as if nothing ever happened.

Before long, the cookout is in full effect, and everyone is having the time of their lives.

Dale wanders by the DJ booth, where he and his roommate spend most of their time. From time to time, he and the roommate make their rounds to different tables, sneaking unattended liquor and beer, not realizing it's all free.

Winton stands later, frustrated from losing another hand of spades and smiles when Boogey motions him over with hands deep in his pockets; coming up with rabbit ears, when peeling off a hundred and whispering. Winton smiles when taking the money to the DJ booth and whispers and when passing the money to the DJ. He walks off as the song ends and the microphone keys up.

"Alright, everybody! We've got a rap contest coming up soon, so please sign up. Please write your song down or provide your CD, if you have one. You..., you, and..., you, please come up and be judges," the DJ utters pointing to two women he has been checking out while talking to a man he knows.

Dale stares at the few hands reaching for the clipboard when a real big smile grows. He turns, jostling into a few people, and rushes to the car for his backpack.

The DJ waits for people to grab a bite, then returns to the mic. "Alright, folks!" He turns the volume up to a dope beat, calling the first young guy's name and watches the guy makes his way to the booth, reaching for the mic when the beat fades in.

The seventeen-year-old rocks his head, smoothly flowing in with a nice freestyle when over half the people look in laughter and cheer as the concrete pad fills quickly with dancers.

An hour later, and after the fifth person performs, the DJ looks over the board. "Judges, one more, and then we will tally the score," the DJ utters, winking at his female companion, standing next to him, who gives him a glowing smile.

Dale hands the DJ the CD and then looks at the crowd with bloodshot eyes until pulling his shades from his head over his eyes.

A few people get others' attention when they find the old, collar-popping, shade-wearing, cool Dale with the mic.

The DJ puts on Dale's stolen CD, and everyone stands, screaming. Dale's head slightly bobs like a cool youngster as the DJ fades Dale's CD in as he did with the others when the crowd stands and goes suicidal over the dopiest beat ever.

Several guys in the back wild out until the first line of Dale's freestyle has them scrambling to see his flow and moves.

The women continually yelp loudly until the yard sounds like a small, filled stadium.

All of the judges applaud, except one, who gets up and starts dancing, while the other two dance in their seats.

A well-dressed guy reaches for his backpack, pulling out a miniature microphone and recorder, when furtively recording the beat and Dale's lyrics.

Dale ends the rap with a standing ovation, something the others had not managed to accomplish in their flows.

A roar echoes over the neighborhood when the DJ ends the session, and looks at the roster.

People grow quiet, mumbling, as the judges, stand and the DJ call the first rapper when the judges raise their fingers, scoring.

Everyone scores five through seven, and a drumroll plays when calling Dale's name.

The judges stand; all three showing ten fingers, with the crowd going crazy.

The DJ reaches for the wrinkled hundred, waving it high before passing it to Dale. "Hey, how about a track from your CD and a rap to close out?" the DJ asks, easing on headphones when moving to another track when Dale begins freestyling.

The well-dressed man with the recorder looks around excitedly, smiling when grabbing a chair next to the DJ, getting quality reception from the crystalline speakers.

Three hours later, the cookout comes to a near end when over half the people leave.

The DJ and his female companion begin wrapping up some of his gear.

All of a sudden there's a fracas out front with a female and the DJ's best male friend, which escalates to the side of the house and then the backyard.

"Ugh..., ugh..., who the hell is this damn, skeezer?" A beautiful, thick-bottomed, heavy breathing ex. screams, pointing at the DJ's new woman, who stands in shock. "Naw…, naw…, naw…, who the hell is this, tramp, Skeet! Somebody better tell me something!" the woman yells, pushing the DJ's best friend's hand down and swinging on him when he forces her back.

"Girl, you better gone (get out of here) with that mess! I done (already) took out a restraining order, so you best leave!" the DJ yells, motioning for his new female companion to run like hell when she moves closer, thinking he will protect her.

The DJ continues quickly and fearfully wrapping up and accidentally slips Dale's CD under the turntable.

The crazy ex boldly stares at the crowd then the DJ, rushing to the far end of the house.

The DJ's male friend follows closely when the ex-girlfriend rushes past a steel baseball bat, and then slows. She bobs and weaves, then fakes right, doubling back, and scooping up the bat when he screams, veering off around the trailer as fast as his feet can carry him.

"Run!" the DJ squawks, looking into his new female companion's wide eyes while backing up when his ex-girlfriend runs to the booth with the bat drawn overhead.

The DJ's new companion drops low, low-crawling to the other side of the stand, closer to the DJ.

The ex-girlfriend takes a swing at the DJ's fast-ducking head, then another, missing. She screams, wide-eyed as if crazy when smashing his equipment with four good whacks when looking at the DJ with bloodshot eyes when his face transforms.

The DJ's new companion peeks out from under the stand, looking for the DJ, who is nowhere in sight until looking toward the house, finding his shiny shoes fading alongside. She eases out, kneeling and pleading for her life until on her feet with her hand shielding her face, in tears.

The ex-girlfriend ambles up with the bat sprung back, taunting her with derogatory words and forcing her back into the platform.

Winton pops up out of nowhere, taking a stance when leaning back, aiming his shotgun high, and firing a shot straight up in the air.

Everyone screams, ducking and scrambling with many covering their heads in fear of falling buckshot when running off screaming with some slamming against houses when hearing the light sound of pellets spraying the area when more screams come.

The ex-girlfriend drops the bat's base, dragging it backward while backing away, then slowly turns, finding Winton's gun to her head.

"Girl, if you don't get off my property with this bull…, I'll pump enough lead in you to send you off the face of God's green Earth!" he screams with one eyebrow slightly raised.

The girl nervously drops the bat, staring at Winton with a smirk while slowly backing away until at the edge of the house, looking out front, then mischievously back at Winton, smiling when falling back in a deep turn.

The DJ sits nervously, patting his feet, lightly revving the engine, and looking for his new companion when his ex-girlfriend fades into view like a jaguar on its prey. His eyes grow wide, and his mouth drops open when tires squeal, burning deep rubber when bailing out, almost hitting a few scurrying bodies.

Dale finally crawls out of the doghouse, scrambling to his feet, looking over the damaged equipment. He glances inside the broken mixer, finding a jammed, busted CD, and feels weak when falling in a seat, sadly staring around when tears fall as he thinks about the CD.

Nattie walks up out of nowhere, lifting the busted CD player. "Is this what you're looking for?" Nattie asks, handing him the undamaged CD when a big smile comes over him.

Boogey and Nattie load up, bidding Nelle and Winton a goodnight.

Distant sirens soon fade in when Dale and his roommate jump inside, and Boogey pulls through the path behind the trailer, heading for the convalescent center.

# CHAPTER TEN

### State Fair Extrava Without The Ganza

On Monday, over at Boogey's house, around noon, Dale bathes, listening to a radio, and grows excited when hearing the announcer advertising a new hit that he can't wait to hear. He turns up the volume, adjusting the clothes hanger antennae, when the prerecorded session from the cookout fades in, and his name comes across the air, clearly. Dale's eyes bulge, skittishly springing from the tub, naked. He heads for the door, reaching back, yanking the cord, and dropping the radio in the tub; mildly shocked by the over splash when the power goes out and the bathroom lights up from sparks. Dale's shocked body trembles, slowly falling back into the cabinet with his eyes closed tight with radiant hair when Boogey shoots up from the couch.

"Dale, what the…!" Boogey shrieks, still rocking to the silent beat.

"Oh…, nooootthhiiiingggg!" he nervously responds with bright, fearful eyes.

Boogey runs to the fuse box, resetting the power, which instantly shorts out, followed by fizzing when Boogey slams the power level down again hearing a thump. He runs for the door, throwing the bathroom door open, and finds Dale half-naked; low-crawling toward him with a smoking, blown-out hairdo and trembling hands.

Throughout the day, Boogey notices that he seems more coherent, responsive, playful, and mature.

Time goes by, and Dale finally walks in later, sitting on the couch next to Boogey, watching television.

Boogey stares at him from time to time, noticing an attentive and worried look.

"Shucks, I forgot my meds, but I'll be doggone…, I feel a lot better without them," Dale utters, yet not so cheerful while looking around and surprisingly moving his head and arms while staring at them as if they are foreign objects. Dale goes into a higher level of conversation, indulging in the news and world events, until surprising even Boogey.

Nattie stands in the kitchen, listening for a while, and then walks to the door, peeking until her shadow unknowingly extends across the living room floor.

"Boy…, is your wife still nosy as hell, Boog!" Dale utters, watching Nattie's shadow barely move back and then quickly fade off to one side.

Outside the general store, Crackhead Tom stands, looking at the twenty-thousand-dollar, reward poster again, until easing off to the side of the store. He sneaks inside, walking over by the window with an eager eye on everyone.

The female clerk turns for a second, and the sign fades along with Tom, who appears out front with the folded big sign sticking from his back pocket. He sits, stopping folks, and asking about the reward to see if they knew the amount. He even questions a teen who had just scrolled up, combing his hair. "Yeah..., well, there is a twenty-dollar reward for information, so if you know anything or anyone who does, I'll double the reward," he utters, still picking dirt from under his nails.

Over at Boogey's, an unfamiliar voice calls the house, advising Boogey that the word is out that he and Nattie hit the mega jackpot, then immediately hangs up.

Boogey freezes with his mouth dropped open, until without warning he frantically screams, and Nattie bursts out of the room, running into him. "Grab some things! People think we hit the dang jackpot! Oh, man! This place will be swarming like flies on stank in no time!" Boogey yells, slamming the phone down and throwing busted luggage on the foot of the bed.

Dale struts out of the junky bedroom, sitting on the couch in a daze, and begins playing with Bud. He goes into a daze, subconsciously shaking his head while nervously rocking to clear his mind of the visions of the mean rapper that won't go away.

Boogey and Nattie rush out within minutes, loading up, quickly. They return Dale to the center and then get a cheesy hotel room on the outskirts of town.

Within hours after sunrise, the news team stands on Boogey and Nattie's porch early Tuesday morning, knocking or peeking through dirty screened windows.

Before long, the lawn fills with all sorts of spectators.

The streets grow crowded as other television crews set up satellite equipment or other teams adjust huge, satellite dishes.

Meanwhile, Boogey and Nattie are coming into a changed game plan when checking into a more luxurious hotel.

Upon arrival, Nattie rushes to the mirror, straightening her scarf then reaching for the remote. She flips through channels, stopping on an old Western until Boogey comes out then goes to shower, tightening her robe when easing the door shut.

Boogey eases into the recliner flipping through channels until stopping on a news channel when seeing Winton's corpulent head in an interview. He watches in awe, noticing Melissa, Davillier, and the grandkids standing off to the side, smiling and waving. "Nattie, quick!" he screams, slightly turning up the volume.

Nattie sprints in minutes later, easing onto the foot of the bed as the kids and grandkids pop up on the screen again; all with big smiles, right down to the baby.

The director and his assistant finally pull up at Boogey's house, fanning dust when jumping out with a big poster-size check with two hundred thousand scribbled in bold, black lettering.

Winton rushes up on the porch and to the door again, banging then pounding until turning with glistening eyes, when finally glancing over at the poster, smiling. He bursts into a silly laugh spitting out a thick wad of tobacco with the wind throwing spit back onto his white shirt when rushing down the steps fast. "Who the heck do you think you're fooling? Hell..., did Boog put you up to this?" he whispers in the director's ear.

"Fooling? By all means..., what do you mean, sir?" the director asks curiously, adjusting his spectacles.

Winton excitedly draws closer, until snatching the poster, then strains with all his might, trying to rip the thick laminated board but can't when loud laughter bursts out from watching veins popping out of his head and neck. Winton begins over excitedly dancing in circles when throwing the poster down, stomping it, then fumbling for his pocket, brandishing a blade, and continually stabbing the poster.

A bigger outpour of laughter comes with more news teams shuffling to get a good shot of the drama.

Winton jumps to his feet, pissed, when expressly sticking his index finger in the director's face. "This hea (here) is bull!" Winton shrieks. "I know for a fact that my cousin, Boogey Johnson, hit for the biggon (big one)!" Winton screams when several more reporters rush up.

"What..., what..., what the..., no..., no..., no, Wint!" Boogey shrieks, slightly rising from the recliner and shaking his head while Nattie stares at the wide-screen in disbelief.

The director picks up the bigger pieces of the poster, frowning and motioning to his assistant, who walks slowly closely behind him. The two walk faster until running for the car with nervous eyes still over their shoulders.

Winton sprints back up the steps, passing Melissa and Davillier, knocking but even more excited with all, thirty-two teeth showing.

"Did it ever occur to you that maybe they're not here?" Melissa tries whispering to Winton when it amplifies through the high-keyed mic.

The cameraman zooms around, taking close-ups of the porch and hole-ridden, busted roof before targeting prospective people to question. One newscaster deviously points to some of the most busted and disgusting-looking characters she can find; the first being a young girl with home-maid, aluminum foil hair wrappers.

The newscaster and cameraman rush up, interviewing her; a crackhead and then a drunk man then move on to others but the most dignified folks they intentionally pass. They quickly move on to those having a bad day or those making themselves readily available; a nuisance or a sight for sore eyes.

A smile grows on Nattie's face for a brief second when the camera zooms in on Freddy, who proudly leans back against an old pickup, running his comb through his long, slicked-back, cold, and black, permed, linty hair.

Boogey instantly cuts his eyes at Nattie, staring at the side of her face; growing pissed when finding her cheeks round until growing flat when cutting her eyes back over at Boogey.

Over at the convalescent center, the famous rapper, his best friend, and his grandfather head for Dale's room, kicking in the door and finding the room empty. The three search the whole facility then burst through the electronic security side door, climbing into the running SUV.

The rapper lays into the engine, bringing the SUV up to seventy, when his hand goes to the radio, tweaking it. Instantly, he hears his unreleased beat bleed through from yet, another radio station when his foot rises high, slamming on the brake, and bringing the truck to a screeching halt.

An immediate, heavy thumb comes when his unbuckled grandfather's head slams into the dash, breaking up the wood grain with the friend flung forward and head-butting the grandfather when his head slams back against the head-rest. "Ouooah!" the grandfather screams in a frown with a few tears.

The grandson eyes shoot to the grandfather, who eases back, rubbing his aching head.

The grandfather soon runs his hand into the indention in his forehead, then slowly over the broken-up wood grain, and then slowly buckles up.

"I knew that clown stole one of my CDs!" the rapper shrieks, turning sharply and speeding away. "Here! Here!" he screams, pointing at the glove box when the grandfather drops the compartment door open. The rapper leans, looking in the glove box, pointing for his gun. "We're doing a drive-by on this old fool!" the rapper shrieks, looking into his grandfather's nervous eyes and then his trembling hands, finding his grandfather's head shaking 'no' with hands coming tightly at his side, in a flash.

"Hmm..., heck naw! You get it yourself. A gun will get you an automatic ten years, but a body can get you a life sentence," he responds, still staring at the shiny gun and shaking his head, negatively.

Hours later, a cameraman receives a reliable tip on Boogey's and Nattie's location. He notifies his newscaster, and they wrap up their gear, speeding off.

Other news teams replicate their actions, and before long, there's a caravan of fast moving vehicles on the back roads.

The fifth truck exits and a man yell out the hotel's name on a live feed and before long, folks and beggars jump in cars, trucks, or anything else with wheels to get to the hotel.

Seconds later and out of nowhere, a man shoots out into the middle of the street on a bicycle with another guy on a skateboard, holding on to the back seat.

Another man floats into the street in a motorized wheel chair bringing several cars to a screeching halt with black rubber burning to avoid hitting him. The man swerves the side of the road with wide eyes peeled back over his shoulder until looking around. He eases his helmet from the lower carriage, strapping it on tight when flipping a switch with his head dropping back and the chair taking off like a rocket, with him screaming with a fist held high.

Those without transportation stay, but some walk off and head home for sleeping bags and tents.

Realizing they've been tipped off, Boogey anxiously grabs things, loading them while Nattie slips on more clothes.

Nattie soon rushes out the side door near the lobby and the engine revs a few times.

Boogey pulls up to an intersection, finding the distant, approaching small band of vehicles when veering down a side street and then other streets until cutting into an adjacent garage. He squeals tires going up several levels until shooting out on the roof and over by the low-cut wall, watching the caravan pull into the hotel lot.

Boogey and Nattie sit until dark, when Boogey exits and turns down a side street, taking the back roads leading to Sam's place.

Twenty minutes later, Boogey makes one last turn and hits the high beams, turning into Sam's long driveway, finding Sam walking to his house when speeding up and pulling alongside.

Sam smiles noticing the car and then bursts into great laughter. He bends over, slapping his hand on one thigh while laughing even harder. "You really done (have gone and) outdone yourself, Mr. Boogey! Two big ones..., huh? Man, you and Nattie must be the happiest folks in Fikesville right now," he says, relying on the director's award check figures vice Big mouth Winton.

Boogey and Nattie smile as the car creeps alongside Sam, who is still making his way up the dirt path.

Boogey stops, and Sam climbs in the back. "You've seen all the commotion, huh?" Boogey asks, looking ahead then instantly into the rearview.

"Ahhh, man…, the heck with that…, just go on home and be proud of yourselves!" Sam utters, looking into the rearview and then into Boogey's bulging eyes.

"Shucks! Are you crazy? No way in hell, am I going around there with their hands out; begging with hands looking like cups. Huh…, half of them are on that wacky tobacky (tobacco)." Boogey smiles when pulling up, and off to the side of Sam's house.

Sam jumps out, hurrying over to the barn.

Boogey and Nattie curiously sit until hearing a tractor engine as it comes into view, with Sam parking alongside the barn and motioning Boogey to pull inside.

Sam rushes past, directing Boogey into a secret, underground car compartment, then waits for them to get out when sealing the door with hay.

Boogey and Nattie camp out at Sam's; watching various news flashes, which eventually turn into a mystery news clip called: 'Where are the Johnson's?'

Boogey strikes up a few financial conversations, seeing how Sam is a small-time, retired, financial investor and advisor.

Sam indulges in their intentions with the new wealth, and then spends hours on stocks, bonds, and other investments until offering other options. He eventually dusts off his old roll-away, pulling out old financial software he had created and tried marketing years before being fired from an investment firm for too many bad investments.

Before dark, Sam fears that the sheriff may come by, so he gets creative and dresses Boogey and Nattie as very old people and later, they go to the market a few counties over and return with food, wine, and liquor.

Sam breaks out a couple of cold beers, pouring Nattie a chilled glass of wine, then grabs a cold beer for himself, and begins toasting.

"I sure wish I had some of my moonshine!" Boogey utters, beaming at Sam.

Sam rushes to the kitchen, reaching in his cupboard, pulling out a jar of store brought moonshine. He walks away fast, and the door accidentally swings open wider when easing the jar on the counter and hasting to the restroom.

Boogey steps in the kitchen and looks down in the cabinet with bright eyes, doing a double-take. He leans forward fast with eyes frequently over his shoulder when taking a swig and instantly recognizes his special blend when his bucked eyes and cocked head excitedly points Nattie to the two familiar looking jars.

Nattie rushes up with her mouth dropped open while Boogey leans, whispering.

Their heads shoot back over their shoulders, hearing the toilet flush when rushing for the couch with Boogey's face automatically transformed into pure evil. "This mother..., been stealing my...!" He whines. "I thought it was you and Wint's trifling tail all along, but it was this mother...," Boogey murmurs until quieting when the door squeaks.

"Me?" Nattie says with evil eyes. "Shh! Just forget about it; just forget about it, Boogey! He has always been a good neighbor, and let's not forget he saved you from that crooked tail sheriff who was about to do you in," Nattie utters, staring deep into Boogey's cocked and settling eyes when thinking back on the sheriff.

Sam comes out whistling and heads for the kitchen with his whistling expressly cut short, finding the jars visible with eyes cut back over his shoulder when whistling off-tune. He begins loudly rattling pots and pans, when starting dinner.

Later, they retire to the front porch, sitting and eating vanilla ice cream with apple cobbler while watching the full moon. They indulge until three sheets to the wind, feeling good after polishing off jars of ABC brand, apple-cinnamon moonshine; something they had never tasted. Before long, they are feeling themselves with feet tapping against the wooden porch while oldies but goodies pour out of the old, busted transistor radio.

Sam tunes into another station, and they cheerfully sing at the top of drunken voices when Boogey stands, dancing in circles, until slipping his hands in both pockets, lifting one pocket at a time, in some highly questionable dance. Sam looks cheery, until immediately noticing Boogey when frowning and quickly looking away, shaking his head, when Nattie bursts into laughter, continually pointing at Boogey when he looks then looks away even faster.

Nattie looks at Sam's stale face and eyes that continually wander to and away from Boogey's dancing hands, tapping his feet slower then slower. "Boogey, you know you need to gone (stop) wit (with) that ole trifling-ass dance!" Nattie finally utters, bursting into a burst of deep, drunken laughter.

Boogey sees that it is annoying Sam, so he intentionally continues a little longer, until pissing off Sam. His favorite song comes on, and he sings and soon thereafter, a few dogs come out front, howling while trotting like Drysdales in circles. The song finally ends, and Boogey throws back another swig. "Man, I'm buzzing like a biiaaatch, hawg..., I mean, dawg!" he utters, following up with the longest burp, when looking at his watch until holding it up to the light. "Everyone is probably gone," Boogey says, looking at Sam, who looks down in a daze.

"Well..., let's walk the path and check," Sam finally says, swaying but looking somewhat sober.

Nattie stumbles over toward the swing, and then stumble a few more times before sitting and watching them fade around the house.

Sam and Boogey stumble through the thick, wood trail, making their way up the hill until their heads barely appear, finding the yard covered with floodlights, candle lights and tents, as far as the naked eye can see.

Sam stands in awe. "Well, I'll be a freakin' monkey's daddy. You were right not to go home, Boog! Man..., they are on your lawn like flies on stank, like a hoe (whore) on a pimp!" Sam utters, drunkenly giggling. "Hell, man, I didn't even think you had that many friends." He pats Boogey on the back and then gently pulls on his sleeve to motion him back.

Boogey and Sam rush up onto the porch seconds later, finding Nattie fast asleep and snoring when Boogey stomps loudly, knocking mud off, and waking her.

The three sit a spell longer until the mosquitoes begin biting and then go inside.

Sam straightens up the messy, spare room and then walks into the living room, finding them nodding. "The master suite is ready," he utters, and then repeats it a little louder when waking them.

"Can I borrow your phone?" Nattie asks, thinking about the kids and grandkids.

"Nattie, don't..., they'll only draw folks over here," Boogey utters when a tear rolls to her cheeks.

"I need to see my babies..., my babies!" Nattie cries in a soft, drunken whisper.

"He's right, Natt..., but you two have to decide if you're ready for the overwhelming crowds of beggars." Sam walks over to the dining room removing dirty dishes from the table.

Boogey stares at her a spell longer and finally agrees; shaking his head to let her know it's alright. "Just don't tell them where we are," Boogey utters, realizing it's a grave mistake.

Davillier, Melissa, and the grandkids sit at home with eyes glued on the broken-down television when the phone rings.

Melissa answers halfway through the first ring. "Mama, Daddy!" Melissa cries with tears of joy.

"Yes, precious, how are my chillins (children) doing?"

"We're fine, Mama! Where are you guys? We came by the house about twenty times. Have you seen the yard? It's a mess over there,

Mama! There are so many people camping out, and I only know about three of them, if that!"

They continue talking until Melissa hears a door slam in the background when Sam steps onto the back porch, whistling to his hogs. She listens closely, waiting for Sam to call the wild boar by its first name, and he does when the phone goes dead.

"Load up!" Melissa shrieks with a big smile.

"What? You know where they are?" Davillier asks, excited when easing in the doorway and looking around.

Nattie calls out to Melissa for seconds, and then calls back, continually clicking the phone until checking the junction box when calling again, but there's no answer.

Melissa's oldest daughter grabs the baby, who is still strapped in the wooden car seat. "Soo wee!" Melissa shrieks when the phone rings again, refusing to answer.

Nattie clicks the receiver when the dial tone grows in her ears again. She makes several more attempts but still gets no answer.

"What is it?" Boogey asks, finally walking up and looking confused.

"I was talking to Melissa, and we lost connection, I guess," Nattie utters, placing the phone down and growing weary.

Deep in the woods, several eyes gaze through darkness onto Davillier and Melissa's porch.

Winton and Nelle sit backed in, deep in the cut, staring at the well-lit house with fast dancing shadows at several windows.

The last shadow runs past the picture window, and the house grows dark when Davillier hits the breaker.

Five dark silhouettes creep out when a flashlight charges inches from the car; the lights dancing around until still when the hood stays up and light begins dancing around in the engine compartment.

Winton and Nelle watch them scurry about until they lift the baby's seat inside.

The hood slams down, and Davillier climbs behind the wheel with the headlights still off. The brake lights light up the front of the house as Davillier turns and eases out to the dirt road. The park lights finally come on then high beams that shine into the woods and unknowingly into Winton and Nelle's glowing eyes.

"Aww..., look at the little does in front of the car," the middle child utters, pointing at the somewhat tree-covered, camouflaged car when four red eyes fade when Winton and Nelle's heads speedily drop low.

Davillier hits the paved highway, watching Melissa's fast pointing hand when stepping into the gas pedal, barreling forward with loud thrust mufflers waking two of Winton's kids.

Winton cranks up and step into the gas, taking off like a jet.

The other two kids wake up when Winton comes off the dirt and mud, hitting the paved highway, fishtailing and kicking up thick mud.

Winton and Nelle scream with wide eyes, when swerving hard, missing a tree, and spinning in several doughnut turns.

Everyone on the passenger side and middle screams with their faces against the driver's window until instantly slung away when Winton finally gains control.

Winton slows down, keeping an eye on Davillier's car as it pulls away, and the taillights vanish around a thin then thick tree line. He goes faster, burning more mud from the tires until seeing their taillights again then slows, approaching a four-way; stopping quickly then speeding off. Winton turns in a sharp curve, slightly swerving until plowing through an intersection, ignoring the stop sign then slowing down. He notices one of Davillier's taillights disappear and reappear twice while pulling away.

Winton steps into the gas, and everyone screams at the top of their lungs when seeing him swiftly closing in on a tall six-pointer, slamming into the deer broadside and lunging the buck twenty-five feet forward. He hits the second unseen deer and, more screams come, when riding high until seeing sky only then the ground with everyone thrown around on the pitch-black road when the tires come to a screeching halt.

All eyes scroll around and Winton rolls down the window, cursing while pushing and pulling on the light switch, but nothing.

Winton sprints out, nervously peeking around the front, finding the bumper mangled and the grill demolished. He slowly pulls on a busted light bulb hanging by frayed, sparking wires and nervously jumps back when hearing a loud pop. He looks over the bloody car and then back at the near-pitch, dark road, whining in tears.

"Is it that bad, Wint?" Nelle nervously screams, looking ahead then squinting until spotting other bucks converging around the injured deer, which kicks and jerks, trying to stand, but keeps falling until not moving. Other deer look off at the dead deer, then the wounded deer, slowly lowering their heads.

"Winton!" Nelle shrieks, seeing two, big deer stare toward the car and then look back down at the one wounded and then the one dead.

Nelle's mouth drops open to call Winton again when Winton looks back, discovering over ten bucks standing around; and two of the biggest slowly walking toward him until in a slow then mild trot with others in the field, converging.

Winton takes a nervous step forward then sprints with metal taps sparking when sliding and breaking his stride.

Nelle and the kids' mouths drop open, leaning forward in fear, screeching.

Winton slips again then jumps up, accidentally bumping and closing the door when hearing loud growing, swift hoofs when springing up and diving through the window with feet dangling.

Nelle's scream comes again, and her eyes grow wide when snatching Winton in the collar, pulling him in when a big buck shoots past the door, ripping off the driver's side mirror with its mouth.

Winton's head swiftly moves in Nelle's lap, fanning his hand to free the dress and fighting to sit up when jumping and rolling up the window, quickly.

Other deers converge quickly; moaning in an agonizing and irritating tone with heads thrown back as if howling at the moon.

Winton nervously throws the car in drive not moving, when feeling Nelle's nervous hands tighten at his thigh.

The kids' eyes grow wide when almost continually taking turns screaming.

The road instantly grows darker when the moonlight dips behind a few thick clouds and when brightens again finding the field covered with forty or more deer, with more tailing each other out of the thick woods.

Winton nervously churns on the ignition, but nothing; then tries two-three more times when the engine finally turns with instant, loud shouts of joy.

Everyone finally tones down, and a loud, unfamiliar noise rises from the fan blade clicking while slightly jammed by the fan's housing.

Winton inches forward when two, big deer come to the front, not budging unless pushed by the busted hood pressing hard against their bodies and forcing them back almost inches at a time.

Soft cries continually fill the car with trembling bodies drawing closer.

Swiftly and out of pure darkness pierces a deer's fat head; fading inbound fast when the car jerks and wobbles when timed, loud bangs come. The door takes the brunt of the hits when smashed in by the raging deer with its antlers crumbling and blood splattering against the car and onto the road.

Winton leans into the horn, with no effects on the bucks, but small deer jump around and take a stance in the next round of attacks, denting the car at all angles.

Something finally catches Winton's attention in the rearview when finding a clear path. He times the next attack, backing down quick, and looking forward when three deer unintentionally butt heads where the car once stood, almost passing out. Winton looks forward, and eyes the path ahead, cutting through deer, and swerves slightly off then back onto the highway.

The biggest deer give chase, paralleling the car and banging his head into mirror brackets until breaking it off.

Winton floors the engine, finding a deer veering toward the car, and everyone watches it careen toward the rear door, missing the collision when fading across the rear and slamming into a deep ditch.

The last deer collides with the front-end, falling back, when the front bumper falls off, puncturing the two front and then two rear tires, with crumbled-antlers fading in the rearview.

Winton brings the car to top speed, wobbling with sparks pouring from four rims.

Outside the general store, a man with coke-bottle glasses stands, adjusting his glasses, hearing a loud horn when turning, finding bright sparks flying along the tree line. "I will be...! What in the...!" he screams, cutting his language short upon seeing a child, when pointing, staring and causing others to look.

Winton cruises forward like a meteor, tumbling. He speeds past the store, dropping off the road and into the dirt with tires smoking like crazy and the burnt smell of rubber growing heavier.

Everyone's eyes stay bucked as if they've seen a ghost.

Several people amble over, finding smoking tires and burning rubber trails when fanning and backing away fast, yet still continually looking.

Winton sprints into the field, looking at Boogey's pitch-dark house and then over the yard. "Where did the car go?" he asks, walking up to the short man with coke-bottle glasses and grabbing the timid man in the chest. "I said where did they go?" Winton screams, slightly lifting him and knocking off his hat.

"Put me down! Put me down!" the midget shouts, kicking until drawn closer. "You freakin' bully! I went through this crap when I was little kid," he utters, struggling to get free.

Winton's arms instantly tremble, growing weak from the man's heavy weight when his belly shakes in laughter, registering the comment about him being little when beginning to lower the midget more.

The midget draws back at the right level, inches from the ground, kicking Winton in his groin hard and forcing him to his knees with a raised vein in his forehead as Winton bows in pain.

The midget's foot hits the dirt quickly, drawing back and kicking Winton in the stomach while he's bent over, then picks up his hat, dust it off, and walks away.

Nelle stumbles over in a mean stare as laughter grows. She sees several people pointing while helping Winton up and guiding him to the car, where he rests on raised, busted hood.

Within minutes, the laughter tapers off with folks staggering back into the store or the field.

Boogey and Sam see headlights against the front porch that fades off fast.

Sam grips his rifle, easing onto the front porch with Boogey peeking from behind curtains. He aims down the trail, squinting until seeing what looks like three adults and one kid as they materialize out of the darkness when the car seat swings forward. "Melissa?" Sam squints again recognizing Davillier's funny walk.

"Yes," she utters, seizing the baby seat and running toward the house with the others close in tow.

Winton finds another man on a bench and strolls up to him, finding him listening to a man who is known for tall, tall tales (lies).

The man with the tales, wearing shades, sits telling a story of pouring hot grease on a man in a botched robbery: 'Man, I put that hot grease on him, and he ran screaming with smoke coming from his hind parts,' the man utters, ending his tale with a loud laugh when Winton chuckles, marveling as to whether it's true when shaking his head.

Winton wipes away the smile, looking down at the man with a mean look.

"Now you look here..., the midget was easy, but with me, I can promise you it will be somethin' to tell the damn captain!" the lying man utters, finally looking up at Winton under-eyed then back over at his hungry tall tale, listening audience.

"Yeah, yeah, yeah! Just tell me: How long have you been sitting here?"

The lying man slowly looks around at his attentive audience, winking then cuts his eyes over at Winton. "Well, I'd say..., that's none of your damn business!" the man rudely utters with his chest stuck out while trying to intentionally provoke a fight and have one more story to add to his portfolio, but a true one this time.

"All I need to know is has anyone seen a station wagon come past?" Winton asks with eyes roving over a few smiling and mean-face bystanders.

The lying man squints at Winton and begins to act nicer, finally recognizing it's Boogey's cousin. "Oh..., you mean Boogey's daughter's station wagon?"

"Yes! Yes!" Winton responds upbeat. "Which way did it go?" he asks, almost out of breath.

"Well, huh..., that depends on how much it's worth to you."

Winton reached deep in his pockets. "Here... here's twenty, now which way?" Winton holds out the money, tightly clenched.

"Ah, man, that's chump change; raise the stakes, seeing how your cousin is the richest man in town, now" he utters, spitting tobacco and looking under-eyed.

"Name it, you sorry son of a...," Winton says, looking over and finding kids running past.

"Ah, ah...," he utters, shaking his head. "How about a thou, for starters," he utters, looking off before slowly looking back up again.

"A thou? Hell, man..., don't talk silly all your freakin' life! How 'bout I get a quick kiwi-shine outcha (out of) your bottom? A thousand?" Winton chuckles looking at the hungry-looking, tall tale, listening crowd. "Look..., ok..., deal." Winton holds his hand out with fingers crossed behind his back.

The lying man spits more tobacco juice when a long drool extends from his mouth, and he tries breaking it off, but can't. He cuts his eyes at Winton, embarrassed, finding several folk's eyes glued to the long slobber. "Turn your head! Turn your freakin' head, I say!" he shouts with Winton slowly looking away, then back and away. The man snatches a handkerchief from his pocket, wiping his mouth with his right hand, and then extends the same hand to Winton as he turns back around.

Winton grasps the man's hand, sliding his hand in the lying man's warm, gummy tobacco juice then snatches back when the man cuts his eyes over, smiling until rotten teeth show. He points Winton to the intersection, motioning to the left, in a whistling sound then left again, in a whistle.

Winton walks to the car and stands by the passenger door in deep thought, wondering where they could be, until finally setting his eyes toward the tall barn in the background, and then the old, thick path, when smiling. He rushes over, opening Nelle's door and then all of the doors, quickening the kids out. They work their way through the crowd, standing off to the side of the porch, and then inch closer and closer to the cornfield, until fading into tall stalks, believing no one is watching.

Winton takes off running with the baby seat in hand, and his family falls in behind him. They draw close to the bottom of the hill, jumping over a stump when someone screams, pointing, and a mob charges, yelping. "Over here! They're over here!" mixed frail voices screams.

Handheld floodlights, flashlights, car and truck lights shine through the wooded trail when the mufflers grow louder as vehicles close in until high overhead high-beam lights come on as they barrel down upon Winton and his family.

Sam hears the fracas rushing Boogey and his family inside, pointing to the floor basement door covered with carpet. "Quick, get down, deep inside the cellar!" Sam yells, chambering a round in his shotgun, and running out the front door.

Boogey and his family fight to get the heavy door open. They rush inside the cellar and slowly close the secret door, with the carpet securely attached, leaving it undisturbed.

Sam turns and sprints out, meeting Winton and his family alongside the house, motioning them to the front. "On the freakin' porch, you idiots! Why did you bring these goons here!" he shouts, when taking off and running faster to the swing gate; swinging it shut and firing off two shots with the crowd backing up fast.

The crowd grows quiet, mumbling, and then gets louder as they close in on the gate again.

Two deputies take off fast, rushing to the front of the crowd, shoving folks aside when coming up on the big 'no trespassing' signs, drawing their firearms while skittishly looking back into the rowdy crowd.

"Get the hell off my property, you clowns! Deputy..., I want these goons off my property right now!" Sam raises his rifle like a warrior about to go into battle.

"Look here..., you just put your rifle away before someone gets hurt, Sam!" the tall deputy utters, finding the sheriff at the top of the hill in a slow jog and almost out of breath.

The sheriff works through the crowd and up to the fence, eye to eye with Sam. "Woo!" he utters, breathing hard. "Now look here, Sam; all these lovely folks want is to see the town's celebrity," the sheriff utters, eye to eye, when leaning into Sam, lightly sniffing with one eyebrow slightly high.

"What freakin' celebrity?" Sam asks, pretending to be dumbfounded.

Crackhead Tom walks up, eating greasy fries saturated in ketchup. He makes his way around a few folks, coming close to the fence, peeking around a few heads.

"Come on, Sam! You don't think we know Boog and Natt are in there?" the sheriff utters, observing Sam's nervous eye movement.

Instantly, the crowd grows rowdier, and some have their hands on the fence, lightly pulling or pushing when Sam fires off another round over his shoulder and in the air when Crackhead Tom dips his finger in the ketchup.

Tom quickly dabble spots on his temple, and then jumps around as if he's lost his mind, screaming that he's been hit.

Those around him back up, perceiving him to be bleeding, while Tom frantically dances around longer then clenches his fries tight, falling to the ground. He begins kicking then goes around in circles until accidentally smearing horse turd on his back and frowning then slowing from the heavy stench.

The crowd backs off quickly and grows quiet with most looking ahead while a few look away, shaking their heads.

A midget kneels, calling Tom, until his face frowns, seeing then smelling fries. He sees the open ketchup packet, then his ketchup-covered fingers when his little fingers swipe across Tom's forehead, until nervously smelling and tasting ketchup when drawing back a foot, kicking Tom until he screams and jump up, giving chase to the dwarf.

A few drunks point at Tom, bursting into laughter when finding a deep, dark, wide brown stain on his shoulder and back. They pinch their noses when Tom's face frowns harder as he runs in circles, shaking off the dung patty when fading behind the crowd and pulling off the shirt.

"It's ketchup! It's ketchup!" the midget finally shrieks, still licking his lips when the quiet crowd grows louder.

"Ok, Sheriff, either you round up these nuts and get them off my land, or you'll be carrying these sucker out in body bags..., it's your choice!" Sam shouts with his face turning bright red.

Without warning, the sheriff's long arms jerk stealthily forward, snatching Sam deep in his collar and pulling him into the fence hard while staring deep into his eyes. "Now, you look here, you silly somebi...!" he says cutting it short when finding the pastor off to one side. "One more threat and I'll run your slew-footed tail in for communicating threats." He quickly shoves Sam back with a mean stare.

"Communicating a threat? Well..., I didn't direct it to anyone," Sam mutters, stepping back a few feet.

"I tell you what..., you let me and my deputy check the place, and if they are not inside, I will clear these folks out quicker than a cat can lick its ass," the sheriff utters, slightly tilting his hat back.

Sam continues trying to convince him, until swallowing hard when looking back at his house. "All..., righty; you've got yourself a deal." Sam unlatches the gate and swings it open wide enough for the deputy's car to pass. He walks fast, vanishing around the shed, running with his head thrown back when his hat falls backward and rolls around with him going faster.

A deputy pulls up, and the sheriff jumps in, banging against the side of the door for the deputy to go. "Hurry it up!" the sheriff shrieks, looking around the property and then around for Sam.

Sam slows down near the porch, looking back when the deputy's car pulls around the front fast, and he fades inside through the back door.

"Come on! Let's get in here before he tries something flaky!" the sheriff utters, expressly jumping out.

The sheriff and deputy rush to the porch, slowing when they discover Winton and his family backing up with wide, nervous eyes.

The sheriff cuts an eye over at Winton, and when at arm's length, he jumps at Winton, making him fall against the house and bump his head.

Sam sprints to the secret door, flipping back a piece of raised carpet, then eases into a chair, jumping up and heading for the front door when hearing heavy boots pounding against the screen door's kick plate.

Two more heavy kicks come when the door springs wide open and the screen door slams shut behind the sheriff.

Sam rushes in view, almost out of breath. "Five minutes, then you're out of here…, you hear me?" Sam mutters staring at the sheriff who is stands in the middle of the room, sniffing high in the air, like a hungry hound.

"Yeah, yeah, yeah…, so…, when would you say was the last time Boogey was here?" he asks, sniffing again but higher when coming up slightly on tiptoes then higher, until looking almost like a ballerina.

Sam lightly sniffs, finally smelling Boogey's strong hair pomade. "Earlier this morning, for coffee, like always. Why…, is that against the law?"

"Shucks naw…, not against the law, but sure as hell, against the truth. Huh…, yeah, I bet he was here but not that long ago. Hell…, I can smell the stink from his greasy head; you know, dirt and grease of some sort," the sheriff utters, sniffing again and then pointing for the deputy to check a room when lightly hearing a door shut.

The sheriff draws his gun, rushing to the bedroom door, staring around the seal when hearing a door shut again. He puts his ear to the door, listening, then looks back at Sam, who leans forward, surprised, until finally recognizing it's just the radio. A smile and mischievous look grow on the sheriff's face when his foot goes high, fast.

Sam lunges, screaming when the sheriff's foot expressly slams into the knob. "Cloooocck! Cloooocck! Cloooocck!" Sam's frail voice shrieks, fizzing out as he slows his pace with eyes roving over the floor, following the demolished pieces of the locking mechanism.

The sheriff lunges in a dive, flipping, rolling, and coming up on his feet fast when training his gun around, slowly looking over the clean room and then the closet.

The sheriff and deputy manage to check the whole house within twenty minutes, and then come back into the dining area, finally noticing an attic opening. They look back, discovering Sam motioning their excited eyes from the attic to the front door.

Sam walks toward the door and the sheriff reaches, quietly sliding the long, dining room table over, jumping up in the chair, and quickly stepping on the white, pristine table cloth.

"The hell you will!" Sam utters, finally registering the heavy shift when turning back in a double take, staring at black heel marks on the cloth chair and tablecloth. "My dead mother gave me this set!" he utters with angry, raised eyebrows.

The sheriff stays tall, on tiptoes, with his head fading inside the square panel, and looking around, until turning three-hundred and sixty degrees; heavily scuffing the tablecloth.

Sam hears something fall to the floor and looks away, keeping an eye on the nosy deputy, until inching up to the table in a man stare.

In a flash, he jerks, grabbing a thick handful of the tablecloth, snatching it back as hard as he can.

Immediately, the sheriff's feet continually dance backward; double-timing, until flying toward the ceiling when a loud crash comes, and he falls flat on the table, on his back; breaking it into two pieces while rolling to the floor. He springs to his feet as if never down, drawing his gun to Sam's forehead quick, when frowning with high eyebrows raised. "Uh huh…, try that crap again and I'll be burying you with this hea (here) tablecloth and the furniture," the sheriff says, still in a leaning stance.

Boogey and Nattie flinch, looking up and then at the other closed compartment where the kids are well hidden.

"Yeah…," he says, with and even meaner face and in deep thought. "Try it again, and they will wrap your dead body in this tablecloth and bury you in the same coffin as your stankin' mammy!" the sheriff utters, staring deep in Sam's eyes then off when a funny sound comes.

The sheriff slowly look over his shoulder until finally bringing the giggling deputy into view, and finding his so weak that he comes to his knees and slides to the floor, laughing even harder, and crazier.

The sheriff spins around and his face turns to an even brighter red when slamming his boots hard into the deputy's back. He inches his foot quickly to his neck, cutting his air supply short until the deputy's tears begin falling down his cheeks. "Yak, yak, yak! Always laughing at something," the sheriff utters, smashing the deputy's upper back even harder until supporting his balance when the deputy chokes, until finally drawing his foot back.

The deputy rolls over quickly, gagging while slowly climbing to his feet.

Sam shakes his head in disbelief when heading for the front door and opening it wide. "Enough of this nonsense…, now get the hell out of here…, now!" he shrieks, rushing from the door and over, helping the deputy, who leans against the wall, still continually coughing.

The sheriff ambles out, jumping at Winton again; making him and his whole family flinch before stepping off the porch. He comes to the edge of the house, waving high for other deputies to get the people off Sam's property.

Sam rushes the deputy out, coming up next to the sheriff, and passing the house when the barn boldly comes into view.

The sheriff stops, staring at the barn with one raised eyebrow and in deep thought. "You see…, I'm a man of my word." The sheriff looks off and in Sam's mean face then back over at the barn again.

"Now let me tell you something…, you can just get your mind off that dea (there) barn! Yeah…, you'll find Boogey's car there because I'm working on it but at the end of the day, who in the heck is going to pay for my crap you done busted up in my house?" Sam asks to distract him when releasing the deputy and turning, motioning Winton and his family to the gate as well.

"Just come down and put in a claim for that cheap-tail furniture, and your nappy head mama's belonging which ain't worth a darn dime!" The sheriff hacks up thick phlegm, when spitting in the wind, and then looking down to find the thick, gel-looking wad on his shirt. "Come here, boy!" the sheriff utters, grabbing the weeping deputy by the head and smearing the side of his head in the wet, thick phlegm, to clean his shirt. "You know I wouldn't hurt you, now don't you, boy," he utters, holding the young man's head back and then looking at his shirt when rubbing his head more before flinging him away, and off to the side, fast.

The deputy smiles clueless, looking up at the sheriff smiling, then runs toward the cruiser, where another deputy stands looking at him. strangely. "Man…, what is all that yellow and green crap on the side of your head?" he asks, backing up fast, and disgusted.

The deputy runs his hand through his head, pulling out a long string of phlegm between his fingers when snatching his shirt off. He wipes his head with a discussed look until looking back at the sheriff, who is bent over to his knees in tears of silent laughter until screaming in uncontrollable laughter.

The rapper pulls up fast outside the general store, sticking his head out and looking at people dispersing. "Hey…, do you know where Dale lives?" he asks a female who ignores him while veering her son off in another direction.

A group of teens ambles by when one notices the famous rapper. "Hey, aren't you TC?" the young man utters, smiling hard. His friends hear the name and stop in their tracks, scurrying over to the SUV.

"Yeah, but raise up off the paint job, shawty (shorty)!" he utters, inching up while looking at the hot chick standing, holding her books in her bosom, starry-eyed and beaming.

Two guys quickly back away, patting their pockets for pen and paper.

"Where can I find Dale?" the rapper asks again, looking into their clueless faces.

"Well…, I think he lives in that old, broken-down shack, or at least his grandson does," the tallest kid utters, squinting when pointing toward Boogey's house.

"Yeah…, yeah, that's it," the grandfather screams, pointing a shaky finger at the house with an exciting look after remembering the house sitting back from the road.

"Who wants to know?" an elderly man nosily asks, walking up and staring with one weak eye burning from the short, smoldering cigar smoke.

"I do..., because I'm looking for that thieving bastard! Why..., do you know him?"

"Yeah, I know ole Dale well, and well enough to know he's not a thief, so maybe you have the wrong, Dale." The elderly man relights his cigar and takes a few puffs, heavily blowing into the rapper's SUV, with the rapper and grandfather heavily waving.

The rapper drops back with faster fanning hands. "Yeah, and you must be smoking crack! I know for a fact that Dale's nothing but a liar and thief! Hell, he's so slick, he can steal grease outta (out of a) biscuit, and sugar out of Kool-Aid, for sure." The rapper watches the man carelessly wave him off and walk off.

"Can we get an autograph?" an overweight kid asks interrupting when pick-pocketing another teen's pen, when the teen doubles back, snatching his pen and slapping the overweight kid in the back of the head.

The rapper presses the gas pedal, squealing wheels, then stops, laughing at folks jumping out of the way. He pulls off slowly, easing through the crowed, clearing them, and then burns rubber, fading off and looking in the rearview, finding a deputy looking back at the SUV before running for his cruiser.

Sam makes several trips through the path, checking to see if the folks are gone then makes a final trip, closing all the blinds and letting everyone out of the cellar.

Boogey and his family stay until 3 AM and then load up in two cars, heading to a hotel, where they have Sam reserve adjoining rooms.

Wednesday morning, well before sunrise, Boogey and his family check out.

Upon arriving home, Davillier drops them off on a back road and they cautiously approach from the backyard out of the cornfield.

Nattie goes into the kitchen, and Boogey sits listening to Bud sing before heading for the shower.

Boogey hears Nattie stirring around in the kitchen until getting quiet when sitting, watching the news until easing up, peeking and finding Nattie with her back to him, giggling. Boogey creeps up on her, coming high on his toes with eyes growing slow and wide. "What in the..., helllll! What do you think that is..., Mr. Jangles, from the darn Green Mile, woman? If you don't get rid of that nasty tail-rodent, you better!"

Nattie turns slowly, looking back at him with a mean stare while picking up the little mice, stroking its back more. "You just jealous because he's more handsome than you," she utters, running her hands up and down the mouse's back when Boogey waves her off and walks out.

Boogey shows up at a condemned, steel manufacturing factory, later greeted by Reggie, then Mack's ex-girlfriend, who strolls up, handing him a cold beer.

Rev finally appears from behind a wide beam.

"Thanks," Boogey utters, with wandering eyes when walking over to the counter where the map is laid out. "See, that's what I'm talking about, putting those minds in play with serious planning!" Boogey utters, pulling up a seat.

Reggie walks up. "Ok, look..., Mack is set to meet us in an hour and a half. I convinced him that there's a gun supplier from out of the area that is serious about doing big business."

"Do you think he'll come alone?" Mack's ex-girlfriend asks, a little concerned.

"Well..., he knows the baller calls the shots and feels comfortable with me being here," Reggie utters, looking into their questioning eyes.

"Ok, so here's the plan," Rev utters, pressing the rolled map down more when showing the expanded section of the old factory.

"So, how did you guys handle the balloons?" Boogey asks, looking at Mack's ex-girlfriend's friend and then her girlfriend when she appears from a dim corridor.

"You just wait and see, honey. We got that room hooked up with more balloons than the law allows," the girlfriend's female friend utters, smiling.

"Everyone get your things, and let's man up. We have to be ready if this thing is going to work as planned," Rev utters, with wandering eyes confirming that everyone hears.

They rehearse until an hour passes, then nervously jump when hearing a car horn. Everyone puts on a ski mask except Reggie, who heads for the main level.

"Hold up," Rev utters, walking and then hurrying to catch Reggie.

Boogey stands in the background looking at Rev until vanishing around a corner, and then backs under a concealed staircase.

"This better be a sweet event," the woman driver utters, rushing inside the balloon-filled room and coming out as fast as she went in.

Reggie swings the tall steel door open, and Mack steps in, nervously looking around.

"Look, Reg..., I don't have time for nonsense because I'm a very busy businessman," Mack utters in his cool voice, when trying to be cooler in his new, proud pimp walk.

"The supplier isn't here yet but should be any moment," Reggie utters, walking him up a level and fiddling with his phone.

Mack and Reggie reach the top floor, and masked Rev steps out from behind a concrete pillar, pointing the twelve gauge sawed-off shotgun at the back of Mack's head. Reggie looks back, faking being surprised when both his hands go up fast.

Mack jumps, reaching for his gun when feeling the shotgun tighter at his skull.

"Don't even, or there will be blood all over these walls." Rev says in a heavily disguised voice.

Reggie's hands go even higher, pretending he's shocked while backing up.

Mack turns, trying to slip his other hand in the back of his pants, when more cool steel presses against the other side of his skull when Boogey pushes his barrel forward. "One wrong move and you will be employed in pushing up daisies in the new world," Boogey says in a deep and convincing voice when Mack's other hand jerks high.

Boogey pulls Mack's gun from his waistband, stuffing it in his pocket, then gets the other gun and adjusts his mask.

The driver's girlfriend rushes up out of nowhere blind folding Mack.

Rev reaches for the metal bin, grabbing a roll of tape and cloth straps. "Here, tie this chump up!" Rev utters to the driver in an overly disguised voice.

The female driver ties Reggie up and Rev pretends as if he's checking the tightness. "Tighter!" Rev shrieks, watching her pull on the straps when Boogey snatches Reggie by the collar, roughly yet playfully pulling him around the corner, kicking with shoes soon dragging.

Boogey pulls off his belt and within seconds, begins slapping it loudly together, making it sound as if he's slapping Reggie when fist sounds come as if beating him, with Reggie loudly responding to each. Boogey sprints back around the corner, running into Mack, punching him in the gut; folding him and tying him up, then checks the blindfolding while Rev stands off to the side, pointing the gun.

Boogey drags Mack into the darkroom filled with three hundred or more balloons, sitting him in the middle, in a wooden chair.

Rev ties Mack's hand with another long rope, throwing it to the floor, before tying another long rope to the back of the blindfold.

Boogey turns a chair in front of Mack, easing into it. "So, you're Mack, huh? They say you're tough..., real tough, but hey..., you don't look so darn tough, chump!" he utters, running his hand across a balloon until it screeches and then pops from him, gripping it tighter in heavily calloused hands with Mack jumping.

Mack tenses in fear; sweating when hearing the too familiar sound, and trembling with a few tears dropping. "I ain't ever harmed you, so why are you screwing with me?"

"You're right, not me, but a lot of people, I'm sure, so here's what you're going to do. Now…, I've meditated on killing you for what you did to a friend of mine."

"What? Who? What friend?"

"Never mind, that's irrelevant, but you better get out of dodge because if I see you again, there are no odds to gamble," Boogey utters in a deep, mean voice when leaning, digging deep and brandishing a sharp knife which he puts to his throat. Boogey tightens the blade with a light cut and sweat begins to burn.

"Name your price," Mack utters with more tears finally dripping from under the blindfold when thinking of the balloon again with his mind drifting to the kid's party he shot up. "Anything, just name it," he utters, shaking in fear when hearing another slow, screeching sound from a balloon that the female driver is slowly churning in the corner.

Boogey loosens the ropes from his hands, leaving them on when stretching out two ropes and motioning Rev over.

Boogey and Rev exit; leading the two ropes through a barred window and shutting the door halfway.

Mack begins whining until crying. "Hey…, don't leave me! Please…, I beg you!" Mack skittishly cries, looking at the minuscule, faint beam of light underneath the blindfold when the door slams shut.

The lock clicks, and the steel bars seal, closing out all light sources except under the door until a piece of cardboard slides underneath, making the room pitch black.

Boogey grips the rope tight, yanking hard and jerking Mack's hand and head, unraveling the blindfold and his hands as the cardboard is slightly drawn away.

Boogey, Rev, and Reggie stand with ears against the steel door, snickering when hearing the chair slide back, quickly when Mack instantly screams. A death cry comes with Mack's vision crystalline when finding a roomful of balloons. Loud yelping comes again when covering his eyes, crying, and then dropping down in the chair, yelping louder.

He jumps up, and cardboard fully flies from underneath the door, bringing in a full source of light when Mack jumps, screams, seizing the chair with a death grip, continually slams it into the wall, bursting balloons nonstop until exhausted. After taking a breather, he continues screaming and smashing more balloons until backed into a clear corner, still screaming at the top of his lungs.

The five giggle, quietly laughing like crazy hyenas until their laughter tapers off.

Boogey reaches for the panel covering the bars in the door and opens it, throwing a key to the far side and closing it.

Everyone heads for the ground floor, scurrying to the far side of the huge building, until entering a concealed garage. They load up in separate cars, and exit through a chain-link fence.

Reggie breaks off, heading down a long hallway leading to the front, where his and Mack's rides are parked.

Boogey arrives home an hour later, hits the moonshine, and then makes it to the kitchen, accidentally knocking over clothes. "What you need to do is clean this nasty tail house, Natt! Huh..., a mouse for a friend..., now ain't that some crap, if there ever was carp!" He giggles, flipping on the light, finding the mice on the counter when his wandering eyes anxiously look for the broom. He backs up slowly, gripping the handle tight until raised high when swiftly slamming it into the counter with all his might, but missing.

The mouse scurries over the counter with Boogey taking a few more good whacks, continually missing and becoming so mad that he grabs his rifle from the corner, training it fast, and trips, accidentally blowing a hole in the wall.

Nattie bursts into the kitchen, screeching when grabbing a skillet from the counter's edge, hitting Boogey square in the back of the head, and dropping him cold. She stands over him, looking until nervously checking for a pulse, then his breathing when cutting off the kitchen light and going into the bedroom, slamming the door.

Hours later, the rooster crows, and Boogey opens his eyes, sitting and then gaining his balance. He drops down in the kitchen chair, looking around in a daze.

Nattie enters the kitchen, staring at him and shaking her head until pulling out pots and pans, cooking. She soon engages with him, smoothing things over in mild chat.

Before noon, Boogey and Nattie have spent most of the morning riding around, paying off debts to show off before those who had continually oppressed them.

The following morning, Boogey enters the room with a mail brochure from a dealer. "I sure would love heated seats," he utters, reading over the overrated ads.

"Huh..., oh yeah, and you'll be riding alone. Can you imagine heating those seats with those sticky drawers? It definitely would be something to tell the captain; that's for sure. Ok, look..., let's go over this once more. You're doing what with your money?" she asks, picking up his long list, and scrolling down the sheet with paint-peeled, index fingernail. "Hmm...; the neighbor for investing, Rev's church, Winton's restaurant..., Stinky's or Big Baby's nightclub, and let's see..., something for Melissa's wedding..., trailer down payment, and then some for the community," she utters, shaking her head. "Have you done plum lost your cotton-picking mind? Don't think you're going to dip into mine, Baby!" she utters with a mean stare when standing.

"Look..., we must share and plant seeds to reap a good harvest!" He looks back at her.

"Well, sew-on, bubba, but if you don't reap, then don't creep, meaning trying to get to some of mine," she utters, reaching for her purse. "Come on; let's get going because I've got to meet Bev and dem (them) later."

"Bev? Bev who?" he asks, reaching for the keys.

"You know, Beverly Anne..., Boogey, I know you remember Beverly Anne."

"Beverly and who?"

"Beverly Anne..., you know Beverly Anne," she repeats, staring with a frown.

"Hell, I don't remember either of your crazy friends, Beverly or Anne."

"What? Man, you're a straight nut! Beverly Anne is one person, dang!" she laughs, walking into the bedroom, shutting the door while looking in the closet.

Boogey strolls into the kitchen, freezing in his tracks with eyes gazing around fast. He looks for anything he can get his hands on when finding the mouse on the kitchen counter, eating cheese and drinking water from a lid, so neatly placed. He looks around more then back over his shoulder, finding the mouse on hind legs when grabbing the broom with a death grip, easing it from behind stacked boxes.

"Ahh!" Boogey shrieks, quickly bringing the broom up and squealing with each heavy slam into the counter. He takes firmer whacks, bursting open a big bag of flour and knocking over a big pot of chicken grease in the sink then onto the floor.

Nattie bursts out of the bedroom, slamming into a tall stack of clothes, knocking them over, and springing up fast. "What in the Sam Dilbert Jenkins are you doing, Boogey?" she shrieks, holding her head when the broom straws; still in motion accidentally slams into her face, knocking her back.

"Sorry! Sorry!" Boogey shrieks with a handheld out to her when dropping the broom in shock.

Nattie quickly pushes his hands away, staring at him when finally finding the mess sprawled all over the kitchen.

"The mouse," he sadly utters, pointing backward. Look..., I'll clean this mess up," he utters, stepping toward the sink when she pushes him in the back, making him stumble forward a few feet with his feet heavily slapping the floor to break his fall.

"You just get out of my kitchen! Go on now..., get!" she shrieks, walking behind him and motioning the zipping of her lips to let him know not to say another word each time he looks back.

Boogey walks out the back door and stands on the porch.

Nattie watches him fade around the house and turns, cleaning. She finishes thirty minutes later and goes into the bathroom sitting on the edge of the bed, in deep thoughts until the phone rings, startling her.

She rolls over, picking up, and a manly voice rises, as a big smile comes over her when stretching the cord toward the window, discovering Boogey at the edge of the house. Nattie stays at the window, talking and giggling like a girl on her first date when Freddy asks a question that leaves her blushing and in silence.

"Oh, so you're just gonna (going to) play that question off, huh?" he utters, still waiting while looking around the rowdy room.

"What? Nattie asks, rushing from the bedroom to the bathroom window with eyes wandering over the yard for Boogey until finding him near the car.

"You heard me..., when you gone (going to) leave that clown?" he asks, laughing and finally causing her to laugh.

"Real soon, and tomorrow would not be soon enough, but it won't be long because we're always at each other's throats; mostly stemming from you," she utters, nervously peeking out the window again.

"Me? How so?" he utters, proudly riding on the chair's hind legs. "Oh, man! Dang!" he shrieks, falling flat on his back with a full room of laughter bursting out.

"Hello! Hello?" Nattie looks out the window and then closes the curtain when hearing pipes vibrating under the house when Boogey charges the water hose.

Freddy climbs up fast, and laughter grows but settles from the store workers seeing his mean face.

"What was that noise?" Nattie presses the phone tighter to her ear.

"Oh, just these cats playing around at work," he utters, rubbing the back of his slightly knotted head.

Nattie hears the water turn off and nippily ends the call, turning up the TV.

Boogey walks off a ways, feeding the pigs, and then walks back looking in the field, scratching his head. He ambles alongside the house, pulling out wood, nets, and a rope, then looks high in the tree, scratching his head again before getting the ladder and rigging a netted contraption. He pulls the top ropes about thirty minutes later, testing it before spreading out the net and covering it with leaves and dust.

The DJ puts on the anonymous CD again at a radio station, belonging to the famous rapper when the main entrance flies open, and the rapper charges for the broadcast room.

The receptionist lays sprawled out, clinging onto the rapper's dusty cowboy boots, being drug past the picture window and through the studio door.

"Turn it off, and I mean right now before I sue you so bad that your boss' toupee spins off his bald, fat head! That is my music, and rights are fully reserved!" the rapper shrieks, pulling the certifiable copyright letter from his coat liner when the CD scratches and then halts with hungry listeners reaching for volume knobs.

Over at Boogey and Nattie's house, Boogey leaves the house for animal feed and is a fourth of the way there before realizing he left his wallet. He cruises into his driveway five minutes later, finding the crop duster making low-flying runs on the neighbor's field, when hearing the phone ring.

Nattie soon picks up, whispering seductively, and her voice grows louder as he passes the window, peeking with her not seeing him or his vehicle.

Boogey stops, backing up to the house when creeping closer, listening until figuring out its Freddy, when she asks about him living with Bea.

Nattie immediately goes deep into tears of laughter about something then the conversation changes to something business-like. Finally, they discuss the lottery and then instantly dive into pure eroticism until dwindling to small talk again.

Boogey takes off for the front door, and rushes up the steps, slamming the door against the side of the house when rushing inside.

Nattie jumps, nervously slamming the phone down with eyes over her shoulder.

Boogey stares with a mean frown and bloodshot-red eyes, not saying a word for minutes.

Nattie turns, pretending to be straightening the top of the cupboard.

"So this goes on all day, huh?" He continues staring at the back of her head.

"What?" she asks, pretending to be clueless yet fidgety when stepping a few feet away.

"You heard me! So you and Freddy have been going at it behind my back for some time now, huh?" He stares at her nervous, furniture dusting hands and hair that sways as she nervously dusts even faster.

"Man, go head (on) with that nonsense. Freddy, Freddy, Freddy..., Man, Freddy gone (is going) to be the death of you!" She nervously jumps when the phone rings.

"Probably where most of my money and moonshine has been going. You round here fattening that dang fat frog for snakes," Boogey utters. "Go on, answer it! Answer it, I said!" he shouts, turning fast and grabbing the phone.

Nattie nervously ducks, compensating for his fast turn, then comes up with her fists balled; rocking in her fighting stance when swiftly and nervously settling down with hands still up and tensed.

"Hello? Hello! Speak up like you got a pair; you no-good-for-nothing, sorry excuse for a man!" Boogey screams with his face torn up. "Say something, you jerk!" Boogey shrieks, pushing the phone closer.

There is silence but distant voices of many people in the background.

"I know you're there, you freakin' coward!" Boogey shrieks, finally noticing Nattie lowering her hands. "I know this you, Freddy! Your mama ain't nothing but a low-down, tow-timing, dirty tramp, whore, and a filthy trifling slut!" Boogey shrieks, hearing the mouthpiece being covered.

Freddy's face turns red until looking like he's about to burst. "Don't talk 'bout (about) my mama!" Freddy utters fast, gripping and covering the mouthpiece tighter.

"You can have her!" Boogey shrieks, seizing her arm when she slips away in tears. "Come pack her crap up..., naw, naw..., never mind..., I'll pack it for you, just come and get this two-timing, and cheating tail women!"

"Stop it, just stop!" Nattie finally screams, whacking Boogey across his arm when he blocks her the second time.

Boogey drops the phone, turning as she backs up. "Don't put your hand on me! I don't hit you..., because the day I do, you gonna (are going to) be sucking soup through a straw the rest of your natural-born life!" he shrieks with a mean stare.

"Come on! Come on, dangit! I'd rather be hit than put up with all that mouth of yours!" Nattie yells, teary-eyed, when rocking in her favorite fighting stance with tightly balled fists.

"Well, I know for sure I can't trust you now, so I need to go out and find me some new, new!" he utters, boldly staring when picking up the phone and hanging it up.

"Huh, like you said something! If you were half the man as Freddy, you would have some new, new right here!" she utters with a devilish look, walking up to him with her chest out and provoking him to hit her so she wouldn't feel so bad.

Boogey leans forward almost cock-eyed, when taking a deep inhale, smelling moonshine on her breath as it grows stronger from her heavy breathing. "Naw, see, you need to get up and out my face with that puke breath. You ain't nothing but an alcoholic," he utters, looking into her teary eyes and walking away.

"I hate you!" she shrieks, crying when slamming her fist hard into Boogey's back, and stealthily backing up when Boogey turns, jumping in a stance and sad stare.

"A drunk mind speaks a sober heart, and you are tanked off that truth serum. No wonder the moonshine barrel is always low!" Boogey shakes his head. "You are pathetic! Look at you! You need to sleep off that high, walking around looking like the Grand Reaper with that freakin' cap on your nappy head. Shoot, you and your nonsense eat at me like a slow cancer," he utters, staring deep into bloodshot eyes.

Nattie goes into a daze, swaying a little. "Yeah, I'm like a cancer, alright..., the darn Boogey Johnson Cancer that's been eating at me for some time now!" she utters, staring back but not blinking.

Boogey strides out the back door, alongside the house.

Nattie rushes to the window, hearing then seeing him rummaging through jars.

Boogey looks down while filling a shot glass then back off the spout, taking three shots back to back with a deeply frowned face when pulling out a silver flask, and filling it.

Nattie eyes stay glued on him until he lifts his head when she fades behind dingy, heavy, swaying curtains.

Boogey finally notices the curtains settling when walking over to the tree stump, sitting on the tree root. One hand falls into the other, and he begins crying like a baby, then drinking and crying, crying and drinking until the flask is empty. He refills the flask, looking at his watch until kneeling in a strain when coming up, and heading toward the general store.

Boogey comes alongside the store, looking at a couple in a car when dipping through the side door, sprinting to the register, patting his pockets. "Let me get an easy pick." He pats his pockets again, digging deep and coming up with rabbit ears.

A different kid waits until Boogey looks back before peeling off a dollar from a thick roll of bills.

Boogey finds the clerk staring, so he shields the kid, quickly opening and closing his hand fast until feeling the dollar touch his hand when closing it faster. He turns, bending as if he dropped something. "Why thank you, young man; you're honest and sincere; your parents will be proud of you," Boogey utters, patting his pockets as if he has more money when nervously turning and passing the dollar to the clerk.

"Sir, that wasn't your dollar; I loaned it to you, but you can repay me with fifty percent interest next week," the kid utters, walking over to the pinball machine where other kids are playing.

Boogey freezes and then tenses, with eager eyes glued on the clerk when cutting his eyes back, slowly. "Well, I'll be a darn donkey's uncle.

How is that puny rascal gonna (going to) pick up my dollar from the flo (floor) and tell me I owe him?" Boogey utters, laughing and feeling stupid, when the clerk shakes her head and stares in disgust.

Boogey walks out and sits on the bench. He pulls out his flask, looking around, and then turns up the moonshine, stuffing the flask in a pocket when hearing footsteps.

People come and go, and Boogey hits the flask between people passing until the last drop hits the tip of his tongue when he swallows hard.

The boy that slipped him the dollar soon exits, finding Boogey plastered with heavily crossed eyes. He pops the top on his drink, taking a sip while looking at the ground in deep thought and then back up at Boogey's strained eyes which are barely open.

"What?" Boogey asks, finally cracking a drunken eye fully open and staring.

"Oh..., oh, nothing," the boy utters, taking another sip when staring at the ground then Boogey again.

"Now you look, here..., you ain't gone be looking at me like I'm some kind of alien," Boogey utters in a slurred speech. "Just spit it out! Spit it on out!" he utters, staring with bulged, bloodshot eyes.

The boy continually chomps on the fresh gum a few more good whacks and then spits it out. "There, now are you happy? Huh..., just when it gets good, you tell me to spit it out; just like an adult to not know when they have a good thing," he utters, staring back.

"What? I meant your words, not the gum, you little knucklehead! Hell..., how was I supposed to know the gum was good to yah (you)?" Boogey asks, frowning.

"It's called effective communication; you ask something and give them time to respond," the kid mutters, looking at Boogey, puzzled.

"Wow! You're too smart for your age and definitely too young to be in as deep a thought as you are," Boogey utters, more attentive when swaying and studying the kid a little closer.

"Answer me this, sir..., what do you know about girls?" the kid asks, sitting and swinging one-foot inches from the ground while balancing on the other.

"I see..., so you have a crush on some little girl, huh?" Boogey utters, when the kid looks up fast with wide eyes.

"That's kinda personal, don't you think?" the kid utters, taking another sip of his pop. "But now that you've opened that can of worms, we might as well dig 'em (dig them) out," the kid utters, setting his cool can down. "Yeah, I guess you can say that there's one girl, but I'm not sure if she's my type."

"Type? Huh..., your type?" Boogey responds, laughing. "And what type might that be, considering you are not too far out of pampers?" he asks, cheery when straightening his posture to lean against the post.

"Slim in the waist, thick in the thighs, and a nice, round bottom," he utters, looking at the door when a patron exits.

"What? No you look hea (here)! You're too young to worry about waists, thighs, and anyone's bottom, young man; you just keep your head in those books, and the rest will come later."

"Hmm..., oh really? Well, I thought this might be a little too heavy for ya (you)," the kid utters in deep thought. "Well, let me ask you this because it's been weighing on my mind."

"What... what might that be?"

"Well..., do you eat light bulbs?"

"I will be da...!" Boogey cuts the cuss word short. "Now there you go..., just when I thought you were smart, you ask a silly tail question like that? You know good and well, you can't eat light bulbs...; well unless you cut your mouth like a fool."

"Oh really? Hmm..., well, I hear my pa some nights, just before the lights go off, telling ma to cut the lights off and he'll eat it; and I ain't never seen his mouth cut," the boy utters in deep thought, too young to realize his father is talking about sex when swinging his feet off balance again. "I sure do wonder if it burns...; you know, eating hot light bulbs and all," the kid utters, staring in thought while trying to make sense of it all.

Boogey chuckles with his mind spinning. "Well, your pa and mama play like that because they know you're nosy and listening to them. They're just trying to throw off, you being nosy," Boogey utters, finally refraining from laughing. "Look..., no one eats light bulbs, kid," he utters, continually giggling at the clueless kid.

"So, tell me this..., are you married?" the curiously kid asks.

"Why, yes, for some time now, I must add," he responds, thinking about his wedding at the old funeral home.

"Well, tell me this..., how much does it cost to get married?"

"Well..., hell, I don't know, but I can tell you this..., I'm still paying for it after all these years," Boogey utters, smiling.

"Well, is it true that you don't know your wife until you're married in some countries?"

"Shii...!" Boogey utters, curving the cuss word and slightly covering his mouth when drunkenly laughing harder. "Heck, it happens everywhere, especially in the good ole US of A." Boogey stands, heavily swaying and holding the post to gain his footing. He takes two steps forward and three backward until sitting, then looks over at the kid, who bursts out in a silly laugh. Boogey stands again, and the kid puts Boogey's hand on his head, supporting his weight.

People walk past slowly, looking at how Boogey walks because he looks to be walking on stilts.

The kid and Boogey finally make it to his porch five minutes later, and Boogey digs deep, handing the kids a handful of pennies before easing to the busted steps.

"Mister, there's one more thing: My brother listens to a lot of rap, and all I hear is bitches and hoes (whores); so are all women bitches and hoes (whores), or just some?"

Boogey's shoulder goes high and then bounces, trying to keep from laughing when bursting into a burst of drunken, uncontrollable laughter that takes time to taper off. "You, my little friend, are very inquisitive. No..., no, no; the only real B's and H's have nasty attitudes and sell themselves; you know..., like your auntie Barbie. Now Barbie, she's a natural-born B and H, but please..., let's keep that little secret between you and me," Boogey utters.

Nattie sits listening until her soft, giggly voice grows louder then fades off.

The following morning, Boogey awakens, uncovering Bud and playing with him before walking into the kitchen. He opens the refrigerator, listening for Nattie, and then turns the water jug up to his lips until his head jerks forward instantly when Nattie slaps him in the back of the head.

Boogey jumps, dropping the jug, and grabbing his throat, when choking.

"That's straight nasty, Boog! It's bad enough you have bad, oral hygiene, but then you gone (are going to) leave the water looking like lemonade with those yellow teeth?" She snatches the half-empty jug, holding it to the light, finding a light yellow tint. Nattie watches him hack, and spit in the sink then cough a few times to clear his throat. She makes her way to the sink, pouring out the rest of the water then throws the jug in the trash.

"Woman, you done lost the last bit of red sense in that nugget of yours? That was a new jug," he mutters, reaching for the trashcan when her foot shoots up fast, smashing it deeper. He backs up, quickly. "Shucks..., you're just an evil-tail woman!" Boogey utters with his index and middle finger to her face. "Come on up out of this ugly-tail woman, Satan! Release your evil spell off this freakin' heffa!" he yells, backing up then coming close when she swings fast, barely missing.

"Keep on playing, and you'll need a new grill to go up in that ugly mug," she utters, backing up and rocking with her fists balled tight.

Later that evening, at the big, annual event, a county over; television and radio stations strongly advertise the big lottery jackpot and State Fair, plus have even heavier advertising for free food, contests, and various booths.

The lottery officials run prominent ads for the two-hundred-and-forty-five million jackpot and a five hundred dollar giveaway.

Winton walks past the pay booth and leans his head back, smelling Chinese food. He finds people in line, so he falls in at the rear, talking to Nelle. Minutes later, he moves to the counter, putting his hand down while asking Nelle what she wants when something hard, warm and wet spanks the top of his hand.

The spatula slides off slowly as he draws his hand back fast, looking into the eyes of the young non-Chinese looking man and then his father, who burst out in a burst of loud laughter; realizing they were both in the wrong.

Winton bursts into laughter, giving high fives until they are all in deep laughter. He places their orders and tells Nelle about the run-in when turning and apologizing while retrieving their food and waving while heading over to the kids.

Winton's oldest son goes for cotton candy, buying two, big bags and eating them fast. He gets a large soda, and his parents fuss, so he slips off, coming back with two more big bags. "Boy, you lost your cotton-picking mind? You out here eating all those sweets..., it's just going to give you a tummy ache, but don't come crying to me all torn up out of the frame, in pain," Nelle utters, staring as if disgusted.

Winton looks off then looks back at his son seconds later, finding him still stuffing his jowls. "Boy..., did you hear your mama?" Winton utters, grabbing his hand when as the son draws back. "What's gotten into you? Can't you hear?" Winton utters, snatching the last bag.

"What? What?" the son says, looking up and down as if sizing up Winton.

After the son's out-of-body experience, the family plays a few games until the son sits on a bench and eventually, sluggishly lay down.

Winton turns and finally sees him, nudging Nelle, when cutting his eyes over at his son who is rolling over in pain.

Winton and Nelle pretend not to see him when fading to the other side of the boots. They go into a deep conversation when their son and his siblings amble up, and the son begins leaning into Nelle, whining.

"Didn't I tell you not to eat all that sugar?" she utters, curiously looking at Winton. "Wint, let's get him home," she finally utters, pissed while looking at his siblings' teary eyes.

"Home? We can't leave now; a couple of the fellas and Boogey are coming," Winton utters, looking around and then back at his son, pissed while shaking his head.

"Then you can just drop us off and come back." Nelle looks at her son and laughs when finding him bent over in more pain. "That's what you get; with your hardhead self!"

Winton drives home and then heads back. He pulls into the fairgrounds parking lot, looking for a closer parking spot, when discovering Boogey and Nattie pulling up.

The three meet, walking to the ticket booth where Boogey pays, and Winton flashes his stamped hand.

Winton steps off, looking at the big tractors then back at Nattie and Boogey who are still standing at the ticket booth until finally walking through the main tent.

Winton walks a few feet away and over to a car display. He goes into a daze and then comes out of it, finding a man handing him a brochure.

Boogey and Nattie walk up beside Winton, and a hand touches Nattie's back.

Nattie turns, looking back into their foreign neighbor's faces, smiling while greeting the woman with a friendly hug and waving to her husband.

Winton flips through the brochure in a trance when Nattie taps him, to introduce him.

Mr. Cho and Winton come eye to eye, and Mr. Cho's face turns bright red with his fist tight.

Winton looks beside Nattie, finding the beautiful, foreign woman who turns up her nose, looking away. His eyes drift to her hourglass shape in a trance until Boogey's eyes buck when he snaps his fingers in Winton's face several times, to bring him out of the trance.

Mr. Cho's voice rise extremely high, screaming disrespectful things with a finger inches from Winton's face.

Boogey tries to calm Mr. Cho, making Winton shut up, and then waves Winton off as Nattie walks the foreign couple in another direction.

Winton passes a small bingo station and the young man from work, with the stained shorts, bends over a counter secretly scribbling something on a card.

The young man runs up to Winton and, out of nowhere, slaps him on his back hard, smiling when coming alongside. "Hey Winton, ole buddy! How are things going?" he excitedly asks, pressing the tape harder.

"What are you doing here?" Winton asks, looking back for Boogey.

"Chillin with my girl," he utters, pointing to a girl at a distance when walking away fast, stopping, and looking back

Two stumbling drunks run up behind Winton with eyes anxiously roving over folk's shoulders and Winton's back.

The short drunk rushes off, still following a crowd behind Winton, reading. He waits until folks pass and other veer off when his foot comes up quickly, kicking Winton in the butt.

Winton jumps and turns with a drawn fist but eases it down when seeing the short man's towering, muscular friend, so he walks away.

This time the tall man sneaks up, kicking Winton in the butt.

Winton jumps, holding his butt. "Hey! That's not nice!" Winton nervously utters, trying to look mean.

"What? It's your note!" the tall man utters, slinging his shirt to one side, peeling off the sticky. "Now give us our twenty dollars!"

Winton growls. "That, dang puny weasel!" Winton shrieks, finding the young man a ways off, laughing hard and pointing.

The comedian, Keyonton strolls up to the cotton candy stand, jumping when finally noticing Iron Ball turning to him yet looking down without making eye contact. He dodges, coming up to top speed, looking back and finding Iron Ball hot on his trail.

Within minutes, Iron Ball boxes him in near the Ferris wheel, but Keyonton jumps over the back of a seat, into the seat with a stranger as it lifts, and he shrieks, missed by a single swipe from Iron Ball's fat, manicured hands.

Winton stands in the Ferris wheel line, and without warning, a wide hand grabs a handful of booty, gripping when Winton looks back with bulging eyes, slowly pulling away.

"Hey boo-boo!" the bouncer utters, grabbing Winton and hugging him. Winton's eyes drift down to the bouncer's steel arms when forced forward.

Keyonton smiles, continually sporting with Iron Ball as the Ferris wheel continually go around, until in a game of cat and mouse.

Winton's eyes stay piercing around looking for Nattie and Boogey while slumped down with his face shielded.

Iron Ball's excited eyes follow Keyonton until the ride begins to slow down.

The Ferris wheel operator begins letting folks off and Winton jumps off quickly, walking off with the bouncer.

The bouncer rushes up to Winton's quick distancing, giving him a deep wedgy.

Keyonton's eyes roam over to where he last saw Iron Ball, no longer finding him when growing more fearful.

The bouncer sees a deputy, who he stops and flirts with for minutes.

Winton vanishes inside a tent and rushes out the backside with his head thrown back, at top speed. He exits past the ticket booth for his car and turns, ducking beside a car when finding the four women who set his car on fire. Winton stays low and then takes off in a fast sprint with shaking hands to get his trunk open.

The woman's car heads down a long row as directed by security, and Winton sees them heading back.

The woman driver laughs when making another turn, unknowingly coming near Winton's car when he closes the trunk and ducks, anxiously twisting fireworks together.

A forklift engine grows and Winton finds an old man jumping off to move concrete barriers.

The old man steps down again and walk off a ways to move a cone and Winton jumps in the seat, gunning the gas pedal.

The old man jumps and shrieks, hurrying down the long aisle, stopping from time to time to catch his breath.

Winton shoots up another aisle, circling to the opposite side, patiently waiting.

The female's tail lights flash, and Winton lights a fuse, rushing towards the car, timing the fuse as his eyes nervously and continually go from his watch to the fuse.

The lift's brake lights go out and the women jerk, finding the high-speed yellow gear rolling up with bright, blinding lights until finding Winton showing all thirty-two teeth, with his head thrown back, screaming.

Winton lunges the fused cherry bombs in the window, raising the lift's forks under the car, when lifting it high and fast until stopping it when throwing the lift's keys.

The forklift driver's eyes follow the keys until they fade in the high grass.

Winton jumps from the other side, running. He backs up fast, looking up at red smoke billowing from the other, fast rolled-down windows.

One female looks down, screaming as the car lights up like the Fourth of July.

Mild to loud fireworks explode simultaneously until an M-80 blows up, sounding like a full stick of dynamite with a few deputy's hands expressly over their firearms, with fast wandering eyes.

Hank and his gang finally show up dressed as clowns, scouring the grounds, quickly. They take out deputies one at a time, subduing them by making fake reports of needed assistance in vacant tents, when overtaking them with guns and tying them up. They round up all of the deputies within two hours when two hoodlums burst out of a tent, going after the sheriff.

Within ten minutes, they lure the sheriff into a tent, drawing their guns when he's out of view of the patrons, disarming him and shoving his face forward into a bale of hay. They throw the sheriff a set of chain gang clothing, wrestling him into them, when binding and gagging him.

Melley watches Dallas check the harness straps and cable. "Here, cover the door, and don't let anyone in unless you hear from me," Dallas utters, handing Melley a stun gun and pistol while staring into Melley's face before walking away.

Hank motions for six hoodlums to follow him, then exits, converging outside in a circle. "You all go with Dallas, and you two come with me," Hank utters, pointing to a man and a woman.

Lil' Bobby passes his wife and kids drinks, looking up to find Winton flashing past him. "Here…, here…," Lil' Bobby utters, anxiously shoving food into his wife's hands fast and expressly taking off.

Winton cuts through a tent, and within seconds, Lil' Bobby taps Winton's shoulder and brandishes a handgun, pointing it at his head.

Winton's eyes grow wide, and his hands go high.

"I got your drug lord tail now! Just wait, the sheriff's going to give you a good thrashing," Lil' Bobby yells.

Winton backs up further, when discovering a tall, built clown who is closing fast. He stares into the clown's face when Lil' Bobby's eyes stare up at the tall, manly shadow on the tent's wall behind Winton.

A hard body drapes over Lil' Bobby, gripping his gun while putting him in a sleep hold when the gun veers, then train back on Winton, who still has his hands high. Another clown appears from nowhere, changing the channel on one deputy's walkie-talkie. "We've got ole Winton! Let's meet up at the big tent, ASAP!

There is no response, but everyone rushes, heading for the tent.

The second clown grabs a blue tarp, covering Lil' Bobby, then grips Winton by the collar, head-butting him and knocking him out.

The clowns grab each of Winton's arms, slinging them over their shoulders, and then walk with Winton's limp body dangling like a rag doll until they come up on a crowd of kids when skipping in unison, as if to a playful beat.

Hank sees them approaching and motions for two men to drag a wood contraption out and a handful of rope. "Here! Bind him facedown!" Hank utters in a mean tone, unbuttoning the clown suit and pulling off his thick, leather, rhinestone-studded belt with the saucer-sized belt buckle.

Dallas finds the men tying the last rope when they disappear into the tent, rummaging through a trunk, and walking out seconds later with a cordless, power-mic in hand.

The mic keys up loudly with background squelch and a few folks grabbing their ears. "Come one…, come all! You've got to see this, folks! A new attraction…, first time ever! For one dollar…, yes, one…, and you can whip the toughest man in the world! See it! He's here..., right here..., right now! He's gone through the best of whippings, even fifteen lashes from Singaporean executioners!" Dallas yells in a deep, vibrating and echoing voice.

A crowd of folks rushes over, shuffling each other while lining up, looking over one another's shoulder when Melley sticks a rubber ball in Winton's screaming, drooling mouth. He straps the leather band to the back of his head and snaps it hard as possible, making folks cringe.

One of the women clowns walks up, pulling out a wad of singles.

"Step right up..., step right here! Three good whacks for five dollars..., yes, a measly five dollars!" Dallas shrieks over the amplifier, when pointing to the stockiest fellow he can find. "Hey..., you look pretty strong so give this your best shot, foorrr frrreee!" he shouts, instantly intimidating a few other patrons. "As a matter of fact..., the first five big men can get in on this for freeeeee!"

After many screaming lashes, Winton tears up badly, and his bloody whelps begin showing through his clothes. "I told you 'bout my money, sucker!" You ain't gone sit for months when I'm done," Hank utters, eye-to-eye when puffing on a thick cigar fast until blowing circles that drift around Winton's head. He soon blows heavier, generated looking smoke into Winton's face.

Boogey freezes, hearing the new attraction announced several times. "Yeah..., I definitely need to take off some frustration; give me a hundred," Boogey utters, looking at Nattie when jerking, flexing, and loosening up. Boogey is the fifth in line still leaning his head from side-to-side, loosening up more. He finally looks around the shoulder of the man in front of him and then back at Nattie with a flummoxed look when finally recognizing Winton's outdated shirt.

"Is that...?" Nattie asks, flapping her hands to her face in disbelief.

Boogey recognizes Melley by his walk when stepping out of line and walking up behind him fast.

"Hey, get back in line! There's no head-of-the-line privilege here, pal!" a heavy-set hippie utters, kicking up dust when coming up on Boogey until seeing Dallas' mean face when he turns.

"Stop this nonsense! What's this all about?" Boogey asks, walking up on Dallas. He grips the microphone, expressly grabbing Dallas in the crotch with a death grip.

Dallas' hands instantly stretch high, and his body stiffens then trembling as he slowly lifts to his tiptoes like a professional ballerina.

Due to more delays, the crowd grows rowdy, with patrons fussing and cussing.

The female clown steps inside fast, screaming for Hank who steps out finding Boogey's mean face. "Untie him, or your brother here starts talking like Donald, yeah, as in the freakin' Duck!" Boogey tightens his grip, pulling mildly to make Dallas climb higher.

"You stay out of this, Boog! Wint has to learn about playing with my moolah (money)!" Hank shrieks over the loud rides in the background while taking another step closer.

"Cut him loose, and I'll pay you yo (your) money right here and now."

Dallas shakes his head in agreement, with tears running down each cheek.

"Two thou, now!" Hank utters, glowering at Winton sneakily and staring into Boogey's firm eyes.

The cock-strong, long line of patrons grows rowdier when using stronger cuss words.

"One thousand now and the rest tomorrow. I know where you are, so I can get it to you," Boogey utters, staring into Dallas' eyes. "What do you say?" Boogey asks Dallas, who trembles and cries even harder until making the ugliest, painful face.

"You want this debt? Seriously think about Boog because I'll be wailing on your fat hind parts with a two-by-four full of splinters next time!" Hank utters, with his index and middle finger clenching the thick cigar held toward Boogey's face.

"I'm good for it; just cut him loose!" Boogey shrieks, easing his grip with Dallas coming off his tiptoes briefly, then speedily up again when Boogey's grip tightens. "The way I see it, you can spend the rest of your life explaining why he can't have kids, or we can close a deal!" Boogey shrieks, swallowing hard when finding four guns pointing outward from the tent's opening.

"Ok..., ok...," Hank utters, directing the female to untie Winton with the guns coming down.

Boogey looks at Nattie, nodding for her to come over then whispers. "Give me a thousand, get the car, and meet me out front, but make it skippy." He looks into her teary eyes.

Nattie counts off the dollars nervously but fast, slipping them in his pants pocket with fast swaying eyes then vanishes as if never there.

Boogey turns to say something else but can't find Nattie anywhere.

The last rope falls to the ground, and Winton falls after taking one step, slowly crawling to Boogey and pulling himself up on Boogey's leg until he is on his feet.

"Ok, now you. Let Dallas go!" Hank utters, nodding to Dallas.

"Not so fast!" Boogey utters, nodding for other goons to drop their guns as they are coming up slow again.

Winton stumbles into Boogey, making Dallas yelp loudly, and everyone cringes.

Boogey leans into Winton, whispering for him to meet near the go-carts, and then looks back, finding the gang forming a circle. He pushes Dallas down and ducks behind a shooting gallery, looking hilarious when zigzagging in a sprint.

Three people lunge forward after Boogey.

"Never mind him, you goons! We've got bigger fish to fry! The collections will leave the fairgrounds and be deposited into the bank if we wait too late," Hank screams.

As Dallas rolls around in excruciating pain, he freezes, looking up at Hank in terror. "Do me a favor and kill Boogey the next time you see him!" he shrieks in a high pitch when two men lift and dust him off. Dallas grabs one man, angrily shoving him back, then head-butts the other. "Get off me, you freakin' idiot!"

"Showtime," Hank utters, looking at his watch. "You and you hit the tiller and meet us at the cars," he utters, looking at a few confused looking clowns when motioning to Melley and Dallas, who slowly follow him inside the tent.

The sheriff and deputies mumble more cuss words with frowns, when getting louder.

"Let's take these suckers on a joy ride!" Hank utters, nodding for Melley to ungag all of the law officials when louder screams come, below the amplifier ride's music.

The sheriff and deputies' screams grow louder, making several threats while Dallas rechecks the cable.

Hank looks at his watch when gunfire blasts, simultaneously. "That there is biiigggg money, payday!" he shrieks, nodding to Melley, who opens the back of the tent, looking at a constantly slowing, fast ride.

Melley holds the bitter end of the cable tightly with eyes studying the ride until the last person exits, then runs over, connecting the hook to the edge of the ride.

The sheriff and deputy's eyes grow wide when drug a few inches seconds later while the ride is being loaded. Their eyes nervously follow the cable and they begin screaming and jerking when slowly drug a few more feet toward the tent's back door.

The ride's operator continues filling the seats and then looks up at pointing patrons who scream while pointing at the bundle of prison-dressed bodies on the other side. The operator ignores the screams as joy and laughter when taking a swig of moonshine in a plastic cup, throwing his numb head back, giggling when throwing up two thumbs, screaming, and hitting the start button.

The ride lifts high and fast then goes ten feet off the ground when the operator bends to put his cup down with the cable and bundle flying past. He comes up hitting the second green button, and the engine revs high when more pointing hands and screams come as the ride spins, rolling the bundle and lifting it higher and several feet above the operator's head.

The operator finally sees something tumbling in the background when his anxious eyes follow it around, and he ducks then falls backward, kicking when the cable and bodies fly by a few times. The operator waits for the next pass when he ducks and dives for the red button, shutting down the ride and staying low until the bundle hits the ground and tumbles in high rising dust, for minutes.

Later that night, Boogey is drinking his fifth beer when he hears bells outside ringing loudly. "Woo-hoo!" he screams, dancing in the junky living room when spring for the corner, grabbing his gun. He meets Nattie at the door, staring into her nervous eyes when handing her the gun. Boogey seizes the flashlight bursting through the screen door, shuffling down the steps. He eases around the house, charging the light and looking up until the man's drunk, scary eyes shine with teeth looking like that of a possum.

Boogey hears bottles clinking when closer. "Woowee!" he shrieks with the flashlight shining over the yard. He begins beating his chest and screaming, almost like an old Tarzan with Nattie standing a ways off, senselessly giggling.

Five people run up from alongside the store, laughing at another man, who Boogey motions to, for his thick, leather belt, which the man unravels fast.

Five more converge, looking and laughing when Boogey folds the long, leather belt, holding it tight on both ends, loudly snapping and popping it a few times with the man in the net screaming after each pop.

Boogey flexes his shoulder as if rocking then screams, hauling off and giving him a few hog wild lashes until he's out of breath.

The people cheer Boogey on in deep laughter until more people converge, laughing.

Boogey staggers off, fumbling around under the house for a treated two-by-four, for minutes then stands, pulling a few flimsy, rusty nails out of the wood. He happens to look back, finding Sam a ways off and running up with a pink slip of paper high over his head, screaming something that he can't make out.

Sam sees the familiar clothing in the net and increases speed, finally screaming Boogey's name.

Boogey stares at Sam with the two-by-four high over his shoulder, and sprung back tight.

"Boogey! Wait, Boogey!" Sam shrieks, running up and pleading for him to stop.

Boogey looks up at the screaming man, slightly swaying, then looks down.

"Look at it!" Sam utters, unfolding the check to get Boogey's attention when looking up at who he thinks is his father. "The investment with your money yielded a great return already."

"Well, that's Great! Great!" Boogey utters, sticking the check inside his front coverall pocket. "You're just in time to see me whip this thieving bastard!" Boogey shrieks, swinging the two-by-four back again until he's standing like he's ready to hit a home run.

"No, Boogey! No! That's my father!" he yells, holding Boogey back at his chest.

Boogey stares up at the man and then at Sam, noticing some resemblance. "Your father? So you two, been stealing my shine?" Boogey utters, confused.

"No, no, no..., just let him down, and we'll get to the bottom of this!" Sam screams over the loud commotion, while patting Boogey on the shoulder and grabbing the two-by-four when lowering it.

Boogey motions to a man standing near the tree to let the rope loose, slow, using slow downward motions.

The man begins lowering the rope then sneakily let go. "Oops!" he yells, looking at the laughing crowd when a plume of dust rises five feet high after the man slams onto the ground.

Sam balls his fist tightly, and his face turns red, closely watching the selfish man near the tree make more clowning gestures to keep the crowd entertained.

Sam's father lies moaning for seconds then slowly crawls to his knees. He comes up with one arm over Sam's shoulder and limps then hops on one leg until resting on Sam's shoulder. "That almost snapped my joint; it did," he utters, wiping the smile away when seeing Boogey's mean face, crossed eyes, and balled fist.

"Now you look hea (here); you better have a good reason for stealing my shine!" Boogey says, stepping to him with a tight fist.

Sam's father motions for Boogey to settle down with a fast flapping hand. "You're right; I had no right to steal, but I'm close to cutting-edge technology, and a company is offering twenty a bottle."

"You mean you're selling this shine for twenty a bottle?" Boogey excitedly says.

"No, it is a part shine mix and other engineered ingredients; here, take a sip," Sam's father utters, pulling out a pint-size, half-empty bottle.

Boogey turns up the bottle, downing almost all of it when the old man snappily pulls the bottle down.

"Easy there, young feller (fellow), it only takes a little to get you ah thumping," he mumbles, shaking his head.

"Man! This is so smooth and easy-going," Boogey utters, taking another swig.

"It's the mixture." Sam's father smiles. "We can go into business if we can seal an honest deal with a reputable distributor," he says, finally standing on his own, smiling.

"Well, that would require me cutting in my supplier, right?" Boogey asks.

"No..., not really; just ask him for a reduced rate. It does not take much of your moonshine to make the potion because most of the additives are organic."

"Look..., let's talk business later, but let's just sample the product since there's an audience. Hey! Anybody wanna party?" Boogey screams at the top of his lungs, looking over the crowd of thirty or more. Boogey digs in his front pocket, giving one of the off-duty firefighters a handful of money for stocking up on cookout food, beer, and snacks.

Suddenly, a continuous, loud thump grows, and folks look near the street, finding the old foreign lady getting out of the backseat of her grandson's car.

Boogey runs up in the foreigner's yard, and the old lady drops down into a karate stance. "Whoa, whoa, whoa, Mama!" he utters with her fingers barely touching his chest, stomach, and then forehead when the three begin to lightly ache.

"Crouching nugget!" she shrieks, bursting into a drunken laugh. "Deployed with force, you would be stretched out right now," she utters, dusting hands together.

"Yeah, yeah, yeah..., what the hell ever!" he utters, senselessly giggling and awaiting the grandson's confirmation.

Boogey sees the old lady perform a few more moves when staggering to the driver's side. "Hey... that thing..., could she really do damage?" he fearfully asks, looking into the foreign boy's bright eyes and confirming stares then confirmation.

"Yep..., as sure as it is night," he utters, finding his mom and dad anxiously running into Boogey's yard.

"Nice system; why don't you pull up and let her rip?" Boogey shrieks, pointing to the cheery crowd when digging in his pocket, slipping him two crisp fifties.

The foreign boy grabs the money, pulling alongside Boogey's house, where guys begin rigging bright lighting.

The music starts low then cranks up, and everyone dances, kicking up dust as the bass goes into overdrive.

The soon drunken crowd unknowingly fades into the high, dark dust with endless, cheerful screams with several flashing cruiser lights flashing by on the main road.

**THE END! :)**